Electronic Commerce: Opportunity and Challenges

Syed Mahbubur Rahman
Minnesota State University, Mankato

Mahesh S. Raisinghani
University of Dallas, USA

IDEA GROUP PUBLISHING
Hershey USA • London UK

Senior Editor:	Mehdi Khosrowpour
Managing Editor:	Jan Travers
Copy Editor:	Maria Boyer
Typesetter:	Tamara Gillis
Cover Design:	Connie Peltz
Printed at:	BookCrafters

Published in the United States of America by
Idea Group Publishing
1331 E. Chocolate Avenue
Hershey PA 17033-1117
Tel: 717-533-8845
Fax: 717-533-8661
E-mail: jtravers@idea-group.com
Web site: http://www.idea-group.com

and in the United Kingdom by
Idea Group Publishing
3 Henrietta Street
Covent Garden
London WC2E 8LU
Tel: 171-240 0856
Fax: 171-379 0609
Web site: http://www.eurospan.co.uk

Copyright © 2000 by Idea Group Publishing. All rights reserved. No part of this book may be reproduced in any form or by any means, electronic or mechanical, including photocopying, without written permission from the publisher.

Library of Congress Cataloging-in-Publication Data

Electronic commerce: opportunity and challenges / Syed Mahbubur Rahman, Mahesh S. Raisinghani [editors]
    p. cm.
   ISBN 1-878289-76-4
    1. Electronic commerce. 2. Internet marketing. 3. Business enterprises--Computer networks. I. Rahman, Syed Mahbubur, 1952- II. Raisinghani, Mahesh S., 1967-

HF5548.32 .E368 2000
381'.1--dc21   99-059766

British Cataloguing in Publication Data
A Cataloguing in Publication record for this book is available from the British Library.

NEW from Idea Group Publishing

- **Instructional and Cognitive Impacts of Web-Based Education**
  Bev Abbey, Texas A&M University/ISBN: 1-878289-59-4
- **Web-Based Learning and Teaching Technologies: Opportunities and Challenges**
  Anil Aggarwal, University of Baltimore/ISBN: 1-878289-60-8
- **Health-Care Information Systems: Challenges of the New Millennium**
  Adi Armoni, Tel Aviv College of Management/ISBN: 1-878289-62-4
- **Evaluation and Implementation of Distance Learning: Technologies, Tools and Techniques**
  France Belanger, Virginia Polytechnic Institute; Dianne H. Jordan, Booz Allen & Hamilton/ ISBN: 1-878289-63-2
- **Human Centered Methods in Information Systems: Current Research and Practice**
  Steve Clarke and Brian Lehaney, University of Luton Business School/ ISBN: 1-878289-64-0
- **Managing Healthcare Information Systems with Web-Enabled Technologies**
  Lauren Eder, Rider University/ISBN: 1-878289-65-9
- **World Libraries on the Information Superhighway: Preparing for the Challenges of the Next Millennium**
  Patricia Diamond Fletcher, University of Maryland Baltimore County
  John Carlo Bertot, University at Albany, State University of New York/ISBN: 1-878289-66-7
- **Social Dimensions of Information Technology: Issues for the New Millennium**
  G. David Garson, North Carolina State University/ISBN 1-878289-86-1
- **Object Oriented Technologies: Opportunities and Challenges**
  Rick Gibson, American University/ISBN 1-878289-67-5
- **Process Think: Winning Perspectives for Business Change in the Information Age**
  Varun Grover & William Kettinger, University of South Carolina
  ISBN: 1-878289-68-3
- **Community Informatics: Enabling Communities with Information & Communications Technologies**
  Michael Gurstein, University College of Cape Breton/ISBN: 1-878289-69-1
- **A Primer for Disaster Recovery Planning in an IT Environment**
  Charlotte Hiatt, California State University, Fresno/ ISBN: 1-878289-81-0
- **Information Technology Standards and Standardization: A Global Perspective**
  Kai Jakobs, Technical University of Aachen/ ISBN: 1-878289-70-5
- **Internet and Intranet Security, Management, Risks and Solutions**
  Lech Janczewski, University of Auckland/ISBN: 1-878289-71-3
- **Managing Web-Enabled Technologies in Organizations: A Global Perspective**
  Mehdi Khosrowpour, Pennsylvania State University/ISBN: 1-878289-72-1
- **Distance Learning Technologies: Issues, Trends and Opportunities**
  Linda Lau, Longwood College/ISBN: 1-878289-80-2
- **Knowledge Management and Virtual Organizations**
  Yogesh Malhotra, Florida Atlantic University/ISBN: 1-878289-73-X
- **Case Studies on Information Technology in Higher Education: Implications for Policy and Practice**
  Lisa Ann Petrides, Columbia University/ISBN: 1-878289-74-8
- **Auditing Information Systems**
  Mario Piattini, University de Castilla-La Mancha/ISBN: 1-878289-75-6
- **Electronic Commerce: Opportunity and Challenges**
  Syed Mahbubur Rahman, Monash University & Mahesh S. Raisinghani, University of Dallas
  ISBN: 1-878289-76-4
- **Internet-Based Organizational Memory and Knowledge Management**
  David G. Schwartz, Bar-Ilan University; Monica Divitini, Norwegian University of Science and Technology; Terje Brasethvik, Norwegian University of Science and Technology
- **Organizational Achievement and Failure in Information Technology Management**
  Mehdi Khosrowpour, Pennsylvania State University/ISBN: 1-878289-83-7
- **Challenges of Information Technology Management in the 21st Century**
  Mehdi Khosrowpour, Pennsylvania State University/ISBN: 1-878289-84-5

Excellent additions to your library!
**Receive the Idea Group Publishing catalog with descriptions of these books by calling, toll free 1/800-345-4332
or visit the IGP web site at: http://www.idea-group.com!**

Electronic Commerce: Opportunity and Challenges

Table of Contents

Preface i

SECTION ONE: Electric Commerce Opportunities, Policies and Case Studies

Chapter 1. Electronic Commerce at the Dawn of the Third Millennium 1
Mahesh Raisinghani, University of Dallas, USA

Chapter 2. Building E-Commerce From Ground Up:
A Study Of The Retail Industry 21
David Gordon, University of Dallas, Texas USA
James E. Skibo, University of Dallas, Texas USA

Chapter 3. Principles of Digitally Mediated Replenishment of Goods:
Electronic Commerce and Supply Chain Reform 41
Robert B. Johnston, Monash University, Australia

Chapter 4. Electronic Trade Scenario for Global Supply Chains 65
Ronald M. Lee, Erasmus University, Netherlands

Chapter 5. Promoting Electronic Commerce in the Defense Industry 85
Charles Trappey, National Chiao Tung University, Taiwan
Amy Trappey, National Tsing Hua University, Taiwan
Thomas Gulledge, George Mason University, USA
Rainer Sommer, George Mason University, USA

Chapter 6. Diffusion of Electronic Commerce in Australia:
A Preliminary Investigation 102
Mohammed Quaddus, Curtin University of Technology, Australia

Chapter 7. Planning E-Strategies for New Zealand Firms:
A CSF Framework for Investing in E-Commerce Projects 115
Liaquat Hossain, Massey University, Albany, New Zealand

SECTION TWO: EDI Applications

Chapter 8. Electronic Commerce Contracting for Open EDI 126
    Andreas Mitrakas, GlobalSign NV, Belgium

Chapter 9. EDI and Small/Medium Enterprises 142
    Rob MacGregor, University of Wollongong, Australia
    Deborah Bunker, University of New South Wales, Australia

Chapter 10. Economics of EDI Investments 152
    Ruhul A Sarker, University of New South Wales, Australia
    Syed Mahbubur Rahman, North Dakota State University, USA

SECTION THREE: Internet-Based Electronic Commerce and Payment Systems

Chapter 11. Internet Business Models For Government Agencies 171
    Mariam Fergusson, University College, University of New South Wales, Australia

Chapter 12. A Model Of Internet Commerce Adoption (Mica) 189
    Joan Cooper, University of Wollongong, Australia
    Lois Burgess, University of Wollongong, Australia

Chapter 13. E-Retailing: New Opportunities In Internet Commerce 202
    L F Sugianto, Monash University, Australia
    S Sendjaya, Monash Mt Eliza Business School, Australia

Chapter 14. Consumer Motivations for Commercial Web Site Use:
Antecedents to Electronic Commerce 218
    Thomas F. Stafford, Texas Woman's University, USA
    Marla Royne Stafford, University of North Texas, USA

Chapter 15. The Retail Payments System and Internet Commerce 233
    Boon-Chye Lee, University of Wollongong, Australia

SECTION FOUR: Agent Applications for Automated Transactions

Chapter 16. Internet-enabled Smart Card Agent Environment and Applications 246
    Teoh Kok Poh, SciNet Systems, Singapore
    Sheng-Uei Guan, National University of Singapore, Singapore

Chapter 17. Supporting Innovative Competitive Strategies as Mass Customization
by Pairing E-Commerce Techniques with Agent Technology 261
    Klaus Turowski, Otto-von-Guericke-Universität Magdeburg, Germany

Chapter 18. Electronic Commerce Based on Software Agent 279
    X.Yi, C.K.Siew, Nanyang Technological University, Singapore
    Syed M Rahman, North Dakota State University, USA
    Robert Bignall, Monash University, Australia

Chapter 19. A Mobile Agent Computation Model for Best Buy Searching 303
    Timothy K. Shih, Tamkang University, Taiwan

**Chapter 20. The Design and Architecture of a Secure Agent Transport
Protocol for E-Commerce** 321
    Yang Yang, National University of Singapore, Singapore
    Sheng-Uei Guan, National University of Singapore, Singapore

Chapter 21. The Evolving Future of Agent-Based Electronic Commerce 337
    T. Deshani Rodrigo, Monash University, Australia
    Peter A. Stanski, Monash University, Australia

SECTION FIVE: Attacks and Legal Aspect of Electronic Commerce

**Chapter 22. The Use of the Internet by Terrorists and Its Impact
Upon Electronic Commerce** 352
    Matthew Warren, Deakin University, Australia
    William Hutchinson, Edith Cowan University, Australia

Chapter 23. The Law vis-a-vis Electronic Commerce 362
    Assafa Endeshaw, Nanyang Technological University, Singapore

**Chapter 24. The Challenge of the Law to Electronic Commerce :
The European Union Initiatives** 383
    Séverine Dusollier and Laetitia Rolin Jacquemyns
    Centre de Recherches Informatique et Droit, (Centre of Research in
    Computers and Law), University of Namur, Belgium

About the Authors 411

Index 419

Preface

"We are on the verge of a revolution that is just as profound as the change in the economy that came with the industrial revolution. Soon electronic networks will allow people to transcend the barriers of time and distance and take advantage of global markets and business opportunities not even imaginable today, opening up a new world of economic possibility and progress."

———Vice President Albert Gore, Jr.

Commerce is the buying and selling of goods and services or the transfer of money in the course of business transactions between sellers and buyers. Taking a broad perspective, electronic commerce (e-commerce) may be seen as the process of conducting commercial transactions using any electronic communication technology to achieve an organizational goal. In such a sense, e-commerce is not totally new and dates back to the days when interaction between buyers and sellers began to occur over the telephone and later via fax. Today e-commerce includes electronic data interchange (EDI), EFTPOS, electronic banking, digital cash transactions and other forms of electronic payment via a closed network or over the Internet.

In recent years, with the emergence of the Internet as a public network infrastructure from its origins as a solely military and academic network, research into and development of electronic commerce technologies have been boosted significantly. World Wide Web based transactions have opened up immense possibilities and electronic commerce is gaining in popularity. "Making purchases" has emerged as the fastest-growing online activity as e-commerce becomes central to the Internet consumer's experience, according to a study released on November 11 1999 at a media briefing by America Online Inc and Roper Starch Worldwide, one of the nation's largest marketing research and consulting firms. According to the 1999 study "Internet Economy Indicators," by the University of Texas' Center for Research in Electronic Commerce, the U.S. Internet economy was worth US$301.4 billion in 1998. International Data Corporation has estimated that the Internet commerce market will exceed $425 billion by 2002, with business-to-business sales accounting for more than 75 percent of those revenues. Consumer sales will exceed US$108 billion by 2003, according to Forrester Research Inc. A recent Pricewaterhouse Coopers survey of Global 1000 companies found that 85 percent see e-business as an investment priority over the next three years. E-commerce has been a catalyst for change as some existing brick-and-mortar companies seek to find the right strategy and structure for their online operations, including buyouts (e.g., Homebid.com), integration (e.g., Prudential California realty), partnerships (e.g., PetSmart), or subsidiaries (e.g., MagazineOutlet.com). Traditional intermediary functions are being replaced, new products and services are appearing, markets are developing worldwide and new relationships are being created between business and consumers. Against this background the need for understanding the opportunities and challenges in e-commerce cannot be overstressed.

Although the Internet provides many opportunities for companies that can leverage the key drivers of business success; that is, information, collaboration, agility and velocity, it also poses tremendous challenges in terms of a lack of comprehensive e-business strategies, rapid and radical transformation of traditional business models, learning curve issues, privacy and security of information, among others. This book is designed to help its readers get a better grip on the opportunities and challenges in e-commerce as it affects business theory and practice in the new millennium.

The opportunities offered and the issues that arise are immense and it is not possible to encompass them all within the scope of a single book. Relevant issues include telecommunications infrastructure and information technology, content of business information, technical standards, a Uniform Commercial Code for electronic commerce, intellectual property protection, privacy, information security, electronic payments, consumer confidence, automated secure transactions and a lot more. This book contains 24 chapters that introduce many of these issues and discuss approaches and technologies to take advantage of the numerous opportunities that exist. The chapters can be categorized into the following very interrelated sections:

* Electronic commerce opportunities, policies and case studies
* EDI applications
* Internet-based electronic commerce and payment systems
* Agents applications for automated transactions
* Attacks on security and legal aspects of electronic commerce

The book will be useful to policy makers, business professionals, academics and students. We expect that the promising opportunities illustrated by the case studies and the technical solutions described in the book will help to expand the horizons of e-commerce and disseminate knowledge to both business and the technical community.

This book could not have been written and published without the help and support of many people, and we would like to acknowledge a few who have been instrumental in bringing it to fruition. We are grateful to our parents who by their unconditional love have steered us to this point and to our wives, sons and daughters who have steadfastly supported us throughout this project. We also take this opportunity to express our sincere gratitude to each of the chapter authors who contributed their ideas and expertise, and also to our Senior Editor Dr. Mehdi Khosrowpour, Managing Editor Ms. Jan Travers and Ms. Amanda Stauffer for their hard work in producing this book. Thanks are also due to many colleagues who have contributed invaluable ideas by thoroughly reviewing the chapters.

Syed Mahbubur Rahman and Mahesh S. Raisinghani
Editors

Chapter I

Electronic Commerce at the Dawn of the Third Millennium

Mahesh S. Raisinghani
University of Dallas

"The future ain't what it used to be." —Yogi Berra

EXECUTIVE SUMMARY

At the brink of the new millennium, in global economy and commerce, there has been a dramatic increase in the role of information technology in markets, both in traditional markets and especially in the emergence of the electronic marketplaces. In recent years, the Internet has grown exponentially and is clearly transforming global markets. This chapter analyzes the fundamentals of electronic commerce and discusses the opportunities and challenges that e-commerce presents for global enterprises with relevant examples from the industry where appropriate. Opportunities of e-commerce are improvements in marketing activities such as one-to-one marketing and communication, better management of product/service support and product/value chain, and cost cuttings due to several electronic payment methods. On the other hand, global enterprises face the challenges of e-commerce, such as adjusting to competition in electronic markets, re-engineering/e-engineering distribution channels, addressing security and privacy issues, and applying strategic management to corporate alliance systems. Finally, the future of electronic commerce is discussed.

INTRODUCTION

On the brink of the new millennium, a number of converging trends are taking the global economy beyond the embryonic stages of the Information Age. Even though electronic commerce (e-commerce) is in its relative infancy, in recent years the Internet has

Copyright © 2000, Idea Group Publishing.

grown exponentially and is clearly transforming global markets (Barua, Ravindran, and Whinston, 1997; Rao, Salam, and DosSantos, 1998). The most important trend is the increasing digitization of business, which is driven by the consumer demand side in which consumers use the Internet for their purchases, and the marketing and supply side in which electronic commerce has emerged as the mission-critical application.

The 21st century projections suggest order-of-magnitude increases in both business-to-business and business-to-consumer e-commerce. The U.S. e-commerce industry ranks as the world's 18th largest economy, behind Switzerland and ahead of Argentina, according to the study conducted by the University of Texas' Center for Research in Electronic Commerce (Murphy and Feldman, 1999). In the same study, researchers also found that the four sectors of the U.S. Internet economy—infrastructure, applications/Web development, intermediaries (including portals, on-line brokerages, travel agents, and advertising), and commerce—generated an estimated $301.4 billion in revenue in 1998. The qualitative and quantitative research methods used to make the projections of e-commerce activity and the valuation of the information technology (IT) industry are predicted to become more rigorous, precise, and useful over the next four to five years by the U.S. Census Bureau, the U.S. Bureau of Economic Analysis and several IT research organizations such as the Gartner Group and Forester Research. The impact of extraneous variables on e-commerce such as mobile, wireless global e-commerce using satellite communication; interactive television as an alternative to Web sites and/or taxation of on-line transactions need to be considered. In addition, new metrics need to be derived for measuring the volume of e-commerce and the tangible and intangible costs and benefits of e-commerce. Specific estimates from private sources are included in this chapter to be illustrative of developing trends. The wide range of e-commerce revenue projections by various researchers from $800 million to over $1 trillion a year by 2002 is due to sampling errors and/or lack of a standard research methodology. In addition, disparities among private estimates result from differences in definitions, methods, data, model and sampling error, and product coverage. Variations also reflect the research needs of customers. While data used for estimates and forecasts are based on a combination of surveys and interviews, the survey questions and answers are not made public, sample sizes vary considerably across surveys, and little information is available on the respondents (*http://www.ecommerce.gov/ede/chapter1.html*).

Even though the elements measured (e.g., consumer transactions on the Web, business-to-business transactions such as corporate procurement from catalogs or Web-based electronic data exchange (EDI) in the virtual supply chain, Web transactions that result in sales through other distribution channels, etc.) and the methods to measure these elements differ, there is no doubt that the e-commerce economy is on a significant rise. Researchers also grossly underestimated the size of the electronic commerce marketplace. In 1995, for instance, Forrester Research projected that the Internet would have a worldwide user population of 34.9 million people by 1998. The real number ended up being in excess of 100 million users. In 1995, Jupiter Communications projected $3.1 billion in annual business-to-consumer revenue for e-commerce by 1998. Forrester predicted $2.3 billion. The real number turned out to be more than $13 billion.

The U.S. Department of Commerce predicts the volume of business-to-business e-commerce will increase from $8 billion in 1997 to $300 billion in 2002, and Jupiter Communications predicts the growth on the consumer side (including travel and tangible goods sold, but not financial services) to be from the current $7 billion to $41 billion by 2002 (Kindel, 1999). By the year 2003 worldwide e-commerce will approach $3.2 trillion and represent nearly 5% of all global sales[1].

The objective of this chapter is to provide a thorough analysis of the fundamentals of e-commerce, discuss the changes it brought in terms of opportunities and challenges to the way the business is conducted, and outline the implications for executives. First, electronic commerce is defined; the organizational model, framework, and taxonomy of e-commerce are examined; and e-commerce business models are described. Next, opportunities and challenges that e-commerce presents for global enterprises are discussed. This is followed by a discussion of best practices and implications for management. Finally, the future of e-commerce is explored and conclusions drawn.

CONCEPTUAL BACKGROUND

The global information infrastructure serves as the foundation for new modes of personal interaction and business transactions in a collection of activities known as electronic commerce (e-commerce). E-commerce is sharing business information, maintaining business relationships, and conducting business transactions by means of telecommunications networks. E-commerce is defined as a variety of market transactions that are enabled by information technology and represents the entire collection of actions that support commercial activities on a network (Zwass, 1999; Applegate et al., 1996). From a *business process* perspective, e-commerce is the application of technology toward the automation of business transactions and workgroups. From an *on-line* perspective, e-commerce provides the capability of buying and selling products and information on the Internet and other on-line services (Kalakota and Whinston, 1997).

Essentially, electronic commerce involves any electronic business action such as an inquiry about a product feature, a purchase order, or an invoice delivery. Although technologies such as fax and telex are extensively used in the business world, they are not considered electronic commerce since they include the use of paper as an output, which hinders the interaction of electronic media and thus prevents data exchange on an electronic basis. E-commerce is a way to open new markets, improve communications, speed delivery times, simplify business processes, streamline supply chains, and maximize customer relationship marketing.

THE E-COMMERCE ORGANIZATIONAL MODEL

E-commerce is a very young field in the context of general management. Since 1952, the year large-scale computers were introduced into the private sector in the United States, technology users have sustained dramatic decreases in cost and changes in the diverse technologies of computing and telecommunications. This has created a continuous explosion of applications opportunities on the one hand and a kaleidoscope of management implementation issues on the other.

The new organizational model for the e-commerce era is best understood by a synthesis of the strategic management literature. The central theme of Mintzberg's (1990) critique of the premises of the strategic design school model is the promotion of thought independent of action and strategy formation as a process of *conception*, rather than as one of *learning*. In the most general sense, it is argued, the design school has denied itself of the chance to adapt. Although no definitive view of the new competitive landscape is possible

for several years, it is currently being shaped, and the advent of the e-commerce-based information model has contributed to the three new imperatives pointed out by Bettis and Hitt (1995) that will increasingly drive the direction of organizational design:
a) decreased transaction costs;
b) increased penalties for mistakes and hesitancy;
c) competition based on knowledge accumulation and deployment.

These three imperatives imply a redefinition of organizations, an increase in the explicit importance of organizations as learning systems, and a new generalized organizational strategic response capability. The new competitive landscape suggests that firms exist in highly turbulent and often chaotic environments that produce disorder, disequilibrium, and significant uncertainty, as well as discontinuous change

A firm's absorptive capacity (the ability to exploit new technological developments) not only enables a firm to exploit new extramural knowledge, but also to predict more accurately the nature of future technological advances. As companies strive to maximize their Inter/Intra/Extranet capabilities to offer innovative products and services valued by customers, the biggest executive challenge is to determine the optimal method to transform a business so it can thrive by using the Internet. The organizational model for the information/knowledge era is based on the optimum level of integration where people share a common goal, possess complementary skills and knowledge, and hold themselves

Table 1: The E-Commerce Organizational Model

The E-Business Model		
Characteristics	**Old Model (Industrial Era)**	**New Model (Information/Knowledge Era)**
Structure	Hierarchical	Integrated, team-based
Creativity	Largely undervalued	Must be nurtured
Orientation	Internal	External
Management gap/difference in perception between levels of management	Large	Small
Learning, experimenting, and creativeness	Important	Essential
Group relationships	Vertically aligned teams	Integrated teams centered around the customer
Virtual corporation acceptance	Downsizing and Rightsizing	Forming strategic organizational alliances and linking of global business core competencies
Primary business organization goal	Dominance	Able to act and adapt quickly
Key success factors	Streamlined and matured internal structure, tight well-organized internal procedures	Change company behavior; change reward structures, externally focused

Source: Adapted from *Corporate Internet Planning Guide: Aligning Internet Strategy With Business Goals* (Gascoyne, 1997)

mutually accountable for results. Its features are outlined in Table 1.

E-COMMERCE FRAMEWORK AND TAXONOMY

The generic framework of e-commerce is illustrated in Figure 1 and can be summarized in three levels (Zwass, 1999; 1996):

1) Infrastructure—the hardware, software, databases and telecommunications that together deliver such functionality as the Web over the Internet, and support Electronic Data Interchange (EDI) and other forms of messaging over the Internet or over value-added networks.
2) Services—messaging and a variety of services enabling the finding and delivery of information, as well as negotiation, transaction, and settlement.

Figure 1: Generic Framework for Electronic Commerce. Source: Zwass (1996).

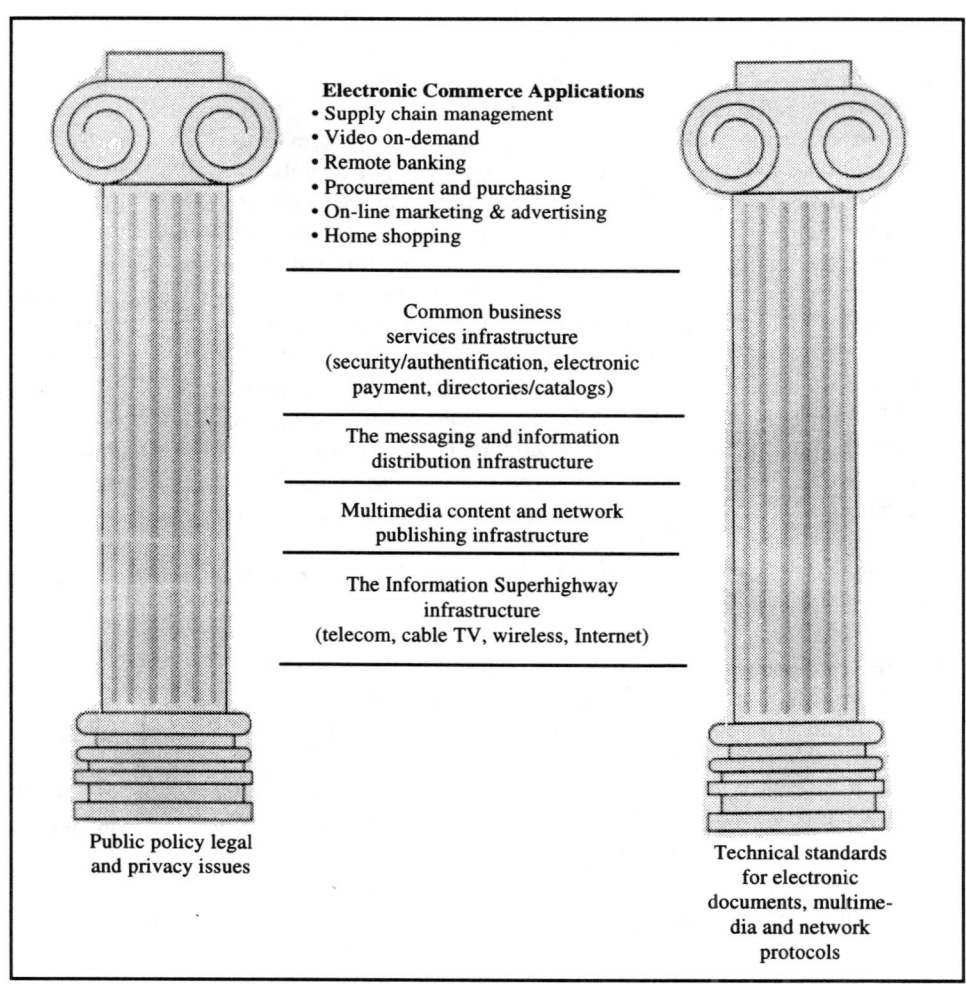

3) Products and structures—direct provision of commercial services to consumers and business partners, intraorganizational information sharing and collaboration, and organization of electronic markets and supply chains.

The Internet can be interactive, has global connectivity, and is relatively inexpensive to use. It is synonymous with innovation, cost reduction, and growth. There are three business models of e-commerce using the Internet infrastructure, i.e., business-to-consumer, business-to-business, and within-a-business e-commerce; which are discussed next.

Business-to-Consumer Electronic Commerce

Business-to-consumer e-commerce can be in several forms, such as electronic shopping, customer support, and product delivery. The old "push" model in which customer preferences were filtered through the supply chain, and the production cycle serving the needs of the suppliers instead of the customers have been replaced by the "pull" model in the business-to-consumer e-commerce model, whereby customers elicit products and services. Using the "pull" model, Dell Computer's on-line sales more than doubled during 1998 rising to more than $14 million per day and accounts for 25 percent of the company's total revenues. During the quarter ended April 30, 1999, on-line sales rose further to an average of $18 million per day and now account for 30 percent of the company's $5.5 billion first quarter revenues. Dell expects this percentage to increase to 50 percent by 2000 (*www.dell.com; www.nua.ie;* and *www.ecommerce.gov/ede/chapter1.html*). Forecasters project online retail sales in the range of $40 billion to $80 billion by 2002.

Business-to-consumer e-commerce can occur in a variety of forms. One form is illustrated by United Parcel Services (UPS) who, through its *www.ec.ups.com* and www.ups.com Web sites, provides Internet-based interactive services to its customers and allows them to track packages, calculate shipping costs, download rate and tracking software, determine UPS package drop-off locations, estimate package time in transit, request supplies and send e-mail messages to customer service. Another form is illustrated by the Internet Service Provider (ISP), NetZero.com (*www.netzero.com*), which offers free access to the Internet; or the on-line superstore, Buy.com (www.buy.com), which was able to set a historic record of $125 million in sales during its first year of operation by underselling rivals, sometimes at or below cost, and making profits through banner advertising on its Web site (Hof, 1999).

Some critical questions that need to be answered before an organization begins selling products or services online are:

- How well suited are your products for selling on the Web?
- What will happen to your traditional sales channel?
- What are your business objectives? For example, do you want to extend your market reach, reduce costs or improve customer relationships?
- How will issues related to order fulfillment, returns and exchanges be addressed? How will you integrate your front-end Web site with back-end database management system/s? How will bills be processed?
- How will you secure the transactions that take place?
- What will you do with the all the personal information you gather on customers? Will you tell them how you plan to use that information?

Business-to-Business Electronic Commerce

According to Forrester Research, while the U.S. business-to-consumer revenues will grow to $108 billion in 2003, the business-to-business revenues will balloon to $1.3 trillion, accounting for 9.4% of total business-to-business sales (*www.forrester.com*, December 17, 1998). There are a variety of technologies that can be utilized in business-to-business electronic commerce. The most important and traditional form is Electronic Data Interchange (EDI). EDI is basically the technology that enables inter-organizational, computer-to-computer exchange of business documents in machine-processable format. "Unibex is a company that offers traditional e-commerce services by partnering with IBM, AT&T, Microsoft, the U.S. Chamber of Commerce, and Chase Manhattan Bank" (Palvia, 1997, p.3). Virtual private networks (extranets) and EDI are the primary services of Unibex. Through its services, Unibex is clearly forming a global e-commerce platform where inter-operations among multi-vendor systems can take place.

Some other examples of business-to-business e-commerce are Dell Computers (www.dell.com) and Be Free (*www.befree.com*). Dell Computer serves over 5,000 large U.S. companies with its Premier Page Program. Each customer's 'Page', which is often linked to the customer's intranet, enables approved employees to configure PCs, pay for them, and track their delivery status online. Premier pages also provide access to technical support and Dell sales reps. Premier Pages of customers that lease PCs from Dell link all the people who need to keep track of leased PCs, and regularly generate lease-management reports. The Pages also tell buyers which Dell models will be discontinued and which will be introduced over the next year (Brown, 1999). Be Free *(www.befree.com)* is an example of an on-line affiliate network technology services provider that receives a royalty payment when a customer hot links from its site to one of its affiliate members like the bookseller, barnesandnoble.com and makes a purchase. Be Free employs collaborative filtering, provides the capability for creating the bookseller's presence on those other sites and also handles the royalties bookkeeping.

One area of growing business-to-business e-commerce is in procurement. Enterprise Resource Planning (ERP) systems of suppliers and buyers are linked via intranets and extranets, enabling every step between the two ends of a transaction to be automated (see Figure 2). Buyers select items from electronic catalogs that are updated by pre-approved suppliers. Purchase requests, approvals, order issues and acknowledgments, tracking shipments, invoicing, and matching invoices to purchase orders all occur electronically (Krapf, 1999). Electronic (E) procurement streamlines the traditional buying process through extensive use of catalog management techniques such as content aggregation, custom catalog, proactive compilation, contingency plans, and cooperative Open Buying Over the Internet (OBI), resulting in cost savings, responsiveness and more strategic supplier relationships.

Forrester Research groups the new business intermediaries under three classes: aggregators, auctions, and exchanges. To enable buyers and suppliers to communicate seamlessly and without a lot of costly infrastructure duplication, a number of companies offer *e-commerce portal* Web sites—also known as *on-line trading communities* (created by aggregators like Chemdex for the geographically dispersed buyer community of research scientists) and *transactive content intermediaries*. Suppliers register their content with the portal, and then any buyer can access that information through the portal. One of these portal providers, www.ariba.com, manages participating suppliers' catalogs, ensuring that they meet buyers' functional demands. Ariba Inc. (www.ariba.com) also offers, for a fee, "value-

Figure 2. An Electronic Procurement System
Source: Krapf, E. (1999). Can Business Find Common Ground for E-commerce? Business Communications Review, *April, pp. 43-46.*

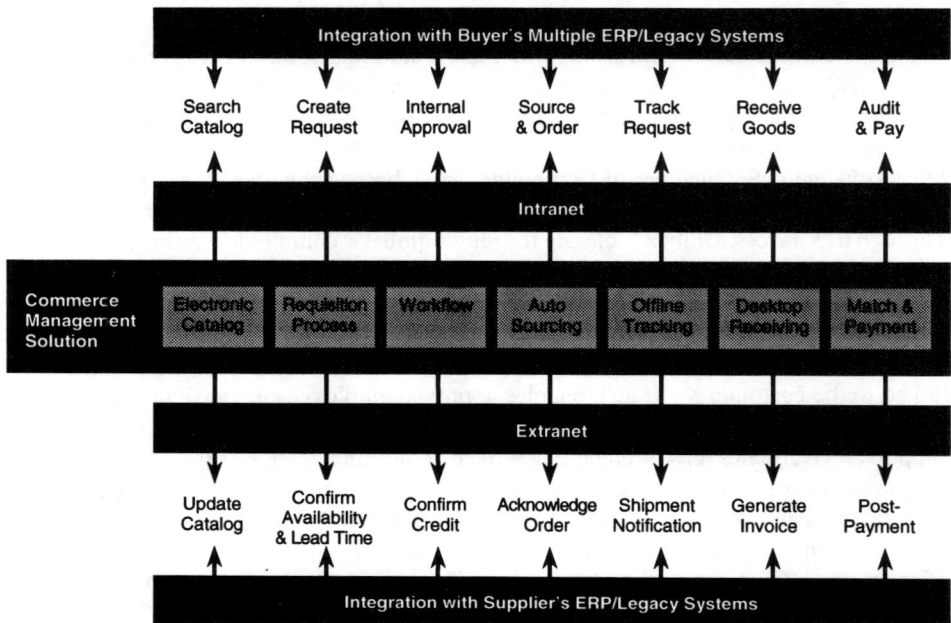

added services" such as translating among EDI and (Internet protocol) IP-related standards such as XML (extensible markup language) (Vigoroso, 1999). Multiple, real time auctions pit buyers against each other to purchase seller surplus–without accruing physical-world search and travel costs. Online exchanges create stable online trading markets that are less expensive to operate than the "brick and mortar" model of the physical world and provide businesses with a trading venue defined by clear rules, industry-wide pricing, and open market information (*http://www.forrester.com; http://www.ecommerce.gov/ ede/ chapter1.html*).

Within a Business Electronic Commerce

Within a business, electronic commerce is basically *e-commerce* within the different subsidiaries or units of an organization using an intranet. This enhances the ability of headquarters to communicate with their subsidiaries and vice versa, and facilitates the sharing of information (e.g., employee manual /medical benefits information) by making it easier, quicker, and hence in greater volume. The intranet also enables headquarters to better coordinate their activities and operations around the world. According to the research organization Ovum Limited, business users around the world will grow from nearly 53 million in 1999 to 180 million by 2004.

Within-a-business e-commerce has contributed to the popularity of intranets at organizations such as Ford Motor Company, Harvard Business School, Morgan Stanley, Tandy Corporation, and many others. For example, Ford Motor Company has a half-million product design resources, production management tools, and strategic information assets residing on its massive intranet. Ford's CIO considers it the backbone of Ford's business today, even more important than the company's mainframe infrastructure (Brown, 1999). The next section discusses the stages of e-commerce evolution followed by the opportunities and challenges presented by e-commerce from a global perspective.

THE STAGES OF E-COMMERCE 'E'VOLUTION

From an ontological perspective at the meta level, e-commerce may have a greater impact on exchanging information and optimizing existing business processes than on generating funds flow. This impact is illustrated by Arthur D. Little's Michael Taylor, who describes the four stages of EC as follows (Varney and McCarthy, 1996):

Stage 1: Companies digitize internal data. It is a publishing model without a significant impact on business processes.

Stage 2: Companies start thinking about reengineering a part of their business process. Integration with back-end systems begins; "flow-through" is the goal, with a hands-off approach to particular processes.

Stage 3: Companies move into original content, which may be highly interactive. With the goal of one-to-one marketing, a company seeks to develop profiles of users accessing its sites so they can be treated uniquely.

Stage 4: Companies that are fully enabled seek to achieve dynamic segmentation, in addition to developing basic user profiles. Specifically, segmentation of site visitors is done in real time, based on user activity. For example, Infoseek targeting ads on its Web search engine to users' interests based on their search tendencies by keeping track of every search made by the user. The Internet's ability to function as a micromarketing channel is also used by other sites that use customizing software to track user behavior and predict future user interests in order to boost sales of goods and services online.

OPPORTUNITIES FOR GLOBAL ENTERPRISES

E-commerce acts as a catalyst for many opportunities which include a radical adaptation of the basic business model, such as the one that a Malaysian company, BizTone.com, is experimenting with in its third year of operation to compete with its rivals. In addition to licensing its enterprise software, BizTone is offering it free to corporate customers and then charging them between 1 cent and 10 cents for each electronic transaction they conduct with the software (Green, 1999).

Customer-Centric Interaction

The Web offers unparalleled opportunities for customer-centric interaction, from data-mining behavioral information to using 'infomediaries', incentives, and loyalty programs to provide mass customization in a "high tech-high touch" approach. According to a recent study of 250 Fortune 500 Web sites by Palmer and Griffith (1998), marketing activities and strategies of corporations have been greatly affected by the Internet. The Internet has created a new marketing environment and a new distribution channel that enable organizations to establish a closer relationship with their customers. For instance, MicroAge Inc., the personal computer distributor, earns customer loyalty by offering customers information on rival distributors' inventory when it is unable to fulfill an order due to being out of stock. Traditionally, there were certain physical constraints placed on commerce, between a customer and the company. However, the Web creates a virtual environment in which customers and companies, buyers and sellers are directly connected.

One-to-One Marketing

Certainly, the Web is changing the business environment and is providing various opportunities for businesses, especially from the marketing perspective. Most importantly, the Internet presents a rare opportunity for companies to create one-to-one relationships with their customers. Personalizing and customizing the Web site are clearly the trends in today's business world. With advancements in technology, businesses gather not only enough but also accurate information about customers' preferences, tastes, and interests (Bakos, 1998).

Neural networks and collaborative filtering are two of the newer systems used by companies to achieve one-to-one relationships with their customers. Neural networks, which are based on mathematical vectors and designed to mimic the human brain, represent the hyperlinks clicked upon by the customer when they visit a Web site, as vectors. As a result, a neural network constantly updates itself with the customer profiles. However, the caveat is that the use of neural networks can sometimes be misleading, since a customer might purchase a product/service and/or obtain information about it only once (http://www.techweb.com/ se/directlink.cgi?INW19981102S0060.htm).

Conversely, collaborative filtering is used for predicting the future behavior of customers by studying the past behavior of customers. Collaborative filtering is based on the assumption that a customer who purchased a certain product will buy the same or similar product in the future. Corporations compare detailed questionnaires completed by customers with their travel patterns and behavior when visiting the Web site in order to predict customers' interests and tastes. However, while companies try to collect the maximum amount of information about their customers, customers can be reluctant to provide information [http://www.techweb.com/ se/directlink.cgi?INW19981102S0060.htm]. This is mainly due to the privacy issue, which will be discussed in the 'Challenges for Global Enterprises' section.

Some examples of companies that employ one-to-one marketing strategy are:
- Federal Express, which lets customers track their shipment online, and even print shipping labels from their Web browser;
- Kraft, which provides cooking recipes via e-mail, along with a shopping list for each recipe;
- NextCard, which lets its customers apply for credit cards and get statements online, and design their own cards with images of family members or celebrities;
- Amazon.com, which makes buying recommendations to customers based on data it has collected discreetly during previous visits, and gives customers the opportunity to read book reviews and, sometimes, even the first chapter of the book.

As the Internet continues to expand explosively, more and more global enterprises will not only realize the importance and opportunities presented by the Web but also practice one-to-one marketing in order to gain competitive advantage.

Communication

Communication is a vital element of successful marketing, and the Internet allows companies to easily reach millions of customers around the world at a very low cost (Rao, Salam, and DosSantos, 1998). Companies can gain significant advantage by utilizing the Web for communication purposes. The information intensity of the product/service is a key element. Highly information-intensive products and services require a higher frequency of contact with customers to achieve effective communication. "The more information-intense the product, the more likely the Web site will utilize promotional activities to stimulate repeat consumer patronage of the site" (Palmer and Griffith, 1998, p. 47). Content management has become a key component for developing a sustainable e-commerce strategy, but properly managed Internet/Intranet data can serve as a valuable "content warehouse" for advanced business intelligence. The integrated information from the sales, marketing, billing, customer service and other departmental databases could also provide a 360-degree database view of all the customers which can help streamline marketing efforts, increase sales, improve internal procedures and serve customers more effectively. Memory-resident databases can help support extraordinary traffic demands like on-the-fly personalization and real-time trading.

Product/Service Support

Palmer and Griffith (1998) state that " the Web is one avenue organizations can use to provide consumers the opportunity to examine or test their products or services and receive technical support" (p. 46). The amount and content of information on Web sites greatly depends on the information intensity of the product/service of the company. For instance, low information-intensive products/services such as cigarettes, food, and utilities can be sold on-line without providing much information for customers, since customers are already aware of these products. Thus, the Web content does not require extensive information or hyperlinks to related information on these products. On the other hand, customers like to have as much information as they can for high information-intensive products/services such as cars and insurance policies. Hence, Web sites of companies providing such products/services should include internal links and hyperlinks to all kinds of related information. For instance, Aon Corporation offers not only its traditional insurance but also a Web-based service that matches recent changes in government regulations with information in its database on each of its clients' operations. The service helps clients better assess and manage their insurance costs, and has generated $25 million for Aon Corp. from new customers in 300 companies (Green, 1999).

Information Value Chain

The Web provides an excellent means of supporting intense value chains though providing sales/marketing, service, and delivery activities. The Internet is a catalyst of pivotal change by facilitating virtual partnership in a much more cost-effective manner than EDI systems, where the cost to install and operate restricted the companies to connect with no more than 20% of its trading partners. Revolutionary concepts for personalized products such as the "five-day car" pioneered by Toyota and other Japanese carmakers in the early 1990s, have become viable with the customer at the center of the entire business universe. Many organizations are investing their resources to stake their claim on the Web as an extension of their current business operations (Bakos, 1998). For instance, since 1995, MicroAge started transforming itself into a service company after realizing that the Internet makes it easier for resellers to bypass distributors. It did so by helping corporations with installation and training.

Web sites provide not only a direct contact between the organization and its customers but also present an opportunity for innovation in both the delivery and selling of products. One factor determining whether the organization will use its Web site for the electronic delivery of its products may be the firm's preexisting distribution structure and channel relationships. "Some innovative organizations are attempting to provide customers greater value by using this technology within their value chain" (Palmer and Griffith, 1998, p.47).

Electronic Payment Systems

Of the 63 billion checks written each year in the U.S., approximately 40 percent originate from a corporate disbursement account, according to Cybercash, a Web based firm specializing in electronic billing. The annual dollar figure for business-to-business transactions, as estimated by Forrester Research will top $1.3 trillion by the year 2003. "The growth of international interconnected computer networks and the pervasive trend in commerce of using these networks as a new field for business operations is stimulating demand for new payment methods" (Panurach, 1996, p. 45). Internet billing promises lower costs and improved cash management benefits to both buyers and sellers. Electronic fund transfer (EFT), electronic checking, and credit or debit cards are some of the electronic payment methods.

Electronic fund transfer is the generic and most widely used electronic payment method. Some examples of electronic fund transfer are paying university tuition fees through ATM, paying utility bills from a bank account, and sending/transferring money overseas. Electronic checking occurs when the buyer begins a transaction with the seller and the seller demands payment by obtaining the unique certification of payment and then provides it to the intermediary/"infomediary" (the buyer's bank). Credit and debit cards are widely used by customers on a daily basis.

Compared to the traditional methods of payment, electronic payment methods offer several advantages. First, there is no clearing period for the transactions to be finished. This allows "large cost reductions and more opportunities in cases of large-sum arbitration" (Panurach, 1996, p. 47). Moreover, corporations can save time since checks no longer have to be cashed and purchased at bank branches. Second, costs for paper handling can be reduced considerably. Third, companies receive cash immediately after the transaction is completed. Therefore, there is no possibility for bounced checks. Finally, companies can eliminate most of the accounts receivable from customers, and thus reduce losses incurred by selling unpaid accounts receivable to a factor.

CHALLENGES FOR GLOBAL ENTERPRISES

E-commerce is analogous to the market in China for companies based outside China that are doing business in China. This is because the market potential is significant even though the short-term profits for most companies (with the exception of a few like Cisco Systems and Dell Computers) are negligible or nonexistent. To realize the opportunities of the age of e-commerce to the full extent, global enterprises need to have the capability to constantly and rapidly assimilate the lessons from the best practices of companies that 'compete on Internet time.' Companies spend an average of $750,000 just for the baseline technology, according to a Gartner Group survey of 100 commerce sites (www.informationweek.com, December 1998), and the annual cost of a major licensing contract on a high traffic portal costs eight figures in U.S. dollars. Thus, to separate fact from fiction, a full scale e-commerce effort that is effective, scalable, and successful is a rather expensive proposition. Leaving cost considerations aside, however, some of the primary challenges of e-commerce are adjusting to the competition in electronic markets, e-engineering distribution channels (i.e., revamping logistics/operations for the Internet era), addressing the security and privacy issues on the Internet, and applying strategic management to corporate alliance systems. These challenges have a profound impact on businesses in a variety of industries such as banking, education, insurance, pharmaceuticals, professional services, and retail, among others, where the routine way of doing business is about to be "fossilized" by the Web.

Adjusting to the Competition In Electronic Markets

Internet access through foreign domains is beginning to approach nearly half of all Web traffic, according to StatMarket, an Internet research firm. International orders have presented challenges in terms of order entry, as street address formats are different across borders. While some U.S. retail sites like the clothing cataloguer Lands' End ships to 185 different countries, its competitor, J. Crew, does not transact business outside U.S. borders via the Internet. One estimate indicates that the amount of non-English language material available on the Web is growing so quickly that by 2003 more than half the content will be in a language other than English, up from 20 percent today (Helm, 1999). In addition, improvements in translation services (by people and machines) and browsers that recognize characters of different languages will greatly expand the amount of content usable by worldwide Internet users (*www.ecommerce.gov/ede/chapter1.html*).

Although in theory anyone can enter any market in e-commerce, leveraging it is quite a challenge. Brand power, trust and consumer confidence built through order fulfillment and customer service contribute to credibility in cyberspace. On the one hand, one of the characteristics of the world of e-commerce is that it eliminates the stability of pricing (Palvia, Palvia, and Roche, 1996; Palvia, 1997). "Electronic marketplaces lower the buyer's cost to obtain information about the price and product features of seller offerings as well as the sellers' cost to communicate information about their prices and product characteristics" (Bakos, 1998, p. 39).

The low margins on products mean that the way to make money is not through the sale of the objects themselves, but in the remarketing of intangibles such as customer information or by selling advertising.

On the other hand, the reduction of "maverick buying" from unauthorized suppliers is a goal of Web-based procurement initiatives at Chevron, Bristol-Myers, Squibb, Ford, General Electric (GE), and other companies. For instance, by pooling purchases over the Web, GE divisions get the price reductions from suppliers of up to 20% on more than $1 billion worth of goods purchased online (Hof, 1999). As markets grow and expand, competition will increase enormously and be more intense (Palvia, Palvia, and Roche, 1996; Barua, Ravindran, and Whinston, 1997). Even niche categories, such as battery retailing, now have multiple venture-backed startups. Global enterprises such as Duracell must be able to quickly find out about changing prices and be ready to respond to any aggressive moves of competitors, especially cut-price suppliers. Under all circumstances, the quality of service and support, as well as competitiveness of the global enterprise should be the same across all the markets that it operates.

From Re-Engineering to E-Engineering Distribution Channels

The emergence of e-commerce has greatly impacted the traditional distribution channels of global enterprises and given rise to the second-generation buzzword "reintermediation." For example, General Motors' BuyPower Web site lets customers configure and order cars online, but the sale is directed to a dealer in the customer's area. Complex, multi-enterprise applications such as supply chain management, which represent more than just "access" to another company's inventory data or getting the shipment status from a carrier, have been enabled by e-commerce. Companies can present their customers greater value by using the Internet to create a high-velocity enterprise within their value chain to reduce cycle times, increase sales and improve operational efficiencies. For example, FedEx and 3Com are early adopters of the "zero-latency" information strategy, which lets them act quickly on new information to outflank their competition. By selling online, companies are reaching their customers directly but are establishing competing channels, which may disrupt existing relationships with their channel partners (Palmer, and Griffith, 1998). The impact of e-commerce on distribution channels might create great opportunities in some industries but present severe threats in others. For instance, the emergence of community logistics systems, logistics intermediaries, and shared service offerings will enable higher velocity, more dynamic logistics processes at lower costs, but creates a challenge in terms of inventory monitoring and optimization across the supply chain.

Most industries with a fragmentation of numerous suppliers have seen the rise of industry- specific Web intermediaries such as Chemdex for chemicals, MetalSite for steel, pcOrder.com for computers, PlasticsNet for plastics, National Transportation Exchange for trucking spot market, GoFish for seafood exchange and Instill Corp. for food services. Many Web intermediaries claim allegiance to buyers rather than products by charging a smaller transaction fee and passing the savings on to buyers. Hof (1999) suggests that the "caveat emptor" (i.e., let the buyer beware) byword of traditional commerce should be "caveat venditor" (i.e, let the vendor beware) in e-commerce.

Even in commodity industries such as gas and electricity, differentiation in the e-commerce marketspace (as opposed to the marketplace)—such as allowing the buyer to customize their bill online and providing other value-added features such as electronic bill payment/ automatic bank withdrawal with summary/detail/exception statements—is critical. Even though marketing to a "segment of one" has long been the goal of database marketing, data mining and telemarketing; the issues of customer acquisition, customization and personalization pose a considerable challenge in the virtual "marketspace," where branding and mass marketing are more important than ever.

Security Issues on the Internet

The main security issues on the Internet include eavesdropping, password "sniffing," data modification, spoofing, and repudiation (Bhimani, 1996). Eavesdropping is a way of illegally entering into a network to steal credit card numbers and customer account numbers. Furthermore, it can be used to obtain information on customers and suppliers. Password "sniffing" is a successful attempt to gain access to a system and steal information that is very significant to the company such as marketing strategy or legal issues outstanding. Data modification is mostly used to change the payee on an electronic check or alter the amount being transferred to a bank account. Spoofing is creating an unreal company (e.g., a company on the Internet) and collecting money for fraudulent transactions. Another example of spoofing can be establishing a financial clearinghouse and collecting payment from buyers or fees from sellers. Repudiation is not an illegal activity, but is rather caused by inability of one party to perform the required activity. For example, a company sends an electronic check to its supplier but the supplier's bank is unable to verify the electronic check's authenticity.

In order to reduce these sensitive security issues to a minimal level, global enterprises need to meet certain requirements in their databases. Basic security requirements are confidentiality, authentication, data integrity, and non-repudiation. Confidentiality is the inseparable part of user privacy. Any transaction between two parties should be confidential and performed through encryption. Authentication allows trading partners to feel secure and comfortable, since the transactions are completed not only through digital signatures but also are certificated. Data sent between parties should be free of modification and attack by outsiders. Finally, both parties should perform the transaction in an authentic and safe environment.

User Privacy Issues On The Internet

As previously mentioned, one of the greatest opportunities that the Internet has provided for global enterprises is one-to-one marketing that results in personalization and customization. However, personalization and customization interfere with the privacy of customers. For instance, the Web site owners of GeoCities were accused by the U.S. Federal Trade Commission (FTC) in summer 1998 of selling members' personal information to outside marketers. However, the U.S. FTC is not yet recommending legislation to force Internet sites to implement and follow privacy policies, even though they acknowledge that more should be done to protect privacy of online users, including children. The onus is on industry self-regulation while the FTC intends to continue monitoring the online industry (*http://www.infoworld.com/scoop/ scx?990714nw3, July 14, 1999*).

According to Alper Caglayan, the president of an agent software vendor named Open Sesame Inc., "the privacy issue is a cost-to-benefit formula. Consumers are asking, 'What are you going to give me in exchange for my information?' And the industry's answer to date has been pretty myopic: better-targeted ads. Consumers don't see much benefit in that trade-off" (Wilder, Caldwell, and Dalton, 1998). Indeed, the invasion of their privacy is the main concern for customers. However, companies cannot boost sales without knowing personal information such as tastes, preferences and interests of customers.

Due to the sensitivity of the privacy issue, companies have been trying to find other ways to track customers' tastes, interests, and preferences. One high-tech company, Firefly Inc., has assisted companies in obtaining information on customers without invading their privacy. Their product was based on collaborative filtering technology. Currently, BarnesandNoble.com uses the beta version of this product. According to Firefly Inc., this product "overcomes many privacy fears by using customers' preferences to group them with other customers who like similar books rather than using their preferences to produce customized marketing pitches" (Wilder, Caldwell, and Dalton, 1998). Furthermore, Firefly's product allows customers to read book reviews written by similar customers or to chat with them. Customers also have an option to receive an e-mail notification of new releases by their favorite writers or their preferred subject. A newer community called CyberSites takes this "commerce plus compassion" approach a step further in order to build a global community and partners with the customer by allowing them to edit their profiles to accommodate shifting tastes, tactfully surveying them before exposing them to ads, and negotiating group discounts on products sold onsite (Gross, 1999).

Applying Strategic Management to Corporate Alliance Systems

Since the mid-1980s, there is an increasing trend in the formation of international corporate alliances (ICAs) (Ostry, 1998). In the age of electronic commerce, these global alliances are actually a response to the increased competition based on innovation. These alliances enable global enterprises to share R&D cost and information systems knowledge as well as strategic management and marketing. By using information technology, global enterprises can better coordinate production networks, which leads to a more flexible and responsive networked global enterprises. "The task of management will become much more similar to diplomacy between sovereigns, but instead of nation states, the player will be parts of virtual enterprises" (Palvia, Palvia, and Roche, 1996, p. 438).

Best Practices in E-Commerce and Implications for Management

The best practices in e-commerce reflect opportunities presented to companies such as first mover competitive advantage of integrating their electronic commerce outreach to new and existing customers. The best practices also help companies overcome the challenges of aligning their internal business processes with those of their suppliers, customers, and strategic trading partners in a seamless manner. The research and practice of information systems/e-commerce often assume that 'best practice' in the application of new technologies is transferable across organizational and national boundaries and expected to lead organizations to adopt new and more effective structures and practices according to 'global' standards. Yet, research has shown that managers often improvise in ways which are meaningful in their context. In practice the reality, according to the IT research firm, Gartner Group's, Bill Roser, is that most companies devote 85 percent of their IT budget to utility functions, 12 percent to productivity enhancement, and just three percent to cutting-edge efforts to gain competitive advantage.

Customers now drive information into the entire length of the supply chain. The actions that occur back in the supply chain, like moving a finished good to the shipping dock, now drive back office activities like billing and payment. These networked, software-driven processes replace the expensive, inefficient paper shuffling of invoices and work orders. As cost gets driven out of these transactions, an organization's back office could be anywhere, even in another organization.

In the digital economy, the Internet is the "front office." Opening it to back office functions is like opening the floodgates. If the two aren't seamlessly connected with interwoven processes, the new demands can create a burden to any company. As much as the lines are blurring between front and back, what's important is that the handoff is done so that the back office can respond to Web-driven front office activity. This is especially hard for traditional companies that put up a Web facade but still handle the process internally the old-fashioned way.

The irony of the Internet is that it is a marketplace with low barriers to new entrants but only if you get there first. According to Forrester Research, the six industries that are feeling the impact of the Internet the most are computing and electronics, telecommunications, financial services, retailing, energy, and travel. There are numerous companies in the the United States and outside United States that have been greatly benefiting from e-commerce. This section briefly provides some examples of companies that have successfully overcome the challenges and adopted their business operations to the age of electronic commerce.

Borders Group, Inc. uses digital technology to augment their existing supply channels by installing Sprout, Inc.'s digital print-on-demand technology in its distribution center which services both Borders.com and Borders stores. This new technology, which Sprout is also marketing to other book retailers and publishers, provides the ability to produce single copies of bound paperback books, not only in distribution centers, but also at in-store production facilities after the book has been sold to the end consumer. This just-in-time production "reduces the cost of storing and shipping books for publishers and retailers, lowers the threshold for keeping slow-moving titles in print, increases the in-store exposure of titles not already on the shelf, and eliminates the risk of returns " (*www.BordersGroupInc.com*).

In the financial services industry, which is one of the fastest growing industries on the Web, Charles Schwab and Co. states that its active on-line accounts were 617,000 in 1996, 1.2 million in 1997 and 1.9 million on July 31, 1998. Its assets have increased by a total of $90 billion from $42 billion to $132 billion since 1996 (*http://www.internetwk.com/trans/tr1e.htm*). Seventy-three percent of Cisco Systems' customer orders are taken over the Internet. Cisco Systems' (with 18,000 employees and annual sales of $10 billion) CFO Larry Carter can call up his company's revenues, margins, orders, discounts given on those orders, and top ten customers—all for the previous day. Financial data that once took weeks to gather and verify are now collected automatically as part of doing business. This makes for a company that reacts more quickly to market shifts and competitive threats. The use of the Internet by Cisco employees to file expense/purchase reports, make travel reservations and hiring decisions, has enabled Cisco to shorten the time it needs to close its books at the end of each quarter from the ten days it took in 1995 to two days, and a projected one day at the end of its fiscal year in July, 1999—while cutting spending on finance from 2% of sales to 1%. The top-down transparency allows for a management structure in which people can make decisions quickly—for example, all Cisco employees are free to fly anywhere on earth without prior approval—but can also expect that somebody will be looking over their shoulder (Brown, 1999).

At a managerial level, the widespread use of information systems has resulted in pressing issues with significant economic effects such as the year 2000 and the transition to the common European currency. Moreover, the issues of optimal configuration and metrics of productivity, efficiency and effectiveness of hardware, software, and personnel all require management attention. In the age of electronic commerce, the two major trends that business managers face are: "1) continued transformation in the structure and operations of global business enterprises, and 2) a rapidly growing use of network-intensive business applications" (Palvia, Palvia, and Roche, 1996, p. 424). These changes greatly shape the global economy and commerce and thus have great implications for global enterprise management.

CONCLUSION — THE FUTURE OF E-COMMERCE

The Internet economy represents the world's next growth engine where increased trade and faster diffusion of information lets companies and countries play on a larger field. There is a common theme that runs through almost all e-commerce innovations: it does not change some fundamental rules of business. As the Internet continues to speed the pace of change in the coming years, many aspects of business will be altered and transformed, but the guiding principles of business will always remain. Being successful at e-commerce requires rapid adaptation and excellent timing, i.e., quick and comprehensive realigning of an enterprise's key elements; not just technology but also processes, strategies and people; and delivering it to the customers when they are ready for it. Successful e-commerce players streamline the customer's entire experience: from researching options, to customization, to ordering, from checking order status, to order fulfillment and delivery, through to payment, billing and after-sale customer service, as well as input into new product development.

As a superhighway, the Internet is well-paved and ready to carry lots of traffic. "Along its path, however, are a great number of partially built shopping centers with parking lots and access roads still under construction" (*http://www.internetwk.com/trends/trends100598.htm*). Although the bandwidth is not that much of a problem on the Internet, access to the Internet in most parts of the world as well as the limited number of well-developed commercial destinations on the Internet, do present problems.

E-commerce is poised for radical change. The emerging enterprise e-commerce model may bring some changes that will transform the current model in as sudden and cataclysmic a manner as e-commerce's rise. So how does e-commerce survive the coming shakeup? The solution lies in persistent Internet connections and capitalizing on the expectations that persistent connections enable, i.e., the relationship sell, as well as, reaching untapped customers with innovative projects through community networking (Gillmor et al., 1999).

Himelstein (1999) warns that like objects in the rear view mirror, Internet competitors are closer than they appear, and suggests that the future of e-commerce could be determined by the investments made by venture capitalists in e-commerce. According to the research firm VentureOne Corp., venture capitalists have invested approximately $3.8 billion into some 530 e-commerce businesses since 1995. For example, the current and future investments of venture capital/"angel" firms such as Kleiner Perkins Caufield and Byers that are backing e-business startups to eliminate inefficiencies in a broad spectrum of industries in virtually every sector of the U.S. economy, could serve as a roadmap for where e-commerce is poised to strike next (Himelstein, 1999). Consequently, it can be stated that the Internet is still really in its formative stages and despite its early and dramatic impact on commerce, its final form is yet to be seen. The technology already developed ensures that this dynamism will continue unabated for at least another decade. Although the effect will be revolutionary, the emergence of e-commerce will be 'e'volutionary.

REFERENCES

Adhikari, R. (1998). E-commerce Impact. *Informationweek*, (693), July 27, 77-81.

Applegate, L. M., McFarlan, F. W. and McKenney, J. L. (1996). Corporate Information Systems Management: Text and Cases. Homewood, IL: Richard D. Irwin.

Armstrong, A., and Hagel, III, J. (1996). The Real Value of On-line Communities. *Harvard*

Business Review, 74(3), 134-141.

Bakos, Y. (1998). The Emerging Role of Electronic Marketplaces on the Internet. *Communications of the ACM*, 41(8), 35-42.

Barua, A., Ravindran, S., and Whinston, A. B. (1997). Efficient Selection of Suppliers over the Internet. *Journal of Management Information Systems*, 13(4), 117-137.

Bettis, R. A. and Hitt, M. A. (1995). The New Competitive Landscape. *Strategic Management Journal*, 16, 7-19.

Bhimani, A. (1996). Securing the Commercial Internet. *Communications of the ACM*, 39(6), 29-35.

Brown, E. (1999). The e-Corporation. *Fortune*, May 24, 112-125.

Dalton, G. (1998). Small World. *Informationweek*, (695), August 10, 38-42.

Gillmor, S., Angus, J., and Gallagher, S. (1999). New Model for E-Commerce, *Information Week Labs*, June 28, 65-74.

Green, H. (1999). Throw Out Your Old Business Model, *Business Week*, March 22, EB12-EB13.

Gross, N. (1999). Building Global Communities, *Business Week*, March 22, EB22-EB23.

Helm, L. (1999). "World Wide Web Living Up to Its Name," *Nando Times News*, March 28.

Himelstein, L. (1999). Log On Boss, *Business Week*, March 22, EB26-EB27.

Hof, R. D. (1999). The Buyer Always Wins, *Business Week*, March 22, EB16-EB17.

Kalakota, R. and Whinston, A. 1997. *EC—A Manager's Guide*. Addison-Wesley Longman, Inc.

Kindel, S. (1999). Reassessing E-Commerce. *Executive Edge*, February-March, 32-38.

Krapf, E. (1999, April). Can Business Find Common Ground for Ecommerce? *Business Communications Review*, 43-46.

Mintzberg, H. (1990). The Design School: Reconsidering The Basic Premises Of Strategic Management. *Strategic Management Journal*, (11), 171-195.

Murphy, K. and Feldman, J. (1999). Study: U.S. Net Industry Ranks As World's 18th Largest Economy. *Internet World*, 5(22), 1 and 41.

O Reilly, T. (1996). Publishing Models for Internet Commerce. *Communications of the ACM*, 39(6), 79-86.

Ostry, S. (1998). Technology, Productivity and the Multinational Enterprise. *Journal of International Business Studies*, 29(1), 85-99.

Palmer, J. W., and Griffith, D. A. (1998). An Emerging Model of Web Site Design for Marketing. *Communications of the ACM*, 41(3), 44-51.

Palvia, S. (1997). The Challenges of Using the Exploding Internet for Global Electronic Commerce. *Journal of Global Information Management*, 5(4), 3-5.

Palvia, P.C., Palvia, S.C., and Roche, E.M. (1996). *Global Information Technology and Systems Management*. Nashua: Ivy League Publishing.

Panurach, P. (1996). Money in Electronic Commerce: Digital Cash, Electronic Fund Transfer, and Ecash. *Communications of the ACM*, 39(6), 45-50.

Rao, H. R., Salam, A. F., and DosSantos, B. (1998). Marketing and the Internet. *Communications of the ACM*, 41(3), 32-34.

Tenenbaum, J. M. (1998). WISs and Electronic Commerce. *Communications of the ACM*, 41(7), 89-90.

Varney, S. E. and McCarthy, V. (1996). E-Commerce: Wired for profits. *Datamation*, October, 42(16), 43-50.

Vigoroso, M. (1999). Ariba portal takes next step in e-commerce. *Purchasing Online*. *http://www.manufacturing.net/magazine/purchasing/archives/1999/pur0617.99/062net.htm*, June 19.

Wilder, C., Caldwell, B., and Dalton, G. (1998). Web Incentive. *Information Week*, (690), July 6, 18-20.

Wilder, C., and Dalton, G. (1997). The World Wide Watch. *Information Week*, (652), October 13, 54-59.

Zwass, V. (1999). *Foundations of Information Systems*. Harcourt Brace Publishing Co.

Zwass, V. (1996). Electronic Commerce Framework, editorial preface to the *Journal of Electronic Commerce*, Vol.1, 1-8.

WORLD WIDE WEB REFERENCES

"Electronic Commerce In The Digital Economy," Patricia Buckley, Office of Policy Development, Chapter I in The Emerging Digital Economy II, June 1999 report. (http://www.ecommerce.gov/ede/chapter1.html).

"E-Commerce an 'Online Earthquake' for American Business," Mary Beth Regan, Cox News Service, Computer News Daily, April 14, 1999.(http://www.nua.ie) and "Dell Earnings Rise 45 Percent on 41- percent Revenue Growth: Internet Increasing Company's Competitive Advantage," Dell Computer Corporation press release, May 18, 1999. (http://www.dell.com).

"U.S. Online Business Trade will Soar to $1.3 Trillion by 2003, According to Forrester Research," Forrester Research, press release, December 17, 1998. (http://www.forrester.com).

"Anatomy of New Market Models," Varda Lief, Forrester Research, February 1999. (http://www.forrester.com).

"Borders to Roll Out Sprout's Print-on-Demand Technology in Distribution Center," Borders Group, Inc. pressrelease, June 1, 1999.(http://www.BordersGroupInc.com).

http://www.internetwk.com/trends/trends100598.htm
http://www.internetwk.com/trans/tr1b.htm
http://www.internetwk.com/trans/tr2b.htm
http://www.internetwk.com/trans/tr3b.htm
http://www.internetwk.com/trans/tr2d.htm
http://www.internetwk.com/trans/tr1e.htm
http://www.techweb.com/se/directlink.cgi?INW19980914S0005.htm
http://www.techweb.com/se/directlink.cgi?INW19981102S0060.htm
http://www.techweb.com/se/directlink.cgi?INW19981005S0020.htm
http://www.techweb.com/se/directlink.cgi?INW19981026S0033.htm

Chapter II

Building E-Commerce from the Ground Up: A Study of the Retail Industry

James E. Skibo and David Gordon
University of Dallas

INTRODUCTION

The selling of goods and services on the Internet has evolved from a hypothetical business concept into a thriving, multi-billion dollar industry which has prospects of sustained double-digit growth well into the first decade of the 2000s. This new market channel is estimated to achieve over $108 billion in sales transactions by 2003 (*Business Week*, Sept. 1999). There are various definitions regarding what is meant by "electronic commerce," however for the purposes of this chapter, we will confine our definition of the term to that segment of the retail industry which comprises sales transactions for products and services consummated via the Internet. This is a critical distinction from the far more vast array of literature devoted to companies' use of electronic commerce such as Electronic Data Interchange for the purpose of reducing operating costs by streamlining productivity and efficiency. In short, we will limit our view of e-commerce to the business of selling goods and services via the Internet.

Within this realm of e-commerce, there are several critical issues that arise for companies seeking to open an e-commerce storefront. In this chapter, we will use the actual experiences of one retailer to highlight various approaches to those issues.

The Electronic Field of Dreams

Conventional new store wisdom states that, if you build it, the customers will indeed come to your storefront. This is why the old adage "location, location, location" is all-important for a store. This is also why one store's success will almost always guarantee that a friendly neighboring store will also be built to capitalize on the first store's traffic. And, with traffic, stores typically realize proportional sales volume. Traditional traffic builders are print advertising, radio and television. Further, depending on whether the store is part of a larger chain or not, traffic can be driven to a new store location by in-store advertising at the other locations. The latter does not simply play a shell game with sales, moving sales from one location to the next, rather it helps build sales because word-of-mouth advertising about the presumably more convenient location starts driving new traffic to that location.

The Company

For an example of what works and what does not, we will use the example of the Army and Air Force Exchange's (AAFES) site www.aafes.com. AAFES is better known by its name of PX® or BX®, standing for Post Exchange (PX) and Base Exchange (BX) depending on whether one is on an Army post or Air Force base. A Post or Base Exchange is a full-line retail department store which is situated on a military posts or base. We chose AAFES as an example because, while AAFES is a part of the United States government, its profile is quite similar to that of a broad cross section of retailers such as Dayton-Hudson Corporation's Target chain of discount stores. As an entity of the federal government of the United States, AAFES' financial operations are also open for scrutiny without violating internal confidentiality that one would typically find with a civilian sector retailer. As such, this chapter delves into detail regarding how AAFES chose to inaugurate its e-commerce, how the site is promoted, and how the operation of the site is meeting expectations. In another respect, AAFES represents a closed environment which makes it ideal for our research.

One needs to understand some basics about AAFES in order to understand why AAFES made some of the decisions it did. AAFES is what is called a "non-appropriated instrumentality of the United States government." That translates: The organization is a Federal entity that does not receive tax dollars to operate. Instead, AAFES operates off of its self-generated revenues derived from retail sales made to authorized military customers. Net sales of more than $6.3 billion in AAFES' fiscal year ending January 1999 make AAFES the eighth largest discount store operator in the United States. Retail operations encompass stores in more than 20 countries throughout the world; essentially, wherever there is a presence of United States armed forces.[1] Operations include more than 190 full-line discount department stores; 300 convenience stores; plus a variety of gas stations, electronics stores, and a full-line direct marketing operation. The latter produces a semi-annual catalog which is distributed to more than a half-million customers around the world.

AAFES also has the distinction of being the second largest Burger King® franchisee in the world with more than 170 restaurants in operation. AAFES provides a wide variety of other services including dry cleaning, optical shops, in-store banking, video rental, pizza delivery and operation of more than 170 movie theaters. AAFES is quite literally "The Company Store." A complete listing of all major business units within the organization and the respective sales for the most current fiscal year given in Appendix A.

There is competition. AAFES has competition both within the military retailing community and external competition from retailers who build large discount stores immediately outside the gates of military installations. Within the military resale community, there are two other similar military retailers: Nexcom, which sells to personnel of the United States Navy and the Marine Corps Exchange System which sells to personnel of the United States Marines Corps. Customers from any branch of the military service may shop at any of the military stores.

The Customers

While AAFES' operation is in many ways a mirror image of various civilian-sector retailers and service providers, a key difference is that AAFES' potential customer base is finite. We use the word "potential" because, while customers may be authorized to shop the military resale stores, there is no assurance they actually do so. The customer base is finite because only active duty military, military retirees, and the National Guard and Reserve are authorized to shop at AAFES' facilities and Internet site. This provides a potential customer base of approximately three million adult military sponsors, and 13 million people when spouses and dependents are included. Customers within a specific branch of the military may tend to shop those military stores of the namesake organization; this is, personnel of the Army and of the Air Force tend to shop the AAFES stores, while Navy personnel tend to shop the Navy stores, and Marine Corps personnel tend to shop either Navy or Marine Corps stores. However the choice is the customers' and, regardless of branch of service, the customers may shop any of the physical stores and Internet site. Because of this, there is some vying for the same customers at locations where the resale systems all have stores in close proximity to one another.

With this knowledge of customers, AAFES has strategic advantage in that it possesses information no other retailer has: The names, addresses, and concise demographic data for every potential customer.[2] While this places AAFES in a unique position in its ability to market to its customers, AAFES saw its customer base decrease over the past 10 years due to the downsizing of the United States military. The decline totaled 23% of the active duty military population during the period 1991 through 1995, from 1.2 million to slightly under 1 million by 1999.

While at first this type of knowledge regarding one's customers seems enviable, one must keep in mind that there are no assurances any of these customers will actually choose to shop in either a physical store or the Internet site. There is no "captive audience."

To determine the potential e-commerce customer base, one would tend to make the assumption that both the sponsors and dependents are customers of the physical stores and are, therefore, potential customers of the Internet store. However, the customer base quickly drops to three million when the e-commerce option is considered, because of the requirement to possess a credit card in order to make purchases on the site. Minor dependents (under age 18) can browse the site, but obviously cannot shop the site because of the credit card requirement.

A Need for Growth

AAFES, like its civilian counterparts, is always seeking revenue growth; however, with the downsizing of the military in full swing in the early 1990s, AAFES felt significant pressure to achieve growth. The reasons were fundamental: The organization's reason for existence is to provide economic support to the Morale Welfare and Recreation (MWR) agencies of the military services. While those agencies receive appropriated funds (tax dollars) for some of their support, they rely on AAFES for 70% of their funding. AAFES, after paying expenses, gives all remaining revenues (80%) to the respective MWR funds where it operates. This forms something of a symbiotic relationship in that the MWR depends on AAFES for income and AAFES depends on the MWR as one of its principle reasons to exist.[3] Since there are certain unknowns as to what Congress will appropriate for any given fiscal year, AAFES feels pressure from the MWR to increase dividends. AAFES had to find growth within its declining market or face the possibility of being legislated out of existence.

AAFES knew that many of its potential customers were not necessarily *actual* customers. In fact, significant sectors were not, namely those customers who lived in locations too remote to shop at the traditional stores. From past customer surveys, AAFES knew that customers willing to drive past the competition to get to a PX® or BX® dropped significantly if they were located more than 50 miles from a store. This segment therefore, represented a significant growth opportunity for the organization, if it could be reached.

For this reason, and to stay abreast of evolving retail technologies, AAFES in 1995 made the decision to establish a Web site for the purposes of conducting e-commerce. The Web site's evolution occurred in two phases. The first phase was designed simply to establish "some" presence on the Internet even though it would not have all of the functionality desired. The second phase would provide for comprehensive e-commerce. In 1995, there were many unknowns; however, the AAFES decision to proceed with the first phase was made. AAFES felt that these concerns could be addressed as they arose:

- Would the organization's legacy systems be able to interface with the Internet site?
- What would it take to build site traffic?
- Could high customer service levels be maintained?

The First Step

In 1996, AAFES established its first Web site www.aafes.com. The site was created using in-house talent and available Web site authoring software. The resulting site was informational only, i.e., it was a static site that only contained non-interactive text which described current customer policies such as those for refunds, price guarantees, some store locations and the like. No promotion of the site was attempted other than word-of-mouth within the military community. This was helped somewhat by the organization's decision to have all of the brick-and-mortar stores' point-of-sale registers print the site's URL at the bottom of every sales receipt. There were an average of two million sales transactions a week, therefore this simple step had the result of bringing in an average of slightly less than 10,000 visitors a month. There was no knowledge of how many customers should have been expected to visit the site, nor how they should perceive it once they were there, therefore 10,000 visitors were viewed as a success.

By the end of 1996, the site had added merchandise samplings taken from the organization's printed mail order catalog. There was no ability, however, for customers to purchase the items online; customers could only view items and descriptive data. To make a purchase, they had to print out and fax, or call in, any order. Without the full functionality of an e-commerce site (described below), the site received some orders, but not enough to maintain economic viability. The site lacked the integration to process orders online. This inability severely hampered the site's growth compared to the functionality and growth seen in 1996's emerging sites like Amazon.com and CDNow.com. However, this first step was viewed as only a stop-gap measure to the ultimate functionality of full-scale e-commerce conducted entirely via the site.

The Next Step

The organization was determined to create a viable shopping venue for its customers. In mid-1996, the organization set the imperative that it would build its e-commerce with the ultimate, and very aggressive, goal of offering not only its compete mail order catalog assortment to customers, but also its complete store stock assortment as well. The initial expectations were to make its stock assortment contained in its semi-annual mail order catalog available for customers to shop and order online. That assortment comprised an average of more than 12,000 unique items not excluding sizes and colors. The ultimate goal, putting the typical brick-and-mortar store stock assortment online, would increase the assortment online to more than 55,000 items, exclusive of color and size.

The next issues the organization had to resolve were significant. AAFES had restrictions on who it could market to, who could see its merchandise assortment and sell prices, a legacy system that could not be modernized in time to fully support e-commerce, and no formal organizational structure to handle the overall management of the Internet. Each of these issues is discussed at length because they involve decisions and actions many companies seeking to enter the world of e-commerce may face.

STOCK ASSORTMENT

AAFES' choice was whether to mirror their current mail order catalog stock assortment, or offer only Internet-unique items such as closeouts and one-time-buys. AAFES chose to do *both* using the logic that, in order to gain commerce from customers too remote to shop its stores, it needed to offer as much of the AAFES brick-and-mortar experience as possible, thereby encouraging customer loyalty, frequency and recency.

An early problem was determining which of the 12,000 catalog items to put on the Internet site. The solution was to simply go for what can be called "low-hanging fruit," the most profitable items in the catalog. Fine jewelry with its higher margins was chosen because it ensured that any items ordered and shipped would be profitable regardless of what efforts were necessary to process the order. This was an elementary decision for the organization, however may not be one a single-line retailer may be able to make. It is essential therefore to have a clear grasp of the order processing costs before an assortment is placed on-line. For example, the organization's cost per order, exclusive of shipping charges, is approximately $1.05. Obviously, assortment items with a gross profit of many dollars are not a concern. However, if the gross profit dollars become cents rather than dollars, then those items are not viable in an e-commerce environment. The organization knew that its general mix of items in a typical mail order environment would ensure profitability.

The next challenge was getting the images for the catalog items onto the site. The organization's plan had been to simply use the digital images it already had for the catalog's printed pages for the Web site. While both venues use digital images, the images for the print medium are typically very large; tens of megabytes, sometimes hundreds of megabytes, in size. Images of that size were not suitable for the typical customer's connectivity bandwidth. Further complicating matters was the fact that all of the catalog images on file were formatted in dimensions suitable for a printed page but not for an Internet site. This meant that all Internet images had to be reformatted one-by-one before any could be used.

A similar challenge came from the need for descriptive text. Again the organization had planned to simply take the text descriptions of the printed catalog and use them for the Internet site. The problem that arose from this was that the printed text used in the catalog was somewhat abbreviated since the costs of printing a catalog are considerable compared to costs for Internet site space. This meant that all text descriptions for the items placed on the site would have to be rewritten.

Because of these problems, the organization lagged in its ability to get items onto the site quickly. Although 12,000 items were intended for inclusion on the Web site, only a few thousand could be viewed by 1997. Items available for sale on the site versus the organization's goal are shown in Figure 1.

Figure 1: Items Available to Customers

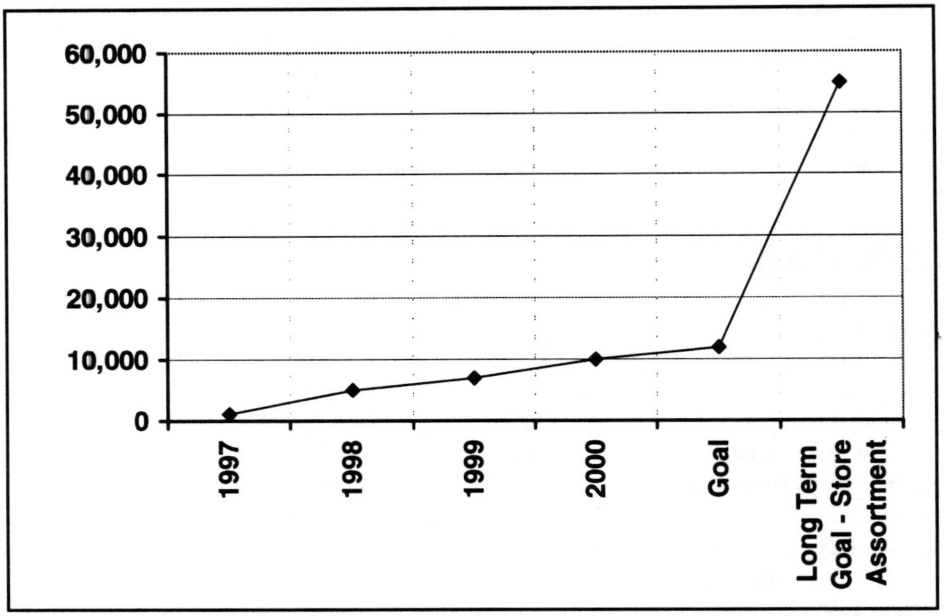

```
60,000 ┤                                              ♦
50,000 ┤
40,000 ┤
30,000 ┤
20,000 ┤
10,000 ┤                              ♦    ♦
       │          ♦    ♦    ♦
    0  ┤    ♦
       └────┴────┴────┴────┴────┴──────────
         1997 1998 1999 2000  Goal  Long Term
                                    Goal - Store
                                    Assortment
```

ORGANIZATIONAL STRUCTURE

From the outset, the organization viewed its Internet site as an adjunct to the direct marketing operation, not as a separate operating entity. This had certain economic advantages in that the existing catalog operation's management and staff could be tasked with much of the duties required to run the site. This was also seen as a way of reducing any internal conflict regarding the use of resources from the direct marketing group to support order processing and telephone inquiries regarding an order's status. Technical support requirements were placed under the organization's MIS department with a scalable budget for necessary hardware and software. The word "scalable" applies in that the budget would rise along with revenues, or clearly "evident" revenues. Every facet of equipment and software acquisition had to have clearly defined ROI or the investment was not made. Figure 2 shows the organizational pattern as of 1997.

As the months passed in 1997 and problems were encountered with both the digital images and descriptive text, the organization added dedicated staff to handle the images and text descriptions[4]. The Internet group was also realigned to report directly to the head of Direct Marketing. This change was made so that the resources needed to support the Internet operation would receive equal footing with the resource needs of the rest of the catalog operations. These changes had the unintended side effect of now making the Internet site a net cost to the organization rather than just an no-cost experiment which is how some naysayers in the organization had tended to view it. The revisions to the organization are shown in Figure 3.

Customer Validation

The need to ensure customers were authorized to shop in a military resale store was

Building E-Commerce from the Ground Up 27

Figure 2: Organizational Chart — Internet Staffing Early 1997

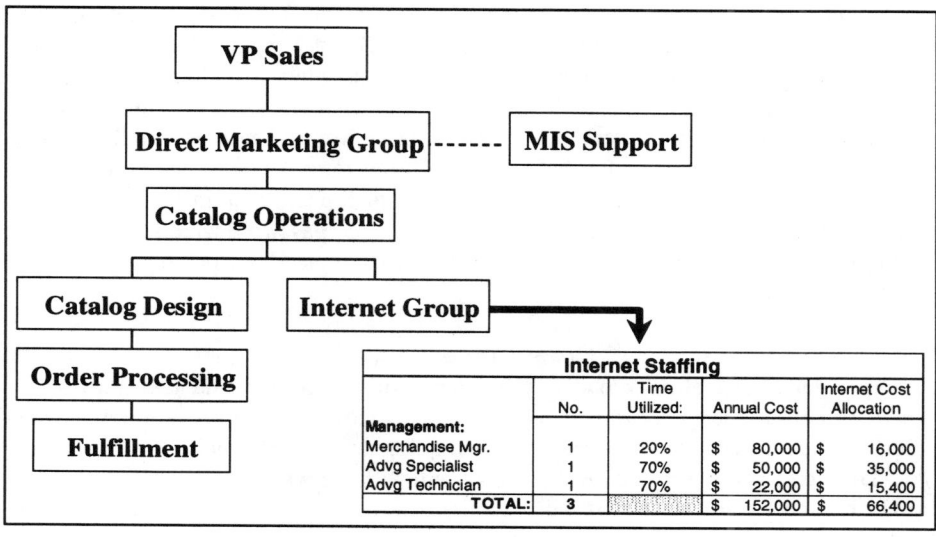

Figure 3: Organization Chart — Internet Staffing Late 1997

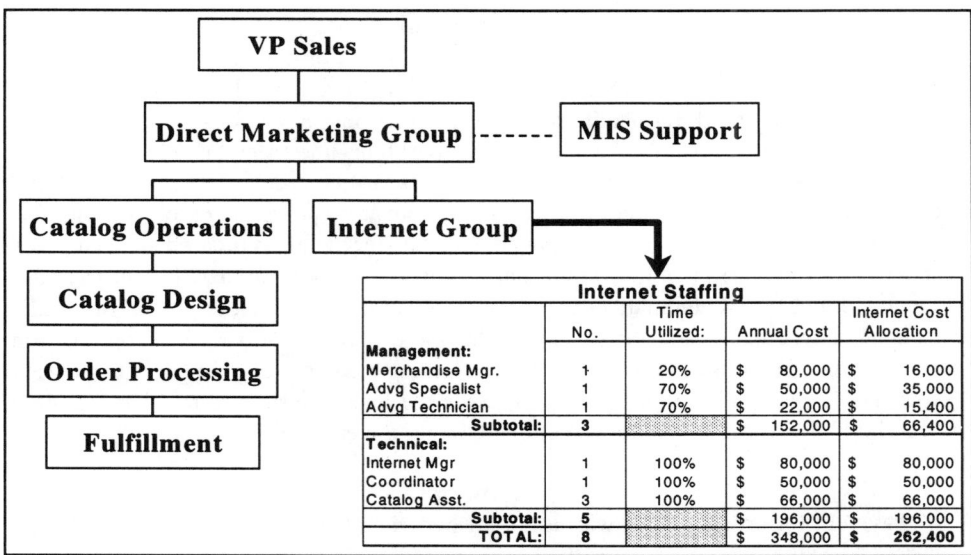

not a new requirement for AAFES; its bricks-and-mortar stores had staff to check customers' ID cards at the entry doors. The challenge to the organization came when it realized it had to devise a way to validate customers in a virtual store that did not have the traditional "front door." This was a unique requirement for the organization. The organization cannot sell its products to anyone other than authorized customers. The question then arose: How could an on-line site limit access? There were several possible solutions. The first would have been to create some form of customer ID and then mail that ID to all of the existing three million possible customers and all new customers who joined the military services. The principle drawbacks to this solution were the expense of the mailings and the administration of the program over time. The second solution, and the one actually utilized, was to use the existing customer data base and validate customers against it. To that end, the main site was made public. However to enter into the mall page, customers were asked to enter their ID which was their Social Security Number, and a password which was their date of birth. The site then validated those entries against the customer database and either provided or denied access.

Order Processing

The organization already had a direct marketing operation and therefore had a complete in-house order processing center in Dallas, Texas. The primary requirement was to interface the on-line order data into the existing legacy system which was done in two stages. The first stage interfaced the on-line system with the warehouse stock availability data. On-line customers were notified if the item was out-of-stock and when expected delivery would occur. Customers were then given the choice of proceeding with the order anyway and having the item shipped when it does become in stock again (putting the item on backorder), or canceling the transaction. As customers placed orders for any given item, the available on-hand quantity was then decreased by the order quantity.

Legacy System

The second stage of order processing required a link of the on-line orders with the legacy system's batch processing. However, the organization's legacy catalog order processing system could not handle real-time transactions. It was designed to be batch updated each evening. Therefore, a representation of all on-line order data had to be placed on a flat file that was built during the business day as on-line orders were placed. The flat file was then brought into the catalog processing system batch processing each evening. The system then created the necessary shipping documents for the items ordered and generated both a written (mailed) and e-mail confirmation message to the customer. This process has the heavy drawback of automatically adding one extra day to the order processing cycle. That is not a desirable characteristic in a world where next-day delivery is an option with most other retailers. It is however, the hazard of linking e-commerce processing to a legacy system. The organization is working to upgrade the legacy system to provide real time processing, however this will not be completed until the early 2000s.

Payment

Payment for orders placed was accomplished via a two-step process. The first step occurred when the customer entered their credit card data. The information was transmitted in real time to the organization's clearing bank and an approval, or declination, was returned. If the transaction amount was approved, the pre-approval code and the order were accepted for processing. If the transaction amount was declined, the customer was offered the choice of reentering the credit card data, entering another credit card's data, or canceling the order.

The second step was processing the charge. This took place during the evening batch processing. The pre-approval code and transaction data were transmitted to the clearing bank for creation of a charge record for that customer's credit card. An inherent flaw in this system was the fact that the credit card was charged at the time of ordering and not at the time of shipment. The latter is the customary business practice. In the case of items shipped relatively quickly, within five days, the charge process was not noticeable to the customers. However, in the case of lengthier times, particularly those associated with some of the drop-ship vendors or for items which are back ordered, the time the charge was processed could become a significant customer irritant. This was an inherent problem with the organization's legacy system and is now under active review at the time this chapter was written.

An additional feature being added in late 1999 is the availability of instant credit. If customers are browsing items within the on-line catalog, and at the time of customer validation it was determined that the customer does not have the organization's private credit card, the customer will be prompted, "Would you like to charge this item on your AAFES credit card?" Similar prompts are also planned if customers enter other than the organization's in-house credit card when completing their order. This is similar to the sales associates in a brick-and-mortar store asking the same questions in order to drive use of the private credit card. The reason for this is that retailers stand to lose merchant fees when transactions are charged on other than their own private credit card or an affinity card.[5]

Fulfillment

Fulfillment takes place at the organization's warehouses in Atlanta, Georgia; Yakota, Japan; and Giessen, Germany. There are also shipments from the many United States locations of the catalog's many drop-shipment vendors. In the case of items stocked in the Atlanta, Yakota and Giessen warehouses, the necessary shipping documents are created on site at each warehouse for same-day processing of the order. For drop-ship vendors, the necessary documentation to process the order is mailed to the respective vendors via overnight delivery. The combination of these methods means that the fastest possible delivery time to a customer would be three days for items stocked in the organization's warehouses and approximately five days for items that are drop-shipped.

RESULTS

By March 1997, the few thousand items were available for purchase on the site and initial orders began to be received. However, the inability to publicly advertise had an effect on the site's growth; there were very limited sales in April and June and none in May. Figure 4 shows the monthly sales volume for the site and complete supporting data for all sales charts is shown in Appendix B.

The effects of adding items throughout the rest of the year and promoting the site within channels available to the organization had a favorable impact on the site's growth for the rest of the year. The fiscal year ended with net sales of $502,665. The downturn seen in January is normal for the brick-and-mortar retail sector and was presumed normal for the Internet site. We show later in this chapter how this assumption was incorrect—the Internet sector does not seem to follow the traditional sales patterns experienced by brick-and-mortar stores.

The number of orders processed and the number of items ordered during this period followed a similar pattern to the dollar sales shown in Figure 5. The increase in the number

Figure 4. Fiscal Year 1997 Monthly Sales

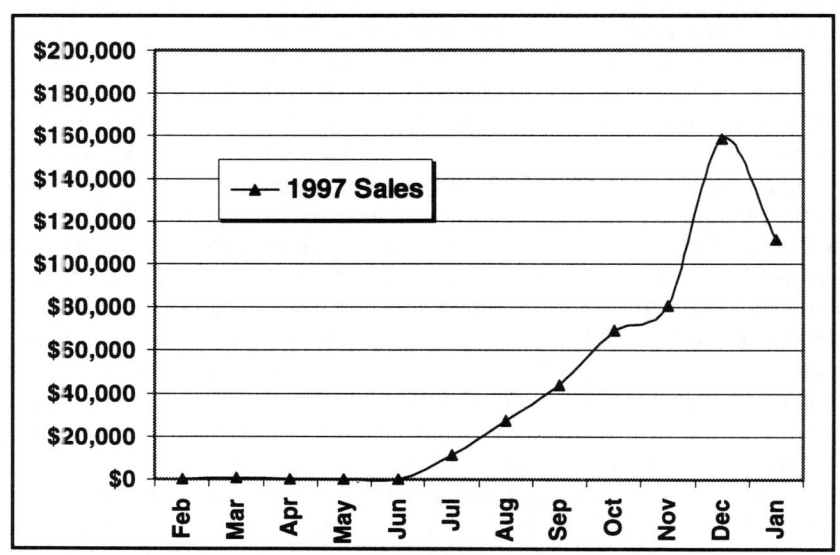

Figure 5: Fiscal 1997 Orders Processed & Number of Items Ordered

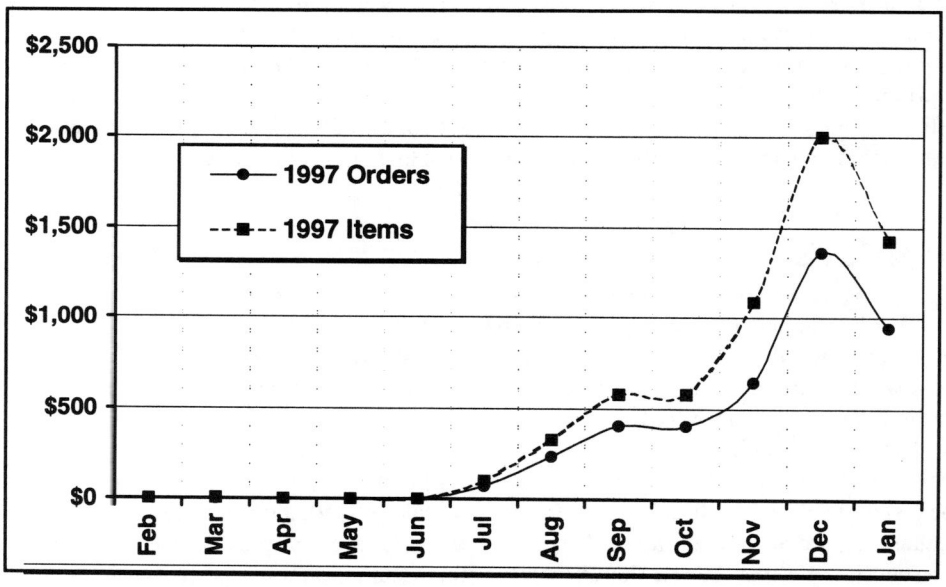

of items ordered versus the number of orders received during the fourth calendar quarter is an indication that the site was being used for holiday orders. The organization's experience is that the norm is multiple items on one order during this period each year since the items tend to be presents for others, rather than the customers making purchases for themselves. This follows the pattern in a traditional direct marketing (printed catalog) business model.

The Promotion Efforts

With sales of a half-million dollars, the Internet site went from zero to approximately 1.5% of the total direct marketing business in less than one year. This piqued more than a casual interest in e-commerce within the organization. By early 1998, the organization was promoting the site heavily in both its weekly sales fliers, its in-store radio broadcasts, and had thousands of store sales associates wearing tee shirts which said in bold letters, "click dot shop at aafes.com". With the promotions came a steady increase in the number of items available on the site. By the end of the organization's 1998 fiscal year, more than six thousand items were available on the site.

Other net-peculiar promotions also attracted attention to the site. The organization created a monthly net sweepstakes that awarded $5,000 in merchandise each month to ten winners. By the end of 1998, this sweepstakes was drawing a steady 20,000 entrants each month. The sweepstakes are funded by both cooperative advertising dollars and merchandise provided by the organization's vendors.

Other promotional efforts included special sales on close-out merchandise that were only available on the Internet site and special discounts for returning loyal customers. Since the organization knows the identity of the customer as soon as they enter their ID, it is possible to provide different merchandise offerings for different people. This especially includes loyal customers from either the brick-and-mortar store, the printed catalog, or the Internet site. AAFES also promoted its site via text links on other Department of Defense sites. Some of the organization's suppliers also chose to include links from their web sites to the organization's site, however this is not something the organization can solicit since

Figure 6: Fiscal Year 1997 & 1998 Sales

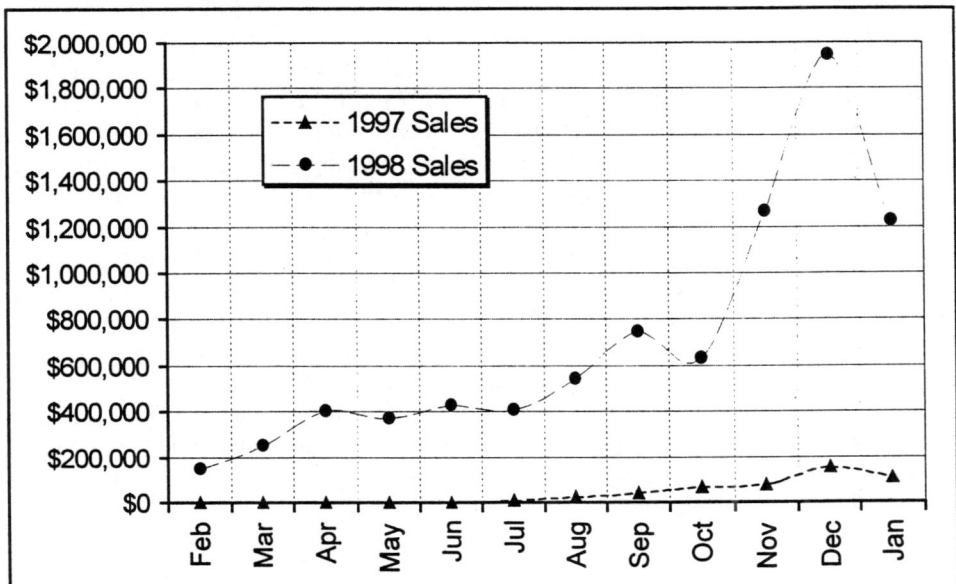

Figure 7: Fiscal Year 1997 & 1998 Orders Processed and Number of Items Ordered

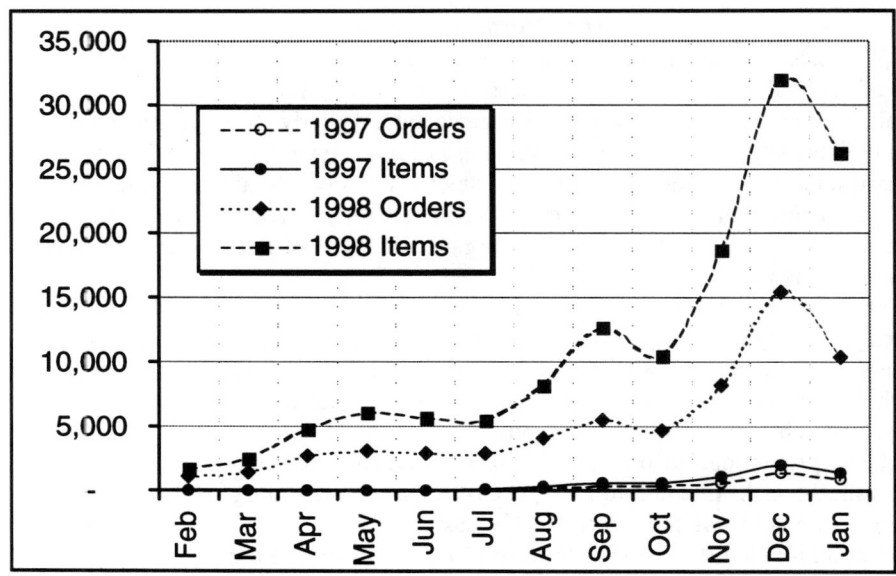

it is a form of advertising external to the controlled channels of the organization.

Combined, the promotional efforts and the increasing stock assortment had a marked effect on sales in the 1998 fiscal year. The normal retail sales pattern has somewhat flat sales throughout the year with some rise in summer to reflect school summer vacation spending and then a rapid rise in the fourth quarter for holiday spending. AAFES' site defied this pattern with continued sales growth throughout the year. This is detailed in Figure 6.

During this period, the number of orders processed as well as the number of items ordered followed the same pattern as the fiscal 1997 results. Interestingly, the number of items being ordered increased as the year progressed. This is thought to be due to the increasing breadth of the stock assortment on the site offering more purchasing opportunities for the customers. Figure 7 compares 1997 to 1998 in terms of orders and items. Again, we see somewhat nontraditional growth during the year. The fourth-quarter results were expected due to the holiday season, however the steady growth throughout the year did not follow a traditional brick-and-mortar store's retail sales pattern. Fiscal year 1998 (ending January 1999) had $8.3 million in sales. Compared to fiscal year 1997, that was almost a 16-fold increase over the prior period. This now meant that the site was generating approximately 25% of the organization's total direct marketing business.

Interestingly, during the same period (February 1998 through January 1999), sales and order volume of the print catalog did not decline in relationship to the growth of the site's e-commerce. In fact, the print catalog's business grew at a rate of 7%, which was well above inflation during the same period.

Figure 8: Fiscal Year 1997-1999 Sales

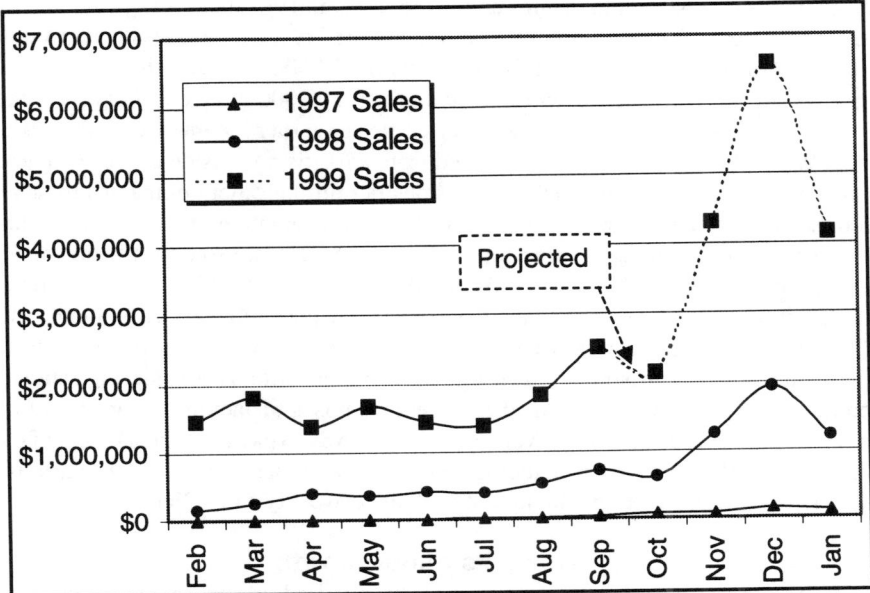

1999 Results

Sales data for the organization's eight months of the 1999 fiscal year discloses the same dramatic sales increases that fiscal year 1998 exhibited over fiscal year 1997. Data for this is illustrated in Figure 8. With this data, it is possible to forecast the remainder of the fiscal year, and net results are expected to be $30.7 million in sales, or a 270% increase over fiscal year 1998. Orders processed have thus far followed a similar pattern compared to prior years and these data are shown in Figure 9.

It is difficult to argue with sales growth of 1,563% one year (1998 versus 1997) and "only" 270% the following year (1999 versus 1998), however, there are some effects the net site is having on other business that the organization started experiencing in early 1999. Sales volume for the printed catalog was ahead of prior years, however it was not following expected growth compared to the same period in prior years. It was thought that perhaps the e-commerce was now beginning to affect the printed catalog's business, although to what degree was not yet known. Data from future operations is needed in order to ascertain what impact the e-commerce is having on traditional sales. There is no evident impact on brick-and-mortar stores' sales by e-commerce at this point. During the first quarter of fiscal 1999, sales in the traditional sectors are 9% above prior year which is above inflation.

Hits, Visitors and Advertising Revenue

No discussion of this site would be complete without commenting on the number of hits and visitors to the site since its inception. While these data tend to follow the sales growth discussed previously, there are always the curious visitors who are potential customers. This site is most unique in that fact, since all visitors to the mall page are indeed authorized customers because they first had to be validated against the organization's customer database before entering the mall page. Other than sales, the most telling argument that the site is successful, is in the hits and visitor data. In 1997, the average number of hits for the site were 10,000 each month with unique visitors averaging less than 1,000 each month. In 1998, the year averaged 2.5 million hits and 50,000 unique visitors a month. Thus far in 1999, the site averaged four million hits and over 100,000 unique visitors every month.

With this visibility came unique opportunities to garner income from advertising on the site. While the organization is prohibited from advertising outside of those advertising channels it controls, it has no such prohibitions permitting other companies to advertise within the controlled portion of its site. In 1999, the organization included banner ads and text links in its corporate advertising rate card. Banner ads were sold for the rate of $5,000 a month, and text links at the rate of $500 a month. It is too early to tell what the total revenues will be from this source, however there have been more takers than space available thus far in 1999. While the organization will not place advertising from competitors, there has been such an interest in advertising on the site that the organization is considering establishing secondary pages within the site for the express purposes of facilitating advertising. The organization sees the advertising revenue stream as a way to pay for all marketing of the site within its channels. That would include the tee shirts mentioned earlier and the various print media the organization has available to it such as its weekly sales fliers.

Thoughts About Growth

When one sees data showing sales gains in the hundreds of percentage points, one must ask the questions like "How long can this continue?" or "What is the place of this business within the organization?" The answers to the latter can be seen by looking at Appendix A. Even with projected sales of over $30 million for fiscal year 1999, the e-commerce business

Figure 9: Orders Processed and Items Ordered

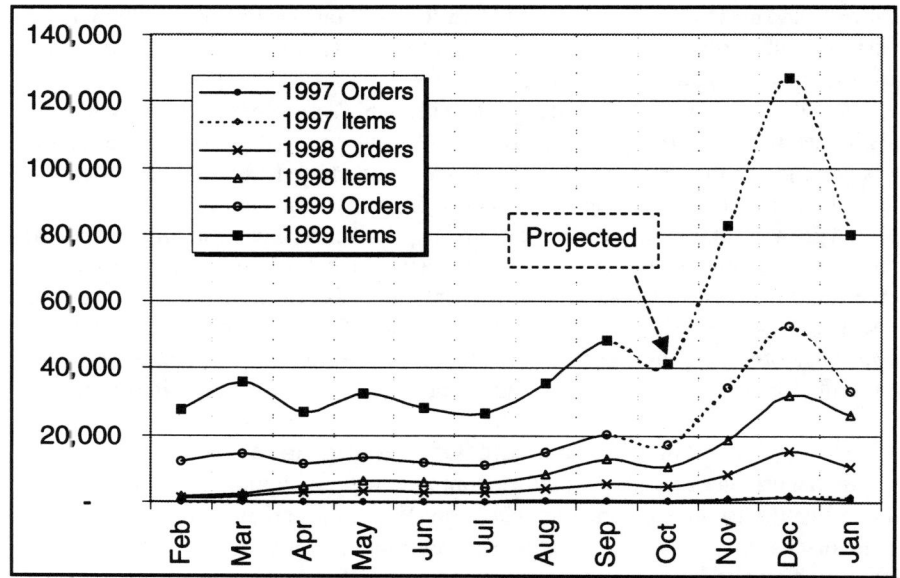

represents only a fraction of the overall business of the organization, less than one-half percent of the total revenue. However, when the total business exceeds six billion dollars, a half percent is not insignificant.

The organization is using a new unit of measure for its e-commerce: store equivalents. The organization's average store has a sales volume of $30 million per annum. With the Internet site's sales data being readily available to the organization's management, managers have started referring to the site as their newest store because the site is projected to achieve almost the same sales volume as one of the brick-and-mortar equivalents. The organization is using conservative sales growth forecasts for the years 2000 through 2001, only 20% per annum growth. Because AAFES is committed to giving its earnings to the MWR, the organization chooses to underestimate future performance and provide the MWR with extraordinary earnings rather than overestimate results and have to revise earnings estimates downward for the MWR contribution. The latter is troublesome to the organization because, in the event of revising earnings downwards, the MWR is then put in a position of not performing all that it has budgeted.

Realistically, how long can this growth continue?[6] For this organization, it is perhaps possible to predict the extent of e-commerce based on the demographics of those customers who do not live close enough to the brick-and-mortar stores to shop. If one establishes a 60-mile driving distance as being the point at which customers will not drive to shop the stores, then one is left with a potential population that is approximately 41% larger than all current active customers. Another limiting factor is PC ownership among this population. Current estimated PC ownership in the military is between 75% and 90%. If we use the lower of the two figures and estimate a market penetration of 10% into those customers living outside a 60-mile radius of brick-and-mortar stores, we derive potential growth demographics that are 3.1% of the current market, or $98.1 million[7].

CONCLUSIONS

There are interesting aspects to this organization's e-commerce and some lessons. With relatively simple methods, the organization was able to promote its site among its customers and, once they were made aware of the site, the customers did come to the site. Unlike this organization's limitations on promoting the site, commercial retailers are unrestricted in their ability to promote their site and may realize similar growth if other factors are also similar. The growth experienced by this organization's site is interesting from the standpoint that, while the initial reaction was slow, certainly the results within the first two years of operation were impressive considering the promotional limitations placed on the organization.

The conclusion one can draw is that the e-commerce is new business. This can be verified when one looks at the demographics of the organization's customers generating the e-commerce. Preliminary results reveal that the majority of e-commerce customers are indeed located more than 30 miles from one of the organization's stores. The data show that the organization has been successful in gaining new customers who are too remotely located to shop the traditional brick-and-mortar stores.

In the section above which discusses growth, we have made some estimates for the future. Based on what we can model for this organization, even with its demographic limitations, we feel that the future growth has great potential to continue to increase. We are not stating, however, that this growth does not come at some cost: chiefly, these customers are shopping *someplace* today, and future growth is going to come from another retailer's revenue.

THE FUTURE

The organization clearly sees the internet site as displacing a major portion of the print catalog business at some point in the future, the only question being "when." With economics of retailing on the Net being superior to those of producing and distributing a mail order catalog, the organization may face a future decision to vacating its position in the mail order business and concentrating resources on its e-commerce business. With a diversity of market segments, there may also be a place for both channels. Any future decision however, will be based on the evaluation of the costs of producing ever-fewer catalogs versus the benefits of sales and customer service gained from those catalogs. Interestingly, the Web site is forecasted to yield one-third of all direct marketing sales by 2000. If the web site's e-commerce erodes the sales of the printed catalog business sufficiently in the immediate out years, then the organization will be facing the decision sooner rather than later.

There are other revenue opportunities that the organization is exploring for the future. One is establishing partnerships in some form with the major automobile manufacturers to lead customers towards financing their cars via the automotive companies' financing divisions and receiving a fee for the referral. This is a novel way to gain income from a commodity the organization cannot sell[8]. Another opportunity is expanding the site to accommodate increased advertising for the purposes of generating revenue.

END NOTES

1 Germany, Belgium, Italy, Kosovo (Yugoslavia), Bosnia, Turkey, United Kingdom, Saudi Arabia, Sinai, Greenland, Puerto Rico, United States Virgin Islands, Panama, Honduras, Columbia, Haiti, Japan, Guam, Okinawa, Korea and Thailand.
2 Demographic data includes Social Security Number, name, complete address data, branch of service, military rank and computed wages, ethnicity, sex, age, birth date, marital status, and any relevant spousal and dependent relationships. We also use the word "potential" because customers may be authorized to shop, but choose not to do so.
3 The MWR activities are appropriated funds and Congress budgets the remainder of funds needs for their operation.
4 Interestingly, the internet site's personnel cost as a percent to total sales is less than 2% even with the additional staff. This compares very favorably with the typical brick-and-mortar store's personnel costs of 9-14% of sales.
5 Affinity cards typically represent .75% to 1% income for the retailer or institution with which they have an association regardless of where the customers use the card.
6 There is no like business model to compare this growth against unless we look at either the Industrial Revolution or seek out similar upheavals in channels of distribution. The closest comparison we find for this type of exponential growth is that of the Industrial Revolution in the nineteenth century, the rapid growth of the industrial capacity of the United States during the period of 1921 and 1925, or industrial production in the United States during World War II, 1941 to 1945. We feel the closer model is that of the 1921

through 1925 period because it was facilitated by similar factors to those we see facilitating e-commerce: The enabling technologies were largely already in place and the periods were ones of great commercial prosperity and growth. Industrial production in the United States increased 53% during 1921-1925 versus wartime industrial growth of 25%. Source: *Wartime Production Achievements and the Reconversion Outlook* (Washington, DC: War Production Board, 1945), 10-13.

7 We have conservatively used the multiplier of 31% times the retail main stores portion of sales, or 31% of $3.2 billion.

8 AAFES may only sell those commodities that the United States Congress approves for resale. Automobile sales in the United States are not one of those commodities.

REFERENCES

Abrahamson, J.(1983). *The American Home Front*. Washington, DC: National Defense University Press.

De Kare-Silver & M. E-Shock (1999). *The Electronic Shopping Revolution: Strategies for Retailers and Manufacturers*. AMACOM, May.

Kalakota, R. (1996). *Frontiers of Electronic Commerce*. Addison-Wesley Pub Co.

Mougayar, W.(1997). *Opening Digital Markets : Battle Plans and Business Strategies for Internet Commerce*. New Jersey: McGraw-Hill; 2nd edition.

Somers, H. M.(1950). *Presidential Agency: The Office of War Mobilization and Reconversion*. Cambridge: Harvard University Press.

Szuprowicz, B. O.(1999). *E-Commerce : Implementing Global Marketing Strategies*. Computer Technology Research Corporation.

Tapscott, D., Lowy, A., & Ticoll, D. (1998). *Blueprint to the Digital Economy: Wealth Creation in the Era of E-Business*. New York: McGraw-Hill.

Vatter, H. G. *The United States Economy in World War II*. New York: Columbia University Press, 1985, 20.

Whinston, A. B., Stahl, D. O. & Choi, S. (1997). *The Economics of Electronic Commerce*. New York: Macmillan Technical Publishing.

Appendix A and B follow on the next pages.

APPENDIX A

Army & Air Force Exchange Service
Fiscal Year 1998 Operations
(February 1998 through January 1999)

RETAIL OPERATIONS	Facilities	Sales
Main Store	197	$ 3,191,396,203
Convenience Store	300	$ 752,945,848
Military Uniform Sales	209	$ 345,909,822
Commissary Sales	210	$ 307,368,064
Limited Assortment Retail Store	182	$ 211,935,746
Wine & Spirits	80	$ 184,437,389
Limited Assortment Store	127	$ 182,772,072
Home And Garden	6	$ 78,207,544
Grocery Store	3	$ 67,910,766
Furniture	27	$ 67,828,071
Four Season	22	$ 62,166,189
Book Store	46	$ 31,268,871
Sports Store	7	$ 16,585,942
Misc. Retail	5	$ 13,608,408
Video Rental	14	$ 7,047,419
Hospital Store	20	$ 6,420,400
Warehouse Sales	105	$ 2,677,545
Sound Centers	1	$ 2,374,614
Sales To Non-AAFES Agencies	123	$ 1,005,842
Subtotal:	1,684	$ 5,533,866,755
DIRECT MARKETING OPERATIONS		
Catalog	1	$ 37,623,789
Internet	1	$ 8,360,842
Subtotal:	2	$ 45,984,631
AUTOMOTIVE OPERATIONS		
Service Station	99	$ 240,225,546
Filling Station	40	$ 42,525,999
Car Care Center	19	$ 31,739,224
Auto Parts Store	69	$ 24,018,600
Misc. Automotive	3	$ 788,441
Subtotal:	230	$ 339,297,810

Army & Air Force Exchange Service
Fiscal Year 1998 Operations
(February 1998 through January 1999)

FOOD OPERATIONS	Facilities	Sales
Burger King	171	$ 184,796,484
Cafeteria	276	$ 59,411,713
Anthony's Pizza	196	$ 55,056,899
Popeye's	43	$ 32,287,416
Robin Hood	109	$ 25,405,928
School Lunch Program	106	$ 12,991,129
Special T's	45	$ 12,683,282
Frank's Franks	113	$ 9,447,996
Snack Stand	83	$ 8,758,969
American Eatery	43	$ 8,154,239
Baskin Robbins	68	$ 8,116,525
Taco Bell Express (Nbff)	35	$ 7,922,596
Mobile Snack Bar	75	$ 7,288,385
Royal Chopstix	17	$ 3,229,225
Sweet Reflections	32	$ 3,123,598
Other Food	151	$ 2,343,171
Casa De Amigos	20	$ 2,328,971
Chicken Loft	13	$ 1,236,916
Church's Fried Chicken	4	$ 792,713
Mealtime Express Food Carts	5	$ 737,123
Manhattan Bagel	6	$ 719,640
Starbucks Coffeee	4	$ 701,892
Food Court	107	$ 497,427
Pepe's	3	$ 278,038
A&W Root Beer	1	$ 218,230
Delicatessen	6	$ 207,091
Subtotal:	1,732	$ 448,735,596
THEATER OPERATIONS		
Theaters	170	$ 17,925,654
Theater Snack Stand	7	$ 1,364,935
Subtotal:	177	$ 19,290,589
TOTAL:	**3,825**	**$ 6,387,175,381**

APPENDIX B

Army & Air Force Exchange Service
Web Site Sales Data

Month	1997 Orders	1997 Items	1997 Sales	1998 Orders	1998 Items	1998 Sales	1999 Orders	1999 Items	1999 Sales
Feb	-	-	$ -	1,090	1,693	$ 147,939	11,962	27,732	$ 1,473,748
Mar	2	6	$ 454	1,441	2,471	$ 249,778	14,359	35,855	$ 1,829,746
Apr	-	-	$ -	2,740	4,760	$ 401,826	11,147	26,822	$ 1,396,506
May	-	-	$ -	3,064	6,099	$ 371,520	13,425	32,304	$ 1,457,671
Jun	1	2	$ 225	2,923	5,750	$ 429,668	11,645	28,020	$ 1,095,780
Jul	72	101	$ 11,299	2,909	5,490	$ 408,734	11,078	26,655	$ 1,042,393
Aug	236	326	$ 27,086	4,067	8,224	$ 543,728	14,736	35,458	$ 1,386,667
Sep	406	577	$ 43,860	5,535	12,702	$ 742,428	20,121	48,416	$ 1,893,411
Oct	404	582	$ 69,286	4,678	10,546	$ 632,718	17,148	41,261	$ 1,613,618
Nov	645	1,089	$ 80,589	8,178	18,667	$ 1,267,299	34,347	82,644	$ 3,231,987
Dec	1,366	2,125	$ 158,245	15,385	32,007	$ 1,941,259	52,612	126,595	$ 4,950,785
Jan	944	1,429	$ 111,621	10,437	26,297	$ 1,223,945	33,172	79,818	$ 3,121,422
Total:	4,076	6,237	$ 502,665	62,447	134,706	$ 8,360,842	245,752	591,580	$ 24,493,733

Fiscal Year = February through January

Data for October through January 1999 is forecasted.

Chapter III

Principles of Digitally Mediated Replenishment of Goods: Electronic Commerce and Supply Chain Reform

Robert B. Johnston
Monash University, Australia

INTRODUCTION

Many authors (Cunningham and Tynan, 1993; Dearing, 1990; Johnston, 1998; Rochester, 1989; Skagen, 1989; Swatman, 1993) now recognize that the significance of business-to-business electronic commerce in the supply chain is not just its ability to reduce direct operational costs (Colberg, 1990; Dearing, 1990), but also as an enabling technology for business process simplification, particularly as part of the over-arching simplification philosophy that goes variously by the names Just-In-Time (Abraham, Holt and Kathawala, 1990; Groenevelt, 1993), Quick Response (Fiorito, May and Straughn, 1995) and Efficient Consumer Response (Kurt Salmon Associates, 1993). There is also increasing recognition that supplier/customer interactions and supply chain performance as a whole are the correct units of analysis of supply chain reforms and their benefits (Buxmann and Gabauer, 1999; Johnston, 1998). Yet few accounts have attempted to define the precise principles by which the various technologies that make up supply chain electronic commerce are able to provide this simplification of business processes and supply chain performance improvement.

This chapter takes up that challenge by describing an increasingly sophisticated series of supply chain reform initiatives with the aim of extracting the underlying principles of digitally mediated replenishment. It is hoped that such an approach will provide a richer, more unified, and more principled account of various EC-enabled supply chain reforms which are often discussed in isolation, but also, by drawing out from diverse supply chain reforms a small set of underlying principles, that it will be possible to more easily generalize from these cases to create other process simplifications appropriate to novel circumstances and business requirements. The chapter begins with fairly well known supply chain reforms analyzed in a new way, but leads on to quite novel issues such as the role of EC in pull as well as push JIT replenishment systems, the use of two dimensional bar code as a medium for EDI, and the use of the new Internet-based business document exchange and presentation products and services. This work is empirically grounded upon a series of case studies

Copyright © 2000, Idea Group Publishing.

conducted in the past four years with some of the largest manufacturing and retail enterprises in Australia, but the reforms described are very much typical of world best practice in supply chain management. The case descriptions are kept brief: greater detail can be found in the references provided.

The chapter concentrates on replenishment of retail goods, component parts, and raw materials along the supply chain of large retail and manufacturing enterprises. It focuses on the interaction between a "customer" enterprise which wishes to replenish goods from a "supplier" that distributes or manufacturers them. For simplicity, certain potential intermediaries to this process, such as third-party transport companies, are ignored. In the next two sections, the pertinent technologies involved are described, and a small number of principles that explain their use and their effectiveness in creating supply chain reform through electronic commerce are stated.

SUPPLY CHAIN ELECTRONIC COMMERCE TECHNOLOGIES

There are a number of technologies which must be used together to achieve digital mediation of the replenishment/remittance cycle (Clarke, 1992; Cunningham and Tynan, 1993; Kalakota and Whinston, 1996; Kimberley, 1991). They are:

1. *Universal product numbering.* For effective digital mediation of the exchange of goods for money, trading partners must use a common system of identifying products. This has led to the requirement for a world-wide, unique product numbering system for individual retail packs, distribution packs of items such as cartons, and shipments of multiple items (Johnston, 1998). Building on the initiative of the Uniform Code Council in the U.S. who developed the 12-digit Universal Product Code, the United Nations-based International Article Numbering Association (EAN International) has provided systems for such unique numbering through the EAN-13 retail item number, the Trade Unit Number (TUN), and the Serial Shipping Container Code (SSCC), respectively (EAN, 1997). They have also produced standards for other product and shipment descriptive data such as batch number, production data, maximum durability date, and so forth.

2. *Automatic Identification.* The ability to mark items, cartons, and shipping containers with a machine readable form of their EAN identification codes is a vital requirement for digitally mediated replenishment. Simple linear bar code is by far the most widespread automatic identification technology (Harmon and Adams, 1990), but there has been recent interest in radio frequency tags and smart cards as additional possibilities for specialized applications. These are more expensive technologies but they have the potential to move beyond mere identification and allow data to be updated in the course of transactions.

3. *Electronic Data Interchange (EDI).* EDI is "the Interorganizational exchange of business documentation in structured, machine-processable form" (Emmelhainz, 1990, p4). In addition, traditionally it is required for the transmission to qualify as true EDI, that the message be structured according to widely disseminated, preferably international *de jure* standards, and that the transfer be from one trading partner's business application to the other's application via independently sourced translation software. The most common approach to distribution has been via store-and-forward

mailbox facilities provided by Value Added Network services (VANs), using private wide-area networks which they often own (Leyland, 1993). As we will see, the Internet is now becoming an alternative transmission means, and many new Internet-based supply chain EC products and services do not conform to the strict traditional EDI definitions. Two-dimensional bar code (Itkin and Martell, 1992; Pavlidis, Swatz and Wang, 1992) is also considered later in this article as a potential transmission means for EDI.

4. *Electronic Funds Transfer.* Settling debts by electronic means, which can be done using the Automated Clearing House system of the banks (O'Mahony, Peirce and Tewari, 1997) and by other means (Lynch and Lundquist, 1996), closes the digitally mediated replenishment loop. Electronic settlement offers a number of direct cost savings to both parties. For the creditor it means prompter payment than traditional check settlement; for the debtor it offers tighter cash management because debts are settled on a precisely known date, but also it means a loss of some "float" characteristic of the check-clearing process. In any case, electronic transmission of money is not such a crucial technology in business-to-business EC as it is in business-to-consumer EC, because in the former the trading partners usually have a credit arrangement which takes payment out of the tight operational loop.

FIVE PRINCIPLES OF DIGITALLY MEDIATED REPLENISHMENT

It is argued in the rest of this chapter that there are a small number of principles that can be seen operating in various approaches to supply chain process simplification using the above technologies and which explain their effectiveness. They are:

1. *The "once-only data entry" principle.* Once data concerning a replenishment requirement has entered one trading partner's computer system it should never need to be manually reentered by another partner;
2. *The "data turnaround" principle.* Data received from a supplier should be derived from data transmitted earlier by the customer;
3. *The "information sharing" principle.* The actions of the customer and supplier should be coordinated through information sharing;
4. *The "synchronicity" principle.* Data relating to physical events should be transmitted, as near as possible, synchronously with those events;
5. T*he "100% compliance" principle.* The reforms with the greatest benefits are not tolerant of partial EC compliance within the supply chain. 100% EC compliance of trading partners should be the aim of large EC players.

The rest of this chapter explains in detail how these five principles can be applied to replenishment systems to achieve the benefits of business process simplification, buffer reduction and throughput acceleration. The approach is to begin with the traditional paper-mediated model for control of the replenishment/remittance cycle as a stating point and in order to define terms. Then a digitally automated version of this model using the above technologies will be described. This is just a digital imitation of the traditional paper-mediated model, and while it uses the "once-only data entry" principle to achieve direct labor savings, it does not yet use the power of the digital technologies to incorporate process simplification. Then a series of variations on this basic EC model will be presented in order to demonstrate the use of each of the other four principles for process simplification.

MANUAL TRADE MEDIATION

First consider the information exchanges that occur in traditional paper-document mediated trade between a supplier and a customer. We consider the process to begin with a purchase order which is triggered by a requirement to replenish goods, although there may be a formalized request-for-quote and quote process preceding this. The purchase order is acknowledged by the supplier, transcribed using internal product nomenclature onto a sales order, and when the due date for shipment is reached, the goods requested are shipped with a delivery document listing the actual products and quantities shipped, which due to contingencies, may differ from those requested. A copy of the delivery docket is signed by the receiver and returned as a receipt of the goods in good order. An invoice is sent demanding payment for the goods, traditionally asynchronously with the actual delivery. Where accounting practice features net monthly credit terms (i.e., all goods received during a given month are paid for at the end of the next month) end-of-month statements are sent itemizing new invoices, due invoices and acknowledging payments received during the month. A check is sent by the customer for due invoices which are itemized on a remittance advice. Figure 1 shows the paper-based information exchanges involved.

The paper-based system involves an enormous amount of duplicated data entry from paper documents and also a number of time-consuming control processes to ensure the correct operation of the system. One is the "invoice matching" control in which the customer checks the items on a supplier's invoice against the original purchase order and the delivery

Figure 1: The Information Exchanges Occurring in Traditional Paper-Mediated Replenishment

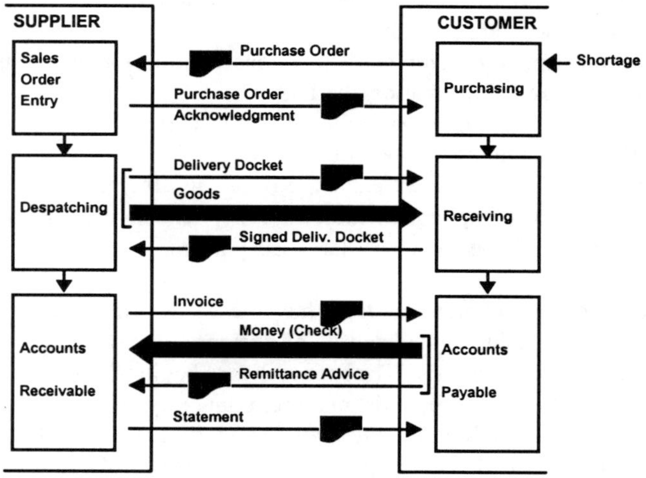

docket to ensure that only goods identical to those ordered are paid for, and at the correct price. This is a major time-consuming process of the traditional accounts payable function and is made more so by the difficulty in identifying parts and the frequent use of different product numbers and description by the customer and supplier. Another is the preparation and processing of statements whose main function, apart from acting as a receipt for money received, is to allow each party to reconcile its accounts with the other's.

These document exchanges are required in traditional trading of goods for money because the notification of a requirement, the transfer of goods, and the transfer of cash are all separated in time and place, which causes control and legal issues to arise. By contrast, when we order goods over a counter, none of these mediating information exchanges need be formalized, although they may have informal counterparts. A major aim of digitally mediated replenishment systems will be to simplify these formalized exchanges, essentially by simulating the simplicity of proximal exchange of goods for money.

AUTOMATING THE MANUAL SYSTEM

Using the supply chain EC technologies described earlier, the manual information exchange system described above can be automated (Johnston, 1998). The principle involved is "once-only data entry": once one trading partner has manually entered a requirement into their purchasing application, there should be no need (or minimal need) for that trading partner or their suppliers to perform data entry relating to that replenishment transaction later in the replenishment/remittance cycle. This first cut at automating the replenishment process is an electronic imitation of the manual process (see Figure 2) where documents are sent by EDI, products and shipments are recognized by bar codes, and money is transferred by electronic funds transfer via the banking system. The description below shows how the EC technologies achieve the once-only data entry ideal.

Once the purchase order is manually entered, it is sent by EDI to the supplier where it replaces the traditional sales order. This process automation depends on universal agreement and recognition of product part numbers, catalogues of which need to be transferred at irregular intervals preferably via EDI. Goods picked for supply are individually bar coded. With simple software a highly accurate electronic delivery document known as an Advance Shipping Notification (ASN) can be constructed from the actual shipment by scanning these bar codes as items are packed. The software can check against the electronic purchase order to insure correct part numbers and quantities are packed. This process is known as "scan packing" in the grocery industry. At the same time stock is automatically relieved from the supplier's inventory system. The ASN is given a shipment number whose uniqueness must be guaranteed (for example, the SSCC) and which can be generated without human input. The electronic document is transmitted by EDI to the customer ahead of the delivery and primes their receiving application with data about the impending shipment. The shipment is bar coded with a machine readable form of the shipment number, either on the cartons or on existing documentation (delivery dockets are often retained in otherwise electronic trading environments). At receiving, the bar-coded shipping number is scanned allowing the pre-loaded ASN to be retrieved. The individual items in the shipment are checked by scanning their product bar codes, stock is updated, and an acknowledgment receipt advice is prepared electronically from this receiving data and sent to the supplier via EDI. An invoice is prepared based on the receipt advice and the

Figure 2. A simple model of the replenishment system automated using EC technologies

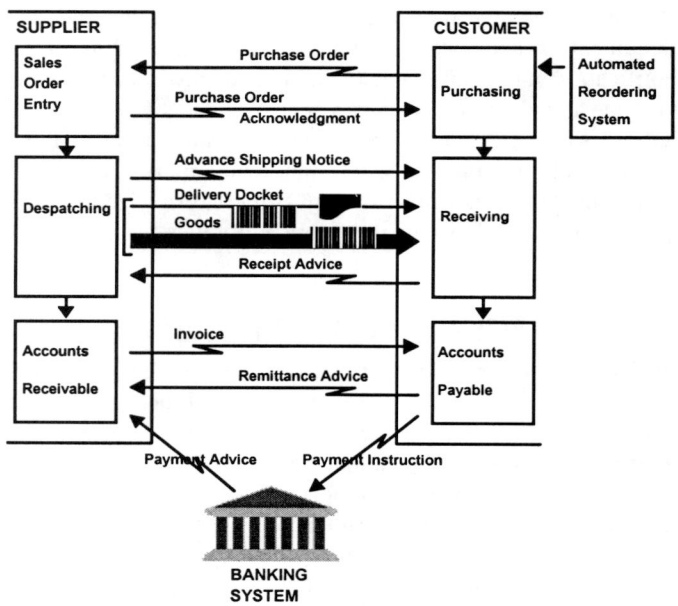

purchase order pricing, and sent to the customer via EDI. When received by the customer, the invoice can be automatically checked against the purchase order and receiving data eliminating the time-consuming manual invoice matching process. At the end of the credit period, data from the due invoices is used to prepare a payment advice and a corresponding electronic remittance advice, which are sent via the bank Automated Clearing House systems to effect electronic funds transfer from customer bank account to vendor bank account. The remittance advice is either passed on to the vendor by the bank with a payment advice or can be transferred asynchronously directly from customer to supplier via EDI.

It will be noted that there is no need for any manual data entry in this transaction cycle after the initial entry of the requirement. In fact the requirement itself might be triggered automatically by a shortage being detected in a computerized inventory system (so-called "event-driven EDI") which is automatically updated by bar-coded receipts and issues. In that case the only manual data entry is theoretically at the low level of maintaining master file data such as product descriptions and prices. In practice one would expect some manual review even in automatic reordering situations.

With the implementation of this level of automation of the replenishment process the main direct cost savings of reduced labor are achieved through the elimination of manual data re-entry, error chasing and correction, and other labor-intensive processes such as postage, document filing, and document matching.

EVALUATED RECEIPTS SETTLEMENT

However, it is possible to go much further than this: the quality of the data used in the digitally mediated automated replenishment enables it to be redesigned, leading to further benefits from process simplification and elimination of non-value-adding processes, or what is generally referred to as Business Process Reengineering (BPR). In particular, the "data turnaround" principle can be used to show that certain processes in the traditional replenishment cycle are now redundant. The Evaluated Receipts Settlement system, pioneered by the Ford Motor Company, and which was used as a prime example of technology-driven BPR in Hammer's early writings (Hammer, 1990), is now described as an example of this approach.

The "data turnaround" principle states that data received by a customer from a supplier has the highest quality when it was ultimately derived from the customer's own earlier

Figure 3. Process simplification under the Evaluated Receipts Settlement system.

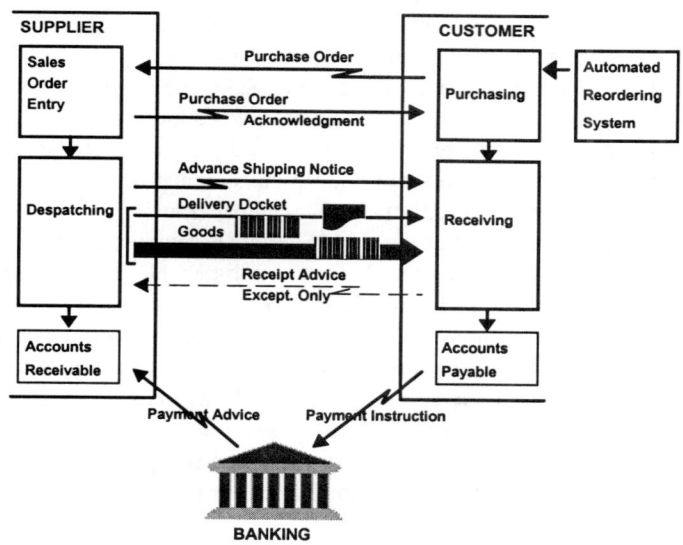

transmissions. In the model of automated replenishment, this is true of the data contained in the ASN. The ASN data has been checked during construction against the original customer purchase order and by bar code scanning against the physical goods. Therefore, provided the customer has trust in the suppliers processes, the ASN must both truly reflect the contents of the shipment and also be a shipment which was ordered by the customer. The usual concerns at receiving are that the products received were not actually ordered, or that those ordered have been substituted with unacceptable variants. Therefore, minimal further processing is required before the ASN itself can become the trigger for payment. The supplier could check every item against the ASN received using bar-code scanning, but according to the principle of "data turnaround" this is strictly an unnecessary process. It may be done as an occasional quality checking process. The ASN simply has to be evaluated using standard or contract prices. Thus there is no need for the supplier to send an invoice or for the customer to perform invoice matching, and the statement is also unnecessary as a control document. In fact, most of the customer's accounts payable and supplier's accounts receivable functions can be eliminated. Figure 3 shows the process simplifications achieved. It is based on data from a case study at Ford Australia (Johnston and Lee, 1997).

VENDOR MANAGED INVENTORIES

The Vendor Managed Inventory concept (Holmstrom, 1998), which is influential in the retail sector, further illustrates how the quality of information provided by the EC technologies coupled with the principles of "once-only data entry" and "data turnaround", allow further simplification of the control systems by reduction or elimination of the purchase ordering function at the customer site. Take the replenishment system of a supermarket as an example. Rather than the supermarket applying their sales transactions, recorded automatically at the point of sale by bar code scanning, to their own inventory system and using reorder triggers to set-off the replenishment process, the supermarket may instead send to each supplier via EDI, the raw inventory transactions (POS data) for their products. Each supplier can then manage, within certain parameters set by the customer, the inventory of their products at the customer's site and initiate replenishment themselves. This effectively eliminates the ordering functions for the purchasing department at the supermarket site. Effectively, the supermarket becomes a provider of end-consumers, shelf space, and infrastructure to the suppliers. Although this innovation makes new system demands upon the supplier, it also provides to them much greater visibility of end-consumer's purchasing patterns which were previously lumped as store level orders. The potential is there for the supplier to market more directly to the end consumer with less intermediation by the supermarket. Figure 4 shows the process simplifications achieved.

INFORMATION SHARING: MATERIAL REQUIREMENT SCHEDULES

Next the principle of "information sharing" is illustrated as a way of achieving supply chain buffer stock reduction and pipeline acceleration. When component parts for a complex assembly operation, such as automotive manufacturing, are replenished by periodic review (order-point) methods, large buffer stocks result (Orlicky, 1975). If each

Figure 4. Process Simplification Using the Vendor Managed Inventory System

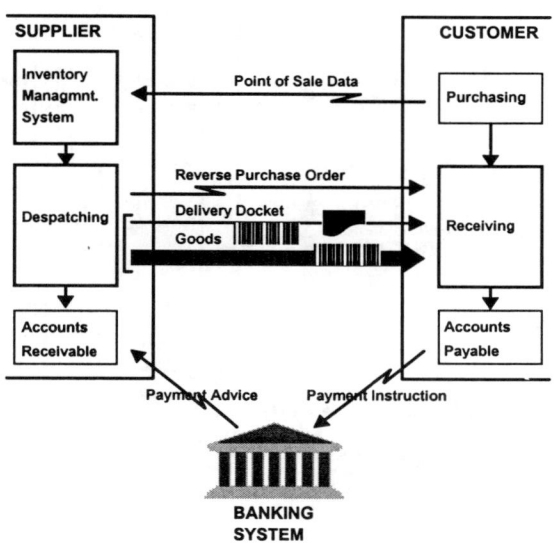

successive upstream supplier replenishes in a similar reactive way, large buffer stocks result at each point along the supply chain. According to Little's Law (Hopp and Spearman, 1996, p231) this results in slow supply chain throughput time. In addition, requirements become increasingly variable and lumpy as they are passed upstream (the Forrester effect (Forrester, 1961)) due to the increasing loss of information about downstream requirements that accompanies these traditional order-point methods (Johnston, 1996).

In the "push" replenishment approach used in many automotive assembly plants in the western world, requirements for locally sourced parts are determined from the future build schedule using a time-phased bill of material explosion process known as Material Requirements Planning (MRP) (Orlicky, 1975). This process produces a precise schedule for each supplier for each part, which if followed will allow the parts to arrive as close as possible before the time that they are required in assembly. This results in a great reduction in buffer stocks of components compared with replenishment triggered by uncoordinated periodic review of component stocks. It is now common for this requirements scheduling technique to extend through several levels of the automotive supply chain (Prajogo and Johnston, 1999) resulting in an overall reduction in supply chain inventory rather than a mere redistribution. This reduction also helps accelerate the flow of materials along the supply chain and dampens the Forrester effect by preserving the lot-for-lot nature of successive replenishment order quantities. The principle at work here is buffer stock and

Figure 5. The Standard "Push" Replenishment Model in the Automotive Manufacturing Industry

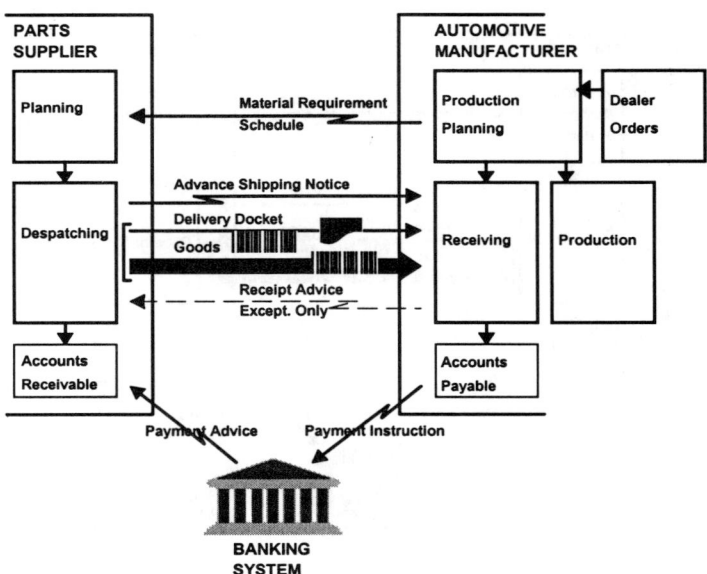

variability reduction through information sharing, or put crudely, the replacement of stock with information.

Although the MRP principle has been in use for many years to coordinate activities *within* companies, extending the concept to a large supplier base requires electronic application-to-application transfer of schedules, particularly if they are updated frequently. Transmission of EDI Material Requirement Schedule transaction sets has been one of the driving forces for EDI adoption in the automotive industry (Mackay, 1995). For instance at Ford Australia (Johnston and Lee, 1997) a Material Requirement Schedule (MRS) is transmitted by EDI to all local suppliers monthly, and weekly to internal suppliers. An amended MRS can also be transmitted at any time. In keeping with general automotive industry practice, the MRS represents a firm commitment to receive parts scheduled in the first month, a commitment to buy for the next two months quantity, and planning forecasts for the following nine months. Since Ford is committed to pay for materials by the MRS, the scheduling is cumulative with any parts not delivered in one month included in the next month schedule. The schedule, which shows for each part, quantities to be shipped every few days for the first month, triggers replenishment at the supplier site on those days. When packed by the supplier, an advanced shipping notice is sent and the rest of the receiving / remittance cycle follows the EC model above including ERS payments. Figure 5 shows the system based on a case study at Ford Australia (Johnston and Lee, 1997) and on the published Chrysler system (Mukhopadhray, Kekre and Kalathur, 1995).

THE PUSH AND PULL APPROACHES TO JUST-IN-TIME

The system described in the previous section can form the basis of a Just-In-Time (JIT) replenishment system. The schedule has to show requirements to be shipped daily or more frequently in smaller quantities, replenishments should be ordered on a strictly lot-for-lot basis with end-item production, and safety lead times need to be reduced as far as possible to zero. Such a JIT conception is an essentially "push" one, and it can be argued (Johnston and Lee, 1997) that most published discussions of the connection between JIT and EC implicitly assume this push conception of JIT. However, by far the greatest success with JIT has been achieved by Japanese automotive companies and their foreign off-shoots using a "pull" approach (Schonberger, 1982). According to the pull principle (DeToni, Caputo and Vinelli, 1988), replenishment activities are initiated by current shortages. Pull systems are thus reactive and activity is authorized and initiated by current shortage, which is often made visible by variations upon the Japanese "Kanban" card system. Kanban is a visual pull replenishment control system that makes use of cards ("kanbans") which travel with parts at all times (Schonberger, 1987). If a kanban becomes freed by the consumption of goods at the production line, it becomes both a signal and an authority to replenish that item in the quantity with which each kanban is associated. By contrast, in the previously described push system, current replenishment activities are initiated in response to a perceived need at some future time. Push systems are thus plan-based and rely upon the creation of activity schedules and despatch lists to authorize and initiate activity. In pull systems information that triggers activity flows in the opposite direction to the physical movement of goods. For instance, the appearance of a free kanban at the customer's production line due to consumption of materials causes a signal to travel from customer to supplier, usually in the form of the physical kanban, that initiates a movement of goods from supplier to customer. In push systems, although customer requirements initiate the supplier's planning of component production, it is the falling due of an item on the Materials Requirements Schedule held by the supplier which is the trigger for replenishment. Information about this replenishment activity travels from supplier to customer in the form of the ASN.

It should not be assumed that companies using pull systems do not engage in forward planning. However, in pull systems execution activity is effectively decoupled from planning activity. Because current shortages initiate replenishment at the execution level, this can precede autonomously from tactical planning systems and any information flow is bottom-up. In push systems by contrast, the control system architecture demands the tight coupling between planning systems and execution systems that is characteristic of top-down, Taylorite, mass production-era management (Johnston, 1995; Womack, Jones and Roos, 1990).

Just-In-Time means simply to produce/replenish the necessary units in the necessary quantities at the necessary time (Monden, 1983). The term Just-In-Time refers to an ideal state of affairs rather than to a particular system for realizing that state (Cowton and Vail, 1994). In fact JIT replenishment is possible using either a push or pull replenishment discipline. In order to achieve JIT delivery in a push environment, the lead time for delivery of parts must be shorter that the firm planning horizon (DeToni et al., 1988), which allows component parts to be ordered lot-for-lot. Therefore, EDI and bar code technologies that promise to reduce order generation and receiving times are frequently recommended, or even claimed to be essential for JIT (Banerjee and Golhar, 1993; Dale, 1991; Ragsdale and Gilbert, 1990; Srinivasan, Kekre and Mukhopadhray, 1994). It appears that the association of EC, particularly EDI and bar coding, with JIT in the EC literature implicitly conceives of JIT within such a push framework. Most reports of successful JIT implementations associated with EC technologies describe push systems (Banerjee and Golhar, 1993; Mukhopadhray et al., 1995; Ragsdale and Gilbert, 1990; Srinivasan et al., 1994).

In Japan and in Japanese-owned companies in the West however, JIT is usually achieved using the Toyota Production System or some variation there-of, which features pull replenishment of parts. Devised by Taiichi Ohno and others at Toyota in the 1950s and 1960s (Monden, 1983), the Toyota Production System, often referred to as Lean Production in the west (Womack et al., 1990), features a whole raft of waste elimination reforms that support the JIT concept and quality improvements (Johnston, 1995). These include production levelling ("Heijunka") to reduce the impact of demand fluctuations on production, improvement initiatives such as early detection and correction of faults, team concepts such as quality circles, cellular plant layout, and visible control systems such as "Andon" lights, which indicate production line problems, and Kanban. Thus, in Japanese companies and western companies influenced by Lean Production ideas, JIT is strongly associated with the pull approach.

Pull JIT and particularly the Kanban replenishment system represents an alternative approach to supply chain buffer reduction and acceleration. It achieves this by insisting on extremely small and frequent reactive replenishments of parts, and again, this replenishment system is ideally extended through several levels of the supply chain to achieve overall improvement. Although information is often shared along pull supply chains using EDI transmitted forecasts (Prajogo and Johnston, 1997; Prajogo and Johnston, 1999), in keeping with the pull philosophy these can no longer initiate replenishment. Furthermore, because of the smaller more frequent deliveries (typically several times per day for each part) required by the pull JIT approach, using EDI to control replenishments at the operations level becomes prohibitively expensive with a delivery every few minutes. This leads to the interesting, and in terms of the existing EC literature somewhat paradoxical, observation (Johnston and Lee, 1997; Lee, 1996) that at least in Australia, the automotive company with the greatest achievement of JIT, the Toyota Motor Company of Australia, is the company with the least use of EDI in its replenishment system. However, it will be seen that, under the definition given in Section Two, it still uses EC technologies to some extent to achieve this. The system in use at this company (Johnston and Lee, 1997; Lee, 1996) is now described as one possible solution to using EC technologies, in the broader sense, in a pull environment.

As with car companies using the push approach, Toyota gathers data electronically from its dealers in order to plan its car build schedule. This schedule is exploded into parts requirements which are sent to suppliers monthly via EDI. However this electronic document is now purely a forecast provided for supplier information and planning, and does not directly initiate replenishment. The signal for replenishment is the appearance of a free kanban from production indicating an immediate shortage. Local parts are delivered in containers with kanbans directly to the production line where they are used. As kanbans are released by consumption of the parts at the production line, they are delivered to a kanban

Figure 6. A Pull Replenishment System Using Kanban and a Bar-coded Turnaround Deliver Docket

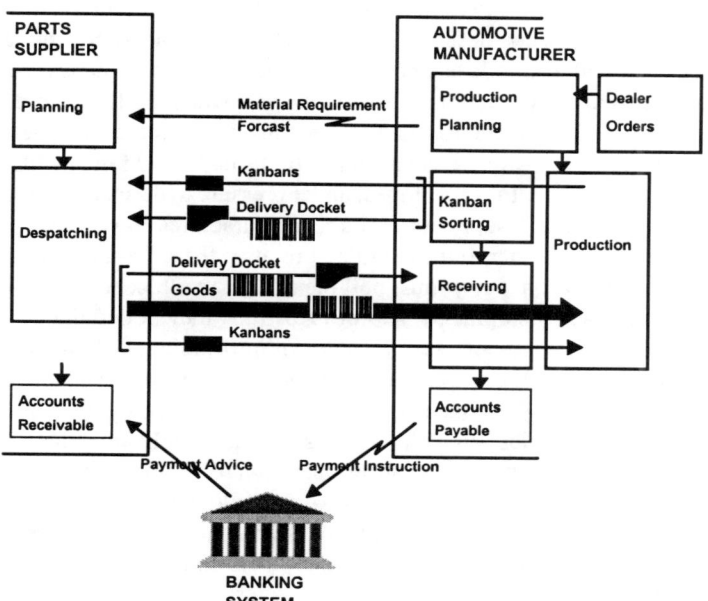

sorting area where they are sorted electro-mechanically into vendor/part number sequence, using bar-coded data on the kanban. The sorting system also produces a paper delivery docket with a bar-coded delivery number, on behalf of the supplier, and transmits the expected delivery records to Toyota's receiving system. The kanbans and the related delivery dockets are picked up by the vendor's carrier upon the next delivery. Each vendor delivers parts at least twice a day. The transport driver must arrive during a preassigned delivery time window, and drop off the present delivery of parts together with the associated kanbans and delivery docket. The shipment number on the delivery docket is scanned by receiving staff with a bar-code reader to recall the expected receipt information which is checked against the goods and the kanbans. The parts are then taken to the production line with their kanbans to complete the replenishment cycle (see Figure 6).

This system neatly illustrates the use of the "data turnaround" and "synchonicity" principles in achieving process simplification through data accuracy. Since the delivery docket was produced by Toyota, it contains the part numbers and quantities expected by them, and the parts actually supplied are controlled by the kanbans which produced the delivery docket and which always travelled with them. The receiving information for the shipment is easily retrieved from the bar-coded shipment number on the turnaround document that travels synchronously with the physical shipment.

TWO DIMENSIONAL BAR CODE AS A MEDIUM FOR EDI

As mentioned in the last section, the traditional accounts of the importance of EC, and especially EDI, for implementing JIT implicitly assume that it is implemented within the push replenishment framework described earlier. Reduced lead times are enabled by automating receiving with bar code technology, and the use of EDI enables reduced order quantities by reducing the fixed reorder costs. However, when the frequent deliveries of parts characteristic of JIT are approached using this push method problems become apparent. The delivery of the ASN asynchronously to the delivery of the goods creates the potential for a timing problem. In recent times, under pressure to delivery frequently and in small quantities, many of the suppliers of large manufactures have moved into close proximity to their major customer. If the manufacturer uses the store-and-forward services of a VAN for economy reasons, they must poll their VAN mailbox at regular intervals to retrieve ASNs for impending shipments. At Ford Australia they polled the mailbox every 10 minutes, but many large suppliers were located within 10 minutes drive of the plant. In order to guarantee that the ASN arrived before the goods, they would need to increase their polling to an unacceptably high frequency, which threatens to destroy the cost advantages of store-and-forward communication with suppliers. On the other hand, if the ASN does not arrive before the physical shipment, this causes operational disruption, and this disruption would be especially acute if delivery windows were employed. Delivering the machine-readable information about a shipment with the shipment itself, in keeping with the "synchronicity" principle, would solve this timing problem and also simplify the process of identifying a message with the shipment to which it refers.

In 1997 a study (Johnston and Yap, 1998; Yap, 1997) was undertaken to investigate the feasibility of using the newly available two-dimensional, high data capacity bar codes as a medium for transmitting EDI messages. Since reversion to a paper-based medium for data transfers would be a retrograde step unless a suitable surface for printing was available within the EC replenishment framework, delivery information was chosen as the most likely transaction set for this "paper-based EDI" approach (Martel, 1992; McCullouck, 1994; Seidman, 1993). In this case the bar codes could be printed in the cartons themselves, but also delivery dockets are frequently retained to identify shipments even in electronic trading environments.

Conventional linear, or one-dimensional, bar codes have been used to automate the identification of products since about 1970 (Harmon and Adams, 1990). An ID scanned from a delivery docket can also be used as a key to retrieve the full record of shipping details from a computer file as described earlier. However, their small data capacity (around 30 characters) limits their usefulness for the direct transmission of business data in machine readable form. For that purpose high density bar codes which use the vertical dimension of the symbol to carry extra information have recently been developed (Itkin and Martell, 1992; Pavlidis et al., 1992). They can hold up to two kilobytes with a single symbol and unlimited data in multiple symbols. The concept is often referred to as a "portable data file."

Two main approaches have been used to extend the data capacity and data density of bar codes: stacked linear bar codes and matrix symbols (Itkin and Martell, 1992; Johnston, 1998; Pavlidis et al., 1992; Yap, 1997). The first approach is to stack a number of conventional (linear) bar code symbols of reduced height above each other. The second approach is to divide the whole area of the symbol into pixels and encode the information in the color (light or dark) of the pixels. The latter matrix symbol systems have generally been developed for special applications, and while they can achieve high data density, they require complex and often proprietary equipment based on Charge Coupled Device (CCD) technology and pattern recognition software.

By contrast, stacked bar codes (Figure 7) can be read by conventional laser scanners and the output signal can be translated using conventional signal processing techniques. Several stacked bar code symbologies have had their symbology standards placed in the public domain (Pavlidis et al., 1992). This is important for large scale EC adoption because it means that a number of independent scanner and printer manufacturers are being encouraged to support these symbologies as standard. The most sophisticated stacked two-dimensional bar code symbology to date is PDF417, developed in 1989 by Symbol Technologies, a significant U.S. bar code equipment manufacturer (Itkin and Martell, 1992). PDF417 appears set to become the dominant two-dimensional bar code symbology for several reasons: it can be read by most new upper range bar code readers, its symbology is public domain, it has high data capacity and density, it has strong error correction as well as error detection and other features which improve its readability, and its use has been incorporated into the standards of a number of important bodies in the U.S. (Yap, 1997).

Both the push approach in use at Ford Australia and the pull approach in use at the Toyota Motor Company of Australia were studied, and it was found that the use of two-dimensional bar code to transfer the shipping data in machine readable form, in the Ford case *instead* of the ASN, and in the Toyota case *in addition* to the conventional printed data, would potentially overcome some existing problems in their replenishment systems. In the Ford push approach, sending the shipment data in this form solved the operational timing problem associated with sending the ASN asynchronously. In the Toyota pull approach, adding the full delivery docket details in machine readable form, rather than just the shipment number, would overcome the problem that their turnaround document system, while elegantly solving their own problem, did not achieve the usual EC aim of data sharing. In addition, at the time invoices were still being received from many suppliers, so providing the opportunity to suppliers to base these on Toyota-sourced data had the potential to improve the accuracy of this data in accordance with the "data turnaround" principle. It is interesting to note the opposite direction of travel of the encoded information in the two cases, which is a characteristic difference of push and pull systems. A demonstration system was also constructed from Windows-based tools and the resulting two-dimensional bar-coded delivery dockets were found to be adequately robust against anticipated types of

Figure 7: A PDF417 Stacked Bar Code Symbol. This symbol encodes Lincoln's Gettysburg Address (1437 bytes of text data) and is reproduced approximately full size.)

Table 1. Typical Layered Approach to Message Standards for Conventional EDI and 2D Bar Code EDI

Layer	Traditional EDI	2D Bar code
Message formatting layer	EDI standards e.g. X.12, EDIFACT	EDI standards eg. X.12, EDIFACT Application specific formats
Message handling layer	Enveloping standards e.g. X400 Addressing standards e.g. X500	N/A since it is point-to-point
Message transport layer	Packet switching standards e.g. X.25	PDF417 symbology standards
Physical layer	Telephone lines, Networks	Paper

physical abuse (Johnston and Yap, 1998; Yap, 1997).

This application of two-dimensional bar code as a medium for EDI illustrates the importance of the "synchronicity" principle. When information exchanges about future planned events, such as planning schedules, purchase orders and so forth, are transmitted between trading partners timing is not crucial. This is because the events of the virtual, simulated world of plans do not occur at actual places and times. The economies of batch transmission via speed of light media on a store-and-forward basis may be the overriding business consideration. However, when the information relates to *actual physical* events, correct timing and simple association of the exchange with the actual event becomes more crucial from a business operations point of view than transmission economies, especially in a tightly coupled JIT environment. There may well be other scenarios where using other physical media, such as diskettes or smart-cards, offers the same synchronicity advantages as two-dimensional bar code. There is no reason why such physical media should not carry fully standardized EDI messages. Such an approach would have advantages for integration with existing EDI systems. In fact, since EDI message exchanges conventionally employ several layers of independent standardization, there is no reason why we should not think of such message exchanges as genuine EDI exchanges which simply employ alternative transport layer standards (Johnston and Yap, 1998). Table 1 shows how the standards used in conventional EDI and 2D bar code EDI compare. We must always avoid being too doctrinaire about valid EC practice and always relate the technology to the critical operational considerations.

100% EC COMPLIANCE—THE ROLE OF THE INTERNET

Large retailers and manufacturers with many suppliers have embraced EDI enthusiastically for its operational and tactical benefits. Many have now succeeded in controlling a high proportion of their replenishment transaction volume using traditional standards-based EDI messages transmitted using the store-and-forward services of VANs to and from their larger EDI-enabled suppliers. From the point of view of direct labor savings, such adoption levels can be considered high. However, the familiar Pareto principle applies: 20% of their suppliers account for 80% of their transaction volume. The remaining 80% are generally small to medium sized enterprises (SMEs) who are usually unsophisticated in their use and knowledge of information technology. The existence of 80% of suppliers who are EC non-compliant represents a barrier to achieving the greatest rewards from EC through business process simplification initiatives. For example, advanced distribution techniques such as Cross-Docking (Andel, 1994), which have the potential to provide immense cost savings, depend on 100% compliance to ASNs and bar coding for smooth operation. In a Cross Docking distribution center, goods received from suppliers are sorted and routed directly to the destination store using information from bar codes and the ASN. This reduces double handling, warehouse space and infrastructure costs compared to traditional "pick and pack" distribution. Therefore, although it is possible to justify EDI on the basis of direct benefits (Buxmann and Gabauer, 1999), it can be argued that the goal for the largest supply chain EC players, with the most to gain, should be EC compliance of *all* their trading partners, rather than simply high levels of compliance among larger technically sophisticated suppliers.

Within the traditional EDI framework it was assumed that high levels of compliance could be achieved through the mutual cost savings that EDI enables, or else through coercion by the larger customers who could threaten "desourcing" (Emmelhainz, 1990; Sarich, 1989; Zinn and Tahac, 1988). However, small suppliers have little to gain from the global connectivity and application-to-application functionality that traditional standards-based EDI offers (Scala and McGrath, 1993), because it is typical of the profile of SMEs (Iacovou, Benbaset and Dexter, 1995; Rodwell and Shadur, 1997) that they are unsophisticated in systems use and generally have few customers (Johns, Dunlop and Sheehan, 1989). At the same time, the operating and especially set-up costs to become EDI capable were high, largely because of the oligopolistic position of the VANs, who usually owned the only suitable wide-area networks for EDI transmission. Due to their high failure rate, SMEs are transient by nature, so it is also difficult for established customers to make use of their superior bargaining power to insist on compliance. It is now becoming clear that the traditional one-solution-fits-all approach of traditional EDI has failed to bring small suppliers into the supply chain EC network.

The large EDI players with the most to gain from 100% compliance are increasingly looking to the Internet as a means to solve this problem. The Internet is a worldwide network of networks with excellent throughput capabilities. Internet transmission charges are low compared to those of VANs and do not depend on the amount of data transferred. More importantly, the Internet provides simple and widely understood new methods for information exchange (Hruska, 1995; Kalakota and Whinston, 1996). Non-EDI-enabled trading partners can use a Web browser to fill in a form-based Web page representing a business document, in order to comply with their EDI-enabled trading partner's information requirements. To access the Internet they need only a personal computer, a modem and an Internet Service Provider (ISP). They require little more computer expertise than is now becoming common knowledge. The new cost structure, the new means of digital document presentation, and a global market for new software products afforded by the Internet have led to the development of a large number and wide variety of new products and services for the distribution of business documents between trading partners over the Internet, many of which are specifically targeted to the inclusion of unsophisticated trading partners in the EC network. Large EDI players are now able to use these new Internet-based products to leverage their investment in traditional EDI through the benefits afforded by 100% supplier compliance (Anon., 1998; Mak and Johnston, 1999).

These new products and strategies have been reviewed by Mak and Johnston (1997; 1998) where a classification of 50 specific products can be found. They can be differentiated along two dimensions. The first is whether they make use of third-party Internet-based digital document handling service providers (Internet Value Added Networks, IVANs), or whether they provide software and infrastructure tools to allow large traders to create their own electronic document distribution solutions. Secondly, they differ in their use or non-use of traditional standards for message formatting. Products that allow for uncoordinated selection of the message handling software by separate trading partners generally use traditional EDI messages. However, many of the new products require the trading partners to use proprietary software products or software development environments at both ends, often using client-server technology and hub-spoke topology, and therefore often use proprietary messages or Web standards for the document exchange. Some of the new products types include:

1. Products that interface to applications through flat-file exchange using traditional standards-based message mapping, but use the Internet as the transport layer. These products mimic the conventional approach, but because the Internet is already capable of any-to-any transfer, these products threaten to bypass traditional VANs;
2. Internet-based third-party EDI services, often run by the traditional VANs, that effectively export the traditional VAN concept to the new medium. These IVANS attempt to add traditional forms of value to the document exchanges, such as secure mailboxes, control measures, gateways to other traditional VANs, plus new value such as support for nonstandard transmissions such as fax and Web forms;
3. Development environments and products that allow large trading partners to design custom electronic document exchange systems tailored to the unsophisticated needs of their small trading partners. Document distribution options include: a Web server at the large trading partner site that can be accessed by a standard browser, and proprietary client-server environments which allow tailored front-end document presentation software to be provided to unsophisticated trading partners;
4. "Intelligent gateway" products that allow large trading partners to route electronic documents to or from their applications to a variety of trading partner types, using a variety of media including private networks, the Internet, and fax, and using message formats appropriate to the functional capabilities of the trading partners. These products give to large players who can afford the development cost the same mixed-media functionality that the IVANs offer as third parties to smaller trading partners;
5. Internet-based third-party sites that enable trading partners to exchange documents entirely using Web forms. These are designed for exchanges between unsophisticated trading partners or to allow wide participation of unsophisticated traders in such things as government tenders.

The new EC infrastructure (Mak and Johnston, 1999) being developed at Coles Myer Limited (CML), Australia's largest retail store chain, demonstrates how these new products can be used to include both traditional EDI-enabled suppliers and unsophisticated small suppliers into a single EC network in order to achieve 100% electronic trading compliance.

CML operates 11 retail brands over 1,800 stores in Australia and New Zealand. CML has various business applications for different retail brands, running on different system platforms using various EDI translators. Eighteen hundred merchandise and grocery suppliers use the traditional VAN-based EDI approach, while the rest (approximately 8,000) use paper-based document processes via regular mail, phone calls or fax, to exchange business data with CML. CML is aiming for 100% compliance to electronic purchase orders and ASNs by using a single centralized EDI system which includes an Internet-based component tailored to the needs of small suppliers.

CML's new EDI infrastructure (Figure 8) adopts the "Intelligent Gateway" concept, using a central EDI gateway system to perform bidirectional any-to-any translation. The intelligent EDI gateway will accept flat-file formats generated by CML's in-house business applications, and translate the flat files into various formatted messages, including EDI formatted messages, fax-based messages, e-mail messages, and E-form messages, based on their suppliers' requirements and vice versa. The central EDI gateway system will also support multiple transmission media for transferring messages to CML's suppliers, for example, the Internet, VANs, and direct connection, using a trading partner profile database to make routing and translation decisions.

An important part of the new infrastructure are the subsystems devoted to transferring data to small suppliers using the Internet ("Internet Server Hub" in Figure 8). CML has chosen an Internet EDI approach which uses software from a single provider to create both the CML hub and the small supplier front-end data entry application. This allows for document exchanges not structured using traditional EDI standards, and facilitates the participation of SMEs in the EC network without the need for them to purchase full EDI translation facilities. Given the limited requirements of their small traders, CML has chosen an Internet EDI system based on client-server technology, which was determined to be most

Figure 8: The New Electronic Commerce Infrastructure at CML

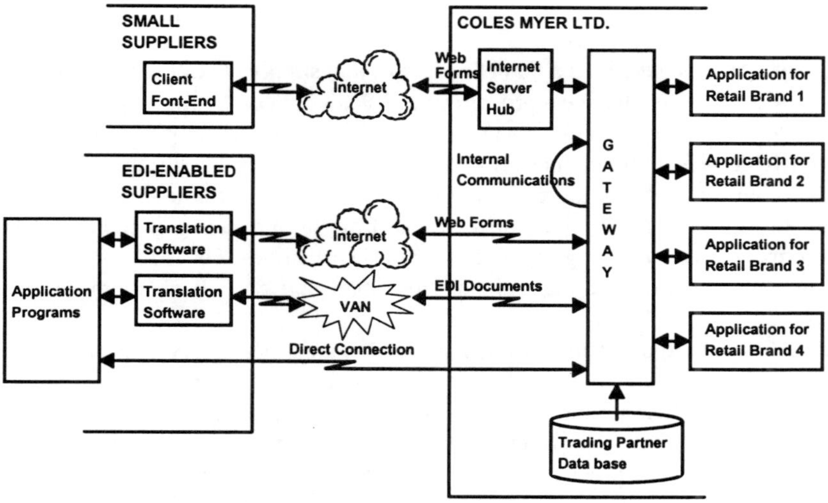

appropriate for application-to-person system integration with hub-spoke connectivity (Mak, 1998).

CML is also using the "data turnaround" principle to increase the accuracy of delivery information from the suppliers. Purchase orders from the main application programs will be routed by the gateway to an Internet-based hub server where they are stored in a web-form file format. Using the front-end provided, the supplier then retrieves these files through the Internet using Secure HyperText Transfer Protocol (HTTPS). The front-end application stores this data in a local database and allows it to be displayed using predefined templates. The supplier then updates this form with the shipping details, by scanning the actual items as they are packed, to create a turnaround ASN. The front-end enforces editing rules specified in the template to validate the supplier's input, and locks certain fields to prevent unintentional data entry from suppliers. This ensures that CML receives error free ASN documents and helps enable advanced distribution initiatives such as Cross Docking with only minimal inspection.

The approach used by CML, which retains a traditional standards-based backbone EDI network with sophisticated trading partners, along with hub-spoke subnetworks catering for the limited functional requirements of unsophisticated trading partners, is arguably the emerging model for achieving 100% compliance to supply chain EC (Johnston and Mak, 1999). CML has opted to set up the gateway system and Internet hub at their own expense for the control it gives them. Others, such as Atkins Carlyle in Perth, Australia (Anon., 1998), will use the services of third parties that provide the same rich mix of delivery modalities. The new solution embodies more realistic notions about the requirements of small trading partners, the power that large players have over them, and a fair distribution of cost and benefits between the interacting parties. It also suggests the emergence of new attitudes to traditional EDI standards: they are vital on the backbone network where global connectivity and application-to-application functionality is desired, but may be relaxed on dedicated small-trader hub-spoke networks, provided a migration path from one type of interaction to the other is available as traders increase their sophistication.

CONCLUSION

This chapter has described a number of ways that supply chain EC technologies can be used to create effective business process simplification, in particular business units, and also to enable buffer reduction and throughput acceleration in the supply chain as a whole. The approach has been to try to uncover a small set of principles that describe the ability of these technologies to achieve these aims. It is hoped that this will allow practitioners and academics to think creatively about new forms of digital mediation of replenishment in novel circumstances by applying and extending these principles. The reader may well have thought of simplifications of the systems described and can check them against the principles.

Internet exchange of business documents is one area that deserves more research. It can be argued (Johnston and Mak, 1999) that we are on the brink of a new era of supply chain electronic commerce that not only makes extensive use of the Internet as a data transport layer, but also uses the new cost structure of the Internet and its new development and data presentation tools to create products and services that cater to a richer mix of trading partner requirements and capabilities. Another area promising new digital mediation possibilities is the decreasing cost of automatic identification technologies such as RF tags and smart cards which can have their data updated, as well as read, during the course of the transaction cycle. Dispute the current glamour and topicality of consumer-oriented EC, it will remain true for some years to come that supply chain EC has far greater potential for economic impact on firms, industry sectors, and national economies.

REFERENCES

Abraham, Y., Holt, T., and Kathawala, Y. (1990). Just-In-Time: Supplier-Side Strategic Implications. *Logistic Information Management, 3*(4), 45-48.

Andel, T. (1994). Define Cross-Docking Before You Do It. *Distribution, 35*(11), 93-98.

Anon. (1998). Technologies to Grow Electronic Trading Communities for Atkins Carlyle. *EC Edge: Newsletter of Tradegate ECA. 3*(4), 13.

Banerjee, S., and Golhar, D. Y. (1993). EDI Implementation in JIT and Non-JIT Manufacturing Firms: A Comparative Study. *International Journal of Operations and Production Management, 13*(3), 25-37.

Buxmann, P., and Gabauer, J. (1999, January 5 - 8). *Evaluating the Use of Information Technology in Inter-Organizational Relationships.* Paper presented at the 32nd. Hawaii International Conference on Systems Sciences, Maui, Hawaii.

Clarke, R. (1992). A Contingency Model of EDI's Impact on Industry Sectors. *Journal of Strategic Information Systems, 1*(3), 143-151.

Colberg, T. P. (1990). The Compelling Case for EDI. *The Financial Manager, 3*(1), 20-26.

Cowton, C. J., and Vail, R. L. (1994). Making Sense of Just-In-Time Production: A Resource-based Perspective. *OMEGA International Journal of Management Science, 22*(5), 427-441.

Cunningham, C., and Tynan, C. (1993). Electronic Trading, Inter-Organisational Systems and the Nature of Buyer-Seller Relationships: The Need for a Network Perspective. *International Journal of Information Management, 6*(3), 73-77.

Dale, C. (1991, June 27-28). *The Use of EDI in a Just-In-Time Manufacturing Environment.* Paper presented at EDICOM'91 The Asia Pacific Conference and Exhibition on Electronic Data Interchange, Singapore.

Dearing, B. E. (1990). The Strategic Benefits of EDI. *The Journal of Business Strategy, 11*(1), 4-6.

DeToni, A., Caputo, M., and Vinelli, A. (1988). Production Management Techniques: Push-Pull Classification and Application Conditions. *International Journal of Operations and Production Management, 8*(2), 35-51.

EAN. (1997). *EAN Numbering and Barcoding of Non-Retail Items: Including an Introduction to EAN Application Identifiers and EAN-128 Barcodes.* Melbourne, Australia: EAN.

Emmelhainz, M. A. (1990). *Electronic Data Interchange: A Total Management View.* New York: Van Nostrand.

Fiorito, S. S., May, E. G., and Straughn, K. (1995). Quick Response in Retailing: Components and Implementation. *International Journal of Retail and Distribution Management, 23*(5), 12-21.

Forrester, J. W. (1961). *Industrial Dynamics.* Cambridge, MA: MIT Press.

Groenevelt, H. (1993). The Just-in-Time System. In S. C. Graves, A. H. G. R. Kan, and P. H. Zipkin (Eds.), *Logistics of Production and Inventory* (Vol. 4, pp. 629-670). Amsterdam: Elsevier Science Publishers.

Hammer, M. (1990). Reengineering Work: Don't Automate, Obliterate. *Harvard Business Review, 68*(4), 104-112.

Harmon, C. K., and Adams, R. (1990). *Reading Between the Lines: An Introduction to Bar Code Technology.* Peterborough, NH: Helmers Publishing Inc.

Holmstrom, J. (1998). Implementing Vendor Managed Inventory the Efficient Way: A Case Study of Partnership in the Supply Chain. *Production and Inventory Management Journal, 39*(3), 1-5.

Hopp, W. J., and Spearman, M. L. (1996). *Factory Physics: Foundations of Manufacturing Management.* Chicago, IL: Irwin.

Hruska, V. (1995). The Internet: A Strategic Backbone for EDI. *EDI Forum: The Journal of Electronic Commerce, 8*(4), 83-85.

Iacovou, C. L., Benbaset, I., and Dexter, A. S. (1995). Electronic Data Interchange and Small Organizations: Adoption and Impact of Technology. *MIS Quarterly, 19*(4), 465-485.

Itkin, S., and Martell, J. (1992). *A PDF417 Primer.* Bohemia, NY: Symbol Technologies.

Johns, B. L., Dunlop, W. C., and Sheehan, W. J. (1989). *Small Busine$$ in Australia.* Sydney: George Allen and Unwin.

Johnston, R. B. (1995). Making Manufacturing Practices Tacit: A Case Study of Computer Aided Production Management and Lean Production. *Journal of the Operational Research Society, 46*(10), 1174-1183.

Johnston, R. B. (1996, July). *From Efficiency to Flexibility: Entropic Measures of Market Complexity and Production Flexibility.* Paper presented at Complex 96: From Local Interactions to Global Phenomena, Charles Sturt University, Albury, NSW.

Johnston, R. B. (1998). *Trading Systems and Electronic Commerce.* Melbourne: Eruditions Publishing.

Johnston, R. B., and Lee, R. P. W. (1997, January 5-8). *The Role of Electronic Commerce Technologies in Just-In-Time Replenishment.* Paper presented at the Hawaii International Conference on Systems Science, Hawaii.

Johnston, R. B., and Mak, H. C. (1999). An Emerging Vision of Internet-Enabled Supply Chain Electronic Commerce. *International Journal of Electronic Commerce*, (Forthcoming).

Johnston, R. B., and Yap, A. K. C. (1998). Two Dimensional Bar Code as a Medium for Electronic Data Interchange. *International Journal of Electronic Commerce, 3*(1), 86-101.

Kalakota, R., and Whinston, A. (1996). *Frontiers of Electronic Commerce.* New York: Addison-Wesley.

Kimberley, P. (1991). *Electronic Data Interchange.* New York: McGraw-Hill.

Kurt Salmon Associates. (1993). *Efficient Consumer Response: Enhancing Consumer Value in the Grocery Industry.* Washington, DC: Food Marketing Institute.

Lee, R. P. W. (1996). *Rationale for Adopting Electronic Commerce in the Australian Automotive Industry.* Unpublished masters thesis, Monash University, Melbourne, Australia.

Leyland, V. A. (1993). *Electronic Data Interchange: A Management View.* London: Prentice Hall.

Lynch, D. C., and Lundquist, L. (1996). *Digital Money: The New Era of Internet Commerce.* New York: John Wiley and Sons.

Mackay, D. (1995). *The Impact of Electronic Data Interchange on the Australian Automotive Industry.* Unpublished PhD thesis, Deakin University, Geelong, Australia.

Mak, H. C. (1998). *Use of the Internet to Facilitate Electronic Data Interchange between Small and Large Enterprises.* Unpublished masters thesis, Monash University, Melbourne, Australia.

Mak, H. C., and Johnston, R. B. (1997, October 3). *A Survey Of Internet Strategies For EDI.* Paper presented at the 1st Annual Collecter Workshop on Electronic Commerce, Adelaide, South Australia.

Mak, H. C., and Johnston, R. B. (1998). Tools for Implementing EDI over the Internet. *EDI Forum: The Journal of Electronic Commerce, 11*(1), 44-56.

Mak, H. C., and Johnston, R. B. (1999, January 5-8). *Leveraging Traditional EDI Investment Using the Internet: A Case Study.* Paper presented at the 32nd. Hawaii International Conference on Systems Sciences, Maui, Hawaii.

Martel, J. (1992). PDF417 Aids EDI in Transportation. *EDI World, 2*(12), 12-13.

McCullouck, B. (1994). 2D Bar-Code Applications in Construction. *Journal of Construction Engineering and Management, 120*(4), 739-751.

Monden, Y. (1983). *Toyota Production System.* Norcross: Institute of Industrial Engineers.

Mukhopadhray, T., Kekre, S., and Kalathur, S. (1995). Business Value of Information Technology: A Study of Electronic Data Interchange. *MIS Quarterly, 19*(2), 137-156.

O'Mahony, D., Peirce, M., and Tewari, H. (1997). *Electronic Payment Systems.* Norwood, MA: Artech House, Inc.

Orlicky, J. (1975). *Material Requirements Planning.* New York: McGraw-Hill Book Company.

Pavlidis, T., Swatz, J., and Wang, Y. (1992). Information Encoding with Two-Dimensional Bar Codes. *IEEE Computer Magazine, 25*(6), 18-28.

Prajogo, N. H., and Johnston, R. B. (1997, November 12-15). *JIT Implementation in Small Manufacturing Enterprises: A Case Study Analysis.* Paper presented at the 2nd Annual International Conference on Industrial Engineering Applications and Practice, San Diego, USA.

Prajogo, N. H., and Johnston, R. B. (1999). A Barriers Framework for Just-In-Time Implementation in Small Manufacturing Enterprises. *International Journal of Technology Management,* (Forthcoming).

Ragsdale, C. T., and Gilbert, J. P. (1990). Is EDI Needed for JIT? A Survey of U.S. Firms Using JIT. *EDI Forum, 3,* 13-16.

Rochester, J. B. (1989). The Strategic Value of EDI. *I/S Analyser, 27*(8), 1-14.

Rodwell, J., and Shadur, M. (1997). What's Size Got to Do with It? Implications for Contemporary Management Practices in IT Companies. *International Journal of Small Business Management, 15*(2), 51-62.

Sarich, A. (1989). *The Outlook for Pan-European EDI.* Paper presented at the Electronic Messaging and Communications Systems, London, UK.

Scala, S., and McGrath, R. (1993). Advantages and Disadvantages of Electronic Data Interchange. *Information and Management, 25,* 85-91.

Schonberger, R. J. (1982). *Japanese Manufacturing Techniques: Nine Hidden Lessons in Simplicity.* New York.: The Free Press.

Schonberger, R. J. (1987). The Kanban System. In C. A. Voss (Ed.), *Just-In-Time Manufacture* (pp. 59-71). London: IFS Ltd. UK.

Seidman, T. (1993). BC Labels Turn High-Tech. *Distribution, 92*(1), 83-84.

Skagen, A. E. (1989). Nurturing Relationships, Enhancing Quality with Electronic Data Interchange. *Management Review, 78*(2), 28-32.

Srinivasan, K., Kekre, S., and Mukhopadhray, T. (1994). Impact of Electronic Data Interchange Technology on JIT Shipments. *Management Science, 40*(10), 1291-1304.

Swatman, P. (1993). *Integrating Electronic Data Interchange into Existing Organisational Structure and Internal Application Systems.* Unpublished PhD thesis, Curtin University of Technology, Perth, Australia.

Womack, J. P., Jones, D. T., and Roos, D. (1990). *The Machine That Changed The World.* New York: Rawson Associates.

Yap, A. K. C. (1997). *The Feasibility of Using Two Dimensional Bar Codes as a Medium for Electronic Data Interchange.* Unpublished masters thesis, Monash University, Clayton.

Zinn, D. K., and Tahac, P. F. (1988). *Electronic Data Interchange in Australia: Markets, Opportunities and Developments.* Melbourne: Royal Melbourne Institute of Technology Press.

Chapter IV

Electronic Trade Scenario for Global Supply Chains

Ronald M. Lee
Erasmus University, Netherlands

This chapter introduces the concept of an electronic trade scenario as an aid to the management of (global) supply chains, and other forms of international, business-to-business electronic commerce. The problem addressed is the following. Competition demands that trade transactions be handled efficiently and securely. However, the same competitive environment also demands flexibility, and the ability to redesign the supply chain as conditions change. Current EDI (electronic data interchange) technologies offer efficiencies, but tend to be quite inflexible, often requiring substantial reprogramming for each modification to the transaction. Furthermore, these revisions need to be made not just for a single company, but for every affected company in the supply chain. In cases where some of the companies in the chain are relatively small, with limited computing staff and skills, such changes are even more difficult and disruptive. Electronic trade scenarios are generic, reusable models of the entire trade transaction. They are stored in a on-line repository, where each member of the supply chain can download the transaction component for their role in the transaction.

*In our proposed solution, the procedural logic of the transaction is designed using a high level, graphical representation called Documentary Petri Nets (DPN). The **InterProcs** system is described as a prototyping environment to support the design and execution of such supply chain transaction models using this DPN representation. A key concern will be the development of trustworthy trade scenarios that have sufficient controls and evidentiary documentation. Various directions of further work are described to improve the quality and flexibility of trade scenario designs.*

Copyright © 2000, Idea Group Publishing.

INTRODUCTION

Electronic linkages to support in global supply chains are typically implemented using Electronic Data Interchange (EDI), which provides a standardized format and structure for business documents in electronic form. While this standardization of the electronic documents provides some independence and generality among the trading partners, the actual implementations, nonetheless, tend to involve a high amount of relationship specific investment.

For industries where change is gradual, this is not a serious problem. But in industries that are more dynamic, e.g., the electronics industry, such relationship specific investments can become a hindrance to change. In these cases, there is a need to make these electronic linkages more generic and reusable. Furthermore, the scope of the modeling needs to encompass not only simple two-party links, but the entire trade or supply chain transaction model, which may include as many as a dozen different parties.

The most complex challenges are in the area of global supply chains. In these cases, trading relationships are not only with other companies, who have similar competitive pressures, but also with a variety of governmental agencies involved in the regulation of import and export. In many cases, the transaction costs of dealing internationally are double or triple those for domestic trading, ranging from 7-10 % of the total transaction value. (On a global scale, this is an added cost of over two trillion dollars per year.)

The focus of this paper is to propose a new technology, called electronic trade scenarios, as a means of reducing the transaction costs of global supply chains, while yet providing increased flexibility to quickly modify and re-configure them in response to changing market conditions. The basic idea is to separate out those aspects of the electronic transaction that are not relationship specific, and represent them in the form of trade "scenarios" that are more generic and reusable.

These electronic trade scenarios can then be made available via publicly accessible repositories that are under, for instance:
   a. proprietary control (e.g. a major manufacturer)
   b. controlled by an industry or sector organization (e.g. insurance industry)
   c. controlled by a local or regional sector, e.g. a port authority
   d. made globally available, e.g. by the International Chamber of Commerce (ICC), or United Nations.

A given supply chain application may in fact draw components from several such repositories, and assemble them (with automated tools) to provide a customized transaction model. Current technology developments in wide area networking (e.g. extranets) and related component technologies make this vision increasingly feasible and practical. Needed, however, are effective design representations and methodologies for representing complex trade and supply chain transactions.

In this paper we examine the requirements for such representations. We then present our own solution to this challenge: Documentary Petri Nets (DPNs), which satisfy these representation requirements in a way that supports both bottom-up and top-down design approaches, and also procedural separation of the business roles. Implementation characteristics of the DPN representation are also examined.

A modeling and prototyping environment, called ***InterProcs***, is presented that includes a graphical design interface based on Documentary Petri Nets, which automatically generates functioning prototype transaction models that operate locally or in distributed fashion over the Internet.

But this is only the beginning of the potential we foresee. Once a formal representation for trade scenarios is adopted, new functionalities may be developed based on that representation. Here, we briefly examine two of these:

- scenario grammars — which allow the sharing and reusability of chunks of procedural knowledge at arbitrary levels of abstraction. For instance, a car loan, a mortgage, and a documentary credit procedure are all special cases of a more generic secured loan. The use of scenario grammars allows computer aided generation of customized procedures by parties with little or no expertise.
- supply chain designer — a high level graphical interface for combining supply chain components (based on scenario grammars).

ELECTRONIC TRADE SCENARIOS

An electronic trade scenario is a computational component that controls the document flow and related constraints and rules for a trade transaction. It also contains specifications for the electronic documents[1] used in the transaction. An electronic trade scenario may be a complete, automatic generic solution for a certain type of trade transaction. As such, it may be downloaded from a public repository by the contracting parties and executed immediately. Alternatively, an electronic trade scenario may be a component, intended to be combined with other components, to perform a transaction. In this case, contracting parties may assemble components from several different repositories to produce a customized trade transaction solution. Electronic trade scenarios are also discussed in the context of Open-EDI (Ahlsen, 1994; ISO, 1991; ISO, 1996).

All of this is technologically feasible using current Java and related component technologies. What is missing is the capability to represent, design and analyze electronic trade scenarios. In order for an electronic trade scenario to be of any value, it must be trustworthy. That is, the parties need to have confidence that it will perform the transaction in a way that is safely controlled from each party's perspective. This is a difficult claim to achieve. But the difficulty is not so much technology as modeling.

Clearly, as for ordinary paper-based transactions, the trustworthiness of the procedure is also an issue. This is usually solved by various experts, such as the lawyers that draw up the contract. Also, problems are sometimes detected by the clerical staff that handle the documents. Their professional knowledge is also part of the manual procedure.

The trustworthiness of an electronic trade scenario depends on the degree to which this legal and clerical control knowledge is incorporated into the design of the electronic trade scenario. This is the knowledge acquisition challenge. However, once acquired and refined, the control knowledge represented in the electronic trade scenario can be reused an unlimited number of times. This is a very important consideration. Thus, while electronic trade scenarios require a great deal more exactness and detail than manual procedures in their original design, it is a one-time learning investment.

Compare this to the usual situation, where there may be wide variations in proficiency among the clerical staff. For instance, studies have shown that in cases of international trade transactions (e.g., documentary credit procedures), some 50% of the transactions contain errors that cause delays and sometimes even void the transaction (Dewitz, 1992). In effect, an electronic trade scenario is able to capture the skills and knowledge of the best clerk on his/her best day.

ARCHITECTURES FOR ELECTRONIC TRADE SCENARIOS

There are various kinds of architectures for electronic trade scenarios. In each of these cases, we assume that the electronic trade scenario is made available by means of a repository that is publicly available to the trading community. Each party (role) in a trade transaction, whether done repetitively or only once, may obtain the electronic transaction sub-procedure for their role by downloading from this repository, as shown in Figure 1.

Hub and Spoke

One architecture is where a single organization dominates the transaction and determines the transaction procedure its clients must follow. This is typical, for instance, of large car manufactures. It might also be used for the purchase tendering procedures of large governmental organizations. In this case the "hub" organization designs the electronic trade scenario and makes it available to its clients from its own repository.

Regional Trade Community

Another architecture is used to support regional trade communities, such as a port. In this case, there may be an independent service organization that provides the electronic trade

Figure 1: Parties Downloading from Electronic Trade Scenario Repository

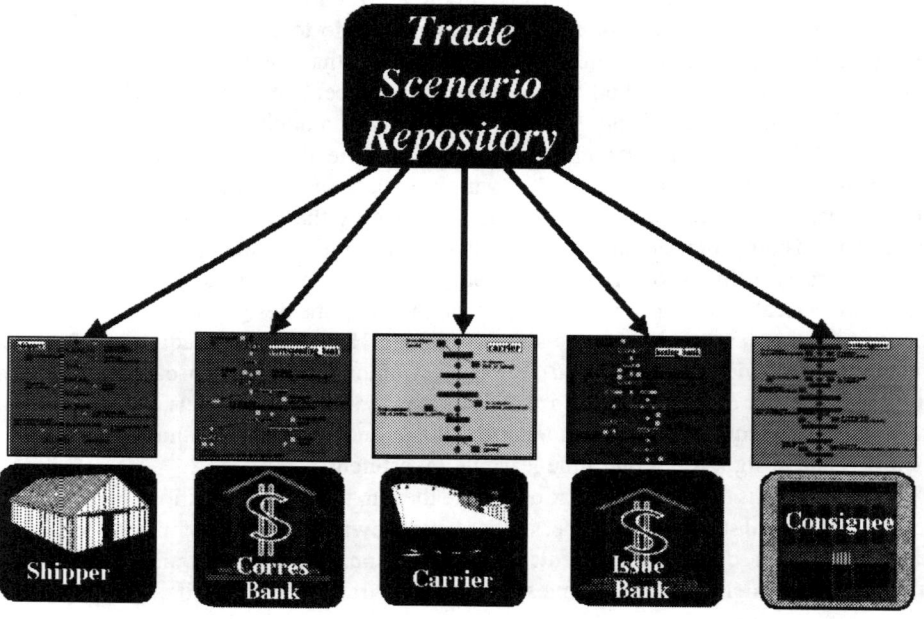

scenarios via a regional registry. New companies that seek to participate in the port's electronic trading need only to download the electronic trade scenarios for the transactions they need.

Industry Sector

Somewhat similar to regional trade communities, certain industrial sectors may develop electronic trade scenario repositories. Here, the parties using the electronic trade scenarios may be geographically dispersed. (However, distance has little importance for electronic networks.) Examples might be textile, construction, and banking industries. In this case an industry organization may develop the electronic trade scenarios and provide the repository.

International, Global Trade

At the global level, the candidate service organization might be the United Nations (CEFACT), WTO or ICC. Here, electronic trade scenarios would be provided for transactions where globally recognized conventions have been established. For instance, the ICC might maintain electronic trade scenarios for documentary credit transactions. Similarly, the World Customs Organization (WCO) might provide electronic trade scenarios for the exchange of control documents among national customs agencies.

FORMAL REPRESENTATION OF TRADE SCENARIOS

A basic issue for this project is how electronic trade scenarios should be represented (a) from the modeler's perspective, and (b) from a computation (inferential) perspective. In the course of our prior research, we have examined a wide number of such representations, including state-transition diagrams, marked graphs, event nets, event grammars, the event calculus, process algebras, temporal and dynamic logics. Eventually, we found Petri Nets (Petri, 1962; Peterson, 1981; Aalst, 1992) to be the most appropriate representation for capturing the temporal/dynamic aspects of electronic trade scenarios, offering both a graphical representation (for modelers) and a formal basis for the verification of various properties (computational). In addition, Petri nets have become popular in a wide variety of problem domains where sequence, contingency and concurrency of activities need to be modeled. This wide acceptance facilitates the training and understandability for electronic trade scenarios. However, Petri Nets by themselves offer only a temporal framework for knowledge representation. For that reason, we have found it necessary to add various extensions to the Petri Net representation, making it more appropriate for the modeling of trade scenarios, what we call Documentary Petri Nets (DPNs). The actions represented in a DPN can include the sending or receiving of a document, goods or funds, or the expiration of a deadline (Lee, 1992; Bons, Lee, Wagenaar, 1995; Lee and Bons, 1996).

Basic petri nets focus on the representation of discrete dynamic systems, including aspects of concurrency and choice. A petri net is a bi-partite, directed graph with two types of nodes: *places* (represented as circles) and *transitions* (typically represented as bars or boxes). Arcs connect places with transitions or vice versa (it is not allowed to connect two places or two transitions). The dynamic behavior of the modeled system is represented by tokens flowing through the net (represented as blackening of a place). A transition is enabled if all its input places (i.e., arcs exist from those places to the transition) are marked. If this

Figure 2a: DPN Transition (Action) Syntax

Figure 2b: DPN Timer Event Syntax

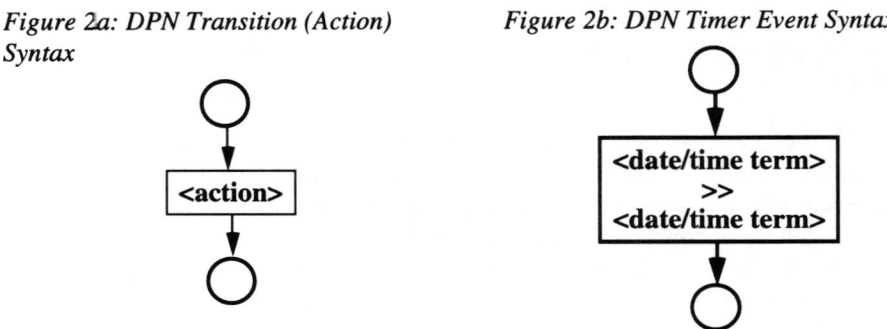

Figure 2c: Example DPN for Deadline

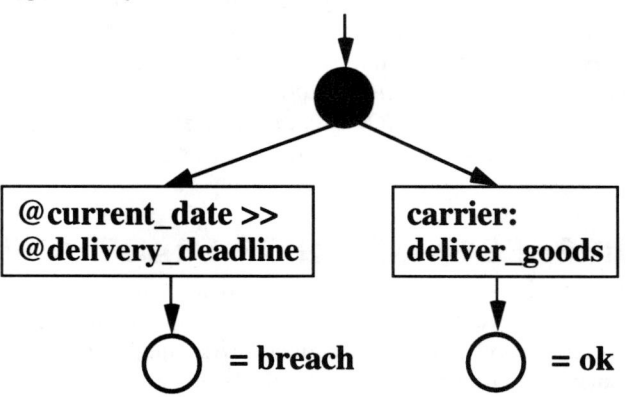

Figure 2d: DPN Document Place Syntax

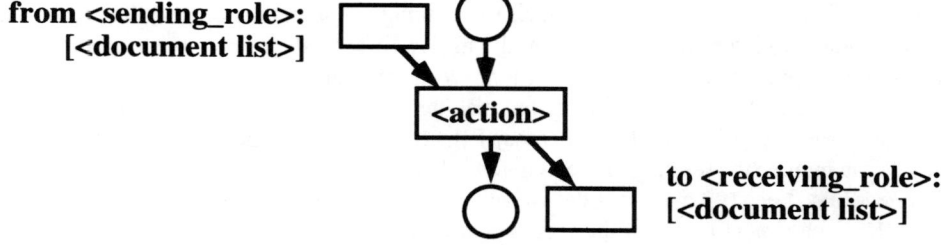

is the case, the transition removes the token from each input place and instantaneously produces one in each output place (i.e., an arc exists from the transition to the place). This is called the *firing* of a transition.

Figure 2e: DPN Physical Goods Syntax

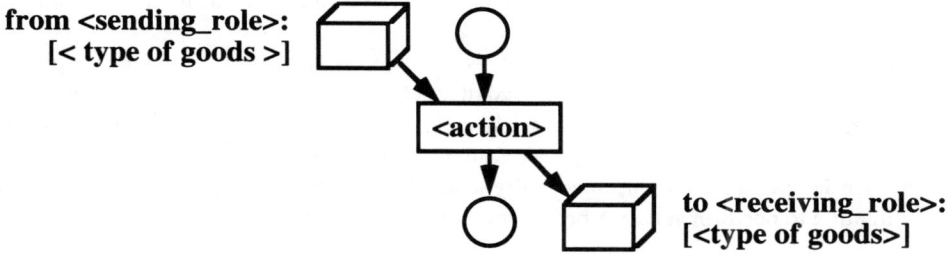

Figure 2f: DPN Example Deontic Status Labels on Control Places

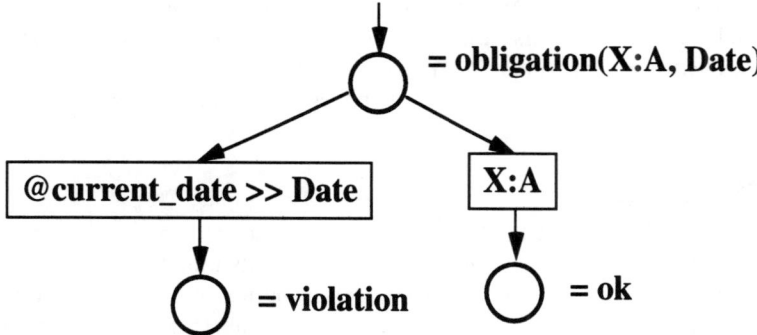

Our extended form of petri nets is called documentary petri nets (DPNs). An important addition we make is the interpretation of transitions as the actions of contracting parties, which are indicated by an associated label of the form[2] shown in Figure 2a. Also, whereas basic petri nets represent relative time, we needed to add certain absolute time notations for deadlines, etc. In DPNs, these are included as a special kind of transition, called a *timer event*, having an associated label of the form (">>" is time ordering), as shown in Figure 2b. Most commonly, these involve a comparison of the built-in parameter, **@current_date**, with a another date such as a delivery deadline. For example, see Figure 2c. In this case, the token will be taken by the first transition to occur. Thus, if the event that the current date exceeds the delivery date occurs before the delivery of the goods, the token will more to the state of breach.

Another important extension to basic petri nets that we have added in DPNs, is a representation of *documents*[3]. Syntactically, these are another kind of place node, called a *document place*, drawn as a rectangle. In the role procedures, each document place has an associated label of the form as shown in Figure 2d. Normally, the document list will be only a single document (type), but this allows also for the sending of bundles of documents as a single documentary communication[4]. A frequent type of documentary exchange relates to the transfer of funds. Often, this is a document sent to a bank, such as a payment instruction. In business-to-business transactions, the exchange of actual cash is fairly rare. However, to model such cash payments we also use the same notation of a document place. (Thus, we would consider paper currency as a special kind of performative document.) A variation of document places that is occasionally used is a *goods place*, indicating the exchange of physical goods. The notation for this is a cube, and it has a similar labeling as for document places[5], as shown in Figure 2e.

In addition to the above described labels, any of the control places, document places or goods places may have an additional kind of label, known as a state predicate. These use the same predicate notation as in Prolog, and are used to indicate additional properties and relations that become true when the place is marked. These are commonly used to indicate changes in deontic status, for instance, **obligation(X:A, Date)** which means that party **X** has an obligation to perform action **A** before the deadline, **Date**[6]. This is illustrated in Figure 2f.

One important aspect of modeling trade scenarios is the ability to model the procedures of each role as a separate documentary petri net. This modeling style results in a clear, visual separation of the various the roles, that also enables their geographical separation. Indeed, it is this characteristic of the DPN modeling technique that allows the automated trade scenarios to be executed in a distributed fashion, by *legally autonomous parties. The only coordination between the various role scenarios is by means of the (electronic) documents they exchange.* This directly parallels the way paper-based trade procedures operate today.

INTERPROCS

The overall objective of this project has been to develop a general framework for electronic trade scenarios, and to demonstrate its feasibility though a realistic pilot system with real transactions based on various model scenarios. This pilot system is called *InterProcs*. This divides into two separate systems, one to aid in the modeling and knowledge base development, called *InterProcs Designer*, and the other, which executes transactions, utilizing this knowledge base, called *InterProcs Executor*.

InterProcs Designer

The development of an electronic trade scenario is done using *InterProcs Designer* (Lee, 1992; Lee and Bons, 1996; Lee, 1999). To design a Documentary Petri Net, the user interacts using a graphical interface. This graph is then compiled into an internal (object-based) representation. This supports the capability of simulating or actually executing these trade procedures.

The simulation mode allows the designer to verify the DPN model, and as well demonstrate it to users and clients. This can be done locally or over the Internet.

The architecture of these electronic trade scenarios assumes that they will be distributed among multiple, distant parties. Thus, the trade procedure is a collection of separate sub-procedures, one for each party to the transaction. The coordination among these role procedures is done exclusively by the (EDI) documents they exchange.

A tiny example[7] of an *InterProcs* model is displayed in Figure 3. Here a Documentary Petri Net is shown for the buyer role, as well as a sample electronic document. Figure 4 shows a sample electronic document in English and Dutch.

InterProcs Executor

In addition to the knowledge engineering tools provided by *InterProcs*, a transaction system has been developed, called *InterProcs Executor*. This is a pilot version for a

Figure 3: Role DPNs (Buyer and Seller) for Simple InterProcs Model

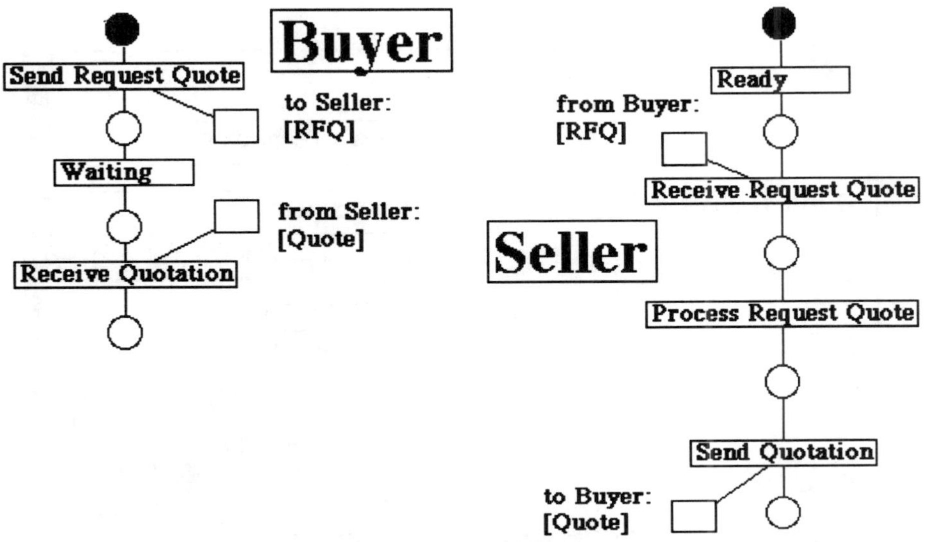

commercial product/service, supporting open electronic contracting (Open-EDI) for multiple concurrent transactions among distant parties. Implemented in Java, it operates over the Internet, and may be executed as an applet, via a Web site, or as a stand-alone application. It has the following three modes of operation:

- Viewer mode — this is single-user simulation of all the roles together; it is normally executed as an applet from a Web site.
- Gaming mode — this is multi-user simulation, also executed as an applet from a Web site; each user executes a separate role of the transaction from a different computer which may be at different locations, and EDI documents are sent among the roles utilizing the Web site as a central post-office.
- Network mode — this is also a multi-user simulation, where each user executes a stand-alone version of the Executor, after downloading his/her role model for the transaction. EDI documents are sent via normal Internet e-mail (POP). This mode is a realistic pilot of actual commercial operation, since transaction results may be stored, and other interfaces to local applications may be introduced.

The *InterProcs Executor* includes an electronic document facility (like other EDI servers), but most importantly, it executes transactions distributed across the various parties automatically based on electronic trade scenarios.

As discussed earlier, these scenarios are of two types: fixed form (manually developed) and parameter driven (expert system). For the fixed form scenarios, users need only select the scenario, and the transaction procedure is determined. For parameter-driven scenarios, a user-dialog is needed to determine the situational characteristics. As with other aspects of contract negotiation, this will proceed from one party to another in an offer, counter-offer, acceptance sequence. Once this dialog is complete, the inference engine will assemble the trade scenario.

Figure 4: Sample Electronic Document: English and Dutch

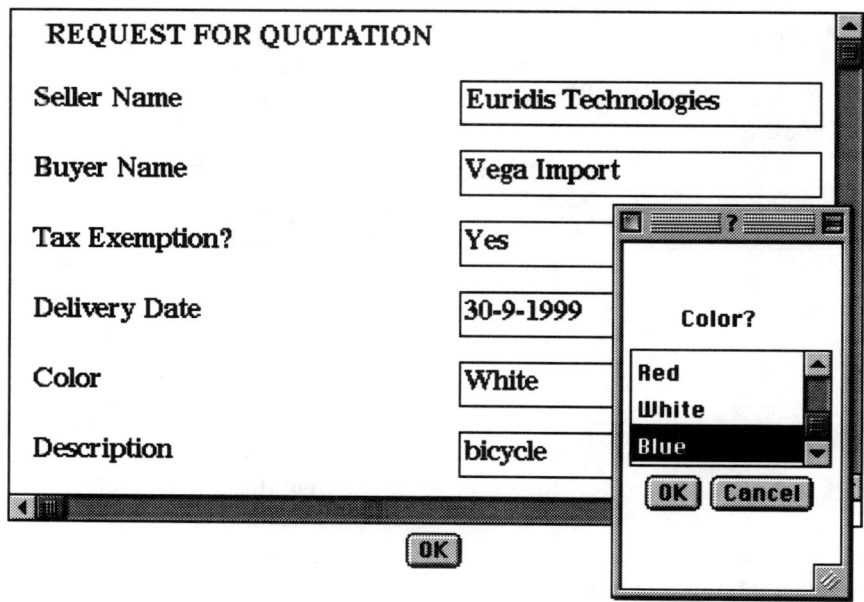

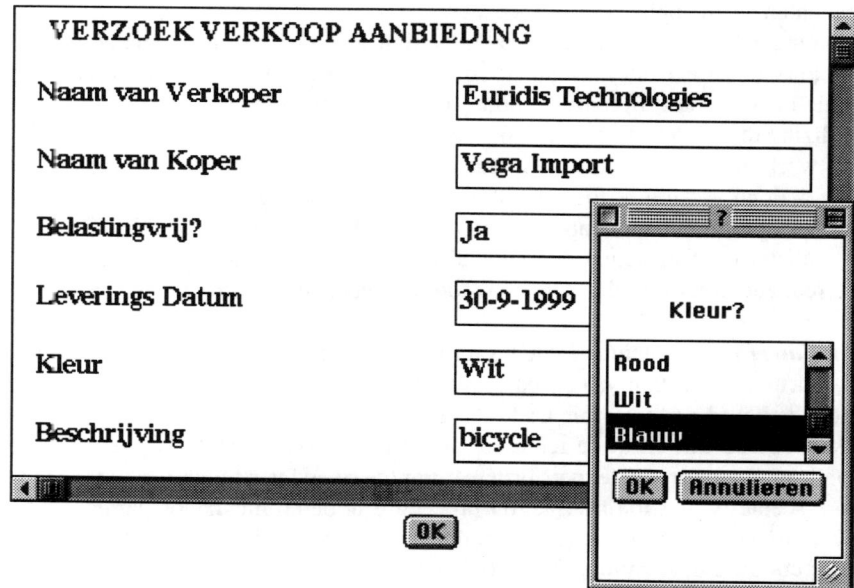

MODELING EXAMPLE

Many global supply chains involve sea transport. Even in this aspect by itself, the transaction model may be quite complex (UN/ITPWG, 1999).

Following is an example electronic trade scenario for import/export, based on procedures used at the Port of Rotterdam. This model was developed (by R. Bons) based on the Port of Rotterdam Executive Game (Wagenaar, 1992; Wrigley, Wagenaar, and Clarke, 1994), developed at Erasmus University, which in turn was based on analysis and interviews conducted at the Port of Rotterdam itself. It is important to keep in mind that each of these snapshots is the graphical display of a separate computer program, operating on the local machine of each of these parties, essentially a distributed software system for the transaction. Each of the party's role scenarios is downloaded from a central site (the 'transaction provider'), in this case probably the port authority, and is immediately executable. In short, it is "point and click" installation of EDI capability.

The first diagram, following, is called an Overview Graph. It summarizes all of the document flows among the parties, but omits the details of the sequencing of these flows (sequential order, contingent branching, concurrency). These detail aspects are contained in the DPN diagrams for each role.

Following, we present the Documentary Petri Ne models for three of these roles: the exporter, the export liner agent, and the export liner agent. (Because of space limitations, only these few could be shown.) We remind the reader that while the procedure is shown graphically, each of these DPNs is actually a separate computer program (in Java), that operates independently at each of the parties' locations.

ONGOING DEVELOPMENTS

Having modeled various international trade procedures using the DPN representation and prototyping them using **InterProcs**, we begin to visualize more advanced kinds of functionality, incorporating more 'intelligence' into the system. Two of these ongoing developments that pertain specifically to global supply chains are discussed here. First is a generalization of the DPN representation, called procedure constraint grammars (PCGs), that allows abstraction of trade procedures into more generic procedural components. The second, supply chain designer, is an experimental application using these PCGs.

Procedure Constraint Grammars

A limitation of the manual design approach (indeed, more generally of other Open-EDI approaches) is that the scenarios produced are fixed; that is, they cannot be adapted or adjusted to meet additional needs of a given situation. In this part of the project, we address this problem with an expert system approach, by which scenario components are broken down into reusable component parts, which can be flexibly reassembled to meet the needs of a wide variety of situations.

The computational formalism employed is called a PCG. As its name suggests, an objective of the PCG representation is to describe procedures by their temporal ordering *constraints,* rather than the absolute sequence of steps (Lee, 1997; Lee 1998). This allows for more flexible recombination of procedural components (doing and control tasks).

Using a procedure constraint grammar, the user interacts with the system, specifying constraints and objectives of the contracting situation. Based on these specifications, the

Figure 5: Overview Graph for Import/Export

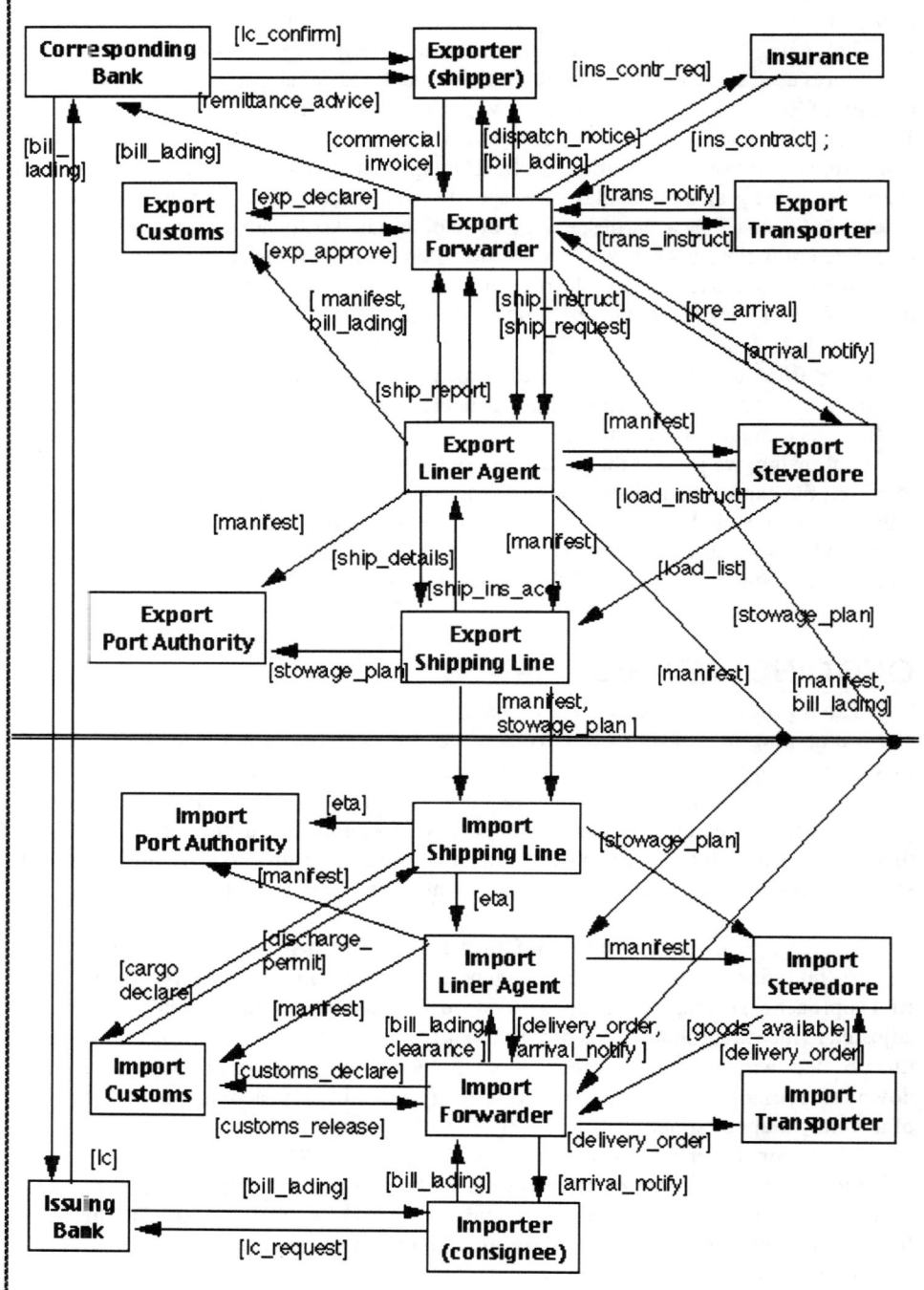

Figure 6a: DPN for Exporter

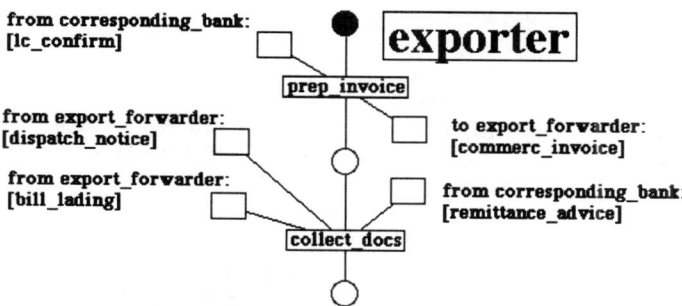

Figure 6b: DPN for Export Forwarder

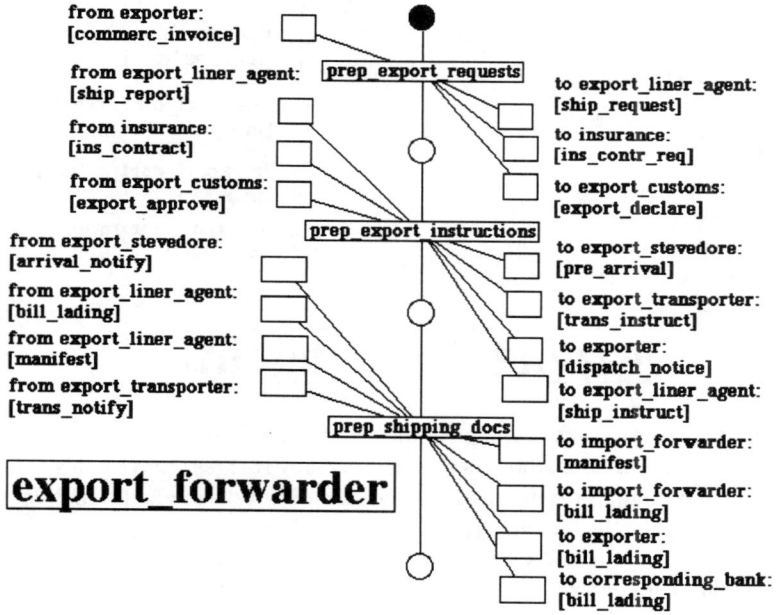

system composes a trade procedure, which is presented in graphical form, and which can then be compiled and simulated. Here, the term 'grammar' is used in the linguistic sense of generative grammars, i.e., a set of rules for generating syntactically correct or well-formed sentences in a language. The objective of PCG rules is to generate procedures that are not only well-formed syntactically, but also from a control standpoint. In this aspect, a procedure constraint grammar operates like an expert system shell that may be used to develop knowledge bases about contracting and associated legal and documentary requirements.

Unlike language grammars, however, which are typically represented as an integrated hierarchy of rules, PCGs are organized as *constraints* on a target procedure. It is the job of the PCG constraint solver to identify a (minimal) solution procedure (according to some preference ordering of the user — e.g. minimal duration vs. minimal risk).

Figure 6c: DPN for Export Liner Agent

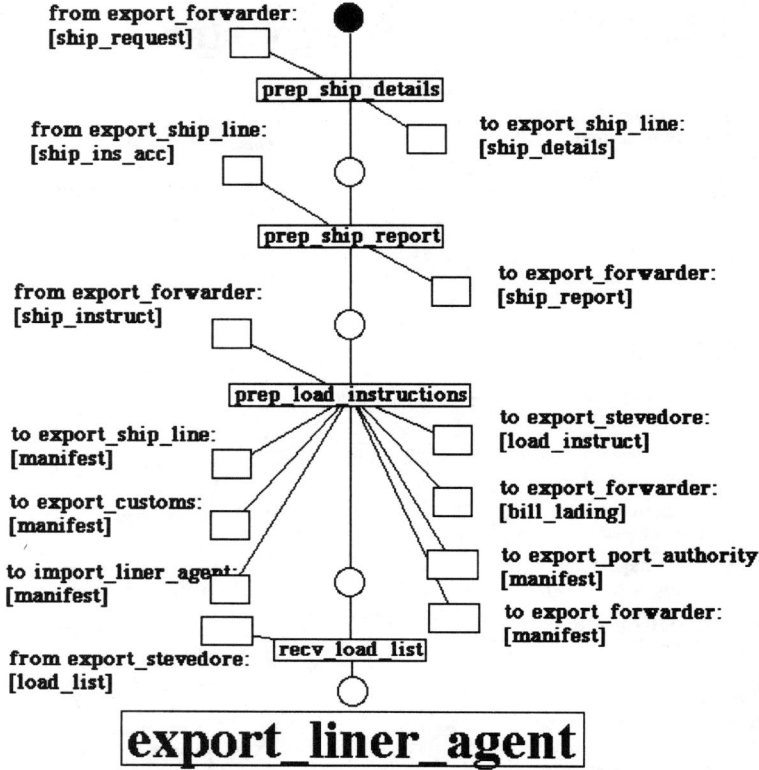

We classify these tasks of the procedure into two broad categories: *doing* tasks and *control* tasks. Doing tasks are those organized to achieve the respective goals of the parties, e.g., building a building or transporting goods. Control tasks are additional documentary actions meant to provide evidence (including an audit trail) of the parties' performance. More specifically, control tasks are means of ensuring that each of the parties conforms to their obligations in the contract. Thus, controls may be either detective — in recognizing that a contractual violation (breach) has occurred, or preventative, in verifying preconditions for activities (e.g., checking that someone has an import license).

In the architecture for procedure constraint grammars, we want to provide a clear separation of specification for these two kinds of tasks, doing and control. The reasons are twofold. First, the sources for these two types of activities in a contract are different: doing tasks represent the goals of the contracting parties, whereas control tasks are often imposed for legal considerations, etc. (Indeed, the interests may conflict to some extent — excessive of control tasks may add overhead that actually impedes the completion of the doing tasks.) Second, the commitments or obligations of the contract (mainly) govern the doing tasks, but not (so much) the control tasks. Thus, in mid-execution of a contract, a control task might be revised or achieved in some other manner without violating the contract terms.

Electronic Trade Scenario for Global Supply Chains 79

Supply Chain Designer

A supply chain is a contractual linkage among various parties, normally to achieve a 'just in time' flow of supplied goods. The purpose of the supply chain designer is to quickly generate the electronic trade scenarios for a new supply chain. In addition to scenario templates, which include the actions of multiple roles, another kind are role templates, which contain the actions of just a single role. The supply chain designer makes use of role templates to produce the links of the supply chain. An interesting feature of the supply chain designer is that the design of the chain can be specified by means of a more aggregate level kind of graphical interface, where the building blocks are not detailed actions, but rather entire roles. An example of this supply chain design interface is shown in the snapshot of Figure 7. The parties of the chain, warehouse0, transporter0, and retailer0, are instances of role templates, Warehouse, Transporter, and Retailer. In the supply chain, there may be multiple instances of a certain template. For instance, there may be more than one warehouse, or multiple carriers (as for multi-modal transport). The links among them represent the flow of goods. However, other kinds of linkages may also be defined.

When the option 'Expand Chain Model' is selected, the trade scenario is generated. For instance, for this tiny demonstration example, the generated scenario is as shown in the snapshots of Figure 8.

Figure 7: Snapshot of Example Supply Chain Design

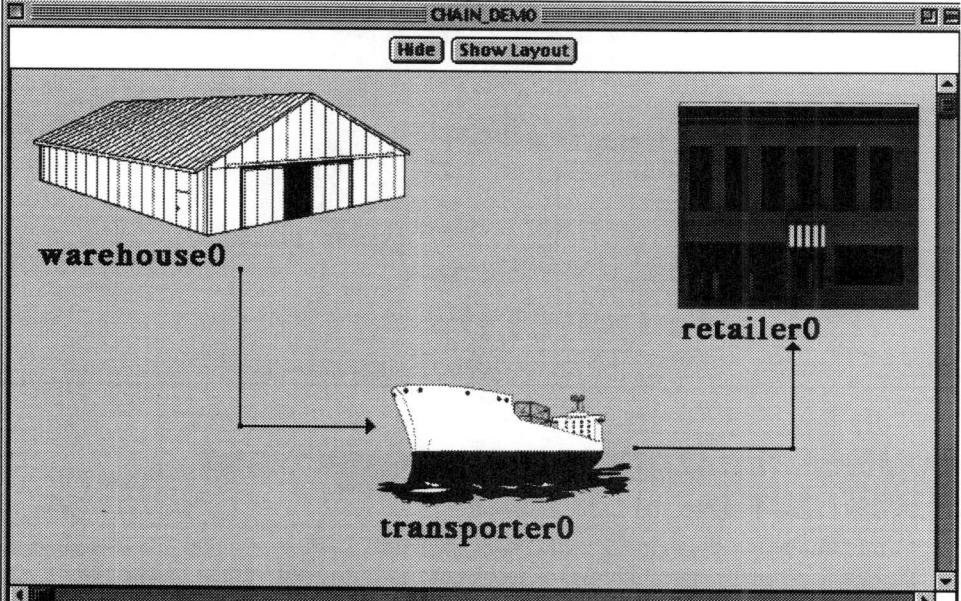

Figure 8: Snapshots of Generated Trade Scenario for Supply Chain Design

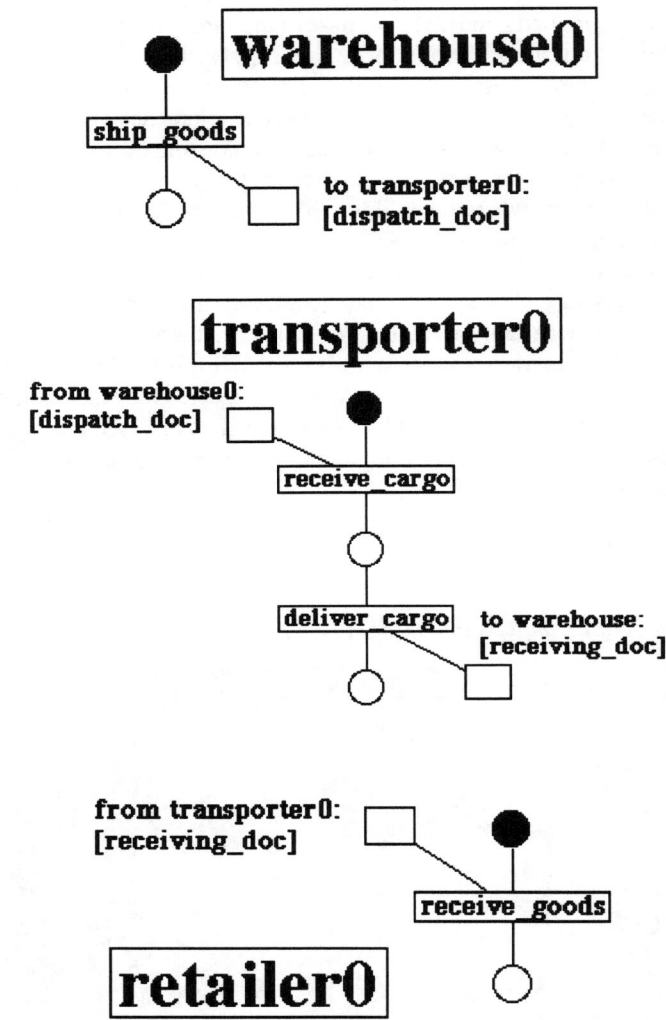

COMMERCIALIZATION PATH: COMPONENT ARCHITECTURE

Up to this point, the value of *InterProcs* is mainly in the design and prototyping of trade scenarios. But, the question that arises is how does this model lead to the implementation of a commercial system? *InterProcs* models are incomplete in two important respects:
  a. interfacing to standard (EDI) document definitions
  b. interfacing to local applications

Building an interface to e.g. UN/EDIFACT document definitions involves parsing the definition syntax into the internal (predicate logic form) used by *InterProcs*. Indeed, such an interface has been designed, and an implementation is planned. However, new forms of document syntax are being developed (e.g. Lite EDI, XML/EDI, FLBC), and presumably separate interfaces would be needed for each new syntax that comes along. However, this problem is hardly unique to *InterProcs*, and one would expect a more general solution to be available.

The second problem, of interfacing to local applications (those internal to a specific company), is far more difficult. Whereas EDI document syntax is subject to agreement and ratification by industry groups and international organizations, there are no restrictions on the way a company chooses to implement its internal systems. A possible solution for this is in the growing popularity of application packages, e.g., those of Baan, SAP, that replace ad-hoc data processing software with off-the-shelf parameter-driven solutions. A by-product of this approach is that these installations have uniform interface by which their applications may communicate with the outside world. Unfortunately, these solutions are (so far) vendor specific.

What is needed is more of an "open systems" approach for application integration. Such an approach is gradually emerging in what is coming to be known as "component-based architectures" (Segev and Bichler, 1998). While this is emerging on several fronts, such as CommerceNet, MicroSoft, the leading innovations (at the present time) appear to be from a consortium (including Sun, IBM, Netscape, Oracle, Baan, and others) focusing on specifications for components based on the Java programming language (O'Niel and Schildt, 1998) and CORBA (Vogel, 1998).

"A component is a reusable software building block: a pre-built piece of encapsulated application code that can be combined with other components and with handwritten code to rapidly produce a custom application ... An application developer should be able to make full use of the component without requiring access to its source code. [Thus,] customized business solutions can be assembled from a set of off-the-shelf business objects" (Thomas, 1997, pp 5-6).

A particular initiative, known as "Enterprise Java Platform" directly addresses the problems of production-level implementation of *InterProcs* models, providing "a standard set of application programming interfaces (APIs) to a core set of enterprise-class infrastructure services, including life cycle, naming, remote invocation, messaging, transactions, database access, and management" (Thomas, 1997, p. 9).

Of course the information technology marketplace is extremely dynamic, and it is yet too early to tell if this particular component solution will succeed. However, enthusiastic industry response seems to indicate that some kind of open systems component architecture will emerge. Further, it appears that Java will play an important role in this architecture. Anticipating this, we are extending *InterProcs* so that scenarios can be saved in component form (separated by role). With this, a local application environment can download a role-scenario component that has been designed by *InterProcs*, and automatically install it to include database access, security, transaction management, etc.

The component approach to be an emerging solution for interfacing to EDI documents as well (Harvey et al., 1998). Rather than being simply data structures, document components will be objects that can dynamically communicate their data contents in a variety of syntactic forms (obtained via object inheritance). Ultimately, these document components will be made available via global repositories, available for applications worldwide.

SUMMARY, CONCLUSIONS

The concept of an electronic trade scenario was introduced as a potential solution to "open" electronic commerce — trade among parties that have no prior trading relationship. The vision is that these trade scenarios would be stored in a publicly accessible electronic library (perhaps a "global repository" maintained by an independent international organization), and downloaded by trading parties as needed for a particular trade. The Documentary Petri Nets (DPNS) representation was presented as a candidate representation for such trade scenarios. The *InterProcs* system was presented as a prototyping environment to support the design and execution of such trading systems using this DPN representation. Features included a graphical design interface for trade scenarios, Internet-based scenario execution, audit daemons for detecting control weakness, as well as scenario grammars and supply chain designer for the automated generation of trade scenarios. Future directions include the output of trade scenarios as object-oriented components for assimilation within emerging business component architectures, to support plug-and-play installation of trade scenarios into production transaction systems.

REFERENCES

Aalst, W.M.P. van der (1992). "Timed Coloured Petri Nets and their Application to Logistics", *PhD thesis Eindhoven University of Technology*.

Ahlsen, M., Pelkonen, H., Walseth, S.(1994). "Concepts and Notations for Open-EDI Scenarios", *Dedicate Project Report No 8*, Swedish Institute for Systems Development SISU, February.

Bons, R.W.H., Lee, R.M. & Wagenaar, R.W.(1995). *Modelling Inter-organisational Trade Procedures Using Documentary Petri Nets*, Proceedings Hawaii International Conference on System Sciences (HICSS) 28, Hawaii, USA, pp. III/189-198.

Dewitz, Sandra (1992). *Contracting on a Performative Network: Using Information Technology as a Legal Intermediary*, PhD Dissertation, University of Texas at Austin,.

Harvey, B. Hill, D. Schuldt, R. Martin, B., Thayer, W. Raman & D. Webber (1998). "Position Statement of Global Repositories for XML", The XML/EDI Group, July, (www.eccnet.com/pub/xmledi/xml-rep.htm)

ISO (1991). *The Open-edi Conceptual Model*, ISO/IEC JTC1/SWG-EDI, Document N222,.

ISO (1996). *The Open-edi Reference Model*, IS 14662, ISO/IEC JTC1/SC30.

Kimbrough, S. (1998-99). Sketch of a Basic Theory for a Formal Language for Business Communication, *International Journal of Electronic Commerce*, 3(2), 23-44.

Lee, R.M. (1992). "Dynamic Modeling of Documentary Procedures: A CASE for EDI", *Proceedings of Third International Working Conference on Dynamic Modeling of Information Systems*, Noordwijkerhout, NL, June.

Lee, R.M.(1997). "A Messenger Model for Navigating Among Bureaucratic Requirements", *Proceedings of the Hawaii International Conference on System Sciences*, January, Vol IV, 468-477.

Lee, R.M. (1998). "Automatic Generation of Electronic Procedures: Procedure Constraint

Grammars" Proceedings of the Eleventh International Electronic Commerce Conference, Bled, Slovenia, 8-10 June, II: 49-85.

Lee, R.M. (1999). "Distributed Electronic Trade Scenarios: Representation, Design, Prototyping"*International Journal on Electronic Commerce* : Special Issue on Formal Aspects of Digital Commerce, eds. S. O. Kimbough and R.M. Lee, 3(1).

Lee, R.M. & Bons, R.W.H. (1996). *Soft-Coded Trade Procedures for Open-EDI*, International Journal of Electronic Commerce,1(1), 27-50.

O'Niel, J. and Schildt, H.(1998). *JavaBeans Programming*, McGraw Hill.

Peterson, J. L.(1981). *Petri Net Theory and the Modeling of Systems*, Prentice-Hall.

Petri, C.A.(1962). *Kommunikation mit Automaten*, PhD thesis University of Bonn, Germany.

Segev, A. & Bichler, M. (1998). *Proceedings of the International Workshop on Component-Based Electronic Commerce*, Berkely, CA, 25 July (www.haas.berkeley.edu/~citm/CEC/index.html)

Thomas, Anne (1997). *Enterprise JavaBeans — Server Component Model for Java*, Patricia Seybold Group, December 1997 (ww.psgroup.com)

UN/IPTWG. United Nations / International Trade Procedures Working Group (see www.unece.org/trafix/)

Vogel, A. and Dukky, Keith (1998). *Java Programming with CORBA*. 2nd ed. Wiley.

Wagenaar, R. W. (1992). "Business network redesign - Lessons from the Port of Rotterdam Simulation game", *Proceedings Conference on interorganizational systems in the global environment*, Bled.

Wrigley, C.D.(1992). EDI transaction protocols in international trade, *Proceedings Conference on interorganizational systems in the global environment*, Bled, Slovenia, September.

Wrigley, C.D. and Wagenaar, R.W. and Clarke, R.A.(1994). "EDI in International Trade: Frameworks for the Strategic Analysis of Ocean Port Communities", *Journal of Strategic Information Systems*, 3(3).

ENDNOTES

1 Electronic documents might use different kinds of syntax, for instance ANSI/X12 EDI, UN/EDIFACT, XML/EDI, FLBC. An electronic trade scenario might be narrowly defined to assume one specific syntax, or be more general, to accept different kinds of syntax.

2 Here we are presenting the notation for role DPN's, where all the actions in the procedure refer to the same agent. Another form of DPN is possible, called a joint DPN, that models the coordinated actions of some or all of the parties together in a single graph. In that case, the form of the action labels for transition nodes becomes:
   <role(s)> : <action>
and the form of the labels for documents places (incoming or outgoing) becomes:
   <sender role>to <receiver role> : [<document list>]
and similarly for physical goods:
   <sender role> to <receiver role> : [<kind of good>]

3 Typically, these documents will be in a structured format such as UN/EDIFACT or XML/EDI. However, they could equally well be in a logic-based format such as

Kimbrough's Formal Language for Business Communication (FLBC) (Kimbrough, 1999). The only requirement is that selected data needed by the procedure be retrievable from the document.

4 Computationally, the data in these documents is persistent; that is, once a document has been received by a role, it is recorded in the role's local database, and remains there even though the document place may cease to be marked. Functionally, this is similar to the way electronic documents are handled in actual practice. An alternative approach would be to use coloured petri nets (Aalst, 1992), where data would be carried through the petri net by means of structured tokens. We found this latter approach to be unnecessarily complicated for our modeling needs.

5 Automated trade scenarios, operating over digital networks, obviously do not handle or transport physical goods directly. The use of this notation is usually to describe the larger system, where physical as well as electronic actions are modeled.

6 This example also illustrates the use of logical variables (as in Prolog) within a DPN. The scope of these variables is the DPN procedure where it appears. By contrast, parameters, which begin with "@" (e.g., @delivery_deadline) may be global in the entire model, or refer to data elements in documents within the role.

7 This and other more complex models can be seen in operation at the Euridis Web site: http://www.euridis.fbk.eur.nl/Euridis/.

Chapter V

Promoting Electronic Commerce in the Defense Industry

Charles V. Trappey
National Chiao Tung University

Amy Trappey
National Tsing Hua University

Thomas Gulledge and Rainer Sommer
George Mason University

INTRODUCTION

Beginning in 1993, when the U.S. Federal Government proposed the "framework of electronic commerce (EC)," the call went out for the wide-scale deployment of EC solutions in government. The Department of Defense immediately became the center of attention since it has the largest procurement budget of all. Initiatives were launched to move from a paper-driven procurement process to an electronic, on-line concept satisfying federal mandates. However, the defense industry consists of thousands of small and medium sized enterprises (SMEs) that were far from ready to conduct business with the government electronically. In order to help the Department of Defense (DoD) and its suppliers to comply with the EC mandates, 17 Electronic Commerce Resource Centers (ECRCs) were established across the U.S. to transfer process improving and enabling EC technologies to small and medium sized businesses and government agencies. Each ECRC comprises business partners (and several university partners) that provide EC outreach, training and technical support to DoD supply chains. The goal of the nationwide network of centers is to facilitate the transition from paper-dependent supply chains to fully electronic-based procurement environments. In order for SMEs to do business with the U.S. government electronically, the mission of the ECRC must grow beyond training and outreach to hands-on implementation and intervention in SMEs.

In this chapter, the key issues, approaches and challenges of bringing EC to defense supply chains are described. The chapter first discusses the complexity of defense supply chains and the efforts underway to make the procurement processes EC compliant. The related government laws and regulations are outlined to set the legal foundation for EC implementation. Then, the elaboration of the ECRC model provides a detailed view of the collaboration between industry, academia, and government to improve defense industry supply chains. Details of a local ECRC's operations are provided to demonstrate its functions and accomplishments. Case examples of the center's operations and technical support are provided to show how the technology is transferred to the SMEs. The chapter concludes with a description of future directions in EC promotion, education and support necessary for the defense industry to change and to do business electronically.

BACKGROUND AND GOVERNMENT EFFORTS

The nationwide network of ECRCs are designed to assist the transfer of information technology (IT) and specifically EC technologies to defense supply chains. The specific tasks and the organization of the national network are defined and orchestrated through a series of government efforts and initiatives. In this section, the background of the defense supply chains, EC-related government legislation and regulations, and DoD initiatives provide a view of why the ECRCs have been opened across the United States.

The Defense Industry Practice

The means and methods by which the United States Government adopts information technology are different from and often slower than the American commercial sector (DoD, 1997a). Whereas U.S. businesses realign management practices, corporate knowledge, and information systems as the result of competitive forces (Davenport and Prusak, 1998), the Department of Defense is unique in the way it restructures the organization. Sullivan (1996) and Kelly et al. (1999) write that the DoD proceeds for long periods of time without significant change and strives to keep the organization "as-is." Keeping the organization as-is allows for continuous change at the component level (among the services, the joint chiefs, etc.) but maintains unnecessary infrastructure.

The impetus to change the organization, particularly defense industry supply chains, tends to come from outside the organization rather than from within. For example, changes in national resource requirements or in national military strategy will lead to top-down directives from senior DoD leadership or Congress, but often these directives are met with arguments and resistance (Graham, 1998). Even though individuals within the organization may recognize a need to migrate toward new strategies, enterprise-wide organizational change is resisted and is difficult to manage.

The culture of the DoD is paper-driven, with as many as 13 copies of a contract printed and sent to multiple offices. The Defense Reform Initiative Report (DoD, 1997b) notes that in 1996, the Defense Finance and Accounting Service Center processed over 5.6 million contractor invoices, made payments against 387,000 major contracts, and disbursed over 84 billion dollars. The paper-bound system for the Service Center has generated over 15 miles of paper files and operations have become increasingly costly and difficult to manage. Electronic commerce solutions are the means of choice to improve efficiency and reduce paper in procurement, weapon systems programs, and personnel administration.

E-Commerce Related Laws and Regulations

The e-commerce efforts in the defense industry are initiated through laws and legislative acts (Table 1). As a result of mandates and public laws, the DoD has implemented electronic commerce solutions to increase the efficiency of the acquisition process. Legislation in 1990 led to the creation of the Chief Financial Officers Act (Public Law 101-576, 1990). Under this Act, President Clinton (1993a) mandated executive branch agencies and departments to use electronic commerce and electronic data interchange (EC/EDI). Government agencies were also required by law (Government Performance and Results Act of 1993) to develop strategic plans and link performance measures to processes (Public Law 103-62, 1993). Subsequently, a law entitled the Federal Acquisition Streamlining Act of 1994 required the entire government to begin using electronic data interchange via the Federal Acquisition Computer Network (FACNET). Public Law 104-106 (1996), i.e., the Clinger-Cohen Act of 1996, established the position of Chief Information Officer (CIO) in each executive agency to coordinate IT purchases, to increase use of modern information technology, and to perform an annual assessment of information resource management. Finally, the Defense Reform Initiative (DoD, 1997b) mandated that the best business practices of the private sector must be applied to the business of defense. The highlights of the target practices are:

- By January 2000, all aspects of contracting for major weapons systems will be paper free.
- By the fiscal year 2000, 90% of DoD purchases under $2,500 will be made using an IMPAC purchase card (similar to a credit card) and these purchases will account for almost one half of all DoD purchases.
- The DoD will expand the use of Internet-based electronic catalogs and electronic shopping malls.
- The DoD will create paper-free systems for weapons support and logistics and will discontinue printing on paper all regulations and instructions.

IT and the Defense Logistics Agency

The Defense Logistics Agency (DLA) was established in 1961 to provide centralized management of consumable items of supply, manage the federal supply catalog, maintain the DoD industrial plant equipment reserve, and operate the surplus disposal program (DoD, 1997b). The DLA has evolved into a logistics combat support agency with broad complex obligations to the DoD and other government organizations. The DLA is one of the world's largest logistics operations covering global military operations and emergency relief. The DLA coordinates the purchase and delivery of equipment, weapon systems, services, and supplies whenever needed, anywhere in the world, at the lowest possible cost. Purchasing is handled by the Defense Contract Management Command and the Defense Logistics Support Command is responsible for materiel management. The DLA maintains five supply centers, one distribution center, three service centers in addition to the two administrative centers. On a continuous basis, it must maintain and manage tiers of centers and activities in a complex supply chain structure and ensure their efficient, accurate and reliable operations among member organizations.

Most government agencies are expected to conduct 75% to 80% of their purchases using EC/EDI within the next two years (DoD, 1997c), and the DLA's simplified acquisitions (commodities and services valued under $100,000) will be the first to require that suppliers use EC and EDI. Suppliers unable to use EC/EDI will not be able to sell to the DLA. As a result, the newly imposed laws, mandates, and schedules have created a tremendous

Table 1. Government-Related EC Laws and Regulations.

Legislation	Intent
Chief Financial Officers (CFO) Act of 1990	A bill to improve the financial management of the federal government by establishing a Chief Financial Officer of the United States within the Office of Management and Budget. Establishes a Chief Financial Officer within each executive department and within each major executive agency and requires the development of systems that provide complete, accurate, and timely reporting of financial information (Public Law 101-576, 1990).
President's "Framework for Electronic Commerce" (1993)	The framework calls for the wide-scale deployment of electronic commerce solutions in government, driven by commercial industry with a minimum of government regulation (Bridges et al, 1997; Clinton, 1993a). President Clinton said EC "will make our antiquated paper-based procurement system accessible to anybody with a personal computer. It will open up a world of possibilities to small businesses in America and drive down costs to taxpayers" (Clinton, 1993b).
Government Performance and Results Act	The Government Performance and Results Act provides for the establishment of strategic planning and performance measurement in the Federal Government (Public Law 103-62, 1993).
Federal Acquisition Streamlining Act of 1994	A bill to revise and streamline the acquisition laws of the federal government. The act established the Federal Acquisition Computer Network (FACNET). FACNET will reduce paperwork through the introduction of EDI processes, provide a single electronic face to industry, and increase interoperability between agencies (Public Law 103-355, 1994; Moeller et al., 1998).
Paperwork Reduction Act (PRA) of 1995	A bill to further the goals of the Paperwork Reduction Act requires federal agencies to become more responsible and publicly accountable for reducing the burden of federal paperwork on the public (Public Law 104-13, 1995).
Clinger-Cohen Act of 1996 (IT Management Reform Act)	A bill to establish the position of chief information officer (CIO) in each executive agency to coordinate IT purchases, to increase use of modern information technology, and to perform an annual assessment of information resource management (Public Law 104-106, 1996).
Debt Collection Improvement Act of 1996	Requires the use of Electronic Funds Transfer (EFT) by all federal government agencies by 1999. EFT should be used to pay and reimburse expenses for all federal employees, to handle all interagency payments, to make payments to state and local governments, and to pay for purchases from the private sector (Gore, 1993; Public Law 104-134, 1996).
Defense Reform Initiative of 1997	The reform initiative mandates paperless contracting processes throughout DoD. Electronic links between procurement and payment processes will reduce acquisition cycle times, lower costs, and improve operations. The DoD will define policy, process flows, and technical solutions to facilitate an electronic buyer/supplier interface to exchange procurement and payment information and automate these processes (DoD, 1997b).

need for education and training across the defense industry supply chain. The Defense Logistics Agency provides related education and training through two national programs called the Procurement Technical Assistance Centers (PTACs) and Electronic Commerce Resource Centers (ECRCs). The Procurement Technical Assistance (PTA) Program was established by Congress to assist state and local governments and other nonprofit entities to provide procurement education activities and to help business firms market their goods and/or services to federal, state and local governments. The role of ECRCs is to help industrial and government organizations enter the world of electronic commerce, but with special emphasis on helping SMEs.

EC FOR SUPPLY CHAIN MANAGEMENT

Electronic commerce, according to the official DoD definition, is the paperless exchange of business information using Electronic Data Interchange (EDI), electronic mail, computer bulletin boards, FAX, Electronic Funds Transfer (EFT), and other similar technologies (DoD, 1997c). Electronic Data Interchange (EDI) is the computer-to-computer exchange of business information using an agreed-upon standard. EDI is a supporting electronic commerce mechanism because it enables large organizations with firmly established trading partner agreements to exchange business information electronically much faster, cheaper and more accurately than is possible using paper-based systems.

Supply Chain Management

A supply chain is a collection of interrelated activities that must be executed among business entities to accomplish a business objective. Using retail supply chains as an example, consumers order goods from a retailer that must work with under-links to ensure sufficient quantity and variety of goods at the store to satisfy the customers' demands. Thus, a retailer must work closely with its suppliers, which in turn work with other component suppliers and manufacturers to ensure the delivery of goods. These interrelated activities are performed by retailers, distributors, manufacturers and even raw material providers, which form a multi-tier of supply chain systems to fulfill end-customers' orders (Kalakota and Whinston, 1997).

Kalakota and Whinston (1997) point out that supply chain management (SCM) is the general concept of coordinating and administering the order generation; order taking; production; and order fulfillment/distribution of goods, services or information. As the business world becomes more complex and competitive, the research and development (R&D) in making one's SCM efficient, accurate and reliable represents a significant effort in enterprise reform and business process re-engineering. A typical supply chain infrastructure consists of three basic flows. Within the DoD there are physical flows, information flows, and financial flows. These flows encompass commercial suppliers, DoD procurement and logistics officials, and DoD end users (Bridges et al., 1997).
- The physical flow is the flow of goods and services through various tiers of the supply chain from raw materials, components, or end products to the end customers. This aspect of SCM includes inventory management, distribution, and transportation.
- The information flow consists of the transmission and exchange of information regarding products, orders and related activities. The business transactions include purchase orders, bills of lading, tracking, receipt acknowledgments, and invoices.
- The financial flow deals with the payment and collection of funds incurred due to

business transactions. The monetary transactions are initiated by the acknowledgment of goods and services delivery.

The ECRCs focus on making information flow more efficiently among supply chain business entities. The efficiency can be improved by increasing communication speeds. This will result in quality goods being delivered on time and more business being accomplished with limited resources. The EC functions can be classified into three main activities (Bridges et al., 1997), i.e., accelerating business communications, facilitating transactions of goods/funds and integrating logistics information into the key processes. These activities serve as the baseline for the mapping of EC benchmarks to the DoD's SCM strategy.

ELECTRONIC COMMERCE RESOURCE CENTERS

The Electronic Commerce Resource Centers are a network of technology transfer centers that are sponsored by the Defense Logistics Agency of the U.S. government (Gulledge, Sommer, and Tarimcilar, 1999a). Prior to 1994, the ECRC network was known as the CALS Shared Resource Center Network and was designed, implemented, and managed by the U.S. Air Force (Lammers, 1992). The ECRC network has grown substantially over the last eight years. Currently, the program is managed by the Defense Logistics Agency and is operated through prime contracts with Concurrent Technologies Corporation (CTC) and CAMP, Inc. (ECRC, 1998).

Since the DoD suggests that suppliers use electronic commerce, the program was designed to accelerate the cooperative use of electronic commerce throughout government and industry. The primary goal of the program is to electronically enable the supply chain so that the DoD and other federal organizations can procure the lowest-cost and the highest-quality goods and services. As stated in the ECRC 1997 Annual Brochure, the program targets small and medium size enterprises that may not have sufficient resources to keep pace with evolving technologies (ECRC, 1998).

The ECRC program is structured as a national network with 17 local centers (Figure 1). The local ECRCs serve DoD suppliers in five regions of the United States. Although each region has a unique mix of suppliers and government agencies operating within its boundaries, a regional model is not used for planning and coordination. Rather, the Defense Logistics Agency manages planning at the national level. Regional boundaries are used to describe the relative distribution of defense industry contractors and the regional structure of the defense force logistics infrastructure.

Each local office has developed programs suited to the major clients in the area. The specific tasks of each center fall into four categories including outreach, education, consultation and technical support.

Specific ECRC Tasks

An ECRC provides consultation and enabling technologies to improve EC implementation processes and methods. However, successful technology transfer requires that the clients understand their business, are committed to change, have sufficient leadership, and are financially capable of supporting change. Outreach is a critical step in identifying potential clients that are willing to support fundamental changes in the way they do business. Potential clients are identified at trade shows, regional economic development conferences,

Figure 1. Five ECRC Geographical Regions and their Corresponding Centers

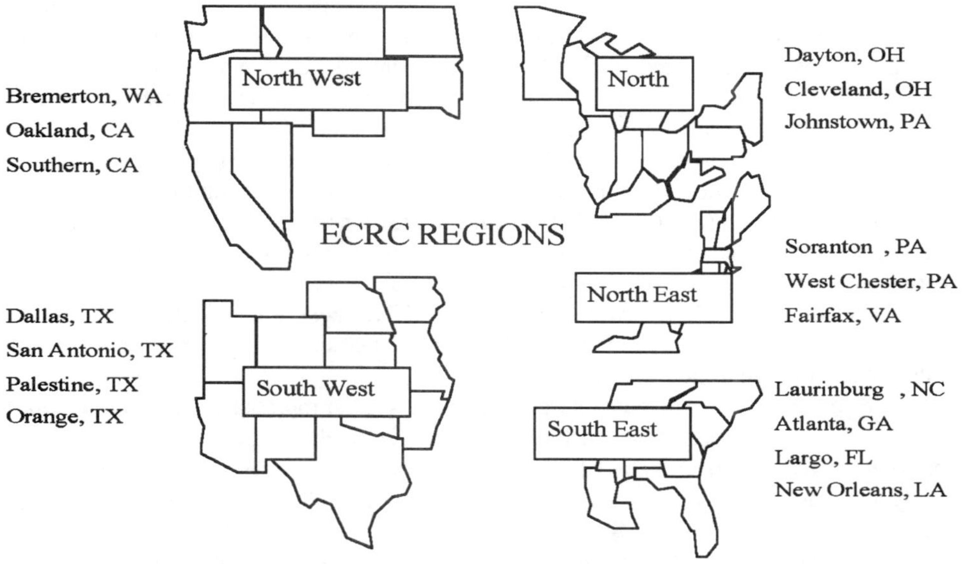

Bremerton, WA
Oakland, CA
Southern, CA
— North West

Dayton, OH
Cleveland, OH
Johnstown, PA
— North

ECRC REGIONS

Soranton, PA
West Chester, PA
Fairfax, VA
— North East

Dallas, TX
San Antonio, TX
Palestine, TX
Orange, TX
— South West

Laurinburg, NC
Atlanta, GA
Largo, FL
New Orleans, LA
— South East

and government-sponsored events. Outreach contacts are encouraged to attend ECRC training courses, but on occasion, clients require more than training. The ECRC provides consultation and training and for some cases will organize specific teams to work directly with the client. The primary tasks of the ECRCs are detailed below:

Outreach – Outreach promotes recognition of the center and identifies potential clients. Each ECRC provides seminars that promote the functions and services offered and coordinates outreach efforts at trade shows and occasionally at client sites. Outreach is an educational effort as well, providing information about the latest electronic commerce technologies, federal government laws, policies and programs.

Training – The goal of training is to provide a basic level of knowledge about the EC technical domain. Clients attend classes where formal course materials are presented in a multimedia environment. The class participants are drawn from business, government and the military and may attend classes in mixed groups or separately if requested. Classes are intended to inform, increase knowledge, and provide direction. Students are expected to participate in class discussions and to seek additional information that will enable the implementation of electronic commerce in their organization. If the information needs are significant, then the client is asked to apply for additional consultation or technical support.

Consultation and Technical Support – The ECRCs are committed to provide technical information and assistance in response to specific questions and requests for help. Each client comes to the center with unique problems and difficulties. Thus, consultation is provided on a one-to-one basis if the efforts will enhance implementation of the EC technology. Consultation cannot be used as a substitute for dedicated in-house efforts to apply a working solution, which are also provided by the ECRCs in the form of in-depth technical support.

Courses taught at the ECRCs are divided into two groups. The first group consists of the standard offering provided by every ECRC. These courses are planned, coordinated, and archived at the program office by the education and training working group. The second group consists of specialized courses adapted by local ECRCs to match the needs of their clients. Each of the 17 local ECRCs is free to adapt the standard courses to the local environment or to develop new and specialized courses.

Sixty-four percent of the official courses offered fall into the categories of electronic commerce and electronic data interchange (Figure 2). Electronic commerce courses (10 courses, 40% of the curriculum) hold the largest share of the official curriculum and the next largest segment consists of electronic data interchange courses (six courses, 24%). The official electronic commerce course listing covers topics such as getting started with electronic commerce, EC hardware and software, EC for government workers, the internet as a business platform, marketing on the Internet, Internet business operations, HTML, Internet security, and the use of e-malls.

The official electronic data interchange courses cover topics such as EDI orientation, issues in EDI implementation, business opportunities with the DoD, EDI software, and Internet-based commerce. The official business process courses cover business needs analysis, concurrent engineering, and data management. The official technical data exchange courses focus on CALS and integrated manufacturing.

At least half of the official courses have been adapted to meet local requirements. The courses most frequently adapted to local needs are the basic and introductory level courses. Since each region of the country tends to have different groupings of defense contractors, suppliers, defense industries, and military specialties, the courses are tailored to meet the needs of the target audiences. The most common changes to course content concern differences in business opportunities and the differences in clients across regions. Centers also develop courses that reflect the specialties of their teams (e.g., information security) or demonstrate real world applications and solutions derived from technical support projects.

Linking the Regional Sites

Regional ECRCs, government agencies, and defense industries identify, evaluate, demonstrate, validate, and transfer electronic commerce solutions to suppliers. E-Link is the

Figure 2: Education and Training Working Group Official Course Categories

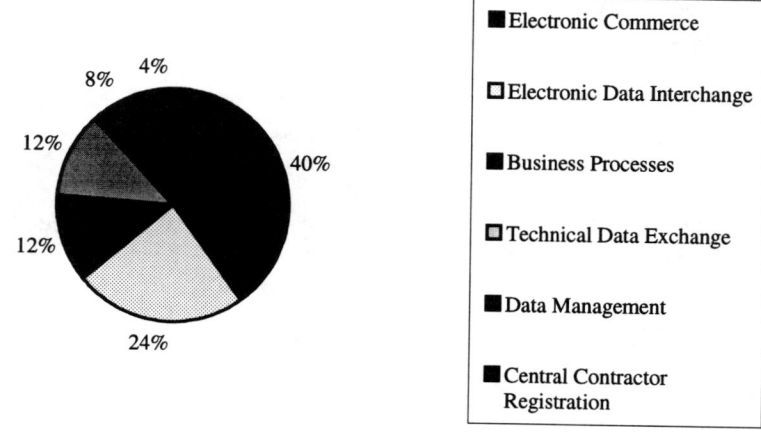

Figure 3. The linkage among nation-wide ECRC's (ECRC, 1998)

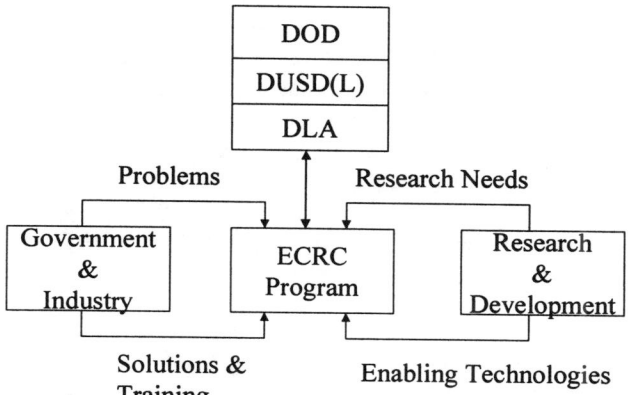

web-based site that provides members of the ECRC program with a central repository of files, activity schedules and communications tools such as threaded messages. The site contains URLs, class materials, minutes and agendas, case studies, success stories, and news of upcoming events. The site is the official program distribution site and posting board for related technology to be shared and disseminated among local ECRCs and to their SME customers (Figure 3).

Taking the Fairfax ECRC (FECRC) as an example, the technical staff helps SMEs assess their EC requirements, develop transition plans, evaluate EC product and service decisions, train in-house and trading partner staff, and implement EC solutions. Specific areas of Fairfax ECRC expertise include requirements definition modeling and implementation planning, Internet-enabled electronic commerce, information technology for integrated electronic commerce, enterprise resource planning and supply chain integration, and process costing and business case development.

CASE EXAMPLES FROM THE FAIRFAX ECRC

Three cases are presented to illustrate how electronic commerce is applied in the defense supply chain and how the FECRC provides the technology necessary for the transition. The first case describes a small defense supplier's LAN/WAN-enabling efforts. The second case describes a company's network upgrade to ensure better business opportunities as a government contractor. The third case discusses efforts put forth by the ECRC to help a shipbuilding supply chain implement EDI.

Case 1: Introducing EC to SMEs

A DoD supplier was required to submit bids via EDI within a year and was struggling to understand and identify the necessary technology solutions that are required to proceed with an EC/EDI implementation. The supplier recognized that choosing the right EC/EDI solution would not only satisfy the DoD requirements, but would also develop EC/EDI capabilities that could be leveraged with other customers and suppliers. Management reasoned that a sound EC/EDI strategy, coupled with Internet-based World Wide Web technologies, could increase their market share by reaching customers outside of their immediate business area. In order to achieve these goals, the company had to modify the stand-alone PC environment and develop in-house technical expertise. Before the EC/EDI and WWW technologies could be implemented, the DoD supplier needed basic low-level IT capabilities including a technology assessment, an upgrade of existing computer equipment, a network plan, and an EC/EDI strategy. Once the basic IT solutions were implemented the company could begin to deploy the higher level EC/EDI and WWW software technology layers.

Solution and Result

The DoD supplier participated in an in-depth ECRC technology assessment. Based on this assessment, the ECRC developed a time-phased implementation plan that included an EC/EDI requirements analysis. The analysis emphasized a new integrated accounting and inventory package, a manageable LAN\WAN topology (Figure 4), a configuration management plan, pre-designed configuration management templates, and a detailed cost analysis of the implementation.

Using the implementation plan, management contracted a local integrator to implement the initial FECRC network design. Since the FECRC-designed network was to be managed by the company's personnel, costs would increase but less than if the network were managed by an integrator on a monthly fee basis. The FECRC plan provided more functionality by including WWW and WAN support as well as a shared modem pool. In an effort to build upon the new IT infrastructure, management evaluated and selected several EC/EDI software options provided by the ECRC.

Figure 4. A LAN/WAN Topology for a Small DoD Supplier

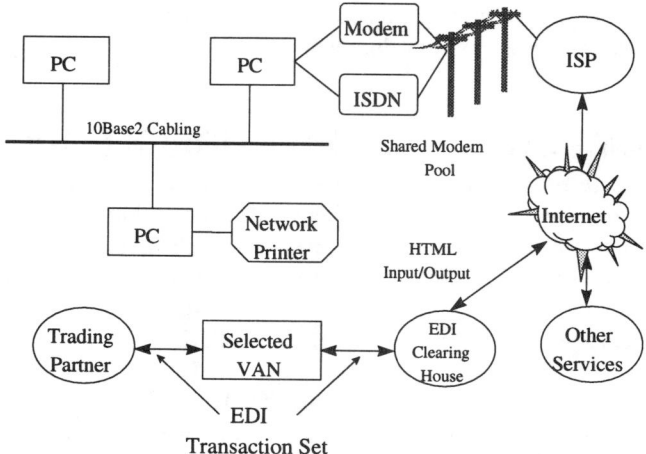

Case 2: Designing for Growth

A defense supplier was actively seeking to expand the volume of its government contracts by pursuing more leads on the Internet. The supplier wanted to search for Requests for Quotation (RFQs) from all government departments and to actively monitor as many sources of potential business as possible. The technology needed by the supplier included:
- Web exposure through a self-maintained home page
- Web-based EC for Internet online transaction processing
- Basic EDI capabilities

Solution and Result

Since these goals must be supported by a basic IT infrastructure, the ECRC technical support team provided the following:
- A network plan (Figure 5)
- A technology assessment to upgrade existing computer equipment
- A EC/EDI strategy (after the basic IT solutions are implemented)
- A configuration management plan with preconfigured management templates

The ECRC worked with the office manager to deliver a preliminary report, a candidate solution, and a customized product selection and pricing guide. The client used the ECRC documentation to guide the work of a local systems integrator. The integrator implemented the recommended network topology, the LANtastic small business network solution, and the ECRC-designed ISDN connection to a local Internet Service Provider. The infrastruc-

Figure 5. A Network Plan for a Defense Contractor's Office and Warehouse Facilities

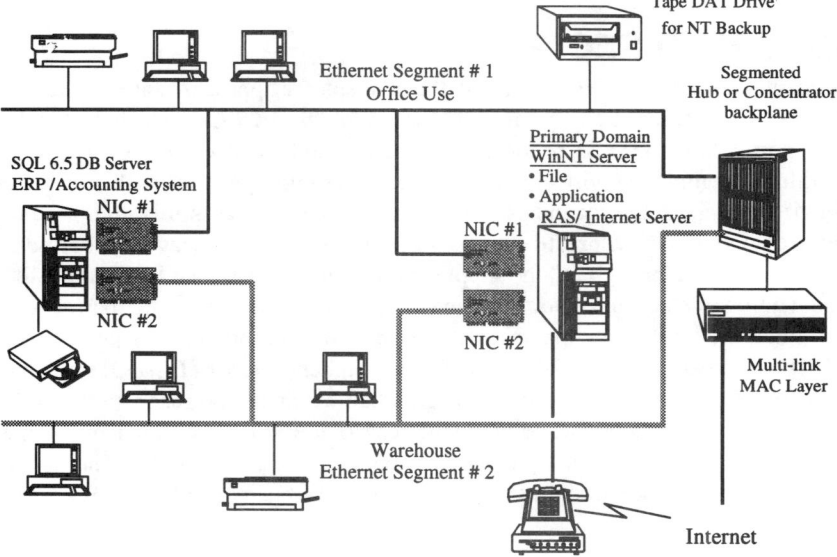

ture was documented with configuration management templates provided by the ECRC. This new network topology allowed the company to bid on government contracts electronically, to provide e-mail services to all its employees and to host its own Web page on internal computers. The company also selected a Web-based e-commerce solution in order to move basic business transactions from a paper-based format to HTML forms.

Case 3: Realizing EDI for Shipbuilding Supply Chains

The objective of this ongoing project is to assist a DoD shipbuilding prime contractor and its suppliers to implement VAN-based Electronic Data Interchange (EDI).

Solution and Result

The project deliverables were implemented in several stages. First, training sessions were conducted to promote supplier awareness of VAN-based EDI implementation issues. In this task, 45% of the top 1,000 suppliers that account for more than 50% of the total purchase order (PO) volume attended FECRC-sponsored training sessions. The second step of the project offered technical support to suppliers needing assistance in EDI implementation. The third project task established an effective evaluation criteria.

The criteria evaluated supplier coverage, efficacy of training, and integration of EC objectives. Since the suppliers in the chain have a wide range of characteristics and concerns, it is critical to understand what they need, what they can afford, and what they are capable of accomplishing. This case has helped the center gain access to a large number of SMEs that are critical links in U.S. shipbuilding supply chain. Through continued analysis of their needs, the center gains a better understanding of the needs, capabilities and decision patterns of SMEs as well as general knowledge of how to improve the supply chain via EC/EDI implementation.

TRENDS AND DIRECTIONS

This chapter focuses on the background, the concept, the approach, and the execution of ECRC support processes. The primary objective of the ECRCs is to help the U.S. government, particularly the DoD, become lean, efficient and effective through its business practices within a complex supply chain structure. After eight years of collective effort, most of the first tier and some second tier DoD suppliers have successfully complied with government-regulated EC/EDI practice. However, there is still a long way to go before true EC/EDI is implemented through out the supply chain. This is to say that SMEs are still far from the realization of electronic commerce in comparison to their upper tier partners, and it is unlikely that the smaller companies will ever be able to economically justify VAN-based EDI. The future direction for ECRCs requires a higher-degree of EC/EDI implementation in the supply chain system and will necessitate extensive outreach to the SMEs. Extensive outreach will promote the common interests of the SMEs, provide new inexpensive solutions, and assist their compliance with DoD EC/EDI practices. The specific guidelines will require international extension, business-to-business EC, and Web-based EC/EDI.

Extending Support to SMEs

The ECRC's most critical mission is to work from the SME's perspective and to serve their interests in developing EC capabilities for conducting business with suppliers, the DoD, and other customers. This objective via the DoD initiative intends to improve the competitive edge of the government by lowering acquisition costs. However, there is an inconsistency in the mission since businesses succeed not only by doing business with government, but also by competing in the global marketplace. All ECRCs should focus more on introducing standard commercial solutions, and not proprietary, expensive and one-of-the-kind solutions that are required by government and the DoD in particular.

Business-to-Business EC

According to a recent EC study, the majority of business transactions are between businesses, and a much smaller proportion of the transactions are conducted between businesses and end-users (business-to-consumer EC). The ECRC functions in education, training and technical support must focus on providing solutions that will result in the development of business-to-business EC. Historically, business practices target the vertical integration of activities within a single functional domain and result in the creation of "stovepipes" (Gulledge, Sommer, and Tarimcilar, 1999b). Stovepipes create barriers that limit the sharing of information and necessitate the duplication of data and information systems. A successful EC implementation takes horizontal integration into consideration where business processes' cross functional or departmental boundaries. The result is the design and development of information systems that follow the most efficient and effective process flows to achieve true electronic commerce with enterprise integration (Kirchmer, 1998).

Internet-Based EC/EDI

The Internet is progressively becoming the standard interface and connection mechanism for users, in both industrial and consumer markets. The ECRCs should follow the commercial trend in promoting Internet-based (and Web-based) EC/EDI solutions so that the very-same technology transferred to SMEs can be applied across many application-domains. Off-the-shelf solutions can be acquired readily with affordable costs and can be implemented by all members of the supply chain – not just the largest players. For instance, XML has been rapidly developed by the Internet industry consortiums as a Web-enabled standard markup language (XML/EDI, 1998). Business-to-business electronic data interchange using XML as the common data representation is a promising way to achieve several EC objectives. First, XML/EDI enables real time business transactions with multiple business partners using basic Web technology. Second, the transferred data are form-based documents that follow an industry de facto standard. An enterprise and its partners can interchange and integrate data easily and automatically with enterprise information systems (Figure 6). Third, XML/EDI allows batch operations for the large volume transaction environment. The most recent EC/EDI trend goes one step beyond XML/EDI and calls for an any-to-any EDI transformation (Mercer, 1999). The principle underlying any-to-any EDI translation engines and management tools assumes that supply chains will never agree on a universal standard for electronic data exchange. For example, the United States is using ANSI X12 and the rest of the world is adapting UN/EDIFACT as the EDI standard set. An eventual solution is to provide enterprises that need to do business with many companies worldwide a flexible tool that will in-bound and out-bound "any" type of data while satisfying the requirement of internal and external data formats.

Figure 6: The Structure of XML/EDI Transmission

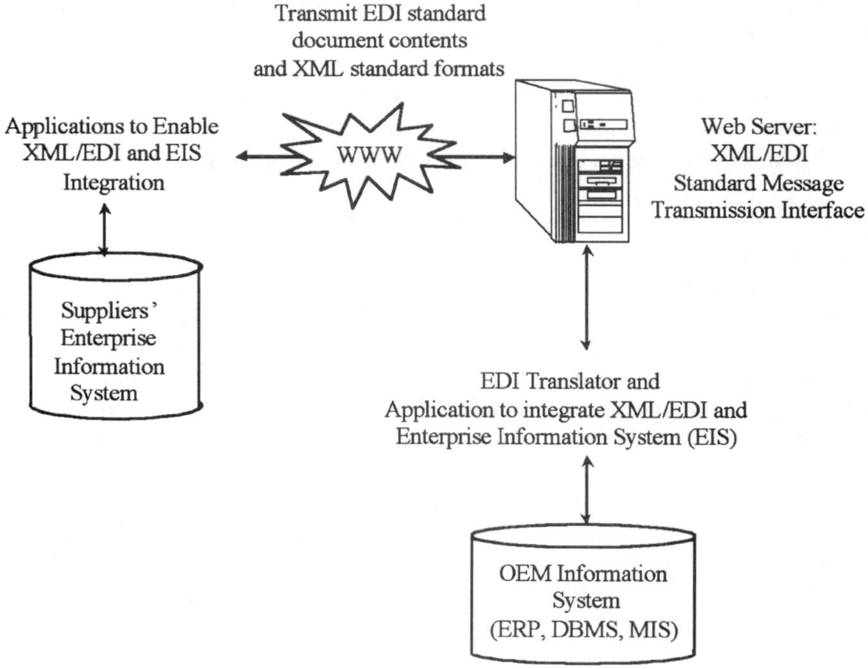

CONCLUSION

The question remains whether the ECRCs designed and dedicated to enhance the U.S. defense supply chain are useful to all SMEs. Judging from the nature and characteristics of the defense industry, the solutions may not be suitable for both commercial and defense environments. However, some of the ECRC concepts and methodologies can be applied directly to industries with global supply chains, such as the electronics industry. The reason why the ECRC model applies so well to this sector is that the electronics industry has a fairly large supply chain network that requires efficient and effective logistic management. The second reason is that time to market and rapid product obsolescence make business-to-business EC (B2B EC) a fundamental requirement for competitive advantage. Finally, the electronics industry is the sector most knowledgeable of and most willing to accept IT applications such as B2B EC.

The U.S. is unique in the development of an information infrastructure based on defense technology and funding. Other nations that want to implement EC/EDI face the formation of an information infrastructure without the assistance of strong defense industries. National strategies for development become increasingly critical (Wong, 1998) as does the leadership of government, the private sector, and universities to address new problems. The literature targets several areas of research for the successful deployment of EC/EDI:

- Research is needed to forecast the needs of a national EC/EDI network and its hardware and software components.

- Commercial enterprises, government agencies and research institutes need to access placement of key EC/EDI gateways and connections (Jo, Pottmyer and Fetzner, 1995).
- Internet commerce, as it spans international boundaries, is redefining the fundamental definition of money. Businesses must be willing to accept EC/EDI as a new medium of exchange and be willing to restructure business processes to insure privacy, reliability and security (Camp and Sirbu, 1997; Yam, 1998).
- The effect caused by EC/EDI on market channel relationships and economic development must be studied carefully (Vijayasarathy and Robey, 1997).
- The reach of EDI needs to be broadened so that every company can become a trading partner. The challenges that lay ahead include enabling firms to use EDI and provide more channels for trade on the Internet and not only through VANs (Senn, 1998).
- There remain many legal issues concerning EC/EDI and questions about what legislation is needed to make local EC laws and regulations internationally compatible (Chen, 1997).

The development of electronic commerce for the U.S. defense industry supply chains has been a long and expensive struggle involving lawmakers, soldiers, business leaders, and academics. The U.S. ECRC efforts and results provide a means for other economies and industry sectors to learn from and avoid the pitfalls inherent to this emerging technology.

REFERENCES

Bridges, W.M., Kapusta, D., Pirko, K., Pope, D.B., Rhode, D., Wall, A., & Young, E. (1997, June). DoD Electronic Commerce Prototype Program Final Report — Electronic Commerce Benchmarking Study. Available Internet: *http://www.acq.osd.mil/ec/library_frame.htm.*

Camp, L.J., & Sirbu, M. (1997, May). Critical issues in internet commerce. *IEEE Communications Magazine*, 58-62.

Chen, G.C. (1997). Electronic commerce on the Internet: Legal developments in Taiwan. *Journal of Computer & Information Law, 16* (1), 77-123.

Clinton, W. (1993a). Framework for Global Electronic Commerce. Available Internet: *http://www.whitehouse.gov/WH/New/Commerce/index.html.*

Clinton, W. (1993b, October 26). Remarks by the President in Re-inventing Government Announcement. Available Internet: *http://www.pub.whitehouse.gov/white-house-publications/1993/10/.*

Davenport, T.H., & Prusak, L. (1998). *Working Knowledge — How Organizations Manage What They Know.* Boston, MA: Harvard Business School Press.

DoD (1997a). *Configuration Management Guidance, Military Handbook MIL-HDBK-61.* Washington D.C.: Deputy Under Secretary of Defense (Logistics)/CALS Office, Department of Defense.

DoD (1997b, November). Defense Reform Initiative Report. Available Internet: *http://www.acq.osd.mil/ec/ECDAY/ec_day.htm.*

DoD (1997c, October). *Introduction to Department of Defense Electronic Commerce, A Handbook for Business* (Version 2). Washington D.C.: Department of Defense, developed by Hughes Training, Inc.

ECRC (1998). National Website for Electronic Commerce Resource Centers (ECRCs). Available Internet: *http://www.ecrc.ctc.com.*

Gore, A. (1993). National Performance Review — Summary of Savings. Available Internet: *http://www.pub.whitehouse.gov/uri-res/I2R?urn:pdi://oma.eop.gov.us/1993/9/7/15.text.1.*

Graham, B. (1998, November). Retired admiral pushes Pentagon to run a tighter ship. *The Washington Post*, November 6.

Gulledge, T.R., Sommer, R.A., & Tarimcilar, M.M. (1999a). Electronic commerce resource centers: an industry-university partnership. *Industry and Higher Education*, April, 127-134.

Gulledge, T.R., Sommer, R.A., & Tarimcilar, M.M. (1999b). Cross functional process integration and the integrated data environment. in *Business Process Engineering: Advancing the State of the Art*, D.J. Elzinga, et al. (Eds). Boston, MA: Kluwer Academic Publishers.

Jo, K.Y., Pottmyer, J.J., & Fetzner, E.A. (1995, November). DoD electronic commerce/ electronic data Interchange systems modeling and simulation. *Proceedings, Military Communications Conference, MILCOM'95, 2*, 479-483.

Kalakota, R., & Whinston, A.B. (1997). *Electronic Commerce, A Manager's Guide.* Reading, Massachusetts: Addison Wesley.

Kelly, L., D. Olson, & Sullivan, L. (1999). Defense enterprise planning and management. in *Business Process Engineering: Advancing the State of the Art*, D.J. Elzinga, et al. (Editors). Boston, MA: Kluwer Academic Publishers.

Kirchmer, M. (1998). *Business Process Oriented Implementation of Standard Software.* Berlin, Germany: Springer-Verlag Publishing Co..

Lammers, M.S. (1992). CALS shared resource centers. *CALS Journal, 1*, 36-37.

Moeller, D., & McCulloch, H. (1998). *Electronic Contracting*. Vienna, Virginia: the National Contract Management Association, in connection with the NCMA 1998 National Education Seminar Series.

Mercer, R. (1999), Technical Reference Manual — EDI EX*tender, Oracle Corporation, Reston, Virginia.

Public Law 101-576 (1990). Chief Financial Officers (CFO) Act. Available Internet: http://thomas.loc.gov/cgibin/bdquery/L?d101:./list/bd/d101pl.1st:551[1650] (Public_Laws)|TOM:/bss/d101query.html, November.

Public Law 103-62 (1993). Government Performance and Results Act. Available Internet: 0.ENR: *http://thomas.loc.gov/cgi-bin/query/z?c103:S.20.ENR:.*

Public Law 103-355 (1994). Federal Acquisition Streamlining Act. Available Internet: *http://thomas.loc.gov/cgi-bin/query/z?c103:S.1587.ENR:.*

Public Law 104-13 (1995). Paperwork Reduction Act (PRA). Available Internet: *http://thomas.loc.gov/cgi-bin/bdquery/z?d104:SN00244:|TOM:/bss/d104query.html.*

Public Law 104-106 (1996). Information Technology Management Reform Act, Public Law 104-106. Available Internet: *http://thomas.loc.gov/cgi-bin/query/C?c104:./temp/~c104GHrpx8.*

Public Law 104-134 (1996). Information Technology Management Reform Act, Public Law 104-134. Available Internet: *http://thomas.loc.gov/cgi-bin/query/C?c104:./temp/~c104GHrpx8.*

Senn, J.A. (1998). Expanding the reach of electronic commerce – The Internet EDI alternative. *Information Systems Management, 15* (3), 7-15.

Sullivan, L.M. (1996). *Defense Enterprise Planning and Management: A Guide for Managers.* Washington D.C.: Office of the Secretary of Defense, ASD (C³I), March 11.

Vijayasarathy, L.R., & Robey, D. (1997). The effect of EDI on market channel relationships in retailing. *Information & Management, 33*, 73-86

Wong, P.-K. (1998). Leveraging the global information revolution for economic development: Singapore's evolving information industry strategy. *Information Systems Research, 9* (4), 323-341.

The XML/EDI Group (1998), *Electronic Data Interchange on the Internet,* .netscape.com/maps/vs_menu.map *http://developer.netscape.com/maps/vs_menu.map.*

Yam, J. (1998). The impact of technology on financial development in East Asia. *Journal of International Affairs, 51* (2), 539-553.

Chapter VI

Diffusion of Electronic Commerce in Australia: A Preliminary Investigation

Mohammed A. Quaddus
Curtin University of Technology, Australia

Diffusion is the process by which a new technology spreads in its usage among a population. This chapter analyses the diffusion process of one aspect of the consumer-to-business electronic commerce (EC) in Australia, namely Internet shopping. The chapter first reviews three popular logistics diffusion models from the literature and then applies them to the EC diffusion data. Results show that the most flexible model is not significant, while the simple diffusion model (Blackman's) is. It was also found that the past diffusion process had been mostly influenced by the "internal" interactions between the adopters and the potential adopters of EC. Further analysis of the Blackman's model revealed some high level policy guidelines to enhance the diffusion process further into the future. Limitations of the study and future research directions were also identified.

INTRODUCTION

Electronic commerce (EC), both Internet-based or by some other networks, is changing the way organizations perform their tasks, interact with the customers and in general do their business. Among the myriad of computer and telecommunication-based applications of the modern era, the advent of EC is having the biggest impact on organizations and its customers. EC is not only changing the business processes, it is also changing the organizational structure to support the new processes. EC is not only "buying and selling" of products via electronic means, it involves all other activities to support the sale process (Applegate et al. 1996).

Although the term electronic commerce is wide spread and well accepted in the academic and business community, Wigand (1997) points out that "the term electronic commerce is poorly understood and frequently used to denote different meanings." Taking a broad perspective the author defines EC as the seamless application of information and communication technology to the entire value chain of business processes, conducted electronically, in order to achieve an organizational goal. Wigand (1997) highlights the need for supporting an organizational goal by electronic means. Nath et al. (1998) review various definitions of EC, which vary from pure use of technologies (e.g., e-mail, EDI, etc.) to supporting organizational needs to searching and retrieving information for corporate decision making. The authors summarize two key points of EC, which are: (i) to simplify and streamline business processes by electronic means, and (ii) to enable and facilitate the formation of electronic markets.

Kalakota and Whinston (1997) provide the most comprehensive definition of EC. The authors take four perspectives as *communication*, *business process*, *service*, and *online* to define EC. From the *communication* perspective EC is meant to support the communication needs of various tasks (delivery of products/services, payments, etc.) via various electronic means. From the *business process* perspective the primary goal of EC is to automate the business transactions and workflows (Kalakota and Whinston, 1997). From the *service* perspective EC is meant to cut the service costs of the organization and provide better service to the customers. The *online* perspective assumes the primary goal of EC to support the product buying/selling via Internet and other online means. It is observed that the four perspectives taken by Kalakota and Whinston (1997) are not discrete. They overlap to a great extent. For example, automating the business process would result in better communication and reduce the service costs of the organization. Similarly, online product buying/selling would improve the service to the customers/suppliers and result in better communication and streamline the corresponding business processes.

Research on EC had been diverse. This chapter, however, concentrates on the research on the adoption and diffusion of EC by organizations. It is interesting to note that most of the research on EC, in some way or other, deals with the opportunities and problems with EC. These opportunities and problems, of course, act as the factors of successful (or unsuccessful) adoption and diffusion of EC by organizations. Based on the interview with 10 executives Nath et al. (1998) concluded that benefits of the Internet-based EC are broad, ranging from global reach to image enhancer. The authors also found major perceived problems with EC as security, costs, legal issues, maintenance, etc. Auger and Gallaugher (1997) concentrated their study on small business EC adoption and found a number of factors in favour or against the adoption of EC. The study was exploratory in nature. Poon and Swatman (1999) did a longitudinal study on the gap between expectation and realization due to EC by a group of small businesses. The authors found that many of the expectations of the small businesses did not materialize eventually. Behrendorff and Rahman (1999) provided a brief look into the adoption of EC in small to medium enterprises in Australia. The authors found the organizational, technological and the role of government as the main factors of adoption of EC. Opportunities and problems with EC have also been studied, among many others, by Ng et al. (1998), Cunningham and Tynan (1993), Bolisani et al. (1999), Palmer (1997), and Giaglis et al. (1999).

Background

Theoretical background to technology diffusion in general and EC in particular is presented in a later section. However, we briefly highlight here some related studies to put our current research in perspective. Two important phases of technology acquisition by organizations are *adoption* and *diffusion* (in that order) (Rogers 1983). However, without large-scale diffusion any adopted technology will die soon. Kraemer et al. (1992) studied the impact of government policies in information technology (IT) diffusion in nine Asia-Pacific countries. The growth of IT expenditures in these countries showed significant exponential growth. However, the authors found no significant direct impact of government policies on diffusion. The level of economic development was a more significant predictor with IT demand, IT cost and cost of substitutes of IT being the significant variables. Harkola and Greve (1995) investigated the diffusion of technology by cohesion and structural equivalence. The basis of the cohesion model is the interaction of prior and potential users of technology, whereas the structural equivalence model assumes that technology diffuses through indirect information and social comparison. Based on their research in a single Japanese firm, Harkola and Greve (1995) found the cohesion model prevailed at the beginning of the diffusion period, after which the structural equivalence model took over. La Rovere (1996) emphasized the need for detailed supply-and-demand-oriented policies for effective IT diffusion among small and medium-sized enterprises.

While general technology and IT diffusion-related studies are available in the literature, research on the diffusion of EC is almost nonexistent, with the exception of the study by Dos Santos and Peffers (1998). The authors studied the diffusion of one of the earliest EC applications, the automated teller machine (ATM) system, using three modelling approaches. These approaches are: external, internal and mixed. While all three models fit the data quite well, careful examinations revealed that the mixed influence model fit the dataset meaningfully. The authors thus concluded that both communication/imitation among the competitors and vendors' push were significant for the diffusion of ATMs.

Research Objectives

Most of the research on the adoption of EC had been exploratory in nature. The researchers primarily investigated the opportunities and problems with EC as perceived by the participants in survey or interview. Suggestions then followed to improve the situation. No comprehensive causal relationships were developed between the adoption variables and other contextual variables to explain the causes of the failed or successful adoption process of EC. The diffusion (spread in usage) phenomenon of the EC was not investigated in any of the study reviewed, with the exception of Dos Santos and Peffers (1998).

The primary objective of this paper is to fill this gap in the literature of EC. In particular, this research aims to study the diffusion process of EC in Australia. In doing so it aims to answer the following research questions:
i) What are the dynamics of EC diffusion in Australia?
ii) What is the influencing source of the EC diffusion process?
iii) What must be done to enhance the EC diffusion process in Australia?

It must be mentioned that this study only deals with Internet-based EC, which is the primary research focus of many recent studies. The paper is organized as follows. After presenting the theoretical foundation of the study, the status of electronic commerce in Australia and the relevant diffusion data are presented. The research design is next presented followed by the analysis of the data, which reveals the best-fitted dynamics of EC diffusion. Next we present comprehensive discussions on the results and their implications. Finally, conclusions and future directions are presented.

THEORETICAL FOUNDATION

Wigand (1997) identifies five conceptual approaches surrounding electronic commerce. These are: (i) transaction cost theory, (ii) marketing, (iii) diffusion, (iv) information retrieval, and (v) strategic networking. It is observed that diffusion is one of the core foundations of EC. In this section a closer look at the theory and concept behind the diffusion process is taken.

Diffusion is defined as a process by which an innovation is communicated through certain channels over time among the members of a social system (Rogers, 1983). Literature on the diffusion process is plentiful, for example see Mahajan and Peterson (1985), Loh and Venkatraman (1992), Rogers (1983), Brancheau and Wetherbe (1990); among many others. Applications range from administrative innovation (soft-tech) diffusion (Teece 1980) to the diffusion of high-tech products (ICs) (Norton and Bass, 1987). Four key elements of the diffusion process are: the *innovation, channels of communication, time,* and the *social system* (Mahajan and Peterson, 1985, Rogers, 1983). Table 1 describes the key elements in the context of EC diffusion, which are self-explanatory.

It has been observed that diffusion of technology over time can be modelled by a logistic or S-shaped curve. The literature suggests that new technology is not adopted all at once. Some early adopters adopt new technology. If they are successful a bandwagon effect takes place and the potential adopters then imitate (Mahajan and Peterson 1985, Rogers 1983). This imitation process grows in the same way as the growth of organisms or population which is S-shaped (Pearl 1925). Figure 1 shows such a diffusion curve. It is noted that the period between points A and B is the growth period of the technology (EC in our case), when the rate of diffusion increases over time. Whereas the period between points B and C is the decline period, when the rate of diffusion decreases over time until the technology is enhanced or replaced by a new improved one. N, in figure 1, is the upper limit of the innovation diffusion, which denotes the "social system" (see Table 1).

The basic differential equation, which governs the diffusion process, can be presented as follows (Mahajan and Peterson 1985):

Table 1: Key Elements in EC Diffusion

Generic Elements	EC Context
Innovation	Internet based EC and its associated software and hardware having significant impact on the adopting organizations and customers/suppliers of the organizations.
Channels of communication	Horizontal channel (e.g. direct interpersonal contacts, indirect observations within the EC user community) and vertical channel (e.g., interaction with outside agents, promotional efforts by the EC vendors etc.) (Loh and Venkatraman, 1992)
Time	The time period of EC diffusion under study.
Social system	Set of organizations (and the customers and/or suppliers of the organizations) leveraging EC to achieve their mission (Loh and Venkatraman, 1992)

$$\frac{dn(t)}{dt} = b(t)\, n(t)\, [N - n(t)] \qquad (1)$$

Where $b(t)$ is the coefficient of imitation and N is the upper limit of $n(t)$. $n(t)$ is the number of technology in use at time t. It is noted that equation (1) is of internal influence type (Dos Santos and Peffers 1998) and provides basic structure of the explicit time dependent diffusion model. It deals with the diffusion process over time. A lot of information about the dynamics of the technology (i.e., behaviour of adopter population over time) are obtained using the dynamic model.

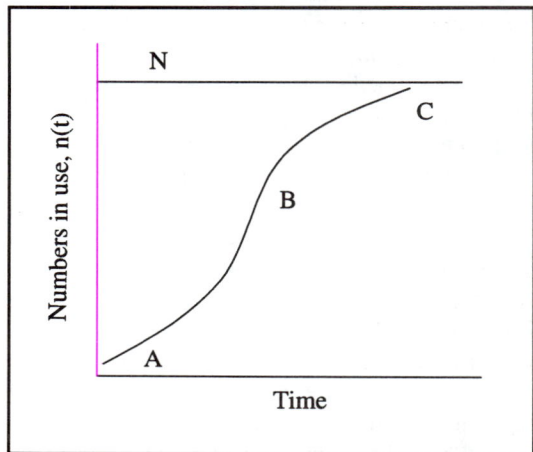

Figure 1: S-shaped Diffusion Curve

In some diffusion studies (for example, Brancheau and Wetherbe 1990; Nilakanta and Scamell 1990; among many others) behaviour and characteristics of the adopter population are investigated at a specific point in time to study different stages of the diffusion process. Conceptual models are first developed for the diffusion process and different hypotheses are then tested. These models are implicitly dependent on time and can, therefore, be classified as stage (or phase) models of IT diffusion.

The scope of this paper is the explicit time dependent dynamic models of diffusion. Literature, however, provides many logistics models (Quaddus 1986, Meade and Islam 1998). In order to study the diffusion of EC in Australia three popular diffusion models have been selected as follows:

Blackman's Model (Quaddus 1986, Meade & Islam 1998):
The functional form is as follows:

$$n(t) = \frac{N}{1 + AB^t} \qquad (2)$$

Where $n(t)$ and N are as defined previously and A and B are the parameters. For this model the coefficient of imitation $b(t)$ is a constant. The nature of $b(t)$ has important implication, which will be explained later.

Gompertz Curve (Quaddus, 1986; Meade and Islam, 1998):
The functional form is:

$$n(t) = NA^{B^t} \qquad (3)$$

Where A and B are the parameters. This model assumes that coefficient of imitation $b(t)$ decreases with time.

The NSRL Model (Quaddus, 1986; Meade and Islam, 1998):
The functional form is:

$$n(t)-n(t-1)=B\left(\frac{n(t)}{N}\right)^D[N-n(t)] \quad (4)$$

Where B and D are the parameters. NSRL is the most flexible logistic model. The imitation coefficient b(t) decreases with time if 0<D<1, and increases with time if D>1.

In our application to the EC data, we shall also use the upper limit N as the parameter and let the model and the data find the most appropriate value for N. We shall also use a simple exponential growth model to experiment with the data. As pointed out by Gurbaxani (1990) when a technology is in its early stage of diffusion, it may well be specified by an exponential model. The functional form of the exponential model is:

$$\ln(n(t))=A+Bt \quad (5)$$

Where A and B are the parameters.

ELECTRONIC COMMERCE IN AUSTRALIA

The history of electronic commerce in Australia goes back to the 1970s when pharmacies began to order inventories from their suppliers by electronic means (Behrendorff and Rahman, 1999). However, modern era of electronic commerce began in early 1990s and got a boost in 1994 with the formation of "Electronic Commerce Australia (ECA)." ECA started promoting and assisting the implementation of various electronic commerce technologies in Australia (Behrendorff and Rahman 1999).

Figure 2: Internet Use and Growth in Australia (Source: Marzbani et al. 1998)

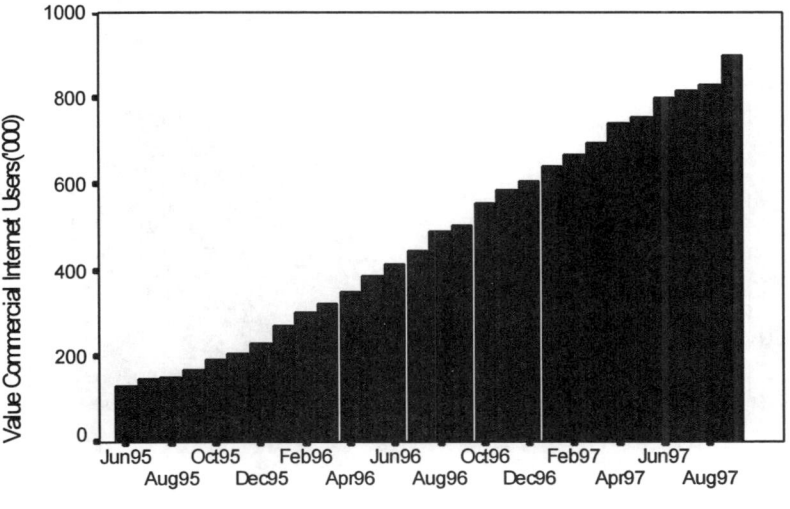

Internet infrastructure is well developed in Australia, and it ranks third in the world in per capita usage of the Internet (DOCITA 1999). However, there is a general lack of diffusion data on electronic commerce in Australia. Marzbani et al. (1998) did a comprehensive survey on the state of electronic commerce in Australia. The authors report that at the start of 1998 there were some 1.6 million Internet users in Australia (consumers, enterprises, and academic), of which some 21% reported Internet shopping as either primary or secondary Internet activity. This represents the aspects of consumer-to-business electronic commerce (Kalakota and Whinston 1997). In the absence of any comprehensive data on electronic commerce growth in Australia, the Internet shopping is used as the measure of electronic commerce for further analysis. Figure 2 shows the Internet use and growth in Australia from June 1995 to September 1997.

Marbzani et al. (1998, pp 13) also reports that online shopping has grown steadily over the years—from 4.5% per month in June 1996 to 8% per month in December 1997 (approximated from six monthly figures). This and other information from Marbzani et al. (1998) have been used to estimate of Internet shopping in Australia as shown in Figure 3.

Data of Figure 3 will be used as the measure of consumer-to-business electronic commerce in Australia for further analysis.

Figure 3: Internet Shopping Growth in Australia (Source: Estimated from Marzbani et al 1998)

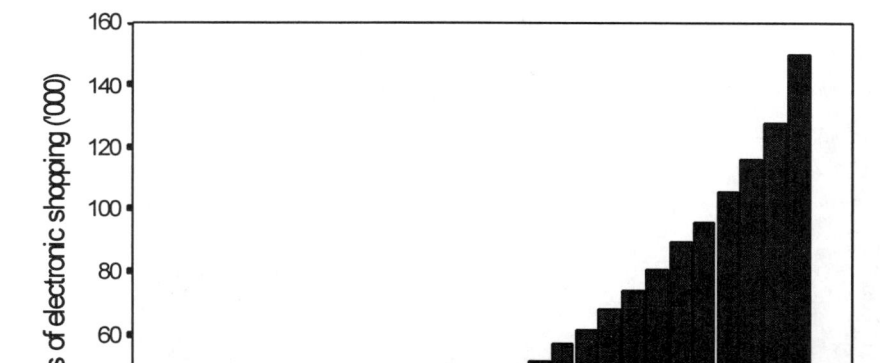

RESEARCH DESIGN

This study investigates the research questions by using the internal influence models presented earlier. While literature provides many similar models (Quaddus, 1985), we have chosen the most popular ones in this study. The characteristics of the models have been presented earlier. The models are time series in nature, where the dependent variable is the number of EC in use, n(t).

It is extremely difficult to obtain real diffusion data in EC domain. Various surrogate measures (e.g. investment in EC) could be used. However, we have used the best estimate of the consumer-to-business EC in Australia (as shown in Figure 3) for the analysis.

Our research design is simple. The three models (presented earlier) are applied to the dataset of Figure 3. Statistical tests are then carried out to select the best model. Based on the selected model, the research questions are analyzed.

ANALYSIS OF THE DATA

In order to answer the research questions, we apply the three diffusion models in this section and find the best-fitted model. Table 2 presents the results of the Blackman's model, NSRL model, and the exponential model. It must be noted that the Gompertz curve did not produce any meaningful result at all.

It is observed that all the models fit quite well in terms of R^2 value. For Blackman's model, all the parameters are significant (high t value). For NSRL model, parameters N and B are not significant (low t values), however, parameter D is significant with reasonably high t value. This model will be discarded in favour of Blackman's model, which has all the parameters as significant. The exponential model fits quite well and all the parameters are significant. However, no diffusion process continues exponentially and hence the exponential model does not provide any meaningful interpretation of the diffusion process. It will be, therefore, discarded from further analysis. The objective was to show that the exponential model does fit well with the early stages of the diffusion process.

DISCUSSION ON THE RESULTS

It's now revealed that Blackman's model is the only popular diffusion model, which fits quite well with the EC growth in Australia. We now address our research questions in light of the data analysis of the previous section.

Table 2: Results of the Diffusion Models

Blackman's Model	NSRL Model	Exponential Model
$R^2 = 0.996$	$R^2 = 0.998$	$R^2 = 0.99$
N = 533.42, t = 3.34	N = 10000, t = 0.02	A = 1.875, t = 48.88
A = 7215, t = 4.11	B = 0.252, t = 0.125	B = 0.115, t = 49.93
B = 0.89, t = 171	D = 1.19, t = 2.5	

Research Question 1: What are the dynamics of EC diffusion in Australia ?

From resource allocation point of view this question is extremely important. It helps the planners to forecast the diffusion process and thus to allocate resources to achieve planned growth in EC. It is observed that Blackman's model is the appropriate model to forecast the dynamics of EC diffusion in Australia. The model forecasts the upper limit N (saturation level of EC growth) as 533,420, i.e., about half a million internet shoppers. As of December 1997, the level of hard-core Internet shoppers was around 50,000 and "sometime" internet shoppers numbered around 200,000 (Marzbani et al. 1998). It is noted that the value of N was the best-fitted value as provided by the model. This provides a food for thought for the planners, who can now compare this value with their hunch or some other logically derived value of N (see Quaddus, 1985) for methods of finding the upper limit N for some real technology diffusion). The Blackman's model (and any other diffusion models) can also be applied with any planned value of N. The model can then be used to forecast the diffusion pattern for appropriate resource allocation.

Figure 4 shows the dynamics of the diffusion of EC from June 1995 until December 2001. Blackman's model also predicts that the maximum rate of diffusion will be achieved at the time when 50% of the upper limit of diffusion is achieved. Given that the upper limit N is 533420, the time of maximum rate of diffusion was achieved around mid-1998. According to the model, from that point on the Internet shopping diffusion rate will decrease gradually if corrective measures are not taken. This becomes an eye opener for the planners. It must be pointed that the numeric values of the model should not be taken as definitive.

Figure 4: Dynamics of EC Growth by the Blackman's Model

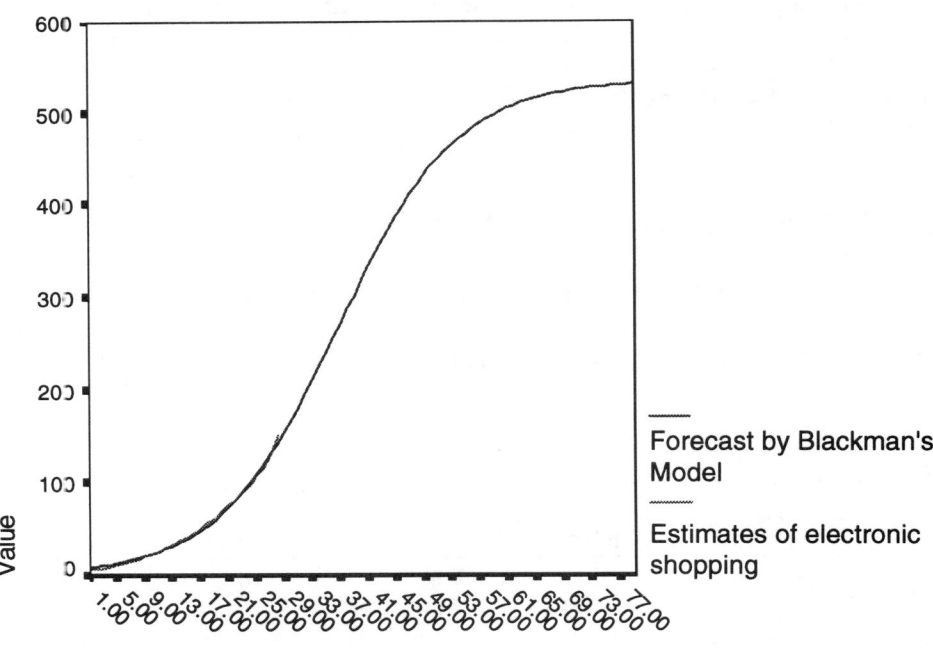

They must be viewed as information providers, which can then be researched from other points of view and appropriate actions can then be taken.

Research Question 2: What is the Influencing Source of the EC Diffusion Process?

The diffusion model also specifies what had been the most influencing force for EC growth in Australia. The governing equation of the diffusion model is provided by equation 1. A careful analysis of the equation reveals that the diffusion process proceeds due to the interaction of the adopted ($n(t)$) and potential adopters ($N - n(t)$) of the EC. This type of model is widely known as the "internal" influence type, i.e., predominant influencing factor is the interaction between the adopters and potential adopters. It is, therefore, observed that EC growth in Australia, thus far, had been influenced by this factor. Potential adopters of internet shopping mostly learned from the experiences of other shoppers and decided to follow them.

As mentioned before the coefficient of imitation $b(t)$ (see equations 1 and 2) also plays an important role in the diffusion process. $b(t)$ indicates a "driving force" which pushes the potential adopters to adopt the EC (Quaddus, 1985). For the Blackman's model $b(t)$ is a constant. This indicates that the "forces" of the imitation process for the diffusion of EC in Australia had been more or less constant during the last several years and had been influenced mostly by the interaction between the adopters and potential adopters.

Research Question 3: What Must be Done to Enhance the EC Diffusion Process in Australia?

Analyses of the Research Questions 1 and 2 provided much information. It is observed that EC diffusion has already achieved its maximum rate of growth. Appropriate policies must be implemented to enhance the diffusion process. Note that Blackman's model assumes a constant level of upper limit N. However, the level of Internet shopping depends on the level of Internet use. Therefore, policies must be adopted to enhance the use of the Internet. Although this might sound like a very trivial policy, the information on the maximum rate of growth and the model assumption on the constant level of N put some urgency in implementing appropriate policies.

It is also discussed above that the diffusion process, so far, had been influenced by some internal interactions. Two top-level policies can thus be addressed to enhance the diffusion process further, which are: (i) campaign to enhance the interactions between the adopters and the potential adopters, (ii) create environment to bring in more external influence. Marzbani et al. (1998) found "cost", "security" and "response time" to be the top concerns which are acting as barriers to EC diffusion. It is noted that all these are "external" influences and must be addressed sooner than later. DOCITA (1999) also presents a number of government-led policies to enhance EC diffusion. It is interesting to note that none of the documents on EC (DOCITA 1999, Marbzani et al. 1998; among others) deal with the issues of the "internal" interactions between the adopters and the potential adopters of EC to enhance the diffusion process. Based on the above analyses, we firmly believe that this must be done in the form of a forum where these interactions might take place.

CONCLUSIONS AND FUTURE DIRECTIONS

This chapter took an inside look into the diffusion process of electronic commerce (EC) in Australia. After a brief review of the problems and opportunities of the EC adoption, the chapter concentrates on the diffusion process and presents the theoretical background to the diffusion process. In doing so it reviews three popular diffusion models, which are subsequently applied to one aspect of the internet based consumer-to-business electronic commerce in Australia, namely internet shopping. Results show that Blackman's model is the appropriate model to describe the dynamics of the EC diffusion process.

Characteristics of Blackman's model were then analyzed in detail to propose a number of policy guidelines. It is observed that the past diffusion was mostly dominated by the "internal" interactions between the adopters and the potential adopters of EC. Government and other relevant bodies should look into this seriously and chalk out formal plans to formalize the internal interactions.

Limitations of this study lie with the limitations of the chosen diffusion models. We have only chosen internal influence type diffusion models. However, literature shows that diffusion might be influenced by internal, external and mixed mode interactions (Dos Santos and Peffers, 1998). Our future research will be continued towards this direction. Also, it is noted that Blackman's model assumes a constant upper limit of the diffusion level. But EC is a pervasive technology and, therefore, the upper limit of diffusion could be time dependent. Our ongoing research effort will also concentrate on this direction.

REFERENCES

Applegate, L M, Holsapple, C W, Kalakota, R, Radermacher, F J, and Whinston, A B (1996). Electronic Commerce: Building Blocks of New Business Opportunity, *Journal of Organizational Computing and Electronic Commerce*, 6(1), 1-10.

Auger, P and Gallaugher, J M (1997). Factors Affecting the Adoption of an Internet Based Sales Presence for Small Business, *The Information Society*, Vol 13, 55-74.

Behrendorff, G and Rahman, S M (1999). Adoption of Electronic Commerce by Small to Medium Enterprises in Australia, In Tan, F B, Corbett, P S, and Wong, Y Y (eds.), *Information Technology Diffusion in the Asia Pacific: Perspectives on Policy, Electronic Commerce, and Education*, Idea Group Publishing, USA, 130-147.

Bolisani, E, Scarso, E, Miles, I, and Boden, M (1999). Electronic Commerce Implementation: A Knowledge-Based Analysis, *International Journal of Electronic Commerce*, 3(3), 53-69.

Brancheau, J.C. and Wetherbe, J.C. (1990). The Adoption of Spreadsheet Software: Testing Innovation Diffusion Theory in the Context of End-User Computing, *Information Systems Research*, 1(2), 115-143.

Cinningham, C and Tynan, C (1993). Electronic Trading, Inter-organizational Systems and the Nature of Buyer-Seller Relationships: The Need for a Network Perspective, *International Journal of Information Management*, Vol 13, 3-28.

Cockburn, C and Wilson, T D (1996). Business Use of World-Wide Web, *International Journal of Information Management*, 16(2), 83-102.

Department of Communications, Information Technology and the Arts (DOCITA) (1999), *Australia's e-commerce Report Card*, Canberra, Australia.

Dos Santos, B L and Peffers, K (1998). Competitor and Vendor Influence on the Adoption of Innovative Applications in Electronic Commerce, *Information and Management*, Vol 34, 175-184.

Giaglis, G M, Paul, R J, and Doukidis, G I (1999). Dynamic Modeling to Assess the Business Value of Electronic Commerce, *International Journal of Electronic Commerce*, 3(3), 35-51.

Gurbaxani, V (1990). Diffusion in Computing Networks: The Case of BITNET, *Communications of the ACM*, 33(12), 65-75.

Harkola, J and Greve, A (1995). Diffusion of Technology: Cohesion or Structural Equivalence? *Academy of Management Journal*, 422-426.

Kalakota, R, Stallaert, J and Whinston, A (1996). Worldwide Real-Time Decision Support Systems for Electronic Commerce Applications, *Journal of Organizational Computing and Electronic Commerce*, 6(1), 11-32.

Kalakota, R and Whinston, A B (1997). *Electronic Commerce: A manager's Guide*, Addison_Wesley, Reading, Massachusetts.

Kraemar, K L, Gurbaxani, V and King, J L (1992). Economic Development, Government Policy, and the Diffusion of Computing in Asia-Pacific Countries, *Public Administration Review*, 52(2), 146-156.

La Rovere, R L (1996). IT Diffusion in Small and Medium Sized Enterprises: Elements for Policy Definition, *Information Technology for Development*, 7(4), 169-181.

Loh, L and Venkatraman, N. (1992), Diffusion of Information Technology Outsourcing: Influence Sources and the Kodak Effect, *Information Systems Research*, 3(4), 334-358.

Mahajan, V. and Peterson, R.A. (1985). *Models of Innovation Diffusion*, Sage Publications, Beverley Hills.

Marzbani, R, Wong, C, Holmes, M, Chick, H, Ghassemi, K and Moore, P (1998). *Stats: Electronic Commerce in Australia*, www.consult and Department of Industry, Science and Tourism, Canberra, Australia.

Meade, N and Islam, T (1998). Terchnological Forecasting - Model Selection, Model Stability, and Combining Models, *Management Science*, 44(8), 1115-1130.

Nath, R, Akmanligil, M, Hjelm, K, Sakaguchi, T, and Schultz, M (1998), Electronic Commerce and the Internet: Issues, Problems, and Perspectives, *International Journal of Information Management*, 18(2), 91-101.

Ng, H, Pan, Y J and Wilson, T D (1998). Business Use of the World Wide Web: A Report on Further Investigations, *International Journal of Management*, 18(5), 291-314.

Nilakanta, S., and Scamell, R.W. (1990). The Effect of Information Sources and Communication Channels on the Diffusion of Innovation in a Data Base Development Environment, *Management Science*, 36(1), 24-40.

Norton, J.A. and Bass, F.M. (1987). A Diffusion Theory Model of Adoption and Substitution for Successive Generations of High-Technology Products, *Management Science*, 33(9), 1069-1086.

Palmer, J W (1997). Electronic Commerce in Retailing: Differences Across Retail Formats, *The Information Society*, Vol 13, 75-91.

Pearl, R. (1925), *The Biology of Population Growth*, Alfred A. Knopf, New York.

Poon, S and Swatman, P (1999). A Longitudinal Study of Expectations in Small Business Internet Commerce, *International Journal of Electronic Commerce*, 3(3), 21-33.

Quaddus, M A (1995). Diffusion of Information Technology: An Exploration of the Stage Models and Facilitating the User's Choice by Systems Approach, *Proceedings of the*

1995 Pan Pacific Conference on Information Systems, 29 June - 2 July, Singapore, 191-199.

Quaddus, M A (1985), On Applying Logistic Models in Technological Forecasting, *Socio Economic Planning Sciences*, 20(4), 201-206.

Rogers, E.M. (1983). *Diffusion of Innovations*, The Free Press, New York.

Teece, D.J. (1980). The Diffusion of an Administrative Innovation, *Management Science*, Vol.26, 464-470.

Wigand, R T (1997).Electronic Commerce: Definition, Theory, and Context, *The Information Society*, Vol 13, 1-16.

Chapter VII

Planning E-Strategies for New Zealand Firms

Liaquat Hossain
Massey University, New Zealand

This chapter examines the risk factors for firms investing in e-commerce or electronic commerce in New Zealand. The relationships between the intra and extra organisational factors that ensure the success or failure of the electronic commerce projects in New Zealand are discussed. The investment risks for electronic commerce projects may rest on the planning, development, implementation and post-implementation phase. This study analyses the success criteria that are to be considered critical for electronic commerce projects in New Zealand. By using the CSFs criteria for investing in electronic commerce, this study suggests an e-strategy planning framework for New Zealand firms involved in electronic commerce. Future directions identifying the need for this proposed e-strategic framework and the need for empirical validation is also discussed.

INTRODUCTION TO ELECTRONIC COMMERCE

E-commerce or electronic commerce can be defined as the electronification of the consumer-supplier value chain as well as the industry chains (Weinstein, 1997). It refers to all commercial-based electronic transactions including the transmission of data, text, sound and image files. E-Commerce includes electronic data interchange (EDI), EFTPOS, electronic banking, digital cash, and other forms of electronic payment systems. Weinstein's (1997) research identified two key emerging trends that are making the development and deployment of a global enterprise network more critical. The first is the evolution of global enterprises and the rise of electronic commerce and the second is the impact of supplier and industry value chains on the business function.

Apparently, it is observed from the present situation of the information industry that there is no implicit criteria which may guide companies investing in electronic commerce

(Weinstein, 1997). The risks in investing in electronic commerce projects are four-fold: *planning, development, implementation and post-implementation* risks. An investigation of the existing literature suggests that critical success factors (CSFs) are the small number of easily identifiable operation goals shaped by the industry, the firm, the manager, and the environment that assures the success of an organisation (Laudon and Laudon, 1988 and 1998).

Rockart (1982) and Rockart and Scott (1984) argue that CSFs are the operational goals of a firm and the attainment of these goals will assure the successful operation. CSFs can also be defined as those few key areas in which things must be correct in order for the firm to remain competitive (Neumann, 1994). Wiseman (1988) argued that the CSF analysis has evolved to a role in which the managers use this in their information-planning approach for identifying opportunities and threats. According to the most widely used CSF technique suggested by Rockart (1982), it is evident that the usefulness and scope of this framework depend on the subjective ability, style, and perspective of the executives.

The shaping of the CSFs evolves from four viewpoints: (i) can be shaped by the industry and its structural changes; (ii) the firm's operational strategies and changes in the products/services offered; (iii) the managers and their perceptions towards the success factors of a firm; and (iv) changes in environment with regard to technology, computer hardware and software, other external factors like government regulation, changes in the policy. CSFs research is receiving considerable attention from both academics and managers. The environmental uncertainty and flooding of the market with changing hardware and software make the manager's investment decisions even more complex.

Research by Daniels (1994) provides us an early foundation of the CSFs investigation for the firm. However, Daniel's definition of CSFs is focusing on the three to six areas that a company must do in order to succeed. Rockart (1982) further argued that the CSFs are limited number factors that ensure successful competitive performance of organisation, if implemented. Furthermore, the fundamental problem that most of companies are facing is to stay on top when technology changes. It is therefore essential for an organisation to develop a comprehensive CSF framework that can guide its future investment and in particular, for the case of electronic commerce investment projects.

An ethnographic approach is used in this study for the purpose of identifying the CSFs for investing in electronic commerce projects in New Zealand. Thus, the investment complexity in New Zealand's electronic commerce projects is addressed. It is apparent that the identification of the CSFs for electronic commerce-based companies will provide a framework for future investors in this sector. Therefore, the overall aim of this chapter is to provide an analysis of the critical risk factors for electronic commerce investment in New Zealand. It then analyses the planning, development, implementation and post-implementation risk factors in the development of an e-strategic framework that will guide future investments of electronic commerce projects.

ELECTRONIC COMMERCE IN NEW ZEALAND

The New Zealand Government has realised the true benefits of the development of electronic commerce for maintaining its economic development over the past few years. New Zealand experienced a significant growth in electronic commerce development among retailing, banking, healthcare and other small businesses like grocery chains. New Zealand's

Ministry of Commerce is also actively involved in monitoring and promoting the electronic commerce development throughout the country. As a part of the monitoring process of electronic commerce development, the New Zealand Government has stressed the importance of critical issues like fair trade and an informed marketplace for ensuring the success of electronic commerce implementation and consumer acceptance (MOC, 1997).

At the government level, consumer protection laws, fair practices and policies affecting consumers to function effectively and equitably in the marketplace are considered to be critical in electronic commerce development and the deployment phase (MOC, 1997). In order to address the aforementioned critical issues, the New Zealand Government under the Weights and Measures Act 1987 and the Fair Trading Act 1986, has initiated proper administration, enforcement of trade measurement and consumer safety functions for monitoring the electronic commerce development and deployment process.

Consumer confidence in electronic payment systems, including the avoidance of fraud are identified by the Ministry of Consumer Affairs as critical for the success of electronic commerce investment (MOC, 1997). In order to enforce and assure the required consumer confidence level, the Ministry of Consumer Affairs in 1997, have initiated three critical steps. The first is to promote the early establishment of a certification process for authenticating New Zealand suppliers for the benefit of the consumers and the business. The second is to have payment systems' operators inform consumers on the capabilities and the terms and conditions of payment systems, and about their liability in the event of disputes. The last is to undertake international cooperation among business, consumers and government agencies in creating electronic payment frameworks, seal of approval schemes and security services such as public keys. However, it is evident from the review of New Zealand's existing electronic commerce literature that the present privacy law does not extend to persons or organisations operating outside New Zealand jurisdiction (MOC, 1997).

Moreover, it is anticipated that the market for global electronic commerce will grow to US$300 billion by 2001. The New Zealand Government is also anticipating that electronic commerce will benefit in minimising the barriers of time and distance to world markets and efficiency gains in business supply chain (MOC, 1998). However, it is observed that electronic commerce development in New Zealand focuses primarily on some government organisations by isolating them from the private sector. Thus, demonstrating the absence of an established policy framework for electronic commerce development (MOC, 1998). Ensuring consistency across all policy sectors, avoiding duplication of effort, ensuring comprehensive consideration of electronic commerce issues and certainty in delivery to business and customers must be addressed by an electronic commerce development policy framework.

Considering the driving force of electronic commerce development from the private sectors and its flexible operations, the New Zealand Government in 1998 decided to introduce '*Self Regulation*' for encouraging the high level of private sectors participation (MOC, 1998). However, it is critical for the New Zealand Government to decide on an appropriate framework for supporting and enforcing a competitive, predictable, consistent, market and technology-driven approach towards the diffusion of electronic commerce technologies in this market.

A lack of understanding of these CSFs may very well hinder the rapid development of electronic commerce in New Zealand. So, what are the CSFs for electronic commerce projects? How can the lack of understanding of these CSFs inhibit the growth of electronic commerce? What are the government strategies for dealing with these CSFs in New Zealand? In order to provide an answer to these questions addressed, it is important to develop an understanding of the CSFs for electronic commerce projects. At this stage, it is crucial to be aware of the apparent differences of CSFs and its definition in the body of literature.

CRITICAL SUCCESS FACTORS FOR ELECTRONIC COMMERCE

Critical Success Factors or CSFs are the small number of easily identifiable operation goals shaped by the industry, the firm, the manager, and the environment that assures the success of an organisation. So, the success of the electronic commerce investment is dependent on the consideration the operational goals of a firm and the attainment of these goals. It can be argued that CSF analysis has evolved to a role in which managers use them in their information planning approach for identifying strengths, opportunities, weakness and threats (Wiseman, 1988). However, past research (Rockart, 1982) also suggests that the usefulness and scope of the CSF framework is largely dependent on the subjective ability, style, and perspective of the executives.

The emphasis of CSFs, in the past, is on the identification of factors that are critical to a company's success and dictated by interviewing only the strategic planning executives. Therefore, it overlooks the CSFs identification from the management and operational control levels. The literature also suggests that by using only the strategic planners as a basis in guiding the firm, it undervalues the true essence of decision making. When this happens, an unreliable identification of CSFs is anticipated. Therefore, this methodology has a major flaw in its validity as it ignores the importance of CSFs identification from management and operational control level.

The existing CSFs methodology lacks the concern of the management control, and operation control of Anthony's (1970) three levels of management function. The environmental changes with regard to the technology, government regulation and changes in the international marketplace have brought about significant changes in the operation and management of organisation in a particular context. This is even more severe for the case of electronic commerce planning, development, implementation and post-implementation phases. The success of the electronic commerce project may rest on the level of management's concern on these four critical issues of electronic commerce project.

The move is towards an efficient and effective information infrastructure. The future of the business will depend more on the technology, hardware, software and the integration of these at the business-level function. However, the fundamental problem that most companies are facing is to stay on top when technology changes. It is therefore essential for an organisation to develop a comprehensive CSF framework that can guide future investments and in particular, for the case of electronic commerce-based investment projects.

As mentioned earlier, the investment risks of electronic commerce projects can be seen from four viewpoints: planning, development, implementation, and post-implementation. The present situation of electronic commerce development reveals that there is no implicit criteria for guiding the investors in the development and implementation phase of electronic commerce project. A study by Viehland and Mitchell (1997) on electronic commerce proposed eight essential challenges for firms considering to enter into electronic commerce. Table 1 summarises the CSFs identification and strategies for electronic commerce development.

Challenges for firms are largely influenced by the interplay of factors mentioned above. It is evident from the summary presented in Table 1 that there are valuable relationships between *intra* and *extra*-organisational factors that need to be considered. This underpins a successful strategy of electronic commerce implementation sought after by future investors. Furthermore, it is important to note that the strategies for dealing with intra-organisational success factors can be dealt with by introducing electronic commerce development planning methodologies. The major difficulty is on managing the extra-organisational success factors, which are to be guided by a well thought policy framework. The development and implementation of this electronic commerce policy framework will ensure the success or failure of electronic commerce development among New Zealand firms.

At present, the New Zealand Government is in the process of formalising a broader policy framework that is expected to serve as a policy mechanism for guiding the future of electronic commerce development (MOC, 1998). This policy framework is crucial for the diffusion of information technologies in creating and sustaining the strategic benefits through electronic commerce. It is evident from Viehland's (1998) study that New Zealand

Table 1. A Summary of CSFs Identification and Strategies for Electronic Commerce Development

E-Commerce Development CSFs	Strategies for Addressing CSFs
1. Confidentiality	Introduction of SET (Secure Electronic Transactions) introduced by VISA and MasterCard in 1997
2. Authentication	Digital signature authenticating identity of sender and receiver of the message or the transaction
3. Infrastructure for multi-media	Government and private sectors' investment in information technology innovation and diffusion
4. Protection of intellectual property	Government laws for protecting intellectual property rights and review of TradeMarks Act., 1953. Technical solutions such as digital watermarks are already in place to serve as a protection mechanism
5. Rules	The New Zealand (NZ) Privacy Act for protecting unauthorised collection and use of personal data. The NZ Consumer Protection Laws for safeguarding NZ consumers in the on-line environment both trader and consumer based NZ as well as trader based outside NZ
6. Ability to be paid and get paid	SET for credit card transaction. Introduction of Mondex smart card for secure on-line payment
7. Better search tools	Development of new search engines as fuzzy-logic for indexing and metadata, first search, and MIRO
8. Management control	Technical solutions for tight coordination and control among participating organisations in electronic commerce

Table 2. A Summary of the Strategic Advantages and Disadvantages of Internet Commerce in New Zealand

Strategic Advantages	Strategic Disadvantages
1. English speaking	1. High cost of Internet access
2. Geographical location	2. Volume-based charging
3. Acceptance of communications technology	3. Immature and unstable Internet service provider market
4. Deregulated telecommunications industry	4. IT skills in workplace
5. An exporter of technology expertise	
6. A history of innovation in software industry	
7. A pioneer in volume-based pricing	

poses many advantages that are to be considered strategic for the deployment of Internet commerce technologies. Furthermore, there are some inherent disadvantages for Internet commerce development and implementation process in New Zealand. Table 2 summarises the strategic advantages and disadvantages of Internet commerce in New Zealand.

It is evident from the KPMG's (1999) study on electronic commerce challenges and opportunities that the deployment of electronic commerce technologies in Australia and New Zealand lags behind the U.S. and the Europe. However, the actual barriers to the widespread acceptance and use of electronic commerce in Australia and New Zealand are more perceived than real (KPMG, 1999). KPMG's (1999) recent study on the identification of the CSFs for electronic commerce business in Australia and New Zealand indicates that there are nine CSFs, which must be considered by the managers of electronic commerce projects. Table 3 summarises the CSFs for Australian and New Zealand firms investing in electronic commerce projects. The identification of these CSFs is based on a recent empirical study conducted among 309 firms in Australia and New Zealand. However, this KPMG report on electronic commerce for 146 Australian and 163 New Zealand firms has failed to address the criticality of planning, development, implementation and post-implementation CSFs for firms investing in electronic commerce.

In order to gain a sustainable competitive advantage from doing business on the electronic commerce, firms must understand the inherent risks factors associated with planning, development, implementation and post-implementation. A framework address-

Table 3. A Summary of the CSFs for Australian and New Zealand Firms Investing in Electronic Commerce Projects

1. Start with a needs-based strategy, not a technology solution
2. Develop an e-commerce strategy for complementing the corporate strategy
3. Aggregation of the disparate investments that are likely to be found in any organisation
4. Avoid layering costs onto the current distribution network
5. Choose the partners and skills carefully
6. Integrate across the entire organisation for large efficiency gains
7. Focus on the transparency of implementation and chaining process
8. Distinguish between striving to win new markets or customers and gaining cost savings from process improvement
9. Develop a benefits register and measure the organisation's achievement against it

ing the aforementioned risk factors for electronic commerce defined as e-strategic framework, is important if a firm wants to make a successful electronic commerce investment and also to employ this for its strategic benefits.

TOWARDS AN E-STRATEGIC FRAMEWORK

E-strategy for the purpose of this study is referred to as a strategy that helps a firm in gaining and sustaining competitive advantage through electronic commerce. The work by Daniels (1994) supports that a successful strategy should have a global vision, both at the national and international levels. As an electronic commerce investment planner, one should think strategically and recognise that managing and investing in electronic commerce projects require new management styles and new approaches of innovation. This is essential for maintaining and keeping pace with the changes in the information technology industry.

Porter's (1987) framework suggests a model to identify new business opportunities for organisational planners. It is, however, important to understand that competitive advantages change over time, and for many companies like in electronic commerce business, the key is not to get stuck with a single strategy. Stalk (1988) argued that the development of a competitive and successful investment strategy should be guided by the strategic thinking as well as keep moving and staying on the forefront. McFarlan's (1984) work states that a strategic organisation requires high dependence on communications.

Over the years, the need for the use of electronic commerce in service sectors has increased significantly. By *'walking through'* the process of Anthony's (1970) business model, electronic commerce investors can identify interdependencies in the process flows and bottlenecks as well as contingencies can be planned for. It is manifested in Nolan's (1987) study that planning, development, implementation and post-implementation has continued to receive a high level of priority for organisational development and its decision-making process for managing the crises in data processing.

Past research in the area of information systems (Parsons, 1983; Porter and Millar, 1985; Porter, 1987; Wiseman, 1988; Primozic et. al., 1991; Hopper, 1991; Neumann, 1994) provides an understanding of the use of information technologies for creating a competitive advantage. Schoemaker (1995) also suggests that the main advantage of strategic CSF planning over conventional is its externality and broader focus, which ensure the challenge of managing technology as well as infrastructural leapfrogging.

Figure 1 provides an e-strategic framework for firms investing in electronic commerce projects. It is highlighted in Figure 1 that an e-strategic framework for competitive advantage should be based on a thorough process involving planning, development, implementation, and post-implementation of electronic commerce. Planning for electronic commerce is the starting point for the identification of CSFs. Identification of the required stages, procedures, and involvement of key decision makers are essential for ensuring the success of electronic commerce projects. Key criteria for measuring the success of electronic commerce investment should be considered in the planning phase. An understanding of the impact of external factors like government regulation, future competition, advancement of technology and changes in the international marketplace are also needs to be considered in this stage of electronic commerce investment, thus, demonstrating the interplay of *intra and extra* organisational factors. Findings from the Bank of New Zealand

Figure 1. An E-Strategic Framework for Firms Investing in Electronic Commerce Projects

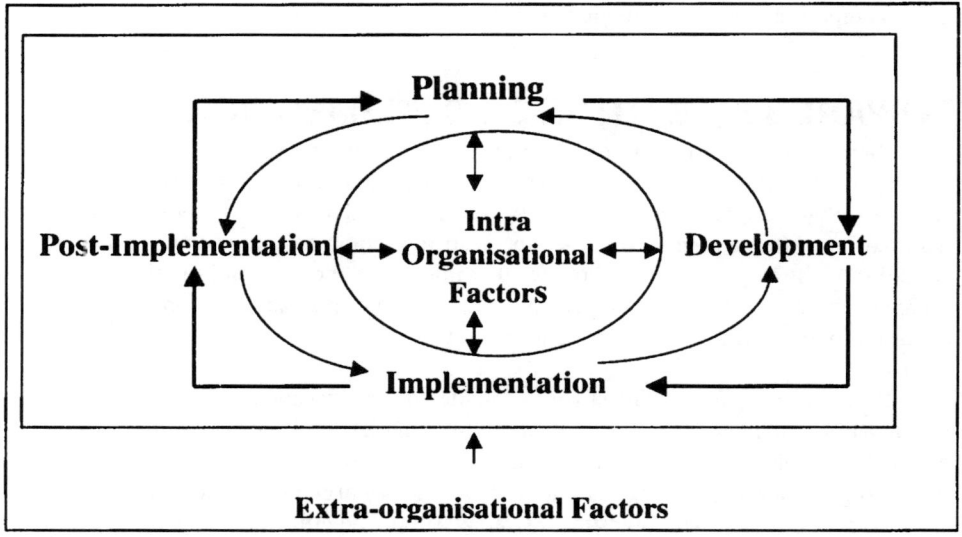

(BNZ) suggests that understanding of your customer's needs and meeting those needs are considered to be most critical at the planning phase of e-commerce (Briant, 1999).

In the planning phase of e-commerce, BNZ studied the strategies for the deployment of e-commerce both domestically and internationally. In this process, BNZ also studied the stability and functionality risk of the technology that is being retired in key markets (Briant, 1999). Scalability and the implications of e-commerce for users are as well studied in details for BNZ. Finally, a clear link between the e-commerce projects and bank's wider strategy was developed in BNZ. Findings suggest that BNZ is a camp of supporters for structured planning. The benefits of structured planning identified from BNZ's e-commerce project management suggests that having a structured planning process provides an order of magnitude and a better chance of delivering what was expected, on time and within the agreed resources.

The second phase of developing e-strategy is the consideration of electronic commerce development risks factors. Understanding the underlying relationship between electronic commerce development methodology and the required measure of success is vital at this stage. It can be accomplished by aligning the required electronic transactions with the existing business processes. A link establishing the relationship between the user and system requirements must be considered.

Findings from BNZ's electronic payment systems development suggests that the fewer new aspects are confronted with the lower the perceived risk of participation and therefore shorter the acceptance time (Briant, 1999). For example, many e-commerce projects use credit cards as their first payment type because the cards are deployed, sellers and buyers are familiar and trust them and processes are in place worldwide to handle the payment. It has been observed from BNZ's e-commerce development that leveraging existing processes greatly reduces the cost for all participants. This has also allowed BNZ to learn while not getting the cost curve too far ahead of the income.

The third is the identification and analysis of the implementation risks for investing in electronic commerce. A feasibility study related to the impact of technological change and instability in electronic commerce project is important at this stage. The strategies for dealing with these at BNZ include the following (Briant, 1999):
1. building solutions that are platform independent or can utilise the key technologies or be adapted to;
2. use of international standards where possible; and,
3. take incremental steps with short focused projects

The last is on the identification of post-implementation risks for electronic commerce. Electronic commerce managers are required to develop appropriate strategy for gaining user commitment in the post-implementation phase. Understanding the expectation of the end user is crucial for the success of electronic commerce. Organisations at this phase need to develop appropriate measures for managing end-user expectations of required level of services to be rendered through electronic commerce. For example, BNZ at present is in a leading position of the implementation of the electronic payment systems for their banking operations. Findings suggest that BNZ is committed towards the delivery of customer services. This has been accomplished through a clear understanding and commitment of the post- implementation factors involved in ensuring the success of e-commerce projects. Table 4 summarises the post-implementation critical factors considered by BNZ. It is evident from the summary presented in Table 4 that BNZ have established a process of gathering customers feedback and incorporating it to the improvement of the electronic payment systems delivery procedure.

FUTURE TRENDS

The use of electronic commerce in business will continue to grow at a significant rate over the next few years. Continuous innovation in information technologies will make the operation of electronic commerce business more feasible and reliable. However, the success or failure of electronic commerce investment in the future will largely depend on establishing a link between the electronification of firms' business with the overall corporate strategy. Establishment of this link is important for ensuring that proper user support and

Table 4. A summary of the post-implementation critical success factors (CSFs) of Bank of New Zealand (BNZ)

1. Gaining external customer commitment is ultimately essential if you are ever to sell your solution
2. Making sure you are delivering a solution that will reach their objectives
3. Keep talking to them, manage and meet their expectations, get their feedback and make changes that make sense
4. Making sure all parties earn a fair share from the activity
5. Appointing an implementation manger to work with them
6. Promoting the success jointly
7. Partnering with innovators who understand the imperfections of new release technologies and who can help mature the solution
8. Building flexible products

user friendly system is in place. Empirical research in the future will be required to validate the e-strategic framework proposed in the previous section. In particular, the relationships between the planning, development, implementation and post-implementation factors identified in the preceding sections with the intra and extra-organisational success factors for investing in electronic commerce need to be investigated.

CONCLUSION

It is to be concluded that the success of electronic commerce investment is largely dependent of the firms' involvement in planning, development, implementation and post-implementation. A broad definition of CSFs together with the limitations of the existing method are addressed in this chapter. It is evident that the collection of data for designing a CSF framework for electronic commerce should be based on identifying the key success factors from operational, management and strategic planning levels. This method of identifying CSFs from three levels of management will ensure that the necessary critical factors are adequately addressed in the e-strategic framework. For the case of New Zealand, it is evident that electronic commerce will have a significant impact on the business and its efficient operation. However, it is necessary for the New Zealand Government to develop appropriate policy mechanisms for guiding the future development of electronic commerce.

ACKNOWLEDGMENT

I would like to thank the editors, reviewers and Theresa V.B. Roldan for their comments in preparing this chapter.

REFERENCES

Anthony, R. (1970). *Planning and Control Systems: A Framework for Analysis.* New York: John Wiley and Sons.

Bergeron, F., Buteau, C., and Raymond, L. (1991). Identification of Strategic Information Systems Opportunities: Applying and Comparing Two Methods. *MIS Quarterly*, 15, 4, 89-103.

Briant. R. (1999). Survey-Product Manager Electronic Payments. *Bank of New Zealand (BNZ).*

Cats-Baril, W. and Thompson, R. (1997). *Information Technology and Management.* IRWIN Publishing, USA.

Daniels, C. (1994) *Information Technology: The Management Challenge.* Addison-Wesely Publishing Company, USA.

Hopper, M. (1991). In Depth Interview. *Computerworld*, August 5.

Jason, D. and Kenneth, K. (1995). National Technology Policy and Computer Production in Asia-Pacific Countries. *The Information Society-An International Journal*, 11(1), 29-58.

KPMG (1999). *Research Report on Electronic Commerce: The Future is here.* Nolan Norton Institute: A Research Organisation of KPMG, Australia.

Laudon, K. and Laudon, J. (1988). *Management Information Systems: A Contemporary Perspective.* Macmillan Publishing Co. Ltd., USA.

Laudon, K. and Laudon, J. (1998). *Management Information systems: New Approaches to*

Organisation and Technology. Macmillan Publishing Co. Ltd. (5th Ed), USA.

McFarlan, F. (1984). Information Technology Changes the Way You Compete. *Harvard Business Review*, May-June, 98-103.

MOC (Ministry of Commerce) (1997). *Electronic Commerce and the New Zealand Consumer: Issues, and Strategies for the Future.* Government Report, August, html://www.moc.govt.nz/mca/.

MOC (Ministry of Commerce) (1998). *Electronic Commerce - The "Freezer Ship" of the 21st Century.* New Zealand Government Report, November, html://www.moc.govt.nz/itpg/ecommerce/ecomm.html.

Neumann, S. (1994). *Strategic Information Systems: Competition through Information Technologies.* Macmillan College Publishing Company, Inc., USA.

Norton, D. (1987). Strategic Vectors: Translating Vision into Action. *Stage by Stage*, 7(3) May-June, Nolan, Norton & Co. Massachusetts, USA.

Nolan, R. (1987). Managing the Crises in Data Processing. *Harvard Business Review*, March-April, 115-126.

O'Brien, J. (1996). *Management Information Systems: Managing IT in the Networked Enterprise.* The McGraw-Hill Co. Ltd., USA.

Porter, M. and Millar, V. (1985). How Information Gives You Competitive Advantage. *Harvard Business Review*, July-August, 149-160.

Porter, M. (1987). From Competitive Advantage to Corporate Strategy. *Harvard Business Review*, May-June, 43-59.

Primozic, K., Primozic, E. and Leben, J. (1991). *Strategic Choices.* New York: McGraw-Hill, USA.

Parsons, G. (1983). Information Technology: A new Competitive Weapon. *Sloan School of Management Review*, Fall.

Ritchie, B., Marshall, D. and Eardley A. (1998). *Information Systems in Business.* Thomson Business Press, USA.

Rockart, J. (1982). The Changing Role of the Information Systems Executive: A Critical Success Factors Perspective. *Sloan Management Review*, Fall, 1-24.

Rochart, J. and Scott M. (1984). Implications of changes in Information Technology for Corporate Strategy. *Interfaces*, 14(1), 84-95.

Schoemaker, J. (1995). Scenario Planning: A Toll for Strategic Thinking. *Sloan Management Review*, Winter, 25-40.

Stalk, G. (1988). Time-the Next Source of Competitive Advantage. *Harvard Business Review*, July-August, 41-45.

Tozer, E. (1996). *Strategic IS/IT Planning.* Butterworth-Heinemann, MA, USA.

Valovic, T. (1993). *Corporate Networks: The Strategic Use of Telecommunications.* Artech House Inc., Boston, USA.

Viehland, D. and Mitchell, L. (1997). Electronic Commerce Challenges. *Chartered Accountants Journal of New Zealand*, December, 12-16.

Viehland, D. (1998). A Strategic Overview of the Internet: What does the Internet mean to New Zealand? *TUANZ Special Report on Including the Internet in your Marketing, Telecommunications Users Association of New Zealand Inc.*, 3-5.

Wiseman, C. (1988). *Strategic Information Systems.* Homewood, Ill.: Irwin, USA.

Weinstein, M.A. (1997). Planning and Building Global Electronic Commerce Networks. *Proceedings of the Global Networking'97 Conference: Interconnecting-Incorporating-Interfacing,* June 15-17, Calgary, Canada, 21-30.

Chapter VIII

Electronic Contracting for Open EDI

Andreas Mitrakas
GlobalSign NV, Belgium

Open EDI is a concept appropriate to address the needs of commercial business-to-business relationships in an open environment. While open EDI, an open electronic commerce technology, can be used for ad hoc commercial transactions, delivering it over public open networks poses a challenge that contains a substantial legal component. How can the pre-transaction delay time be shortened in a way that allows for the speedy conclusion of the commercial part of the deal? Legal shortcomings can pose a potential danger for trading partners if not properly underpinned before initiating business transactions. Dynamic contracting procedures preceding the endorsement of an interchange agreement are a viable alternative to face-to-face negotiations. Recon is an on-line system to make available such a functionality over an open network by means of a repository of negotiated legal terms.

INTRODUCTION

Electronic commerce has created the need for new arrangements in commercial practices in a way that can addresses adequately the regulation of emerging business relations. In the past, replacing the manual ways of business transactions gave rise to legal issues that sometimes threatened to destabilise the legal relations of the parties. The answers to the legal questions should fulfill two basic requirements, that is, security of the transactions and flexibility to accommodate the changing business needs of the trading partners. On one hand security of the transactions means that parties can maintain good long-term business relations. On the other hand, flexibility can allow the parties to negotiate freely and pursue their market goals. In light of open electronic commerce applications, it

Copyright © 2000, Idea Group Publishing.

is essential to discuss the role of bilateral contractual arrangements within trading communities. Interchange agreements for closed Electronic Data Interchange (hereunder, EDI) have been criticised as static for the transactions they are used. Turning interchange agreements to dynamic applications and automating the contract-making process are essential to the deployment of open EDI.

The absence of mutually recognised contracting practices between the trading partners can be an inhibiting factor for electronic commerce. This has been a typical problem of EDI where although the legal and technical complexities have always been alarming many users unaware of the risks opted to operate in an informal manner without using any interchange agreement prior to initiating commercial transactions. It is now known that as far as EDI relationships are concerned, the interchange agreements are the best way to address the legal problems of EDI (TEDIS 1994, 1996).

To address the shift from closed transaction networks to open user communities it is necessary to provide basic legal safeguards that render electronic transactions legal and safe. Transacting in an open electronic trading environment means that a transaction is as legal as the weakest national legislation or the bilateral contractual arrangements of the trading parties allow it to be. Relying on an open electronic commerce transaction network often means that obligations undertaken by any party at any stage of the transaction may reflect on the relationship this party builds further with its business counterparts. Users of public open networks, like the Internet, often underestimate the effect that national legal regimes that are often unfit for bilateral arrangements may have on their business relationships. Fragmented national legislation may undermine electronic commerce users' efforts to reach out to a global user community. In light of the tidal shift towards World Wide Web (WWW) based transactions such questions may also reflect on commercial users. Improving the means to deliver contractual arrangements between trading parties is an issue that requires further attention. In business-to-business relations, paper-based interchange agreements can give way to agreements negotiated over a computer network to improve the trust of the trading parties to the legal framework of electronic transactions and overcome the often-observed legal shortcomings of electronic commerce.

As an electronic commerce application that facilitates the swift conclusion of commercial transactions open EDI may miss out its expected goals if hampered by lengthy negotiations to endorse an interchange agreement. In this chapter we propose a legal repository to dynamically effect on-line negotiations and conclude an interchange agreement with a view to use it as a component in open EDI procedures. We claim that information technology if used in structured contracts, can assist in curbing part of the downside of interchange agreements, such as the lengthy negotiation periods. The remainder of this chapter discusses open EDI as an electronic commerce application, the legal concerns of open EDI, and interchange agreements, and introduces Recon, a repository of legal terms to effect on-line negotiations.

ELECTRONIC COMMERCE TECHNOLOGIES AND OPEN EDI

Applications of electronic commerce can be divided in two broad categories, namely free form and structured. E-mail, the communication of electronic messages between computers, composed as unstructured or free format text may be suitable for humans to understand but it has the disadvantage that limits automated machine processing applications. EDI is the interchange of commercial data structured on the basis of approved standard messages between computer systems and effected by electronic means (TEDIS, 1991a; Emmelheinz, 1993). Data is structured in data elements that include, for example: the name of the customer, the address, the quantity of the goods, the reference code of the goods, etc. EDI succeeds in transmitting messages according to an agreed format that allows the information system of the recipient to process information automatically (Emmelheinz 1993). EDI applications often pre-suppose a trust environment as it is typically used by trading partners who are already known to each other and have had previous business contact. Fukuyama (1995) defines trust as:

> "...the expectation that arises within a community of regular, honest, and cooperative behaviour, based on commonly shared norms on the part of the other members of that community."

The interpretation of this definition should contain no moral notion, since trust is a social phenomenon that does not distinguish between legal activities or otherwise while trust is the result of factors like previous acquaintance or satisfaction from existing transactions (Fukuyama 1995). A basic concern when building a business relationship is to define the level of mutual trust that may exist between the trading partners as a proportion of that relationship.

Electronic commerce transactions are the exchange of electronic messages and interactive on-line communications that have a commercial meaning. One distinguishing goal of electronic commerce is that it enables short-term or *ad hoc* commercial transactions between organisations and individuals (Lee et al., 1995; Kalakota et al., 1996). An open trading environment can contribute to the lowering of entry barriers for new users and establishing links between trading partners by minimising the need for bilateral interchange agreements. Special reference must be made to spontaneous or WWW-based *ad hoc* electronic commerce transactions effected over public open networks, like the Internet.

Electronic commerce appeals to both commercial parties and consumers alike. The boost of electronic commerce technologies has multiplied by the immense possibilities that WWW-based transactions have opened. Business-to-business transactions are often based on EDI relationships over closed networks. In a typical EDI case, before starting transactions the potential business counterparts are asked to exchange the technical and organisational specifications of their systems. These specifications may be negotiated, agreed upon, described, and preferably included in a contract, the interchange agreement that precedes the interchange of commercially meaningful messages. Defining standard trade procedures are one way to reduce negotiation costs. Although EDI messages can be currently structured using international standards like UN/EDIFACT, there is no standard way to describe the semantics and the context of the messages exchanged. For example, a reply to a purchase order can be a purchase order acknowledgment or a shipping notice (Lee et al., 1995).

The open EDI working group of the International Standards Organisation defines open EDI as (ISO, 1994):

> "Open EDI is called EDI among autonomous, multiple participants using public standards and aiming towards interoperability over time, business sectors, information technology systems and data types, capable of multiple, simultaneous transaction, to accomplish an explicit shared business goal."

The main goal of open EDI is to enable short-term or *ad hoc* commercial transactions among organisations (Kalakota et al., 1996). Open EDI also aims at lowering the entry barriers of establishing structured data links between trading partners by minimising the need for bilateral interchange agreements. Industry-wide and cross-sector public open EDI standards are essential to the parties involved in commercial transactions (Bons 1997). These standards can also include formal models of business procedures, known as business scenarios. A scenario is a formal specification of a class of business transactions serving the same goal. Scenarios can be designed for specific situations, but they can also be generic and customisable by the trading parties. A trade procedure is the mutually agreed upon set of rules that governs the activities of all parties involved in a set of related business transactions. A trade procedure stipulates the actions, the parties, the order and the timing constraints on performing actions (Lee, 1996; Lee et al., 1995). Open EDI procedures are envisaged to be publicly available, remotely accessible and directly executable.

Open EDI scenarios rely upon taking into account several commercial parameters of an application in an effort to accommodate needs like changes in the business and legal status of the users, due to unforeseen factors, like a bankruptcy, for example. Open EDI is used between multiple parties, the trading partners, each one fulfilling its role in a commercial transaction. A role refers to the recognised set of activities of each individual party, for example buyer, carrier, bank, etc. Certain roles can be divided to sub-roles to serve the individual requirements of trade for example a bank can be a seller's bank or a buyer's bank. More than one commercial role can be attributed to the same party depending on its involvement in a transaction, for example a seller can also offer carrier services. Open EDI is used for the external activities of trading partners and not for procedures used within an organisation. Open EDI can be seen as a way to facilitate traditional business relationships over public open networks. Tapping the merits of public open networks can be an asset for open EDI users who may expand a network of structured transactions over multiple user communities. Traditional security concerns regarding the mitigation from closed trading relationships to open trading environments can be appropriately met by using digital signatures and Trusted Third Party (TTP) services. Digital signature technology can already be used to address concerns of the trading partners regarding security over public open networks.

LEGAL CONCERNS OF OPEN EDI

Typical of open EDI is a set of largely unresolved legal questions related to the reluctance of several legal systems to appropriately address such concerns across national borders to create a unified legal regime for electronic commerce. Although several countries have been experiencing a substantial review of legal rules and regulations related to electronic transactions, much of the world remains reluctant or inactive in addressing such concerns. Although there are encouraging signals from developing countries eager to accommodate digital signatures for example, others still remain inactive creating bottlenecks to electronic transactions unless a contractual arrangement precedes the conclusion of on-line business transactions. It remains, however, a challenge to effect such contractual negotiations at a speed comparable to the speed of concluding a commercial agreement on-line. The remainder of this section presents a brief overview of the legal issues that outline the substantive regulatory requirements for electronic transactions (Mitrakas, 1997b). Since open commercial transactions are essential to both domestic and international trade, legal regulations should follow suit to accommodate both.

Validity and The Formation of A Contract

Recognising the validity of electronic messages and accepting rules on the formation of electronic contracts are two essential requirements for electronic commerce. Standard form electronic commerce applications remain largely applications for transactions concerning transport, certain governmental agencies, like customs, and most importantly movable goods. To conform to the various national regulations, the trading partners must currently acknowledge bilaterally the value of electronic messages. This recognition, however, does not satisfy all the other types of transactions that still have to be concluded in writing. Real estate contracts, for example, require a notarised approval and they have to be recorded in a public register (TEDIS, 1989; Piette-Coudol et al., 1991). Fulfilling legal formalities like tax requirements, for example, is also an issue that should be examined in light of electronic commerce. Although recognising the validity of electronic messages and accepting the rules on the formation of electronic contracts is an issue that requires a legislated approach, providing a bilateral regulation is necessary to ensure stable trading relationships among trading parties across multiple jurisdictions.

Electronic Messages as Evidence

The admissibility of electronic documents and the weight attached to them as evidence in court may still require reviewing certain national laws. According to the main tendency in the continental European legal systems, for example, courts have the task to decide upon the admission of electronic documents as evidence (Mitrakas, 1997b). A court may deny that an electronically produced piece of evidence is an original. Even if admitted as evidence, an electronic document may be granted a lesser evidential value, than a paper-based equivalent. The parties, however, may choose the favourable laws of a third country to govern their trading relationships in a way that favours electronic communications. Although the admissibility and evidential value of electronic documents are issues that require appropriate legislative approach, where it is an obstacle, the bilateral regulation of this concern can be a remedy where needed. The proliferating digital signature legislation, however, is an incentive to address this issue through appropriate legislative reform while giving legal validity to new forms of electronic and digital signatures. Several laws and draft laws World Wide support prescribed licensing schemes for digital signatures that may be granted the same value as their paper-based alternatives. The Italian Act 59 (15-03-1997) and the German Digital Signature Act (22-07-1997) both recognise the validity of electronic messages and introduce rules on the usage of digitally signed electronic messages.

Liability

Introducing news parties in commercial transactions affected by open electronic commerce may result in new liability requirements. The question of apportioning liability for acts or omissions in the interchange is of particular concern to the users, and possibly third parties to a transaction like trusted third parties, network operators and insurers. Service providers tend to disclaim the alleged errors in the transmission or security of data. Open electronic commerce users may limit their liability to the acts or omissions of their agents while they may not be held liable for any further acts or omissions concerning messages in transit. Liability rules in electronic commerce should be established by appropriately applying objective criteria and interpreting existing liability laws (Galtung, 1991).

We can notice, however, a tendency towards introducing new liability rules especially in providing security services like those described in the draft *European Directive on a Common Framework for Electronic Signatures* (COM 98/297 Final). The European Directive has introduced liability rules regarding the accuracy of information in digital certificates.

Dispute Resolution

The technical nature of open EDI may lead users to adopt a self-supported system for the resolution of technical disputes. Apart from the expected speed to reach a decision, by relying upon experts the users can expect to gain increased accuracy of the settlement of technical disputes. Dispute resolution is becoming an issue of legislative attention with examples like the draft European Directive, *On certain legal aspects of electronic commerce in the internal market* (COM 98/586 final), that addresses the matter by urging trading partners to adopt alternative dispute resolution in their disputes.

Security of Messages

Security is an issue that currently receives appropriate attention through legislation that largely aims at creating a global environment for secure electronic commerce. The subject matter of current security regulations includes provisions on the transmission of data, the storage and the legal value of secure data not necessarily extending to issues involving third parties, like the certification authorities, technical requirements and licensing schemes. Through implemented laws in Italy (DPR 513, 10-11-97 and DPCM 8-02-99) and Germany (Ordinance 1-11-97) security is becoming a centrepiece of electronic commerce regulation in Europe.

Standard Business Scenarios

Open EDI users should be reassured about the technical integrity of the standard business scenarios. Market-driven standardisation initiatives have given the users the ability to participate in the process of proliferating and customising standard scenarios for open EDI. Further improving on these scenarios is a task that should be reserved to international organisations to assure the applicability of the proposed solution. The resulting standard scenarios can be examined and tested for technical integrity and legal consistency and content. As experience has shown standard messages for EDI can hide legal obligations that may often go undetected (TEDIS, 1996). Inconsistencies with the original purpose of open EDI scenarios should be revealed to the users and dealt with accordingly to enhance interoperability and legal certainty. The users can retain the right to perform certain alterations and modifications to the standard scenarios to match the requirements of their respective systems.

Interchange Agreements

Interchange agreements are the typical bilateral regulation tool to effect a customised legal framework between trading parties in an EDI environment. Interchange agreements are paper-based documents to address general legal concerns resulting from shortcomings and incompatibilities among jurisdictions. Recognising the often-observed legal shortcomings, national or international authorities have modelled interchange agreements with a view to assist trading parties in safely deploying this technology and enhance fairness in the transactions (Ritter, 1990). The issues to address in an interchange agreement for open EDI largely include the general legal concerns discussed above. A secondary target is the bilateral concerns of the contracting parties referring to the business side of the transaction. Yet a third category of issues can comprise the specifications of the technical implementation of the application, including references to standard business scenarios as compiled in a technical annex.

Proprietary contract terms with reference to issues not described above may also be included in an interchange agreement. Proprietary contract terms may hamper the notion of fairness prevailing in model interchange agreements. Since EDI relationships have been largely seen as a result of pressure and coercion from the large trading parties rather than cooperation among all parties involved in a transaction, the role of model interchange agreements as an impartial regulation of trading relationships can be grossly overturned (Webster, 1995). Model interchange agreements, however, are appropriate for open EDI since they are fairly standardised and, in the context of open EDI, can be an instrument to create cohesion in a global trading environment.

One further shortcoming of the interchange agreements for open EDI is related to the negotiation time possibly required to negotiate one. Slashing the negotiation time of closing an interchange agreement can have an immediate practical effect on users of open EDI. This, however, would require drastically reducing the need for the physical presence of the trading parties to negotiate an agreement.

Electronic contracting can be used on a performative computer network as an alternative means for regulating the legal questions concerning the interchange (Austin, 1962; Searle, 1969). Electronic interchange agreements can be seen as an effort to bring traditional legal instruments in line with developments in technology. Automated interchange agreements are instruments to facilitate the conclusion of legal transactions in open electronic commerce. Automated interchange agreements use techniques for building legal advisory systems. Open EDI users can take advantage of the full capabilities of a performative network by using certain automated tools that allow for automated contracting.

RECON: A REPOSITORY FOR OPEN EDI NEGOTIATIONS

Electronic contracting is increasingly becoming a necessity at a time when electronic transactions can be easily concluded over a public open network. Legal shortcomings may require bilaterally agreeing on selected issues in addition to existing legal rules in the jurisdictions electronic commerce actors operate from. Open EDI in particular offers an appropriate test case to users to conclude an interchange agreement in a dynamic electronic contracting environment (Mitrakas, 1996b).

Recon (Repository for Electronic Commerce Negotiations) is a proposed application to implement the theoretical concerns described so far. It provides a quasi-negotiated contract and document generation facility for the immediate drafting of an interchange agreement by any two open EDI users. The users are allowed to communicate online and choose appropriate clauses from a pre-drafted pool of contractual terms for interchange agreements. After the parties exchange the respective agreements a utility program compares the two versions and detects any differences between them. The comparing program traces the differences in the text of the two files while a report of the results of this process is sent to both trading partners together with the suggestions on the issues that cause disagreement. A second round of negotiations aims at revising the inconsistencies between the two versions of the interchange agreement and generating the final document. The final version of the agreement can be digitally signed and dully stored in an approved database. In this context, further research can assist the definition of the proper terms for each sector of industry and trade to create appropriate variations. The remainder of this paper outlines a repository for contractual negotiation that focuses on the settling of the legal questions preceding an open EDI transaction.

A Repository of Legal Terms

The centrepiece in the proposed structure is a repository of legal terms. Repositories are widely seen as a way to facilitate electronic contracting in electronic commerce applications, like digital certificates. Public standards, like the X.509 for example, use the concept of repositories to store information concerning the status of a digital certificate. Repositories of legal terms are a way to store and access data on business, contracts, legislative, and other public documents available via public open computer networks concerning electronic commerce transaction terms (Mitrakas, 1997a; 1997b, Mitrakas et al., 1998). Registration of a document in the ICC ETERMS Repository may facilitate legal notice for the purposes of enhancing their enforceability in multiple jurisdictions.

Submitted contract terms are a unilateral declaration of will made available in a remote database for anyone to view. These terms are not to be negotiated as with other contract terms. General conditions are legal terms that are unilaterally drafted by a company to make them available in mass transactions, like for instance when contracting with consumers. General conditions must observe certain regulatory principles like equity, and to the extent that they restrict statutory rights they are unenforceable. An example of such terms in electronic commerce is the certification practice statements publicised by the certification authorities A certification practice statement is a statement of practices, which a certification authority employs in issuing certificates (ABA 1996).

Building on the functionality of legal repositories, Recon is not a mere storage facility for contractual terms but an actual platform for contract negotiation. Recon is also based on using secure server transactions and a network of trust based on certified users. Prior to negotiating an interchange agreement, it may be required to register the users of the system and use digital certificates to sign each communication. Time stamping may also be used to appropriately record the negotiation session. The whole session, a report of the results and the final agreement can further be stored in a secure repository to be made available to the contracting parties for future reference.

Standard Terms and Acceptable Variations

The repository of Recon consists of a database capable of storing and retrieving clauses related to particular electronic commerce applications, like open EDI. The registered clauses receive a unique identifier to facilitate reference. Specific fields may be left open to be further regulated by the transacting parties. The operator of the repository can draft the terms *ad hoc*; however, other possibilities for drafting or submitting legal terms cannot be ruled out.

To support the information stored in the repository, other support material can be made available to the users. Electronic textbooks facilitate the easy retrieval of information, like textbook knowledge, case law and case studies. Using a tree structure to store information and featuring search and hypertext functions to access it, electronic textbooks can provide a real life alternative to legal knowledge-based systems (LKBSs). LKBSs have reached limited success in fulfilling their promise of programs that cover large areas of law where expertise could be represented in computer executable formats that could be widely copied and distributed. Legal knowledge based systems in law typically fail on the presumption that law is a rule-based phenomenon composed of clear rules. Since legal rules require interpretation within a social context rigid criteria cannot be applied. Often clearly stated rules have less-than-anticipated affect over judicial review of administrative and tribunal practice (Leith, 1986).

Figure 1: Repository and Stored Legal Terms

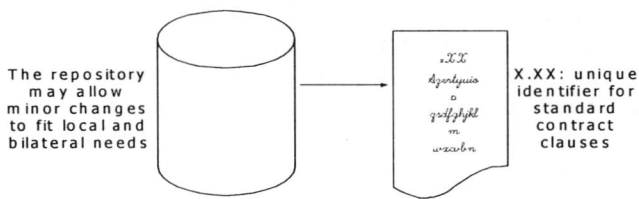

Using standard legal terms has been seen as a solution to moderate the risks in international trade transactions. The International Chamber of Commerce supports the use of standard commercial terms for international trade transactions known as the Incoterms. The high level of standardization and the limited scope of the Incoterms offer a rare example of a set of rules that can be relatively well analyzed and formalized (Tan et al. 1998). Although formalizing statutory legal information stored in a knowledge base is a manageable task, it is impossible to achieve the formalization of the factual element of a case. The limited level of our understanding of how law works is what makes it necessary to study parameters like the empirical side of law before applying that knowledge into knowledge-based systems (De Mulder et al., 1992).

Instead of a standard interchange agreement to sign and approve, Recon can host standard legal terms to cover variations of law to reflect jurisdiction rules or individual preference and current status. The pool of standard legal terms within the repository can be complemented with a function to allow for additions of proprietary terms in selected fields in the standard terms. To validate variations of standard terms, a keyword-based function detects the desired context and allows for the variations to take effect. In this case, rigidity in terminology is a safeguard of impartiality. After the variation is imported in the system, it can be used as a valid term for the comparison function to take effect. An example of a variation of a legal term regards the time and the place of the formation of a contract for which practice has developed the following four rules:

- The declaration rule: according to which a contract is concluded at the time and the place the offeree accepted the contract.
- The postal rule: according to which a contract is concluded at the time and the place the offeree handed his/her acceptance to the post office, or any other independent third

party assigned to deliver mail.
- The reception rule: according to which a contract is concluded at the time and the place where the acceptance was delivered to the premises of the offeror.
- The information rule: according to which a contract is concluded at the time and the place where the offeror actually became informed about the offeree's acceptance.

Choosing the appropriate term has been subject to a long-standing debate that has been partially resolved through the *United Nations Convention on Contracts for the International Sale of Goods* of 1980. According to Article 24 of the Vienna Convention the reception rule is the one that applies in international trade transactions. To facilitate flexibility for local transactions, the repository can also accept approved sets of variations to reflect local practice and customs of trade. Users may also be permitted to include free-form text in the agreement to better describe issues of their unilateral or bilateral interest not otherwise covered in the repository of Recon. Any free-form text additions must be limited to a prescribed range of issues that the system dictates so that it does not overrun issues already covered by the repository clauses.

Figure 2: Negotiations in Recon

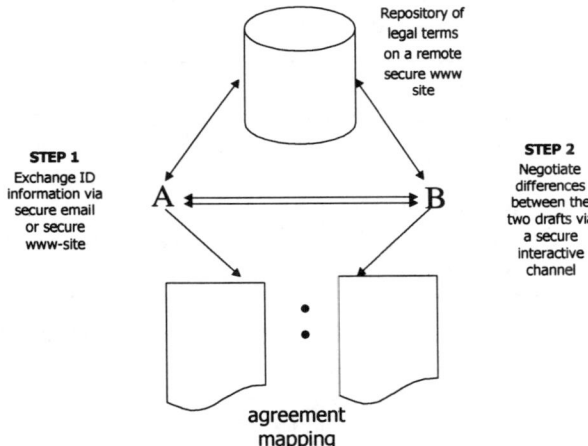

Multilingual Capability

Essential to the purpose of performing electronic transactions over various jurisdictions is the use of a multilingual interface. Constraint interaction between trading partners with respect to choice of language can increase the user understanding of the function of this system while widening the scope of the system to include users without prior experience in international trade. To effect this it is interesting to facilitate a constraint intervention of the user into the text of the clauses combined with a multilingual presentation of the text (Lee 1992, Lee 1998).

The multilingual presentation of the contract clauses can be accompanied by specific legal conditions that apply to the national law of the country in question. For example, a clause on the evidential value of electronic documents presented to a user in a given language e.g. German, can take into account the difficulty imposed by German law on this issue. According to it, the rule on the evidential value of electronic documents in Germany is a rule of public order (*d' ordre public*) that cannot be modified by a bilateral agreement (Mitrakas, 1997b).

To allow for the modular intervention of the user in the final clauses of the interchange agreement, pre-set parameters can be introduced. Pre-set parameters may also be used to limit the ability of the trading parties to make interventions more than required by the transactions. Such conditions can detect the layout of certain clauses or the issues they address. Ontologies can be used to effectively define the parameters used to allow recognition of the differences between national laws and legal systems, and effect compliance with national regulations that deviate from international practice. Disclaimers are necessary to avoid the unilateral introduction of unfair terms in the agreement and limit the scope of the application of the system within the range of the legal issues of the interchange.

An Interface-Based System

Recon uses a menu-based system to support the various functional requirements necessary to conclude an interchange agreement online. After reviewing all outstanding issues the program creates a single output file. This file contains the text of the interchange agreement that the parties have agreed upon. The parties can exercise control on the issues to select, but they cannot influence the contents of the clauses in question. An example of a selection menu in Recon may look as follows:

Underlying transactions

Do you want this agreement to cover open EDI issues only or also include issues on the substance of the transactions?

1. Address open EDI issues only.
2. Address open EDI issues; issues of other means of electronic commerce and issues on the substance of the transactions.

As a response to the user's selection of the first option Recon triggers a clause that is placed in the output file. This clause reads:

The parties' agreement will exclusively address transactions affected by using open EDI.

As a response to the user's selection of the second option, the program fires another clause that reads:

The party's agreement covers all legal issues concerning the use of any means of electronic commerce including open EDI. The scope of this agreement also includes the regulation of the underlying substantial commercial transactions. For this purpose the parties agree to append the relevant provisions to the prescribed space reserved at the end of this agreement. Any other issues not referring to the scope of the underlying transactions addressed in this appendix will be void for the part that does not correspond to the prescribed purpose.

Recon may also feature explanations, examples and cases to give background information with a purpose to assist users with limited legal experience to draft an interchange agreement.

Recon targets mainly open EDI users with limited experience in drafting agreements. Those users are most likely to decline using an interchange agreement at all after having a basic understanding with their trading counterpart on the technical parameters of the interchange. The produced agreement can be a legally safe equivalent to rigid model agreements being more representative of the profiles of the users with respect to jurisdiction they operate from, scope of use of the agreement etc.

The reliability of the performed tasks and the selected legal clauses to include in the system require special attention. This purpose can be better served if the options included in the clauses are checked for legal validity in the legislation of the jurisdiction in question.

Figure 3: Features of Recon

Recon	
Legal Content Features	**Form Features**
Standard contract clauses	Multilingual
Ontology-based clause variations	Jurisdiction customised
Free form text variations	Chat/video conference
Output file comparison	Trade sector customisation

Distribution and Usage

At the user's end a standard browser can be used to access data. A secure server will be appropriate to store the repository and the negotiating centre, while it can be made available through the WWW. This WWW site can provide the necessary support with regard to utility applications like a videoconference capability, chatting and a notice board. These applications can be used to advance negotiations on terms not included in the standard agreement sections or for customisation according to local legislative requirements. Text based applications are good for recording a negotiations session. Video-based applications can be used to emulate the face-to-face way lawyers work (Morison et al., 1992).

The preparation of automated interchange agreements can be a task for groups of expert users. Drafting automated interchange agreements is not fundamentally different from drafting any other kind of model interchange agreements. The process to select the issues and the varying options remain basically unchanged. A major requirement and a serious obstacle is to define the policy of the industrial sectors that use electronic commerce with respect to issues such as the security measures to employ, the kind of arbitration services to use, etc. An expert committee can be used on a temporary basis to provide input on the introduction of new terms related to changing practices and legislative developments in the respective countries.

Security measures may also guarantee that the contents and the provisions of Recon remain unaltered by unauthorised users. Registration of terms is a feature to ensure a unique identity for each alternative term. Recorded sessions can further be used to support trading partners in case of a dispute. Security measures can protect the integrity of the contents of the program. This is a task that can be reserved for an electronic notary to host Recon. The secure site of an electronic notary can offer access to the text of the interchange agreement and additional functions like storage facilities for the resulting agreement.

Assessment and Future Research

Recon brings about an electronic contracting regulation among commercial parties in electronic commerce that are the direct beneficiaries of the contractual regulation they may effect by using this system. The potential users of Recon should recognise, however, that in electronic commerce applications no real life technical solution can succeed without the appropriate regulation of the legal issues in question. With the objective to point out the legal issues of open EDI and propose a methodology to resolve them, Recon can be used as a component in a dynamic on-line electronic contracting system for electronic commerce transactions. The functionality of Recon is to propose a test bed and a solution for electronic contracting focusing less on the transactional matters while stressing the substantial legal questions of a business relationship. Recon can be used in demanding applications as a platform to test the validity of concepts regarding fundamental legal questions by means of a basic electronic contracting infrastructure.

The observations and methodology of this chapter on improving contracting in virtual trading environments by using automated tools for the bilateral negotiation of a commercial relationship can be further exploited and applied in electronic commerce transactions in general. The imbalance created between the projected applications and the potential risks in electronic commerce will create an impetus for improved communications between the legal actors, legal tools to bilaterally regulate commercial relationships and better conditions in the on-line provision of legal information. To better respond to a diversified set of applications, it may be required to create a database of shared terms and concepts to be used in multiple negotiating environments. Ontologies may offer a solution to appropriately analyse fundamental legal concepts (Valente, 1996). Creating automated systems requires the conceptualisation of the building blocks of legal knowledge to form the basis of legal knowledge representation (Visser et al., 1997). Ontologies may be used particularly in the field of obligations. A common definition layer on obligations can be used to define the liability of the parties involved in a transaction. It may be beneficial for the parties involved to compile an index of liabilities with a view to have a concrete picture on liabilities prevailing in a transaction and transfer them from one stage of the transaction to the other.

CONCLUSIONS

Interchange agreements for the regulation of the legal concerns of EDI have been used in trade for a number of years. In spite of their widespread use certain disadvantages associated with them often hamper their perceived role as impartial off the shelf regulation of bilateral relations (Mitrakas, 1996a; 1997b). Open EDI changes the bilateral regulation of the outstanding legal issues by creating an open trading environment that allows for *ad hoc* trade transactions. To improve this contract-making process in an open trading environment automating interchange agreements can be proved to be a viable solution.

Electronic contracting allows for flexible contractual arrangements that also permit open EDI users to refine their core legal concerns in open EDI and better define the ways to put them into practice. Automated interchange agreements are a solution distinct from similar more traditional instruments used to address legal issues, such as paper-based interchange agreements. Automated interchange agreements facilitate structured contract negotiations and they combine it with contractual flexibility.

Using electronic contracting in open EDI is no replacement for the human legal expert since it provides an efficient alternative solution to the lengthy negotiations that precede electronic transactions. Open EDI users can provide the content to build the knowledge base of the system and will subsequently use the system. Electronic contracting, however, can successfully correspond to the scarcity of legal expertise on electronic commerce since it can be extended to the selection of the preferred clauses (contract drafting), the comparison of the different versions of the contracts (simulation of the negotiation process) and the formation of the final document (text generation).

Recon is a test case that extends the functionality of interchange agreements from closed EDI to open EDI environments supporting a fully electronic contracting environment. Recon can also be used in a broader electronic contracting context with a view to settle upcoming legal issues of electronic contracting relationships. A legal advisory system represents the current state of development of the legal rules of open EDI. On the lines of the Recon prototype other types of trade agreements can be planned and concluded. The constrained negotiation of interchange agreements allows for the limitation of the extreme effects of the unilateral declarations of will that are increasingly characterising electronic commerce transactions effected in an open network. Recon puts the negotiation power back to the user while it provides a dynamic environment to match the speed and easiness of open EDI transactions.

Besides bilateral contractual arrangements automated or traditionally affected in a paper contract, it is important to note that the growth of open electronic transactions depends heavily on the number and the type of the legal problems that the trading parties will have to surmount before effecting the actual commercial transaction. The bilateral regulation of issues like the evidential value of electronic documents may provide a valid remedy in some jurisdictions. Still for many other jurisdictions it is an issue that requires decisive legislative action to allow for uninterrupted trading transactions uninhibited by legislative shortcomings. The remarkable growth of electronic commerce and the promising prospects that it creates make it of a paramount importance to take all the necessary legal measures that will render this possibility realistic and allow for electronic transactions in an open virtual marketplace.

NOTE: Part of this research has been carried out at the Erasmus University Research Institute for Decision and Information Systems (EURIDIS) PO Box 1738, 3000 DR Rotterdam, Netherlands, (www.fbk.eur.nl/Euridis) as a Marie Curie project funded by the European Commission.

REFERENCES

American Bar Association (1996). *Digital Signature Guidelines*, ABA, Chicago, "TEDIS".

Austin J.L. (1975). *How to DO things with words*, 2nd edition, Harvard University Press, Cambridge.

Bons, R. (1997). *Designing trustworthy trade procedures for open electronic commerce: A methodology for the automated auditing of interorganisational controls*, Ph.D. dissertation, Erasmus University Rotterdam.

Boss, A.H., Ritter, J.B. (1993). *Electronic Data Interchange Agreements. A guide and a sourcebook*, ICC, Paris.

Dewitz, Donaldson S. (1992). *Contracting on a performative network: Using information technology as a legal intermediary*, (Unpublished PhD dissertation), The University of Texas at Austin, August.

Emmelhainz, M.(1993). *EDI - A total management guide*, 2nd edition, Van Nostrand Reinhold, New York.

Fukuyama F.(1995). *Trust*, Free Press, New York.

Galtung, A. (1991), *Paperless systems and EDI - A survey of Norwegian law*, CompLex 4/91, TANO, Oslo.

International Standards Organisation (ISO/IEC JTC 1/SC 30) (1994). *Working draft of the Open-EDI reference model standard*, Draft document N 075, Paris, 27 October.

Kalakota R. & Whinson A.(1996). *Frontiers of electronic commerce*, Addison-Wesley Publishing Company Inc., Reading Massachusetts.

Lee, R. (1992). DX: A deontic expert system, EURIDIS report No. 92.10.01.

Lee, R. & Bons, R. (1995). Soft-Coded trade procedures for Open-EDI, in GRICAR J., NOVAK J. (eds.), *Electronic commerce for trade efficiency and effectiveness*, 6th international conference on EDI-IOS, Moderna Organizacija, Kranj.

Lee, R. (1996). *InterProcs: Modelling environment for automated trade procedures - User Documentation*, EURIDIS, WP 96.10.11, Erasmus University, Rotterdam.

Lee, R.(1998). *Open electronic contracting using electronic trade scenarios*, Proceedings Caboto '98, EURIDIS Report No. 98.02.04.

Lee, R.(1998), Towards open electronic contracting, *Electronic Markets*, 8(3), St. Gallen,.

Leith, P. (1986). Fundamental errors in logic programming, *The Computer Journal*, 29(6).

Mitrakas A. (1996a). Changes in the interchange agreements, in ADAM"Adam" N., YESHA Y. (eds.), *Electronic Commerce*, Springer Verlag, Berlin.

Mitrakas A. (1996b). *A legal advisory system concerning electronic data interchange within the European Community*, CompLex Series, No. 6/96, Tano-Aschehoug, Oslo, September.

Mitrakas A. (1997a). The proposed ETERMS Repository of the International Chamber of Commerce, *EDI Law Review*, 3(4), Dordrecht, May.

Mitrakas A.(1997b). *Open EDI and Law in Europe: A regulatory framework*, Kluwer Law International, The Hague.

Mitrakas A. & Bos J. (1998). The ICC ETERMS Repository to support Public Key Infrastructure, *Journal of Jurimetrics*, 38(3), Tempe AZ.

Morison J. & Leith, P. 91992). *The barrister's world and the nature of law*, Open University Press, Milton Keynes.

Piette-Coudol T. & Bensoussan A. (1991). *L' echange de donnees informatise et le droit*, (Electronic Data Interchange and the law), Hermes, Paris.

Poullet Y. & Vanderberghe G.P.V. (eds.) (1988). *Telebanking, Teleshopping and the Law*, Kluwer, Deventer.

Ritter J.(1990). *EDI legal Strategies: The ABA model trading partner agreement*, EDI Forum.

Searle J.(1969). *Speech Acts: An essay in the Philosophy of Language*, Cambridge University Press, London.

Steel K.(1994). Another approach to standardising EDI, *Electronic Markets*, No. 12, St. Gallen, September.

Tan Y-H., Mitrakas A. & Thoen W. (1998). *A formal analysis of Incoterms for electronic*

commerce, ITeR Series, No. 12, Kluwer, Deventer.
TEDIS (1991). Commission of the European Communities, *The legal position of the EFTA member states with respect to Electronic Data Interchange*, Brussels, July.
TEDIS (1994). Commission of the European Communities, *Draft on a European Model EDI Agreement*, Brussels.
TEDIS (1996). Commission of the European Communities, *EDICON - Final Report*, Brussels.
Valente A., A.(1996). *Legal Knowledge Engineering*, IOS Press, Amsterdam.
Visser, P. & Winkels, R.(1997). *Proceedings of First International Workshop on Legal Ontologies*, July 1997, University of Melbourne, Law School.
Webster, J.(1995). Networks of collaboration or conflict? Electronic Data Interchange and power in the supply chain, *Journal of Strategic Information Systems,* 4(1).

Chapter IX

EDI and Small/Medium Enterprises

R.C. MacGregor
University of Wollongong, Australia

D.J. Bunker
University of New South Wales, Australia

Small/medium enterprises (SMEs) represent a sizeable proportion of the GDP of most western economies. Not only are they the single largest employer of both skilled and unskilled labour but they make up a large proportion of the supply chain of larger enterprises.

Although there is a strong advocacy for the potential of EDI to improve the performance of those firms involved in the industrial supply chain, Lee, Clark and Tar (1999) suggest that much of the improvement—which includes areas such as: improving the bottom line; working faster and better in the organisation; gaining strategic advantage; strengthening customer relations; preparing for the future in business—benefits the EDI champion rather than those coerced into EDI use. Studies (Kilbane, 1998; Tucker, 1997) have shown that noncompliance to EDI by SMEs can result in larger enterprises being 'limited' in their own business practices often far more than the small business's economic contribution.

A number of reasons have been put forward in the literature as to why SMEs have been slow, or indeed resistant to adopt EDI. These include high set-up costs, poor security and limited EDI partners. While clearly these are important, Harvey (1992) and Mackay (1992) suggest that when attitudes to EDI are being considered, this must be taken in the context of attitudes to IT in general.

Based on the views of both Harvey (1992) and Mackay (1992), this chapter examines two studies carried out in Australia. The first study examined the attitudes of SME managers towards the acquisition of IT in their organisations. 131 small businesses were surveyed, the results suggesting small business managers considered the benefits expressed by EDI advocates (improving the bottom line; working faster and better in the organisation; gaining strategic

Copyright © 2000, Idea Group Publishing.

advantage; strengthening customer relations; preparing for the future in business) as being of little consequence. Rather, their primary considerations for the adoption of IT were cost/benefit, ease of use and performance.

A second study concentrated on 16 of the respondents from the first study who had adopted EDI in order to conduct business with Australia's largest steelmaking company, Broken Hill Proprietary (BHP).

While the second study is, at best, a pilot, both suggest that designers and advocates alike need to examine the small business environment more closely. They need to realise that the operation of SMEs differs markedly from their larger counterparts and that small businesses' managers are more interested in maintaining the operational level of the firm rather than attempting to gain a strategic advantage.

INTRODUCTION

EDI has variously been described as:
The movement of business documents electronically between or within firms in a structured, machine-retrievable, data format that permits data to be transferred, without re-keying, from a business application in one location to a business application in another location. (Hansen and Hill, 1989)

The electronic transfer from computer to computer of commercial or administrative transactions using an agreed standard to structure the transaction or message data (Bamfield,1994).

A collection of standard methods of codifying certain business documents (Tucker, 1997).

EDI involves a number of basic processes. Firstly, EDI passes data to and from different applications processes. Secondly, EDI converts data from proprietary formats into standard format, the process being reversed at the receiving end. Finally, EDI transmits the standard data to and from trading partners.

Early advocates of EDI stressed that its benefits included the elimination of re-keying of errors, faster trade cycles, better customer response, reduction of inventory levels, reduced information and storage, more efficient use of information (Huttig, 1994; Pletsch, 1994; Zack, 1994; Udo and Pickett, 1994; Britt, 1995). When examining the SME environment the EDI World Institute (1995) suggested that benefits included improving the bottom line of the business, working faster and better in the organisation, gaining strategic advantage, strengthening customer relations, preparing for the future of the business. More recently, studies carried out by Tuunainen and Saarinen (1997) and Philip and Pedersen (1997) added the following benefits of EDI: both intra and interorganisational functions can be carried out more effectively and efficiently; the organisation can respond more quickly to global competition, risk, service and cost;l better cash management throughout the organisation; economies of scale can be gained when EDI is used for integration of the value chain; the ability to link and restructure organisations to enhance 'business practices'; and gains in efficiency from functional integration of the organisation.

Yet despite the extensive work which has been done in the area, EDI has failed to live up to expectations, especially in SME implementation (Iacovou, Benbasat and Dexter, 1995; MacGregor, Bunker and Waugh, 1998). A number of reasons have been put forward in the literature (see Chatfield and Alston, 1997; Anson, 1995; Barker, 1995; Higgins, 1995). These include resistance to paperless transactions, difficulty in implementation, lack of adequate security, high set-up costs, limitation of the functionality of SMEs.

If we take the view of Harvey (1992) and Mackay (1992) viz when attitudes to EDI are being considered this must be taken in the context of attitudes to IT in general, it is appropriate to examine the overall use of IT in SMEs prior to examining the specific case of EDI.

As such, this chapter begins by briefly examining the nature of SMEs, in particular their use of IT. A study carried out on 131 Australian small businesses will then be presented. This study shows that despite the promised benefits 'pushed' by the advocates of EDI, small business managers tend to adopt and use computer technology primarily for the enhancement of their day-to-day environment. The chapter will then concentrate on the specific case of EDI in SMEs. Firstly an examination of the literature will be presented, followed by a small pilot study of 16 users of EDI, each of whom responded to the first survey. While the second study cannot at this stage be considered representative of the entire small business EDI user group, it does raise a number of questions concerning some of the claims made by EDI advocates.

THE NATURE OF SMALL BUSINESS

The nature of SMEs has been the topic of both governmental committee findings as well as research initiatives. Brigham and Smith (1967) found that SMEs tended to be more risky than their larger counterparts. This view is supported by later studies (Walker, 1975, Delone 1988). Cochran (1981) found that small business tended to be subject to higher failure rates while Rotch (1987) suggested that small business had inadequate records of transactions. Perhaps most important in any discussion concerning SMEs is the view given by Barnett and Mackness (1983) that small firms are not miniature versions of larger firms, but quite unique in their own right.

A detailed definition of a small business was provided by Reynolds, Savage and Williams (1994). They suggested that the following characteristics make up the organisational environment in which a small business operates. These include:

- small management team,
- strong owner influence,
- centralised power and control,
- lack of specialist staff,
- multifunctional management,
- a close and loyal work team,
- informal and inadequate planning and control systems,
- lack of promotable staff,
- lack of control over business environment,
- limited ability to obtain finance,
- labor-intensive work,
- limited process and product technology,

- narrow product/service range,
- limited market share,
- heavy reliance on few customers,
- decisions—intuitive instead of rational,
- leadership— personal but not task oriented,
- education experience and skill—practical but narrow,
- low employee turnover,
- product dedication rather than customer orientation,
- reluctance to take risks,
- management swayed by personal idiosyncrasies,
- strong desire to be independent and
- intrusion of family interests.

When the introduction of IT into small business is considered, there are marked differences between small firms and their larger counterparts (Barnett and Mackness, 1983). Khan and Khan (1992) suggest that most small firms avoid sophisticated software or applications. This view is supported by studies carried out in the United Kingdom by Chen (1993). Cragg and King (1993) suggest that small firms often lack the necessary expertise to fully utilise IT. This view is supported by the findings of Holzinger and Hotch (1993) and Delvecchio (1994). Indeed, Yap, Soh and Raman (1992) have shown that many small firms use consultant or vendor expertise in the identification of hardware and software as their first critical step towards computerisation. They conclude that ongoing success with IT is positively associated with vendor support, vendor training, vendor after sales service and vendor expertise. This is supported in recent studies (MacGregor and Cocks, 1994; Wood and Nosek, 1994; MacGregor and Bunker, 1998).

Added to the views and findings concerning small business, are the variety of definitions of what actually constitutes a SME. Some definitions tend to be based purely on a quantitative perspective, such as amount of staff or amount of turnover, while others attempt to utilise qualitative definitions, similar to those provided by Reynolds et al. (1994). Meredith (1994) suggests that any definition of a SME must include a qualitative as well as a quantitative component. The quantitative component should examine tangible financial measures, while the qualitative component should reflect less tangible factors such as mode of operation as well as organisational procedures.

Not only is there a myriad of views concerning the nature of small business, but from a governmental standpoint, there are a variety of definitions of SMEs.

In the United Kingdom a small business is defined as:
'having fewer than 50 employees and was not a subsidiary to any other company'

In the United States:
'a small business concern shall be deemed to be one which is independently owned and operated and which is not dominant in its field of operation' (United States Small Business Administration - based on section 3 of the Small Business Act 1953)

While in Australia, a small business is defined as:
 one in which one or two persons are required to make all the critical decisions (such as finance, accounting personnel, inventory, production, servicing, mar-

keting and selling decisions) without the aid of internal (employed) specialists and with the owners having knowledge in one or two functional areas of management' (Meredith 1994, p 31).

STUDY 1 —THE ADOPTION OF IT BY SMEs IN AUSTRALIA

A questionnaire was developed to be administered to SMEs, which sought information concerning the number of employees, the suitability of the computer technology being used, the rationale for computerisation and the practices adopted by the business with the acquisition of the computer.

A mailing list was developed by the Illawarra Chamber of Commerce in Australia. The geographic area covered included the southern suburbs of Sydney, the cities of Wollongong and Nowra (population approximately 500,000). The sampling frame developed included companies with a workforce less than 50, where the company was not a subsidiary of a larger company.

Respondents were asked the amount of time (in hours per week) that was devoted by the organisation to develop new projects for the computer. Respondents were also asked which of the following criteria was the major reason for the acquisition of computer technology: improving the bottom line, working faster and better in the organisation, strengthening customer relations, preparing for the future of the business.

ANALYSIS OF RESULTS

A total of 600 questionnaires were distributed. Responses were obtained from 131 businesses, over a range of market activities, representing a response rate of 21.8%. All respondents indicated that they were using IT in their day-to-day work.

Table 1 indicates the number of hours spent on developing new projects using IT.

As can be seen from Table 1, most small businesses do not spend many hours developing new applications. Indeed, over 65% of respondents indicated that less than two person-hours per week are devoted to this task.

This tends to support a number of previous studies (Khan and Khan, 1992; Delvecchio, 1994; Cragg and King, 1993; Kilbane, 1998) that suggest that there is a reluctance by most SMEs to use sophisticated hardware or software or to enhance these for particular company needs.

Respondents were asked which was the major criterion used in the acquisition of IT.

Table 1: Number of New Project Hours Spent Using IT

No. of Hours	No of Respondents	Percentage
0 - 1	67	51.1
1 - 2	19	14.5
2 - 5	27	20.6
> 5	18	13.7

Table 2: Major Criteria Considered with the Acquisition of IT in the Small Business

Criteria	Number of Respondents	Percentage
Improvement of the Company's Bottom Line	19	14.5
Working Faster and Better within the Org'n	71	54
Strengthening Customer Relations	22	16.7
Preparing the Business for the Future	12	9
Not Sure	7	5.8

Table 2 indicates the findings.

The results in Table 2 would tend to support the views of Reynolds et al. (1994) that for the most part small businesses are not customer oriented, nor are they interested in gaining a larger market share, but rather they are intent on improving their day-to-day efficiency.

THE ADOPTION AND USE OF EDI IN SMEs

Many researchers point to specific tangible benefits of EDI. Tuunainen and Saarinen (1997) suggest that EDI allows both inter and intra-organisational functions to be carried out more effectively. Kava and Van Over (1990) suggest that EDI offers better cash management throughout the organisation, while Tuunainen (1998) suggests a valuable bi-product of EDI is extensive business integration.

It is interesting to note that while these authors advocate adoption of EDI by SMEs, the examples they provide to justify their claims come from larger businesses.

More recent studies (Ratnasingham, 1998; Kilbane, 1998; Iacovou et al., 1995; Evans-Correia, 1994; Huttig, 1994) have begun to examine the adoption and use of EDI in SMEs. In all cases most of the small businesses interviewed indicated that they were forced into EDI by larger trading partners. Most reported difficulties and dissatisfaction with EDI in particular: the number of transactions is too low to warrant EDI, tasks often need to be duplicated as a result of the installation of EDI technology, there are few willing partners to warrant the use of EDI, cost of EDI outweighed the benefits, there are problems attributable to standards incurred when EDI was being used. These studies show that many SMEs have had difficulties arising through lack of technical, financial or administrative resources.

STUDY 2—THE ADOPTION OF EDI IN SMEs IN AUSTRALIA

A pilot study was carried out on a subset of the respondents from the first of the surveys. The pilot survey was restricted to those who used EDI and who were trading with BHP through EDI technology.

The study involved a questionnaire which sought information concerning the number of years the business had used IT as well as EDI. Respondents were asked the number of customers they dealt with using EDI technology, as well as the number of customers overall.

Respondents were asked whether they would use EDI again if they had the choice. Finally respondents were asked if they had difficulties with EDI in any of the following areas: the number of transactions is too low to warrant EDI, tasks often need to be duplicated as a result of the installation of EDI technology, there are few willing partners to warrant the use of EDI, cost of EDI outweighed the benefits, there are problems attributable to standards incurred when EDI was being used.

ANALYSIS OF RESPONSES

Sixty questionnaires were distributed, 16 responses were obtained, giving a response rate of 26.6%.

Respondents were asked the number of years they had been using Information

Table 3: Number of Years Using IT and EDI

	<2 years	2 - 5 years	> 5 year
Use of IT in business	0	2	14
Use of EDI in business	0	3	13

Technology (IT) in general and EDI in particular within their company. Table 3 indicates the findings.

Respondents were asked for the total number of customers they dealt with together with the number of customers dealt with utilising EDI. The data showed that none of the respondent SMEs dealt with more than 15% of their customers using EDI technology, with nine of the 16 responses showing that they dealt with less than 5% of their total clientele using EDI.

Respondents were asked, if given a free choice, would they use EDI again. Nine of the respondents indicated they would not use EDI again.

Finally respondents were asked whether any of the following difficulties had to be regularly dealt with since the inception of EDI:
- Number of transactions too low to warrant EDI
- Tasks often needed to be duplicated since the installation of EDI technology
- Few willing partners to warrant the use of EDI
- Cost of EDI outweighed the benefits
- Problems attributable to standards incurred when EDI was being used

Table 4 indicates the findings.

Table 4: Difficulties Encountered Using EDI

Difficulty	Responses	% Response
Number of transactions too low to warrant use of EDI	10	62.5%
Tasks need to be duplicated	7	43.7%
Few willing partners	10	62.5%
Cost of EDI outweighs the benefit	6	37.5%
Problems with the imposed standards of EDI	5	31.2%

DISCUSSION

Traditional EDI is premised on the ability to carry out many-to-many connections, without the need to coordinate software, one to the next. An examination of the second study would suggest that while a small business may have the requisite technology for EDI trade, most of their trading partners still prefer traditional methods. Not only, then, are the number of transactions carried out through EDI low, but much of the work done using EDI has to be duplicated to fit into existing practices within the organisation.

Recently a number of authors have proposed alternatives to traditional EDI approaches. Kilbane (1998) proposed a 'Web-based EDI' approach, where the EDI champion can still maintain up to 100% of its trading through EDI but where value-added networks will change their role from transmission orientation to service orientation for the smaller trading partners. Tucker (1997) suggests the development of 'EDI boutiques' where outside vendors provide EDI capabilities on the Web which the SMEs accesses for a fee. While these may reduce the set-up costs to SMEs, Tuunainen (1998) suggests that there is a fundamental flaw in the argument. She states that EDI is normally only used by small businesses because it has been forced upon them by a larger firm. Thus, while simpler alternatives may be potentially available, the approach adopted by the SME will always be directed by the larger firm, resulting in a continuation of the difficulties currently encountered as shown in Table 4.

CONCLUSION

Small businesses provide a large 'slice' of most western economies. In many countries they are the single largest employer of both skilled as well as unskilled labour. They are also becoming far more integral to the supply chain of larger businesses.

Most advocates of EDI in small business tend to suggest that the benefits to small business include gaining strategic advantage, strengthening customer relations, restructuring of the business and preparing the business for the future.

The two studies presented in this chapter call into question both the benefits as well as the use of EDI in small business. The first study shows that most small business managers do not carry out long-term planning, nor are they particularly interested in enhancing the market share. Most are interested in the day-to-day activities of their firm and only look to technology from that perspective. The second study seems to support the view that EDI will only be used by a small business as a small percentage of its overall trade. While alternatives such as Web-based EDI and EDI boutiques may be cheaper and easier to use, ultimately SMEs will be dictated to by their larger trading partners.

Perhaps most important is the fact that most advocates of EDI in small business have failed to recognise the true nature of small business, rather they have simply supplanted the aspirations of larger businesses onto the small business environment and assumed that there are no real differences from one to the other.

If EDI is to be applicable to SMEs, designers and advocates alike need to examine the nature of SMEs far more closely, especially in regards to their planning environments. They need to realise that many are product rather than customer based, that most small businesses are interested in maintaining stability of operations rather than attempting to increase market share and that most need to maintain a position of independence from larger organisations they may interact with. The implementation and use of EDI for a SME, therefore, may need to be based more around the ability to derive immediate short-term benefits and savings rather than longer term strategic issues.

REFERENCES

Anson R. (1995). The Shape of Future EDI *Lan Magazine* May, 77 - 80.

Bamfield J.A.N. (1994). Implementing EDI: Problems in Managing Retail/Supplier Relationships by Technology Logistics *Information management*, 7(1), 7 - 10.

Barnett R.R. and Mackness J.R. (1983). An Action Research Study of Small Firm Management *Journal of Applied Systems,* 10, 63 - 83.

Barker P. (1995). Fear, resistance holding back electronic commerce *Computing Canada,* 21(13), 36

Brigham E.F. and Smith K.V. (1967). The cost of capital to the small firm The Engineering *Economist* 13(1), 1 - 26.

Britt P. (1995). EDI/EFT Moves Forward America's Community *Banker,* 4(8), 7 - 8

Chatfield, A.T. and Alston, M. (1997). Small and Medium Enterprises in Electronic Commerce: A Case Study of Barriers to Financial EDI Adoption, *Proceedings of 5th European Conference on Information Systems,* Cork-Ireland, 1219 - 1233.

Chen J.C. (1993). The Impact of Microcomputers on Small Businesses: England 10 Years Later, *Journal of Small Business Management,* 31(3), 96 - 102.

Cochran A.B. (1981). Small Business Mortality Rates: A Review of the Literature *Journal of Small Business Management* 19(4), 50 - 59.

Cragg P.B. and King M. (1993). Small Firm Computing: Motivators and Inhibitors *MIS Quarterly,* 17(1), 47 - 60

Delone W.H. (1988). Determinants for Success for Computer Usage in Small Business *MIS Quarterly,* 51 - 61

DelVecchio M. (1994). Retooling the Staff along with the system *Bests Review*, 94(11), 82 - 83

EDI World Institute (1995). *The WHY EDI Guide for Small and Medium-Sized Enterprises,* EDI World Institute, Canada

Evans-Correia K. (1994). New Company Lets Small Suppliers in on EDI, *Purchasing,* 116(4), 76.

Fallon J. (1988). GM Europe Blaze EDI Trail: Will Link 200 Suppliers in Seven Countries *MIS Week* Dec 19.

Hansen J.V. and Hill N.C. (1989). Control and Audit of Electronic Data Interchange *MIS Quarterly,* 13(4), 403 - 413.

Higgins K.J. (1995). The Internet Beckons EDI, *Information Week,* October 2: 66 - 70

Hinge K.C. (1989). *Electronic Data Interchange: From Understanding to Implementation,* American Management Association, New York

Holzinger A.G. and Hotch R. (1993). Small Firms Usage Patterns *Nations Business,* 81(8), 39 - 42

Huttig J.W. (1994). Big Lessons for Small Business *Secured Lender* , 50(5), 44 - 49.

Iacovou C.L., Benbasat I and Dexter A.S. (1995). Electronic Data Interchange and Small Organisations: Adoption and Impact of Technology *MIS Quarterly* , 19(4), 465 - 485.

Jones M.C. and Beatty R.C. (1998). EDI Benefits and Compatibility: An Empirical Comparison of End User and EDI Manager Perspectives, *Journal of Computer Informa-*

tion Systems, Fall 1998, 51 - 54.

Kavan B.C. and Van Over D. (1990). Electronic Data Interchange: A Research Agenda *Proceedings of the Twenty-Third Annual Hawaii International Conference on Systems Science,* 192 - 197.

Khan E.H. and Khan G.M. (1992). Microcomputers and Small Businesses in Bahrain *Industrial Management and Data Systems,* 92(6), 24 - 28.

Kilbane D.E. (1998). EDI is not going away, *Automatic ID News,* 14(13), 27 - 29

Lee H.G., Clark T and Kar Y. (1999). Can EDI Benefit Adopters, *Information Systems Research,* 10(2), 186 - 195.

MacGregor R.C, Bunker D.J. and Waugh P. (1998). Design of Electronic Data Interchange Systems for Small/Medium Enterprises in Romm C.T. and Sudweeks F. *Doing Business Electronically,* Springer London,151 - 161.

Meredith G.G. (1994). *Small Business Management in Australia* McGraw Hill, 4th Edition.

Phillip G and Pedersen P. (1997). Inter-Organisational Information Systems: Are Organisations in Ireland Deriving Strategic Benefits from EDI *International Journal of Information Management,* 17(5), 337 - 357.

Pletsch A. (1994). Study showing EDI Acceptance Level on the Rise, *Computing Canada* 20(19), 13.

Ratnasingham P. (1998). EDI Security: The Influences of Trust on EDI Risks, *Computers and Security,* 17(4), 313 - 324.

Reynolds W., Savage W. and Williams A. (1994). *Your Own Business: A Practical Guide to Success ITP.*

Rotch W. (1967). *Management of Small Enterprises: Cases and Readings* University of Virginia Press.

Roy Morgan Research (1995). *Link Telecommunications Survey Carried Among 500 Small Business Across Australia,* Roy Morgan Research.

Sehr B. (1989). Levi Strauss Strengthens Customer Ties with Electronic Data Interchange: Levilink Network Carries Order and Shipment Information, *Computerworld,* 30.

Tucker M.J. (1997). EDI and the Net: A Profitable Partnering, *Datamation,* 43(4), 62 - 69.

Tuunainen, V.K. (1998). Opportunities of effective integration of EDI for small businesses in the automotive industry, *Information and Management,* 34(6), 361 - 375.

Tuunainen, V.K. and Saarinen, T. (1997). *EDI and Internet-EDI: Opportunities of Effective Integration for Small Business* Proceedings of 5th European Conference on Information Systems Cork-Ireland June 19-21, 1997, 164 - 177.

Udo G.J. and Pickett G.C. (1994). EDI Conversion Mandate: The Big Problem for Small Businesses, *Industrial Management,* 36(2), 6 - 9.

Walker E.W. (1975). Investment and Capital Structure Decision Making in Small Business in Walker E.W. (ed.) *The Dynamic Small Firm: Selected Readings* Austin Press, Texas.

Yap C.S., Soh C.P.P. and Raman K.S. (1992). Information Systems Success Factors in Small Business *International Journal of Management Science,* 20, 597 - 609.

Zack M.H. (1994). The State of EDI in the U.S. Housewares Manufacturing Industry *Journal of Systems Management,* 45(12), 6 - 10.

Chapter X

Economics of EDI Investments

Ruhul A. Sarker
University of New South Wales

Mahbubur Rahman Syed
North Dakota State University

INTRODUCTION

Electronic data interchange (EDI) technology gives organizations an opportunity to exchange their information and messages electronically, instead of with paper documents, and leads to a new way of doing business known as electronic commerce (EC). The benefits of EDI include less delay in data handling and labour savings in the areas of data transcription, controls, and error investigation and correction. As a result implementation of EDI improves the following:
- the internal operations of a firm by reducing the process-cycle time,
- responsiveness to customers,
- trading partner relationships, and
- the ability to compete, both domestically and internationally.

The documentation requirements and their distribution in either local or international trade add a significant amount to cost of trade. So EDI implementation may save considerable expenses from this sector. The volume of documents that are potentially convertible to EDI usually creates economies of scale, which drives the conversion process.

Most of the EDI-related works found in the literature emphasize the strategic opportunities and organization-specific critical success factors that determine the potential benefits of an EDI implementation (Hoogeweegen and Wagenaar, 1996). Not many authors stressed the actual cost-benefit analysis for EDI project implementation based on the argument that its actual implementation is often a matter of power between the competitors. However, to show the feasibility of an EDI project implementation, like any other project, it should include a cost-benefit analysis as it is easily understood by senior management in the process of their planning decisions. EDI investment analysis is more difficult than many other investment decisions, because the costs and benefits are hard to identify and quantify, and the intangible factors are likely to be significant. We assume that the goal of developing

Copyright © 2000, Idea Group Publishing.

an EDI system in an organization is mainly to increase its net worth. The overall increase of the organization's net worth is measurable. But it is difficult to quantify benefits such as technological experiences and confidence gained by the organization due to adaptation of an initial EDI system that would help to further develop, update and expand other systems in the future and increase its benefits on a continuous basis. This makes new technologies like EDI somewhat different from the conventional projects where continuous improvement or expansion within the project is almost nonexistent. Investment in an initial EDI project can have a significant impact also on the value of future projects. Without the initial exploratory project, the future projects may not even be justifiable (Dos Santos, 1991). This impact (which may not be true for conventional projects) and many EDI technology-specific factors (such as level of technology, system response time, computer expertise required, user friendliness, acceptance to the users, operational complexity, ease of maintenance, accuracy of output produced and ease of system upgrading, etc.) are not easy to quantify. These unquantifiable costs and benefits of EDI projects demand integration of different other factors in the traditional investment analysis. Another major difference of an EDI investment from a traditional IT investment is that EDI should be multi-organizational with the following characteristics, which are part of feasibility analysis:

- EDI is a technology infrastructure that spans multiple independent organizations. As such, EDI investment is meaningful only when trading partners are willing to participate in it.
- The costs and benefits involved in the EDI investment are seldom equally distributed over the participating organization.
- EDI assumes a minimal level of IT maturity among the partners and requires a rather formal way of conducting business.
- In many countries, EDI messages have not yet received the same legal status as their paper counterparts.

So in principle, though the evaluation of EDI investments are quite similar to any other IT investment, several important differences, as indicated above, are necessary to be incorporated in the analysis process for a more accurate feasibility output.

In different literatures there are approaches, in a scattered manner, which may be used in EDI investment evaluation and is necessary to be presented to the EDI/IT forum for the following reasons.

- give an idea how they are different from the conventional projects and
- make popular EDI/IT investment analysis tools easily available to the users.

This chapter is an approach to compile the description and procedure of a few popular investments analysis tools so that the EDI practitioners have an overview to be able to choose the right tools for their organizations. In addition, few possible new parameters have been discussed for inclusion in future research in this area. Since the cost-benefit analysis is recognized by many researchers as a strong factor (though not the only factor) for EDI investment analysis, a few methods for cost-benefit analysis are also highlighted in this chapter for integrating into EDI investment evaluation. The objectives of these integrations are to obtain more accurate information on the following:

- whether or not to invest for an EDI project;
- the expected rate of return on EDI investment; and
- analysis in order to find "*the best*" EDI project.

This chapter is organized as follows. Following the introduction we present an overview of available assessment techniques. In the following section, a procedure for selecting an optimum system is discussed. Decision analysis approach is then briefly described. Decision making for multiple linked projects and multiple criteria analysis are presented in the following two sections. After that, an EDI project evaluation approach with respect to inter-organizational relationships is discussed. A case study regarding EDI implementation is provided in the second to last section. Finally, discussion and future research directions are presented.

AN OVERVIEW OF AVAILABLE ASSESSMENT TECHNIQUES

There may be many users of an EDI system, each with a different set of possibly conflicting benefits. However, it is clear from previous practices and research results that any new system must be evaluated before management decides to accept it for implementation. A sufficiently accurate evaluation may be made using simple techniques and managerial expertise. A few techniques are briefly introduced in this section.

The techniques used to evaluate certain investments can be based on deterministic modeling, stochastic modeling, multiple-criteria analysis, or simulation. Deterministic models provide a set of formulas that produce certain outcomes based on business context-dependent parameters. The same set of parameter values will always produce the same outcome. Stochastic models, on the other hand, incorporate probability as a moderator between the context parameters and the final outcome. Multiple-criteria analysis models calculate outcomes based on a set of weighted scores. These weighted scores are assigned by the decision-makers to a checklist of variables, such as "contribution to strategy," "expected payoff," and the like. There are certain multiple criteria methods which incorporate qualitative factors along with quantitative parameters to produce the outcome. Finally, simulation models reflect a system's current way of working and would allow the EDI decision-maker to change certain parameters to measure their effect on the system's performance.

Whatever method is used to evaluate an EDI investment project, it is necessary to identify all tangible and non-tangible costs and benefits. The general system costs for an EDI system are as follows:

- Initial or one-time setup costs:
  - Hardware
  - Software (system, communication and interface)
  - Manpower
  - Expenses to train users

- Current/ Operational costs:
  - Internet access fee
  - Ongoing system support and maintenance
  - Costs for system upgrading
  - Costs for enhancing the software solution
  - Costs for leased lines (if any)

- Administration
- Any external costs to link the associated organizations

The important factors that must be considered in an EDI investment evaluation process are as follows:
- Level of technology used
- System managing capability
- Overall system performance
- Security issues
- System response time and speed
- Computer expertise required to use the system
- User friendliness
- Overall system acceptance to the users
- Operational complexity of the system
- Ease of maintenance
- Accuracy of output produced
- Ease of system upgrading
- Costs for associated organizations to add new link

The benefits of an EDI system may be as follows:
- Net worth increase due to EDI implementation
- Time savings
- Improved product quality or accuracy of information
- Technological advancement and confidence gained (both company-wise and personal level)
- Benefits of the partners and/or associated organizations
- Customer/ user satisfaction

All these factors, discussed above, may not be relevant for a given organization, and there may be some organization-specific important factors that are not listed above. The mode of connections and type of connections between the trading partners, and the EDI standards are not considered in detail for economic analysis in this chapter. However, interested readers may find them in Johnston (1998).

Table 1 presents several methods available in the literature, used for general information systems investment analysis. In this chapter, we discuss some of these methods, which may be used for analyzing EDI investments. The stochastic and simulation modeling are based on complex and time-consuming techniques and require an in-depth analysis. This makes their application expensive and restricted to academic arena.

Like any other technological projects, management must have some sort of feasibility studies before implementing an EDI project (Hoogeweegen and Wagenaar, 1996). In many cases, management tends to avoid objective evaluation of an EDI system because many of the benefits (and costs) are intangible and difficult to precisely quantify. However, imprecise data can be used to provide an objective evaluation of the benefits of an EDI system. Such an evaluation may serve as an *'initial screening process'* to screen out some unjustifiable systems before any costly analysis is performed (Schell, 1986).

The net present value (NPV) and return on investment (ROI) are the conventional cost-benefit methods (Tersine, 1980). In most cases, the ROI is expressed as the internal rate of

Table 1: Overview of Available Assessment Methods

Methodology	Name of Methods	Reference
Deterministic	Cost-Benefit Analysis	Lay (1985), Dos Santos (1991)
	Financial Analysis	Guimaraes and Paxton (1984), Dos Santos (1991)
	Value Analysis	Keen (1981)
Stochastic	Decision Analysis	Schell (1986) Buxmann and Gebauer (1999)
	Option Valuation Model	Dos Santos (1991)
Multiple-criteria	Multiple Criteria Analysis	Bedell (1985)
	Information Economics	Parker et al (1989)
Simulation	Simulation Modeling	Wikner, Towill and Naim (1991)
	Multiple Criteria Analysis	Bedell (1985)

return (IRR). To evaluate the feasibility of investments, the return on investment (ROI) techniques is used by many organizations with tight financial disciplines. Managements often set a 'hurdle' rate which defines the minimum acceptable ROI for a project (Farbey et al., 1992). The main strength of these methods is that they permit decision-makers to compare the estimated returns on different investments. The weakness is that some good investment possibilities are withheld because the benefits are difficult, as in case of EDI investments, to assess in cash flow terms. The conventional cost-benefit assessment methods subsequently integrated in EDI investment analysis usually include breakeven analysis, net present value (NPV) and internal rate of return (IRR). The detail of these methods can be found in Tersine (1980). Lay (1985) suggested that traditional cost-benefit analyses are inappropriate for evaluating any information systems projects. As long as business measures success in terms of dollars, it will tend to evaluate projects based on quantifiable costs and benefits. However, it is important that IS is evaluated by some objective measure and not only by cost-benefit analysis. Objective measures may include system performance, expertise requirement, risk, user friendliness, and user acceptance.

Schell (1986) proposed a decision analysis approach to determine the value of information systems. A decision analysis approach evaluates the expected payoff under risk. This approach requires specifying the actions that can be taken and the dollar payoffs of those actions. When risk is involved in the attainment of payoffs, probabilities of attaining the payoffs must be specified. He analyzed the benefits of developing information systems for sales forecasting using a decision analysis approach. We have indicated that decision analysis method can be used for EDI investment analysis in a later section.

Chandler (1982) suggested an approach that is appropriate for the set of information systems that have passed through both the initial determination of value and the subsequent determination of net value resulting from the system requirement analysis. The multiple linked project approach allows for objectives such as risk and corporate positioning to be evaluated in conjunction with dollar payoff. This approach is applicable in the EDI scenario. This method is discussed in this chapter.

Multiple criteria methods can be used to evaluate a project that can incorporate factors other than money. This method allows decision-makers to appraise the relative value of different outcomes in terms of their own preferences. They can rank goals by applying a preference weight to each. The end result is to evaluate the project in terms of a utility measure rather than money. The multiple criteria method is best used where there are a number of possible objectives to serve a number of different units or persons in the organization. It is also useful where there are a number of design alternatives and there is difficulty in choosing between them because they do not all provide the same outcome. This approach is useful to deal with the non-quantifiable EDI implementation benefits. Two different multiple criteria methods proposed by Bedell (1985) and Parker et al. (1989) are briefly presented in a later section.

EDI is normally introduced to link the individuals from within and outside an organization. The costs and benefits are not evenly distributed among the players. That means the information exchange costs for conducting business are different with different parties. Buxmann and Gebauer (1999) proposed a technique that is useful to evaluate the EDI system considering the inter-organizational relationships, not as system cost of one organization only. This approach is also discussed in this chapter.

Value analysis attempts to evaluate a wide range of benefits including intangible factors. This method is based on the notion that it is more important to concentrate on value (added) than on cost saved. To get a value the intangibles must be assessed. For example, value analysis may use an iterative approach, such as the Delphi method, to provide answers. Where the proposed system is expected to deliver a variety of benefits, the value analysis method groups the benefits into homogeneous categories using statistical techniques such as cluster analysis. Like multiple criteria method, value analysis permits the calculation of utility scores by attaching utility weights to each category of benefit. The value analysis method can be found in Keen (1981), Melone and Wharton (1984), Money et al. (1988) and Rivard and Kaiser (1989).

In practice, many organizations combine parts of a number of methods and vary the methods to suit the situation. Probably the most frequently used methods might be described as *ad hoc* methods.

OPTIMUM SYSTEM SELECTION

A new system can be analyzed in one of the following two different ways.
- Selecting a system from a number of available alternatives, or
- Assessing a given system based on its cost, return and other relevant factors.

When selecting from a number of available systems, they may vary in terms of their prices and performance measuring parameters. Peaucelle (1998) suggested two parameters for consideration in the process of selection of a system from a number of alternatives. These are (i) cost of acquiring a system and (ii) operating loss due to having a less expensive system. It is assumed that less expensive systems that are under consideration should have reduced operational capabilities. Peaucelle expressed the total cost function of the system as follows:

$$TC(x) = f(x) + g(x)$$

Where, x = technical variable, system's efficiency (range from zero to one)
$f(x)$ = cost function of the system with efficiency x
$g(x)$ = loss function of the system with efficiency x

Figure 1: Total Cost Function of a System

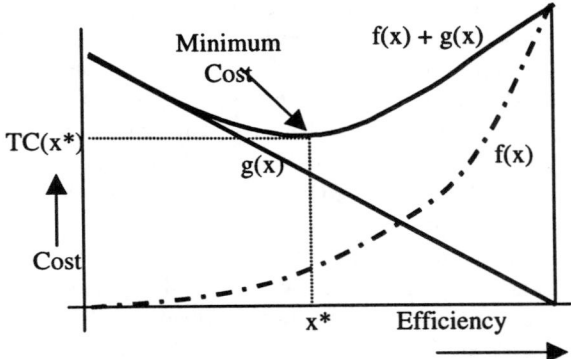

The cost function $f(x)$ increases with the level of efficiency, whereas the loss function $g(x)$ decreases with the level of efficiency. So $g(x=1)$ must equal 0 and $f(x=0)$ must equal 0, $g(x<1)$ must be negative (loss count as cost due to having bad system) and $f(x>0)$ must be positive (system cost). These functions could be either linear or nonlinear. If we assume that these two functions are continuous, and $f(x)$ is nonlinear and $g(x)$ is linear, then the pattern of the total cost function is as shown in Figure 1.

A desired system is that which minimizes the cost minus the loss of the system. Practically, there are usually a finite number of known systems in the market with known costs. The losses can be estimated based on the company's objectives and performance of the system in similar situations. So this is a problem of choosing one out of n systems from the market. The mathematical model of this problem can be formulated as shown in Appendix A.

DECISION ANALYSIS

Decision analysis, mostly using decision trees, is a technique that evaluates the expected payoff of the decision-maker under risk. It requires that the decision-maker be able to specify the actions he can take and the dollar payoffs of those actions. Probabilities of attaining the payoffs must also be specified when risk is involved in the attainment of payoffs. A general introduction on the decision analysis approach can be found in Turban and Meredith (1994).

Decision analysis is most valuable in situations where the majority of the benefits from the system or the project are intangible. The task of analysis should occur early in the evaluation of the system/project so that time and money are not spent for detail analyses of the system/project that does not demonstrate the potential for value. An example of this approach may be seen in Mukhopadhyay et al. (1995).

DECISION MAKING FOR MULTIPLE LINKED PROJECTS

It is a common practice to introduce and implement new technology in a number of stages until it gets popularity and maturity within the organization. The first stage is initiated by a decision to invest in a project involving a new technology (Dos Santos, 1991). Initial projects involving new technologies are exploratory and experimental. Without the initial exploratory project, the future technology-based projects may not be justifiable. A first-stage project can have a significant long-run impact on the organization beyond the short-term benefits of the first-stage project alone, specially where future projects would prove to be extremely valuable. This long-term impact should be considered in order to determine the true return of a new technology investment.

Let us discuss a case of a new technology. It is apparent that the availability of Integrated Services Digital Network (ISDN) services across the United States are likely to make entirely new types of applications economically feasible. Some organizations are considering or have undertaken experimental projects using this technology. Using traditional financial analysis these initial projects may be difficult to be justified on their own. However, the experience gained from such experimental projects could prove to be extremely valuable in future projects. These benefits must be taken into consideration when a new technology, as for EDI, is to justify its investment.

Example:
A firm is contemplating an investment in an application involving the use of ISDN services, a new technology for the organization. It is estimated that the initial ISDN project will incur development costs in the form of an initial outlay (I_0) of $12,000. For simplicity, it is assumed that future cash flows from the first-stage project (F_t) will be received at the end of period 1 (i.e., $t = 1$), and are estimated at $7,000. Assume that the firm uses a discount rate (i) of 12 percent for its investment analysis. The question is: *Should this first-stage project be undertaken?*

Solution:
Using net present value approach, the NPV may be calculated as follows:

$$NPV_{t=0} = -I_0 + \frac{F_1}{1+i} = -12,000 + \frac{7,000}{1.12} = -5750.00$$

With negative NPV this project would be rejected.

The top management may argue that this project will make it possible for the organization to undertake other projects using ISDN technology and that these future projects (referred to as second-stage projects) could be extremely profitable. Therefore, if we were able to capture the value of these future projects, investment in the first-stage project would be justified.

Assume that the firm plans to undertake another ISDN project after the first-stage project is completed. Since the second-stage project would be undertaken in the future after first-stage project, the benefits of the project are likely to be uncertain at this point in time when investment in the first-stage project is being considered. In order to analyze the return on investment, the benefits of the second-stage project, possible outcomes and their probabilities have to be estimated.

Example:
Let us assume that there are two possible outcomes in the case of a second ISDN project. For simplicity, we also assume that all cash inflows from the second-

stage project occur at the end of Period 2, while development costs are incurred at the beginning of Period 2. If the business conditions are favourable, this project is expected to result in a cash inflow of $40,000. Else, it will result in a cash flow of $20,000. The expected development cost of the second-stage project incurred at the beginning of Period 2 is $20,000. Analyze the return on investment for the (i) second-stage project and (ii) two projects together.

Solution:

The inflows and outflows of the second-stage project are shown in Figure 2.

Figure 2: First and Second-Stage Projects with Cash Flows

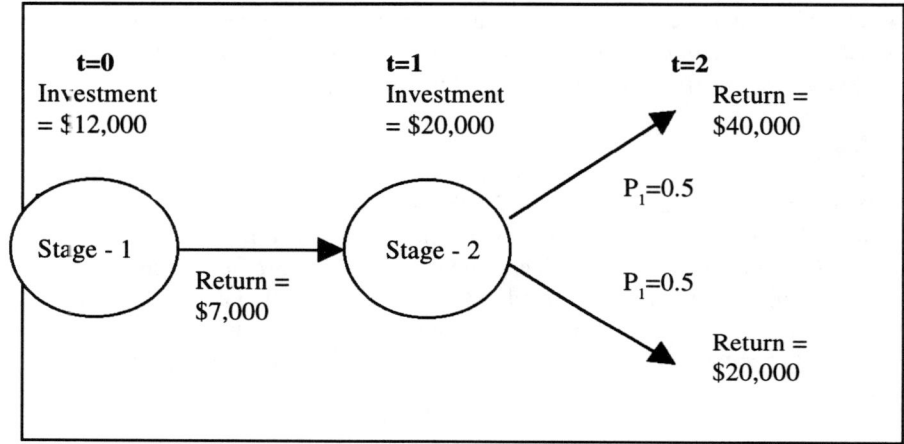

The NVP at $t = 1$ for two probable cash inflows:

$$NPV^1_{t=1} = \frac{F^1_2}{1+i} = \frac{40,000}{1.12} = 35714.29, \quad NPV^2_{t=1} = \frac{F^2_2}{1+i} = \frac{20,000}{1.12} = 17857.14$$

The expected value of the cash flow for the second-stage project, at the beginning of Period 2, can be calculated using the following formula:

$$EV_{ssp} = \sum_{j=1}^{m} p_j \sum_{t=1}^{n} \frac{F^j_t}{(1+i)^t} - I_1 - \sum_{t=2}^{n} \frac{I_t}{(1+i)^t}$$

$$= p_1 \frac{F^1_2}{(1+i)} + p_2 \frac{F^2_2}{(1+i)} - I_1 = 0.5 \left[\frac{40,000}{1.12} \right] + 0.5 \left[\frac{20,000}{1.12} \right] - 20,000 = 6,785.715$$

Where, m = the number of possible outcomes.
F^j_t = cash inflow for outcome j at the end of period t.
P_j = probability that state j occurs.

The NPV of the two projects together is:

$$NPV_{total} = -I_0 + \frac{F_1}{(1+i)} + \frac{EV_{ssp}}{(1+i)} = -12,000 + \frac{7,000}{1.12} + \frac{6,785.715}{1.12} = 308.67$$

The net present value of the two projects together is positive. So the investment in the first-stage project may be justified. Sometimes additional projects, further into the future, must be considered to justify the first-stage investment. This situation presents serious forecasting problems.

The NPV approach does not consider the flexibility that the firm has in managing the assimilation of a new technology. The managerial flexibility is discussed below.

Managerial Flexibility: In reality, investment in a first-stage project provides management a number of options in dealing with the second-stage projects. For example, management has the option to abandon second-stage projects. In addition, a manager may be able to expand or reduce the scope of second-stage projects or delay them, etc. The above method fails to consider the value of these 'real' options that are available to management in dealing with second-stage projects. If such options are available but are not considered in the evaluation, the investment will be undervalued. The true value of the first-stage project, as proposed by Dos Santos (1991), can be expressed as:

$$V_{ntp} = N_{fsp} + V_{ssp}$$

Where, V_{ntp} = the value of the new technology project.
N_{fsp} = NPV of the first-stage project's cash flows.
V_{ssp} = value of the second-stage projects when management options are considered.

If V_{ntp} is greater than zero, the first-stage project is a good investment. However, it is very difficult to calculate V_{ssp} at the beginning for the first-stage project.

Undertaking a first-stage project will give the company the ability to take on second-stage projects that might not otherwise be possible. By investing in a first-stage project, the firm obtains the option to undertake future projects. Experienced management may have the capability to assign a value for V_{ssp}. Since the cost of acquiring (developing) a future project and the revenues from the project are uncertain at the time a new technology decision is being made, Margrabe (1978) developed a model to determine the value of an option to exchange risky development costs for risky revenues. Margrabe's model is presented in Appendix B. Such a model could be complex to the practitioners and may have the problem of data unavailability.

It is well known that benefits, such as improving quality and customer service, creating new markets, improving decision making, meeting legal requirements, etc., are non-quantifiable. Though, the benefits like sales volume, profit, etc. (those are quantifiable) are the results of all benefits, they do not represent the experience and technological advancement gained by the organization which are the key factors for further improvement of the organizational goal. Multiple criteria decision analysis approaches can deal with both quantitative and qualitative information.

MULTIPLE CRITERIA ANALYSIS

So far we have considered the quantitative aspects of investment decisions. To justify the investment of any new technology, both quantitative and qualitative benefits arising due to implementation of this new technology must be considered. Bedell (1985) proposed a scoring system to incorporate all types of benefits into the investment decision process. He listed a number of activities within a system and then defined two indexing system based on: (i) the relative importance of activities within the organization and (ii) the relative

Table 2: Level of Importance of Activities

Factor	Score	Description
Strategic	10	Absolutely essential in achieving significant strategic objectives
Major Support	5	Not absolutely essential but play a vital role
Minor Support	1	Helps to achieve its strategic objectives
Not Useful	0	Not useful

Table 3: Level of Effectiveness

Level of Effectiveness	Score	Description
Highly Effective	10	Functionally appropriate, technically appropriate and cost effective
Moderately Effective	5	Provides reasonable support
Ineffective	1	Support but ineffectively
Not Support	0	Worthless

effectiveness of the activities. Bedell defined the importance of the activities, in numerical scale, as shown in Tables 2 and 3.

In addition to the above index system he defined another system to represent the effectiveness of each activity. Effectiveness means functionally appropriate, technically appropriate and cost effective.

Let, n = number of activities to be considered
SF_i = score of degree of importance for activity i
SLE_i = score of level of effectiveness for activity i

Now, the total system effectiveness can be calculated using the following formula:

$$\text{Total System Effectiveness} = \frac{\sum_{i=1}^{n}(SF_i) \times (SLE_i)}{\sum_{i=1}^{n} SF_i}$$

Example:

A wholesaling company is planning to implement an EDI system to improve its stocking and distribution systems. The top management identified the important activities that will be affected by the new system and decided the scores based

Table 4: Level of Effectiveness

Activity Number	Activity	Score for Degree of Importance	Score for Level of Effectiveness
1	Stock Level	10	10
2	Inventory Planning	5	0
3	Inventory Reporting	5	5
4	Delivery Planning	10	10
5	Customer Service	5	10

on their importance to achieve the company's goal. The management also estimated the score for the level of effectiveness after EDI implementation as in Table 4. Let us find the total effectiveness of the system.

The stock level and product delivery are identified as the strategic factors because:
- the holding cost can be reduced by decreasing the stock level, and
- the transportation cost can be reduced by proper planning.

The EDI system will be implemented, if it does not have the inventory module. As a result, the score for level of effectiveness for inventory planning is assumed as zero. The index for inventory reporting is assigned 5, because this module needs substantial improvement to be effective.

Solution:

$$Total\ System\ Effectiveness = \frac{\sum_{i=1}^{n}(SF_i) x (SLE_i)}{\sum_{i=1}^{n} SF_i}$$

$$= \frac{(10x10)+(5x0)+(5x5)+(10x5)+(5x10)}{10+5+5+10+5} = 6,429$$

Bedell used a common scoring system for both quantitative and qualitative benefits. The quantitative benefits are converted to qualitative scores for assessment. Parker et al. (1989) proposed a new system that incorporates different scoring and weighting scheme for qualitative and quantitative benefits. In addition, they consider the risk and uncertainty involved with the project. Parker et al. identified the following important factors for IS/IT and related projects' investment analysis:

- *Economic Cost Benefit*: Relative score based on return on investment, internal rate of return or net present value.
- *Strategic Match*: Assesses the degree to which the proposed project responds to established organizational strategies and goals.
- *Competitive Advantage*: Evaluates the degree to which the proposed project provides an advantage in the marketplace, for example, inter-organizational collaboration through electronic data interchange.
- *Management Information Support*: Assesses the project's contribution to management's need for information on core activities, e.g., activities directly involved in the realization of the firm's mission.
- *Competitive Response*: Evaluates the degree of business risk associated with **not** undertaking the project.
- *Strategic System Plan*: Assesses the degree to which the proposed project fits into the overall organizational systems direction.
- *Strategic Uncertainty*: Assesses the degree to which the business strategy is likely to succeed.
- *Organizational Risk*: Assesses the degree to which a project depends on new or untested skills, management capabilities, or experience.

Table 5: Scoring Scheme for Different Types of Organization

Factors	Aggressive Company	Regulated Public Utility	Non-profit Service Organization	Private University
Economic Impact	50%	80%	50%	15%
Strategic Match	10%	10%	20%	20%
Competitive Advantage	10%		20%	30%
Management Information Support	10%	5%	10%	-
Competitive Response	5%	-	-	20%
Strategic System Plan	15%	5%	-	15%
Strategic Uncertainty	-	-	-	-
Organizational Risk	-5%	-	-25%	-
Infrastructure Risk	-10%	-	-	-
Definitional Uncertainty	-10%	-10%	-	-
Technical Uncertainty	-10%	-5%	-	-
Maximum possible score	100%	100%	100%	100%

- *Infrastructure Risk*: Assesses the environment, involving such factors as data administration, communications, distributed systems, etc.
- *Definitional Uncertainty*: Assesses the specificity of the user or business' objectives that are communicated to the project personnel. When the user cannot properly describe a problem, the technology department is hard-pressed to supply an answer.
- *Technical Uncertainty*: Assesses a project's dependence on new or untried technologies.

Every enterprise is different considering its size, structure, or strategy. So their scoring scheme should also be different. Parker et al. compared the scoring scheme for four different types of organizations as shown in Table 5.

The relative value of each item must be recommended by the management that suits their organizational goals.

INTER-ORGANIZATIONAL SYSTEM

When an organization introduces an EDI system, its goal is not only to link the key people within the organization but also to link its business partners/ associated organizations and the customers for the greater benefit of the organization. Buxmann and Gebauer (1999) proposed an evaluation approach for an EDI system used for a procurement process on the basis of inter-organizational relationships. The inter-organizational relationships are very important for the success of any EDI system. That means we should look at the integrated EDI system rather an individual organization. Similar inter-relationships may be developed for sales, designing, manufacturing, communication, and other partners.

The approach is based on the discounted cash flow and decision theory, which are discussed in earlier sections. They considered only two factors of the benefits namely, cost savings and time savings. The cost is defined as the information costs that the buyer faces for conducting business with suppliers in a given period. The cost saving is equal to the difference of costs of information before and after EDI implementation. To make the calculation simple, the time savings are expressed in monetary units. The discounted benefit of the buying company for conducting business with a given number of suppliers is calculated. Then decision theory is applied to analyze the 'Investment' or 'No investment' alternatives.

A detailed case study for a procurement process is presented by Buxmann and Gebauer (1999). The price, quality and transportation costs are not considered in this study as they concentrated only on the information exchange part.

BENEFITS OF EDI SYSTEM—A CASE STUDY

Consider a typical capacitated two-echelon supply chain system between a supplier and a retailer. For this system Gavirneni et al. (1999) considered three models/situations to assess the benefits of EDI implementation to the organization. These are:
- *A Traditional Model*: where there is no information to the supplier prior to a demand to him except for past data;
- *Supply Chain Model with Some Information Flow*: the supplier knows the inventory policy used by the retailer as well as the end-item demand distribution; and
- *Supply Chain Model with Full Information Flow*: the supplier has full information about the state of the retailer.

Study of these models enables us to understand the relationships between capacity, inventory, and information at the supplier level, as well as how they are affected by the retailer's inventory policy and end-item demand distribution.

Consider a periodic review inventory control problem. The sequence of events in every period is as follows. First, the supplier decides on his production quantity for the period. Next, the retailer realizes her demand for the period. After satisfying (fully or partially) the demand, if her ending inventory level is below the safety stock (s), she places an order with the supplier to bring her inventory level to maximum stock level (S). This order arrives at the beginning of the next period. If the supplier cannot satisfy the full order of the retailer, it is assumed that the retailer acquires the missing part of the order elsewhere. All this happens with no lead-time. The (s,S) policy is optimal for the retailer, for example, when she incurs fixed plus linear ordering costs, linear holding and backlogging costs. The supplier incurs holding and penalty costs (for the portion of demand not satisfied from inventory). The models are briefly discussed below.

Model 1: The supplier has no information about the retailer, except what is available from past demand data. To forecast the retailer's demand in a period, Gavirneni et al. analyzed past data to fill an order up-to level.

Model 2: At the beginning of each period, the supplier knows the number of periods i that have elapsed since the last order was placed. Since the supplier knows that the retailer follows an (s,S) policy, and since he knows the value of $D = S - s$, he can determine the probability p_i that an order will be generated at the end of the coming period and the order size using the known demand distribution.

Model 3: At the beginning of each period, the supplier knows j = the number of units sold by the retailer since her last order. Now, the supplier can easily determine p_j, the probability that an order will be placed at the end of the coming period and the order size.

After analysis of the above three models, it is found that the total cost for Model 3 is always smaller than that for Model 2, which in turn is smaller than that for Model 1. This leads us to conclude that faster *information exchange is always beneficial*. This information interchange is not possible without appropriate electronic media because the status of inventory will be different with time (little delay of information exchange) and the calculated probability will be useless for that point in time. So the implementation of an EDI system is useful for such situation.

DISCUSSION AND FUTURE RESEARCH

It is a common practice by top management to concentrate on the cost-benefit analysis to evaluate any type of projects before implementing them. However, cost-benefit analysis is not sufficient to evaluate the EDI projects, because many of the benefits of an EDI project, especially for the new projects, are not quantifiable. The experience and technological advancement gained due to undertaking of an EDI project cannot be quantified; this must have a vital role in the decision-making process.

A number of feasibility analysis methods that are reported in the literature are compiled and discussed in this chapter with examples and case studies, which can be integrated to take into consideration the tangible and non-tangible parameters associated with an EDI implementation decision.

It has been pointed out that for selection from a number of alternative systems the decision-maker must consider not only the cost of acquiring the system but also the operating loss due to having a less expensive system. Although this approach does not incorporate the qualitative factors for decision making, it does consider the cost affect of implementing inferior systems. Such a system can also be selected using a mathematical programming model like integer programming (IP). The application of IP models, for any EDI or IT systems selection, is not common in the literature. A representative IP model is proposed and presented in Appendix A. A case study using IP would be an interesting piece of research for an EDI project selection.

The cost-benefit analysis uses deterministic and known cost figures to analyze a system. If the factors/parameters are probabilistic and the overall decision problem is a multi-stage decision process, then the decision tree/analysis concept is useful to evaluate the alternative projects. The net present value concept can also be added in decision tree analysis. The use of utility function in decision tree analysis is a common practice. So a decision tree approach, combining other relevant methods, would be a useful tool for analysing certain EDI projects.

Decision making for multiple linked projects is an useful concept for new technology introduction or implementation processes. Implementation of new technology requires a number of stages until it gets popularity and maturity within the organization and even to make it financially feasible. So the long-term impact needs to be considered in order to determine the true return of a new technology investment. This concept is very much applicable for EDI cases. To analyze the long term impact, multi-stage decision analysis based on expected value, present value concept and decision tree is presented in the section for Decision Making for Multiple Linked Projects.

All of the above methods consider normally one independent objective measure or the simple sum of different objective measures irrespective of their preferences and values. Multiple criteria analysis considers multiple objectives simultaneously to make the decision. This method considers both qualitative and quantitative decision parameters together to get an overall decision score. In this chapter, we discussed two scoring systems from the literature. These scoring systems are popular among the practitioners because these are easy to implement and human judgement can also be incorporated. These scoring systems also work well to compare a number of different alternative systems to choose one. Analytic Hierarchy Process (AHP) is another multiple criteria decision tool that can be applied to EDI implementation decision process. Interested researchers may try to apply AHP for EDI projects selection. The details of AHP can be found in Saaty (1990).

EDI investment evaluation, considering the inter-organizational relationships, is discussed in an earlier section. This approach uses the concept of an integrated system, which includes all the trading partners, rather than analyzing the EDI activities of an individual organization. To calculate the savings this approach considers the cost and time requirements of an organization to do business (specifically for procurement purposes) with it's trading partners. However, the author did not consider the price, transportation, and quality of materials to be purchased and reliability of delivery. We believe there is a scope of doing further research in this direction. For example, an organization may be interested to prepare a short list of its good trading partners based on their quality of materials, price, transportation, reliability, etc. Then the organization may influence the short listed partners to implement a suitable EDI system. Some of these partners may not be interested in implementing an EDI system, as it seems to be expensive and troublesome at the initial stage. In such a situation, a benefit sharing approach may be a consideration by the larger and interested partners. In the literature, similar benefit-sharing approaches are common on other issues like quantity allocation and delivery (Zahir and Sarker, 1991). In this system, the benefits are shared in terms of monetary values giving discount to its trading partners. In the case of EDI, the larger organizations may consider sharing some of their benefits, even in monetary values. Given the nature of EDI implementation, requiring multi-organizational data interchange, this sharing approach may turn out to be viable for the larger organizations to develop a strong network/bond among the trading partners. The tangible and non-tangible benefits resulting from such an inter-organizational relationship associated with EDI give rise to research questions. The identified benefits may be incorporated to the methods discussed in this chapter and provide a more accurate answer to the feasibility question.

REFERENCES

Bedell, E. F. (1985). *The Computer Solution: Strategies for Success in the Information Age*, Dow Jones-Irwin, Illinois, USA.

Buxmann, P. and Gebauer, J. (1999). "Evaluating the Use of Information Technology in Inter-Organizational Relationships", *Proceedings of the 32nd Hawaii International Conference on System Sciences*, IEEE Publications, 1-10.

Chandler, J. S. (1982). "A Multiple Criteria Approach for Evaluating Information Approach", *MIS Quarterly*, 6(1), 61-74.

Dos Santos, B. L. (1991). "Justifying Investments in New Information Technologies", *Journal of Management Information Systems*, 7(4), 71-90.

Farbey, B., Land, F. and Targett, D. (1992). "Evaluating Investments in IT", *Journal of Information Technology, 7*, 109-122.

Gavirneni, S., R. Kapuscinski and Tayur, S. (1999). "Value of Information in Capacitated Supply Chain", *Management Science,* 45(1), 16-24.

Guimaraes, T. and Paxton, W. E. (1984). "Impact of Financial Analysis Methods on Project Selection", *Journal of Systems Management,* February, 18-22.

Hoogeweegen, M. R. and Wagenaar, R. W. (1996). "A Method to Assess Expected Net Benefits of EDI Investments", *International Journal of Electronic Commerce,*1(1), 73-94.

Johnston, R. B. (1998). *Trading systems and electronic commerce,* Eruditions Publishing, Emerald, Victoria, Australia.

Keen P. G. W. (1981)."Value Analysis: Justifying Decision Support Systems", *MIS Quarterly,* 5(1), 1-15.

Lay, P. M. Q. (1985). "Beware of the Cost-Benefit Analysis for IS Project Evaluation", *Journal of Systems Management,*36(1), 30-35.

Margrabe, W. (1978). "The Value of an Option to Exchange one Asset for Another", *Journal of Finance,* March,177-186.

Melone, N. P. and Wharton, T. J. (1984). "Strategies for MIS Project Selection", *Journal of Systems Management, 35,* 26-33.

Money, A. , Tromp, D. and Wegner, T. (1988). "The Quantification of Decision Support Benefits within the Context of Value Analysis", *MIS Quarterly,* 12, 223-236.

Mukhopadhyay, T., Kekre, S. and Kalathur, S. (1995). "Business Value of Information Technology: A Study of Electronic Data Interchange," *MIS Quarterly,* June, 137-156.

Parker, M. M., Trainor, H. E. and Benson, R. J.(1989). *Information Strategy and Economics: Linking Information System Strategy to Business Performance,* Prentice Hall, New Jersey, USA.

Peaucelle, J-L (1998). "The Paradox of Cost Reduction within A Support Department", *Proceedings of the 6th European Conference on Information Systems,* June 4-6, France, 967-983.

Rivard, E. and Kaiser, K. (1989). "The Benefits of Quality IS", *Datamation,* 35, pp53-58.

Schell, G. P. (1986). "Establishing the Value of Information Systems", *Interfaces,* 16(3), 82-89.

Saaty, T. L. (1990). "Multicriteria Decision Making, The Analytic Hierarchy Process: Planning, Priority Setting, Resource Allocation," Vol. 1, RWS Publication, Pittsburgh, PA, USA.

Tersine, R. J. (1980). *Production/Operations Management: Concepts, Structure & Analysis,* North-Holland, New York, USA.

Turban, E. and Meredith, J. R. (1994). *Fundamentals of Management Science,* Irwin McGraw-Hill, New York, USA.

Wikner, J., Towill, D. R. and Naim, M. M. (1991). "Smoothing Supply Chain Dynamics", *International Journal of Production Economics,* 22(3), 231-248.

Zahir, S. and Sarker, R. (1991). "Joint Economic Ordering Policies of Multiple Wholesalers and a Single Manufacturer with Price Dependent Demand Functions", *Journal of the Operational Research Society,* 42(2), 157-164.

APPENDIX A
An Integer Programming Model

Minimize $$Z = \sum_{i=1}^{n}(f_i + g_i + a_i)y_i$$

Subject to
$$\sum_{i=1}^{n} y_i = 1$$

$$\sum_{i=1}^{n}(f_i + g_i + a_i)y_i \leq B$$

$$y_i \in \{0,1\}$$

where
- f_i = cost of system i
- g_i = operating loss (negative) of system i
- a_i = additional cost (technical support, manpower and other) for system i
- B = budget of the firm to develop the system
- n = number of alternative systems available
- $y_i = \begin{cases} 1, & \text{if system } i \text{ is selected} \\ 0, & \text{otherwise} \end{cases}$

The objective is to minimize the total cost of the system development. The first constraint indicates that we must select only one system, and the second constraint ensures that the system development cost must be within the budget. This is a binary integer program that can be easily solved using Excel solver or any other optimization packages.

APPENDIX B

Margrabe's Model

The value of an option to exchange risky development costs for risky revenues can be expressed as follows:

$$V_{opt} = B_1 N(d_1) - C_1 N(d_2)$$

Where

- B_1 = current value of the expected benefits fo the second-stage project
- C_1 = current value of the expected development cost of the second-stage project
- $N(\cdot)$ = the cumulative standard probability density function
- $d_1 = \dfrac{\ln(B_1/C_1) + \sigma^2 t/2}{\sigma\sqrt{t}}$
- $d_2 = d_1 - \sigma\sqrt{t}$
- ln = natural logarithm function
- σ^2 = instantaneous variance of the ratio B_1/C_1, computed as

$$\sigma_{B1}^2 + \sigma_{C1}^2 - 2\sigma_{B1}\sigma_{C1}\rho_{BC}$$

- σ_{B1}^2 = variance of the rate of change of development costs of the second-stage project
- σ_{C1}^2 = variance of the rate of change of revenues of the second-stage project
- ρ_{BC} = correlation between development costs and revenues for the second-stage project

In order to use this model, it is necessary to estimate B_1, C_1, σ_{B1}^2, σ_{C1}^2, ρ_{BC}, and t. The V_{opt} plus the benefits from the first-stage project should be compared to the proposed initial investment in the first-stage project.

Chapter XI

An Internet Business Framework for Government Agencies

Mariam Fergusson
University of New South Wales, Australia

INTERNET COMMERCE

The Internet offers enormous potential as a means of communication, doing business and providing channels for service delivery. The most striking feature about the Internet as a technology has been its very high rate of growth compared with other modern communication technologies such as the telephone, television and facsimile.

The trend over the last few years of increasing uptake of the Internet is evidenced by host counts doubling approximately every two years (http://www.nw.com/zone/WWW/top.html), the number of people connected, and to a lesser extent the dollar amount of trade activity generated. In addition to the sheer number of hosts and people is the amount of traffic that is being generated. The traffic level on the Internet is doubling every 100 days (International Telecommunications Union [ITU], 1999). Forecasts of the on-line trade of goods in the U.S. are in the order of $1 trillion, and revenue generated by Internet electronic services alone is of the order of $220 billion by the year 2003 (http://www.forrester.com/ER/Research/Report/0,1338,5417,FF.html). These measures of the growth of Internet participation and predictors of future uptake suggest that the Internet "revolution" is more than journalistic hype. This is underlined in a provocatively titled article "Use Net or Die, Travel Agents Told," reporting advice from the Australian Tourism Commission (ATC) to travel agents that Internet travel sales are doubling every six months (Southgate, 1999). The ATC is predicting A$13 billion in net-based business in the Year 2000. Ansett Airlines expects 50% of its sales to be online by 2005, up from 1% today. Travel agents, like other 'middlemen' face significant threats from disintermediation as hotels and others who sell their wares through intermediaries work out effective strategies to use the Internet to sell direct to end consumers. Some hotels, for example, are using the commission (typically 10%) they pay to an agent to deliver lower room costs to consumers who transact directly with them over the Net. Businesses, and to some extent, governments that choose to ignore the Internet as a medium for doing business may be doing so to their detriment.

Copyright © 2000, Idea Group Publishing.

In this chapter, the Internet is viewed as an electronic market environment: a virtual space for buyers and sellers to meet and to conduct a transaction (traditionally this would be that of buying and selling), as well as an electronic shopfront environment for public service delivery. To date, much of the literature has focussed on identification of the critical success factors for effective implementations of Web-enabled technologies in the commercial sector in a relatively generic sense.

The term "Internet commerce" covers a wide range of business activities, so it becomes important to place some boundaries around the concept to get a working understanding of what these business activities are. The definition of Internet commerce that is used in this chapter is fairly broad: it is an activity that involves some form of obligation between two or more parties, or some type of exchange that occurs over the Internet. Electronic commerce is a broader term that covers all electronic communications channels. An electronic marketplace is the term used to refer to the virtual space on the Internet.

This chapter is divided into three sections. The first explores some of the "models" or frameworks of Internet commerce proposed in the literature that try to explain the shape and the expected gains of the electronic marketplace. Most models were developed within the context of private sector activity, so they provide few pointers or useful information for where the public sector should look to capitalise on the opportunities offered by Internet commerce. The second section develops a framework for government on-line service delivery on the Internet that incorporates the lessons learned from the commercial sector. The purpose of the framework is to provide a migration path towards more efficient service delivery, and to open the door to new ways of conducting government business. The chapter ends with an application of the framework using two real world case studies and examines some of the practical issues revolving around on-line government service delivery. The examples and cases studies are drawn from the Australian experience.

MODELS OF INTERNET COMMERCE

A simple way of classifying the commercial activity that we see on the Internet is as either business-to-business or business-to-consumer. Of the business-to-consumer market, there appears to be two classes of purchases that stand out as being acceptable to the consumer. The first is a conventional buying activity for low value physical goods such as books, CDs, flowers, personal computer peripherals and software (Department of Foreign Affairs and Trade [DFAT], 1999a). The other class is the service provision of simple, product-like services such as the travel services and on-line auctioning. It also covers "Internet-enabled" businesses such as search facilities for information archives, search engines for Web pages and other information-centred activities. On-line services are becoming increasingly prevalent, and there is some evidence that an unmet demand for these services exists (Putnam, 1999).

Commonly acclaimed advantages of doing business via the Internet include: the removal of time and space barriers (to yield a global marketplace and 24-hour-a-day, seven-days-a-week trading); the efficiency gains in the supply-chain due to process automation and reduced cycle times; and the changes in the industry market value chain with the removal of conventional intermediaries (Choi, Stahl, and Whinston, 1998; Wigand and Benjamin, 1995). Large efficiency savings are attributed mostly to the business-to-business Internet commerce sector rather than to business-to-consumer transactions (see for example, Anders, 1998; Anderson, 1997). The experience in electronic business for these two classes, however, has been quite different. The largest volume of transactions occurs in business-to-business commerce. These typically larger organisations have been using the older, more established technology of electronic data interchange (EDI) in the electronic commerce paradigm. Internet commerce thus represents a "shift" towards a different technology for some business-to-business transactions, whereas it represents a completely new way of doing business for many of the business-to-consumer transactions.

The most often cited barriers to Internet commerce uptake is the lack of security including problems with payments, lack of authentication mechanisms (Coffee, 1998), and privacy and confidentiality issues (see for example, Ratnasingham (1997) for a discussion of Electronic Data Interchange security, and Camp and Sirbu (1997) for payment security). Other barriers include a paucity of technology know-how, and the general lack of awareness and understanding of Internet commerce issues, particularly among the small to medium size enterprises (SMEs). One of the key requirements, which seems to attract less attention than security and privacy issues is that of standardisation (Farquhar, Langmann, and Balfour, 1998). We have seen a plethora of electronic payment schemes come and go, we are beginning to see some security "standards" emerging, but it is still an evolving and unstable environment.

Electronic Markets

A more aggregated view of Internet commerce is gained by considering the Internet as an electronic marketplace representing a virtual space for buyers and sellers to meet. The application of transaction cost theory can be used to understand the development of the electronic market place (Wigand, 1997). The emphasis here is on the transaction being the formal communication process between the buyer and seller or provider that occur within the marketplace itself. It specifically excludes the part of the business that is concerned with the production of the goods and services (actually manufacturing a good or physically providing a service). This is not to deny that there is a good case for suggesting that Internet commerce has particular attributes that enables the production of information goods in a more efficient way than using traditional commerce, or that the Internet provides for unique ways of "producing " information.

Theoretical predictions are that the adoption of electronic commerce for most firms will lead to transaction cost reductions, and this is why electronic markets can deliver efficiencies over and above traditional markets (Garcia, 1997). The discussion in this chapter pertains to the information management and information systems considerations of electronic markets and their relative costs rather than the economic considerations (see for example Picot, Bortenlanger, and Rohrl, (1997) for a theoretical exposition of transaction cost economics and electronic markets). The main thrust of the argument is that using the Internet for commercial transactions allows for efficiencies in the transactions themselves, rather than in the production of goods. This holds for the provision of services as well, and it is relatively easy to distinguish the delivery of a nonelectronic service from the transaction involved in acquiring the service in the first instance. Where the service involves information, and in particular in electronic form, it is a little more difficult to draw the line between the production and the transaction elements.

Within the context of an electronic market and transaction cost economics, three phases of a transaction are described (Schmid and Lindemann, 1998). These are: information costs; agreement (also called negotiation and contracting or ex ante transaction costs);

and settlement (or maintenance or ex post transaction costs).

Information costs are attributed to the gathering of data by buyers and sellers that are considered to be relevant. This could be about the product or service itself, or about the market to gauge demand. For some physical products, electronic markets will increase this cost since it is not possible to physically examine a product (Dominique, 1998), nor is it possible to engage in the same type of dialogue as one would in a real shop. Information products on the other hand are easier to "sample" on-line. There are claims that the Internet reduces the search costs because of the ease and speed of browsing. Studies on consumer behaviour, however, suggest that information costs are not necessarily reduced, although consumers acknowledge that there is potential for time savings and reduction in effort (Jarvenpaa and Todd, 1997). For much of the business-to-business commerce that already occurs remotely, the move to the Internet represents a cost reduction and a time reduction.

The Internet as a virtual market space affords a huge opportunity to accumulate data and information. It is relatively easy to access information (so lowering the cost of obtaining information) and to distribute it to those requesting it (so lowering the cost of providing information). This is predicated on the assumption that the cost of hardware and software to connect to the Internet is not an issue, that the searching technology and skills are available, and that there is no need to attempt to verify the information that is discovered. There is little empirical evidence to support or refute claims of cost reductions in the information cost component.

Agreement phase costs are those incurred in drawing up a legally binding contract include drafting and negotiating. In an electronic market, the most visible "contracts" include ordering from a catalogue where the price is pre-set, and there is no negotiation at all, and an on-line auction situation where prices are bid. The range of agreement options available electronically is reduced, and a high level of specification is needed up front. It is argued that this degree of automation in negotiations is a key to the cost reductions afforded by EDI.

The settlement phase is perhaps one of the more difficult aspects of transaction cost reduction when it comes to Internet commerce. It is essentially the fulfillment of the terms of the contract, and includes follow-up costs after the event (see Schmid and Lindemann (1998) for a fuller discussion of these costs). The type of activity that is Internet enabled includes automatic order tracking, although once again, there is scant evidence to suggest that such Internet transactions result in cost reduction.

Despite the arguments that point to large reductions in transaction costs, there remain a number of limitations to the application of transaction cost theories to electronic markets. One of these is in establishing the requisite degree of trust between contracting partners, in particular at the initial encounter. The degree of confidence in the virtual market mechanisms will be reflected by the attendant costs of bearing the risks by both parties. As was the case with EDI, Internet commerce currently appears to be limited to a niche market of those organisations which already trust these technologies either by being very technically oriented themselves, or can afford the cost of securing them.

Electronic Business Models

There are few generic business models described for Internet commerce. Timmers (1998) identifies 11 possible types of business model within an electronic market which include: the e-shop, e-procurement, e-auction, e-mall, third-party marketplace, virtual community, value chain service provider, value chain integrators, collaboration platforms, and information brokerage, trust and other services. What is particularly interesting is the measurement of the models against their degree of innovation and level of integration. The implication is that the "easiest" to achieve is at the low end of both scales. There is an implicit "evolution" from the simplest e-shop to the more sophisticated integrators and on-line brokerage services.

Electronic markets as business models are increasing in number, though their viability, and ability to attract a sufficient critical mass remains unproven. A factor in their viability is the high cost of setting up electronic markets, and also in the lack of standards, particularly for product catalogues (Segev, Gebauer, and Ferber, 1998). A vertical market study suggests that success factors are closely related to having a critical mass, and becoming a part of the existing market value chain rather than attempting to replace it (Fong, Fowler, and Swatman, 1998).

A distinction can be made between "transplanted real-world business models" and "native business Internet models" (Bambury, 1998). The former are activities that existed in the real world and transposed onto the Internet, such as mail-order businesses, whereas the latter are those that exist because of the Internet. It is reasonable to expect these two to have different structures and for the transaction cost components to be reflected in this discrepancy.

Despite the huge "success" attributed to Internet commerce, its uptake has been slow in two sectors: governments, and small to medium sized enterprises SMEs). The implications behind many studies and government reports (see for example DFAT, 1999b) is that SMEs stand to gain by adopting Internet electronic commerce because of the global Internet reach, as well as the relatively low cost of advertising. However, the actual uptake of the Internet by SMEs is still slow. For example, retail sales over the Internet in the U.S. are still under 1% of total retail (U.S. Government Working Group on Electronic Commerce [USGWGEC], 1998).

Benefits that are touted as being so significant in the private sector appear at first glance to apply to the public sector, though this is not reflected in practice. Establishing electronic commerce channels up until very recently was limited to a few government agencies requiring a considerable effort in systems development. Although systems that encompass a range of electronic commerce activities are commercially available now, they are typically targeted at the retail sector (Lincke, 1998), and there is little, if any, parallel in functionality that suits the public sector.

It is likely that a significant inhibitor is the perceived cost of participation and the associated risks. Electronic commerce applications have unique attributes, and failing to recognise and understand these is a major contributor to the risk (Murchland, 1995). The cost of establishing an Internet commerce site is very high, according to a recent report, in the order of millions of dollars (http://www.computerworld.com/home/news.nsf/all/9905274gart). The requisite development effort may of itself be an inhibitor to the government's uptake of Internet commerce. The implication here is that the benefits from electronic commerce do not outweigh the costs in the public sector. West (1998) takes a theoretical perspective of the role of information technology relative to transformation of governments and suggests that "traditional restraints on the activities of governments actually lead to inefficient investment in information-producing activities…"(p.24), but that the further application of information technologies may in fact redress this problem.

The next section proposes a model for describing government services and a strategy for migrating them online. Government service delivery, while sharing some similarities with commercial on-line transactions, requires a different approach. The model is based on the premise that the motivation for providing government services online is either to increase the level of public good or welfare, or to deliver a more efficient and effective service. It takes into account risk factors and attempts to minimise the risk of a failure in service delivery. Procurement activity that government engages in is deliberately excluded from this discussion. Procurement does not fall into the ambit of "service provision" and very closely mimics the buying and selling transactions of the private sector.

GOVERNMENT ON-LINE SERVICES FRAMEWORK

Governments have taken various attitudes towards electronic commerce, ranging from a very hands-off approach to a highly regulatory one. Regardless of the government's position with respect to its overall policy toward electronic commerce, there are advantages to be gained in the way that it transacts business that parallels those accruing to the private sector, at least in terms of cost reduction.

We have seen how transaction cost economics can be applied in the private sector to explain the emergence of electronic markets. Services and products are viewed as being similar within this context, and the characteristics of a government service per se need not have particularly distinguishing features from a commercial market service. It is the notion of *selling* a service, together with the sets of transactions surrounding this that distinguishes the public sector from the private sector. The exchange characteristics of a government service as an electronic transaction are thus quite different from a commercial one. For example, there are "services" that are mandated, removing any notion of "competition." In addition the provision of information is driven by different motivations in private and public sectors (for example required by regulation, or in the interest of the public good respectively).

Rather than look at the three phases of transaction costs, (information, agreement, and settlement phases), or look at the enablers and inhibitors separately, a new framework for government service delivery is illustrated. Transaction cost theory phases describe the processes that are involved in a "transaction." This is predicated on the concept that an activity is about the exchange of goods and services. Government services, however, are not based on this same premise. Although the notion that it is possible to reduce the overall price of a product or service by increasing the efficiency of the transaction through the application of information technology (rather than the production of the good or the delivery of the service) is applicable, the nature of "transactions" for government service delivery needs to be explored in greater depth.

The proposed framework incorporates an identification scheme to better understand what the equivalent to these transactions are. The specific question addressed is: What are the specific generic activities that are required in order to describe government services? The objective is to decompose the services into discrete activities that are defined by business function and to identify a potential set of services that represent a suitable starting point for migration to Internet delivery. A service can then be matched against the available technology to get a handle on what is actually feasible, what the costs are, and to provide a baseline comparison with the equivalent non-electronic delivery of service. The framework sets a basis from which to build a migratory path from traditional service delivery through to end-to-end electronic service delivery and to understand the potential inhibitors and enablers.

This incremental migratory approach does not preclude revolutionary changes to doing government business on the Internet, and there is no reason that the two cannot coincide. A proposition is that it is more appropriate for the "revolutionary" approach to be linked to new legislation and regulation. These are being fashioned in ways that are technology free (USGWGEC, 1998), but at the same time to take into account the capability and potential of current technology not previously available.

Government On-line Services Model

The on-line services framework provides for a way of modelling of a government service and a strategy for evaluating services to be migrated on-line. The model defines discrete atomic 'activities' on the basis of a single business function. Revenue collection is an example of a discrete activity and forms an essential component of many "services." Activities may need to be aggregated together in order to deliver a complete service. For example obtaining a new car registration may require three activities: proof of purchase, proof of identity, and payment. The discrete activities that describe a generic Internet service are:

- provision of information;
- verification of the ownership of the object of the transaction;
- verification of the identity of a person or entity;
- receipt of a payment; and,
- recording the transaction (for example: maintain a register, issue a registration certificate or sticker or license).

This list is not intended to be exhaustive, nor prescriptive, rather it represents a functional grouping of activities that underpin services and can be adapted for any particular government agency. The generic activities suggested can be replaced by agency-specific activities. What is important is that they are defined by business objectives, not by technology, and that each service provided can be described by one or more of the discrete activities.

These discrete business functions are aggregated together in an additive manner to provide a service. In Bambury's (1998) terms these services are most likely to be "transplanted real-world business models." The normal range of services offered is very wide, and in some instances the end-to-end delivery means that all of the discrete activities set out above are necessary, but not sufficient. On the other hand there is a class of "service" that requires only one of the above discrete activities such as the payment of land rates and the payment of traffic and parking offence fines. In this case the Internet service need only receive a payment against a particular "notice to pay" (a bill) for a specified service (payment of land rates).

An illustrative case of driver licensing given in Table 1 shows the necessary discrete activities. It should be noted that not all aspects of the service are explicit, though they are implicit. For example, a driving test result implies that a test has been conducted. The test itself may or may not be a service delivered by the government. If it is, then the summation of activities below are necessary but not sufficient for the completion of the service.

Information provision is a special case of a service and merits attention in its own right. Information is often the "product" that is being sought from a government agency. There is little doubt that the ability of the Internet to deliver information as WWW pages to the public

Table 1. Discrete business activities

Activity	Example: New drivers license
information provision	drivers handbook, logbook, traffic rules
verification of object/ownership	driving test result
verification of personal identity	birth certificate or equivalent
revenue collection	full payment
recording transaction	drivers license issued

is unsurpassed by any other technology. The more difficult questions here are to do with information management (how information is organised and cross-referenced, what search facilities are available, what type of information is available to the public), equity of access to information (for example public kiosks or Internet connections in public libraries), and privacy of information.

As in the physical world, there is a "band of tolerance" for each discrete activity and a hierarchy of stringency that can be applied. For example, verifying an identity can range from recognising a conventionally accepted form of identification, to requiring a number of particular types of identification. At one extreme "sufficient" identification may be a biometric measure, or it may be a photographic identification on an official document that is recognised internationally such as a passport. At another extreme sufficient identification may be a public library card. A normal business expectation is for very stringent levels of identification only if the implications of incorrectly identifying a person are very serious. Correctional and policing services normally require biometric identification such as fingerprints for incidents involving a legal offence.

It is interesting to note the type of information that is currently offered on the Internet. A fairly cursory examination suggests that a considerable portion of the government Web pages comprise material that is already published in paper form. Increasingly there are attempts at providing information in a more integrated fashion taking into account the capability of Internet technology and with the consumer needs at the forefront of the design. An example of a fledging interactive development is the Victorian government's site (http://www.maxi.com.au), and an example of consumer-oriented design is the Australian Capital Territory government's Internet site (http://www.act.gov.au). A major information initiative is the placing of all legislation onto the Internet making it readily and easily accessible at no cost to the consumer (http://www.austlii.edu.au/).

Government On-line Services Strategy

Government services are moving onto the Internet, albeit slowly. The model above provides a way of describing services. What is needed now is a way of roughly evaluating which of the myriad of services should go online in order to reduce the cost of providing the service. A migration strategy can be charted by measuring the service against two criteria: the number of discrete business activities that make up that service; and the extent to which the technology is available to support the required functions. The relative merits of moving government services onto the Internet can be eyeballed by examining their relative position on a two-dimensional chart. Figure 1 illustrates business models that encompass a large number of government services. The two axes represent the ease of implementation of a technology to meet the service, and the number of discrete activities required to deliver the

Figure 1: Internet Commerce Business Model Evaluation

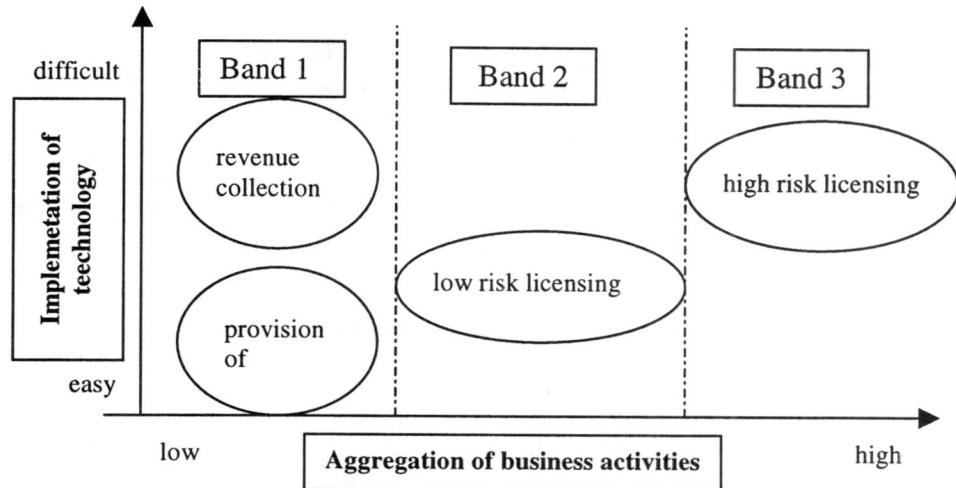

service.

The three bands shown in Figure 1 represent a crude measure of the effectiveness of migrating services to the Internet. Within each band, there are different technology implications. Band 1 is the most readily analysed since the technology options are being considered for one or two activities only. These need to be examined on a case-by-case basis. Band 3 represent those services to be migrated last, after a level of expertise has been acquired, and once single activities have been mastered as stand-alone services. Band 2 services are those that are most likely to lend themselves to radical change in the way in which services are delivered. For example vehicle registration renewals could be changed from actively requiring an owner to renew, to actively requiring an owner to de-register. Band 3 services are likely to present significant challenges in terms of radical change. For example, medical practitioners need not be licensed if sufficient information is easily available to the consumers about the credentials of the medical practitioner (West, 1998). This is a revolutionary and potentially controversial proposition. Even though it may be economically rational and technically feasible, it poses a new set of technology problems, and certainly requires social and professional acceptance.

Returning to the example of issuing a drivers license, the service is placed in the top right hand area of the chart, under Band 3, as a high risk licensing service. The extent to which the person involved in the transaction must be identifiable, the requirement to provide "proof" of having passed a test, the requirement to make a payment, and the need to issue a license places this service high on the aggregation scale. Implementing Internet technology for this purpose can quite safely be described as "fairly difficult."

The model and the strategy are proposed as starting points only. They enable a discrete activity to be costed roughly, and provide a guide for a migration strategy. There are other dimensions that will colour the choice of on-line public service delivery. One factor is the extent to which the technology is enshrined in existing legislation. A number of statutory requirements prescribe particular methods with terms such as "by your own hand," or phrases requiring a piece of paper. Another factor is the extent to which the transaction departs from a traditional mode of conducting business with the attendant socioeconomic change implications. This is a complex issue that merits consideration, though outside the scope of this discussion.

In the next section, two case studies are presented. The government services on-line framework is applied to two very different models of service delivery: an existing service (the payment of land rates); and an innovative service (Internet industry licensing). These models were both implemented as pilot systems in a real-world scenario. By identifying the components of the transactions as discrete activities it was possible to make an assessment of the desirability and the associated risks of government participation in the electronic marketplace.

CASE STUDY 1: ELECTRONIC REVENUE COLLECTION

The cost of revenue collection for the government is significant. For third-party commission-based payments, the cost to the government is a percentage figure of the total dollar value collected, in the order of 1-5%. Government shop front collection of a single payment is in the order of $3-$6 regardless of the amount of payment and is set by the overhead cost of the shop front, the salaries of the staff, and varies according to the mode of payment. The cost of receiving electronic payments are an order of magnitude less, with the additional advantage of avoiding a delay in the receipt of funds (Westland and Clark, 1999). Governments stand to benefit considerably from efficiencies of electronic revenue collection across a range of services that they provide.

A pilot study grounded in real-world operating constraints was conducted using two commercially available payment schemes for the collection of land rates (Fergusson and Boo, 1998). The objectives of the pilot included mapping out the processes required to implement Internet payments, evaluating cost effectiveness of the services, and gauging consumer opinions and likely uptake. It also identified some of the technological, legal and social issues that need to be addressed in implementing the two payment schemes.

In terms of the government on-line services framework presented above, the service involved a single discrete activity: collection of revenue. Rates collection represents the simplest form of revenue collection activity as it depends only on a unique bill identifier. The main potential benefit of migrating this service onto the Internet is to reduce the cost of revenue collection. The use of commercially available payment schemes in the pilot meant that the technology already existed, was in use (albeit to a very limited degree) and therefore the implementation of the technology fell at the "easy" end of the scale. The framework predicts that this service is ready for migration onto the Internet and theoretically would yield cost efficiencies.

A recent survey on general usage of the Internet reported that the volume of Internet payments was well behind the telephone, Electronic Fund Transfer at the Point of Sale (EFTPOS) or automatic teller machines (ATMs) (Australian Bureau of Statistics [ABS], 1998). Less than 1% of adult Australians had used the Internet in the three months prior to August 1998 to pay bills or transfer funds. The question begging to be asked then is, "why are there so few services in place to take advantage of the potential savings?"

Based on the discrete business activity framework described above, we can challenge the premise that the technology is simple or that the activity is singular. The latter is easily

established since identification of the person making the payment is not needed, nor is it necessary to show a relationship between the paying entity and the owner of the land. This leaves the matter of the ease of implementing the technology. There were two payment options trialed:
- eCash, a proprietary electronic token scheme specifically created for the Internet, available from a single Australian Bank only (see http://www.stgeorge.com.au/ecash/ or http://www.digicash.com/index_e.html). (As a point of interest, though not central to this case study, towards the conclusion of the pilot on the 4th November 1998, DigiCash (US) filed for bankruptcy and Mark Twain bank formally ceased its eCash trading.)
- BPay, a centralised third-party billing option available from a consortium of major Australian banks (see http://www.stgeorge.com.au/epayments/Bpay/Default.asp, or http://www.anz.com.au/australia/persbnk/prdsrv/phone_BPay.htm).

BPay can be used to pay a range of bills directly from bank accounts held at participating banks with "registered" BPay merchants, and works in a similar way to the credit card system. It is implemented predominantly as a telephone and across-the-counter payment system. Customer access to Internet BPay is through bank-owned proprietary solutions for Internet banking. The prerequisite to using BPay is an account at one of the participating banks and an Internet banking facility connected to the account.

At the time of the pilot (March - December 1998), only two banks offered an Internet BPay service, though more recently other major banks have made the facility available to its customers. For the purpose of future developments, it is reasonable to assume that the remaining participating banks will offer BPay services once they have established Internet banking services.

The pilot study carefully traced the processes required by the customers to use both of the payment options and logged all problems reported by the customers, as well as the technical implementation problems. The latter were effectively minimal. It documented the various interactions needed between the five distinct players in the Internet payment scenario. These were:
- the customer (the paying public)
- providers of payment products and services (DigiCash and BPay Pty Ltd)
- banks (customers' bank, payment model issuing bank, government's bank)
- the merchant (government agency)
- Internet Service Provider (government provider, customer provider)

A survey of 19 merchants in an electronic shopping mall that supported eCash prior to the start of the pilot confirmed the "ease of implementation" of the technology. The results of the survey suggested that the initial uptake appeared to be as a one-off experiment by curious consumers, and that there had been no other activity since. There was no commercial BPay Internet activity against which to benchmark the pilot results.

The pertinent findings of the pilot included the following:
- There is a distinct difference between the trust that people are willing to give government-backed systems and commercial systems. This level of trust does not appear to be technology dependent, rather it is levelled at the entity providing the service.
- Although 87% of the respondents stated their willingness to pay their government

bills on the Internet, less than 1% used the pilot Internet payment service.
- There is a latent demand for an Internet payment facility not currently being met by existing commercial solutions that are totally reliant on Internet banking software.
- The number of processes that the consumer had to navigate through to make a simple payment was very large.

The case study is useful in providing an understanding of how to measure the criteria of the framework. In particular it highlights the importance of including the ease of implementation of the technology to all parties involved in the activity. Without getting drawn into a discussion of electronic payment systems per se, there is an important lesson to be learned from the study. Third-party billing options for the Internet are still in their infancy, and they depend on the banking system to provide the front-end for the consumer. The problem lay in the poor usability measure for the consumer, rather than the fact that the technology was difficult to implement. The needs of all the major players must be taken into account. The electronic token system suffers from the same drawback, along with many others.

What at face value appears to be a single discrete activity turned into a labyrinth of screens and processes for the consumer. There must be a close coupling between the transactions involved in the execution of the activity and the level of aggregation of activities to deliver a service. Ideally the consumer selects a simple button which accepts payments, not unlike the options available on an Interactive Voice Response system. Simple government revenue collection services can be provided on the Internet in a cost-effective manner, but they need to look and be simple for the person making the payment. By extension, all services that fall into this activity type must have the same look and feel to maintain simplicity and familiarity.

CASE STUDY 2: ELECTRONIC LICENSING

Internet commerce offers very real opportunities for innovation in the way that governments transact regulatory and quality assurance business (Fergusson and Quinton, 1997). This case study describes a prototype called the eLicence that effectively represents a new form of industry "regulation". It relies on the Internet to communicate best practice between the public sector, industry and consumers that would not otherwise be possible. It permits truly "public" dissemination of, and access to, official and commercial information. This type of model challenges existing legislative objectives, and utilises the opportunity presented by the Web to enable a better way of meeting new business objectives.

Government agencies throughout Australia have been examining laws that foster anti-competitive conduct to ensure that they comply with published legislation review timetables under the National Competition Policy (1995). Many anti-competitive laws will be repealed; however, policy objectives of some (that meet a stringent new public benefit test) will need to be retained. The motivation for the development of a new on-line service comes as part of the review process involving consideration of cost-effective alternatives to existing regulatory mechanisms. Legislation that deals with licensing and regulation is a major target of legislative review.

The case study on electronic licensing illustrates the migration of the framework's Band 2 activities from traditional methods to innovative Internet applications. The industry regulation service consists of a number of discrete activities, including the provision of information, the verification of identity, and a collection of payment.

The business objectives of regulatory schemes have, traditionally, been limited by the delivery mechanisms and administrative constraints available at the time that the legislation was drawn up. The eLicence case focussed on an industry sector which was moving from being unregulated to a government and industry co-regulated one. The traditional approach to providing this service is using "gatekeeping" techniques and providing permission to participate in an industry. It requires the industry participants to provide proof of fitness to participate. Registers are kept of "approved" participants, and a policing regime is used to enforce the regulation. The cost of the gatekeeper approach is expensive, in particular the latter part.

The innovation involved taking a limited paper-based registration scheme and transforming it into an electronic marketplace. The principle advantage of the scheme is that it capitalises on significant consumer and regulatory benefits which flow from an informed marketplace. The scheme provides, for the first time, a register that can be truly "public." It extends the traditional "register" of persons entitled to trade by allowing open communication between government agencies, industry members and the public.

The Internet prototype provides a registration form for any entity wishing to participate in the industry. The first section of the eLicence involves making a public and legally binding undertaking to conform to industry-set requirements that are formally "legislated" as an industry Code of Conduct. Having made this commitment and a payment, all

Figure 2: A Diagrammatic Representation of the eLicence

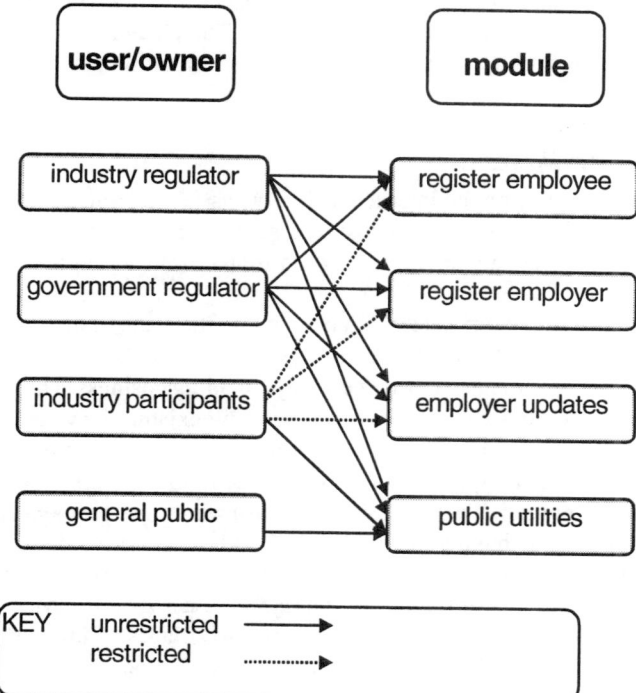

participants are displayed in a public register on the Internet. The participants are either employers or employees, and both need to register. This concept of openness enables the move away from needing permission to participate in an industry. Further, it eliminates the need for formal policing. In this model, problems with the industry are dealt with under the Consumer Protection and Fair Trading umbrellas, as well as by an industry co-regulator.

The Web prototype of the eLicence is best visualised as a virtual building, with a shopfront as the first port of call. The objective was to provide as much visibility as possible to public utilities, and so engender the "marketplace" ambience. All "rooms" leading from the shopfront (industry register, registration inquiries, industry information, complaints to Consumer Affairs) are accessible to the public except for the inquiry on the industry employee register. Figure 2 shows the major functions encapsulated in the prototype, and the key players.

The prototype was developed in tandem with the development of the Codes of Conduct with both industry and government regulators. The degree of acceptance of the prototype by all the parties concerned was very high. Benefits provided by the eLicense prototype far exceeded those available using traditional government quality control technique, and in fact open the possibility to having new objectives in the interest of the public good, at reduced cost.

Although the Codes of Conduct were implemented, the Internet prototype was not. A reason for this was a requirement for "stringent validation" of identity by the government regulator. Implementing the technology required to match this need meant that the solution was perceived as being too "difficult." The notion of creating a virtual marketplace was resisted by some industry participants because of a perception that it would be government driven, and that it was not the place of government to be promoting these sorts of activities. Although this was not raised as an issue by the industry, the general unfamiliarity with the Internet might well have been a demotivating factor. The element of mistrust of Internet commerce came through quite strongly, though it was a small minority-held view.

THE NEXT PHASE?

Government presence on the Internet is largely passive information provision. There is a trend away from this one-way "broadcast" presence to a more interactive style of service provision where consumers are able to engage in transactions with government agencies over the Internet.

The two case studies described give an insight into the some of the challenges that are present for governments in adopting the Internet as a medium to conduct business. A greater challenge exists for governments to foster new ways of doing business. The government on-line services model provides a useful way of describing existing services, as well as new services. This can be charted against the ease of technology implementation to provide a viable starting point for assessing the relative ease and merits for classes of service that can be migrated onto the Internet. It also helps to provide a whole government approach to on-line delivery of services by having them described as discrete activities that which can be shared across a number of agencies. The case study for an activity as simple a making a payment brought to light a perturbing trait that is found across all service provision: the applications for Internet technology are in the very early stages of infancy, and it will be some time before an obvious "standard" or set of standards emerge.

The model of government business provides a practical perspective on what actually needs to be done, and provides a delineation between the physical service delivery, and the activities (or the transaction, to use the terminology of transaction cost theory) surrounding it. The more difficult cases are those where the services to be delivered are information based, and so it becomes very difficult to separate the physical service itself from any other activity.

The framework as it stands applies to both "transposed" models of electronic commerce, and those that are Internet "native," that is, only feasible because of the technology. A number of research questions that surround this difference include: What, if any are the unique discrete activities for electronic commerce initiatives that are "native"? What kinds of models can we use to help us evaluate the relative cost efficiency of moving on to the Internet, or redesigning the business model to become an Internet native? From the government's perspective an equally important issue that needs to be addressed is that of equity of access. How can equity be assured for those services that are available on the Internet only? Does this mean that parallel, non-Internet systems need to exist? Alternatively, what are equitable public access mechanisms to the Internet?

The rate of Internet uptake around the world, though it appears to have levelled (ITU, 1999), is not to be ignored. There is little doubt that the Internet provides unique opportunities for businesses and governments alike. There is a growing amount of evidence to show that the cost of transacting business over the Internet can yield substantial efficiencies. This needs to be balanced against the creation of a critical mass to achieve those efficiencies and also the need for standardisation in the available technology.

Government can have a major influence in both of these areas, without having to proscribe or prescribe on behalf of the private sector. The adoption of Internet commerce in an evolutionary way by the government will facilitate a number of things, including:

- Build up confidence across the public sector, which by implication will also build up the confidence in the private sector and so boost the Internet market and in particular the SME market. Governments are in a position to "lead" by virtue of the fact that they already have a trust relationship with the general public, and that they are bound to work in the interest of the public good.
- Develop business models that are modular in design and defined by their functionality, with identified levels of consumer risk, meaning that the agencies can leverage from one another without the need to reinvent the wheel. The reusability of commerce modules will minimise the development cost and will also have the advantage of providing a uniform interface for the public.
- Anticipate the problems that are relevant to the private sector that are under government control and take remedial action (for example, modify legislation as required).

The Internet has enabled the delivery of services and information in ways that were not possible a short time ago. The characteristics of the electronic services and information are markedly different to their physical counterparts. In the same way as we are seeing new market structures in the private sector, it is likely that new government structures will emerge in the future to take advantage of the efficiencies and innovations enabled by Internet commerce.

The government on-line services framework was developed primarily for public sector service delivery, though there is no reason why it cannot be translated for use in the private sector. A number of case studies would need to be used within an industry sector in order to define the "discrete activities." A complicating factor in the private sector is the less tangible factors that need to be incorporated into the framework such as like the value placed on competitive advantage and the global reach issue.

CONCLUSION

This chapter has explored the provision of government services online. It reviewed models of Internet commerce in the private sector and derived a theoretical framework for government services. Two case studies, one on revenue collection (a component of many existing services) and another of an innovative licensing service were explored within the context of the framework to explore viability of these services. Problems with implementation of interactive systems that contain an element of complexity remain as a barrier given the lack of standardisation of the technology. One of they key findings is that governments can do a great deal to encourage Internet commerce—they can take the lead because the trust barrier does not apply to them! What they cannot do however, is afford any mistakes, and going down paths which are already available to large organisations that are trading successfully is not necessarily a useful avenue.

The issues surrounding the uptake Internet commerce are complex and cut across many different levels, including technological, social, legal and economic. There is however, a growing body of evidence that confirms the efficiencies delivered by Internet commerce, and the challenge to the public sector is to capitalise on these efficiencies, while at the same time delivering a reasonable choice to the consumer.

In an era of increasing consumer expectations, high accountability and the demand for ever more transparency of government processes, it is appropriate for governments to take a more significant role with respect to Internet commerce, and to start delivering some of the more easily attained efficiencies. It is hoped that the proposed framework makes a very small contribution towards this goal.

REFERENCES

Anders, G. (1998, 7 December) Click and Buy. *Wall Street Journal.* Retrieved 5 February 1999 from the World Wide Web: http://interactive.wsj.com/public/current/articles/SB912719949440084500.htm

Anderson, C. (1997, May). Electronic Commerce: In search of the perfect market. *The Economist,* 4-9.

Australian Bureau of Statistics. (1998). *Use of the Internet by Householders* (Catalogue No 8147.0). Canberra, Australia.

Bambury, P. (1998). A Taxonomy of Internet Commerce. *First Monday.* Retrieved 22 February 1999 from the World Wide Web: http://firstmonday.dk/issues/issue3_10/bambury.

Camp, L. J., and Sirbu, M. (1997, May). Critical Issues in Internet Commerce. *IEEE Communications Magazine,* 58-62.

Choi, S.-Y., Stahl, D. O., and Whinston, A. B. (1998). Intermediation, Contracts and Micropayments in Electronic Commerce. *Electronic Markets, 8*(1), 20-22.

Coffee, P. (1998, 2 February). Authentication risks weigh against rewards. *PC Week* Online. Retrieved 15 December 1998 from the World Wide Web: http://www.zdent.com/

pcweek/sr/0202/02auth.htm

Department of Foreign Affairs and Trade, (1999a). *Creating a Clearway on the New Silk Road*. Canberra, Australia.

Department of Foreign Affairs and Trade, (1999b). *Driving Forces on the New Silk Road*. Canberra, Australia.

Dominique, N. P. (1998). Exchange Costs as Determinants of Electronic Market Bearings. *Electronic Markets, 8*(1), 3-6.

Farquhar, B., Langmann, G., and Balfour, A. (1998). Consumer Needs in Global Electronic Commerce. *Electronic Markets, 8*(2), 9-12.

Fergusson, M., and Boo, C. T. (1998). *ePay: A Trial of Internet Payments* (Report of Information Services, ACT Department of Urban Services). Canberra: University College, UNSW.

Fergusson, M., and Quinton, P. (1997, December). *Pioneering the eLicence: a Methodology*. Paper presented at the Collecter'97, Adelaide, Australia.

Fong, T., Fowler, D., and Swatman, P. (1998). Success and Failure Factors for Implementing Effective Electronic Markets, *Electronic Markets*. 8(1), 45-47.

Garcia, D. L. (1997). Networked Commerce: Public Policy Issues in a Deregulated Communication Environment. *The Information Society, 13*(1), 17-31.

International Telecommunications Union. (1999). *Challenges to the Network: Internet for Development*. Geneva.

Jarvenpaa, S., and Todd, P. A. (1997). Consumer Reactions to Electronic Shopping on the World Wide Web. *International Journal of Electronic Commerce, 1*(2), 59-88.

Lincke, D.-M. (1998). Evaluating Integrated Electronic Commerce Systems. *Electronic Markets, 8*(1), 7-11.

Murchland, P. (1995). Inhibitors to Adoption of Electronic Commerce. *Electronic Markets, 16-17*(Nov 95), 11-12.

Picot, A., Bortenlanger, C., and Rohrl, H. (1997). Organization of Electronic Markets: Contributions for the New Institutional Economics. *The Information Society, 13*(1), 107-123.

Putnam, M. (1999). *Business Services on The Net* : Forrester Research.

Ratnasingham, P. (1997). EDI Security - Re-evaluation of Controls and its Implications on the Organizations. *Computers and Security, 16*, 650-656.

Schmid, B., and Lindemann, M. (1998, January). *Elements of a Reference Model for Electronic Markets*. Paper presented at the 31st Hawaii International Conference on System Sciences, Hawaii.

Segev, A., Gebauer, J., and Ferber, F. (1998). *Internet-base Electronic Markets* (Working Paper 98-WP-1036). Berkeley: Fisher Centre for Management and Information Technology, University of California.

Southgate, L. (1999, 25 May). Use Net or Die, Travel Agents Told. *The Australian*, pp. 24.

Timmers, P. (1998). Business Models for Electronic Markets. *Electronic Markets, 8*(2), 3-8.

U.S. Government Working Group on Electronic Commerce. (1998, April). *The Emerging Digital Economy*: US Department of Commerce.

West, L. (1998). Electronic Markets and Electronic Governments. *International Journal of Electronic Commerce, 2*(2), 5-28.

Westland, J. C., and Clark, T. H. K. (1999). *Global Electronic Commerce: Theory and Case*

Studies: MIT Press.

Wigand, R. (1997). Electronic Commerce: Definition, Theory and Context. *The Information Society, 13*(1), 1-16.

Wigand, R. T., and Benjamin, R. I. (1995). Electronic Commerce; Effects on Electronic Markets. *Journal of Computer Mediated Communication, 1*(3). Retrieved February 22, 1999 from the World Wide Web: http://www.ascusc.org/jcmc/vol1/issue3/wignad.html

Chapter XII

A Model of Internet Commerce Adoption (MICA)

Joan Cooper
University of Wollongong, Australia

Lois Burgess
University of Wollongong, Australia

INTRODUCTION

The commercialisation of the Internet has led to widespread usage of on-line services and being connected to the Internet has become a high priority for both large and small to medium size enterprises (SMEs) (Wai-Pun, Farhoomard and Tunnainen, 1997). Internet usage around the world is doubling every 10 days, with the number of people on the Internet expected to increase ten-fold from 100 million to 1 billion by 2005 (Network Wizards, 1995). The biggest transformation is in the area of e-commerce, which is expected to boom from (US) $6 billion in 1997 to more than $300 billion in 2002 (NOIE, 1998b). There is no doubt that it will be an imperative for any business to be part of the global Internet commerce community.

Doing business online provides new opportunities for business, as well as presenting new business opportunities, facilitating new forms of e-commerce across industries in both the business to consumer and business to business context. It also provides new one-one as well as the more traditional one-many customer relationships and greater opportunities for customer-supplier interaction (Rayport and Savioka, 1995). The result will be more open economies and a levelling of opportunities for all businesses. This will enable small companies to overcome the main advantages (such as economies of scale and greater access to resources) of their larger counterparts.

The proliferation of e-commerce and the exponential growth of the Internet as a commercial medium has resulted in the development of a number of frameworks that seek to enable a better understanding of what businesses are doing on the Web.

New forms of e-commerce are emerging across industries in both the business-consumer and business-business arenas. In addition there has been numerous studies and surveys undertaken to report on the status of e-commerce within SMEs (Anderson Consulting, 1998; Dowler, 1998; Poon and Jevons, 1997; Poon and Swatman, 1997; Telstra Small Business Index, 1998; Wai-Pun et al., 1997; Wales Information Society, 1998).

However, these studies have failed to address the e-commerce evolution process, that is, the way in which organisations' Web sites develop and evolve over time.

Recent research contends that "business Web site development typically begins simply and evolves over time with the addition of features as the site takes on more functionality and complexity" (Sumner and Klepper, 1998). Past empirical research of commercial web sites supports this notion. The literature reports that firms imitate what others do on the Web, partially in a desire to keep pace with competitors or to gain an advantage over competitors in one's own industry by replicating what firms have done in other industries (Sumner and Klepper, 1998; Timmers 1998). However there is a lack of academic enquiry in regard to the evolutionary process followed by SMEs in the development of commercial web sites. A Model of Internet commerce Adoption (MICA) was designed in an attempt to explain the different stages of e-commerce that SMEs pass through in the process of developing their web sites. MICA is a tool for both locating the position of an industry on the Internet Commerce Road Map and how it has progressed to that location.

In this chapter, the model, MICA is outlined. A discussion of MICA's two functions is provided: one, for identifying the stage of Internet Commerce an organisation or industry sector is at; and two, to describe the evolutionary process of development followed by organisations in reaching that stage. The Metal Fabrication Industry Sector is analysed using MICA and the results of a longitudinal study on this sector are reported. Justification for MICA's viability as a suitable model for such a study is provided and the results compared with other recent studies of SMEs and Internet commerce developments.

Figure 1: What is Internet Commerce?

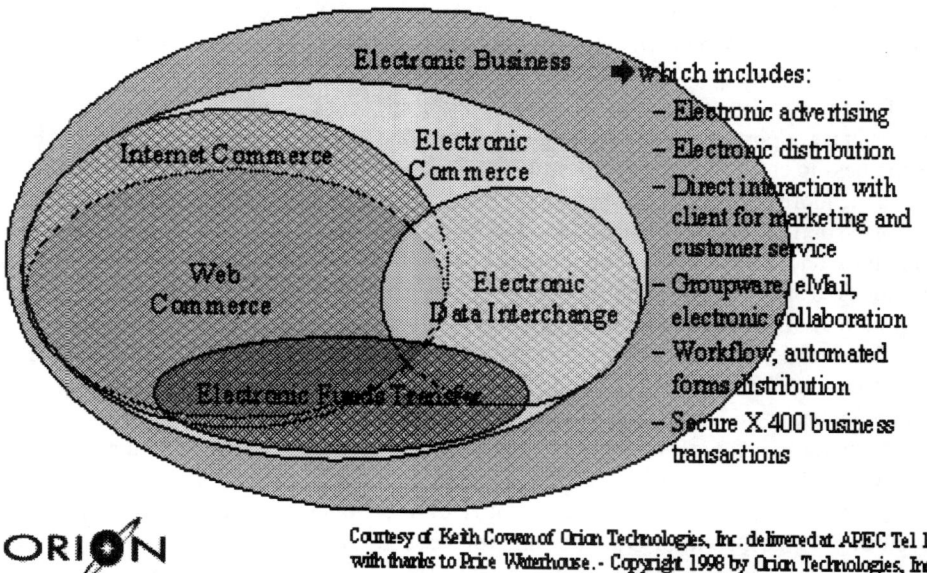

BACKGROUND

Computer-based commerce is not new, however, the application of the Internet to this electronic business process is having rapid and far-reaching effects. A new business paradigm is emerging, based on the utilisation of the Internet's open systems architecture as the transmission medium. This is in comparison to current methods that use closed systems such as proprietary networks and VANs (Value Added Networks). Figure 1 shows both the old and new computer-based business processes that comprise the larger concept of e-commerce and their relationship with respect to one another.

Internet commerce (IC) is defined as "the buying and selling of information, products and services via computer networks, today and in the future using anyone of the myriad of networks that make up the Internet" (Kalakota and Winston, 1996). It includes the delivery of information, products/services and payments over the Internet.

INTERNET COMMERCE AND SMEs

Small to medium-size enterprises make an invaluable contribution to the economy, forming an integral part of the renewal process that pervades and defines market growth. In fact, recent research contends that SMEs play a much more important role in economic growth than previously acknowledged (see for instance Storey, 1994; Admiraal, 1996).

In Australia, SMEs make up 97% of all enterprises (ABS, 1997), and more than 56% of private sector employment (Behrendorff, Fisher and Goldsworthy, 1996). Statistics on SMEs contribution to other major economies such as the USA support these figures. In the USA the number of small businesses lodging tax returns in 1995 grew by 2.3% and reached almost 22.6 million. From 1981 to 1994, the number of small businesses grew at a compound rate of 3.8% per annum (The Annual Report on Small Business and Competition, U.S. Government, Small Business Administration, Office of Advocacy, 1997).

Technological change, combined with microeconomic reform and general globalisation trends is creating a global marketplace. However, estimates state that only 1% of Australian SMEs are globalised to a major extent with a further 2-3% to a limited extent (OECD, 1997). As the argument for electronic business moves from competitiveness to survival (Crawford, 1997), it is imperative that Australia's SMEs recognise the opportunity offered by Internet Commerce as:

"Australia's' future employment, growth and prosperity depend upon it" (DIST, 1997).

The Internet provides the opportunity to increase current participation rates and consequently for the Australian SME sector to "…create wealth, develop trade and deliver services…" (DFAT, 1997; Australia.com, 1997).

At a national level it is vital that the business sector recognise the change created by information-intensive business practices and the impact this has for traditional industries. This is especially pertinent to regional areas that have depended on industries like agriculture and manufacturing. Unlike previous paradigm changes, such as steam and electricity, there is limited time for this trading opportunity to be embraced and used for the advantage of Australian business (DIST, 1997).

However, despite its potential for SMEs, recent reports centering on the adoption of Internet commerce have identified a number of barriers to uptake by this sector (Small Business Index, 1998; 1999; Anderson Consulting, 1998). One of the major barriers identified is lack of technical skills and/or expertise (Small Business Index, 1998; 1999). Other major barriers include lack of knowledge/understanding of what Internet Commerce can deliver at the business level, and cost.

JUSTIFICATION FOR THE STUDY

The impetus for the study arose from the outcome of a number of Australian Government investigations and e-commerce initiatives (DFAT 1997; NOIE 1998a, 1998b). The objectives of the study are:
1. to identify how the Metal Fabrication Industry Sector compared with national and international figures in relation to the adoption of e-commerce; and
2. how an SME organisation in this industry sector can leverage on this situation to gain a competitive advantage by incorporating an Internet trading strategy into its overall business strategy.

In order to address the objectives of the study, existing e-commerce frameworks and models were analysed and investigated as to their viability as a tool for explaining the status of Internet commerce and the process by which businesses' Web sites develop over time. Deficiencies in these models were identified and based on existing models, MICA was developed. The model was then used to analyse the Metal Fabrication Industry Sector. This industry sector is of particular importance to the Australian economy, as BHP (Australia's largest steel producer) has been at the forefront in the adoption of leading-edge EDI technologies during the 1980s and e-commerce initiatives in the 1990s. In addition, many of the studies undertaken, relating to e-commerce research and resultant models have concentrated on the service sector and other sectors where the product can be readily delivered digitally to the customer (e.g., software). In contrast, the difficulty of engaging in Internet e-commerce when a large physical good is involved is well documented particularly when the organisation needs to add-value to the physical good before shipping. The logistics of shipping large physical items are far more complex to that of shipping items such as books (the common quoted example of success on the Internet is Amazon Books). In addition, the metals industry organisations' manufacturing schedules (for adding value) are often tied to the supply chain in terms of production runs of their suppliers. Thus moving to Internet e-commerce requires considerable thought and planning with much consideration given to the possible strategic advantages to be gained.

FRAMEWORKS FOR E-COMMERCE

The proliferation of e-commerce and the exponential growth of the Internet as a commercial medium has resulted in the development of a number of frameworks that seek to enable a better understanding of what businesses are doing on the Web.

While there are a number of frameworks proposed for understanding what businesses are doing on the Web (see for instance, Quelch and Klein, 1996; Chang, Arnett, Capella and Beatty, 1997; Cappel and Myerscough, 1996; Ho, 1997; Timmers, 1998; Hoffman, Novak and Chaterjee, 1995; and APT Strategies, 1998) there is a lack of evidence and academic enquiry in regard to the evolutionary process followed by firms in the development of commercial web sites. Furthermore, there are a limited number of studies that investigate what factors determine the optimum level of functionality incorporated into Web sites.

An examination of EDI adoption models (Iacovou, Benbasat and Dexter, 1995; Ramamurthy and Premkumar, 1995; and Senn, 1996) provides a useful starting point for understanding what factors influence the adoption of Internet commerce technologies. From these models more recent research conducted by Lim, Gan and Wei (1998) has resulted in the development of the Integrated Model of Internet commerce which has been used to assess the level of adoption of Internet Commerce technologies in organisations. This model centres on the factors influencing the organisation's adoption of innovative web technologies.

Timmers (1998), in his study of commercial Web sites identified 11 business models: e-shop; e-procurement; e-auction; third-party marketplace; virtual community; value chain provider; value-chain integrator; collaborative platforms and information brokerage. Timmers proposes that some of these sites are merely simple electronic implementations of traditional business models, while others are 'value-add' sites facilitating information management incorporating high level functionality.

Ho's (1997) study of business use of the Web utilised a 3 x 4 dimensional matrix model. Ho dimensioned his model by business process: promotion, provision and processing, and by value creation for the customer. The customer value dimensions include timely, custom, logistic and sensational. Ho then evaluated 1,800 Web sites according to his model and concluded that at least 24% of the sites surveyed were engaged in some form of business processing.

Quelch and Klein (1996) proposed two types of web site, based on content. According to Quelch and Klein (1996), Web site functionality incorporates either information support or transaction processing. Their study found that information support sites were clearly evident on the Web; however, sites supporting business transaction processing were embryonic in their development.

Cappel and Myerscough (1996) in contrast to Quelch and Klein (1996) proposed that 5 types of sites were evident and categorised these as marketplace awareness, customer support, sales, advertising and information provision.

The APT Strategies (1997) research found that the organisations they studied were using their Web site for multiple business applications. Evidence of at least six business models was found and further, that an average of 2.7 of these models were selected by each organisation.

In a study of Fortune 500 company Web sites, Chang et al. (1997) found that only two-thirds owned a Web site. Functionality of the sites maintained was limited to three categories: promotion of the company (86.1%), provision of product and/or services via the Web (93.2%) and on-line business transactions (26.6%).

An analysis of the different methods of classifying Internet e-commerce Business Models identified weaknesses with each. For example Ho's (1997) model was too complex for many of the sites investigated in the study. A majority of the web sites studied would have fallen into the top left-hand corner of Ho's matrix. The APT (1997) model appeared too simplistic in nature. It did not provide an indicator of the level of maturity of the industry with regard to Internet e-commerce activities. In addition, it includes model options not relevant to all industry sectors (for example, subscriptions). Thus, the strengths of some models were combined to define MICA. While MICA does not incorporate as much complexity as Ho's model, it is easier to understand and it can be used to reflect more accurately the level of maturity of Internet e-commerce both from an industrial sector and a single business perspective.

MICA proposes that in developing commercial web sites, organisations typically start simply by establishing a 'presence' on the Web and build on functionality over time (as the level of technical skill/expertise in the use of Internet technologies increases). In addition, as web sites build on complexity, so will the number of modules incorporated into the site increase. Notions proposed by Sumner & Klepper (1998) and Timmers (1998) support this concept. Cisco Systems Global Networked business model (Cisco On-line, http://www.cisco.com/) is a good example of this approach to Internet commerce development). MICA (Burgess and Cooper, 1998) was developed to explain how business's Web sites develop to incorporate aspects of Internet commerce. MICA (Figure 2) consists of three layered stages and incorporates the three levels of business process of Ho's model (promotion, provision and processing) and is similar to the classification applied by Chang et al. (1997). The stages of development also incorporate some of the attributes of APT's model and provide a roadmap that indicates where a business or industry sector is in its development of IC applications.

As sites move through the stages of development from inception (promotion) through

Figure 2: Model of Internet Commerce Adoption (MICA)

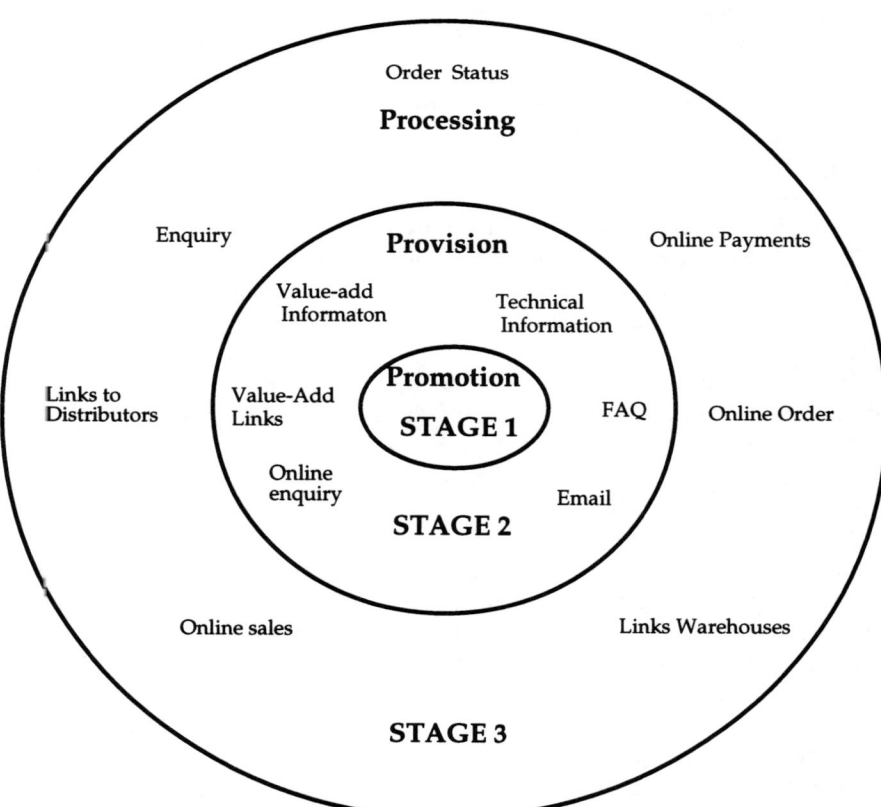

Figure 3: Internet Commerce (IC) Roadmap

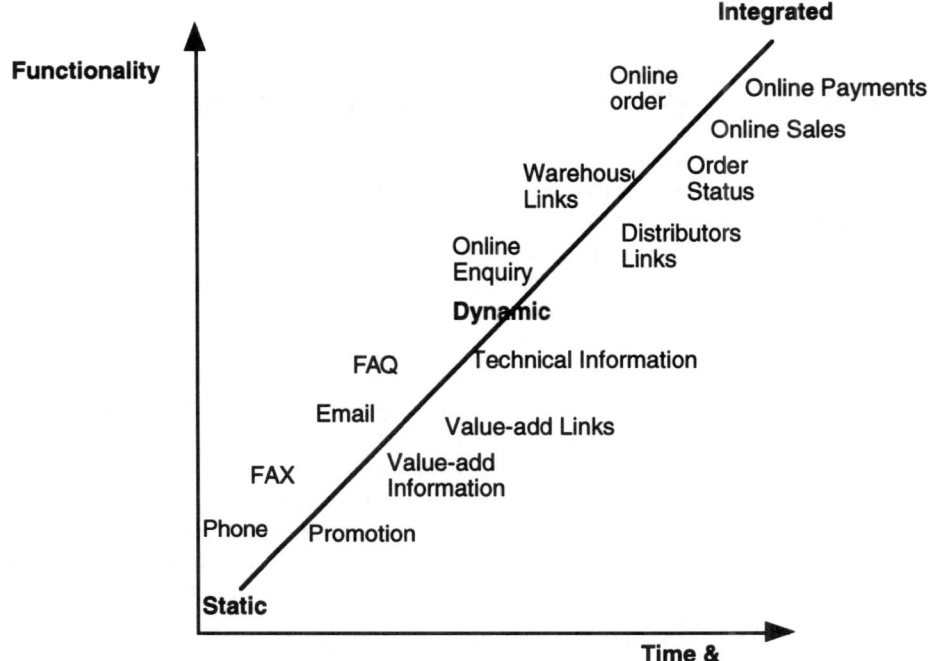

consolidation (provision) to maturity (processing) layers of complexity and functionality are added to the site. This addition of layers is synonymous with the businesses moving from having an Internet presence (static), basic information provision, to embracing Internet Commerce fully (dynamic) with a site incorporating value chain integration and innovative applications to add value through information management and rich functionality (Timmers, 1998). At this stage the organisation has a fully integrated site that includes online ordering, order status tracking, online sales and online payments.

MICA's staged approach to the development of commercial web sites is an approach well accepted within IS history that is growth occurs by adding functionality. However, the increase in complexity of functionality as sites move from Stage 1 to Stage 3 is also a reflection of the enhancement of customer service, a concept supported by recent literature that suggests growth occurs through focusing on customer needs. (Lawrence, Corbitt, Tidwell, Fisher and Lawrence, 1998; Sterne, 1996). BHP Steel Australia provides an excellent example of this approach in that they have fostered customer involvement throughout the design process (BHP Steel, http://www.bhp.com.au).

Figure 3 provides an alternative representation of MICA. It more clearly depicts the evolutionary process of Web site development. The horizontal axis represents time and complexity and the vertical axis represents functionality. At inception firms usually have a static flat site mainly containing promotional material. Over time the site develops in complexity and functionality, evolving from static pages to dynamic pages.

MICA can be used to position both an organisation and a whole industry sector on the IC Road Map. It also provides a clear map of the evolution process, that is, the way in which organisation's Web sites develop and evolve over time to reach a position on the IC Road Map.

SURVEY OF THE METAL FABRICATION INDUSTRY SECTOR

An extensive Internet search was conducted from March to May 1998 to ascertain the stage of adoption of Internet commerce in the Metal Fabrication Industry sector. The search entailed seeking firms globally that either manufactured and/or distributed metal, steel, stainless steel, pipes and other steel products. A total of 186 commercial Web sites were identified as meeting the criteria. MICA was then used to assess the level of development of these commercial Web sites.

The aim of the study was to provide a point-in-time 'snapshot' of this industry sector's stage of adoption of Internet commerce. Table 1 provides an indication of where the 186 firms pages evaluated fit into each of the stages represented in MICA. All sites incorporated the functional attributes of the first stage of development

The study also revealed that the metal fabrication industry sector had firms represented at all stages of Internet commerce adoption. While many of the firms surveyed were clearly operating in Stage 1 and others were moving toward Stage 2, a very small proportion only were located in the outer circle, Stage 3.

Table 1: Results of All Pages Surveyed

	Percentage
Stage 1	100
Stage 2	55.9
Stage 3	4.8

The results of the survey clearly demonstrated that a number of organisations in the metals manufacturing/distribution industry sector were just beginning to embrace Internet commerce. These firms are located either in the centre of the MICA, Stage 1, or just outside the perimeter of the first circle, that is, just entering Stage 2. Those organisations at the centre (Stage 1) mostly had a one-page Web site with their company name and contact details, which in a small number of cases was an e-mail, but well over 50% had contact details that were not online, that is, a phone and fax number (static sites). These results are consistent with Quelch and Klein's 1996 findings.

The data collected from the study clearly indicates that all sites had some form of promotion. However, this varied from 5% of pages utilising simple one-page advertisements with a contact, usually not on-line to a large majority, more than 90%, having basic company profiles with some product details and an e-mail for contact for further information. Often "further information" involved provision of a facility for ordering a hard copy of catalogues. Some sites were extremely sophisticated in design, but still only provided information (albeit very rich and detailed) on the company.

Those firms whose pages were classified at Stage 2 of development had all of the above, but also provided value-add in terms of feedback on enquires (both technical and products), access to technical assistance, full product descriptions, FAQ, on-line quotes and links to related sites and industry associations.

The 4.8% that were classified in Stage 3 included full on-line services, such as on-line ordering, sales, payments and order status tracking. It was difficult to evaluate the extent of the full on-line processing capabilities as most (95%) Stage 3 sites had this functionality secured behind login and password-protected access. Only one of these sites was found to have on-line processing functions accessible. This included order payment and order status tracking facilities.

ANALYSIS OF METAL INDUSTRY SURVEY RESULTS BY CONTINENT

Table 2 contains results of the evaluation of pages by continent. It is interesting to note that all the companies listed in the Asia region basically fit into Stage 1 of the MICA. Some very large and well-known steel producers appeared here (Nippon, Krakatau, Kobe). While they had extremely sophisticated graphics and extensive information about their company and activities, their sites had no interactivity or functionality. Most contacts for these sites were via the Webmaster, which in most cases was not in the form of direct contact to the organisation, but to the company that had developed and maintained the Web pages. This is in stark contrast to the USA, where 7.3% of the sites had full on-line services including ordering, sales and payments. It is interesting to note that these large steel producers in Asia, like BHP Steel (Australia), also trade via VAN's utilising EDI. However, unlike BHP Steel (Australia) and some companies in the USA, the Asian companies have not yet ventured into Internet e-commerce.

As can be seen from Table 2 some firms (64.3%) throughout Europe have moved from Stage 1 of the MICA into Stage 2. All regions accept Asia and others had over 50% of sites developed to Stage 2 level. The extent to which these sites provided features classified at Stage 2 varied greatly. Many (more than 80%) organisations provided minimum value-add services, indicating that the industry sector still has a significant way to go before reaching maturity.

Of the sites found in the USA engaged in Stage 3 Internet commerce (maturity) only 1 had an open environment allowing for assessment of the functionality available. The remainder have chosen a "closed-shop approach." To gain access to the on-line trading facility, customers must register and obtained a login and password.

Table 2: Sites Surveyed by Continent

	Stage 1	Stage 2	Stage 3	% Stage 2	% Stage 3
USA	110	68	8	61.8	7.3
Africa	3	2	0	66.7	0.0
Europe	28	18	1	64.3	3.6
UK	6	3	0	50.0	0.0
Asia	18	0	0	0.0	0.0
Australia	16	13	0	81.3	0.0
Other	5	0	0	0.0	0.0
Total	186	104	9	55.9	4.8

COMPARISON OF SURVEY RESULTS WITH OTHER RECENT STUDIES

The findings from the study indicate that this industry sector is lagging behind other industries in Internet e-commerce adoption. The findings of a number of recent studies lend support to this result. Sumner and Klepper's (1998) study of the Web sites of 23 organisations in the Midwest region of the US (of which six were manufacturing firms) found that out of the 16 firms that responded to their survey only one firm provided on-line transaction processing on their site. Dowler (1998), in his study of SME organisations in regional NSW, Australia found that for the manufacturing industry sector, only 14% of the 30 firms studied having Web presence provided transaction processing facilities, placing them at varying levels of stage 3 of MICA. His study also concluded that 100% of firms engaged in Internet Commerce were engaged in promotion (Stage 1) and 57% in provision (Stage 2).

The Small Business Index (1999) survey of SMEs and Internet commerce developments found:
- 9% of all small businesses and 13% of all medium businesses indicate that they are already purchasing from their suppliers via E-commerce;
- 17% and 24% respectively, have already used e-commerce to buy goods and services, such as books, computer software, videos/CDs and computer hardware;
- 14% and 29% respectively, have been prompted by their customers to consider adopting e-commerce;
- as already noted, 12% and 18% respectively, have established facilities to sell over the Internet; and
- a further 14% and 20% respectively, report that they are extremely or very interested in e-commerce.

Ho's (1997) survey involved surveying 40 different industry categories in the USA from accounting, to electronics, construction and wine/spirits. The sector that most closely related to the metals/steel sector was the construction sector. In this sector, Ho found at least 8% engaging in some type of business processing online. This compares favourably to the 7.3% US firms found at Stage 3 development in this survey. Service industry categories or categories where "goods" could be provided online or distributed easily had much higher percentages of processing on-line. Such categories as newspapers/magazines were as high as 56% while music was 32% and software 44%. The reason for this disparity may be that in contrast to the music and software industries, the nature of manufacturing in terms of the logistics of adding value to manufactured products and the distribution of large shipments of goods does not lend itself to a simple Internet commerce solutions.

LONGITUDINAL STUDY OF THE METAL INDUSTRY SECTOR

Although this study was limited to a single industry sector, and involved a point-in-time study, the results provide a useful 'snapshot' of the process businesses follow in the development of commercial Web sites. It also provided a useful mechanism for positioning this industry sector on the road map of IC and for comparison with other industry sectors.

To validate MICA, an additional study was undertaken in April 1999. As many as possible of the original 186 sites visited in April 1998 were revisited. The intention of the second study was to document the progress of Web site development in the Metals Industry Sector over the past 12 months.

In April 1999 a total of 75 sites were reanalysed. For a variety of reasons only 75 of the original sites were reevaluated. Some of the original 186 sites were pages listed by industry associations; these were not reanalyzed. Some of the original URLs could not be found. This may be due to relocation of the URLs or closure of the sites. Some of the sites were "UNDER CONSTRUCTION," meaning they were being upgraded, an assumption being that they were not only being redesigned, but that functionality was being increased.

Of the 75 sites analysed, 90% had a range of the Stage 2 functions implemented, this compared with 56% of sites in 1998. More importantly, while the 1999 survey only revisited five of the original 18 Asian sites all, five had progressed to Stage 2 and one site displayed evidence of the first signs of Stage 3. Given the 18 sites were all at Stage 1 in 1998 this provides strong evidence to support MICA.

Only 13 of the original 28 European sites were reanalysed. All 13 sites had Stage 2 functionality implemented and three also had evolved to Stage 3. By comparison, in 1998 only one of the European sites had reached Stage 3. The seven Australian sites revisited were all Stage 2 capable and one had evolved from Stage 2 in 1998 to Stage 3 in 1999.

In the USA only 48 sites were reanalysed, 42 were Stage 2 capable and eight were fully operational in Stage 3. The longitudinal study indicates that a number of the organisations initially reviewed in 1998 have progressed from Stage 1 to Stage 2. In addition, a smaller number have progressed from Stage 2 to Stage 3. These results validate MICA as a suitable model for describing the process followed in the evolution of organisations' (in the metal fabrication industry sector) Web site IC capabilities.

CONCLUSION AND FUTURE RESEARCH

The outcome of the research clearly supports the staged approach to development of commercial Web sites as proposed by MICA. Additionally, the results of the studies conducted in 1998 and 1999 demonstrate the value of MICA as a tool to position either an organisation or an industry sector on the Internet Commerce Road Map. It also serves as a tool for comparative analyses between organisations or industry sectors.

Although this study was limited to a single industry sector, it provides a valuable 'snapshot' of the process followed by organisations in the development of commercial Web sites. Future research could extend the use of MICA across a range of industry sectors and organisations (for example larger businesses) to further validate the model

REFERENCES

(ABS) Australian Bureau of Statistics (1997). *Characteristics of Small Business.*
Admiraal, P.H. Ed (1996). *Small Business in the Modern Economy.* Blackwell, Oxford, UK.
Anderson Consulting (1998). *eCommerce: Our Future Today, A review of eCommerce in Australia.*
APT Strategies (1997). *Strategic Internet Business Study*, December. (URL: http://www.apstrategies.com.au/review/researchmethod.htm).

Australia's Future Online (1997) (URL: http://www.acsi.au/publicat/australi.htm)

Behrendorff, G., Fisher, J. &Goldsworthy, M. (1996). *Advice on Electronic Commerce Programs for Small to Medium Enterprises*. Prepared for the Department of Industry, Science and Tourism by the Centre for Electronic Commerce, Monash University.

Burgess, L. and Cooper, J. (1998). The Status of Internet Commerce in the Manufacturing Industry in Australia: A survey of Metal Fabrication Industries. *Proceedings of CollECTeR'98*, 65-73.

Cappel, J. and Myerscough, M. (1996). World Wide Web uses for Electronic Commerce: Toward a Classification Scheme, *AIS Conference Proceedings,* August.

Chang L., Arnett, R. P., Capella, L. M. and Beatty, R.C. (1997). Web Sites of Fortune 500 Companies: Facing Customers through Home Pages. *Information and Management*, 31, .335-345.

Crawford, J. (1998). *Networked Enterprise Web Strategy: A Project to Get Smaller Enterprises On-line*. Report written for The Department of Industry, Science & Tourism and Tradegate ECA. (URL: http://www.dist.gov.au/infoind/busonline/gbo.pdf)

(DFAT) Department of Foreign Affairs and Trade (1997). *Putting Australia on the New Silk Road: The Role of Trade Policy in Advancing Electronic Commerce*. (URL: http://www.dfat.gov.au/bookshelf/html/silk_exec.htm)

(DIST) Department of Industry, Science and Tourism (1998). *stats. electronic commerce in Australia*. (URL: http://www.dist.gov.au/infoind/stats/ecostat.pdf)

Dowler, B. (1998). *Internet Based Electronic Commerce and SMEs in the Illawarra Region*. School of Information Technology and Computer Science, University of Wollongong, Australia, November.

Ho, J. (1997). Evaluating the WWW: A Global Study of Commercial Sites. *Journal of Computer Mediated Communication*, 3(1), June. (URL: http://www.ascusc.org/jcmc/vol3/issue1/ho.html).

Hoffman, D.L., Novak, T.P. and Chaterjee, P. (1995). Commercial Scenarios for the Web: Opportunities and Challengers. *Journal of Computer Mediated Communication*, 1(3). (URL: http://www.ascusc.org/jcmc/vol1/issue3/hoffman.html).

Iacovou, C.L., Benbasat, I. and Dexter, A.S. (1995). Electronic Data Interchange and Small Organisations: Adoption and Impact of Technology. *MIS Quarterly*, Dec.

Kalakota, R. and Whinston, A.B. (1997). *Electronic Commerce - A Managers Guide*, Addison Wesley, USA.

Lawrence, E., Corbitt, B., Tidwell, A., Fisher, J. and Lawrence, J.R. (1998). *Internet Commerce: Digital Models for Business*. John Wiley and Sons, Brisbane.

Lim, L, Gan, B and Wei, K (1998). An Integrated Model on the Adoption of Internet for Commercial Purposes. *Proceedings of IEEE Thirty First Hawaii International Conference on Systems Sciences*, Hawaii.

Network Wizards (1997). *Internet Domain Survey*. (URL: http://www.nw.come/zone/www/report.html).

(NOIE) National Office for the Information Economy (1998a). *A Strategic Framework for The Information Economy*, December. (URL: http://www.noie.gov.au/docs/strategy/strategicframework.html)

(NOIE) National Office for the Information Economy (1998b). *Report on EC Summit'*, Canberra, April 16-17.

(OECD) Organisation for Economic Cooperation and Development (1997). *Globalisation and Small to Medium Enterprises (SMEs)*, Vol.2, Country Studies.

Poon, S. and Jevons, C. (1997). *International Entrepreneurship Opportunities For Small Business Using the Internet*, Swinbourne University of Technology.

Poon, S. and Swatman, P. (1997). *Internet-based Small Business Communication: Seven Australian Cases*. Department of Information Systems, Monash University Australia.

Quelch, J. and Klein, L. (1996). The Internet and International Marketing. *Sloan Management Review*, Spring.

Storey, D.J. (1994). *Understanding the Small Business Sector*. Rutledge, London, UK.

Ramamurthy, K. and Premkumar, G. (1995). Determinants and Outcomes of Electronic Data Interchange Diffusion. *IEEE Transactions on Engineering Management*, 42(4), Decca, pp 325-347.

Rayport, J. F. and Savioka, J. J. (1995). Exploiting the Virtual Value Chain. *Harvard Business Review*, Nov-Dec, 75-851.

Senn, A. J. (1996). Capitalizing on Electronic Commerce: The Role of the Internet in Electronic Markets. *Information Systems Management*, 13(3), Summer.

Sterne, J/ (1996). *Customer Service on the Internet: Building Relationships, Increasing Loyalty and Staying Competitive*, Wiley Computer Publishing, NY.

Sumner, M. and Klepper, R. (1998). Business Strategy and the Use of Web Sites. *Proceedings of First International Conference on Telecommunications and Electronic Commerce* (ICTEC) November.

Telstra Small Business Index, (1998). *Survey of Electronic Commerce in Australian Small and Medium Businesses*, April. (URL: http://www.pacificaccess.com.au/sbi/).

Telstra Small Business Index (1999). *Survey of Electronic Commerce in Australian Small and Medium Businesses*, May. (URL: http://www.pacificaccess.com.au/sbi/)

Timmers, P. (1998). Business Models for Electronic Markets. *Electronic Markets*, 8(2).

US Government, (1997). Small Business Administration, Office of Advocacy, *The Annual Report on Small Business and Competition*.

Wai-Pun, M., Farhoomard, A. and Tuunainen,V. (1997). A Preliminary Investigation of Business Opportunities. *Proceedings of PAWEC '97*, Brisbane, Australia. (URL: http://www.collecter.org/paweccpg.html).

Wales Information Society (1998). *E-ssential for Business, A survey of the use of Information Technology in Welsh Firms*. (URL: http://www.wis.org.uk).

Chapter XIII

E-Retailing: New Opportunities in Internet Commerce

Ly Fie Sugianto and Sen Sendjaya
Monash University, Australia

Internet commerce has brought forward a new spectrum of business practice. It radically changes the way we do business. These changes have been fairly impulsive and inevitable. Limitations caused by traditional commercial practices, such as barriers to reach the whole target market due to geographical distance, and high transaction costs due to engagement costs for attorney, agent and broker involvement, are no longer major issues as businesses become adept at identifying mechanisms to create and deliver value. In view of this new trend, a critical question to be answered is, what is the implication of Internet commerce on the conventional way of conducting business? Has Internet commerce changed the retailing market by eliminating the intermediaries out of the transaction chain? Or, has it defined new roles for the retail industries and intermediaries? This chapter attempts to reveal the impact of Internet commerce to discover new opportunities and identify challenges, in particular, for the intermediaries. It presents a physical and virtual model of business environment and highlights the business areas which would have been affected the most by the introduction of on-line services. The discussion in this chapter is aimed to enable the reader to evaluate the trends, the gains and the losses resulting from Internet commerce in today's competitive business environment.

THE EMERGING TRENDS OF INTERNET COMMERCE

Over the course of four years since 1996, the number of worldwide Internet users has grown from three to 50 million, and by the year 2000, it is expected to reach 100 million (PriceWaterhouseCoopers, 1999). Internet and its inherent possibility to be exploited as a commercial means ought to be taken into consideration very seriously by business organizations. Indeed, most companies plan to engage the Internet technology in their businesses, although their approaches and levels of implementations vary in degrees. Some companies only embrace e-commerce in business-to-business activities, bypassing all paper-based transactions. Others which concern with business-to-customer Internet commerce dealings establish their presence on the Internet – by having a simple corporate homepage to inform the prospective customers about the business, or by having a Web store, which includes e-mail and purchase order forms for the customers to interact with the customer services or product sales departments.

Thus, it can be expected that the number of transactions made on the Internet would increase rapidly, especially with the evolvement of various enabling technologies to support Internet commerce. Moreover, the infrastructure of the information superhighway enables the trading of a group of commodities readily, for instance in transactions that only involve exchanging documents or data and transferring knowledge. Despite the potential growth in the use of the Internet as a powerful information-trading place, Internet commerce has also becoming very popular for the other type of commodity: the physical goods. The fact is that we do not live out of knowledge and information alone, and therefore, it is not surprising that the Internet would be exploited as the trading place for physical goods.

Consequently, a primary element in the value chain which makes Internet commerce feasible is the logistics support. In fact, restructuring of logistics supports to deliver the product to the customers is a field of opportunity upon realizing the e-commerce significance. Imagine the number of cars parked at the parking lot of a giant bookstore; now, that is roughly the number of deliveries which ought to be done if the customers of the bookstore choose to do their shopping from home. Thus, when dealing with physical goods, the critical constraint in any commercial system is the delivery of the product to the buyer. Companies must realize that their e-commerce strategy should not only be focused on utilizing the Internet merely to accept orders, but they must aim to ensure product availability and meeting schedule of delivery accurately. This is a challenge to those companies. But, it also has created new opportunities for delivery firms to cater for better inventory management, routing and delivery services; likewise, the suppliers are also demanded to have more flexible production systems, robust inventory management and prompt delivery services to the retailers.

It is both interesting and useful to appraise the forthcoming challenges brought by Internet commerce, in particular, for the retail industry and others in their roles as intermediaries.

SCOPE OF THE DISCUSSION

Internet Commerce – The Definition

It is necessary to distinguish the terms e-commerce, e-business and Internet commerce at the very start of the discussion. This is in order to set a thinking framework in the mind of the reader.

There is a range of definitions for e-commerce relative to its perspective, may it be communications, business process, service or in the context of on-line business (Kalakota, 1997). Kalakota (1996) defined e-commerce as "the buying and selling of information, products and services via computer networks". An extension to the definition is given by Bloch et al. (1999) as "support for any kind of business transactions over a digital infrastructure." While e-commerce encompasses business activities that is conducted electronically, such as using the World Wide Web, the multimedia interactive component of the Internet, telephone lines, leased lines and wireless, e-business can be understood as a superior set which extends the understanding of e-commerce to reflect the vision of the organization, including the philosophy, the markets and the value of the organizations. Internet or the information superhighway, has been well understood as the enabler or the enabling technology. Subsequently, Internet commerce refers to the marketing, selling and buying of products and services on the Internet. In this chapter, the term "e-commerce" is sometimes used interchangeably with "Internet commerce".

Frame of Reference

Having presented the above as our point of departure, the discussion in this chapter will be confined on the identification of opportunities and impacts on the retail industries and intermediaries caused by the Internet, in particular, those which arise upon the introduction of on-line trading or the World Wide Web component of the Internet.

In order to probe the emerging trends in the retail industry, it is helpful to set a frame of reference to characterize the nature of the business environment. Figure 1 depicts a frame of reference with two extreme ends, namely the physical world and the virtual world (Choi et al., 1997). The three components which constitute a business model: players or agents, products and processes, are the variables in the marketplace. In this frame of reference, the conventional way of doing business is represented by the extreme left of the axis. The introduction of the electronic medium, including the Internet, extends the domain of the three variables. Therefore, the three business components can be virtual in nature. Table 1 lists the examples of the physical and virtual natures of these components which have taken place today.

As portrayed in Figure 1, we can identify two extreme sectors in today's market. One is the conventional business where the three variables occupy the left hand side of the axis; this is when the players, products and processes are all physical. The other scenario is when

Figure 1. Frame of Reference Portraying the Nature of the Business Environment

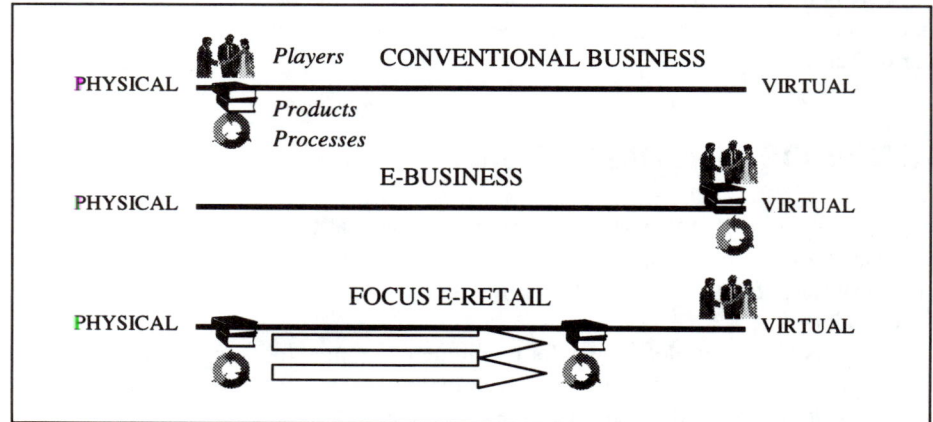

the three variables are at the other extreme representing on-line trading. The last scenario in Figure 1 signifies the business sectors which have adopted the e-commerce enabling technologies in business practices. Note that in the last diagram in Figure 1:
- The players are all online because the sellers and the buyers meet on the Internet
- The products can be physical products, commodity-like products or information-rich products, but not purely digitised. In the diagram, the axis has been marked with an arrow. As pointed out earlier, this chapter limits the discussion and excludes the impact of e-commerce on digitised products which can be fully supported by virtual processes.
- The processes have been defined to include both physical process as well as online because we wish to examine the impact of online retailing, including retailing of physical products, in which the delivery and stock control are carried out in physical world.

The above becomes our area of interest since, in real life, most of commodities in trading are mainly physical or tangible goods.

Some Implications

The implications of the distinguishing nature of the three business components can be summarised as follows:

How prevalent the Internet would be in the business practice of an organization depends on the nature of the **products**, that is whether the products and services are information-rich or commodity-like, the **players** in the business arena, that is whether or not the target market is among the primary users of the Internet, and the business **processes**, that is whether or not the business activities can be fully supported by the Internet.

The deployment of the e-commerce enabling technologies is very advantageous for the **information-rich** products and services. The whole business practice of organizations which trades information-rich products and services would have been impacted by this

Table 1. Examples of Physical and Virtual Players, Products and Processes

	Physical	**Virtual**
Players or agents –		
Buyers	*Shoppers*	*On-line buyers*
Sellers	*Shops in department stores*	*Web stores*
Intermediaries	*Newsagent, Supermarket*	*Search service*
Products -		
Commodities	*Newspapers, Magazines*	*On-line newspapers, E-zines*
Processes -		
Product Selection	*Browsing through the supermarket aisles*	*Browsing through the internet using search engines*
Advertising	*Billboard*	*Homepage*
Payment	*Cash money, Credit card*	*Cybercash, E-cash, Millicent*

trend. For **commodity-like products**, the Internet can be perceived as an alternative distribution channel. The less commodity-like the product is, the more attractive the Internet can be used as a business vehicle.

Some Experiences in Internet Commerce

This subsection includes a series of success stories as well as discouraging experiences of a number of companies in their e-commerce practices. They will be examined as case studies using the frame of reference introduced earlier. (Note that in some cases, "online buyers or players" refer more accurately to "avid computer users," not merely buyers who use the Internet to shop.)

- Case 1: Dell has been among the top ten companies which have reaped huge profit on Internet Commerce. As published in the NUA Internet Surveys (1999), in the first quarter of 1999, Internet sales at Dell Computers exceeded US$18 million per day. Internet sales accounted for 30% of the total revenue.
- Case 2: Kambil in IEEE Computer (1997) reported that in January 1997, Cisco Connection Online received 13% of the company's product orders online and sold products at a rate of more than $200 million a year. The leader in networking products projected US$3 billion in 1998 on-line sales through its innovative connection online Web site, which tied suppliers and customers in a highly integrated value chain (Ticoll & Tapscott, *Outlook Magazine*, 1998). The investment in leveraging the suppliers-partners-customers relationships delivers a phenomenal $585,000 in revenue per employee.
- Case 3: Online share trading has become so popular in the U.S. that there are now several Internet services to help investors simply select best stockbroker to use. Brokers, varying from Suretrade, Ameritrade and Stocks4less, at the cheap end, to Schwab, Fidelity WebXpress, Etrade and JB Oxford at the top, saturate television business channels with their advertisements (Deans, The Australian Financial Review [TAFR], 30 March 1998). Lombard, a discount broker, once offered a discount in commission when the transaction was done via the Internet (Sterett & Shah, Sams Advanced Management Journal [SAMJ], 1998 winter).
- Case 4: Using the E-Cash system, Stamps.AU ensures secure e-commerce transactions offering Internet shoppers the entire range of Australian stamps and philatelic accessories online. Since its establishment in January 1997, a $6,000 investment has generated over $8,000 in sales revenue in the first year (Phillips, 1997).
- Case 5: Choi et al. (1997) and Crawford (TAFR, 30 March 1998) reported that areas of opportunity also exist for travel agencies and on-line pharmacies to utilize the Internet as their consumers' access.
- Case 6: In contrast to the above, Ernst & Young reported that only 7 percent of U.S. households had made purchases online. They also found that the majority of retailers and manufacturers had no plans to sell their products online (Davidson, TAFR, 30 March 998).
- Case 7: Grover (Business Review Weekly [BRW], 9 April 1999) reported that Borders, U.S. second largest chain of bookstores went online in May 1998, but its overall operation is rather pessimistic and that web profit may never come.

Some remarks are listed in Table 2. The most profitable sector of e-commerce is taken up by those organizations which deal with digitised products since the trading of such products is fully supported by the technology. However, the case examples indicate that organizations that trade physical goods commercially to the on-line buyers are among those that earn huge profit. Several articles (Phillips, 1997; Davidson, 1998; Crawley, 1998; Andersen Consulting, 1998) reported that the most common items bought on the Web are computer-related products, books, entertainment and travel. Hence, when the target market is avid computer users, businesses have good opportunities to succeed (Case 1 and Case 2, in contrast to Case 6); whether or not they sell digital or physical products; although, the information rich product has bigger chance to sell successfully in online trading (Case 3 and Case 5). Still, the two factors identified above: whether or not there are online buyers and whether or not the products can be sold online are not the only prerequisite for success trading as shown in Case 7. There are other factors to be considered, as revealed later in the Amazon vs. Barnes & Noble case.

In view of business process, the Internet can be perceived as the enabling technology. Some even argues that the technology is entirely the business driver. Again, these two arguments may both be correct. For the market segment coinciding with the core of the e-commerce, the role of the technology is the driver, whereas for the opposite extreme, the technology may accomplish the role of supporting tool, a new distribution channel. Internet as a new business channel has been a common and widely accepted concept because it offers organizations unique ways to enhance operating efficiency and reduce costs. This is especially true for the majority of the business sectors. Although it may not be profitable instantly, as experienced by many, it is believed that companies will be unprofitable not to be on it. The Internet can be a threat to established companies if it is not utilized.

On that note, it is worth pointed out that the frame of reference has also exhibited an interestingly changing characteristic of today's market: that of physical to a virtual one, as shown in Figure 2. Some opportunities and challenges identified from this trend are highlighted below:

- Internet Commerce enables new markets, a new way of on-line buyers and sellers meet and exchange transactions.
- Johnson & Schreck (Outlook Magazine, 1997) stated that for most industries, e-commerce will ultimately redefine how they create new products and bring them to market, how they acquire customers for these products and then support them, and

Table 2: Remarks on the case studies

Case 1 :	successful, target market exist online (online players), physical goods, semi online process.
Case 2 :	successful, online players, physical goods, online process.
Case 3 :	successful, online players, online process, information (intangible) product.
Case 4 :	successful, online players, physical goods, semi online process.
Case 5 :	potential to be successful, online players, online process, information (travel agency) and information rich (pharmacy) products.
Case 6 :	unsuccessful, target market is household shoppers, physical product, semi online process.
Case 7 :	unsuccessful, online players, physical product, semi online process.

Figure 2. Physical Market and Virtual Market

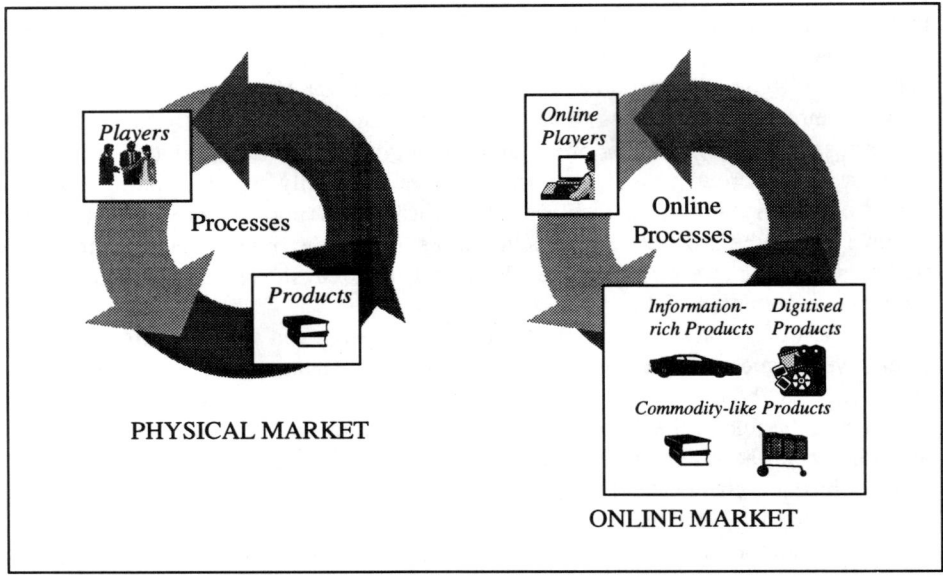

how they engage with end-customers, suppliers and alliance partners.
- For information-rich products and services, Internet commerce forms new product lines employing electronic media as part of the business vehicle, such as the search engine Yahoo, Alta Vista and other Internet directories. Thompson-Sun Interactive has introduced technologies that enable the development and delivery of interactive applications for digital broadcast television (Johnson and Schreck, Outlook Magazine, 1997). Blockbuster Video aimed for long-term strategic benefit by experimenting with high-speed communication links to VCRs with fast recording capabilities so that customers who want to rent an out-of-stock video can get a newly recorded version in minutes from Blockbuster's headquarters (Lipoff and Jens, Telecommunications, June 1996). Blockbuster's business strategy would not only build customer loyalty and reputation, but also enhance the convenience in their service. Ultimately, this would lead Blockbuster one step ahead in the electronic marketplace.
- With the emergence of the "Third-Party Marketplace" and "Cyber Shopping Mall" as the virtual place of trading and the "Virtual Communities" as the buyers and the sellers, the "Value Chain Service Provider" (VCSP) is a virtual entity (agent) which offers specific service, such as for electronic payment, stock management and logistics. The VCSP has been perceived to have a distinctive advantage in Internet commerce.
- Adaptation to the e-commerce area is not that simple and may result in a huge penalty if organizations are not careful in their planning. For example, an establishment of an Internet channel instead of EDI may be advantageous in terms of customer service channels as it enables the development of a corporate Web site. However, companies must also be aware and responsive to the advancement of the technology and be prepared to update and compete according to the trend. This often demands more resources which should not be overlooked by organizations.

- Lipoff and Jens (Telecommunications, June 1996) compiled a list of barriers of employing e-commerce and how to address them. They present examples of technological, institutional, regulatory, economic, social and structural barriers and recommended actions to cope with these barriers.
- Forrester Research, a popular seer of e-Commerce, estimates consumer driven online sales will grow to US$7.17 billion by 2000, up from US$530 million in 1996. Davidson (TAFR, 30 March 1998) predicted that Business to Business transactions will grow from US$600 million in 1996 to US$55.47 billion by 2000. This is a very attractive indicator for online businesses.

INTERNET FOR ELECTRONIC RETAILING

Previously, the Internet was only used for noncommercial activities, such as military, communication, education, research and entertainment sectors. It was not long before the technology infrastructure was exploited for commercial purposes.

Internet commerce indeed appears to be very promising for E-retailing. Grover (BRW, 9 April 1999) reported that in four years, almost 90,000 online merchants have opened up online business in the United States. Online sales reached US$8 billion last year. Examples of innovative strategies applied by online retailers include pricing strategy which offers "extra savings" and "instant rebate" on some products, special price for online orders, sign-up membership facility which offers exclusive members' savings, tracking on previous ordering history, listing of retail stores, superstores and stores in other countries (*http://www.officemax.com*).

In the following subsections, we present some anticipated roles that intermediaries would undertake and the increasing importance of logistics support as the outcome of Internet commerce. The trend is inevitable since the limitations caused by traditional commercial practices, such as barriers to reach the whole target market due to geographical distance and high transaction costs, will not necessarily be primary issues.

Significance of Intermediaries in Conventional Business Processes

In conventional (physical) market, the primary function of intermediaries is to minimize transaction costs. Figure 3 compares the potential cost savings in transaction cost by having intermediaries as part of the distribution channel. This is especially true when the target market is out of reach (by distance).

In Figure 3, the total transaction cost when distribution channel includes intermediary is given by Equation (1).

$$\text{Total Transaction costs} = T1 + (n \times T2) \tag{1}$$

where T1 = transaction cost between the producer and the intermediary
T2 = transaction cost between the intermediary and the consumer
n = number of customers purchasing the product (via the intermediary)

But note that the transaction cost to the producer is only T1 while the (n X T2) component equals the expenses carried by the intermediary.

The dotted line in Figure 3 represents the transaction cost if the producer deals directly

Figure 3. Comparison of Transaction costs with and without intermediary

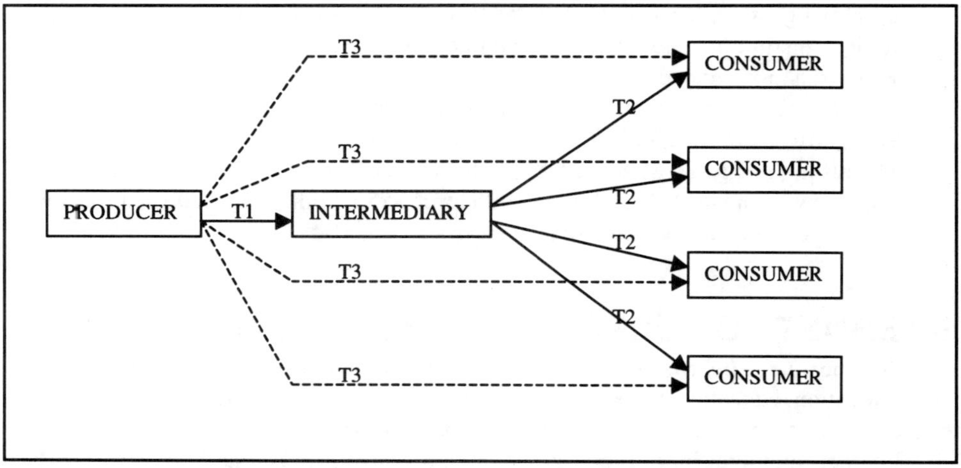

[Figure: Diagram showing PRODUCER connected to INTERMEDIARY via T1, INTERMEDIARY connected to four CONSUMERs via T2, and PRODUCER connected directly to each CONSUMER via T3 (dashed lines).]

with the consumer and the distribution channel excludes the intermediary. The total transaction cost can be calculated using Equation (2).

Total Transaction Costs = n X T3   (2)

where T3 = transaction cost between the producer and each consumer
       n = number of customers purchasing the product (from the producer)

Distribution channel bypassing the intermediary will incur more transaction cost to the producer. And this is the main reason why intermediary has been part of the distribution channel in conventional business processes.

In reality, the distribution chain incorporates a number of intermediaries. Figure 3 would have several blocks of intermediaries before the products reach the consumers. Therefore, the market is inefficient since the intermediate transactions become costly.

E-Retailing vs. Disintermediation

One possible impact of Internet commerce is the disintermediation in the business chain. With the existence of the two-way window of communication through the Internet, producers can interact directly with the customers. This is especially true for the trading of digitised products.

Convenience is also highly valued by the consumers. Buyers do not need to leave home, carry the shopping bags, or be hassled by the trouble of finding a parking spot in order to shop. They can do it anytime, anywhere, at their own convenience. Disintermediation enhances the efficiency of the market because intermediaries incur additional costs and it is possible when market players have enough information about the product. Disintermediation can occur in the market segment which trades commodity-like products – the type of products which can be described as "what you see is what you get." Typical examples are books, musical CDs and travelling tickets. Producers of the commodities will have deployed e-commerce technologies to support the business. This implies that retailers will have to compete against the giant producers on the pricing strategy as well as on the delivery of the goods.

An exceptional case where an E-retailer wins the market is that of Amazon.com, as reported by Sterett and Shah (SAMS, 1998). The firm exploited the technology-driven media "to write the rules of competition in the book of retailing industry." Amazon.com has been the most popular success story quoted ever since the Internet has been used for commercial purposes. However, the latest Bloomberg report (NUA Internet Surveys, 20 May 1999) informed that while first-quarter revenue at Amazon.com exceeded US$293.6 million, up from US$87.4 million in 1998, the Net's largest retailer announced losses of US$61.7 million. Revenue exceeded the original forecast of US$260 million. Despite the increase of the share price from $40 on June 1 1998, escalated to $80 within 22 days, then hit $100 on June 24 and closed at $139 on July 6 1998, as recorded by McLean (Fortune, 3 August 1998), Amazon.com has not reached the break-even point.

Note that Internet commerce has changed the profitability model of retailing businesses. For online retailing, the transaction costs described in the previous section is simply outweighed by the ability to reach global market. In conventional business, a retail shop can only reach the consumers within the vicinity of a store location. The Internet opens a new horizon for the retailing market. Utilizing this technology, Amazon.com, for example, can reach the consumers despite the geographical distance. In order to cater for the same number of customers reached through the Internet, physical retailers must cover numerous costs, such as warehousing, store rental, labor, not to mention the locked asset in the inventory.

The survival of e-retailing industry depends to some extent on the concentration level of the industry. The book industry, for example, is highly concentrated, highly fragmented and makes it ripe for disintermediation (Alsop, 1999). In the case of Amazon.com, although it appears to be a small e-retailer, it has grown to be an e-superstore. The level of disintermediation is, of course, not cutting intermediaries out absolutely. Rather, the e-market would find an equilibrium point as far as the number of competing e-superstores is concerned. Further, there is an anticipation that in the same way the role of intermediaries are reduced in concentrated markets, the Internet will also enhance the role of intermediaries in complex markets (Alsop, 1999).

E-Retailers and producers compete not only in their pricing strategy, but also, in ensuring security, convenience and excellent customer service. Companies which go online must be responsive and establish their "brand names" seriously because customer loyalty is indeed crucial. Quick e-mail form reply and proving the delivery of the value promised is a must. Economies of scale is no longer the sole measure because on the Internet, an established superstore and a newcomer in the business can appear comparable on line. In short, the key word is "responsiveness".

Increasing Importance of Logistics Support

Responsiveness is a real challenge in the world of Internet commerce. Consequently, one aspect for e-retailers to ensure responsive customer service is to enhance its logistics and delivery supports.

Amazon.com, which has succeeded in leveraging the internet's capabilities and establishing its predominant brand name, previously, has not incurred rental costs. Instead, the wholesalers and suppliers ship the products directly from their warehouses to buyers. By eliminating the retail facilities and intermediate warehouses, more cost savings are gained and lower transaction costs are made possible. This is a common approach to inventory management used by e-retailers, i.e., to maintain small inventories of the most popular products, while making direct arrangement with suppliers for more specialized products. Up to this present time, Amazon.com still operates in loss due to the company's reinvestment of revenue, such as building warehouses to support its marketing and distribution channel. Unless otherwise, it can be crushed easily by Barnes & Noble, which has gone online, and the battle has been won by the $3-billion-a-year Goliath. Barnes & Noble's winning ticket is its speedy service. The winner of the contest is determined by who has the most books physically on hand. While Amazon stocks just a limited number of bestsellers, Barnes & Noble outstocks Amazon by having real-world stores and becoming its own giant wholesaler. It deals directly with publishers, cuts out the middlemen, and stocks its central warehouse in New Jersey with 400,000 frequently ordered titles (Stross, 1997).

With the orientation of today's business environment, which extends to a global market, traditional logistics management can become an obsolete approach. Cost reduction and efficiency in value chain services has been the main issue addressed ever since the adoption of e-commerce by many trading organisations. Traditional logistics management has been found to be inadequate to support the growth of e-commerce. Poor inventory management or excessive inventory can be a costly penalty. Online retailers definitely cannot afford to lock their assets away, for example, by keeping products that sit on the warehouse shelf. They must also be careful in their demand forecasting because the penalty of back-order situations, including transportation and delivery time, can be very costly. Traditional logistics can be way too slow to cope with the speedy service demanded by online consumers. Brand loyalty is very much depended upon responsiveness; on the contrary back order situation is a major disadvantage in this case.

Third-Party Warehousing Firms

A third-party warehousing firm is a partial solution to improve the logistics support demanded by the global economic climate. Third-party warehousing firms offer services to companies that wish to outsource the inventory management of their businesses. In 1994, Microsoft Corp. reengineered their logistics supply chain and integrated the logistics management with the manufacturing plan of the company. This move was triggered upon the realization that the inventory cost was excessive. Their cutting cost strategy was to relocate the distribution facility, outsourc the operation and employ a third-party warehousing firm to operate the shipment of returns and slow-moving inventory. Their strategy to outsource some of their logistics support and to relocate the distribution centre worked very well. In 1995, they could reach the majority of their consumers in the Midwest and the East Coast of America from their Seattle Headquarter (Harrington, 1996). Services offered by third-party warehousing firms are a worthwhile alternative for businesses which target the global market, especially for online retailers.

Implications on Product Delivery

This lucrative outlook for warehousing management also applies in delivery services. The impact of e-commerce on logistics support is both to have sufficient warehouses to store products and to have enough vehicles to transport and deliver the products to the consumers. Companies would be required to prove the quality of their service by prompt delivery. Transport and fleet management becomes an important issue. Consequently, this opens ample opportunities for delivery agents to compete and improve their services. Established delivery service companies are readily in the best position to reap opportunities but they have to remain alert and be responsive towards demands.

In previous years, many courier services offered next-day delivery but only Federal Express (*http://www.fedex.com*) provided the customers with an electronic tracking system that enabled customers to track their parcels or packages 24 hours a day. As more and more agents establish their presence on the Internet, electronic tracking systems become their common feature. Currently, delivery and distribution companies like DHL (*http://www.dhl.com*), UPS (*http://www.ups.com*) and Airborne (*http://www.airborne.com*) provide the electronic tracking systems for their customers.

Value Chain Service Providers

FedEx estimated that the value of goods and services traded over the Internet will grow from US$440 million in 1996 to US$165 billion in the year 2000. With such a profound figure, it is not surprising that some restructuring in the distribution channels will take place. The supply chain service will reshape itself to cater to the demand of the services.

An emerging trend in the transportation and distribution services is "virtual fulfillment" services (Kalakota, 1997). FedEx has launched a new organization called Federal Express Logistics Services to outsource telemarketing, warehousing and transportation services from companies, including online retailers. This service aims to eliminate the lagging of product delivery caused by transportation process by shipping product components from their manufacturing sites straight to the customer's home or business without storing them at warehouses. FedEx keeps track of the product components and synchronize their delivery so that they arrive at the destination simultaneously.

This trend indicates a reshaping of the supply chain service: in FedEx's case from a pure delivery service to a distribution company. In fact, this trend appears not only in logistics, but also in other specific services, such as electronic payment and stock management, in which Value Chain Service Provider (VCSP) has been perceived as a distinctive advantage in the context of e-commerce. Established VCSPs, such as FedEx and UPS, operate on the basis of fee or a percentage-based scheme.

Reshaping the Role of Intermediaries

Intermediaries as Information Providers

Interestingly, the increasing popularity of Internet commerce triggers competition among the producers even more vigorously because they have to compete in both delivering values as well as quality of the product. In fact, the role of intermediaries has shifted from transporting, distributing, promoting and advertising the products for consumers to obtain assurance and certainty of the product quality they wish to purchase. A new role of retailers as an element of distribution chain is unique since they may become a service provider, which attracts consumers based on the quality of the information that they can provide.

Furthermore, intermediaries as information providers operate in certain types of markets – where the difference between low quality and high quality products is large, giving a larger profit margin from the two expected prices (Biglaiser, 1993). The justification for the service is when there are more low quality products than high quality products. In short, this unique role of on-line retailers would be in high demand for the trading of information-rich products.

A motor vehicle is an example of an information-rich product. People are very careful and reluctant to buy cars through the traditional channels because most of the time they feel inadequate and disadvantaged in terms of lack of information. E-retailers can assist car buyers by supplying them with the information they need so that they are confident in their purchase.

The competitive edge of online retailers as information providers would be the provision of reliable information about the product quality. Credential of the e-retailers would be a crucial factor in surviving the competition.

Intermediaries as Facilitators

Intermediaries can also take up the role of agents who facilitate and add value to the traded products. Some examples are advertising agents, insurance companies, banks, delivery agents and motor vehicle dealerships. As an illustration, let us examine the car dealership: in conventional business, car dealers display and accommodate car buyers who visit their showroom. If car manufacturers deal directly with car buyers, car dealers may take up the role of a facilitator who brings the car for test-drive to the prospective buyers. The intermediaries in this case facilitate the consumer and adds value to the product by delivering the car to the consumer.

Another example which demonstrates innovative services of an intermediary is that of Aucnet USA, Inc. (Kalakota, 1996). Aucnet *(http://www.aucnet.com)* sets up an inter-dealer network and offers used car buyers a guarantee: product quality as well as low price advantage. Aucnet staff inspected and graded the used cars and provided detailed information to the buyers. In addition to that, Aucnet guaranteed its quality evaluation and invited used car dealers to join its network. Aucnet also conducted auctions as its price-discovering mechanism that mediates access of supply and demand of its members.

Virtual Intermediaries

Virtual intermediaries are entities which not only perform intermediary functions by mediating transactions, but also provide services to organize and present the products in a flexible manner. Among those virtual intermediaries are education brokers, namely educational institutions which offer flexible learning and distance education program, video on demand providers who can transmit and deliver films on video upon demand, and intelligent software agents to assist consumers with their on-line shopping.

SOME RELATED ISSUES AND BARRIERS TO OVERCOME

Last but not least, this chapter highlights some common issues concerning the on-line retailing.

Challenge to Capture Larger Marketshare

Organizations which have been responsive and reshape themselves to embrace e-business would have been profitable and remain competitive in the on-line market. It was shown in the previous section that new players and new products emerge as a result of e-commerce. Those offering products with competing costs and added value would soon find niche position in the market.

Nonetheless, the force to get the whole mass market to adopt the idea of online trading is just at its early stage. The momentum would continue to grow and many factors (see below) would need to be resolved.

Like in any other case of change, on-line players, as well as on-line buyers, are taking very careful steps in embracing the concept of e-commerce. A survey conducted by Andersen Consulting (http://bf.cstar.ac.com) indicated that producers and suppliers are reluctant to use automatic shopping agents for audio CDs since they are not ready to compete solely on prices (Bloch et al., March 1999).

Technology Support

On-line shopping can be a frustrating experience, especially for those unfamiliar with the process – navigating, browsing and searching for the wanted information or product can be time consuming. To manifest an ideal virtual marketplace, the communication bandwidth needs to be upgraded, in particular to cope with the multimedia Web pages; the efficiency and the effectiveness of current search engines must also be improved.

Customer Relations

The consumer behaviour online may appear differently compared to that in the conventional market. One factor which cannot be over emphasized is responsiveness. In order to build reputation and gain credibility, on-line traders must prove that they can indeed deliver the value they promise online. The nature of online product searching is very powerful. On-line search enables consumers to compare prices of many different sellers in a reasonably short time. Hence, to be the winner of the price war, online traders must have strong inbound and outbound logistics supports to deliver the products promptly. Furthermore, they have to be innovative in creating added value to their services. The implication of on-line trading is a less and limited interaction between the buyers and the sellers. This would be a challenge for sellers to develop proactive mechanism to understand and cope with the buyer's demand.

Security of Payment

Another major hurdle for on-line traders to overcome is to ensure the security of the transaction. At present, a majority of potential on-line consumers withdraw from revealing their credit card for payment through the Internet. Development of a better system, such as protocol level security, would help to overcome the reluctance. Obviously, consumers need to be assured about the reliability of on-line payment by continually educating and promoting the security issue. The security issue has also been addressed by the government and its mediation is facilitated by a third party such as the certification agent. Alternative mechanisms of payments have been introduced, including electronic money.

CONCLUSIONS

It is probably too early to predict the ultimate impact of Internet commerce on the retail industry. Yet, this chapter has identified some emerging trends in the identification: the discovery of new opportunities as well as the challenges that lie ahead. A frame of reference which encompasses the physical world and the virtual entity, and incorporates three variables—the players, the products and the processes, has been presented. This is useful for us to gain an understanding of how businesses fit into the world of e-commerce and vice versa.

Indeed, Internet commerce offers a promising outlook for online retailers in some market segments. Depending on the nature of the products, information rich or commodity like, retailers must be prepared to reshape themselves in order to take up the opportunities leveraged by the technology. For information-rich products, new roles of intermediaries and retailers have emerged. Some examples of the renewing and shifting roles of intermediaries have been highlighted in this chapter.

For retailers and intermediaries, in most cases, the impact of the competitiveness brought forward by Internet commerce is largely on improved pricing strategy, being responsive and being innovative in providing added value to the products and services. Consequently, warehousing and delivery services should be very well managed and ideally ought to be integrated to the business value chain.

REFERENCES

Aldridge, D., (1998). Purchasing on the net – the new opportunities for EC. *Electronic Market, 38* (1), 34-37.

Alsop, S. (1999, January 11). Is there an Amazon.com for Every Industry? *Fortune*, (139)1. Retrieved on May 1999 from the World Wide Web: *http://cgi.pathfinder.com/fortune/technology/alsop/1999/01/11/index.html*

Andersen Consulting. (1998, June). Consumers in Control – an interview with Esther Dyson, *Outlook Magazine*. Retrieved on 29 April 1999, from the World Wide Web: *http://www.andersen.com/overview/Outlook/6.98/over_currentf1.html.*

Biglaiser, G. (1993). Middlemen as Experts. *RAND Journal of Economics, 24*(2), 212-223.

Bloch, M., Pigneur, Y. & Segev, A. (1999, March). On the road of electronic commerce - A business value framework, gaining competitive advantage and some research issues, pp.1-18. Retrieved on 3 May 1999, from the World Wide Web: http://www.stern.nyu.edu/~mbloch/docs/roadtoec.ec.html.

Bottoms, D. (1995, October). Making the net pay off. *Industry Week*. 57-58.

Bulkeley, W.M. (1996, December 9). How can you make money from the web? *The Wall Street Journal*, R18.

Choi S., Stahl, D.O. & Whiston, A.B. (1997). *The economics of electronic commerce – The essential economics of doing business in the electronic marketplace.* USA: Macmillan Technical Publishing.

Crawford, P. (1998, March 30). Electronic travel bookings increasing. *The Australian Financial Review*. Special Report, 12.

Crawley, T. (1998, March 30). Web shopping choices are improving. *The Australian Financial Review*. Special Report, 8.

Datamonitor. (1997, -). Business to business electronic commerce: Exploiting market opportunities in the extranet age. *Datamonitor*.

Davidson, J. (1998, March 30). E-shopping: an idea whose time has nearly come. *The Australian Financial Review*. Special Report, 30.

Deans, A. (1998, March 30) Traders happy putting their business on the line. *The Australian Financial Review*. Special Report, 12.

Grover, M.B. (1999, April 9). Electronic retailing's big earnings remain elusive. *Business Review Weekly*, pp.88-89.

Harrington, L. (1996, July 15). Untapped Savings Abound. *Industry Week*, 53.

Johnson, S.J. & Schreck, E.M. (1997, April 1). Electronic Commerce – Seizing Opportunity in the Third Wave. Andersen Consulting. *Outlook Magazine*. Retrieved on 29 April 1999, from the World Wide Web: http://www.andersen.com/overview/Outlook/over_1apr97.html

Kalakota, R. & Whinston, A.B. (1996). *Frontiers of electronic commerce*. USA: Addison Wesley.

Kalakota, R. & Whinston, A.B. (1997). *Electronic commerce – A manager's guide*. USA: Addison Wesley.

Kambil, A. (1997, May). Doing Business in the Wired World. *IEEE Computer*, pp.56-61.

Lipoff, S.J. & Jens, J.H. (1996, June). Ten Steps to Success in Electronic Commerce. *Telecommunications*, pp.45-48.

McLean, B. (1998, August 3). What's Really Going On with Amazon. *Fortune*. Retrieved on May 1999 from the World Wide Web: *http://www.pathfinder.com/fortune/investor/1998/980803/str.html*

NUA Internet Surveys. (1999, May 20). Dell Computers: Dell Sells USD18 Million Per Day Online, Weekly Editorial, Computer Industry. Retrieved on May 21 1999, from the World Wide Web: *http://www.nua.ie/surveys/*

Phillips, M. (1997). Stamps.AU. *Successful e-commerce – 10 case studies to show small business how to profit from online commerce*. Australia: Bookman., 70-78.

PriceWaterhouseCoopers. (1999, May). Electronic business outlook: A guide to seizing the opportunities, meeting the challenges, and implementing e-business solutions [Abstract], *Surveys & Studies,* pp.1-31. Retrieved May 3 1999, from the World Wide Web: *http://www.e-business.pwcglobal.com/feature/surveys.asp*

Staff. Report on electronic commerce. (1998, February) 5.

Sterett, C., Shah, A. (1998 winter) Going global on the information super highway. *Sam Advanced Management Journal, 63*(1), 43-48.

Stross, R.E. (1997, September 29). Why Barnes & Noble May Crush Amazon. *Fortune*. Retrieved on May 1999 from the World Wide Web: *http://www.pathfinder.com/fortune/digitalwatch/0929dig3.html.*

Ticoll, D. & Tapscott, D. (1998, June). A strategy for ecommerce transformation, *Outlook Magazine*, pp.1-5. Retrieved on 29 April 1999, from the World Wide Web: *http://www.andersen.com/overview/Outlook/6.98/over_currente6.html.*

Chapter XIV

Consumer Motivations for Commercial Web Site Use: Antecedents to Electronic Commerce

Thomas F. Stafford
Texas Woman's University

Marla Royne Stafford
University of North Texas

INTRODUCTION

The purpose of this chapter is to explore theoretical background and previous research on new media uses and motivations as an avenue to understanding consumer motivations to use commercial Internet resources. This chapter will explore the communications theory of uses and gratifications, and will report and discuss the implications of a descriptive research process that establishes the domain of consumer motivations for Web site use. Building from a series of on-line focus groups conducted with the HotWired Internet site, the research discussed in this chapter includes the construction of an inventory of descriptive terms used to indicate the various areas of utility and enjoyment represented by the on-line experience.

The objective of the chapter is to expose the reader to a theoretical perspective that is useful for understanding how consumers are motivated to use the Internet, by exploring and describing what consumers enjoy and seek in the on-line experience of Web sites. Knowledge of what consumers seek from a medium (uses), and what they enjoy about a medium (gratifications) prepares the reader to understand and utilize the tremendous communications and marketing resource represented by the World Wide Web. Research from previous studies of new media introductions provides a unique historical perspective available for grounding the conceptualization of the Web as a communications and marketing channel. The theoretical perspective developed from this research has been robust – applied over time to the introduction of television in the late 1940s and early 1950s, as well as to the innovations of video recording and time-delayed media exposure and media control through electronic remote devices.

Copyright © 2000, Idea Group Publishing.

Although the World Wide Web is not much like television, nor computers much like video recorders and remote controls, the approach that has been developed for constructing an understanding of new media innovations of the recent past appears to be applicable to the situation represented by the Web in today's society. To that end, an additional perspective of this chapter is to help the reader ground his or her understanding of what the World Wide Web represents in terms of a useful commercial medium in an understanding of how new media generally are perceived and how consumers are subsequently motivated to attend to them. Knowledge of this sort can enhance the efforts of electronic marketers to more fully utilize and enhance the communicative properties of the new communications channel represented by the Web, and a critical component in the success of any electronic commerce effort will be the marketers' understanding and utilization of the factors which bring the consumer to the Web in the first place.

To that end, the reader can expect three specific benefits from reading this chapter:
1) To gain a working knowledge of the theoretical perspective of uses and gratifications, useful for the investigation of motivations leading to commercial Web site use.
2) The beneficial knowledge of the specific results of a U&G study of Web user motivations.
3) Managerial implications, related to such results, useful for improving performance of commercial Web sites.

The chapter begins with a discussion of the Web as an instance of commercial media, and this is followed by a brief introduction to the uses and gratifications concept as a useful theoretical tool for investigating consumer motivations for using commercial Web sites. A review of uses and gratifications theory is provided in preparation for a discussion of the specific application of U&G perspectives to Web media, which is followed by a detailed explication of the distinctions between the two main classes of gratifications: process and content. The design, execution and results of an on-line uses and gratifications study are presented, which is then followed by discussion of issues and problems related to the application of U&G to Web media. The chapter concludes with a discussion of Web-based trends which imply further usefulness for the U&G research tradition, and several specific recommendations are provided for improving the effectiveness of commercial Web sites.

THE INFORMATION SOCIETY

Any discussion of the Web as a commercial medium requires an understanding of media's place in modern society. An evolutionary process has formed a new societal structure based on information and communication (Ball-Rokeach and Reardon, 1988; Rogers, 1986). This popularly-labeled "information society" has evolved from mass exposure to interactive communication media, with interesting implications for commerce. The World Wide Web gives customers the opportunity to *self-select* themselves as potential prospects for market offerings, which might obviate the need for traditional segmentation practices, but which also implies the need for a greater understanding of the motivations which attract customers to attend to commercial offerings.

Companies have traditionally reached customers through promotions carried on broad-reach media; in the information society, customers can use Web sites to gather the product and company information which matches their interests. Not only is there a new information society, but the flow of commercial information is in the process of reversing from marketer-consumer to consumer-marketer (Sheth 1992). If the new information order mandates that promotional communications are *accessed* by consumers (as opposed to the old model of mass exposure), the important implication is that marketers will have to understand the motivations that bring consumers *to them*.

Web Use Motivations

Previous research on motivations for use of media indicates a rather dichotomous preference for media content versus the experiential aspect of media process (e.g., Stafford and Stafford, 1996); some people prefer to use new media technologies for the sheer joy of playing with the technology ("flow" — Hoffman and Novak, 1996), whereas some people use the new media to access content-specific information. The uses and gratifications research perspective is now being applied to the Web as a medium (for a perspective on corporate Web site use see Eighmey, 1997a; 1997b), and in answer to calls for such research (Newhagen and Rafaeli, 1996; Rafaeli, 1988), the current study proposes to begin the process of developing Web-specific descriptors of consumer usage motivations.

Understanding the motivations for accessing the Web and specific sites can help advertisers, retailers and other Web site operators produce more interesting and effective sites, resulting in more effective communications and transaction outcomes. The Internet has recently been estimated to be growing at a rate of between 10 percent (Rubenstein, 1995) and 20 percent per month (Thomsen, 1997); while the likely current audience for Internet programming ranges to 50 million users (Fox, 1995; Kambil, 1995), this audience will be closer to 150 million by the millennium (Barker and Groenne, 1997). The continuing growth of this new medium warrants considerable scholarly study of its effects and potentials.

Since the uses and gratifications appear to be useful for understanding Web user motivations, a brief overview of the theory is in order. Understanding the general theory can prepare the reader for an applied example, where the theory-based research perspective is used as an investigative tool to determine the motivations for commercial Web site use; in the next section, we review and discuss the theoretical perspective upon which this chapter is based.

USES AND GRATIFICATIONS THEORY

Uses and gratifications (U&G) is a research paradigm that seeks to uncover motivations for media use. One of the earliest theorists of the U&G approach, Klapper (1963), focuses on what people *do with* the mass media. Individual media choices are motivated by particular self-defined uses and goals (Lin, 1977), and a key challenge in learning the motivations of Web page users lies in determining the users' self-defined motivations. Active audiences are selective and make individual choices (Levy and Windahl, 1984), and while the "active audience" assumption of U&G theory was part of the emerging understanding of media use in decades past, audience activity is axiomatic in emerging Internet media; Web sites are designed for active use. Care must be taken to find ways of allowing users of Web pages to express their motivations, rather making assumptions about these motivations, for this active involvement in the Web site is a crucial aspect not only of Web use, but of the commercial activity that might arise from such use.

One of the basic assumptions of uses and gratifications theory is an active audience

(Katz, Blumler and Gurevitch, 1974; Rubin, 1981); this is particularly important when investigating the emerging Internet medium. In this new medium, communication is best conceptualized as a *reversed* flow, where the user (known in classic theory as the "receiver" — the converse of the communicator or "sender") controls the process by simple virtue of access. Heretofore, advertisers have been accustomed to selecting mass-exposure media and "aiming" it toward audience segments of interest. However, the paradigm of the new information order involves audience *self-selection*. This has very much the flavor of, "don't call us, we'll call you," with regard to audience access motivations. Thus, initial exposure to a Web site could be by chance, but the motivations leading to continued use of Internet sites could be very important to establish both the site's continuing viability as a communication source and credibility as an advertising vehicle.

Given the rich and useful nature of the U&G tradition, this research paradigm seems to represent an easily-applied logical template for understanding the motivations for audience use of new and emerging media. In particular, understanding the use of Web sites as a new mass medium is probably a very good application of U&G theory (Eighmey, 1997; Newhagen and Rafaeli, 1996), particularly since pointed comparisons of the Web to television have been made, with regards to the growing similarity in effects and uses in marketing (Eighmey, 1997; McDonald, 1997).

Uses and Gratifications for Web Media

If one subscribes to the futuristic view of the "segment of one," knowing how to attract and keep agglomerations of single person segments will be a success characteristic. Indeed, the segment of one is probably not — as currently explicated — the immediate course of Web-based promotional vehicles; current economic and socio-political trends augur against it (see Burke, 1997; Deighton, 1997). As Rogers (1986) noted, academics and researchers are part of the new information age elite, and it is a sobering thought that the equipment and software necessary to access the Web is fully one-fifth of the federal income poverty level for an individual (Deighton, 1997). So, while the Web will eventually diffuse through the population (Burke, 1997), it is far more likely that traditional segmentation approaches will have continued use (see Peterson et al., 1997) and that the Web will be *integrated* with more traditional media and promotional vehicles in the near term.

It is well established that individuals have particular motives that drive media use (Katz, 1959). Although some Web researchers have not favored U&G as a research tradition (e.g., Hoffman and Novak, 1996), others have observed that what we learned from studying new media in the past can be applied to inquiries about emerging media (e.g., Eighmey, 1997b; McDonald, 1997; Newhagen and Rafaeli, 1996; Peterson et al., 1997). Certainly, McGuire's (1974) concern for motivations that lead to *continued exposure* are just as easily generalized to the emerging Web medium as the channel surfer is to the "flowing" Web surfer (e.g., Eighmey, 1997b). As noted, initial Web site exposure most certainly could be due to browsing. Yet, continued and sustained page user traffic is the key to success, and current researchers echo the concern for increasing the ability to hold the attention of Web site users (Barker and Groenne, 1997), much like the previously researched need to hold television viewers beyond the first few seconds of a television commercial break. It appears that this ability to attract and hold attention will come from a better understanding of the motivations underlying Web site use.

Information Gratifications: Search and Consumption

As we apply the general theory of uses and gratifications to an understanding of Web site user motivations, it is worthwhile to consider two general aspects of activity and benefit-related gratification that consumers might seek from the Web. Within the U&G tradition, two key types of gratifications have generally been identified: content and process (Cutler and Danowski, 1980). Content gratification resides *in use of* the messages carried through the medium. This is analogous to site content, over which there is considerable concern (Drèze and Zufryden, 1997; McDonald, 1997). Process gratification results from the actions involved in *searching for* information; this comes from being involved in the communication process, itself, and is directly comparable to the *flow* experience described in Hoffman and Novak (1996).

It seems that the medium of a Web site might be characterized at the basic level in terms of process gratifications, in recognition of the experience of "Web browsing." As noted earlier, initial exposure is likely due to some random browsing effect, but content gratifications seem more likely to represent the reason for continued site access. Process gratification could be related to use of the Web, in general, where content gratification could be more related to specific and repeated site use—to wit, "bookmarking." With this in mind, it is possible that content gratifications may be somewhat more important to site operators, since content might have implications for real, sustained gratifications for regular users.

In the study reported here, we attempt to discern at an exploratory level whether it is more likely that Web site users seek process or content gratifications. Intuitively, this process might require meeting or contacting Web site users at a site in order to obtain data from users who are familiar with the medium and for whom the use of the medium is momentarily salient. To that end, we have designed and executed an on-line uses and gratifications study to examine user motivations at a prominent commercial Web site. In the next section, we discuss aspects of the study and its results.

UNDERSTANDING WEB USER MOTIVATIONS

Previous research on Web user motivation utilized existing scales adapted from television U&G studies (e.g, Eighmey, 1997a; 1997b); thus, a key consideration of the present study is to begin the process of developing Web-specific measures. In the U&G paradigm, there are accepted methods for compiling motivational profiles of media use. The typical approach is to compile an inventory of descriptive terms for use in establishing the domain of motivational constructs, followed by some form of data reduction to determine broad dimensions of motivations. An initial step in that process is establishing a domain of descriptive terms, which is the process that is reported and discussed here. A first step is the collection of descriptive adjectives corresponding to specific motivations of Web site users. That was the approach utilized in study.

Questionnaire Design

A brief questionnaire was developed to capture self-reported uses and gratifications of the World Wide Web. Because this study was exploratory, it seemed appropriate to utilize open-ended questions in an attempt to develop a fairly complete list of uses and gratifications. Such a list would be useful not only in providing an initial understanding of motivations for Web use but also as a framework from which to build a continuous research stream in this area. To that end, four open-ended questions were developed.

Word association techniques have been suggested for research that seeks to build an understanding of consumer's cognitive structures (Friedmann and Fox 1989; Szalay and Deese 1978. A key advantage of word association is that the respondent's first thoughts are most likely to be highly representative of his/her true opinion on a matter (Weeks and Muehling 1987). For this reason, our subjects were asked to indicate in one word the first thing that came to mind when they thought about what they enjoyed most about accessing the Web. Follow-up probes were used to elicit additional descriptive terms as well as to determine specific uses consumers had for the Web and important on-line activities they engaged in.

Sample

HotWired — a major Internet-themed Web site — agreed to participate in the study, and put the questionnaire in a sign-on space for users; a total of 98 individuals responded over a period of a week. Since participation was self-selecting and based on a potentially world-spanning audience, it proved impractical to calculate any meaningful response rate. Further, information gathered was limited to expressions of gratifications and uses; to encourage participation, no personal information was solicited, so demographic characteristics of the pool of respondents is not available. However, a recent survey of users characterized the average Web site visitor as having a college degree (67%), reasonably affluent ($69,000 average income), and married with children (Gupta, 1997).

Although this method is exploratory in its focus, and has few of the controls normally associated with descriptive and causal research, one must remember that the Internet medium is unlike any other previously-studied medium with regard to specific characteristics: it is both interactive at an individual level *and* self-selected. Researchers cannot necessarily choose who will and will not engage in an Internet survey placed on a Web site; response is purely a function of the individuals who happened to self-select the site the day of the survey. On the positive side, self-selecting participants are demonstrably engaged *with* the medium, and can be presumed to be capable of insightful and accurate discernment of their feelings *about* the medium. That is, they are currently using the medium and have a basis from which to respond to questions about the nature of their use. Also, there is merit in using an exploratory approach with experienced users in order to begin the process of determining what characteristics of medium use are important.

The most important consideration is that 98 separate contact points were established with HotWired users, and this represented an opportunity to learn more about user motivations. Results of these 98 contacts are reported herein.

The HotWired Study

Four specific questions were presented over the HotWired site as stimuli for trait term elicitation. The questions were:
1) What is the first thing that comes to mind when you think about what you enjoy most about accessing the Web?
2) What other words describe what you enjoy about interacting with the Web?
3) Using single, easy-to-understand terms, what do you use the Web for?
4) What on-line activities are most important to you?

Responses were analyzed for frequency of response, and were also qualitatively

Table: *Response Categories*

Response	#1	#2	#3	#4	Total	Type
Information	29	31	40	14	114	Cont.
Email	3	2	15	29	49	Cont.
Research	1	4	31	9	45	Cont.
News	0	5	20	16	41	Cont.
Software	0	4	18	9	31	Cont.
Chatting	2	4	7	11	24	Proc.
Entertainment	0	6	18	0	24	Proc.
Communication	1	8	12	2	23	Cont.
Fun	4	8	8	0	20	Proc.
Access	3	11	2	1	17	Proc.
Work	0	0	13	2	15	Cont.
People	0	6	7	0	13	Cont.
Web Sites	0	2	4	6	12	Cont.
Speed	6	6	0	0	12	Cont.
Updates	0	0	8	4	12	Cont.
Freedom	4	4	0	3	11	Proc.
Interaction	2	7	1	1	11	Proc.
Games	1	1	6	3	11	Cont.
Knowledge	1	4	6	0	11	Cont.
Surfing	0	1	6	4	11	Proc.
News	3	5	0	2	10	Proc.
News Groups	0	0	0	9	9	Cont.
Technology	1	5	2	1	9	Proc.
Resources	1	2	5	1	9	Cont.
Education	0	2	6	0	8	Cont.
Interesting	2	5	1	0	8	Proc.
Easy	2	6	0	0	8	Proc.
Stocks	0	1	4	2	7	Cont.
Answers	0	1	4	2	7	Cont.
Browsing	1	1	1	3	6	Proc.
Variety	2	4	0	0	6	Proc.
Learning	1	3	2	0	6	Cont.
Weather	0	0	3	3	6	Cont.
Progressive	0	5	0	0	5	Proc.
Friends	0	1	3	1	5	Cont.
Shopping	0	0	4	1	5	Proc.
Search Engines	0	0	0	5	5	Proc.
Relaxing	0	1	2	1	4	Proc.
Sports	0	1	2	1	4	Cont.
Ideas	0	3	1	0	4	Cont.
Money	0	1	3	0	4	Cont.
Searching	0	1	0	3	4	Proc.
Current	0	1	2	1	4	Cont.
Homework	0	0	3	1	4	Cont.
Government	0	0	4	0	4	Cont.

analyzed in a categorization scheme that grouped by motivations related to content (what's on the site) and process gratifications (the experience of using the site). This categorization scheme has been demonstrated previously and found to be useful in initial stages of U&G research (e.g., Cutler and Danowski, 1980; Stafford and Stafford, 1996).

Analysis and Results

A number of trait terms were elicited in the experiment, and these responses were both counted and categorized — tabulated by the specific question that stimulated the response. Word counts helped to identify the most commonly-voiced uses and gratifications. Analysis of responses by individual questions allows for the distinction between initial and follow-up responses (e.g., Weeks and Muehling, 1987). A graduate student unaware of the purpose of the study completed the simple counting task, and results are presented in the Table with response items displayed by frequency of occurrence.

The response items are also coded as either a content or process gratification (e.g., Cutler and Danowski 1980; Stafford and Stafford, 1996). Two graduate students were provided with both oral and written descriptions of each of the two gratification types and were instructed to code each item as a content or process item based on a description derived from Cutler and Danowski's (1980) study. Coder instructions are presented in the Appendix.

Disagreements were resolved by a third coder who received identical coding instructions. The intercoder reliability coefficient (Perreault and Leigh, 1989) was .70, indicating an acceptable level of reliability. Results of this coding process are included in the last column (Proc. = process, Cont. = content) of the Table.

In examining the Table, several useful findings are evident: first, by far the most commonly stated use and gratification for the World Wide Web is *information*. The term "information" was the most frequent response to three of the four questions asked, and was also the overall frequency leader. Question 4, the only one that failed to elicit "information" as the most common response, specifically asked about activities, and it is logical to believe that information may be perceived as more of a commodity than an activity by a number of people.

Of particular note, responses to the *initial* question — which is probably the most useful and important probe in a free-elicitation task (Weeks and Muehling, 1987) — indicated that nearly 30% (29 out of 98) of the participants responded that information was the first thing they thought of when considering what they enjoyed most about using the Web. This is a clear indication of the importance this modern commodity plays in motivating use of commercial Web sites.

It is important to realize that the remainder of responses to the initial probe were quite diverse, so a 30% response level for this particular quality (which may seem modest by some measures) is actually quite important, given the range and variety of response terms. Essentially, one-third of our respondents readily supplied the term "information" in response to an initial free-elicitation probe. The next most frequently mentioned word (speed) in response to the initial probe was only offered by six respondents.

Information was also the leading response to the follow-up probe (the second question), and for this question, the next most frequent item was "access," with a count of 11. Thus, information seems to emerge as the clear response with regard to gratifications from the World Wide Web — serving as the first, most important quality to come to mind for a significant fraction of respondents, and then serving as the second or third thing that came to mind for a great deal of those who failed to note it first.

Our third question probed for specific uses and allowed for unlimited responses. Here, too, information arose as a primary use and gratification. Following information, the second most common response was the related term "research" (31 mentions), followed by "news," "software" and "entertainment." Question Four, probing for specific Web uses, identified e-mail as the most important activity to respondents. News and information followed, with total responses of 16 and 14, respectively.

With respect to the process and content classification, about 55% of the specific items listed were classified as content gratifications, indicating that individuals using the Web find content to be more useful and enjoyable than the processes associated with Internet use. Even more interesting is that *information* was categorized as content, as were the next four of the most frequently identified items, lending additional support for the finding that content gratifications are strongly preferred to process gratifications. However, with 45% of listed responses categorized as process gratifications, there does appear to be reasonable motivation and enjoyment sought from process gratifications. It appears that flow is important (Hoffman and Novak, 1996), but not as important as *content*. An additional point worth considering is the need to focus on *quality* of content (Thomsen, 1997; information that is useful or valued) or *value* of content (Eighmey, 1997b; information that is easy to access and utilize) in Web page design.

DISCUSSION

This study serves the specific purpose of generating a list of descriptive adjectives indicative of the qualities users find most important and compelling in Web pages. The exploratory results presented herein are the basis for beginning media-specific analyses of gratification and usage dimensions in accordance with accepted methodology (e.g., Bantz, 1982; Levy and Windahl, 1984), and this list of adjectives forms an important contribution to the evolving stream of research on Web use motivations precisely because the terms developed here come from Web users responding to questions *about* Web use. Further, the initial exploratory analysis reported here provides reasonable support for a working hypothesis that information is the key motivator for World Wide Web use.

While this suggests that marketers should strive to provide valuable and easily-accessible information content in their commercial Web sites, it is also important to note that the specific term, "Web Sites," ranked fairly far down on the list in analysis, and was never the initial item that came to mind in response to the initial probe. Are we taking too much on faith with regard to the potential attraction and efficacy Web sites offer as a marketing channel medium? Given the informational gratifications sought, perhaps a better conceptualization of the commercial Web site is as an analog to a newspaper, magazine or other source of objective information and news, interspersed as they traditionally are in the mature print media with commercial messages and offers, rather than the new high-tech direct sales vehicle that many companies seem to be making of it?

In any case, it seems that marketers who do wish to use the Web as a sales vehicle must create informative sites with drawing power. Because information can include many types of data (e.g., stock quotes, addresses, product information, etc.), there is no way to indicate from the current results how often individuals are actually seeking product information, as opposed to other forms of information. Moreover, the relatively low levels of response for the gratifications of "entertainment," "fun" and "games" suggest that while many marketers may be using such creative approaches to attract visitors, these creative qualities may not be key uses and gratifications sought by Web users. While the results of this study provide only preliminary support for recommendations to Web marketers regarding the potential desirability of relevant content versus high-tech artistic mechanisms, they do form provocative working hypotheses for research that continues to build from this beginning. Such findings seem to be mildly in conflict with the viewpoint of Hoffman and Novak (1996), who posit that *flow*, or the act of browsing the Web is gratifying, in and of itself. That is, while there are certainly process gratifications identified in this exploratory study, they do not appear to provide the *key* uses and gratifications sought by Web users; rather content gratifications related to information sought seem to be the key motivators for consumer Web access and use.

Bearing in mind McGuire's (1974) cautions about [user] retention, as paraphrased by Stafford and Stafford (1996) with regard to channel surfing on television, it is important to realize that the "flow" experience of aimless browsing for the relief of boredom is likely an Internet phenomenon that is *less* related to site use than to use of the *infrastructure*, itself. For advertisers, the more important consideration should be not why users are logged on to the Internet, or even why they navigate it, but what might cause them to either seek out or, once found, spend time with *their specific site*. This is where our key contribution lies: not in explaining the motivations that lead individuals to use computers attached to the Internet, but the specific motivations that cause users to attend to specific commercial messages and offers at single, specific commercial Internet sites.

Although the theoretical perspective we use here is robust and has a history of successful use in studies of new commercial media, it is not without potential drawbacks and problems. In the next section, we present for the reader's consideration several issues which could potentially mitigate the usefulness of the approach discussed here.

ISSUES, CONTROVERSIES AND PROBLEMS

A key concern with the theoretical perspective discussed here is its age and heritage. Uses and gratifications theory has been useful several times in the recent past, as new media innovations have been examined; yet, there is some controversy as to how *current* such a perspective may be with regards to something as new and unique as the World Wide Web. Our perspective of the U&G approach is that it is dated, given its history in application over the past four decades, but that its use in the past has generally been with regard to *new* media innovations. From this viewpoint, U&G research is a tried-and-true method for understanding any new medium, and one which can be immediately applied to the Internet since it is well-developed and documented in the literature.

However, it seems quite clear that the Web is qualitatively different from previous media innovations and there is little doubt that uniquely tailored research paradigms will arise in response to these unique characteristics. Our goal in discussing U&G approaches to understanding Web use is to provide a *starting point* from which researchers and practitioners can begin to evolve specifically tailored research programs that take into account the unique nature and rich characteristics of this important new commercial medium.

The typical U&G approach involves identifying a descriptive domain (as is done here), followed by data reduction to identify underlying and broad dimensions of media use motivation; a positive aspect of this process is the link to measure development. As researchers begin to apply more comprehensive and sophisticated research designs in Web research, these initial studies using U&G theory will have already supplied a reasonably objective benchmark of descriptive terminology which can become the basis for the development of measurement inventories for use in more sophisticated models of cause and effect.

An unanticipated development in Web research might well prove to have synergy with the U&G perspective. Bakos (1997) has described the evolution of the Web commerce market as moving from hierarchies (which are structured and segmented groupings not unlike current mainstream market segments) to electronic markets (which are much like the undifferentiated states of perfect competition envisioned by economic theorists). Bakos' theoretical perspective arises from the recognition that the free and ready access to information about marketers and products available on the Web acts to remove limitations on consumer information that might have previously led to market inefficiencies which give some marketers advantages over others simply due to consumer lack of knowledge about viable alternatives for commerce.

The question we pose is whether consumers are *motivated* to use the Web to its full commercial potential. Moreover, in realization of the economic forces posited by Bakos, promotion-based differentiation leading to competitive advantage and company loyalty will become more difficult for on-line marketers to achieve. In studying uses and gratifications for the use of commercial Web sites, researchers may well be able to confirm, disconfirm, or qualify Bakos' perspective on the Web-based "commmoditization" of commercial enterprise related to the increased availability of competitive information.

As such, future research should seek to determine how motivated consumers are to make extensive information searches, make extensive and detailed product comparisons, or (as an alternative) how willing consumers might be to utilize Web-based information search and search reduction utilities such as meta-lists and intelligent agents to reduce the potential overload of information that is readily available online. The key question seems to be whether consumers are actually willing to give up the hierarchical loyalty and preference relationships with certain known and favored marketers (known as brand loyalty, arising from experience with marketers differentiated by the lack of complete information, in the Bakos view), or whether consumers are more motivated to engage in the detailed and extensive information search that is already available online, in making the sorts of extensive competitive comparisons that Bakos suggests reduces differentiation in electronic markets? Given the sheer weight of available information online, a related question is whether consumers are motivated to accept mediated information searches, by forming quasi-hierarchical relationships with on-line search providers and agents?

As we consider issues related to the use of U&G theory in electronic commerce research, future trends should be considered. In the next section, we discuss our view of events that may take place in the near future, and which may impact the application or usefulness of theory and results presented here.

FUTURE TRENDS

One argument that can be made against U&G approaches to understanding Web user motivations is that it is a methodology that has been substantially perfected in the study of television. This is a legitimate concern, in as much as the Web is not much like TV (at least, currently). However, trends suggest that U&G may be more and more applicable to the Web in the future, as the Web begins to evolve into a "rich" medium that is *more* like television. There has been speculation about the likely channel of video service delivery in the near future, and while little has been concluded with regards to the choice between cable companies, telephone companies or the more egalitarian Internet as a delivery channel for household entertainment services, pundits are predicting that, in the near future, the Internet will be capable of replacing both telephone and cable delivery channels, in addition to providing the already critical Web link.

Broadband digital services delivered to the home may differ from location to location as to which transmission medium is utilized (coaxial cable, twisted pair lines, wireless technology, etc.), but the trend appears to be toward media integration, such that whatever transmission form is used, the home is likely to be receiving integrated telephony, entertainment and Web navigation utilities in a bundled service at some point in the future. In this sense, the Internet service that we are currently familiar with is very likely to be a lot like the television service we currently receive, and U&G perspectives discussed herein will be all the more useful in that regard.

RECOMMENDATIONS FOR WEB SITE DESIGN

As a result of the research reported here, it appears that Web information content is the primary gratification sought from use of the medium. For electronic commerce considerations, this implies that Web sites should be designed to *deliver*. That is, with users motivated primarily by information-related content, commercial Web sites will probably do better providing rich and easily-accessible sources of product and company information than by attempting to dazzle users with fancy graphics, ornate designs, or flashy offers. It is very likely that a simple site design that is rich in utility (i.e., easily delivers the information sought by users about a company and its products) will prove far more gratifying than the site that seeks to amaze and astound visitors with its technical expertise and leading edge design.

This concept of streamlined site design roughly parallels the traditional promotional principle of K.I.S.S., which mandates essentially the same philosophy: consumers seek product-related benefits, and are most interested in direct messages or communications that clearly communicate about a marketer's provision of those benefits. No one disputes the entertainment potential of the Web medium; the point is that for sites which do not deliver that entertainment as a primary product or benefit (like a game site, for instance), informational content should be the primary consideration driving design and execution.

CONCLUSION

This chapter serves the specific purpose of discussing motivations for Web site use, and reports the results of a study that develops descriptive terms indicative of the qualities users find most important and compelling in Web sites. The results and discussion presented here are the basis for beginning media-specific analyses of gratification and usage dimensions in accordance with accepted methodology, and form an important contribution to the evolving stream of research on Web use motivations precisely because the motivational scheme developed here comes from Web users responding to questions about Web use.

It seems, based on the HotWired study, that marketers who wish to use the Web as a commercial vehicle must create informative sites with drawing power. Because information can include many types of data (e.g., stock quotes, addresses, product information, etc.), there is no way to indicate from the current results how often individuals are actually seeking product information, as opposed to other forms of information. However, the relatively low levels of response for the gratifications of "entertainment," "fun" and "games" suggest that while marketers may be using such creative approaches to attract visitors, these creative qualities may not be key uses and gratifications sought by Web users. The results discussed in this chapter form provocative working hypotheses for research that continues to build from this beginning.

The most important consideration appears to be not why users are logged onto the Internet or even why they navigate it, but what might cause them to either seek out or, once found, spend time with *a specific site*. Our key contribution lies not in explaining the motivations that lead individuals to use computers attached to the Internet, but in the specific motivations that cause users to attend to specific commercial messages and offers at single, specific Internet sites.

REFERENCES

Ball-Rokeach, S. J. & Reardon, K. (1988). Monologue, dialogue and telelogue: Comparing an emerging form of communication with traditional forms," in R. Hawkins, S. Wieman & S. Pingree (Eds.) *Advancing Communication Science: Merging Mass and Interpersonal Processes.* Newberry Park, CA: Sage.

Bakos, Y. (1998). The emerging role of electronic marketplaces on the Internet. *Communications of the ACM,* August, 35-42.

Bantz, C. R. (1982). Exploring uses and gratifications: A comparison of reported uses of television and reported uses of favorite program types. *Communication Research,* 9 (July), 352-379.

Barker, C. & Groenne, P. (1997). Advertising on the Web. *http://www.samkurser.dk/advertising/research.html.*

Bellenger, D. N. & Korgaonkar, P.K. (1980). Profiling the recreational shopper. *Journal of Retailing,* 56 (Fall), 77-92.

Bellinger, D. N. & Moschis, G.P. (1981). A socialization model of retail patronage. In A. Mitchell (Ed.) *Advances in Consumer Research, Vol. 9.* St. Louis: Association for Consumer Research.

Bellinger, D.N., Robertson, D.H. & Greenberg, B.A. (1977). Shopping center patronage motives. *Journal of Retailing,* 53 (Summer), 29-38.

Darden, W., Darden, D.K., Howell, R. & Miller, S.J. (1980). Consumer socialization factors in a patronage model of consumer behavior. In K.B. Monroe (Ed.), *Advances in Consumer Research, Vol. 8.* Arlington: Association for Consumer Research.

Dawson, S. & Wallendorf, M. (1984). Associational involvement: An intervening concept between social class and patronage behavior. In E. Hirschman and M. Holbrook (Eds.), *Advances in Consumer Research, Vol. 12.* Provo, Utah: Association for Consumer Research.

Eighmey, J. (1997). Profiling user responses to commercial Web sites. *Journal of Advertis-*

ing Research, 37 (May/June), 59-66.

Fox, B. (1995). Retailing on the Internet: Seeking truth beyond the hype. *Chain Store Age*, 71 (September), 33-46, 68, 72.

Gerbing, D.W. & Anderson, J.C. (1988). An updated paradigm for scale development incorporating unidimensionality and its assessment. *Journal of Marketing Research*, 25 (May), 186-192.

Gutman, J. & Mills, M.K. (1982). Fashion life style, self-concept, shopping orientation and store patronage: An integrative analysis. *Journal of Retailing*, 58 (Summer), 64-86.

Kambil, A. (1995). Electronic commerce: Implications of the Internet for business practice and strategy. *Business Economics*, 30 (October), 27-33.

Klapper, J.T. (1963). Mass communication research: An old road resurveyed. *Public Opinion Quarterly*, 27, 515-527.

Korgaonkar, P.K. (1981). Shopping orientations of catalog showroom patrons. *Journal of Retailing*, 57 (Spring), 78-90.

Levy, M.R. & Windahl, S. (1984). Audience activity and gratifications: A conceptual clarification and exploration. *Communication Research*, 11 (January), 51-78.

Lin, N. (1977. Communication effects: Review and commentary. In B. Ruben (Ed.), *Communication Yearbook 1*. New Brunswick, NJ: Transaction Books.

McDonald, S.C. (1997). The once and future Web: Scenarios for advertisers. *Journal of Advertising Research*, 37 (2), 21-28.

Moore, C.T. & Mason, J.B. (1969). A research note on major retail center patronage. *Journal of Marketing*, (July), 61-63.

Newhagen, J. & Rafaeli, S. (1996). Why communication researchers should study the Internet: A dialogue. *Journal of Communication*, 46 (1), 4-13.

Rogers, E.M. (1986). *Communication Technology: The New Media in Society*. New York: Free Press.

Rubin, A.M. (1981). An examination of television viewing motivations. *Communication Research*, 8 (April), 141-165.

Rubinstein, E. (1995). The retail superhighway: Take a ride on the Net. *Discount Store News*, 34 (August), 79-81.

Sheth, J.N. (1992). *Marketing's Sacred Pigs*. Presentation to the Marketing Ideas Consortium, Athens, GA.

Stafford, M.R. & Stafford, T.F. (1996). Mechanical commercial avoidance: A uses and gratifications perspective. *Journal of Current Issues and Research in Advertising*, 18 (Fall), 27-38.

Stafford, T.F. & Stafford, M.R. (1998). Uses and gratifications of the World Wide Web: A preliminary study. *Proceedings of the 1998 American Academy of Advertising Conference*.

Thomsen, M.D. (1997). Advertising on the Web. *http://www.samkurser.dk/advertising/thomsen.html*.

APPENDIX

Coder Instructions

Content Gratification: In this case, satisfaction is sought from the message communicated through the medium — to *gain information* from a Web site. The content of the message, itself, provides satisfaction, from increased knowledge or the reduction of uncertainty.

Process Gratification: In this case, satisfaction stems from being *involved* in the communication process, itself. In this case, browsing Web sites just for the sake of something to do or for variety is probably distinct from accessing Web sites to get specific information from content.

Adapted from Cutler and Danowski (1980).

Chapter XV

The Retail Payments System and Internet Commerce

Boon-Chye Lee*
University of Wollongong, Australia

INTRODUCTION

The payments system is a linchpin of the modern economy. Transactions involving non-cash payment for goods, services, or the transfer of asset ownership rely on the payments system to effect payment. The development of electronic commerce as an extension of the way in which people carry out transactions will depend crucially on the development of efficient and secure payments methods capable of supporting electronic delivery. At the same time, the preferences of consumers regarding different payment methods, whether it is cash, credit cards, debit cards or stored-value cards, are determined by a complex mix of economic, behavioural, cultural, and institutional factors. Consumer preferences and attitudes towards different payment methods are an important factor that must be taken into account by firms offering their products and services on the Internet.

Payments may be divided into two broad categories. The term "wholesale payments" is used to refer to very large value payments, typically interbank transfers related to the clearing and settlement functions of banks. "Retail payments" refers to all other payments, including consumer-to-business as well as business-to-business payments. While wholesale payments have been electronic since the 1960s, retail payments remain predominantly based on cash and paper (primarily cheques). In this chapter we focus on developments in the retail payments system, and particularly on its capacity to serve the requirements of consumers in Internet commerce. Because the development of electronic commerce technologies has been driven in large part by considerations of efficiency, it is essential that the supporting payments system be able to match the efficiency of the underlying transactions.

The attitudes of consumers to the various payment methods in the physical world have important implications for their use on the Internet. These attitudes will to a large degree determine the relative frequency of use of alternative payment methods on the Internet. It is therefore instructive to look at the different payment methods that are currently available,

Copyright © 2000, Idea Group Publishing.

which we do in the next section, and at trends in the patterns of use as well as the factors that affect the decision to use a particular payment method.

We then move on to examine the implications of the developments in the retail payment system for Internet commerce before summarising.

BACKGROUND: PAYMENT METHODS

The payments system consists of a network of services that both complement and compete with each other to provide those services. It has evolved over time into a highly efficient system offering a wide range of choices of payments media to users, both individuals and institutions. The range reflects the diversity of transactions, each payment method having evolved to serve the needs of a subset of possible transactions. Thus, for example, low-value, everyday consumer purchases are predominantly paid for in cash, while higher-value transactions may be settled by cheque or credit card.

The basic model of a payment method envisages the transfer of value from the payer to the payee without the involvement of intermediaries. This may be called the "direct transfer" method of making payments (Ledingham, 1996). In the case of currency (notes and coin), the transfer takes the form of currency being handed from the payer directly to the payee.

When money is represented by physical objects, the storage and transfer of monetary value involves a logistical as well as a security problem. The costs of holding and transferring money with an adequate level of security would constitute a significant proportion of the costs of conducting any transaction paid for with money, and it is not difficult to see why physical forms of money have evolved down the ages towards progressively less cumbersome forms.

Variations on the method of direct transfer involve some other form of value which substitutes for currency and which is accepted as payment for a range of goods and/or services. This range may in fact be quite limited, as in the case of telephone cards and travel passes; or it may be virtually as wide as that for currency, as with some "stored value cards" (SVCs) whose acceptability is limited only by the availability of merchants with the appropriate card-reading devices. The substitute value is purchased from an issuer who assumes the responsibility for redeeming it.

A less direct means of effecting payment involves at least one financial intermediary which manages an account on behalf of the customer (the payer or payee in a transaction). This may be termed the "account transfer" system of making payments (Ledingham, 1996). When people's holdings of money are stored in bank deposit accounts, the holding costs are correspondingly reduced — money having taken the form of an entry in the bank's records. The cost of transferring that value has also fallen: all that is required is a debit of the payer's account balance and a corresponding credit of the payee's account balance. The instructions to effect the transfer may vary — e.g., the writing of a cheque, which is an instruction to the payer's bank authorising the transfer to the payee's account; a telex or fax instruction; or some other form of communication. Transfer of value therefore relies on a transfer of information from the payer to the financial intermediary. When a payer wishes to make a payment to another party, the payer sends an instruction to his or her financial intermediary authorising the release of a specified amount of value from the payer's account in favour of the payee's account. The payer's financial intermediary, of course, is not necessarily the same as the payee's, in which case another set of instructions (between financial intermediaries) is required.

From the payer's point of view, one important difference between direct transfer and account transfer payment systems is the possibility of anonymity in the former. Direct transfer payment methods are good for immediate value, and there is no further requirement to link the payment with an individual or company. This is not the case with account transfer systems, where the availability of funds in the account has to be verified before payment can be authorised, and indeed the necessity for an on-line link between the merchant and financial institution adds to the cost of such transactions, and is a significant impediment to using such payment methods to settle low-value transactions. In a variety of situations, anonymity may be desired by the payer. On the other hand, account transfer systems provide proof of payment and a record of transactions, features which may appeal to people in other situations.

The availability of a range of payment methods therefore serves a variety of needs. There is no suggestion that different payment methods cannot coexist. However, what we are likely to see is the continuing evolution of payment methods towards less costly, more efficient ways of effecting payments some of which are more suited to particular situations than others. As a result of this process, consumers today are presented with a wider range of choices than has been the case before. Apart from currency and cheques, the choices include credit cards, debit cards, and stored-value cards. In addition, most of these methods are accessible by telephone banking and Internet banking. We focus our attention on the applicability of these methods to Internet commerce.

Cheques

In essence, a cheque is an instruction from an account holder to his or her financial institution authorising payment to a third party. While cheques are overwhelmingly of the physical variety, some schemes involve electronic cheques comprising an e-mail instruction with an electronic signature attached. Cheques, however, do not play a significant part in Internet commerce, and are unlikely to do so. In the range of physical-world transactions for which they have traditionally been used, alternative payment methods (mainly card-based methods) are proving more efficient and are increasingly being preferred over cheques, as discussed below. It is likely that this preference will extend to Internet transactions.

Credit Cards

The main impediment to the more widespread use of credit cards as a means of payment for Internet transactions has been the concern that such communications lack security. However, encryption technology is now routinely being employed in Internet commerce sites which renders the transmission of credit-card details a relatively safe procedure. Credit cards seem likely to remain the principal means of making payments over the Internet for medium- to high-value transactions for the foreseeable future, and card readers may well become a standard feature of personal computers in the future. On the other hand, the relatively high cost of making credit-card transactions means that this is not a suitable means of payment for low-value transactions. In addition, there is a lack of anonymity for people choosing this method.

Debit Cards

Debit cards such as those used at electronic funds transfer at point-of-sale (EFTPOS) terminals offer another potential means of making payment on the Internet, using, for example, personal computers equipped with card readers. Debit card transactions are functionally similar to cheque transactions: when a transaction is paid for using a debit card, the buyer essentially authorises a transfer of funds from his or her account to the seller's. Like credit cards, however, debit cards are a relatively high-cost means of payment because of the need for on-line authentication of the payment instruction. As with credit cards, debit cards also do not offer users anonymity.

Electronic Money

The term "electronic money" denotes digitally-encoded currency balances which represent floating claims on a bank or other issuer. Consumers purchase the claims with conventional money and exchange them for goods and services with merchants who are willing to accept them as payment.

In the search for more efficient means of effecting transactions, the evolution of electronic forms of money is in the forefront of current developments. Electronic money, indeed, is just the latest stage in an evolutionary process towards more efficient media of exchange that began thousands of years ago when people first began using money as an improvement over barter arrangements in trade. It also represents a significant shift from concrete, more tangible forms of money, to a much more abstract medium consisting in its essence of an instruction. In what has come to be known as the Information Age, money has itself become an aspect of information.

Electronic money takes two forms. In the first, it is typically stored on a "stored-value card" (SVC) (also known as a prepaid card or electronic purse); in the second, known variously as "network money", "electronic tokens", and "digital cash," it is software-based and is stored in the hard disk of a computer.[1] SVCs can be classified in two ways. The first, focusing on their coverage of goods and services, classifies them as single-purpose (as with telephone cards) or general purpose, or anything in between. The second, focusing on a more geographic coverage, classifies them as closed (e.g., within a university campus or theme park) or open systems. SVCs are increasingly being combined on a "smart card", using more sophisticated computer chip rather than magnetic strip technology, with other features such as library borrowing rights, personal identification, and health records.

In both forms of electronic money, transfer of value can take place with or without intermediaries, depending on the system. That is, electronic money is not necessarily linked to any particular account, and hence anonymity is possible. This is an important feature of electronic money systems. Furthermore, some systems allow user-to-user transfers of value, in much the same way that cash can be passed from one individual to another without having to go through a third party, and without the need for one of the individuals to be a merchant, as is the case with credit card payments. Very small payment amounts are economically feasible and security is extremely good.[2] To the extent that electronic money offers anonymity, ease of use, and convenience, it is a substitute for currency — indeed, it may be argued, it is an improvement over currency because of (among other things) the negligible storage and transportation costs associated with its use.

The extent and the speed with which electronic money is adopted for Internet payments will depend partly on how quickly people adopt SVCs in their everyday habits, since there will be flow-on aspects of that behaviour on to the Internet. The growing popularity of card-based payment means (see next section) may be a precursor to wider acceptance of SVCs; note that SVCs may be regarded as a substitute for debit cards, although the latter are more advantageous and convenient to consumers. While SVCs are typically not currently linked to the Internet, the technology to do so certainly exists. It is a simple matter for card-readers used for credit and debit cards to be modified to take SVCs as well. A personal computer equipped with such a card-reader could be used to connect to the Internet and payments made using an SVC.

In functional terms, the two forms of electronic money are identical. Each represents a means of effecting value transfers without the use of bank accounts. As well, it is not farfetched to imagine the establishment of links between SVCs and network money so that value can be transferred from one medium to the other. For this reason network money and SVCs can be discussed under the common term electronic money.[3]

Mair (1999) has made some rough estimates for Australia of the costs of alternative payment methods (see Table 1). While the exact cost estimates are "ball park" figures, Mair points to a broad consensus on the *relative* figures. These may reasonably be presumed to be indicative for other industrialised countries as well. The estimated costs include both direct and indirect costs such as forgoing interest on cheque-account balances, processing time, postage (in the case of some cheque payments), and merchant fees (in the case of credit card payments).

The figures reveal a significant cost advantage of more than 88 percent (seven cents compared to 60) that SVCs have over the cheapest card-based alternative, debit cards. These figures are in line with the findings of Harper and Leslie (1995), who report a similar cost advantage of at least 70 percent.

While cost is obviously an important consideration in the choice of alternative payment methods for any transaction, it is not the only one. In a survey of people's attitudes towards the use of money on the Internet, conducted in 1995 by researchers at Imperial College London, respondents were asked to rank several attributes of money in order of importance. The results are illuminating. The attribute considered by far the most important was "wide acceptability". This was followed, in order, by "simplicity of use", "portability", "security", and "interoperability."[4] As the authors of the survey report note, "It should be noted that these [other] attributes facilitate wider acceptability of money, which is the prime concern of its users."[5] Of particular interest is the fact that security was ranked lower than

Table 1: Estimated Costs of Alternative Payment Methods for Australia

	Cost to Service Providers	**Cost to Customers***
Cash	$0.15	$0.30
Cheque	$3.00	$6.00
Credit Card	$0.80	$2.50
Debit Card	$0.40	$0.60
Direct Entry (credit/debit)	$0.10	$0.20
Stored-Value Cards	$0.07	$0.07

*Direct and/or indirect costs, including bank costs
Source: Mair (1999)

Table 2: Characteristics of Main Payment Methods

Payment Method	Typical/ Best Payment Size	Physical World or Internet Use	Simplicity of Use	Portability	Anonymity	Certainty of Transfer
Currency	Small to Medium	Physical	High	High	Yes	High
Cheques	Small to Large	Both	Medium	High	No	Medium
Credit Cards	Medium to Large	Both	High	High	No	High
Debit Cards	Medium	Both	High	High	No	High
SVCs	Very Small to Small	Both	High	High	Yes	High
Network Money	Very Small to Large	Internet	Medium	Low	Yes	Medium to High

wide acceptability, although security seems to be a prerequisite for acceptance: 51 percent of the 204 respondents indicated that they were prepared to use an Internet payment system only if it was secure.[6] Considered of least importance were the availability of small denominations, backing by a government or central bank, and anonymity, in that order.

A comparison of some of the characteristics of the main payment methods is given in Table 2. It is worth drawing particular attention to the third column, which relates to the usability of each payment method in the physical world or Internet domains. With the exception of currency and network money, all the payment methods can be used in both domains. This emphasises the fact that patterns of use in the physical world have important implications for choice of payment methods on the Internet.

RECENT TRENDS IN THE USE OF PAYMENT METHODS

Of the various payment methods, cash remains the most popular in the industrialised countries, typically making up around 80 percent or more of the total volume of all transactions, both wholesale and retail (Humphrey, 1995). In terms of value, cash transactions have been estimated to constitute around 65 percent of all retail transactions around the world.[7] Figures published by the Bank for International Settlements (BIS) indicate that, in the case of non-cash payments, there has been a migration towards electronic means of effecting payments (see Tables 3 and 4).

While in general the industrialised countries have advanced furthest down this path, there are marked differences in their relative use of the various payment methods. However, two trends are broadly discernible. The first is the relative decline in the use of cheques, measured in terms of both volume and value of transactions. This reflects the relative

Table 3: Relative Importance of Cashless Payment Methods, Selected Industrialised Countries (% of Total Volume of Cashless Transactions)

Country	1991	1992	1993	1994	1995	1996	1997
Cheques							
Belgium	21.6	18.8	16.0	11.7	10.6	9.4	8.0
Canada	64.8	62.4	58.7	52.8	46.9	41.0	36.1
France	52.2	50.6	49.1	46.9	44.8	43.6	41.7
Germany	9.6	8.8	8.1	7.9	7.0	6.4	5.7
Italy	41.6	40.0	37.2	34.0	32.8	30.5	28.0
Netherlands	14.3	12.3	8.1	6.0	4.0	4.2	3.0
Switzerland	5.4	4.4	3.3	2.6	2.0	1.6	1.3
U.K.	48.5	45.4	43.0	40.2	36.7	33.1	30.5
U.S.	81.6	81.1	80.1	78.9	77.4	74.8	73.2
Cards							
Belgium	13.3	15.6	16.5	18.0	19.7	21.3	23.4
Canada	27.8	28.9	31.1	35.3	40.0	4.8	48.8
France	14.5	15.0	15.7	16.3	17.3	18.3	19.5
Germany	1.8	2.1	2.6	3.1	3.6	4.2	4.1
Italy	3.1	3.7	4.1	5.2	6.6	8.6	11.2
Netherlands	1.8	2.6	4.1	7.9	13.6	15.1	18.2
Switzerland	9.7	11.8	13.8	16.2	18.4	20.7	22.8
U.K.	16.4	18.8	21.0	23.3	25.9	28.9	31.1
U.S.	16.0	16.2	16.9	18.0	19.1	21.5	23.0
Credit Transfers							
Belgium	57.0	56.9	58.5	60.9	60.2	59.4	58.0
Canada	3.9	4.4	5.2	6.4	7.3	8.1	8.4
France	15.2	15.4	15.4	15.7	16.0	15.7	15.7
Germany	51.3	49.8	45.6	48.7	49.5	49.2	48.2
Italy	40.9	42.1	44.6	46.8	45.9	42.6	41.6
Netherlands	61.3	61.3	66.4	64.2	60.6	54.0	51.7
Switzerland	82.7	81.3	80.1	78.1	76.3	74.4	72.3
U.K.	20.9	20.6	20.4	20.1	19.7	19.9	19.6
U.S.	1.6	1.8	1.9	2.1	2.3	2.4	2.5
Direct Debits							
Belgium	8.2	8.8	9.0	9.4	9.5	9.7	9.8
Canada	3.5	4.3	5.0	5.5	5.8	6.2	6.7
France	9.3	10.2	10.6	11.7	12.2	11.8	12.1
Germany	37.3	39.3	43.7	40.3	39.9	40.2	42.0
Italy	3.8	4.1	4.4	4.7	5.4	7.3	8.6
Netherlands	22.6	23.9	21.5	21.9	21.8	26.8	27.1
Switzerland	2.3	2.5	2.8	3.1	3.3	3.3	3.6
U.K.	14.2	15.1	15.6	16.5	17.7	18.1	18.7
U.S.	0.8	0.9	1.0	1.1	1.2	1.3	1.3

Source: BIS (1996b, 1998)

Notes to Tables 3 and 4: (1) Card payments include payments by credit card and debit card; (2) credit transfers are those initiated by the payer in which funds are sent directly to the payee's account through the banking system without the payee's involvement; figures include paper-based and paperless ones; (3) direct debits are pre-authorised payments by which the payer gives the bank authority to debit his/her account on the payee's instructions; (4) the total for some countries may not sum to 100% because of other payment methods which are not included in the categories above.

Table 4: Relative Importance of Cashless Payment Methods, Selected Industrialised Countries (% of Total Value of Cashless Transactions)

Country	1991	1992	1993	1994	1995	1996	1997
Cheques							
Belgium	5.4	6.2	5.4	4.6	4.3	3.2	2.9
Canada	99.0	98.8	98.8	98.7	98.1	97.2	97.1
France	7.3	6.4	4.6	4.4	4.7	4.8	4.4
Germany	2.8	2.4	2.3	2.3	2.1	1.8	1.6
Italy	9.1	7.1	5.4	4.5	4.5	3.6	3.2
Netherlands	0.2	0.2	0.1	0.1	0.1	0.1	0.0
Switzerland	0.2	0.1	0.1	0.1	0.1	0.1	-
U.K.	16.1	11.6	9.4	7.6	5.3	4.9	4.2
U.S.	13.7	13.1	12.6	12.2	11.9	11.2	10.5
Cards							
Belgium	0.1	0.2	0.1	0.1	0.2	0.2	0.2
Canada	0.3	0.3	0.3	0.3	0.5	0.8	0.8
France	0.2	0.2	0.2	0.2	0.2	0.2	0.2
Germany	0.02	0.02	0.02	0.02	0.03	0.04	0.03
Italy	0.04	0.04	0.03	0.04	0.05	0.05	0.06
Netherlands	0.0	0.0	0.0	0.1	0.1	0.1	0.2
Switzerland	-	-	-	-	-	-	0.1
U.K.	0.2	0.2	0.2	0.2	0.2	0.3	0.3
U.S.	0.1	0.1	0.1	0.1	0.2	0.2	0.2
Credit Transfers							
Belgium	94.3	93.4	94.2	94.7	95.2	96.3	96.6
Canada	0.6	0.7	0.7	0.7	1.1	1.5	1.5
France	89.9	91.2	93.5	94.0	93.3	92.7	93.3
Germany	95.4	95.5	95.7	95.7	95.8	95.7	95.9
Italy	88.6	91.1	93.2	94.2	94.1	95.0	95.4
Netherlands	98.4	98.6	98.8	98.7	98.6	98.7	98.8
Switzerland	99.8	99.9	99.9	99.8	99.8	99.8	99.8
U.K.	82.5	87.1	89.5	91.2	93.4	93.7	94.6
U.S.	85.4	85.8	86.4	86.8	87.0	87.7	88.5
Direct Debits							
Belgium	0.2	0.2	0.3	0.5	0.3	0.3	0.3
Canada	0.1	0.2	0.2	0.2	0.3	0.5	0.6
France	0.7	0.6	0.7	0.8	0.9	1.0	1.0
Germany	1.8	2.1	2.0	2.0	2.1	2.5	2.5
Italy	0.3	0.2	0.2	0.2	0.2	0.2	0.3
Netherlands	1.4	1.2	1.1	1.1	1.2	1.1	1.0
Switzerland	-	-	-	0.1	0.1	0.1	0.1
U.K.	1.2	1.1	1.0	1.0	1.0	1.1	1.0
U.S.	0.8	1.0	0.9	0.9	0.9	0.9	0.8

Source: BIS (1996b, 1998)

inefficiency of cheques as a means of transmitting payment instructions.

Second, in terms of volume of transactions, card payments (involving both credit and debit cards) have increased in importance, in some cases (e.g., in Canada, Italy, the Netherlands, Switzerland, and the United Kingdom) quite dramatically. While the Bank for International Settlements (BIS) figures for most countries do not distinguish between credit and debit cards, there are three exceptions: Canada, the U.K. and the U.S. Relying partly on figures for these countries and partly on Australian data[8], Laker (1999) reports that the usage of credit cards, a reasonably mature product in the four countries by the start of the decade, has grown rapidly during the 1990s. In these countries, credit card usage per head in 1999 is between 60 and 100 percent higher than in 1990.

This development would appear to warrant closer scrutiny. As Laker (1999) argues: Why would a relatively mature product suddenly get a new lease of life? The use of credit cards might have been restrained by the difficult economic conditions of the early 1990s, but the subsequent surge in their popularity seems too large to be attributed to macroeconomic developments. The more likely explanation is that credit cards are being used for new classes of payments, including remote payments — theatre tickets, mail order and, increasingly, utility bills. The Internet could provide another boost to popularity before too long.

Laker (1999) appears to have overlooked an even more remarkable development. The BIS figures for Canada, the UK and the US (reported in Table 5) reveal that, although credit card usage has increased by 44-61 percent by volume and by 88-103 percent by value in these countries since 1991-92, the increase in debit card usage has been even more dramatic: in the UK by 318 percent by volume (374 percent by value), in the U.S. by 693 percent by volume (941 percent by value), and in Canada by a staggering 9,646 percent by volume (8,760 percent by value). Furthermore, the figures indicate that, with the exception of debit cards in Canada, the average value of transactions using cards has increased during this period, even taking inflation into account. This may reflect greater confidence in these payment methods.

These trends, taken together, indicate a broad move away from relatively inefficient paper-based systems towards more efficient card-based and electronic media. While all the nine countries in our sample of industrialised countries in Tables 3 and 4 began the decade of the 1990s with cheques being the most favoured non-cash payment method, card

Table 5: Percentage Increase in the Use of Credit and Debit Cards, Selected Industrialised Countries, 1991-1997

Country	Debit Cards		Credit Cards	
	% Increase by Volume	% Increase by Value	% Increase by Volume	% Increase by Value
Canada	9646.6	8760.0	53.7	88.0
U.K.	318.7	374.7	61.4	103.1
U.S.*	693.0	941.7	44.3	102.4

*U.S. figures are for 1992 and 1997.
Source: Adapted from BIS (1996b, 1998).

Table 6: Worldwide Distribution of General Purpose SVCs (%)

Region	Furst et al. (1998)	Greenstein & Feinman (2000)
Asia-Pacific	24	8
Europe	68	90
United States and Canada	6	}2
Latin America and the Caribbean	2	

Note: Furst et al. (1998), figures for 1997; Greenstein & Feinman (2000), figures for 1995.

payments have since overtaken the use of cheques in five of them (Belgium, Canada, the Netherlands, Switzerland and the UK).

The adoption of stored-value cards has been more mixed. The evidence is that they have had a better reception in Europe and the Asia-Pacific (particularly in Hong Kong and Singapore) than in North America (see Table 6). The balance is expected to change, however. Greenstein and Feinman (2000) report estimates by a marketing firm, Dataquest, that by the year 2001 North and South America combined, which in 1995 was estimated to make up just 2 percent of the market for smart cards, will make up around 20 percent of the market, while Asia will account for 40 percent.

Interestingly, these developments have taken place against a background of more or less stable currency holdings as a percentage of GDP (see Table 7), although again there are individual differences between countries. While a few countries (in particular Japan and the United States) have seen an increase in the ratio of currency in circulation as a percentage of GDP between 1991 and 1997, some (including Belgium, the Netherlands, Sweden, and Switzerland) have exhibited declines, while for still others (France, Italy, and the United Kingdom) the ratio has been more stable. The rise in currency holdings in some countries during this period, it may be noted, may be due partly to the general fall in inflation rates and nominal interest rates, and a corresponding decline in the opportunity cost of holding currency.

Table 7: Notes and Coin in Circulation as % of GDP, Selected Countries

	1991	1992	1993	1994	1995	1996	1997
Belgium	6.2	5.9	6.0	5.2	5.3	5.2	5.1
Canada	3.1	3.3	3.4	3.4	3.4	3.4	3.4
France	3.7	3.6	3.5	3.4	3.3	3.3	3.2
Germany	6.0	6.5	6.7	6.8	6.9	7.0	6.8
Italy	5.4	5.7	5.8	5.9	5.5	5.3	5.5
Japan	9.4	9.0	9.5	9.7	10.4	10.9	11.6
Netherlands	6.8	6.5	6.5	6.3	6.0	5.7	5.5
Sweden	5.3	5.1	5.3	5.0	4.7	4.8	4.7
Switzerland	8.0	8.0	7.9	7.9	7.7	8.1	7.8
U.K.	2.7	2.9	2.8	2.8	2.8	2.8	2.9
U.S.	4.6	4.8	5.0	5.2	5.2	5.2	5.3

Source: BIS (1996b, 1998)

Overall, the developments outlined above indicate that, somewhat contrary to predictions of a move to a "cashless economy", the transition to card-based means of payment has taken place at the expense of cheque payments rather than currency.

ELECTRONIC PAYMENT METHODS AND INTERNET COMMERCE

The relative rates of diffusion of electronic payment methods have implications for the development of Internet commerce. The Imperial College survey of consumer attitudes towards payment methods on the Internet, referred to earlier, indicates that an important area of concern inhibiting Internet transactions is the security of payment methods. The development of the Secure Electronic Transaction (SET) protocol by Mastercard and Visa was aimed at providing a secure payment environment for the transmission of credit card information. It is considered to be a stronger security mechanism than other transmission protocols, such as the Secure Sockets Layer (SSL) protocol because of its stronger authentication features (Greenstein and Feinman, 2000). However, these features come at a higher cost: they cannot be implemented without additional infrastructure and processing capabilities.

In general, fraud abatement measures require system developers to confront the tradeoff between the benefits of such measures and their cost. The cost of such measures will render the use of credit cards uneconomical for a wider range of lower-value transactions. While this will restrict the usefulness of credit cards, it will also create opportunities for the use of both forms of electronic money, which are more suited in any case to low-value transactions, as well as the development of "micro-transactions", transactions of small-value (as low as a fraction of a cent) items.[9]

Another obstacle to more widespread acceptance of electronic money systems is the lack of interoperability between systems (Mair, 1996). This is true not just among the different network money systems and among different smart cards, but also between smart card systems and network money systems. As long as this situation persists, there remains a barrier to the realisation of the global Internet market, as markets will tend to remain fragmented. There is general agreement that it is crucial to ensuring the acceptability of electronic money for vendors offering systems that operate on different technical standards to cooperate to ensure interoperability. The issue of interoperability has important implications for the use of SVCs, not just in the physical world but also on the Internet, since this means that "cardholders will be able to conduct international transactions without having to leave their homes."[10] As Van Hove (1999) puts it, interoperability of electronic purses "in the virtual world ... should generate a significant network effect." In other words, where individual card vendors have been unable to generate sufficient critical mass to ensure the economic viability of their products, interoperability can help to overcome these difficulties.

SUMMARY

In this chapter we examined the different retail payment methods available to consumers today. Recent trends in the retail payments system include a shift away from the use of relatively inefficient cheques to more efficient card-based methods. These developments are significant for Internet commerce because patterns of use in the physical world will have flow-on effects to transactions on the Internet.

While credit cards are likely to remain the principal means of making payments on the Internet, security concerns remain a key obstacle to more widespread use of the Internet for transactions. The need to build in costly security features to alleviate consumer concerns will narrow the range of transactions that can be settled with credit cards, and this opens the way to the development and use of electronic money for lower value transactions, as well as the possible development of a market characterised by "microtransactions".

At the same time, a significant obstacle to more widespread acceptance of both forms of electronic money is the lack of interoperability among the various systems. Achieving a sufficient degree of interoperability among vendors is a crucial precondition to the acceptance of electronic money.

ENDNOTES

1. We will use the term "network money" in this chapter for this form of electronic money, while explicitly recognising that a variety of terms is in use.
2. One network money system "allows payment of amounts as low as one cent, and all payments are made with the security technology currently used by large financial institutions for international money transfers" (DigiCash, 1996).
3. The reader is referred to Lynch and Lundquist (1996, Chapter 2), for a survey of existing vendors and electronic money systems.
4. Interoperability refers to the ability of different proprietary systems to function using the same equipment. This obviously requires service providers to cooperate with each other to agree on common standards for their equipment.
5. Imperial College (1995).
6. For a discussion of security and fraud issues, see Bank for International Settlements (1996a), Roberds (1998), and Greenstein and Feinman (2000).
7. Connors (1998), citing figures from the Ovum research group. The figure is likely to be lower for industrialised countries as a whole. For example, Good (1998), citing the Congressional Budget Office, reports the corresponding figure for the U.S. of 20 percent.
8. The BIS figures do not include Australia.
9. See *The Economist* (1997) for a discussion of alternative views on the viability of microtransactions as an economic model.
10. Visa International press release, June 22, 1998, quoted by Van Hove (1999).

REFERENCES

Bank for International Settlements (1996a). *Security of Electronic Money*. Report by the Committee on Payment and Settlement Systems, August.

Bank for International Settlements (1996b). *Statistics on Payment Systems in the Group of Ten Countries*, December.

Bank for International Settlements (1998). *Statistics on Payment Systems in the Group of Ten Countries*, December.

Connors, Emma (1998). The Smart Card Wasn't So Clever. *Financial Review*, December

31. Australia.

DigiCash (1996). Press release, 24 October.

Economist, The (1997). Cash Poor, 10 May.

Financial System Inquiry (FSI) (1996). Inquiry into the Australian Financial System. Discussion Paper, December.

Furst, K., Lang, W.W., & Nolle, D.E. (1998). Technological Innovation in Banking and Payments: Industry Trends and Implications for Banks. *Quarterly Journal, U.S. Office of the Comptroller of the Currency*, 17(3), September, 23-31.

Good, B.A. (1998). *Will Electronic Money Be Adopted in the United States?* Working Paper 98-20, Federal Reserve Bank of Cleveland.

Greenstein, M. & Feinman, T.M. (2000). *Electronic Commerce: Security, Risk Management and Control*. McGraw-Hill.

Harper, I.R. & Leslie, P. (1995). Electronic Payments Systems and Their Economic Implications. *Policy*, Autumn, 23-28.

Humphrey, D.B. (1995). *Payment Systems: Principles, Practice, and Improvements*. World Bank Technical Paper No. 260. Washington, DC: The World Bank.

Imperial College London (1995). *Survey on Internet Money*. At http://graph.ms.ic.uk/analysis.

Laker, J.F. (1999). The Role of the Payments System Board. Talk to the AIC Conference on "Australian Payments System Evolution", Sydney, 16 June. At http://www.rba.gov.au/speech/sp_ag_160699.html.

Ledingham, P. (1996). *The Policy Implications of Electronic Payments*. Presented to the Consumer Payment Systems Conference, Auckland, May.

Lynch, D.C. and Lundquist, L. (1996). *Digital Money: The New Era of Internet Commerce*. John Wiley.

Mair, P. (1996). *Smart Cards: The Issues*. Financial System Department, Reserve Bank of Australia, October.

Mair, P. (1999). *The Australian Retail Payments System: Some Unresolved Issues*. Discussion Paper.

Roberds, W. (1998). *The Impact of Fraud on New Methods of Retail Payment*. Economic Review, Federal Reserve Bank of Atlanta, First Quarter, 42-52.

Van Hove, L. (1999). Electronic Purses, Interoperability, and the Internet. *First Monday*, 4(4).

AUTHOR NOTE

* I am indebted to two anonymous referees and to Peter Mair for valuable comments on an earlier version of this paper.

Chapter XVI

Internet-Enabled Smart Card Agent Environment and Applications

Teoh Kok Poh and Sheng-Uei Guan
National University of Singapore

INTRODUCTION

The introduction of smart card technology offers an alternative for user authentication and storage medium for data that require both high security as well as location transparency. With a considerably large storage that can be protected from unauthorized access and tampering, and the ability to compute custom software routines including cryptographic algorithms, smart card represents a trusted medium for self-identification and secured information storage that we can carry around with us (Effing and Rankl, 1996).

On the other hand, intelligent software agents represent a new software methodology that starts to gain wide acceptance. While they are possibly the best candidates as an end user's personal assistant in the computer world, they usually are not designed with high security and location transparency in mind. This has greatly limited their ability to function as 'personal representatives' in the world of the Internet.

The proposed smart card agent environment is an effort to bridge these two technologies to produce a viable solution for personalized Internet-based services and solutions. Introduction of software agent technology into traditional smart card applications will bring in new intelligence to make it smarter. The level of security and location transparency in the smart card technology will greatly enhance the usability of agents in the Internet world. With the combination of these two technologies, many Internet-based applications can provide a personalized services with minimum user interactions. This will promote the utilization of Internet-based services and solutions.

BACKGROUND

Smart Card

Since the introduction of smart card in the 1970s, it has been used in many applications, including pay phone, access control, loyalty program, mobile phone, e-commerce and many

Copyright © 2000, Idea Group Publishing.

Figure 1: Typical Smart Card Architecture and System View

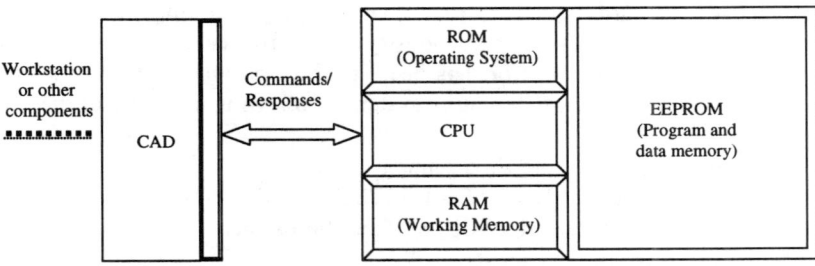

others. The possible applications are growing with the increasing computing power and storage capacity. In a broader scope, smart cards include memory cards with secured and non-secured memory as well as microprocessor cards. However, in the scope of this chapter, we only consider the microprocessor cards in the smart card family.

The basic smart card architecture consists of a communication interface, memory, and a CPU for data processing and calculations. In order to be useful, a smart card needs to interact with a Card Acceptance Device (CAD) or reader through a communication interface. The Card Acceptance Device serves as a conduit for information into and out of the card (Sun Microsystems, 1998). Figure 1 shows a typical smart card architecture and system view.

a) Communication Interface

A smart card is a 'passive' microprocessor that has no power supply and other peripherals like keyboard connected. The only external interface it has is the eight electrical contact points. In order to be useful, a Card Acceptance Device (CAD) is required to provide the power supply and serial communication link.

b) Card Acceptance Device (CAD)

A Card Acceptance Device is required to activate the smart card and perform useful tasks with the smart card. It can be a stand-alone device or link up with other computers in various ways like serial communication port, PCMCIA slot, floppy disk drive, and ISA bus.

c) Smart Card Microprocessor

Smart card microprocessor has limited computation power and memory resources due to the cost and physical constraint. Generally, there are 8, 16 or 32 bit processors operating at a speed of below 5 MHz, with user memory range from 1Kbytes to 64 Kbytes and RAM of 1Kbytes or less.

d) Smart Card Memory

Generally, there are three main types of memory for its respective purpose:
- ROM—Contains code and data that cannot be modified once burnt in. Mainly for the operating system with general-purpose software routine.
- RAM—Fast and volatile memory used as working memory and temporary storage.
- EEPROM—Non-volatile memory that allows both read and write actions at a slower speed compared to RAM. It can be used as application and data memory.

Generally, most smart card architecture supports multi-applications. However, until recently most smart cards issued are based on proprietary operating systems used for single application. As the focus of smart card industry moved from card manufacturers to software and system suppliers, much effort has been made to provide facility to support multi-applications on open standard operating systems. Following are some of the standards or systems proposed (Russell, 1998):

1) Application Processing Environment
- Personal Computer/Smart Card (PC/SC) by Microsoft
- Open Card Framework (OCF) by Sun Microsystems

2) Flexible Card Environments
- Java Card by Sun Microsystems
- MULTOS by MasterCard and Alliances
- Smart Card for Windows by Microsoft

Java Card

In the design of the smart card agent environment, Java Card is used as the operating environment for the smart card. As an open standard platform, Java Card promotes platform independence of chips architecture and object-oriented programming in smart card (Sun Microsystems, 1998). Also, it is inherently designed for multi-applications and dynamic updates of applets and data. This has greatly enhanced the system flexibility while the development and maintenance efforts are reduced.

Java Card security comes from both software and hardware as described in the following (Schlumberger, 1998):
- Smart card hardware provides a tamper-resistant medium.
- Java is well known as a secure programming language.
- It has cryptographic capabilities to perform encryption, digital signature and authentication.

There are several versions of Java Card available in the market for application developers. The following are typical hardware configurations:
- 16/32 bits RISC microprocessor
- 24-32 Kbytes of ROM
- 16/32 Kbytes of EEPROM
- 1 Kbytes or less of RAM

This typical platform is sufficient to install various applets for smart card agent applications with its critical data stored within.

Intelligent Software Agent

Software agents have been around for more than one decade. However, they can be considered as a new software paradigm that is making its way to mainstream application software. Software agents are small software artifacts that have some form of intelligence and autonomy with a metaphor of personal assistants (Huhns and Singh, 1998). It is an active software artifact that would simplify the process of performing tasks through computer software and might exhibit learning abilities to learn its user's habits and preferences. In a multi-agents environment, the learned profile and work pattern can be exchanged among the agents to provide personalized services. This provides customized software services in a new way.

With proper implementation, a software agent has the following potential benefits (Chorafas, 1998):
- Providing a simple-to-use interaction style
- Ability to provide friendly and helpful advice
- Hiding process and software complexity from the users
- Taking care of things that the users would rather not have to do themselves

Internet-Enabled Smart Card Agent Environment

The Internet has realized a connected world with a great degree of openness. The degree of openness for the Internet and its users mobility suggest that a reliable user identification and data security together with location transparency are crucial for any successful Internet-based implementation.

The built-in cryptography capabilities and high resistance towards tampering have made smart card an excellent candidate as a 'personal representative' for Internet users. Many applications can be and have been derived from these key features. Some obvious examples are smart card-based network or service access, e-cash for Internet commerce, electronic wallet for sensitive data like passwords and PINs, digital signatures and certificates. Since the sensitive data are stored inside smart cards and not within the Internet-connected computer, it is relatively distant from security attacks initiated from network or Internet users.

There are already works on the agents as personal assistant, mobile agents and smart card for Internet. The smart card agent environment is an initiative to design a 'personal representative' that will function as a personal assistant that can accommodate user mobility and perform actual transactions. Figure 2 illustrates a typical architecture for Internet-based smart card applications.

DESIGN OF SMART CARD AGENT ENVIRONMENT

The main objective of this design is to explore the agent environment with smart card as an enabling technology for unique features. The key characteristics of such an agent environment are location transparency, security and privacy. Therefore, the major aspect of the design would be reflected on agents as personal assistants that their users can bring along and truly trust.

Figure 2: Typical Architecture of Internet-Based Smart Card Applications

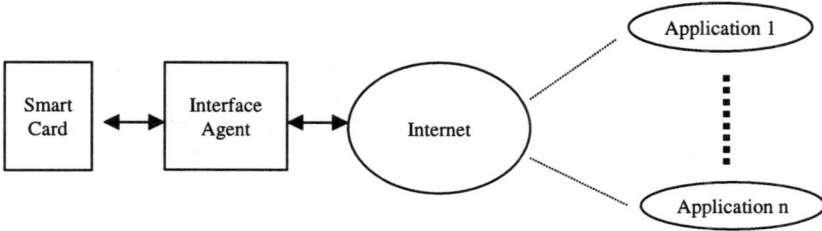

Overview of Smart Card Agent Environment

In this design, the software agent functionality is implemented in three key components to meet the practical consideration of data security, location transparency and usability. Figure 3 illustrates the system overview of the smart card agent environment.

Key Components in a Smart Card Agent Environment

a) On-Card Agent

- Implemented as an applet in Java Card, an open platform smart card that accommodates multiple applications and portable program codes. It is one of the three components of a smart card agent where secured and portable data can be stored and managed. The on-card agent is able to access and manipulate the data stored in the smart card, and response to the requests from off-card agents. With proper software routines, it can exhibit some form of intelligence.
- Smart card's built-in cryptography capabilities allow secure authentication, data encryption and digital signature to be carried out with its data.
- The basic building blocks of an on-card agent are the OnCardAgent applet and several securely managed files.
- The OnCardAgent applet is responsible to handle external requests, security and data management and interfaces with other data files.
- Data files installed within an on-card agent include parameters file, off-card agent parameters file, user file and agent related record files. All the files are protected by an access scheme using PIN or authentication. The interactions between on-card agent applet and other components are illustrated in Figure 4.

Figure 3: System Overview of a Smart Card Agent Environment

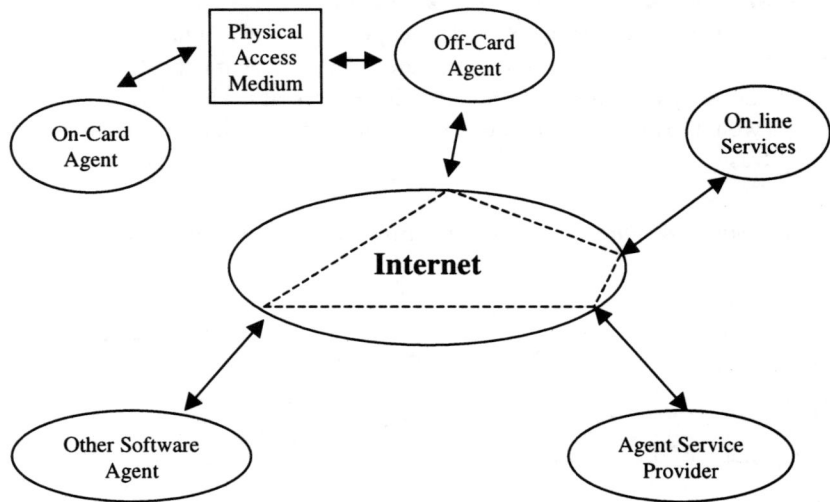

Figure 4: On-Card Agent Interaction Block Diagram

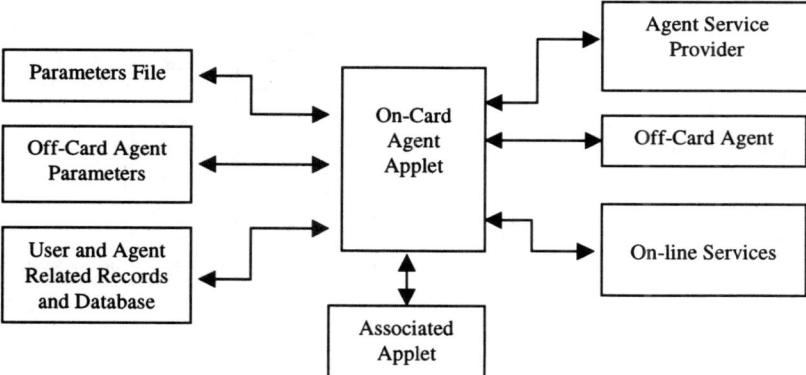

- Parameters file: To store system parameters for the on-card agent, including PIN, ID, and links to associated applets.
- User and agent-related records and database: Including personal profile file, habit and preferences index file, ID record file, personal data record file, registered agent file, custom agent data file, current activities file, and e-data file. This is the key information used by the off-card agents, agent service providers, and on-line services to provide personalized services.
- Off-card agent parameters file: User-customizable software parameters and setting preferences. This will ensure the user getting the same software environment regardless of which copy of the off-card agent is being used.
- Associated applets: Applets that contain customized routines and applications within the card that can communicate with the on-card agent. These are the smart card applications like network access or loyalty programs that are known to the on-card agent.
- The registered user will be provided with a smart card reader, a Java Card and a setup program to set up the on-card agent. After that, the administration and data backup for the on-card agent are handled by the off-card agent in the standard mode (please refer to "off-card agent").
- Similarly, the associated applets and data files can be installed and removed through the off-card agent.

b) Off-Card Agent

- Provides the user interface for user interaction and as an entry point for all agent services.
- The off-card agent will provide all the intelligent software agent features as described in the Services and Features Section using data or software routines from the on-card agent.
- When on-line services are required, the off-card agent will connect to the agent service provider in standard terminology. Agent service provider will be responsible to solve the ontology problem by matching these standard terms to various on-line services

Figure 5: Basic Relationship of Smart Card Agent Components and On-line Services

standards.
- Learning algorithms for usage patterns, habits, and preferences will be implemented in the off-card agent. With these learning algorithms, the off-card agent will be able to capture how the user uses certain services and optimizes the services accordingly. It will accumulate experience and fine-tune the learned indices as the user activities go on. As storage spaces are limited, most on-card agent data are indexed and will be interpreted by the off-card agent once it is retrieved.
- There are three modes of operation for the off-card agent:
  a) Standard mode —In this mode, users can use the entire agent services and functions. Agent data administration and backup is performed using this mode.
  b) Web-Access mode—When the standard off-card agent is not installed in the user's computer, he can access the off-card agent at the agent service provider web site. In this mode, the off-card agent offers the same functionality as in the standard mode except the agent data administration cannot be carried out and performance might be affected if the connection is slow.
  c) Simplified mode—It is a subset of the standard mode to implement on certain features of the off-card agent. It allows on-line services to access on-card agent without going through the agent service provider. Also, it can be implemented on embedded system like PDA and GSM mobile phones.
- As the off-card agent serves a user, statistics on his usage pattern and user profile will be compiled. With these statistics, a relationship between the usage pattern and user group can be established to allow the service provider to provide more focused services. These data can be uploaded to the agent service provider's server to be compiled as master statistic data. These master statistic data will help any off-card agent that requires a reference. As most activities are on the Internet, these data can be well maintained through proper planning.

c) Agent Service Provider
- Offers a center to link the user to the smart card agent environment and other on-line services; maintains the most recent database and on-line services for various agents.
- There are many agents within the agent service provider that might be maintained by several parties with respective domain expertise. Some examples of agents are travel agents, shopping agents for various good types, healthcare agents, investment agents, etc.

- The agent service provider will accept requests from the off-card agent and interface to other on-line services using their own format based on the translated data. Feedback and confirmation will be sent back to the off-card agent after being translated into the standard agent term.
- It is also a resource center for a user to download software like new applets and index database, e.g., habit and preferences index, upgrade software and upload statistic data.
- As an added service, each registered user will be allocated a 'Web house' that contains a secure private area for personal data and a public area for exchange of messages and data between members. While the home page provides a showroom function to its owner, a 'Web house' is more like a private estate on the Internet where the owner can perform some personal transaction and allows others to know and contact him as a certain personality. The private area would allow a user to store significantly larger documents and data that cannot be stored within the smart card. The exchange of messages in the public area allows announcements and exchange of ideas etc. within some defined member groups. A user will be classified under certain member groups based on his personal profile and usage pattern of certain services. Therefore, the same user may be classified under several member groups as long as he meets the requirements.
- To ensure security and privacy, all data in the private area will be encrypted using a user-supplied secret key from its on-card agent. In this case, even the agent service provider cannot access the data. In this context, the agent service provider's role is to provide a storage area that is fully controlled by the user. This will promote the usage of secured Internet-linked data storage.

d) Online Services
- When a transaction is performed through software agent services, it is normally through the interface of an agent service provider.
- An online service provider can play a more active role by implementing the simplified mode of the off-card agent in the server. This will allow direct interaction with the on-card agent to perform automated user data entry, user authentication and custom configuration.
- The major advantages of interfacing on-line services to an on-card agent are the increased security and usability. Also, user databases can be used to provide more personalized services, e.g., on-line membership, online shopping, Internet searching, on-line healthcare etc.
- The key functions would be user authentication, digital signature, digital certificate for membership access, and automatic mapping of secured data and personal data for services that require such input.

e) Access Medium
- The basic level of access medium is the smart card reader that bridges the on-card agent and the off-card agent.
- The off-card agent can be installed on various hardware platforms including PC, notebook and PDA.
- The Internet is the access medium for linking the off-card agent, on-line services and agent service provider.

Application Scenario

Basically, a smart card system would required a smart card and its reader yo keep intact during the transaction and updating of data. While one of its key features is location transparency, it is not actually a "mobile agent" as the applet is not able to move out of the card and continue it duties. It is rather more transactional based, as it will handle requests and responses accordingly.

As for transaction security, a smart card system seldom uses purely software-based protocol like SET as inherently it is easier to implement a secure electronic purse like Visa Cash and Proton based on its built-in cryptography capabilities. Crypto-controller based smart cards are available for financial application and applications that require high security. It has build-in hardware to perform DES and RSA encryption efficiently.

The other advantage of using smart card in an agent environment is the possibility to install other smart card applications in the same card we use for the agents and provide an integrated service. Examples of smart card applications are electronic cash, personal healthcare record, bonus point program, access control and many more.

A typical application scenario of smart card agent environment is illustrated in Figure 6. Following is the description of some of the key events in typical applications:

- A user request or off-card agent autonomous request will be forwarded to the agent service provider together with associated personal and customize data from the on-card agent.
- The selected agent service will query all related on-line services and perform necessary transactions to fulfill the request. Most data needed for transactions can be obtained from the on-card agent, which needs to be unlocked once by entering a user PIN. If confirmation or user selection is required, the information will be forwarded back to the off-card agent for further actions.

Figure 6: Typical Application Scenario of Smart Card Agent Environment

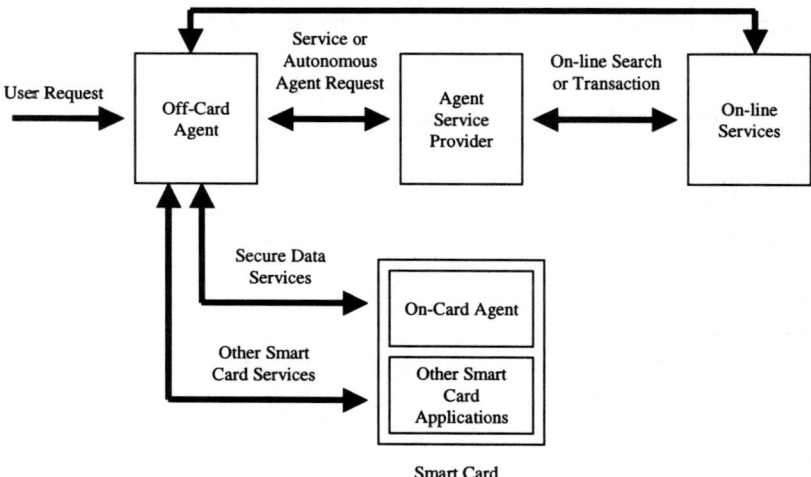

- If secure data like membership ID or credit card number are required for a transaction, the digitally signed data will be obtained from the on-card agent and verified by the agent service provider or on-line service provider.
- Other smart card applications like electronic cash and loyalty program can be accessed during transaction for payment or loyalty point updating purpose.
- The off-card agent will monitor the on-going activities and capture necessary data to update the personal profile, user habits and other on-card agent files. It is rather difficult to catch up with the personal profile and preferences in real time. However, if the applications of this environment are more related to the Internet, we still can come out with a rather useful profile as the fact that most activities online help keep the profile current.
- A mobile user can have the on-card agent installed in the SIM (Subscriber Identification Module) card. However, it is not feasible to implement the complete version of off-card agent in the GSM mobile handset, but we still can have the similar agent services by connecting to the agent service provider that provides the functionality of the off-card agent and as an interface to the Internet services.

On-Card Agent Implementation

In terms of software development technology, off-card agents and agent service providers can be implemented using current architectural framework of software agents and on-line data management services. In order to prove the feasibility of the smart card agent environment, some implementation details for on-card agents are described in this section.

A prototype of an OnCardAgent applet has been implemented using the Java Card Workstation Development Environment (JCWDE). Once completed, the applet can be implemented into actual Java Card like Gemplus's GemXpresso RAD series or Schlumberger's Cyberflex series. Table 1 summarizes the key components of the on-card agent.

Following are some of the application scenarios of an on-card agent:
- A new Java Card is installed with the OnCardAgent applets and all the files with empty or default data.
- The user will fill up the form for personal biography and preferences with the off-card agent. The data will then be transferred to the on-card agent and stored in the personal profile file, and habit and preferences file.
- Along the way, the user can store some important personal data in the personal data file or e-data file. Also, the user can sign up for agent services where it is registered in the registered agent file and the customization data can be stored within the custom agent data file. Any software agent that wants to make use of the secured portable data of the smart card can make an offer to allow for registration.
- The user can sign up to on-line services with the digital certificate for authentication stored in the ID record file.
- When the user makes use of an agent service, this activity with its details will be stored in the current activities file.

Services and Features

The unique features of the smart card agent environment offer an infrastructure for many Internet-based applications. The following shows some of the possible implementations to provide new applications or improvement over existing software-based solutions:

Table 1: On-Card Agent Applets and Files

Item	Descriptions
OnCardAgent Applet	As an interface to external requests and internal files, it will install, register, select an applet or file, process commands, and manage files and data.
Parameters File	Contains parameters like on-card agent ID, expiry date, PIN, and associated applet configurations.
Personal Data Record File	Includes personal biography and data like name, date of birth, driving license ID, and credit card number with critical data digitally signed.
Habit and Preference File	Maintains an index of personal habits and preferences.
ID Record File	Contains custom certificate for on-line authentication purpose.
Registered Agent File	A table to store all the registered applets used by the user.
Custom Agent Data File	Any registered agent can store its custom configurations or data as a record within this file.
Current Activities File	Contains all the active activities carried out by the agents or the user. This file gives a general overview of on-going events.
E-Data File	This is a user data file for the user to store his personal data or any data he wants to keep.
Transaction Log	A log file to record all the transactions of the on-card agent

a) Personalized searching or information filtering —Personal profiles and indices can be used to enhance Internet searching and information filtering. This will greatly increase the search engine hit rate and reduce the browsing time. The search results can be ranked according to the popularity of the information among those with a personal profile closest to the user.

b) Personal E-Wallet—To store personal data, PIN number, password and digital certificate. The information can be retrieved through the off-card agent or agent service provider. With a proper protocol, the data can be mapped to online services' web site for online transactions. This will reduce the number of user interactions required to get a task done.

c) On-line Membership Authentication—For on-line membership or subscription, normally a login ID and user password will be provided. However, the password can be exposed, shared and used by many other users. To improve this, the service provider can issue a digital certificate (to be stored in the on-card agent) for each registered user for a better control and security.

d) Automated Web-Based Transactions—Current Web-based transactions involve heavy data entry from the user side, this forms the unpleasant part of the Web-based services and e-commerce. With a proper protocol, most of the data entry by the user can be replaced by data retrieval from the smart card. To further improve security, financially

sensitive data like credit card numbers can be installed and digitally signed by a trusted organization. The benefit of such a scheme is to minimize user interactions and hence realize the complexity of Web-based transactions and e-commerce. This will help to improve the general public acceptance of Internet technology.
e) Online services based on user group classification—A standard to classify users to groups and types based on their user profiles can be developed to facilitate customized on-line services. With the group classification and user preferences, a user would automatically logon to the service and presented with the most wanted services. This can be fine-tuned later and also linked with other services.
f) Custom setting for desktop and Internet applications —The on-card agent together with the 'Web-house', would be able to allow the user to work within his/her preferred environment and allow access to personalized data like e-mail address book, Web browser bookmark, newsgroup setting and others. When a user logs in to an Internet-enabled workstation and wishes to customize the environment, the data can be downloaded from his own 'web house' in the agent service provider server and the system will be customized. This would be a useful feature as we are increasingly mobile and a consistent environment is a crucial part of work productivity.
g) Virtual communities based on 'Web house'— A virtual community can be created with each member's 'Web house' as a basic unit. A group of 'web houses' with similar profiles will form a community estate where services targeted to a specific group can be developed. Each virtual resident can interact, exchange messages, and perform transactions for services available within the virtual community. The coordination effort will be carried out by the agent service provider or some trusted organizations. The possible activities in the virtual community would greatly depend on the coordinating organizations and their members' effort.
h) Integrate transactions with other smart card applications like electronic purse, membership and bonus point program to perform actual transaction. With a smooth integration of such applications, Web-based transactions like e-commerce would possibly be a pleasant experience.
i) Personal agents will alert a user of important events and appointments like expiry date of personal documents and schedules or arrangements by Web transactions.

ISSUES AND CONTROVERSIES OF SMART CARD AGENT ENVIRONMENT

Issues and Controversies

The smart card agent environment represents a viable solution to serve the need of personalize services in the Internet world. However, there are issues and controversies that need to be sorted out before widespread implementations are possible. Following are some of the possible issues and controversies:
- Agent technology—While smart card represents an excellent system component, the true intelligence of many implementations still comes from the agent technology. Agent technology has been implemented in many applications. However, it is still in the infancy state for implementation as a personal assistant. A mature technology is required to bootstrap the implementation of the smart card agent environment.

- Availability of the access medium—Up to now, the smart card reader is not a common computer peripheral as a floppy drive. In order to facilitate the implementation, the smart card reader would need to be a default computer peripheral.
- Interoperability of various smart cards and readers—Smart cards and readers in the market are not interoperable. Some form of join effort from various players is required in order to implement the distributed environment.
- Lack of industrial standards for interfacing between major components in the environment.
- Security and trust level of the on-card agent as a self-identification unit is a major concern. A trusted organization is required to validate the financially critical data like credit card information.
- Security attacks that focus on the technology weakness as compared to the brute force attacks. A good example is the recent attacks on smart cards using Simple Power Analysis (SPA) where an encrypted key can be extracted by analyzing the power consumption patterns of the chip when the encryption routine is being executed.
- Private statistic data collected when using a smart card might end up in the wrong hand.
- Limited memory size and computing power of smart cards are the limiting factors to more powerful routines.

Solutions and Recommendations

- Although agents as personal assistants have not been truly intelligent, implementation based on current techniques would be sufficient to handle basic requirements with more enhancements being done along the process.
- Smart card has started to gain acceptance as part of the mainstream in the computer industry. Some computer manufacturers have started to ship smart card readers together with their new systems. Furthermore, Microsoft's and others major software vendors' plans to include support for smart card in their products have further promoted its utilization. Hence the availability problem would be solved in the near term.
- Efforts on the open standard platform like Java Card for the operating system and PC/SC for the interface are expected to alleviate the problems.
- A consortium should be formed to develop a standard for smart card agents and their interface protocols. Before such a standard is formed, agent service providers would need to develop a protocol for such a purpose.
- On-card agents should be issued and digitally signed by a reputable and trusted organization so that they can be used as a trusted self-identification unit.
- Most attacks on technology weakness can be solved or contained by modifying the card operating system once this weakness is known. Therefore, field upgradable card operating systems would be needed to handle these problems.
- Practically, personal data have already been used for demographic and others statistics. As long as the exposure is minimal and contained, a smart card agent environment will not make things worse.
- The advancement of semiconductor technology has increased the computing power and memory size of chips used for smart card. There are already 16-bit and 32-bit microprocessors for smart card and continued research aims for better chips.

FUTURE TRENDS

The future of electronic commerce from the perspective of smart card and agent technology actually relies on the social aspects of the technology. Following are some of the future trends and their impact:
- The emerging of electronic commerce has actually enabled personalized goods and services within a reasonable price range. The smart card agent technology would be able to play a key role in this area. For general goods, on-line comparison of product features and price is part of the process where an intelligent software agent can play an important role to minimize the efforts required.
- With more and more people on the move, integration of electronic commerce and smart card agent technology into gadgets like mobile phones and personal digital assistants (PDA) would be inevitable. Smart card agents would play a complementary role as far as this technology is concerned.
- As more and more people start to get involved in the Internet and electronic commerce, agent technology would be widely used to filter the technical details from a general user.
- Smart card would evolve into a powerful personal computing unit that bridges human beings to the networked computing world.

CONCLUSIONS

The integration of smart card and agent technology represents an effort to achieve intelligence amplification through a microprocessor, i.e., smart card that we can carry along. Smart card is probably the first successful attempt to equip the general public with microprocessors in their wallets (Effing and Rankl, 1996). With the increasingly higher computing power, smart card would be the best candidate as a 'personal representative' in the digital world. It has bridged the transactional gap between humans and computers to allow a new level of 'human' computer interaction. This would open up huge application possibilities.

In the context of e-commerce, much effort has been focused on the infrastructure and transactional technology to ensure a smooth transaction from goods selection to the final payment and goods delivery. However, in order to gain widespread acceptance from the general public, the execution of these processes must be seamless with minimum user interactions while the payment security is ensured. Hence, a tight integration among these processes is required.

The Smart Card Agent Environment is designed to address execution issues. The agent technology can be used to greatly enhance the selection process while the transaction, payment and goods delivery information can be exchanged within the multi-applications smart cards. Also, the smart card ability to meet the security and mobility requirement has made this a viable solution.

However, in the practical sense, there are major standardization issues that need to be resolved before a practical implementation can be deployed.

REFERENCES

Alberda, M.I., Hartel, P.H. & Jong Frz, E.K. (1997). Using formal methods to cultivate trust in smart card operating systems. *Future Generation Computer Systems, 13*, 39-54.

Allen, C.A., Barr, W.J. & Schultz, R. (1996). Smart cards: Seizing strategic business opportunities.

Chorafas, D.N. (1998). *Agent technology handbook.* McGraw-Hill.

Dale, J., DeRoure, D.C. (1997). *A mobile agent architecture for distributed information management.* University of Southampton.

Dreifus, H. & Monk, J.T. (1997). *Smart cards: A guide to building and managing smart card applications.* Wiley Computer Publishing.

Effing, W. & Rankl, W. (1996). *Smart card handbook.* London: John Wiley & Sons.

Sun Microsystems Inc. (1998). Java Card applet developer's guide revision 1.12.

Ferrer, J.D. (1997). Multi-applications smart card and encrypted data processing. *Future Generation Computer Systems, 13*, 65-74.

Huhns, M.N. & Singh, M.P. (1998, September-October). Personal assistants. *IEEE Internet Computing*, pp. 90-92.

Jennings, N.R. & Wooldridge, M. (1998). *Applications of intelligent agents.* Queen Mary & Westfield College, University of London.

Nwana, H.S., Ndumu, D.T. (1999). *A perspective on software agents research.* British Telecommunications Laboratories.

Quisquater, J.J. (1997). The adolescence of smart cards. *Future Generation Computer Systems, 13*, 3-7.

Russell, J.F. (1997). *Compatibility and conflicts: PC/SC, OCF, Java Card Multos.*

Schlumberger. (1998). *Cyberflex Access Java programmable smart card.*

Sun Microsystems Inc. (1998). *Java Card 2.1 reference implementation user's guide.*

Sun Microsystems Inc. (1998). *Java Card applet developer's guide.*

Chapter XVII

Supporting Innovative Competitive Strategies as Mass Customization by Pairing E-Commerce Technologies with Agent Technology

Klaus Turowski
Otto-von-Guericke University, Magdeburg, Germany

The Internet has created a tremendous opportunity to conduct business electronically. By this, innovative business concepts—such as virtual enterprises, supply chain management, or one-to-one marketing—and advanced competitive strategies—such as mass customization which encompass these business concepts—may be followed up much more efficiently. However, competitive strategies like mass customization require sophisticated information infrastructures to support the indispensable business-to-business electronic commerce—even for small and medium enterprises taking part in a virtual enterprise that pursues mass customization (MC). Especially electronic data interchange (EDI), understood as a means to exchange business data, is crucial to set up and maintain virtual enterprises. Thus, there is a high demand on software that provides an inter-application system exchange of business data between companies, and which is inexpensive as well as easy to install and use. In this contribution we propose an approach to support distributed, but logically integrated inter-company business processes by applying e-commerce techniques paired with agent technology. Doing so, inter-company data exchange, procurement, and coordination of production in case of MC are improved by means of a multi-agent system. After discussing specific business requirements of companies that cooperatively produce a specific good or service, we show how an automated inter-company communication can be provided, and how this further develops into an agent-based system that automates procurement and inter-company coordination of production. By using the extensible markup language (XML) as an important cross-section technique, together with common business communication standards, we show how the border of heterogeneity between different (distributed) application systems can be overcome. With this, the business communication protocol is set up. Taking this protocol as a basis, we further present a component framework, which is implemented using the JavaBeans technology, that supports an efficient inter-company communication. In addition, we show how this approach may further develop to a means for inter-company coordination.

ENABLING INNOVATIVE COMPETITIVE STRATEGIES USING E-COMMERCE TECHNIQUES

E-commerce may be defined as "any form of business transaction in which the parties interact electronically rather than by physical exchanges or direct physical contact" (ECOM, 1998, p. 2). It "refers to business activities involving consumers, manufacturers, service providers, and intermediaries using computer networks such as the Internet" (Adam, Dogramaci, Gangopadhyay and Yesha, 1999, p. xi). The scope of e-commerce reaches from simple *World Wide Web* (WWW) presence to shared business processes connecting different companies, and it aims on saving time and costs of business transactions. By this, innovative concepts such as virtual enterprises, supply chain management, or one-to-one marketing, and advanced competitive strategies such as *mass customization* (MC) may be followed up much more efficiently.

MC requires a synthesis between mass production and the production of highly specialized and individualized products. It aims at the production of individual products with high quality at cost factors typical for mass production and comparable short delivery times (Pine II, 1993, p. 48). Originally, MC was discussed as a marketing concept, which, following the paradigm of customer orientation, automatically results from a constant market segmentation (Kotler, 1989, p. 13). Starting from a mass market, products for specific market segments are offered to satisfy the needs of special customer groups. A further differentiation of markets leads from micro markets and niche markets to individual markets, which contain the single customer. Above all, small and medium manufacturers were forced so far to follow a strategy of differentiation, as the production of small series was predominant. The number of pieces was not high enough to become a cost leader. Hence, small and medium enterprises, willing to pursue MC, have to focus on a more efficient production process, being customer oriented. On the other side, large manufacturers have to reach a higher flexibility and a higher degree of customer orientation.

Looking at empirical studies, five instances of MC can be classified (Reiß and Beck, 1994): service customization, self customization, splitting of the production process, speed management, and modularization. A variety of cases concerning companies pursuing MC may be found in Piller (1998).

MC as a *competitive strategy* requires (dependent from its concrete instance) that different production types are employed simultaneously—especially single-item production with is usually high demand of inter-company interactions. The approach presented in the following aims at an improvement of these (mandatory) business to business interactions, especially in case of MC. Hereby, we address the problem of an automatic inter-

Figure 1: Networked production process

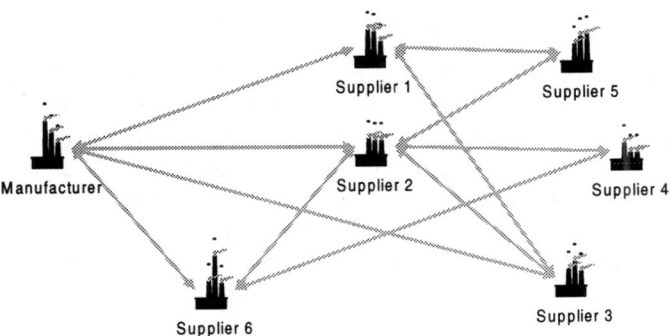

company collaboration involving (legacy) application systems of manufacturers and suppliers, which are often incompatible. By using e-commerce techniques paired with agent technology, we show how data exchange between manufacturers and their suppliers can be handled efficiently and in a timely manner. Furthermore, we point out how this approach develops into a technique to coordinate distributed production processes.

Business Scenarios to Support

The description of the underlying business process is fundamental for understanding the proposed approach. At first, we explain it at a macro level. Next, we pick out a specific scenario, which is used to explain improvements going together with our approach.

The lower part of Figure 2 depicts the MC macro process as introduced in Rautenstrauch (1998, pp. 25-26). It starts with the *configuration* of the desired product by the customer. After that, it is necessary to check which parts or assemblies can be produced by the manufacturer and which must be *acquired*. For parts that must be acquired individual attributes may possibly also have to be taken into account. In such a case, the manufacturer becomes a customer with individual requirements with regard to certain suppliers. The same may happen to some of these suppliers with regard to their suppliers. This leads to a nesting of procurement activities, and finally, to a networked production process that covers multiple companies and plants (cf. Figure 1).

Procurement follows the *production* of individual products by flexible, or respectively partly-automated groups. Ad hoc generated bills of materials and work schedules provide the data basis. This implies that long- and mid-term overall planning in the usual sense is impractical for MC, since realistic parameters cannot be determined due to high uncertainties with regard to products that must be produced in a longer planning period. Production also includes quality assurance. The process is completed through the physical *distribution*.

The upper part of Figure 2 illustrates a concrete instance of the MC macro process. It depicts main interactions between customer, retailer, manufacturer, and suppliers necessary to sell, produce, and distribute an individualized product in a special case. For this example, we assume that the manufacturer pursues splitting of the production process as instance of

MC. In this case, production is split into two pieces: a customer neutral, standardized part, and a part, where individualized products are manufactured. The customer is integrated in the individualized part of the production process, e. g., customer-specific production of utility vehicles. For a better understanding we omit suppliers of suppliers and depict interactions for one supplier only.

The business process starts with a customer, willing to buy an individualized product, contacting a retailer. Then the customer (guided by the retailer) customizes the product. As soon as the product is individualized, the retailer sends an order to the manufacturer. In case of expensive products, or in case of critical time conditions, the customer may demand an offer before he launches an order. If this happens, the manufacturer has to be able to assure a certain delivery date, a certain price, or a certain quality. To do so, the manufacturer has to process the data that he gets from the retailer concerning the configuration of the product. The manufacturer then calculates which parts he will have to produce, which parts he will have to buy, and how long it will take to fulfill the order. If the parts needed are in stock, real-time planning can occur and an offer or a confirmation including information concerning delivery date, price, and quality may be generated currently and sent to the customer. This will not be possible, if parts have to be ordered, especially if these parts are not standardized. In this case, the manufacturer has to negotiate with his suppliers (Figure 2 (1)) whether or not his demand could be covered in time. Thereafter he is able to send an offer to the customer. If the customer accepts the offer, he releases an order, and the manufacturer may have to negotiate for final conditions (Figure 2 (2)) before he finally releases his orders.

Figure 2: MC macro process and a concrete instance

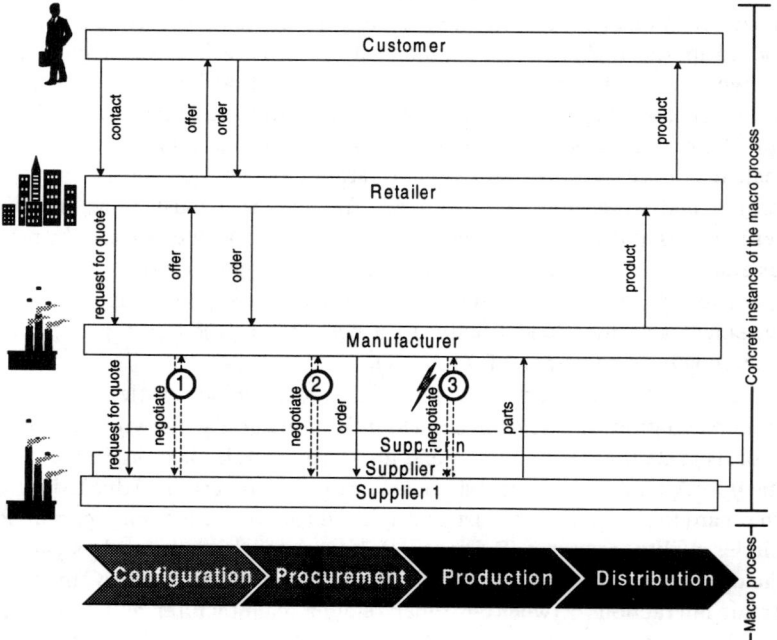

Then the production occurs. In case of machine breakdown or general delivery problems another negotiation between the manufacturer and some, or even all of his suppliers (due to possibly nested production processes (cf. figure 1)) may be necessary – the so-called *coordination* of production (Figure 1 (3)). After all parts are manufactured and delivered by the suppliers, final assembly can occur, and the individualized product may be delivered to the customer.

In the following, we address the question of how e-commerce techniques can improve the described process, and especially, how the respective negotiation tasks can be supported efficiently.

E-Commerce Techniques for MC

E-commerce can be divided into four categories: business-to-business, business-to-consumer, business-to-administration, and consumer to administration e-commerce. From these categories, business to business e-commerce, which covers all transactions between companies, has been well established. Referring to MC this concerns all transactions between retailers, manufacturers, and suppliers, which may especially be improved by *electronic data interchange* (EDI). Business-to-consumer e-commerce expands with the advance of the WWW. With respect to MC it offers opportunities in the area of tool supported configuration of individual products and one-to-one marketing. Business-to-administration e-commerce and consumer-to-administration e-commerce have not yet emerged broadly.

A successful implementation of the MC macro process requires access to a network of suppliers who ideally offer just-in-time shipment and an information network with specially trained retailers offering customized products (cf. Kotha, 1996, pp. 447-449). Other requirements, dealing with the implementation of suitable information systems, are mentioned in Moad (1995, p. 35). Moad emphasizes the importance of application systems for *product configuration, integration of suppliers, coordination of cross-organizational production processes*, and *support of demand-oriented logistics*.

First, customers need a way to describe what exactly they want to purchase. Among time limits and quantities, this encompasses product characteristics such as colors, performance, or geometry. This information has to be translated into terms that can be understood by production planning, manufacturing, and engineering. Configuration tools that are based on (WWW-based) *electronic product catalogues* may support the respective tasks. Configuration tools display all available components and permitted changes of a product's characteristics. Some are already applicable online (Birkhofer and Büttner, 1995). If an order forces an engineering change, software for *engineering data management* (EDM) (Abramovici & Bickelmann, 1993) allows quick changes of design data. EDM-systems may be integrated with systems for *enterprise resource planning* (ERP), such as SAP R/3, BAAN IV, or Oracle Applications, which are responsible for production planning and control.

The coordination of procurement activities (*supply chain management* (Houlihan, 1992)), up to and including the founding of *virtual enterprises* (cf. e. g. Arnold, Faisst, Härtling and Sieber, 1995, p. 10), can occur in various ways on worldwide networks, and here especially on the Internet. Promising approaches for the support of cross-organizational MC activities (Kurbel, 1996) include the establishment of *electronic yellow pages*, e. g. the Enterprise Integration Network (EINet), through which manufacturers and suppliers can locate one another, and in which middlemen mediate between producers and suppliers worldwide via the Internet.

However, the main remaining problem that a business to business e-commerce solution in case of MC should solve is to support an efficient, flexible, and responsive coordination between manufacturers and suppliers, as the integration of suppliers as well as the coordination of cross-organizational production processes are critical success factors for MC. Having technology-enabling communication across organizations using different (heterogeneous) application systems, such as protocols (e. g. transport control protocol (TCP), hypertext transfer protocol (HTTP)), or platform-independent programming languages (e. g. Java), are necessary, but not sufficient conditions. Only combining the so far mentioned e-commerce techniques with EDI makes the links between manufactures and suppliers more efficient and responsive, as manual interfaces can be omitted and costs reduced.

Figure 3 shows a possible information infrastructure to support our MC scenario (in fact, it is the first birds eye view on our approach). In this example, it is conspicuous that there is no direct need for a retailer. In fact, the retailer may be omitted if not needed as an intermediary expert. The customer may use a Web-based product catalogue or product configuration tool himself, maybe together with an expert system that gives explanations and which helps in case of problems. Since we put the emphasis on business to business interactions, we assume that the data describing the individualized product is somehow

Figure 3: Information infrastructure to support the MC scenario

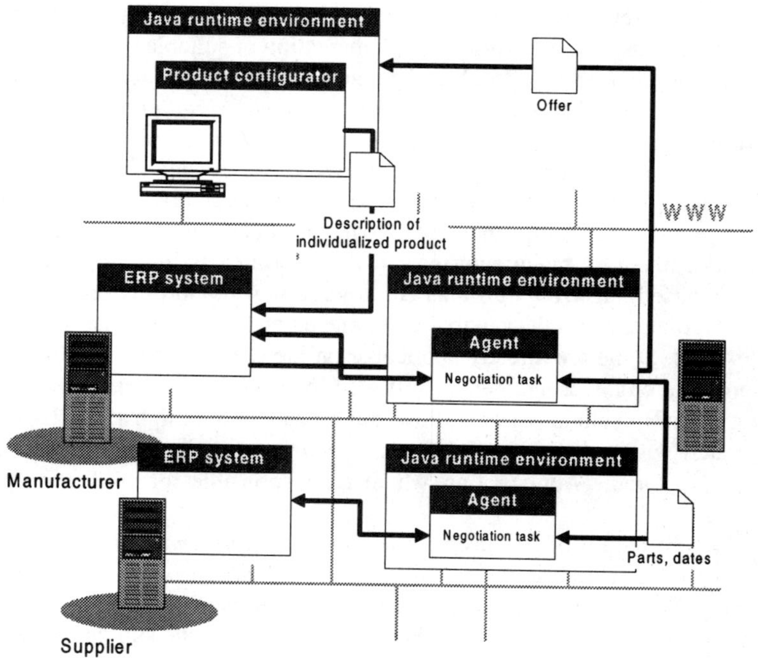

transferred into the ERP application of the manufacturer. In the next section, we show how to handle the data exchange between manufacturer and suppliers.

AUTOMATING INTER-COMPANY COMMUNICATION

Electronic Data Interchange (EDI)

Implementing EDI leads to organizational information-based surplus values (cf. Kuhlen, 1996, esp. p. 90), e. g,. an improved organizational and operational structure as well as time and cost savings. The most important standard for cross-organizational data interchange was established by the United Nations with UN/EDIFACT (*electronic data interchange for administration, commerce, and transport*) (UN, 1995). It standardizes electronic exchange of structured information, e. g., orders or invoices, thus permitting a direct communication between different business application systems. Due to fundamental drawbacks, like the missing of semantic rules, e. g., for quantity or packaging units, the implicit assumption that each organization uses similar business processes and scenarios (cf. Zbornik, 1996, pp. 92-93), and economic (e. g., high implementation costs) as well as organizational (e. g. slow adoption to changing business processes, complicate adjustment of established business process and rules) (cf. Goldfarb & Prescod, 1998, pp. 106-110) causes, that UN/EDIFACT did not win the expected recognition and implementation extent.

Open-EDI/object oriented-EDI (TMWG, 1998), Universal Data Element Framework (UDEF) (Harvey et al., 1998, pp. 25-26), Basic Semantic Repository (BSR), and its successor BEACON (Steel, 1997) are efforts, that address the problems mentioned first. They focus on establishing uniform business scenarios and semantic rules.

The XML/EDI-Initiative (Peat & Webber, 1997) on the other hand concentrates on economical and organizational drawbacks of UN/EDIFACT using the *extensible markup language* (XML) (cf. Bray, Paoli, & Sperberg-McQueen, 1997) to lower implementation costs and increase flexibility of EDI.

The basic idea of the XML/EDI initiative, which is to encapsulate business data between XML tags, will be taken up in the following to support a flexible and efficient inter-company data interchange by means of an agent-based system. The system supports communication and negotiation as depicted in Figure 2 in the phases configuration, procurement, and production of the MC macro process.

XML-Based EDI

XML is a subset of the *standardized generalized markup language* (SGML). In contrast to the *hypertext markup language* (HTML), it allows the creation of custom tokens and custom document structures. Each XML document and each element of a XML document is an object with its own properties. These features allow expressing existing EDI mechanisms using XML, and further, new and more flexible methods may thereby be created. To define custom tokens (tags) and custom document structures *document type definitions* (DTD) are used, which are a part of XML. DTDs serve as templates that explain syntax and content of a document that is based on a specific DTD.

Taking the basic idea of the XML/EDI initiative and the approach given in Turowski (1999, pp. 6-9), we propose to use UN/EDIFACT segment names as a *standardized term set* for business transactions between MC participants, and to encapsulate business data, which has to be exchanged in XML tags that are named according to this term set. This does not implicate any restrictions, since all efforts mentioned above regarding standardization of uniform business scenarios and semantic rules provide backward compatibility to UN/EDIFACT.

Table 1: Part of a Message Generated to Request Whether a Certain Bicycle Saddle is Available

```
<MESSAGE>
 <TYPE>Request for quote</TYPE>
 <REQUEST-DATE>22.4.98</REQUEST-DATE>
 ...
 <PRODUCT>
   <EAN>230239844531</EAN>
   <DESCRIPTION>Bicycle saddle</DESCRIPTION>
   <COLOR>blue</COLOR>
 ...
 </PRODUCT>
 ...
</MESSAGE>
```

By encapsulating business data in XML tags with a given standardized meaning, messages from other business application systems become understandable. Furthermore, only important parts of a message may be processed.

Table 1 shows a typical example of an XML-based EDI message. With this example it is easy to understand how data encapsulated in XML tags get a meaning, and how relevant data only may be extracted by the receiver. If the receiver would need the article number to process a request for quote, it would be enough to extract the data that is encapsulated in the EAN tag. Another receiver might need the description and the color as well to process the request. In this case, he would search for the DESCRIPTION and the COLOR tag.

Table 2: UN/EDIFACT Segment Names

```
DTM DATE/TIME/PERIOD
 To specify date, time, or period.
 ...
 2005 Date/time/period qualifier, M, an..3
 ...
 137 Document/message date/time
 Date/time when a document/message is
 issued.
 ...
 2380 Date/time/period, C, an..35
 ...
 2379 Date/.. format qualifier, C, an..3
 ...
 102 CCYYMMDD
```

```
Calendar date: C = Century;
Y = Year; M = Month; D = Day.
...
```

However, the tag names in Table 1 are not standardized, as they were arbitrarily chosen to be understood by human readers. In order to support an automated inter-machine communication, we use UN/EDIFACT segment names as tag names as given in Table 2 and Table 3. Table 2 shows a part of the UN/EDIFACT definition of a date. Segment names are printed bold. Table 3 shows the corresponding XML message, which substitutes the REQUEST-DATE tag from Table 1. Its meaning is that the request for quote was issued at April 22, 1998. Other approaches to standardized term sets for business transactions may be found in CEN/ISSS (1998).

Table 3: Corresponding XML/EDIFACT Message for <REQUEST-DATE>

```
<DTM DTM2005="137">
 <DTM2380>19980422</DTM2380>
 <DTM2379>102</DTM2379>
</DTM>
```

The names of the XML tags are directly derived from UN/EDIFACT definitions. The main tag name DTM corresponds to the main segment name DTM. Subordinated segment names as 2005, 2380, or 2379 are connected to the main segment name DTM to get subordinated tag names, e. g., DTM2005, DTM2380, or DTM2379. Mandatory attributes

Figure 4: Interactions between software agents during configuration

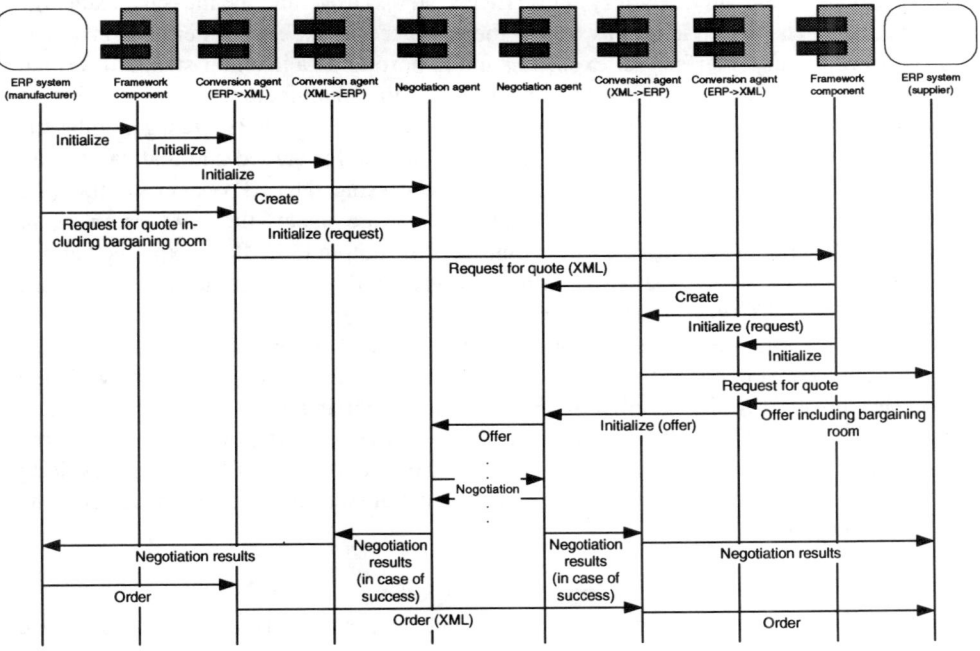

like the date's type qualifier 2005 become parameters of the main tag, conditional attributes such as 2380 or 2379 are processed as subordinated tags.

PAIRING E-COMMERCE TECHNIQUES WITH AGENT TECHNOLOGY

Agent architectures are widely discussed since the late 1950s as a means to automate tasks within the computer's world. Tasks like exchanging information for communication purpose or to coordinate production processes, as needed for the proposed approach, are well-suited to be executed using software agents (Jennings and Wooldidge, 1998, pp. 11-15). In common, a *(software) agent* is defined as an autonomous problem solving unit that may collaborate with other agents, and that tries to come to optimized results for its own problem area. For an indepth discussion, see Bradshaw (1997, p. 5-11). Software agents themselves consist of several different elements. Corsten and Gössinger (1998, p. 176) identified three main parts, constituting the minimal set-up for agents used in the area of production planning and control: a *communication processor*, a *local knowledge base*, and a *problem solver*. We will describe their implementation later, as these kinds of agents are relevant for implementing the negotiation tasks depicted in Figure 2.

Conversion Agents

In the following, we use figure 4 to describe the proposed agent approach. Figure 4 is related to Figure 2. It shows agents and their interactions that are necessary to fulfill negotiation tasks (1) as depicted in Figure 2, according to the business scenario described there.

Figure 4 illustrates which software agents are used by the manufacturer and his supplier, the business application systems (ERP systems) used, and the message exchange between them. The manufacturer as well as the supplier uses an ERP system that provides at least a proprietary interface for exporting and importing data in a non-standard format. After product configuration through the customer, the manufacturer is responsible to procure all necessary parts from suitable suppliers. Therefore, his ERP system generates the resulting demand reports. Ideally, these reports should be forwarded automatically to all suitable suppliers using EDI. To enable automatic processing, the ERP system's output (the request for quote) is initially transferred to a software agent, the *conversion agent* (Conversion agent(ERP -> XML), which translates the output to XML as explained above (cf. Figure 5). Afterwards, the XML output is transferred to the supplier using standard Internet protocols (TCP/IP). There, the supplier's conversion agent (Conversion agent(XML -> ERP)) transforms the request for quote in the format required by the supplier's ERP system. This conversion agent matches the content of the XML document with the arguments needed by the supplier's ERP system by parsing the XML document and interpreting it according to the standardized XML tags which categorize each transferred information. Next, the request for quote is processed by the supplier's ERP system resulting in an (automatically) generated offer, which is finally transferred to the manufacturer using the same mechanism.

Negotiation Agents

Besides this base communication process between manufacturer and supplier there

Figure 5: Converting an ERP System's Output to XML

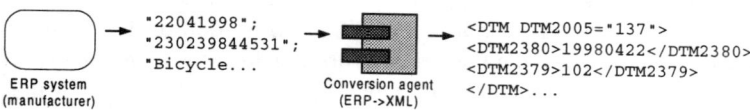

can also exist more complex processes, including additional information influencing the request for quote's processing. So far we have assumed that information, e. g., date of shipment, quantity, deadlines, or prices, is fixed, or at least known to all participating parties. In real-world processes, this information is most likely the subject of negotiations as depicted in Figure 2 (1), (2), or (3). To include and automate these negotiation processes, we introduce an additional type of software agent: the *negotiation agent*. Negotiation agents use and are based on conversion agents. In fact, they are specialized conversion agents that share the same software architecture, use the same information infrastructure, and reuse major parts of the conversion agent's code. We will explain this later.

Objects of negotiation processes are parts that have to be produced in order to assemble a customer individual product as well as terms and conditions under which they are to be delivered. Negotiation agents do not need to know much about these objects. They do only need an identification and certain constraints, e. g., due dates or quantities. According to figure 4 this information is created by conversion agents (Conversion agent(ERP -> XML)) based on data that they initially receive from the supplier's ERP systems or from the

Figure 6: Different Parallel Negotiation Tasks with Manager/Contractor Contract Nets

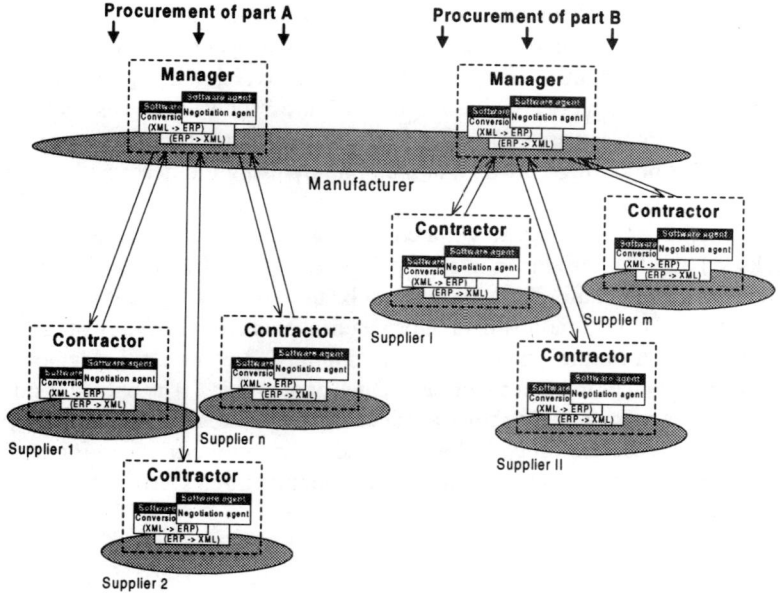

manufacturer's ERP system respectively.

As a result, negotiation agents output terms and conditions on which one or more suppliers agreed, but also the corresponding suppliers. In order to get the best offer, or an offer at all, the manufacturer generates in the first step an additional request for quote with negotiation ranges for several parameters, e. g. price or due date, to initialize the negotiation agent with a bargaining room. After this request for quote was translated by the conversion agent (Conversion agent(ERP -> XML)), the output is passed on to initialize the negotiation agent. On the supplier's side, the supplier's negotiation agent generates an offer that (somehow) matches the manufacturer's request for quote. The manufacturer's negotiation agent waits for the offer(s), extracts all relevant (negotiable) information, and generates counter-offers, accepts a certain offer, or terminates the negotiation process. If the negotiation is completed, the results are passed on to the negotiating parties. Before, the results are translated by the corresponding conversion agent (Conversion agent (XML -> PPS)). If an offer is acceptable, the manufacturer's ERP system generates an order based on the negotiated offer.

If the initially received constraints are violated, the functionality of the attached ERP system is used to evaluate the practicability of the received offers. This is done by generating temporary orders, which are scheduled by the ERP systems. Due dates and float times calculated by ERP systems are in the following passed on to the corresponding negotiation agent via the respective conversion agent. In this case another negotiation process starts.

The described *multi-agent system* is based on the *contract net* paradigm (Smith, 1980). In particular, we employ *manager/contractor contract nets* (cf. e. g., Zelewski, 1993, pp. 20). All participants in a manager/contractor contract net are represented by an agent. The agent that represents the manager asks for a specific output by sending messages directly to the contractor agents. The contractor agents respond by sending offers. Finally, the manager agent informs each contractor agent whether he accepts his offer or not.

By applying the manager/contractor contract net to the negotiation task described above, the manufacturer's negotiation agents act as manager agent, and the negotiation agents of the suppliers act as contractor agents. Precisely, conversion agents together with negotiation agents act as manager or contractor agents. Figure 6 shows agents as well as their communication relationships necessary for two different negotiation tasks (one for procuring Part A, and one for procuring Part B) that are done by using the described manager/contractor contract net approach.

After all shipment conditions are negotiated and corresponding orders are triggered, negotiation tasks (1) and (2) introduced in Figure 2 are supported by the described agent approach. Besides, the same multi-agent system can be used to coordinate the production process itself (Figure 2 (3)), e. g., adjustment of production plans in case of any failure. The ERP system that reports a failure (manufacturer or supplier) creates a suitable software agent to negotiate any changes to agreed shipment dates or quantities. The opposite side, of course, has to initialize a corresponding software agent. Initialization, communication, and negotiation take place as described above. However, the information necessary for negotiation is not provided by the procurement module of the manufacturer's ERP system, but by the production module.

SYSTEM DEVELOPMENT

Software Architecture – The Underlying Component Model

So far, implementation of agents took place in special-purpose programming languages and environments resulting in proprietary systems (Bradshaw, 1997, pp. 377-378) (for an overview of programming software agents (Shoham, 1997)). In case of MC, where systems of the manufacturer have to communicate with systems of different suppliers, maybe unknown at implementation time, an *open*, flexible, and *cost efficient* implementation of agents is necessary. This can be done by using open software development environments, which lead to highly portable systems, by reusing major parts of the written software, and by making this software freely available for suppliers. Consistently, we follow-up a component-oriented implementation of agents that communicate with each other by using the Internet (Fellner, Rautenstrauch and Turowski, 1999). Figure 7 shows the core *component model* of the agents we use. Software components are conversion agent, negotiation agent, communication processor, problem solver, and knowledge base.

In Figure 7 we use the *Unified Modeling Language* (UML) (Rational Software et al., 1997) to model components and their relationships. In particular, we apply the proposal described in Kruchten (1998). Definitions of what exactly constitutes a component vary in the literature. For definitions and an overview of definitions given in the literature cf. (Szyperski, 1998, p 164-168). In common, *software components* are mostly understood as self-contained units with contractually specified interfaces and functionality. They may be sold independently, and be composed by third parties (e. g., to form new application systems) in combinations not assumed by the component's manufacturer.

Software components normally contain domain-specific functions. Application systems made up of software components need therefore an additional cross-domain component, which enables coordination at the technical *and* the business level. A *component (application) framework* encapsulates the services and tasks mentioned. A component application framework may even encompass major parts of the application itself, e. g. San Francisco from IBM (1997). Furthermore, a component framework itself may be implemented as a component. According to Szyperski (1998, p. 275) we call a component framework a component.

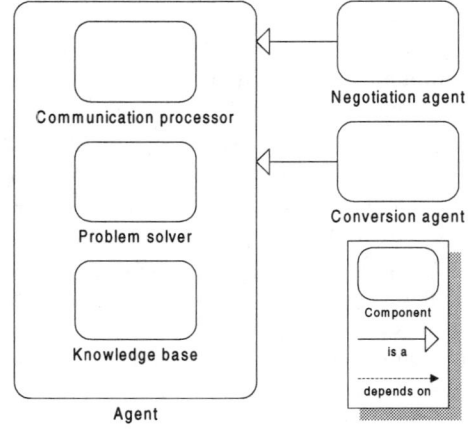

Figure 7: Core Component Model of an Agent and Specializations Used

We propose the component architecture given in figure 8 to solve the described problems of inter-company coordination, and call the component implementing our component framework, *framework component*. The framework component together with the respective agent components constitutes a *component application framework*.

Dependent on business rules for a concrete object of negotiation the agent

Figure 8: Framework component

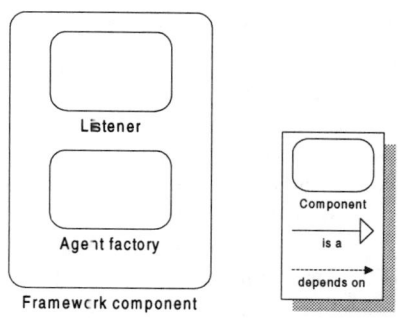

factory within the framework component creates suitable negotiation and conversion agents for every new negotiation process. The implementation of the respective components as well as the implementation of the agents will be discussed later.

The component framework must be applicable in configurations with almost any existing ERP system as well as negotiation method. To avoid repeated implementations of the mentioned components, the framework component that implements the framework has to provide some kind of a *factory* (Gamma, Helm, Johnson, and Vlissides, 1997, pp. 115-125) for application-specific components. The factory component (which is called *Agent factory* in Figure 8) is therefore responsible for creating the right negotiation and conversion agents (e. g. conversion agent (ERP -> XML) or conversion agent (XML -> ERP)).

Implementation – How the Software Components are Implemented

We choose Java as prototype language. Above all advantages (e. g. object-orientation or platform-independence), Java comprises a component model, *JavaBeans* (Sun Microsystems, 1997), providing the features enabling a straightforward implementation of the approach. By definition, JavaBeans are implementations of self-contained components, since a single component can be distributed and used alone as well as in combination with others. In addition, functionality needed to implement inter-agent communication is part of the standard Java API (application program interface) (java.net) (cf. Sun Microsystems, 1998).

We implemented each agent as a stand-alone component (JavaBean) consisting of several JavaBeans: the communication bean, the problem-solving bean, and the knowledge base bean. The JavaBeans correspond to the components described in the component model (cf. figure 7). This allows extensive reuse of different components. The negotiation part (problem solver) for example was reused in conjunction with a different knowledge base as well as a different communication bean. They only have to provide the information that the negotiation agent needs for calculation. On the other hand, the knowledge base and the communication bean may be reused in a configuration using a different kind of negotiation.

The factory itself is implemented as a JavaBean according to the factory pattern presented in Gamma et al. (1997, pp. 115-125). Based on provided parameters (e. g. by the application system or the end-user) and the information in the knowledge base, the matching conversion and negotiation beans are chosen.

The framework component serves as coordinating unit that is responsible for initialization and creation of other agents as required. Several different instances of one agent may act parallel, carrying out different negotiation processes or conversion tasks. Whereas instances of framework component and negotiation agent may be reused in different system environments without any change, conversion agents (Conversion agent (ERP -> XML), Conversion agent (XML -> ERP)) have to be adapted for each new application (ERP) system's interfaces (ERP system).

The complexity of conversion agents (Conversion agent (ERP -> XML)) depends on the interface to the ERP system. A simple conversion agent may parse a text file generated by the ERP system and add the corresponding XML tags to the contained data fields. A more complex agent may access the necessary information directly using function calls of the ERP system, e. g., using the business application programming interface (BAPI) of the R/3 ERP system from SAP (1997). In general, programming of these interfaces may be further simplified by using a *Web interface definition language* (IDL) as proposed by Merrick and Allen (1997).

Additionally, conversion agents executing the transformation from XML to an ERP system specific format (Conversion agent (XML -> ERP)) have to be adapted. Since several XML parsers are available free, e. g. XML4Java from IBM or XMLParser from Sun, the remaining effort to adapt these parsers to produce the desired output is low.

The communication component, which is responsible for the communication between negotiation agents, includes an additional XML parser to interpret the received documents for the problem solver. The output of the XML parser depends on the used problem solver. Hence, it is reusable together with the problem solver. The problem solver implements negotiation mechanisms (e. g., auction based negotiation). The extent of its reuse depends on the number of application scenarios where the same negotiation mechanism may be applied. After configuring the agents with organization specific information and the adaptation to the information infrastructure (e. g., ERP system, etc.) the agents are usable for both, the manufacturer and the supplier.

Besides communication itself, the communication component has to handle security issues. For this reason, it offers different (secure) transfer methods to its communication partner, e. g., RMI, TCP (with RSA), or IIOP (with RSA). According to his security demand, the respective communication partners then choose one of the offered transfer methods. Communication is further done using the chosen transfer method. However, communication itself is totally transparent for other components that use the communication component.

The knowledge base, as the third component of an agent, holds the specifications for ERP systems as well as all carried out negotiation results. It implements the methods setERP and getERP, which are responsible for delivering the target values to and from the given ERP system (e. g. setSAP and getSAP). The methods addOffer, searchOffer, and getOffer are used to manage saved offers. If a new offer arrives, it is stored in the knowledge base. The negotiation component may search and classify (classifyOffer) offers stored in the knowledge base.

Following a simple method, the search for the best offer is done. As a starting point, the best offer is calculated using *linear scalar transformation*. The offers are therefore scaled between 0 and 1 (worst to best) based on the satisfaction of *a priori* defined goals. The results are then weighed according to the importance of the goal. This method is implemented as a stand-alone component, which is used by the negotiation agent in conjunction with the knowledge base to gather the best offer. The negotiation component therefore implements two central methods: getOptimum and setOptimum. The method getOptimum is responsible for collecting the offers for a given inquiry from the knowledge base and finding the best one. When the best one is identified, it is marked in the knowledge base using setOptimum. It is possible to customize getOptimum to collect counteroffers, which leads to a restart of the process with new parameters.

To show the integration of a real-world application system we used SAP R/3. As we used Java, we needed a bridge between our components and the SAP system. The InfoBus technology from Lotus/IBM (available from Sun Microsystems, 1999) and the Enterprise Access Builder (EAB) for SAP R/3 included with IBM VisualAge for Java were therefore used. Of note, the EAB from IBM allows a seamless integration of enterprise data into Java applications. Through EAB, BAPI objects are accessible as standard Java objects and can be encapsulated in JavaBeans.

OUTLOOK AND CONCLUSION

E-commerce is a means to enable organizational changes that support pursuing MC. It enables companies to be more flexible and efficient while processing customer orders, and to be more responsive to customers needs. By blurring and lowering the barriers between companies, manufacturers and suppliers can work together more closely. This simplifies electronic procurement and supports shared business processes, which includes multiple companies up to building and maintaining virtual enterprises.

Deploying an efficient and effective information logistic is a key success factor for organizations implementing competitive strategies like MC. We support this by the proposed multi-agent system. Where available, we use public standards (e. g., XML or TCP) or open-industry standards (e. g. Java) for implementation. Implementation costs are reduced since essential software components are reusable, platform independent, and easily adaptable to certain needs. Furthermore, the proposed techniques may be implemented step by step, e. g. starting with communication agents to support inter-company communication, followed by a multi-agent system for negotiation, and last a multi-agent system to coordinate cross-organizational production process.

Particularly small and medium enterprises pursue MC or try to install MC, as shown by empirical studies in Germany (Piller and Schoder, 1999, p. 21). Especially these enterprises profit from a low-priced, flexible, and open approach to an improved EDI, as they often can't afford investments necessary for installing application systems allowing traditional UN/EDIFACT EDI, or even their suppliers can't. Since investing in EDI pays out only when almost all business partners use it (Goldfarb and Prescod, 1998), market penetration is a critical factor. In general, in the related research area of computer integrated manufacturing (CIM), it has been shown that communication effort can be reduced from quadratic to linear complexity (cf. e. g. Becker and Rosemann, 1993, pp. 20-23) by using *CIM interface systems*. CIM interface systems allow to exchange design data between different companies based on a common interface language, and may be mentioned here to further estimate the use of the proposed approach.

REFERENCES

Abramovici, M., & Bickelmann, S. (1993). Engineering Data Management (EDM) Systeme: Anforderungen, Stand der Technik und Nutzenpotentiale. *CIM Management, 9*(5), 21-28.

Adam, N. R., Dogramaci, O., Gangopadhyay, A., & Yesha, Y. (1999). *Electronic Commerce: Technical, Business, and Legal Issues*. Upper Saddle River: Prentice Hall.

Arnold, O., Faisst, W., Härtling, M., & Sieber, P. (1995). Virtuelle Unternehmen als Unternehmenstyp der Zukunft? *HMD, 32*(185), 8-23.

Becker, J., & Rosemann, M. (1993). *Logistik und CIM: Die effiziente Material- und Informationsflußgestaltung im Industrieunternehmen*. Berlin: Springer.

Birkhofer, H., & Büttner, K. (1995). On-line-Produktkataloge. *ZWF, 90*(11), 558-561.
Bradshaw, J. M. (1997). An Introduction to Software Agents. In J. M. Bradshaw (Ed.), *Software Agents* (pp. 3-46). Menlo Park: AAAI Press.
Bray, T., Paoli, J., & Sperberg-McQueen, C. M. (1997). *Extensible Markup Language (XML)*. Available: http://www.w3.org/TR/PR-xml.html [1998, 06-12].
CEN/ISSS. (1998). *Interim Report for CEN/ISSS XML/EDI Pilot Project*. Available: http://www.cenorm.be/isss/workshop/ec/xmledi/interim.html [1998, 12-23].
Corsten, H., & Gössinger, R. (1998). Produktionsplanung und -steuerung auf Grundlage von Multiagentensystemen. In H. Corsten & R. Gössinger (Eds.), *Dezentrale Produktionsplanungs- und -steuerungs-Systeme: Eine Einführung in zehn Lektionen* (pp. 174-207). Stuttgart: Kohlhammer.
ECOM. (1998). *Electronic Commerce - An Introduction*. Available: http://ecom.fov.uni-mb.si/center/ [1998, 05-15].
Fellner, K., Rautenstrauch, C., & Turowski, K. (1999). *A Component Model for an Inter-organizational Agent-based Coordination*. Paper presented at the 1999 Information Resources Management Association International Conference (IRMA'99): Managing Information Technology Resources in Organizations in the Next Millennium, Hershey.
Gamma, E., Helm, R., Johnson, R., & Vlissides, J. (1997). *Entwurfsmuster: Elemente wiederverwendbarer objektorientierter Software*. Bonn: Addison-Wesley.
Goldfarb, C. F., & Prescod, P. (1998). *The XML Handbook*. Upper Saddle River: Prentice-Hall.
Harvey, B., Hill, D., Schuldt, R., Bryan, M., Thayer, W., Raman, D., & Webber, D. (1998). *Position Statement on Global Repositories for XML*. Available: ftp://www.eccnet.com/pub/xmledi/repos710.zip [1998, 12-01].
Houlihan, J. B. (1992). International Supply Chain Management. In M. Christopher (Ed.), *Logistics - The Strategic Issues* (pp. 140-159). London.
IBM. (1997). *San Francisco Project Technical Summary*. Available: http://www.ibm.com/Java/Sanfrancisco/prd_summary.html [1998, 06-16].
Jennings, N. R., & Wooldidge, M. J. (1998). Applications of Intelligent Agents. In N. R. Jennings & M. J. Wooldidge (Eds.), *Agent Technology: Foundations, Applications, and Markets* . Berlin: Springer.
Kotha, S. (1996). From Mass Production to Mass Customization: The Case of the National Industrial Bicycle Company of Japan. *European Management Journal, 14*(5), 442-450.
Kotler, P. (1989). From Mass Marketing to Mass Customization. *Planning Review, 17*(5), 10-13.
Kruchten, P. (1998). *Modeling Component Systems with the Unified Modeling Language*. Paper presented at the 1998 ICSE Workshop on Component-Based Software Engineering (CBSE).
Kuhlen, R. (1996). *Informationsmarkt: Chancen und Risiken der Kommerzialisierung von Wissen*. (2 ed.). Konstanz: Universitätsverlag Konstanz.
Kurbel, K. (1996). *Multi-project Management Support for Virtual Suppliers in Global-sourcing Business Processes*. Paper presented at the Proceedings of IACIS '96 - Annual Conference of the International Association for Computer Information Systems, Las Vegas, Nevada.
Merrick, P., & Allen, C. (1997). *Web Interface Definition Language (WIDL)*. Available: http://www.w3.org/TR/NOTE-widl-970922 [1998, 06-07].
Moad, J. (1995). Let Customers have it their Way. *Datamation, 41*(6), 34-39.
Peat, B., & Webber, D. (1997). *Introducing XML/EDI: "The E-business Framework"*. Available: http://www.geocities.com/WallStreet/Floor/5815/start.htm [1998, 12-01].
Piller, F. (1998). *Kundenindividuelle Massenproduktion: Die Wettbewerbsstrategie der Zukunft*. München: Hanser.

Piller, F., & Schoder, D. (1999). Mass Customization und Electronic Commerce: Eine empirische Einschätzung zur Umsetzung in deutschen Unternehmen. To appear in *ZfB*.

Pine II, J. B. (1993). *Mass Customization: The New Frontier in Business Competition*. Boston: Harvard Business School Press.

Rational Software, Microsoft, Hewlett-Packard, Oracle, Sterling Software, MCI Systemhouse, Unisys, ICON Computing, IntelliCorp, i-Logix, IBM, ObjecTime, Platinum Technology, Ptech, Taskon, Reich Technologies, & Softeam. (1997). *UML Notation Guide: Version 1.1, 1 September 1997*. Available: http://www.rational.com/uml [1999, 04-17].

Rautenstrauch, C. (1998). *Mass Customization - A Relevant Concept For Small and Medium Enterprises?* Paper presented at the First International Conference on Stimulating Manufacturing Excellence in Small & Medium Enterprises, Sheffield.

Reiß, M., & Beck, T. C. (1994). Fertigung jenseits des Kosten-Flexibilitäts-Dilemmas: Mass-Customization als Strategiekonzept für Massenfertiger und für Einzelfertiger. *VDI-Z, 136*(11/12), 28-30.

SAP (Ed.). (1997). *BAPIs - Einführung und Überblick*. Walldorf: SAP.

Shoham, Y. (1997). An Overview of Agent-Oriented Programming. In J. M. Bradshaw (Ed.), *Software Agents* (pp. 272-290). Seattle: AAAI Press/The MIT Press.

Smith, R. G. (1980). The Contract Net Protocol: High Level Communication and Controll in a Distributed Problem Solver. *IEEE Transactions an Computers, 29*, 1104-1113.

Steel, K. (1997). *The Beacon User's Guide: Open Standards for Business Systems*. Available: http://www.cs.mu.oz.au/research/icaris/beaug1.doc [1998, 12-01].

Sun Microsystems (Ed.). (1997). *JavaBeans: JavaBeans API Specification 1.01*. Mountain View: Sun Microsystems.

Sun Microsystems (Ed.). (1998). *JDK 1.1.6 Documentation - Java Development Kit*. Mountain View: Sun Microsystems.

Sun Microsystems (Ed.). (1999). *InfoBus 1.2 Specification*. Mountain View: Sun Microsystems.

Szyperski, C. (1998). *Component Software: Beyond Object-Oriented Programming*. (2 ed.). Harlow: Addison-Wesley.

TMWG. (1998). *Reference Guide: "The Next Generation of UN/EDIFACT": An Open-EDI Approach Using UML Models & OOT (Revision 12)*. Available: http://www.harbinger.com/resource/klaus/tmwg/TM010R1.PDF [1998, 12-01].

Turowski, K. (1999). *A Virtual Electronic Call Center Solution for Mass Customization*. Paper presented at the 32nd Annual Hawaii International Conference On System Sciences, Maui, Hawaii.

UN. (1995). *United Nations Directiories for Electronic Data Interchange for Administration, Commerce and Transport*. Available: http://www.unece.org/trade/untdid/Welcome.html [1998, 12-01].

Zbornik, S. (1996). *Elektronische Märkte, elektronische Hierarchien und elektronische Netzwerke: Koordination des wirtschaftlichen Leistungsaustausches durch Mehrwertdienste auf der Basis von EDI und offenen Kommunikationssystemen, diskutiert am Beispiel der Elektronikindustrie*. Konstanz: Universitätsverlag Konstanz.

Zelewski, S. (1993). *Multi-Agenten-Systeme für Prozeßkoordinierung in komplexen Produktionssystemen. Ein verteiltes Problemlösungskonzept auf der Basis von Kontraktnetzen* (Arbeitsberichte des Seminars für Allgemeine Betriebswirtschaftslehre, Industriebetriebslehre und Produktionswirtschafts, Arbeitsbericht 46). Köln: Universität zu Köln.

Chapter XVIII

Electronic Commerce Based on Software Agents

Xun Yi and Chee Kheong Siew
Nanyang Technological University, Singapore

Syed Mahbubur Rahman
North Dakota State University

Robert J. Bignall
Monash University, Australia

ABSTRACT

Because electronic commerce provides customers with more convenient and more money-saving services than conventional trading, it has seen explosive growth in recent years and will have a major impact in shaping future markets. Certainly, it will be very advantageous for customers if electronic commerce is capable of being more automated and secure than is currently the case, since the time and energy they spend will be dramatically reduced. This paper focuses on applying software agent technology together with cryptographic technology to automating and securing the information gathering, and payment procedures, which are the principal and most time-consuming steps in electronic commerce, especially on the Internet.

INTRODUCTION

Electronic commerce is emerging as one of the most important applications on the Internet, with the potential to revolutionize the whole structure of retail merchandising and shopping. By providing more complete information to purchasers and cutting transaction costs, it is reducing market friction and making markets more perfect.

With the development of electronic commerce on the Internet, the amount of business information available on the Internet has become so large that it is becoming infeasible for customers and merchants to manually visit each site on the Internet, to analyze the information there, and thus to make sound business decisions regarding the trading of goods or services. In addition, electronic purchase transactions are still largely non-automated. While information about different products and vendors is more easily accessible and orders and payments can be dealt with electronically, a human buyer is still responsible for collecting and interpreting information about merchants and products, making decisions about them and finally entering the necessary purchase and payment information.

Software agent technology offers a new paradigm for electronic commerce, especially on the Internet. A software agent is a software program that uses agent communication protocols to exchange information for automatic problem solving. Unlike "traditional" software, software agents are personalized (incorporating cooperation, negotiation and conflict resolution), continuously running and semi-autonomous (Maes, 1994). Software agent technologies can be used to automate several of the most time consuming stages of the buying process. A software agent might have service capabilities, autonomous decision making and commitment features. These qualities are conducive to optimizing the whole buying experience and revolutionizing commerce as we know it today (Moukas et al., 1999).

Notwithstanding the fact that software agents are able to simulate the entire person to person trading process, customers are wary about employing them to trade on their behalf, largely because of concerns about unknown risks they may face. The key to alleviating many of these concerns—to mitigating the risk—is the security of agents. In order to run, a mobile agent has to expose its code and data to the host environment that supplies the means for it to execute. Thus the agents are at risk of being tampered with, scanned or even terminated by malicious servers.

In this chapter, software agent technology and cryptographic technology are combined with a view to automating and securing electronic commerce on the Internet. The chapter is organised as follows. Firstly, the fundamental cryptographic technology concepts needed to explain secure electronic commerce systems are introduced. An agent-mediated information-gathering system, in which an agent automatically roams the network and gathers relevant trading information is then proposed. An agent-mediated secure electronic transaction protocol is elaborated and the main security issues for mobile agents are reviewed. The implementation of mobile agent systems is then discussed and some conclusions are drawn at the end.

CRYPTOGRAPHIC TECHNOLOGY

Cryptographic technology is used to ensure the privacy and authentication of data on a network. To implement a mobile agent security policy, we need public key algorithms to provide data confidentiality, digital signature schemes for non-repudiation and to confirm data integrity, and authentication schemes to give assurance of an agent's identity (that is, the identity of the agent's owner). This section will briefly review these cryptographic principles.

Public-Key Cryptosystem

The concept of public-key cryptography was invented by Whitfield Diffie and Martin Hellman, and independently by Ralph Merkle. This contribution was the notion that keys could come in pairs —an encryption key and a decryption key. Since 1976, numerous public-key cryptography algorithms have been proposed. Only a few algorithms are both secure and practical. These algorithms are generally based on some computationally hard problem, such as the problem of factoring large numbers or the problem of calculating discrete logarithms.

Named after Ron Rivest, Adi Shamir and Leonard Adleman, the three inventors who first introduced the algorithm in 1978, RSA has since withstood years of extensive cryptanalysis. RSA gets its security from the difficulty of factoring large numbers. The public and private keys are functions of a pair of large (100 to 200 digits or even larger) prime numbers. To generate the two keys, choose two large prime numbers p and q. Compute the product: $n=pq$. Then randomly choose the encryption key e such that e and $(p-1)(q-1)$ are relatively prime. Finally, use Euclid's algorithm to compute the decryption key d such that $ed=1 \ (mod\ (p-1)(q-1))$. In other words, $d = e^{-1} \ (mod\ (p-1)(q-1))$. Note that d and n are also relatively prime. The numbers e and n are the public key; the number d is the private key. The two primes, p and q, are no longer needed. They should be discarded, but never revealed.

To encrypt a message m, first divide it into numerical blocks such that each block has a unique representation modulo n (with binary data, choose the largest power of 2 less than n). That is, if p and q are 100-digit primes, then n will have just under 200 digits, and each message block m_i should be just under 200 digits long. The encrypted message c will be made up of similarly sized message blocks c_i of about the same length. The encryption formula is simply: $c_i = m_i^e \ (mod\ n)$. To decrypt a message, take each encrypted block c_i and compute: $m_i = c_i^d \ (mod\ n)$. Because $c_i^d = (m_i^e)^d = m_i^{ed} = m_i^{k(p-1)(q-1)+1} = m_i \, m_i^{k(p-1)(q-1)} = m_i \cdot 1 = m_i \ (mod\ n)$, the formula recovers the message.

Digital Signatures and Hash Functions

Handwritten signatures on paper-based documents have long been used as proof of authorship of, or at least agreement on, the contents of such documents. We would like to do this sort of thing with electronic documents and information, but there are problems. Firstly, a bit stream is easy to copy. Even if a person's signature were difficult to forge (a graphic image of a written signature, for example), it is easy to move a valid signature from one document to another document. The mere presence of such a signature therefore means nothing. Secondly, documents are easy to modify after they are signed, without leaving any evidence of modification.

There are public-key algorithms that can be used for digital signatures. In some algorithms—RSA is an example—either the public key or the private key can be used for encryption. By encrypting a document using your private key, you have a secure digital signature. The basic protocol is simple:

- Alice can generate her signature on a document by encrypting it with her private key.
- Alice sends the document with her signature to Bob.
- Bob can use Alice's public key to verify the signature.

In practical implementations, public-key algorithms are often inefficient to encrypt long documents. To save time, digital signature protocols are often implemented using a one-way hash function. A one-way hash function, denoted as $H(M)$, operates on an arbitrary-length message M. It returns a fixed-length hash value h, where $h=H(M)$. There are many functions that take an arbitrary-length input and return an output of fixed length, but one-way hash functions have additional characteristics:

- Given M, it is easy to compute h.
- Given h, it is hard to compute M.
- Given M, it is hard to find another message M' such that $H(M)=H(M')$.

Instead of signing a document, Alice signs the hash of the document. In this protocol,

both the one-way function and the digital signature algorithm are agreed upon beforehand.
- Alice produces a one-way hash of a document.
- Alice signs the hash with her private key, thereby signing the document.
- Alice sends the document and the signed hash to Bob.
- Bob produces a one-way hash of the document that Alice sent. He then decrypts the signed hash with Alice's public key and compares it with the hash he generated. If they match, the signature is valid.

Authentication and Certificates

Authentication gives assurance of identity. It is the means of gaining confidence that people or things are who or what they claim to be. In other words, authentication relates to a scenario where some party has presented its identity and claims to be that party. Authentication enables some other party to gain confidence that the claim is legitimate.

The ISO authentication framework provides authentication across networks. The framework is certificate-based. Each user has a distinct name. A trusted certification authority assigns a unique name to each user and issues a certificate containing the name and the user's public key.

An X.509 certificate looks like:
Certificate :: = SIGNED SEQUENCE (
  signature AlgorithmIdentifier,
  Issuer Name,
  validity Validity :: = SEQUENCE (
    notBefore UTCTime,
    not After UTCTime)
  subject Name,
  subjectPublicKeyInfo SubjectPublicKeyInfo :: = SEQUENCE(
    algorithm AlgorithmIdentifier,
    subjectPublicKey, BIT STRING))

A Certification Authority (*CA*) signs all certificates. If Alice and Bob want to communicate, each of them has to verify the signature of the other person's certificate. If they use the same *CA*, this is easy. If they use different *CAs*, this is more complicated. Think of a tree structure, with different *CAs* certifying other *CAs* and users. On the top there is one master *CA*. Each *CA* stores the certificate obtained from its superior *CA*, as well as all the certificates issued by it. Alice and Bob have to traverse the certification tree, looking for a common trusted point.

Throughout the following discussion, each participant X in the framework has a pair of keys associated with it, one being publicly known (Xp, X's public key), the other one only known to X (private or secret key Xs). X's public key is used to encrypt message M, meant to be read by X. The encryption is represented as $C=Xp(M)$. X can decrypt the result using its private key: $M=Xs(Xp(M))$. In this way, X can use Xs to create a digital signature, which can be verified by any party using Xp.

For simplicity, we assume only one certifying authority is involved in the framework. It provides each participant X with an X.509 certificate $Cert(X)$, while the public key of the certificate authority (CAp) is known to all participants in the framework.

A simple example of authentication for access is given here. When Alice wants Bob to allow her to get access to Bob's computing resources, Alice can present Bob with her certificate obtained from the *CA* in advance with her signature on her access request. After receiving this information, Bob can verify the certificate with the *CA*'s public key and then Alice's signature with her public key retrieved from her certificate. Once she is validated, Alice is permitted by Bob to access his computing resources.

INFORMATION GATHERING BASED ON SOFTWARE AGENTS

The vast amount of trading information available today on the World Wide Web (WWW) has great potential to improve the quality of decisions and the productivity of consumers. However, the WWW's large number of information sources and their different levels of accessibility, reliability and associated costs present human decision makers with a complex information gathering and planning problem that is too difficult to solve without high-level filtering of information. In many cases, manual browsing through even a limited portion of the relevant information obtainable through advanced information retrieval (IR) and information extraction (IE) technologies (Callan et al., 1992; Fisher et al., 1996; Larkey et al., 1996) is no longer effective. The time/quality/cost trade-offs offered by the collection of information sources and the dynamic nature of the environment lead us to conclude that the user cannot (and should not) serve as the detailed controller of the trading information gathering (IG) process. The current potential solution to this problem is the utilization of software agent technologies to help consumers with information gathering for electronic commerce on the Internet.

Overview of Information Gathering Agents

The WWW has become an invaluable information resource but the explosion of information available via the Web has made Web searching a time-consuming and complex process. Index-based search engines, such as AltaVista or Infoseek help, but they are not enough. The problem stems from the volumes of information available via the Web and the generality of the term frequency approach to searching. For any given query, there are often simply too many relevant documents about the requested topic for the human client to efficiently search through and process the information.

The solution, as one researcher so aptly put it (Etzioni, 1996), is to "move up the information food chain," in other words, to build high-level information processing engines. One class of work toward this end is the meta search engine. Meta search engines typically issue queries to multiple search engines like AltaVista and Infoseek in parallel, customizing the human client's query for each search engine and using advanced features of the search engine where available. Examples of this include SavvySearch and MetaCrawler (Etzuini, 1996); commercial meta search products (http://www.inforia.com/quest/iq.htm and http://www.zurf.com) are also available. Some of these tools supplement the IR technology of the search engine—for example, if a particular advanced query technique, such as phrase matching, is missing from the search engine, MetaCrawler will retrieve the documents emitted from the search engine and perform its own phrase techniques on those documents. Other features include clustering candidate documents according to similarity and combining redundant URLs. These tools build on the services of the search engines, but processing done on the retrieved documents is typically limited to the same techniques used to implement the search engines. This often results in wider Internet coverage, but the output is simply a list of URLs for the human client to process. Thus this approach also suffers from the same problem as the search engines themselves — too much data.

A closely related class of work is the personal information agent (http://www.robosurfer.com). Rather than simply making single queries to a large number of sites, these agents will actively pursue links to find other relevant information. They are concept driven, obtaining their area of interest either through hard-coded rules, explicit questionnaires or a simple learning technique. These systems are not as fast as the meta search products, but their design goal has a somewhat different focus. Personal agents are typically used to obtain a small number of highly relevant documents for the user to read, either all at once or continuously over an extended time period. Thus, the user sacrifices speed for document quality.

Another class of work targeted at moving up the food chain is the shopping agent class. Shopping agents typically locate and retrieve documents containing prices for special products, extract the prices, and then report the gathered price information to the client. For example, the original BargainFinder (Krulwich, 1996) and the more recent ShopBot (Doorebbos et al., 1997) both work to find the best available prices for music CDs. These tools often differ from meta search engines and personal information agents in that they typically do not search the web to locate the shopping sites; instead, the system designers develop a library containing known shopping sites and other information such as how to interact with a particular store's local search engine. Some shopping agents also integrate some of the functionality offered by personal information agents. For example, the commercial Jango (http://www.jango.com/) shopping agent locates reviews as well as extracting prices and very specific product features from vendor Web sites.

Lesser et al.'s solution (1998) to this problem is to integrate different AI technologies, namely scheduling, planning, text processing, and interpretation problem solving, into a single information gathering agent, BIG (resource-Bounded Information Gathering), that can assume the role of the human information gatherer.

In the following section, we propose a new information gathering architecture for electronic commerce based on software agents.

Architecture of an Information Gathering Agent

Components of the proposed architecture: The proposed architecture for agent-based information gathering comprises the following components:
- Clients (*C*) —generate requests for information gathering.
- Agent Service Center (*ASC*) - generates information gathering agents (*IGA*) according various requests from clients, launches the *IGA* to traverse a list of Online Shopping Centers, retrieves gathered information brought back by the *IGA* and satisfies the requests from those clients by providing them with a series of comparison charts. The *ASC* is a trusted party of the architecture.
- Information Gathering Agent (*IGA*) - gathers information according to its goals as specified by the *ASC*.
- Online Shopping Centers (*OSC*)—each provides an Agent Meeting Place (*AMP*) for the *IGA*s to run and they provide information requested by the *IGA*s. They are denoted by *OSC(1), OSC(2), ..., OSC(n)*.

In addition, we suppose all participants of the architecture have already obtained their certificates from one certification authority (*CA*) in advance and know the public key of the

Figure 1. Construction of an Information Gathering Agent (IGA)

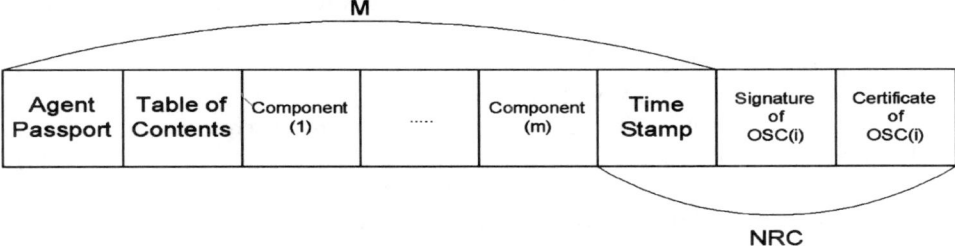

CA, i.e., *CAp*.

Structure of Information Gathering Agents: The Information Gathering Agent defined here is a kind of mobile agent. Therefore, the *IGA* possesses the same structure as that of a general mobile agent. An *IGA* is designed for gathering information from a list of servers on the Internet. Each component of an *IGA* has a specific significance. When an *IGA* traverses a list of *OSCs* to gather information relevant to some goods, the *IGA* generally has the following kind of composition:

- Agent Passport— consists of the basic information required to permit the agent to flow from *AMP* to *AMP*. It includes the certificate of the agent's owner, error actions and addresses (i.e., the action that the *AMP* should take should an error occur while processing the agent), and goal and status information (i.e., a representation of the agent's goals and status). The route of the *IGA* is specified in the goals.
- Table of Contents (*TOC*)—provides a map of the structure of the agent. Each component has a size, type and importance. The size, as expected, is the size of the component. The type field contains a simple representation of what is required to process the component. The importance field describes whether the component is necessary for the agent to be instantiated at the *AMP*. This permits agents to carry obscure components through *AMPs* which do not support these components, and to avoid unpacking components which will not be used at any *AMP*.
- Code and Data Component (*CDC*)—contains code and data executed on the list of *OSCs*. There may be a different code and data for different *OSCs*, but here we simply assume that the same code and data is specific to all *OSCs*.
- Gathered Information Component (*GIC*) — contains the information gathered from a certain *OSC(i)*. The information gathered from the *OSC(i)* should be firstly signed with the secret key of the *OSC(i)* and then encrypted with the public key of the owner of the *IGA* (i.e., the *ASC*) to ensure its integrity and confidentiality, namely, $ASCp\,(OSC(i)_s\,(GIC)\,)$, where *ASCp* is the public key of the Agent Service Center and $OSC(i)_s$ the secret key of the *OSC(i)*.
- Non-Repudiation Component (*NRC*)—contains the signature and certificate of some *OSC* and the time stamp. It usually occupies the last component of the *IGA* and attaches right behind the corresponding *GIC*. For example, when the *IGA* is launched from *OSC(i)* and roams into *OSC(i+1)*, the *NRC* is the certificate of the *OSC(i)* with the signature of the *OSC(i)* on the part *M* and time stamp (as shown in Figure 1).

In Figure 1, the signature of *OSC(i)* on *M* (denoted as $Sign_{OSC(i)}$) is generated and verified in the following way:

- $OSC(i)$ produces the hash value of M, $H(M)$.
- $OSC(i)$ signs the hash value $H(M)$ with its secret key to generate its signature on the IGA, i.e.,

$$Sign_{OSC(i)} = OSC(i)s\ (\ H(M)\ ) \tag{1}$$

where $OSC(i)s$ is the secret key of $OSC(i)$.

- The signature can be verified to be genuine if the following equation holds,

$$OSC(i)p\ (Sign_{OSC(i)}) = H(M) \tag{2}$$

The public key $OSC(i)p$ of the $OSC(i)$ can be retrieved from the certificate $Cert(OSC(i))$ of the $OSC(i)$.

Procedure for Information Gathering

In this scenario, we suppose a client C wants to buy some commodity by utilizing Internet trading services. Of course, C firstly needs to investigate the trading information relevant to this commodity, such as the price, quality, specification, and even the payment method of the commodity. C can gather trading information about the commodity as shown in figure 2.

The procedure can be described in detail as follows:

1. **Request Initiating:** The client gets access to a device connected to the ASC and submits his request for gathering trading information relevant to a commodity to the ASC. Of course, the client has to register with the ASC in advance. Here we suppose

Figure 2: Procedure of Information Gathering Agent Roaming

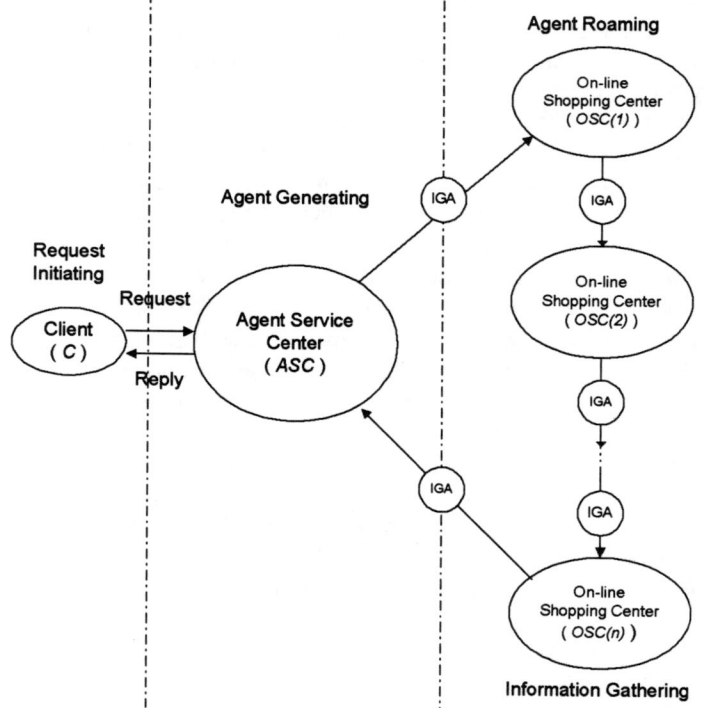

that C has registered with the ASC previously and has gained access to it in accordance with a password-based access policy.

2. **Agent Generating**: On receiving the request from C, the ASC looks up its Yellow Pages to find a list of Online Shopping Centers which may satisfy the request and generates an IGA structured as shown in Figure 1. The route of the IGA is specified in the goal of the agent. At this stage, the Non-Repudiation Component (NRC) of the IGA as shown in Figure 1 is filled with the current time t, the signature of the ASC on H(M) and the certificate of the ASC.

3. **Agent Roaming**: In order to simplify the description, we regard the ASC as OSC(0). Therefore, we only need to deal with the general case in which the IGA is launched by the Agent Meeting Place of OSC(i-1), enters the Agent Meeting Place of OSC(i) (where $i=1,2,......, n$) and later exits from it. The execution process of the IGA at the AMP of OSC(i) is illustrated in Figure 3.

The communication portals of the OSC(i)'s AMP are responsible for managing the arrival and departure of mobile agents. For inbound services, they extract the arriving mobile agent IGA and pass it to the mobile agent concierge. The mobile agent concierge acts much as a concierge does in a full service hotel.

With the help of authentication services, the concierge can verify the following items:
a) Is Cert(ASC) (from Agent Passport) issued by the CA?
b) Is the signature ASC on the original IGA (from the NRC of the ASC) genuine?
c) Is the time stamp of the original IGA (from the NRC of the ASC) valid?
d) Is Cert(OSC(i-1)) (from the NRC of the OSC(i-1) issued by the CA?
e) Is the signature OSC(i-1) on the current IGA (from the NRC of the OSC(i-1)) genuine?
f) Is the time stamp of the current IGA (from the NRC of the OSC(i-1)) valid?

Figure 3: Execution Process of the IGA *at the* AMP *of* OSC(i)

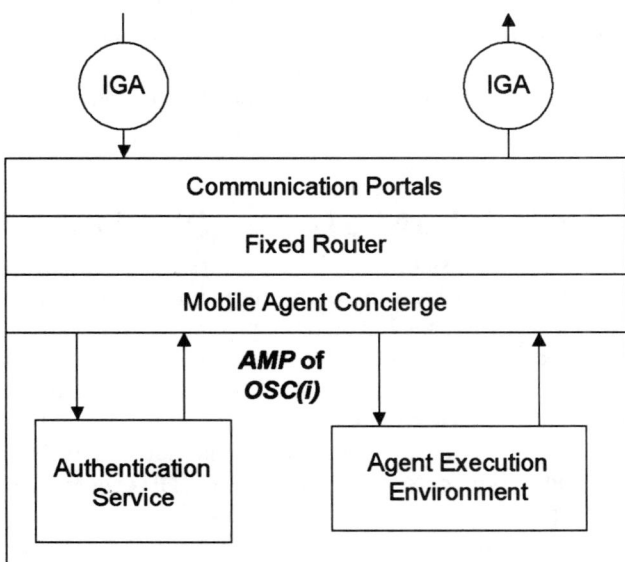

Note that all signatures are verified based on equation (2).

If each answer is yes, the concierge needs to give *OSC(i-1)* a reply with *OSC(i)s(H(M))* and *Cert(OSC(i))* so as to announce that *OSC(i)* has correctly received the *IGA*. *OSC(i-1)* will keep this as non-repudiation evidence. Then the concierge extracts the Code and Data from the *IGA* according to the *TOC* and then sends it to an agent execution environment for it to run. Once the *IGA* resides and runs its code in the agent execution environment, it may ask the *OSC(i)* the following questions:

a) Do you have the commodity for sale?
b) If so, can you provide the price, quality, specification and payment approach for this commodity?

After the *IGA* is supplied with the trading information relevant to this commodity, it may present the following requests:

a) Please firstly encrypt the provided trading information with *OSC(i)s*, reencrypt the intermediate result with *ASCp* and then attach the final result behind the *IGA* as a Gathered Information Component (*GIC(i)*).
b) Please sign the updated *IGA* as per Formula (1) and then attach the current time, the signature and the certificate right behind the updated *IGA* as a Non-Repudiation Component (*NRC(i)*) of *OSC(i)*.

Once the goal of gathering information in the *OSC(i)* has been fulfilled, the *IGA* will ask the concierge to launch it to the next destination, i.e., *OSC(i+1)*.

If *OSC(i)* does not have the commodity for sale, the provided trading information may be only one word—No. The *OSC(i)* is still required to do as above.

If the *IGA* does not pass the verification check, the concierge handles the *IGA* in accordance with the information in the Error Actions and Addresses part from the Agent Passport.

After the *IGA* returns to the *ASC*, the *ASC* extracts the trading information relevant to the commodity from all *GIC*s and verifies their authenticity by all *NRC*s. On the basis of the gathered information, it draws some comparison charts and supplies them to the client.

The software agent based information gathering process terminates with the client viewing these explicit comparison charts and formulating the purchase conditions under which he or she may buy the commodity.

PAYMENT SYSTEM BASED ON SOFTWARE AGENTS

The Internet is now considered to be the preferred environment for electronic commerce. Yet, there is still some resistance from the public to buying products and services on-line and paying for them over the Internet; for example, by browsing a company's Web server, ordering a product and paying for it by filling a form that includes credit card information. The main difficulty is that almost every Internet user has heard of credit card fraud performed by hackers eavesdropping connections used to send transaction data—despite the fact that very few of those attacks have actually succeeded. Even the deployment of secure servers based on protocols such as SSL or S-HTTP is not enough, since the credit card information is deposited in the server where it can easily be read by anyone with access to it (or even by unauthorized hackers).

Overview of Secure Electronic Transaction (SET)

The concern for protecting users' credit card information led VISA and MasterCard, in association with major software and cryptography companies, to the development of the SET protocol (Visa International and MasterCard International, 1997). SET provides important properties like authentication of the participants, non-repudiation, data integrity and confidentiality. Each player knows only what is strictly necessary to play their role, for example, the selling company never knows the buyer's credit card information, and the financial institution authorizing the transaction is not aware of the details of the purchase, including the nature of the products, quantities, etc. Paying for something using a credit card under the SET protocol is clearly much more secure than doing it, say, in a restaurant, where the card is normally taken out of the customer's sight.

SET is expected to give buyers and sellers the necessary confidence to launch Internet commerce definitively (despite some technical and nontechnical problems that still exist). From the buyer's point of view, SET should be very attractive, both to use (there will be many SET-compliant software tools to help the users with their credit cards on the Internet) and to trust (if we assume the financial institutions interested in its success are able to explain and convince users of its benefits).

Each participant X in the SET protocol has two types of certificates: one is the signature certificate $Cert_s(X)$ containing the signature public key of entity X, another is the key-exchange certificate $Cert_k(X)$ containing the key-exchange public key used to distribute session keys for a symmetric cryptosystem. On the assumption that cardholders and the merchants have registered and obtained their certificates from the issuer, the purchase request phase of SET can be outlined as follows (see Figure 4):

- **Step 1:** A cardholder (C) looks at a catalog (printed on paper, supplied on a CD-ROM, or available online on the Web) provided by a merchant (M) and, after deciding to purchase something, sends a request to the merchant's server. The request includes the description of the services or the quantities of the goods, the terms of the order and the brand of the credit card that will be used for payment.

Figure 4: SET Purchase Request Transaction

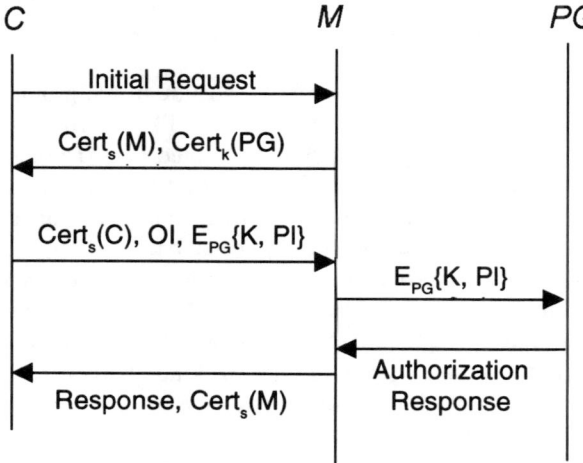

- **Step 2:** The merchant receives the request and sends back its own signature certificate $Cert_s(M)$ and the key-exchange certificate $Cert_k(PG)$ of a payment gateway (PG). The merchant also sends a unique identifier, assigned to this transaction.
- **Step 3:** The cardholder (i.e., his or her software) verifies the certificates by traversing the trust chain to the root key (the public signature key of a certificate authority (CA)) so as to assure itself of the authenticity and integrity of the data (the merchant had digitally signed it), and creates two pieces of information:
  a) The Order Information (OI), containing control information verified by the merchant to validate the order, card brand and bank identification. The OI also includes a digest of the order description, which includes the amount of the transaction and other elements such as quantity, size and price of the items ordered, shipping and billing addresses, etc. This data, not included in the OI, will be processed outside the scope of the SET protocol.
  b) The Payment Instructions (PI), containing the amount of the transaction, the card account number and expiration date, instructions for installment payments (if that's the case) and a couple of secret values to prevent guessing and dictionary attacks on the data, among other elements. The PI is encrypted with a randomly generated symmetric key K.

Both elements will contain the transaction identifier and are dually signed, so they can later be linked together by the payment gateway. Then, the encrypted PI (i.e., $E_k(PI)$) and the key (k) used to encrypt it are encrypted into a digital envelope (E_{PG}), using the payment gateway's public key. Finally, the OI and the digital envelope are sent to the merchant, along with the cardholder's signature certificate $Cert_s(C)$.

- **Step 4:** The merchant verifies the cardholder certificate and the dual signature on the OI. The request is then processed, which includes forwarding the digital envelope to the payment gateway for authorization (the details of this operation are outside the scope of this description). After processing the order, the merchant generates and signs a purchase response, and sends it to the cardholder along with its signature certificate. If the payment was authorized, the merchant will fulfill the order by delivering the products bought by the cardholder.
- **Step 5:** The cardholder verifies the merchant signature certificate, checks the digital signature of the response, and takes any appropriate actions based on its contents.

The software responsible for the cardholder's side of the protocol manages a data structure called a digital wallet, where sensitive data like certificates, private keys and payment card information are kept, usually in encrypted files. The merchant will have a more complex system composed of several parts, doing different jobs: managing the dialog with cardholders, signing messages and verifying signatures and certificates, asking payment gateways for payment authorizations, and so on.

SET is a very complex protocol, and may not be suitable under some technical conditions, such as mobile computing environments. Generally, the devices used in these environments have limited computational capacity and use slow and expensive connections to the Internet. SET may be too demanding for this kind of equipment and connectivity, preventing on-line transactions for mobile users.

SET/A, guided by the SET rules and based on the mobile agent paradigm, is proposed by Romao et al. (1998). With SET/A, the computational burden is taken away from the user's device, so it can be disconnected while the transaction is running. However, SET/A depends on a secure execution environment at the merchant's server to protect an agent's confidential data (i.e., credit card information) against a malicious merchant. In our opinion, the solution is high cost for merchants and the required security is not easy to ensure.

In the next section, we propose another agent-based SET protocol, which avoids the security limitations on the agent's execution environment in the merchant's terminal.

Purchase Request Transaction Based on Software Agents

Generation of a Payment Agent: A purchase request transaction under the agent-based SET protocol has a few more steps than in SET, since a payment agent has to be generated by a cardholder.

This section will continue to refer to the scenario shown in Figure 2. Without loss of generality, we suppose that only the first j Online Shopping Centers (i.e., *OSC(1), OSC(2), ..., OSC(j)*) have the commodity for sale. All of them have already provided the Agent Service Center (*ASC*) with their trading information about the commodity.

A cardholder (*C*) (actually, the client at the information-gathering stage) inspects the trading information gathered about the commodity and supplied by Agent Service Center (*ASC*) and formulates the purchase conditions (*PC*) under which it will be acceptable to buy this commodity. The conditions may include: (1) the expected price of the commodity, which is determined by the lowest offer of the j Online Shopping Centers; (2) expected delivery time of the commodity; (3) expected payment method (in this case, only credit card payment is available to *C*) and so on..

Based on the purchase conditions, *C* creates a payment agent structured according to Figure 1, i.e.,

- The cardholder's signature certificate (*Certs(C)*) is placed in the certificate portion of the payment agent.
- The route of the payment agent is specified in the goal and status of its passport. The order of the route is arranged from the best Online Shopping Center to the worst one among the j Online Shopping Centers. In this case, we suppose the order is from *OSC(1)* to *OSC(j)*.
- The code portion is taken up by a program. The description of this program is outside the scope of this chapter.
- The order information (*OI*) (including the purchase conditions), the digest of the payment information *PI* (i.e., *H(PI)*), the dual signature of the cardholder on *OI* and the payment information *PI*, respectively are placed in the data portion.
   a) Both *OI* and *PI* contain a unique transaction identifier I_c assigned by *C*.
   b) The dual signature of the cardholder on *OI* and *PI* is the signature of the cardholder on the message *H[H(OI) || H(PI)]*, where the symbol "||" denotes the concatenation of two messages. The dual signature is denoted as $Sign_c(H[H(OI) || H(PI)])$ which is generated in the following way:

$$Sign_c(H[H(OI) || H(PI)])=Cs(\ H[H(OI) || H(PI)]\ ) \qquad (3)$$

   where *Cs* is the signature secret key of the *C*.
- A random number *R* is generated and placed in the date portion of the payment agent.
- The current time *t* is recorded in the time stamp portion.
- The signature of the cardholder on the message *M* is placed in the signature portion as shown in Figure 1.

Protected Payment Information to ASC: Besides the payment agent, C needs to prepare for the provision of protected payment information to the ASC as follows:
- The PI is encrypted with a randomly generated symmetric key k, i.e., $E_k(PI)$.
- $m_{ASC} = ASC_p(k + I_c \cdot t + R, C_s(I_c \parallel t \parallel H[H(OI) \parallel H(PI)]))$ (4)

where Cs is the secret (signature) key of the cardholder, $ASCp$ is the public key of the ASC, R is the random number generated by the payment agent and t is the current time.

The information for the ASC comprises $E_k(PI)$ and m_{ASC}. This information is sent to the ASC when the payment agent is launched from C.

It should be pointed out that the ASC cannot retrieve k from m_{ASC} and then reveal the payment information PI because R is absent from the protected payment information provided to the ASC.

Payment Agent Roaming: Once the payment agent is created, it is launched from C into $OSC(1)$ initially, and then migrates from $OSC(1)$ into $OSC(2)$ and so on. The payment agent's roaming is illustrated in Figure 5. In this scheme the Agent Service Center (ASC) acts as a trusted verification center, whose public key is known to all participants in the payment system.

When the payment agent enters an Online Shopping Center, almost the same procedure as in the information gathering stage is carried out. The procedure differs after the concierge sends the payment agent (PA) to an agent execution environment for it to run. Once the PA resides and runs its code in the agent execution environment, it may ask the OSC whether the purchase conditions are acceptable. If so, a purchase request transaction similar

Figure 5: Procedure of Payment Agent Roaming

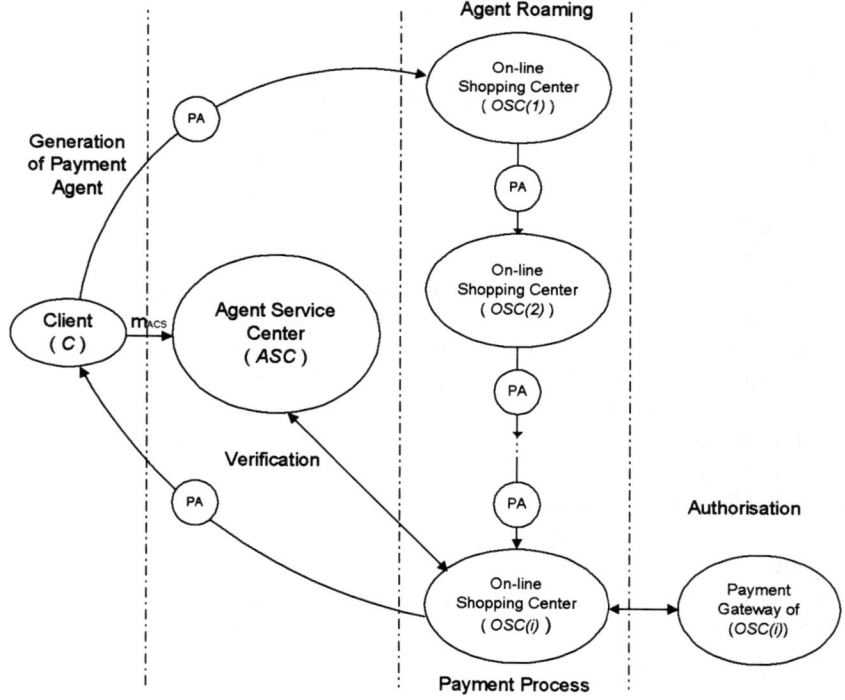

Figure 6. Purchase Request Transaction Based on Software Agents

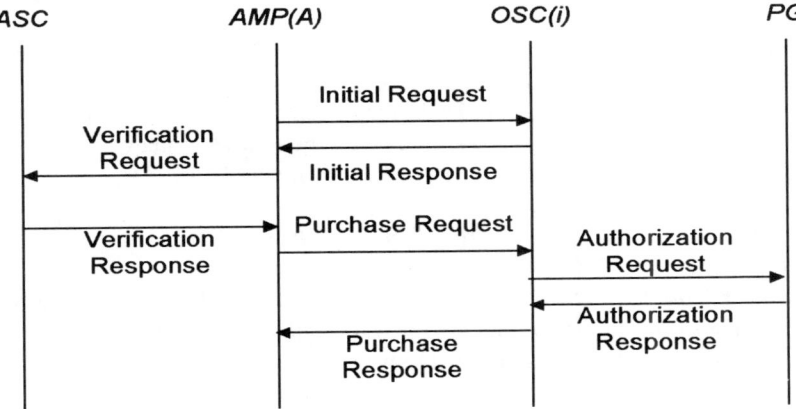

to the SET protocol is initiated (this will be dealt with in next section). If the *OSC* cannot satisfy the payment conditions, the *PA* asks the concierge to launch it to the next destination.

In this case, we suppose that *OSC(i)* (i £ j) is the first Online Shopping Center that can accept the purchase conditions (*PC*) of *C*.

Purchase Request Transaction: Since *OSC(i)* has already accepted the purchase conditions, a purchase request transaction between the payment agent (denoted by *AMP(A)* in this phase) and *OSC(i)* can proceed as follows and shown in figure 6.

Initial Request: The agent *AMP(A)* resides in the environment and sends (now locally) an initial request to the *OSC(i)*. The message indicates which payment card brand will be used for the transaction and which *ASC* will be used for certificate and signature verifications (i.e., $Cert_s(ASC)$), and requests a copy of the gateway's certificate. In addition, I_C, t and $H[H(OI) \parallel H(PI)]$ are also sent to the *OSC(i)*.

Initial Response: When the *OSC(i)* receives the request, it assigns a unique transaction identifier I_M to the message. It then provides the agent with an initial response, which ranges over the *OSC(i)* signature certificate ($Cert_s(OSC(i))$), payment gateway key-exchange certificate ($Cert_k(PG)$) that corresponds to the payment card brand indicated by the agent and $OSC(i)s(I_C \parallel I_M \parallel t \parallel H[H(OI) \parallel H(PI)])$, where $OSC(i)s$ is the secret key of *OSC(i)*.

Verification Request: The agent contacts the *ASC* by transmitting a verification request, which is composed of:

$$Cert_s(C), Cert_s(OSC(i)), Cert_k(PG), OSC(i)s(I_C \parallel I_M \parallel t \parallel H[H(OI) \parallel H(PI)]) \quad (5)$$

After verifying $Cert_s(C)$, $Cert_s(OSC(i))$ $Cert_k(PG)$, the *ASC* decrypts m_{ASC} (see (4)) with its secret key-exchange key into

$$k + I_C \cdot t + R, C_S (I_C \parallel t \parallel H[H(OI) \parallel H(PI)]) \quad (6)$$

and decrypts $C_S (I_C \parallel t \parallel H[H(OI) \parallel H(PI)])$ with the public key of *C* into:

$$I_C \parallel t \parallel H[H(OI) \parallel H(PI)] \quad (7)$$

and decrypts $OSC(i)s(I_C \parallel I_M \parallel t \parallel H[H(OI) \parallel H(PI)])$ with the public key of *OSC(i)* into:

$$I_C \parallel I_M \parallel t \parallel H[H(OI) \parallel H(PI)] \quad (8)$$

The *ASC* then compares the corresponding terms of (7) and (8). If there is no problem, it replies to the agent with a confirmation that includes:

$$PGp(((k+I_C \cdot t+R)+I_M \cdot t), E_k(PI) \tag{9}$$

where PGp is the payment gateway's public key obtained from the key-exchange certificate $Cert_k(PG)$.

It should be noted that R cannot be exposed to the ASC even though the ASC is a trusted center. The reason is that the ASC can retrieve the private key k if R is given.

Purchase Request: After receiving the above confirmation, the agent creates a digital envelope E_{PG} for the payment gateway, containing the following items:

$$E_{PG} = \{ PGp((k+I_C \cdot t+R)+I_M \cdot t), I_C, I_M, t, R, E_k(PI) \} \tag{10}$$

The purchase request including:

$$Cert_s(C), OI, H(PI), Sign_C(H[H(OI) \| H(PI)]), E_{PG} \tag{11}$$

is then sent to the $OSC(i)$.

Authorization Request: After checking the certificate $Cert_s(C)$, in order to ensure that the order is signed using the cardholder's private signature key, $OSC(i)$ verifies the dual signature of the cardholder in the following way:

- Because OI is known to the $OSC(i)$, it can compute the digest of OI, i.e., $H(OI)$;
- Because $H(PI)$ is known to the $OSC(i)$, it can calculate the digest of $H(OI) \| H(PI)$, i.e., $H[H(OI) \| H(PI)]$;
- The $OSC(i)$ can finally check the signature of the cardholder on $H[H(OI)\|H(PI)]$ with Equation (2).

The purchase request is then processed, which includes forwarding the information

$$Cert_s(C), E_{PG}, H(OI), Sign_C(H[H(OI) \| H(PI)]) \tag{12}$$

to the payment gateway, for authorization.

Authorization Response: If I_C, I_M, R and t are compatible, the payment gateway should be able to obtain the correct k and then PI from $E_k(PI)$. If OI and PI agree, the dual signature can be verified with $H(OI)$, PI and $Sign_C(H[H(OI) \| H(PI)])$ in a way similar to that outlined in the previous step. If there is no problem, this ensures that the PI has not been tampered with in transit and that it was signed using the cardholder's private signature key.

Next, the PG formats and sends an authorization request to the issuer via a payment system. Upon receiving an authorization response, the PG generates and digitally signs an authorization request message, which includes the issuer's response and a copy of the PG signature certificate. Then the PG sends the authorization response to the $OSC(i)$.

Purchase Response: This step is the same as that of the SET protocol. After the OI has been processed, the $OSC(i)$ software generates and digitally signs a purchase response message, which indicates that the cardholder's order has been received by the $OSC(i)$. The response is then transmitted to the agent.

If the payment is authorized, the $OSC(i)$ will fulfill the order by shipping the goods or performing the services indicated in the order.

Agent Return: After obtaining the purchase response from $OSC(i)$, the agent stops roaming on the Internet, records the signature certificate of $OSC(i)$, the purchase response and the digital signature of $OSC(i)$ on the purchase response and then migrates back to the cardholder's device. The cardholder's software then proceeds as in SET's final step. After this, the agent-based SET protocol terminates.

SECURITY ISSUES FOR MOBILE AGENTS

Agent technology has received growing interest from the research community and has matured significantly in the last few years. However, the number of applications using this technology is still small. Electronic commerce is generally seen as one of the most promising application areas for mobile agents. For example, a buying agent leaves its host with the mission of querying several vendors about a certain product, determines which one offers the lowest price (or some other kind of preferred feature), buys the product from that one and pays for it. Clearly there is a perception that agents are suitable for this kind of activity and that the ability to pay is one of the desired properties they should have. A major concern is always how to do this in a secure way, in particular without revealing confidential information to the outside world.

Mobile agent security can be split into two broad areas (Chess et al., 1995). The first involves the protection of host nodes from destructive mobile agents, while the second involves the protection of mobile agents from destructive hosts.

Protection of Hosts from Malicious Agents

A mobile agent system is an open system (Tarado et al., 1996). Therefore, just like in any open system, the host nodes are subject to a variety of attacks, both old and new. Attacks on host security fall into four main categories:

1. Leakage: acquisition of data by an unauthorized party.
2. Tampering: alteration of data by an unauthorized party.
3. Resource stealing: use of facilities by an unauthorized party.
4. Vandalism: malicious interference with a host's data or facilities with no clear profit to the perpetrator.

The traditional methods of attack include eavesdropping, masquerading, message tampering, message replay and viruses. A mobile agent can employ any of these methods of attack, which in turn, can be guarded against using standard techniques such as cryptography, authentication, digital signatures and trust hierarchies.

However, a mobile agent is unique in that its code is executed by a host. Thus an executing mobile agent has automatic access to some of a host's resources. With this level of access a mobile agent can mount attacks by altering other local agents, propagating viruses, worms and Trojan horses, impersonating other users and mounting denial of service attacks (Tardo et al., 1996). The standard approach to this problem is to reject all unknown code from entry into a host. This is not a viable solution in a mobile agent environment (Green et al., 1997). Telescript (White, 1994; 1995; 1996) provides three mechanisms that can be applied at various degrees of granularity.

Some research systems provide only partial protection for the hosts. Tacoma (Johnsen et al., 1995) provides hooks so that a developer can add their own encryption subsystem, but does not provide secure execution environments for all of its supported languages. Ara (Peine et al., 1997) enforces restrictions on the CPU time and memory usage, but does not yet protect resources such as the file system and network. Both Tube (Halls et al., 1996) and SodaBot (Coen, 1994) execute their agent inside secure interpreters that enforce some access restrictions. Since a high security level only can be achieved by the sacrifice of flexibility and increased expense, it is important to choose carefully the trade-offs among these factors.

Protection of Agents from Malicious Hosts

In comparison to the protection of host, protecting a mobile agent from attacks by malicious hosts is much more difficult. Since mobile agents are executed by hosts, they have to expose their data and code to the host environment. Thus the agents are at the risk of being tampered with, scanned or even terminated by malicious servers.

Some efforts have been made to solve the problem. However, current results are still far from satisfactory. The simplest method of protecting agents is to avoid supplying them with any important data. A noncritical agent will be free from the concern of being attacked. Obviously, such an agent will not be very useful in most cases. Limiting the confidential data that agents have usually limits the utility of these agents at the same time. Berkovits et al. (1998) try to establish different degrees of trust among different parties and keep agents in secure routing zones to avoid them getting into malicious hosts. The problem is that this severely compromises the concept of an open agent system where new servers can join the system as new needs show up and the interests of the server owners may change dynamically. Tacoma (Minsky et al., 1996) uses replication and voting schemes to handle malicious machines that either terminate an agent outright or provide the agent with incorrect information. Although this scheme prevents many kinds of attacks, it also has several drawbacks. Sander et al. (1997; 1998) came up with a very promising approach which exploits cryptographic functions. In this case, the mobile code performs an algorithm that, given some external inputs, computes a cryptographic value. The site has no clue about which function is actually computed and therefore cannot meaningfully tamper with algorithm execution and computation results.

In addition to the software approach, the use of tamper-proof hardware has been suggested (Wilhelm, 1997). Such devices are processors that execute agents in a physically sealed environment. The system internals are not accessible even by its owner without disrupting the system itself. While these systems can provide a high level of protection, they require dedicated (expensive) hardware. Therefore, they are not easily deployed on a large scale.

Protecting programs against attacks coming from the interpreter responsible for their execution is a challenging problem. Current consensus is that it is computationally impossible to protect mobile agents from malicious hosts. Instead of tackling the problem from a computational (difficult) point of view, current research (Rasmusson et al., 1996) is looking at sociological means of enforcing good host behavior.

A Non-Repudiation Approach to Achieve Security of Mobile Agents

In this section, we combine cryptographic technology and sociological means to propose a non-repudiation approach to securing mobile agents. We take the proposed agent-based information-gathering system as the underlying object. The following approach is similarly suitable for the agent-based payment systems proposed above.

Login Data Bases (LDB): In the proposed agent-based information gathering architecture, each Online Shopping Center (*OSC*) needs to set up a Login Data Base (*LDB*) reserving some information from passing mobile agents in order to provide non-repudiation evidence when any problem occurs.

Because there are probably a lot of mobile agents entering an *OSC* to gather trading information every day, it is impossible for an *OSC* to keep full copies of passing agents in its records, since the *LDB* will then occupy a great deal of storage space. In view of this, the

Figure 7. The record structure of a Login Data Base (LDB)

Agent Certificate	Time Stamp (0)	Previous Node	Time Stamp (1)	Signature (1)	Provided Trading Information	Destination Node	Time Stamp (2)	Signature (2)

record structure of the *LDB* need to be optimized. Our solution to this problem is as follows in figure 7.

The record structure of a Login Data Base (*LDB*)
In the above structure, the meanings of all symbols used are as follows:

- Agent Certificate—the certificate of the agent, obtained from the original agent;
- Time Stamp (0)—the time when the agent is generated, obtained from the original agent;
- Previous Node—the certificate of the previous *OSC* from which the agent launches, obtained from the non-repudiation component of the previous *OSC*;
- Time Stamp (1)—the time when the agent is exits from the previous *OSC*, obtained from the non-repudiation component of the previous *OSC*;
- Signature (1)—the signature of the previous *OSC* on the agent, obtained from the non-repudiation component of the previous *OSC*;
- Provided Trading Information—the trading information provided to the agent by the present *OSC*;
- Destination Node—the certificate of the next *OSC* to which the agent has gone, acquired from the reply of the next *OSC*;
- Time Stamp (2)—the time when the agent migrates to the next *OSC* from the present *OSC*;
- Signature (2)—the signature of the next *OSC* on the agent, acquired from the reply of the next *OSC*.

Protection of Hosts against Malicious Agents: In the agent-mediated information gathering architecture, the Code and Data Component (*CDC*) is signed by the Agent Service Center (*ASC*). No other parties can forge this signature on the basis of cryptography. Therefore, the *CDC* provides not only the code and data which will be executed by all *OSCs* to achieve an information-gathering mission, but also non-repudiation evidence, so that the *ASC* cannot deny having generated the *CDC*. Once any problems such as a virus altering other local agents, propagating viruses, worms and Trojan horses occur when an *OSC* runs the *CDC* on its agent execution environment, the *ASC* is probably malicious and will be accused. So if the *ASC* is a trusted party, no malicious agents will be generated.

Protection of Agents against Malicious Hosts: With the help of the *LDB*, the proposed agent-based information-gathering architecture can provide protection for agents against a malicious *OSC* in the following respects:

On designing the architecture, each Gathered Information Component (*GIC*) is protected by firstly encrypting it with the secret key of the information provider and then encrypting the result with the public key of the agent owner. Except for the information provider, others cannot do this because they do not know the secret key of the information provider. In addition, except for the agent's owner, others cannot retrieve the *GIC* because they do not know the secret key of the agent's owner. In this way, we can prevent a malicious

OSC from scanning or modifying a GIC belonging to others.

Although an OSC is permitted to put the GIC and Non-Repudiation Component (NRC) into an agent, any malicious manipulation (such as cutting or manipulating another $OSCs'$ GIC) will be detected by the ASC (because the ASC will be conscious of any malicious action if an agent has taken an error action, or if any GIC cannot produce significant trading information or even completely disappears). In this case, the ASC will carry out the following check procedure and identify the malicious host.

1. The ASC asks each $OSC(i)$ on the route list to commit their records (denoted as $Rec(i)$) about the agent with $OSC(i)s(GIC(i))$ ($i=1,2, ..., n$), where $GIC(i)$ represents the gathered information from $OSC(i)$. The motivation to prove themselves to be innocent drives all $OSCs$ except a malicious one to provide true records about the agent.

2. On basis of initial agent and $Rec(i)$, $OSC(i)s(GIC(i))$ ($i=1, 2,......, n$), the ASC can reconstruct the Gathering Information Agent (GIA) in all stages in a recursive way.

3. Suppose $OSC(i)$ ($i=1, 2,......, m-1$ ($m <= n$)) have no problem, the ASC checks whether $OSC(m+1)p(Signature(2))$ is equal to $H(M)$, where $Signature(2)$ is extracted from $Rec(m)$. If so, $OSC(m)$ has no problem. If not, $OSC(m)$ will be identified as malicious because it cannot provide the non-repudiation of receipt from $OSC(m+1)$ which states $OSC(m+1)$ has successfully received the correct GIA. $OSC(m)$ should repeatedly have transmitted the GIA to $OSC(m+1)$ until $OSC(m+1)p(Signature(2))=H(M)$ or delivered an error notification to the ASC.

If a GIA is killed by a malicious OSC, the above check procedure can also be carried out to uncover the culprit. The first OSC which cannot provide a correct record about the GIA will be identified as malicious.

IMPLEMENTATION OF MOBILE AGENT SYSTEM

All of the above proposed agent-based architectures for electronic commerce can be implemented with the Aglets Software Development Kit— an environment for programming mobile Internet agents in Java™ (it used to be called the Aglets Workbench).

Java and applets have revolutionized the Web, and executable content has become a common term in the Web glossary. Applets are essentially sets of program code that can be downloaded, instantiated, and executed in Web browsers. Recently, this concept has been matched by the introduction of the servlet. The servlet moves program code in opposite direction to the applet, that is, it allows the client to upload additional program code to a server. The servlet's code is then instantiated and executed in the server.

Aglets represents the next leap forward in the evolution of executable content on the Internet, introducing program code that can be transported along with state information. Aglets are Java objects that can move from one host on the Internet to another. That is, an aglet that executes on one host can suddenly halt execution, dispatch itself to a remote host, and resume execution there. When the aglet moves, it takes along its program code as well as its data. A built-in security mechanism makes it safe to host untrusted aglets.

The Java Aglet Application Programming Interface (J-AAPI) is a standard for interfacing aglets and their environment. J-AAPI defines the methods necessary for

- aglet creation;
- message handling in the aglet;
- initialization;
- dispatching;
- retraction;
- deactivation/activation;
- cloning;
- disposing of the aglet.

J-AAPI is simple, flexible, and stable. Internet agent developers can write platform independent aglets and expect them to run on any host that supports J-AAPI.

J-AAPI is intended for Internet agent programmers. It allows for the development of platform independent mobile agents written in the Java programming language.

TheAglets Software Development Kit (ASDK) is free software from IBM. Anybody can download it at http://www.trl.ibm.co.jp/aglets/download.html. Aglets are intended to do the following.

- Provide an easy and comprehensive model for programming mobile agents without requiring modifications to the Java VM or native code.
- Support dynamic and powerful communication that enables agents to communicate with unknown agents as well as well-known agents.
- Design a reusable and extensible architecture.
- Design a harmonious architecture with existing Web/Java technology.
- Provide security mechanisms that are comprehensive and simple enough to allow end users to trust mobile agents.

Aglets use an organizational approach whereby all agent systems in a certain domain are deemed trustworthy, and the authenticity of the agent is evaluated depending on the domain in which it has been roaming around. A user first authenticates himself/herself to the system, and then issues the credentials of the user's agent. The agent system then evaluates the authenticity of the credentials, to determine whether or not they were issued within the same domain. It may downgrade the authenticity or simply deny access, depending on conditions such as where the agent has traveled and so forth. Host authentication is used to identify the domain to which the communicating host belongs.

There are several scenarios for building an application using aglet technology. While a server can host running aglets, a client can create and control an aglet remotely without any aglet context. Applets can be on either a server or a client, although it is impossible to dispatch an aglet to an applet.

A client application has no server facility; it only has communication facilities for creating and controlling an aglet remotely, or for sending a remote message. Therefore, this configuration requires fewer resources for using aglets and reduces security threats, because it does not download any byte code, although it can still take advantage of mobile agents on the server side.

For example, the console of a massive network management system may not have to install the server facility. The console application, which typically has a client capability, can create a monitor aglet on a machine and let a detective aglet roam multiple machines and send information back to the console.

CONCLUSION

Today's first-generation agent-mediated Internet trading systems are already creating new markets (e.g., low-cost consumer-to-consumer and refurbished commodities) and are beginning to reduce transaction costs in variety of business tasks. However, we still have a long way to go before software agents transform the way in which businesses conduct business. This change will occur as software agent technologies mature to better manage ambiguous content, personalized preferences, complex goals, changing environments and disconnected parties. The greatest change may occur, however, once standards are evolved and adopted to unambiguously and universally define commodities and services, consumer and merchant profiles, value-added services, secure payment mechanisms, interbusiness electronic forms, etc.

During the next generation of agent-based electronic commerce, agents will enhance customer satisfaction and streamline business-to-business transactions, reducing transaction costs at every stage of the supply chain. At some critical threshold, new types of transactions will emerge in the form of dynamic relationships among previously unknown parties. Agents will strategically form and reform coalitions to bid on contracts and leverage economies of scale—in essence, creating dynamic business partnerships that exist only as long as necessary. It is in this next generation of agent-based electronic commerce where companies will be at their most agile and markets will approach perfect efficiency.

In order to narrow the gap between the today's first generation and the next-generation agent-based electronic commerce systems, we have in this chapter proposed an agent-based information-gathering system and an agent-based payment system so as to automate and secure electronic commerce on the Internet.

We are also interested in keeping the agent as intelligent and autonomous as possible, allowing it to make its own decisions (even if very simple) when needed. As part of our future work, we intend to use an Aglet language to implement the agent-based framework for electronic commerce, with agents capable of negotiating with their hosts on the basis of the knowledge they carry as they migrate from one server to another and pay for goods on behalf of their owner.

REFERENCES

Berkovist, S., Guttman, J.D. and Swarup, V.(1998). Authentication for mobile agents. *Mobile Agent and Security*, LNCS 1419.

Callan, J. P., Croft, W. B.and Harding, S. M. (1992). The INQUERY retrieval system. In *Proceedings of the 3rd International Conference on Database and Expert Systems Applications*, pp.78-83, 1992.

Chess, D., Grosof, B., Harrison, C., Levine, D., Parris, C. and Tsudik, G. (1995). Itinerant Agents for Mobile Computing. *IEEE Personal Communications*, 2(3), 34-49.

Coen, M. H. (1994). SodaBot: A software agent environment and construction system. In Proceedings of the CIKM Workshop on Intelligent Information Agents, *Third International Conference on Information and Knowledge Management* (CIKM94), Gaithersburg, Maryland.

Diffie, W., Hellman, M.E., (1976). New direction in cryptography, *IEEE Trans. Information Theory*, vol. IT-22(6), pp.644-654, Nov.1976.

Doorenbos, R., Etzioni, O. and Weld, D.(1997). A scalable comparision-shopping agent for the world-wide-web. In *Proceedings of the First International Conference on Autonomous Agents*, 39-48, Marina del Rey, California, February 1997.

Etzioni, O.(1996). Moving up the information food chain: Employing softbots on the world wide web. In *Proceedings of the Thirteen National Conference on Artificial Intelligence*, 1322-1326, Portland, OR.

Fisher, D., Soderland, S., McCarthy, J., Feng, F. and Lehnert, W. (1996). Description of the UMass systems as used for MUC-6. In *Proceedings of the 6th Message Understanding Conference*, Columbia, MD.

Green, S., Somers, F., Hurst, L., Evans, R., Nangle, B., Cunningham, P. (1997) *Software agent: A review*. May 1997.

Halls, D., Bates, J. and Bacon, J. (1996). Flexible distributed programming using mobile code. In *Proceeding of the Seventh ACM SIGOPS European Workshop*, 225-231, Sept.

Johansen, D., Renesse, R. V. and Scheidner, F. R.(1995) Operating system support for mobile agents. In *Proceeding of the Fifth IEEE Workshop on Hot Topics in Operating System* (HTOS), 42-45, May 1995.

Larkey, L. and Croft, W. B. (1996). Combining classifiers in text categorization. In *Proceedings of the 19th International Conference on Research and Development in Information Retrieval* (SIGIR '96), 289-297, Zurich, Switzerland.

Lesser, V., Horling, B., Klassner, F., Raja, A., Wagner, T. and Zhang, X.Q. (1998). BIG: A resource-bounded information gathering agent. In the *Proceedings of the Fifteenth National Conference on Artificial Intelligence* (AAAI-98).

Krulwich, B. (1996). The BargainFinder agent: Comparison price shopping on the Internet. In *Bots and Other Internet Beasties* by Joseph Williams, SAMS.NET publishing.

Maes, P. (1994). Agents that reduce work and information overload. *Communications of the ACM*, 37(7), 31-40.

Minsky, Y., Renesse, R., Schneider, F.B. and Stoller S.D. (1996). Cryptographic Support for Fault-Tolerant Distributed Computing. In *Proceedings of the Seventh ACM SIGOPS European Workshop, Connemara*, pp.109-114, Ireland, September.

Moukas, A., Guttman, R., Maes, P. (1999). Agent-mediated electronic commerce: an MIT media laboratory perspective. To appear on *Proceedings of the International Conference on Electronic Commerce*.

Peine, H. and Stolpmann, T. (1997). The architecture of the Ara platform for mobile agents. In *Proceeding of the First International Workshop on Mobile Agents* (MA'97), LNCS 1219, Berlin, April 1997.

Rasmusson, L. and Janson, S. (1996). Simulated social control for secure Internet commerce, In *Proceedings of New Security Paradigms'96*, ACM Press, September 1996.

Rivest, R.L., Shamir, A., Adleman, L. (1978) A method for obtaining digital structures and public-key cryptosystem, *Commun.. ACM*, vol.21, no.2, pp.120-127, Feb. 1978.

Romao, A. and Mira da Silva, M (1998). An agent-based secure Internet payment system for mobile computing. In *Proceeding of TrEC'98*, LNCS 1402, Hamburg, Germany, June 1998.

Sander, T. (1997). On cryptographic protection of mobile agents. In Proceedings of the *1997 Workshop on Mobile Agents and Security*, University of Maryland, Oct. 1997.

Sander, T. and Tschudin, C.F. (1998). Protecting mobile agents against malicious hosts. *Mobile Agent and Security*, LNCS 1419.

Tardo, J., and Valenta. L. (1996) Mobile agent security and Telescript. In *Proceeding of*

IEEE COMPCON'96.

Visa International and MasterCard International (1997) *Secure electronic transaction (SET) specification.* Version 1.0, May 1997.

White, J. E. (1994). Telescript technology: The foundation for the electronic marketplace. General Magic White Paper, General Magic, Inc.

White, J E. (1995). Telescript technology: An introduction to the language. General Magic White Paper, General Magic, Inc.

White, J. E. (1996). Telescript technology: Scenes from the electronic marketplace. General Magic White Paper, General Magic, Inc.

Wilhelm, U. and Defago, X.(1997). Objets Protégés Cryptographiquement. In *Proceedings of RenPar'97*, Lausanne, Switzerland, May.

Chapter XIX

A Mobile Agent Computation Model for Best Buy Searching

Timothy K. Shih
Tamkang University, Taiwan

The Internet changes our shopping style. With the growing popularity of Web browsers, electronic commerce (EC) has become a trend of next-generation shopping style. EC software applications are written as Web document control programs, which run on service providers. The techniques used including information retrieval, network communication, database management, communication security and others. Due to the huge volume of data transmitted on the Internet, and the number of electronic commerce shoppers, currently the Internet is overloaded on its limited communication bandwidth. Research contributions are proposed to overcome this problem. Mobile agents are computer programs that can be distributed across networks to run on a remote computer station. The technique can be used in distributed information retrieval which allows the computation load to be added to servers, but significantly reduces the traffic of network communication. Many articles indicate that this approach is a new direction to software engineering. However, it is hard to find a theoretical base of mobile agent computing and interaction over the Internet. We propose a graph-based model, with a simulation design, for the mobile agents, which evolve over the Internet. Based on the concepts of food web (or food chain), one of the natural laws that we may use besides neural networks and genetic algorithms, we define agent niche overlap graph and agent evolution states for the distributed computation of mobile agent evolution. The proposed model can be used to build an environment for many electronic commerce applications, such as advertisement agent or survey questionnaire agent.

Copyright © 2000, Idea Group Publishing.

INTRODUCTION

Communication over the Internet is growing increasingly and will have profound implications for our economy, culture and society. From mainframe-based numerical computing to decentralized downsizing, PCs and workstation computers connected by Internet have become the trend of next-generation computers. With the growing popularity of the World Wide Web, digital libraries over the Internet play an important role in the academic, business, and industrial worlds. In order to allow effective and efficient information retrieval, many search engines were developed. However, due to the limitation of now-a-day network communication bandwidth, many researchers suggest that distributed Internet search mechanisms should overcome the traditional information retrieval technologies, which perform the controls of searching and data transmission on a single machine. Mobile agents are software programs that can travel over the Internet. Mobile search agents find the information specified by its original query user on a specific station, and send back search results to the user. Only queries and results are transmitted over the Internet. Thus, unnecessary transmission is avoided. In other words, mobile agent computing distributes computation loads among networked stations and reduces network traffic.

A mobile agent, in general, can be more than just a search program. For instance, a mobile agent can serve as an emergency message broadcaster, an advertising agent, or a survey questionnaire collector. A mobile agent should have the following properties:
- It can achieve a goal automatically.
- It should be able to clone itself and propagate.
- It should be able to communicate with other agents.
- It has evolution states, including a termination state.

The environment where mobile agents live is the Internet. Agents are distributed automatically or semi-automatically via some communication paths. Therefore, agents meet each other on the Internet. Agents which have the same goal can share information and cooperate. However, if the system resource (e.g., network bandwidth or disk storage of a station) is insufficient, agents compete with each other. These phenomena are similar to those in the ecosystem of the real world. A creature is born with a goal to live and reproduce. To defend their natural enemies, creatures of the same species cooperate. However, in a perturbation in ecosystems, creatures compete with or even kill each other. The natural world has built a law of balance. Food web (or food chain) embeds the law of creature evolution. With the growing popularity of the Internet, where mobile agents live, it is our goal to learn from the natural to propose an agent evolution computing model over the Internet. The model, even applied only in the mobile agent evolution discussed in this chapter, can be generalized to solve other computer science problems, for instance, the search problems in distributed artificial intelligence, network traffic control, electronic commerce, or any computation that involves a large amount of concurrent/distributed computation.

We propose a logical network for agent connections/communications called agent communication network (or ACN). ACN is dynamic. It evolves as agent communication proceeds. It also serves as a graph theoretical model of agent evolution computing. Our research purposes include:
- Provide a model for agent evolution and define the associated rules
- Construct simulation facilities to estimate agent evolution

- Suggest guidelines to write intelligent mobile agent programs
- Suggest strategies to construct efficient ACNs
- Ensure network security in the simulation environment

Given an ACN, the model finds which agent evolution policy produces the maximum throughput (i.e., the goal of agents achieved). Or, changing the structure of an ACN, the model is able to find out how to adjust the agent evolution policy in order to recover from the change (or how is the throughput affected).

We have surveyed articles in the area of mobile agents, personal agents, and intelligent agents. The related works are discussed next. Terminology and definitions are then given, where we also introduce the detail concepts of agent communication network. In our model, an agent evolves based on a state transition diagram, which is illustrated in this chapter. Then, a graph theoretical model, which describes agent dependencies and competitions, is given. Following is a section on agent evolution computing algorithms, which we used to construct our simulation. And finally, we discuss our conclusions and possible extensions.

RELATED WORKS

The concept of agent-based software engineering is discussed in a survey paper Genesereth, 1994). The author presents two important issues: agent communication language and agent architecture. Agent communication languages allow agents to share information and send messages to each other. Agent architecture, on the other hand, includes network infrastructure and software architecture that ensure agent computing. An open agent architecture for kiosk-based multimedia information service is proposed in Charlton et al. (1997).

Survey of different types of agents can be found in Petrie (1996) and Annunziato (1995). Petrie (1996) indicates that Web-based intelligent agents are necessary and should be a trend of new engineering applications. However, application designers need to resolve the conflict between the client-server-based designs and the peer-to-peer protocol. The Java Agent Template (JAT) is proposed, which allows application designers to write Java programs run on heterogeneous computer environments. Agent programs developed in this technique can send KQML messages to each other. In our simulation, we use JATLite which is a version of JAT, on Windows NT-based environment. In Annunziato (1995), the author summarize three types of agents: intelligent autonomous agents, mobile agents, and cooperative agents. Agent applications and development tools are also discussed.

A personalized agent system, BASAR (Building Agents Supporting Adaptive Retrieval), maintains Web links based on personal bookmarks is proposed in Thomas and Fischer (`997). The system is able to support information updating, providing that the content of Web site where the user marked is changed. The system also reduces the number of links by deleting ones that are seldom used. And, new links can be added by using search engines.

A Web-based information browsing agent is proposed in Dharap and Freeman (1996). Using KQML as the communication language, the proposed system significantly reduces network load by pushing the computation to the server. Structured meta information is also used to decrease the complexity of browsing. A multi-agent system supporting intelligent information over the Internet is proposed in Odubiyi et al. (1997). The system incorporates technologies from intelligent software agents, natural language understanding, and conceptual search mechanisms to access Earth and Space Science Data.

The concept of mobile agent is discussed in several articles (Magedanz and Eckardt, 1996; Sapaty and Borst, 1996; Krause et al., 1997; Lingnau and Drobnik, 1996). Agent Tcl, a mobile-agent system providing navigation and communication services, security mechanisms, and debugging and tracking tools, is proposed in Kotz et al.(1997), Gray et al. (1997, and Gray (1997). The system allows agent programs move transparently between computers. A software technology called Telescript, with safety and security features, is discussed in Tardo and Valente (1996). The mobile agent architecture, MAGNA, and its platform are presented in Krause et al. (1997). Another agent infrastructure is implemented to support mobile agents (Lingnau and Drobnik, 1996). A mobile agent technique to achieve load balancing in telecommunications networks is proposed in Schoonderwoerd et al. (1997). The mobile agent programs discussed can travel among network nodes to suggest routes for better communications. Mobile service agent techniques and the corresponding architectural principles as well as requirements of a distributed agent environment are discussed in Krause and Magedanz (1996). The evaluation of several commercial Java mobile agents is given in Kiniry and Zimmerman (1997).

AGENT COMMUNICATION NETWORK

Agents communicate with each other since they can help each other. For instance, agents that share the same search query should be able to pass query results to each other so that redundant computation can be avoided. An ACN serves this purpose. Each node in an ACN (shown in Figure 1) represents an agent on a computer network node, and each link represents a logical computer network connection (or an agent communication link). Since agents of the same goal want to pass results to each other, they are modeled as a complete graph. Therefore, an ACN of agents holding different goals is a graph of complete graphs. In Figure 1, there are six types of agents (i.e., species **A** to **F**). Since agents can have multiple goals (e.g., searching based on multiple criteria), an agent may belong to different complete

Figure 1: Agent Communication Network

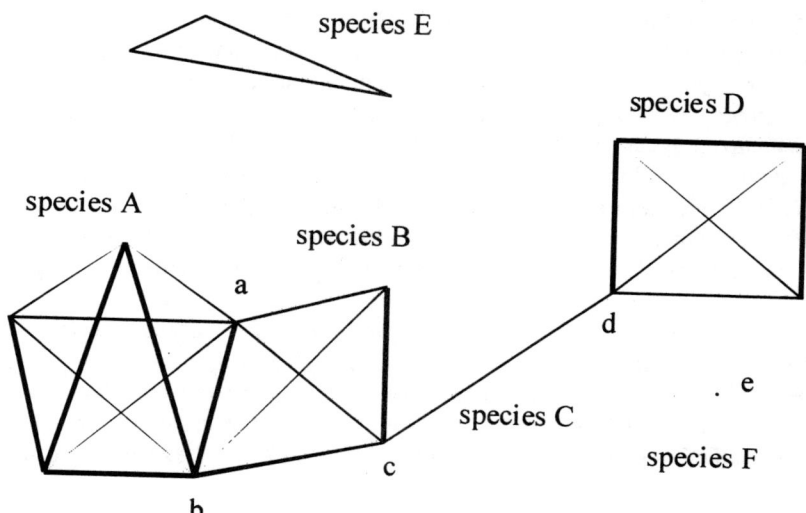

graphs. For instance, agents **a** and **b** both belongs to the complete graphs of species **A** and **B**. On the other hand, agents may have a unique goal (e.g., agents of species **E** or **F**). Agent **e** of species **F** is the only one of its kind.

We define some terminology used through this paper. A *host station* (or *station*) is a networked workstation on which agents live. A *query station* is a station where a user releases a query for achieving a set of goals. A station can hold multiple agents. Similarly, an agent can pursue multiple goals. An *agent society* (or *society*) is a set of agents fully connected by a complete graph, with a common goal associated with each agent in the society. A goal belonging to different agents may have different priorities. An agent society with a common goal of the same priority is called a *species*. Since an agent may have multiple goals, it is possible that two or more societies (or species) have intersections. A *communication cut set* is a set of agents belonging to two distinct agent societies, which share common agents (e.g., {**a**, **b**}, {**c**}, and {**d**} in Figure 1). The removing of all elements of a communication cut set results in the separation of the two distinct societies. An agent in a communication cut set is called an *articulation agent* (e.g., agents **a**, **b**, **c**, and **d** in Figure 1). Since agent societies (or species) are represented by complete graphs and these graphs have communication cut sets as intersections, articulation agents can be used to suggest a shortest network path between a query station and the station where an agent finds its goal. Another point is that an articulation agent can hold a *repository*, which contains the network communication statuses of links of an agent society. Therefore, network resource can be evaluated when an agent checks its surviving environment to decide its evolution policy.

It is necessary for us to give formal definitions of the terminology to be used in our algorithms. In the following definitions, "= =" read as "is defined by" and "*Set_Of(X)*" represents a set of object *X*:

Host_Station == *URL* ✕ *Resource* ✕ *Set_Of(Agent)*
Resource == *Network* ✕ *CPU* ✕ *Memory* ✕ *Information*
Agent == *Set_Of(Goal)* ✕ *Policy*
Goal == *Query_Return_URL* ✕ *Query* ✕ *Priority*
Agent_Society == Set_Of(Agent)
Species ⊂ *Agent_Society*

A *Host_Station* has a uniform resource locator (i.e., *URL*)[1] which represents the station's unique network address. A host station has system resources (i.e., *Resource*) and can hold some agents (i.e., Set_Of(*Agent*)). *Network* represents the network facility available to a station. *CPU* represents the computation power of a station. *Memory* represents the storage of a station. It could be the main memory or the secondary memory. *Information* is available on a station. Each *Agent* has some *Goal*s and a *Policy*, which is a set of application-dependent factors the agent depends on to perform its evolution computation. *Query_Return_URL* is the URL where an agent should return its query results. *Query* is an application-dependent specification, which represents a user request to the agent. *Priority* is an integer represents the priority of a goal. The larger the integer, the higher the goal priority. *Agent_Society* is a set of agents, which share a common goal. *Species* is an *Agent_Society* of the same goal priority.

We use a simple notation to obtain a component of an object. For example, in our algorithm, if agent A is used, then *A.Goal* represents the goals of that agent, where A is unique in its belonging agent society (or species). We will discuss the usage of these terms

308 Shih

in algorithms later in the chapter. But first, we should address the concepts of agent evolution states and species food web respectively.

AGENT EVOLUTION STATES

An agent evolves. It can react to an environment, respond to another agent, and communicate with other agents. The evolution process of an agent involves some internal states of an agent. As shown in Figure 2, an agent is in one of the following states after it is born and before it is killed or dies naturally:

- **Searching**: the agent is searching for a goal
- **Suspending**: the agent is waiting for enough resource in its environment in order to search for its goal
- **Dangling**: the agent loses its goal of surviving, it is waiting for a new goal
- **Mutating**: the agent is changed to a new species with a new goal and the agent survives in a new host station

An agent is born to a *searching state* to search for its goal (i.e., information of some kind). All creatures must have goals (e.g., search for food). However, if its surviving environment (i.e., a host station) does not contain enough resource, the agent may transfer to a *suspending state* (i.e., hibernation of a creature). The searching process will be resumed when the environment has better resources. But, if the environment lacks resources badly (i.e., natural disasters occur), the agent might be killed. When an agent finds its goal, the agent will pass the search results to other agents of the same kind (or same society). Other agents will abort their search (since the goal is achieved) and transfer to a *dangling state*. An agent in a dangling state cannot survive for a long time. It will die after some days (i.e., duration of time). Or, it will be reassigned to a new goal with a possible new host station,

Figure 2: Agent Evolution State Transition Diagram

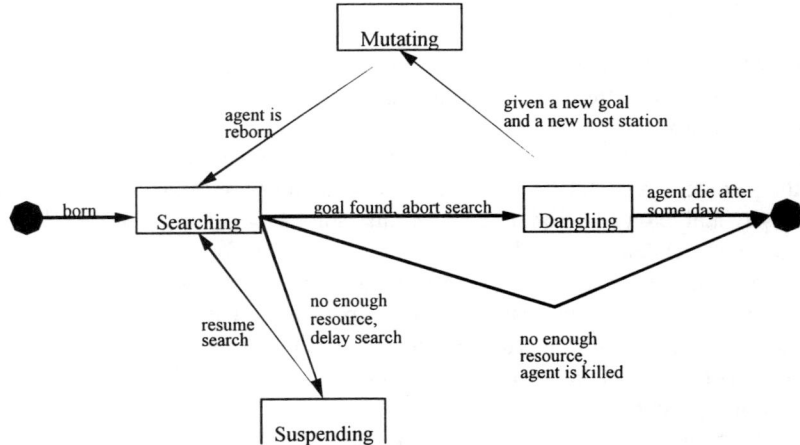

which is a new destination where the agent should travel. In this case, the agent is in a *mutating state* and is reborn to search for the new goal.

The agent evolution state diagram shows how we keep the status of an agent. In order to maintain the activity of agents, in a distributed computing environment, we use message passing as a mechanism to control agent state transition. These agent messages are discussed and will be used in our algorithms.

Agent Messages

Agent evolution computing is performed via actions response to agent messages. There are two categories of messages. The first type of agent messages are sent from a source agent to a destination agent. Agents of the same species are looking for the same goal. When an agent finds its goal, there is no reason for others of the same kind to keep on searching.

Agent Messages

Messages from an Agent	Actions
abort_search(DestAgent, Search_results)	The search process of DestAgent is aborted. The search results are also passed to the DestAgent. After that, the source and the destination agents both transit to the dangling state.
new_goal(DestAgent, Goal)	A new search Goal is assigned to DestAgent.
new_host(DestAgent, Host_station)	The DestAgent is relocated at Host_station.

Therefore, the agent sends an **abort_search** message to other agents of the same species. The message also includes the search results found by the source agent. After that, agents are ready to process a new goal. They can be relocated at a new host station, or stay at the original location.

The **new_host** message is used in conjunction with the **new_goal** message. After a **new_goal** message is received, the destination agent transits to a mutating state.

Host Station Messages

Messages from a Station	Actions
suspend_search(DestAgent)	The agent DestAgent is suspended.
resume_search(DestAgent)	The agent DestAgent is resumed.
kill_agent(DestAgent)	The agent DestAgent is killed.

The second type of agent messages are sent form a host station. Upon resources available at a host station, the host station may suspend and later resume the search process of a specific agent. In the case that the resources are lower than a water mark, the host station may kill an agent.

SPECIES FOOD WEB AND NICHE OVERLAP GRAPH

Agents can suspend/resume or even kill each other. We need a general policy to decide which agent is killed. By our definition, a species is a set of agents of the same goal with a same priority. It is the priority of a goal we base on to discriminate between two or more species.

We need to construct a direct graph, which represents the dependency between species. We call this digraph a *species food web* (or *food web*). Each node in the graph represents a species. All species of a connected food web (i.e., a graph component of the food web) are of the same goal. We assume that different users at different host stations may issue the same query. Each directed edge has an origin represents a species of a higher goal priority and has a terminus with a lower priority. Since an agent (and thus a species) can have multiple goals, each goal of an articulation agent should have an associated food web.

For instance, in Figure 3, the agent communication network has three species. Species A has six agents (i.e., agents **a** to **f**). Species B has agents **d, e, f, g,** and **h**. Species C has agents **d, e,** and **i**. The graph also shows that species **A** and **B** have common goals **g1, g2,** and **g3** at agents **e, d,** and **f,** respectively. Species **A** and **C** have common goals **g1** and **g2**. Species **B** and **C** also have common goals **g1** and **g2**. In the food web of **g1**, the goal priority of **g1** at species **A** is 3 (shown as the subscript of **A**). But, **g1** is of priorities 2 and 1 at species **B** and **C** respectively. Similarly, the food webs of goals **g2** and **g3** are constructed. Based on the directed edges of these webs, agents of a species can send messages to suspend or kill other agents of a different species.

Each food web describes goal priority dependencies of species. From a food web, we can further derive a *niche overlap graph.* In an ecosystem, two or more species have an *ecological niche overlap* (or *niche overlap*) if and only if they are competing for the same resource. A *niche overlap graph* can be used to represent the competition among species. The niche overlap graph is used in our algorithm to decide agent evolution policy and to estimate the effect when certain factors are changed in an agent communication network. Based on the niche overlap graph, the algorithm is able to suggest strategies to rearrange policies so that agents can achieve their highest performance efficiency. This concept is similar to the natural process that recovers from perturbations in ecosystems. Figure 3 also shows the niche overlap graphs of goals **g1, g2,** and **g3**.

AGENT EVOLUTION COMPUTING

We have described how an agent evolves and how agents compete. The algorithms proposed in this section use the agent evolution state diagram and the niche overlap graphs discussed for agent evolution computing. First, we present some naive approaches, which also explain the basic concepts of agent searching and agent distribution. We then present a set of agent evolution computing algorithms over an ACN.

Agent Searching Versus Agent Cloning

An agent wants to search for its goal. At the same time, since the searching process is distributed, an agent wants to find a destination station to clone itself. Searching and cloning essentially exist as a *co-routining relation*. A co-routine can be a pair of processes. While one process serves as a producer, another serves as a consumer. When the consumer uses out of the resource, the consumer is suspended. After that, the producer is activated and produces the resource until it reaches an upper limit. The producer is suspended and the

A Mobile Agent Computation Model for Best Buy Searching   311

Figure 3: An Agent Communication Network and its Species Food Webs

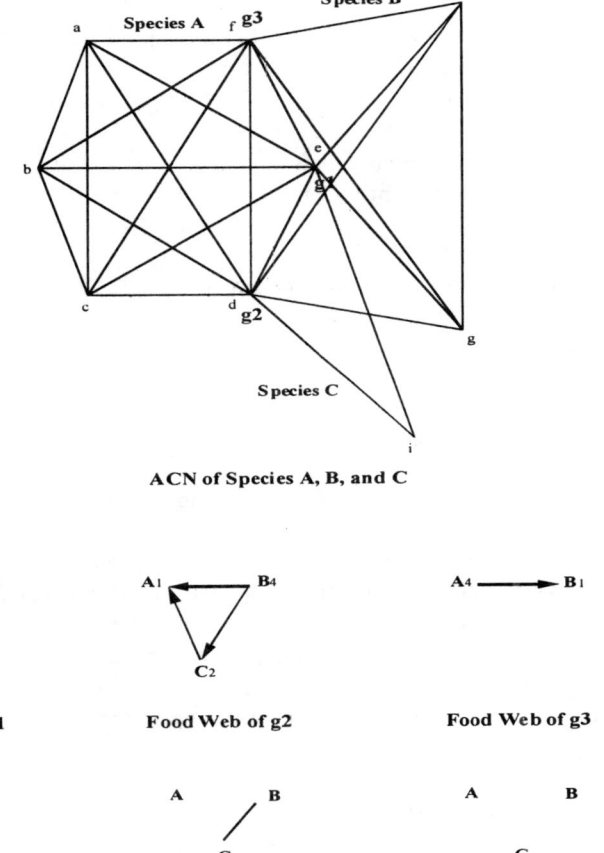

consumer is resumed. If the searching process is a consumer, then the cloning process is a producer who provides new URLs. The following algorithms describe agent searching and cloning:

Co-routining algorithm

Algorithm Search:
  given a goal G
    repeat
      if goal G is found then
        terminate Search
      else
        if URL_queue is empty then
          suspend Search until Clone returns
        else
          search on a URL for goal G
          and delete the URL from the queue

Algorithm Clone:
  repeat
    if URL_queue is full then
      suspend Clone until Search returns
    else
      find and put next URL in the URL_queue

The co-routining algorithms use a queue to store URLs. When the queue is empty, algorithm **Search** is suspended until **Clone** returns. Otherwise, a URL in the queue is used to propagate the agent. Algorithm **Clone** collects some new URLs via search engine until the URL queue is full. The co-routining processes communicate through the URL queue. However, it is not an efficient approach since **Search** or **Clone** wait for each other until the URL queue is full or empty. The drawback can be eliminated using a concurrent algorithm of two separated processes:

Concurrent algorithm

Algorithm Search_Clone:
  given a goal G
    cobegin
      process Search:
        repeat
          if goal G is found then
            terminate Search_Clone
          else
            if URL_queue is not empty then
              search on a URL for goal G and delete the URL
      process Clone:
        repeat
          if URL_queue is not full then
            put next URL in the URL_queue

coend

The concurrent algorithm searches and propagates at the same time when the queue is not empty or not full. Two processes are used concurrently (specified in between "cobegin" and "coend)". When the agent implemented in the concurrent or co-routining algorithm travels to a station, a local URL queue is used and the computation proceeds independently.

The above two approaches describe the relation between searching and cloning of agents. But, there is no communication among agents. All agents compute for the same goal and multiple copies of the same result will be sent back to the query station. this approach not only wastes CPU time, but also wastes network resources. In the next section, we want to overcome this drawback by using an agent communication network, where agents evolve.

Agent Evolution Computing over an ACN

The co-routining and concurrent algorithms discussed work on a single station. However, agent evolution on the agent communication network is an asynchronous computation. Agents living on different (or the same) stations communicate and work with each other via agent messages. The searching and the cloning processes of an agent may run as a co-routine on a station. However, different agents are run on the same or separated stations concurrently. Algorithm **Agent_Search** is the starting point of agent evolution simulation. If system resource meets a basic requirement, the algorithm activates an agent in the searching state. If the search process finds its goal (e.g., the requested information is found), goal abortion results in a dangling state of all agents in the same society (including the agent who finds the goal). At the same time, the search result is sent back to the original query station. Suppose that the goal cannot be achieved in an individual station, the agent is cloned in another station (agent propagation). The **Agent_Clone** algorithm is then used. On the other hand, the agent may be suspended or even killed upon the availability of system resource. Some auxiliary algorithms, which are self-explanatory, describe these processes.

Agent Searching Algorithm on ACN
Algorithm Agent_Search(A, G, X):
    given a goal G to agent A on station X of society S
        if Resource_Available(A, G, X) > low_requirement then
            agent A searches for G in its belonging station X /* searching */
            if G is found then
                A sends an abort message to all agents in S /* abortion */
                A sends search result to the query station
                Agent_Search is complete /* dangling */
            else
                call Agent_Clone(A, G, S) /* propagation */
                terminate Agent_Search /* dangling */
        else if Resource_Available(A, G, X) > min_requirement then
            call Agent_Suspend(A, G, X) /* suspending */
        else
            call Agent_Kill(A, G, X) /* termination */

Note that low_requirement must be greater than min_requirement so that different levels of treatment are used when the resource is not sufficient. But the resource available factor depends on agent policy, as defined in **Resource_Available**.

Agent Cloning Algorithm on ACN

Algorithm Agent_Clone(A, G, S):
    given a source agent A searches for goal G of society S
    use search engine to find a new URL
        on an arbitrary station X that may contain goal G
    if station X has an agent A' then
        if goal of A' contains G then
        let S' be the society associated with G where A' belongs
        union S' and S
    else
        assign G to A' /* mutation */
        make A' join S
        call Agent_Search(A', G, X) /* reborn */
    else
        copy a new agent A'' of A on station X
        make A'' join society S
        call Agent_Search(A'', G, X) /* reborn */

The cloning algorithm is presented as **Agent_Clone**. When the cloning process finds new URLs to broadcast an agent, two strategies can be used. The first is to broadcast the agent to all URLs found by one search engine. But, considering the network resource available, the second strategy may check for the common URLs found by two or more search engines. The cloning algorithm must check whether there is another agent in the destination URL (or station). If so, the algorithm checks whether the agent at that URL shares the same goal with the agent to be cloned. If two agents share the same goal, there is no need to clone another copy of the agent. Basically, the goal can be computed by the agent at the destination URL. In this case, the union of the two societies is necessary. On the other hand, if the two agents do not have a common goal, to save computation resource, we may ask the agent at the destination URL to help search for an additional goal. This case makes a re-organization of the society where the source agent belongs. The result also ensures that the number of agents on the ACN is kept to a minimum. Whether the two agents share the same goal, the **Agent_Search** algorithm is used to search for the goal again. When there is no agent running on the destination station, we need to increase the number of agents on the ACN by duplicating an agent on the destination URL. The society is reorganized. And the **Agent_Search** algorithm is called again.

Auxiliary Algorithms

Algorithm Agent_Suspend(A, G, X):
    given a goal G to agent A on station X
    wait until Resource_Available(A, G, X) > low_requirement
    call Agent_Search(A, G, X) /* resuming */

Algorithm Agent_Kill(A, G, X):
    given a goal G to agent A on station X
    terminate agent A on station X /* dangling */

Algorithm Resource_Available(A, G, X):
    given a goal G to agent A on station X
    switch A.Policy
        case descrete_sim and network_bound then
            Available = X.Resource.Network
        case descrete_sim and cpu_bound then
            Available = X.Resource.CPU
        case descrete_sim and memory_bound then
            Available = X.Resource.Memory
        case descrete_sim and cpu_bound and memory_bound then
            Available = X.Resource.CPU * $w1$ + X.Resource.Memory * $w2$
        case descrete_sim and ...
            Available = ...
        case internet_sim
            Available = resource available on X
    if G.Priority is low then
        Available = Available * r

Note that, $w1$ and $w2$ are weights ($w1 + w2 = 1.0$). In the **Resource_Available** algorithm, we only describe some cases of using agent policies (i.e., *A.Policy*). Other cases are possible. If the goal priority (i.e., *G.Priority*) is low, we let *r* be a constant less than 1.0. Therefore, resources are reserved for other agents.

The above algorithms describe how an agent evolves from one state to another. The factor that agents affect each other depends on the system resource available. However, in an ACN, it is possible that agents suspend or even kill each other, as we described in previous sections. The niche overlap graphs of each goal play an important role. We revise the **Agent_Suspend** and **Agent_Kill** algorithms to take the niche overlap graphs into consideration. In the revised **Agent_Suspend** algorithm, if there exists a goal that has a lower priority comparing to the goal of the searching agent, a suspend message is sent to the goal to delay its search. The searching agent may be resumed after that since system resources may be released from those goal suspensions. In the revised **Agent_Kill** algorithm, however, a kill message is sent instead. The system resource is checked against the minimum requirement. If resuming is feasible, the **Agent_Search** algorithm in invoked. Otherwise, the system should terminate the searching agent.

    Revised Algorithms for ACN

Algorithm Agent_Suspend(A, G, X):
    given a goal G to agent A on station X
    check the niche overlap graph of G
    for each goal G' in the graph that has a priority lower than G
        send a suspend message to G' to delay search
    wait until Resource_Available(A, G, X) > low_requirement
    call Agent_Search(A, G, X) /* resuming */

Algorithm Agent_Kill(A, G, X):
    given a goal G to agent A on station X
    check the niche overlap graph of G
    for each goal G' that has a priority lower than G
        send a kill message to G' to terminate search
    if Resource_Available(A, G, X) > min_requirement
        call Agent_Search(A, G, X) /* resuming */
    else
        terminate agent A on station X /* dangling */

SIMULATION

JATLite is a software library developed at Stanford University for building software agents which communicate over the Internet. Developed in the Java language, JATLite uses KQML (Knowledge, Query and Manipulation Language) as the agent communication language. KQML is well developed and adapted to the agent research community.

It is difficult to build our agent evolution computing environment or any agent systems from scratch. Therefore, we choose JATLite as the underlying supporting system for our simulation implementation. Another reason for choosing JATLite is that agents written in Java, which can be achieved using JATLite, can run on different computer environments, since Java virtual machine is widely available and Java applet agents can be run from any browser.

JATLite has five layers: the abstract layer, the base layer, the KQML layer, the router layer and the protocol layer. The lowest layer is the abstract layer, which uses TCP/IP protocol. The base layer handles basic communication, which can be extended, for instance, to allow multiple message ports. The KQML layer parses and stores KQML messages. The router layer is in charge of sending and receiving agent messages, as well as agent name registration. The protocol layer supports some standard Internet services, such as FTP, SMTP, HTTP, and POP3. Since our agent evolution model does not rely on any specific low level communication protocol, most of the functions we used are in the protocol layer.

The design of our agent simulation environment is illustrated in Figure 4 Based on JATLite functions, it is convenient to develop agents which pass messages to each other. However, agent cloning is a technique problem. When an agent program (e.g., a search agent) is copied to a remote host station, the agent needs to be "alive" on that station. However, the station where the original agent program lives cannot initiate a process on a remote station. Therefore, in the simulation environment, we have *docking agents* to serve this purpose. A docking agent is an agent daemon run on a host station. The daemon is not part of agent evolution computing, but is designed to support the computing. A docking agent is constructed in JATLite, with the ability to launch another agent program (e.g., a search agent). Search agents are used as an example in our simulation. In our test-bed, we also consider other types of agents. For instance, agents intensively use network resources, such as advertising agents, which deliver multimedia information.

The agent cloning process includes a number of steps. Firstly, when a search agent (see figure 4) is about to clone itself, the search agent sends a query to a commercial search engine. The commercial search engine responds with a set of URLs. Based on these URLs,

Figure 4: A Simulation Environment

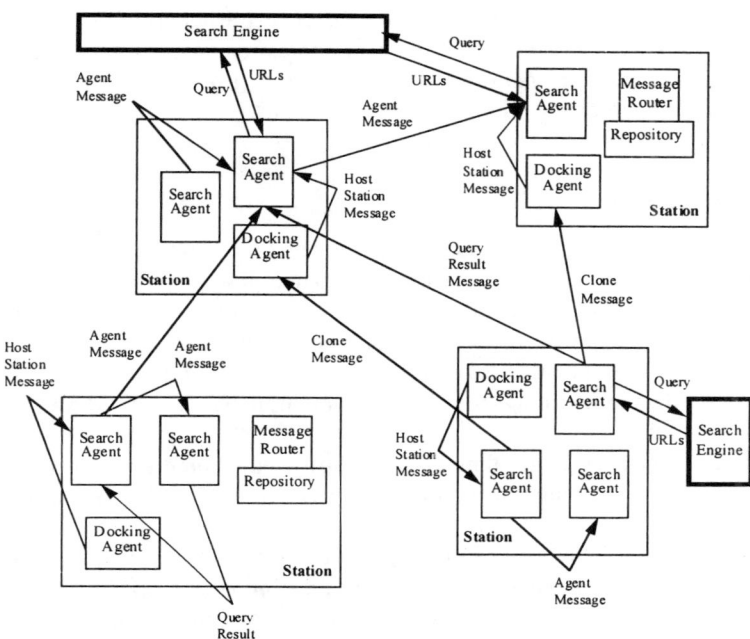

the search agent makes a copy of itself in a remote station through the help of the docking agent on that remote station (i.e., via sending a clone message). After that, the docking agent may start a new process to run the search agent program. Note that, a docking agent is installed in each host station of our simulation environment. One of the reason is that when an agent program is copied, the docking agent can have a write access to the station where the agent program is duplicated.

Docking agents send host station messages to search agents. Thus, a docking agent may kill a search agent if necessary. Search agents may send agent messages to each other. Search results are sent back to the agent who initiate the search goal via query result messages. Each host station may hold some search agents. But, holding a *message router* of a host station is optional. Message routers (or agent message routers) are programs provided in JATLite tool. Their responsibility includes allowing agent name registrations, maintaining agent message queues, and sending/receiving agent messages. A message router in our simulation environment handles the following types of messages:
- Agent Messages
- Query Result Messages,
- Host Station Messages, and
- Clone Messages.

Since a message router should be in an efficient location to deliver messages, it is recommended to install a message router in a station where an articulation search agent lives. Articulation search agents are connected to other search agents of the same societies. Therefore, they suggest efficient routes of communication. A message router, besides holding agent registration information and an agent message queue, also hold a repository which contains useful information such as network status.

CONCLUSIONS

Mobile agent-based software engineering is interesting. However, in the literature we did not find any other similar theoretical approach to model what mobile agents should act on the Internet, especially how mobile agents can cooperate and compete. A theoretical computation model for agent evolution was proposed. Algorithms for the realization of our model were given. Consequently, our contributions in this paper are:
- We proposed a model for agent evolution computing based on food web, the law of natural balancing.
- We developed a set of algorithms for the distributed computing of agent programs.
- We implemented a simulation environment based on JATLite to support our theory.

However, there are other extensions to the evolution model. For instance, species in the natural world learn from their enemies. In our future model, agents can learn from each other. We can add a new state, the "learning" state, to the agent evolution state diagram. When an agent is in the dangling state, it can communicate to other agents via some agent communication languages. Computing methods can be replicated from other agents. And the agent transits to the mutating state to wait for another new goal. In addition, when a station lacks system resources, an agent in the suspending state can change its policy to admit to the environment before it transits to the searching state. These are the facts that agents can learn. On the other hand, in the cloning process, two agents on a station sharing a common goal can be composed into a new agent (i.e., marriage of agents). This agent may have more goals compares to its parents. An agent composition state could be added to the agent evolution state diagram, but, the destination station where this new agent lives should be compromised.

The evolution of computers has changed from mainframe-based, numerical computation to networked stations. In line with the success of Internet technologies, in the future computation and information storage are not limited to a single machine. It is possible that an individual may buy a primitive computer that only has a terminal connected to Internet. Personal data and the computation power are embedded within the Internet. Mobile agent and agent evolution computing will be very interesting and important. Our agent evolution model addresses only a small portion of the ice field, which should be further studied in the societies of network communications, automatic information retrieval, and intelligent systems.

ENDNOTES

1 We could use an IP address. But, since our implementation of agents is based on the Web, a unique URL is used instead.

REFERENCE

Annunziato, Jose G. (1995). "A Review of Agent Technology," in *Proceedings of the First International Conference on Multi-Agent Systems*, San Francisco, California, U.S.A., June 12 — 14.

Caglayan, and Colin Harrison (1997). *Agent Sourcebook: A Complete Guide to Desktop, Internet, and Intranet Agents*, Wiley Computer Publishing.

Charlton, P., Y. Chen, E. Mamdani, O. Olsson, J. Pitt, F. Somers, and A. Wearn (1997). "An Open Agent Architecture for Integrating Multimedia Services," in *Proceedings of the Autonomous Agents 97 conference*, Marina Del Rey, California, U.S.A., 522 - 523.

Dharap, Chanda and Martin Freeman (1996). "Information Agents for Automated Browsing," in *Proceedings of the 1996 ACM CIKM conference (CIKM'96)*, Rockville, MD, U.S.A., 296 - 305.

Genesereth, Michael R.(1994). "Software Agents," *Communication of the ACM*, 37(7), Jul., 48 — 54.

Gray, Robert, David Kotz, Saurab Nog, Daniela Rus, and George Cybenko (1997). "Mobile agents: the next generation in distributed computing," in *Proceedings of the 1997 2nd Aizu International Symposium on Parallel Algorithms/Architecture Synthesis*, Fukushima, Japan, 8 — 24.

Gray, Robert S. (1997). "Agent Tcl," *Dr. Dobb's Journal of Software Tools for Professional Programmer*, 22(3).

Kiniry, Joseph and Daniel Zimmerman (1997). "Hands-on look at Java mobile agents," *IEEE Internet Computing*, 1(4), 21-30.

Kotz, David, Robert Gray, Saurab Nog, Daniela Rus, Sumit Chawla, and George Cybenko (1997). "Agent Tcl: targeting the needs of mobile computers," *IEEE Internet Computing*, 1(4), 58 — 67.

Krause, S. and T. Magedanz (1996)."Mobile service agents enabling intelligence on demand in telecommunications," in *Proceedings of the 1996 IEEE Global Telecommunications Conference*, London, UK, 78-84.

Krause, Sven, Flavio Morais de Assis Silva, and Thomas Magedanz (1997). "MAGNA - a DPE-based platform for mobile agents in electronic service markets," in *Proceedings of the 1997 3rd International Symposium on Autonomous Decentralized Systems* (ISADS'97), Berlin, Germany, 93-102.

Lingnau, Anselm and Oswald Drobnik (1996). "Making mobile agents communicate: a flexible approach," in *Proceedings of the 1996 1st Annual Conference on Emerging Technologies and Applications in Communications*, Portland, OR, USA, 180 -183.

"Learning and Revising User Profiles: The Identification of Interesting Web Sites", Machine Learning, Vol. 27, 1997, 313 — 331.

Magedanz, T. and T. Eckardt (1996)."Mobile software agents: a new paradigm for telecommunications management," in *Proceedings of the 1996 IEEE Network Operations and Management Symposium* (NOMS'96), Kyoto, Japan, 360 - 369.

Odubiyi, Jide B., David J. Kocur, Stuart M. Weinstein, Nagi Wakim, Sadanand Srivastava, Chris Gokey, and JoAnna Graham (1997). "SAIRE - A Scalable Agent-Based Information Retrieval Engine," in *Proceedings of the Autonomous Agents 97 conference*, Marina Del Rey, California, U.S.A., 292 - 299.

Petrie, Charles J. (1996). "Agent-Based Engineering, the Web, and Intelligence," *IEEE Expert,* 11(6), 24 - 29.

Sapaty, Peter S. and Peter M. Borst (1996). "WAVE: mobile intelligence in open networks," in *Proceedings of the 1996 1st Annual Conference on Emerging Technologies and Applications in Communications,* Portland, OR, USA, 192-195.

Schoonderwoerd, Ruud, Owen Holland, and Janet Bruten (1997). "Ant-like agents for load balancing in telecommunications networks," in *Proceedings of the 1997 1st International Conference on Autonomous Agents,* Marina del Rey, California, U.S.A., 209-216.

Tardo, Joseph and Luis Valente (1996). "Mobile agent security and telescript," in *Proceedings of the 1996 41st IEEE Computer Society International Conference (COMPCON'96),* Santa Clara, CA, USA, 58-63.

Thomas, Christoph G. and Gerhard Fischer (1997). "Using Agents to Personalize the Web," in *Proceedings of the 1997 ACM IUI conference* (IUI'97), Orlando Florida, U.S.A., 53-60.

Chapter XX

Intelligent Mobile Agents for E-Commerce: Security Issues and Agent Transport

Yang Yang and Sheng-Uei Guan
National University of Singapore

INTRODUCTION

With the proliferation of Internet, electronic commerce (e-commerce) is beginning to take the center stage in the commerce world. Transactions via electronic means have been growing rapidly over recent years, both in terms of turnover amount and volume. It is estimated that the trend will continue, as more and more businesses have already started or have plans to put their products/services online.

However, the development of e-commerce is hindered by several factors. One of them is the lack of intelligence. Today, there is little intelligence in the World Wide Web. Users cannot delegate jobs to 'agents' that autonomously perform the desired tasks for their owners. One way to resolve this is through the introduction of 'smart software programs', or intelligent agents. With an agent architecture in place, users can delegate tasks to agents. An agent can help its owner to search for and filter information, negotiate with other agents, and even perform transactions on behalf of its owner. It is predicted that agent usage will become the mainstream in the future, not just in the field of e-commerce, but in the World Wide Web as well (Guilfoyle, 1994; Corley, 1995).

Due to the nature of e-commerce, security becomes a primary concern for any architecture under this category. In fact, the threats to e-commerce come mostly from the area of security. Credit card companies lose billions of dollars every year on card frauds. Bank networks are broken into and millions are transferred out without the administration's immediate knowledge. In order to fight against these electronic crimes, it is necessary to protect our architecture with a solid security framework.

Besides the security needs, it is desirable for agents to have roaming capability as well. Roaming extends the agent's capability well beyond the limitations imposed by its owner's computer. Agent operations should not be affected by factors such as the availability of network, the limitation on bandwidth, or the lack of computing resources. Roaming agents should be able to physically leave their owners' machines and perform their operations using the computing resources on hosting machines.

In view of the various needs above, SAFE (Secure-roaming Agent For E-commerce), an agent architecture covering on security and roaming capability, is being developed for e-commerce applications. One of the core elements in SAFE is the agent transport protocol, which allows intelligent agents to roam from one host to another in a secure fashion.

SAFE aims to provide a framework for the development of intelligent agent systems, so as to facilitate intelligent agents' roaming from hosts to hosts to fulfill electronic commerce-related missions. As will be discussed in this chapter, security issues incurred from roaming agents and related agent transport protocol lay a secure foundation for mobile agents. With its powerful roaming capability and strong security feature, SAFE is suitable for use as a middleware layer in the next generation of e-commerce applications.

BACKGROUND

Intelligent agent is not a new area of research. Over the years, there has been a lot of research on intelligent agents, resulting in various agent systems being proposed. Efforts on standardization are also under way to establish a universal basis for intelligent agent development. One of the most widely accepted standards is KQML (Finin, 1993; 1994) (Knowledge Query and Manipulation Language), developed as part of the *Knowledge Sharing Effort*. Despite being a high level language for run-time exchange of information between heterogeneous systems, KQML is not designed with security in mind as there is no security mechanism built in KQML to address the common security concerns, not to mention those introduced by roaming. Agents using KQML still need to implement their own security mechanism to protect themselves. Secret Agent (Thirunavukkarasu, 1995) is one of the security architectures designed for to fill in the gap for KQML.

Secret Agent provides a security layer for agents systems using KQML. However, it has a number of shortcomings and is restricted by the nature of KQML. Firstly, Secret Agent requires every agent that implements the security algorithm to possess a key (master key). If the key is based on a symmetric key algorithm, the authors suggest every agent have additional master keys for each agent that it wishes to communicate with. The prerequisite for an agent to communicate with another is that both of them have the knowledge of a common master key, which is exclusive to the two of them. This requirement may restrict the agent's capability and efficiency if it wishes to communicate with many other agents. At the same time, the maintenance as well as protection of the master key database may pose additional security threats to agent systems. For example, if the key database of agent 007 is compromised, all agents corresponding with agent 007 will be compromised. The point of failure is at every agent's database, which is highly undesirable in the field of security.

Furthermore, if the agent intends to talk to an agent with whom it has no common master key, a central authentication server is required to generate such a key. The use of a central authentication server introduces many issues into the architecture. Among them are potential attacks on the authentication server, key transport/exchange algorithm, key database management etc.

If the master key is based on a public key algorithm, the agent identity must be tightly tied to the key pair. This was not carefully addressed in the Secret Agent design, subjecting the algorithm to man-in-the-middle attack. For example, when agent A and B start a handshake, if a third agent C can intercept all messages between A and B, agent C can pretend to be agent A while talking to agent B, and pretend to be agent B while talking to agent A. If key and ID are not tightly integrated (like that in digital certificates), there is almost no way agent A or B can detect this attack. In the SAFE transport protocol, the integration of agent identity and key pair is achieved through the use of digital certificates.

Due to the limitations of KQML, the authors of Secret Agent acknowledge the following limitations on their architecture (Thirunavukkarasu, 1995):

Limitation 1: Message delivery must be reliable and in order. This is because KQML assumes the message delivery is robust. In the SAFE transport protocol, there is no such assumption so the system can operate across unknown systems.

Limitation 2: It does not support non-repudiation on receipt of messages due to the asynchronous nature of KQML. A receiving agent can safely deny the receipt of messages. However, there is no way an agent can deny similar events in the SAFE transport protocol.

Limitation 3: There is no support for exchanging credentials. Agents are unable to present their credentials to each other for verification. On the contrary, under SAFE transport protocol, digital certificate exchange is frequently used inthe agent handshaking process.

Limitation 4: There is no support for replay detection if the message ID method is not used in Secret Agents. The design of SAFE messages prevents such attack from taking place.

Another prominent transportable agent system is Agent TCL developed at Dartmouth College (Gray, 1997; Kotz, 1997). Agent TCL tries to address all areas of agent transport by providing a complete suite of solutions. Its security mechanism aims at protecting resources and the agent itself. Since some existing agent systems are already very strong in this area, Agent TCL 'seeks to confirm their sufficiency and either copy or redesign as appropriate' [Gray, 1997]. In terms of agent protection, the author acknowledges that 'it is clear that it is impossible to protect an agent from the machine on which the agent is executing… it is equally clear that it is impossible to protect an agent from a resource that willfully provides false information' (Gray, 1997). As a result, the author 'seeks to implement a verification mechanism so that each machine can check whether an agent was modified unexpectedly after it left the home machine' (Gray, 1997). In other words, it addresses agent integrity and provides a certain level of traceability to the agents. The other areas of security, like non-repudiation, verification, identification, are not carefully addressed. Other research focuses on Agent TCL are not on security (Rus, 1997; White, 1998; Gray, 1997).

Besides Agent TCL, TACOMA is another agent system. It is jointly developed by the University of Tromsø, Cornell University and the University of California, San Diego. The security focus of TACOMA is on fault tolerance. Agents are protected against faulty hardware under two protocols. However, these protocols are based on assumptions of common secret or prior knowledge in source and destination. The use of hardware solution and requirement for pre-established shared secrets is not easy to achieve in the Internet environment. In terms of protecting a host from malicious agents, three approaches are proposed, one based on hardware, one using sandbox restriction, and the other using proof-carrying code. While the hardware-based approach is almost impossible to enforce in the multi-vendor environment, the other two approaches are purely software based. They will be refined and enhanced in the SAFE transport protocol.

Different from the various agent systems discussed above, SAFE is designed to address the needs of e-commerce. The other mobile agent systems are either too general or too specific to a particular application. By designing SAFE with e-commerce application concerns in mind, the architecture is suitable for e-commerce application since most general concerns in e-commerce have been addressed. Some of these concerns are security, mobility and interoperability. In addition, the design allows certain flexibility to cater for different needs of different applications.

INTELLIGENT AGENT AND ITS FUNCTIONALITY

Software agents are programs to which one can delegate (aspects of) a task (Finin, 1993). More specifically, an intelligent agent is a piece of computer software that has certain intelligence, autonomy, and is capable of performing distributed computing.

Although an intelligent agent is a piece of software just like any other computer software, it distinguishes itself from other software by its intelligence. Traditional software only responds to human inputs in a fixed and predictable manner. Some of the typical examples are word processors, spreadsheets and calculators. Intelligent agents are capable of 'thinking' and producing feedback intelligently. For example, a medical intelligent agent should be able to diagnose a patient by symptoms and suggest to the doctor a proper prescription based on its diagnosis.

Furthermore, agents have the ability and freedom to choose different approaches to solving the same problem. The autonomy is part of the agent intelligence.

Besides its intelligence, an agent should not be restricted to executing in the machine it is generated. Like a computer worm, it should be allowed to 'crawl' from machine to machine and 'live' in other machines in order to achieve distributed computing. For example, in order to perform a very complicated calculation, an agent may decide to break the task into many pieces and distribute them to other cooperating agents to perform the task simultaneously, or even spawn off some child agents to perform the task.

On the other hand, most agents designed will be friendly intelligent agents. This is the main difference between agents and viruses. Strictly speaking, viruses are intelligent agents that perform destructive tasks. In order to prevent the agent designed from behaving like a virus, security measures are implemented to limit the agent's capability while not preventing it from performing legitimate tasks. A mechanism is implemented to monitor and track the agent's activities at all times. In case an agent attempts any illegal operations that may cause damage to the hosting machine, the agent must be stopped and the operation logged. In this way, the intelligent agent designed is similar to a Java Applet. (A Java Applet is a program that executes on a surfer's workstation and does not harm the surfer's workstation in any way.)

MOBILE AGENTS

Introduction

Roaming refers to the ability for intelligent agents to travel from one workstation to another and use the computer resources from the hosting machines. It is one of the most important features not just in SAFE, but in many agent systems.

With roaming capability, an agent distinguishes itself from a traditional program. Its execution is no longer limited on a local machine but extended to the network world so as to take full advantage of the new era of network computing. The client no longer needs to wait hours for agents to complete a complex task. The agent should be smart enough to break the task into smaller pieces and delegate them to its cooperating partners around the globe. In a fraction of time, the task that would take a computer days to complete may be tackled within a few minutes. This is the power of distributed computing.

Security-Related Issues to Agent Roaming

Roaming, despite being a highly desirable feature, does introduce security issues in the agent architecture. Since SAFE is designed for e-commerce, it is of crucial importance to address these issues in SAFE.

The security and its related issues in agent transport identified are destination identification/authentication, safe transmission, traceability, efficiency and interoperability.

Destination Identification/Authentication

One fear is that an agent might be hijacked/lured to a spoofed destination. If the agent proceeds to execute on this spoofed destination, the agent's execution will be closely monitored by hackers and its behavior analyzed. This may lead to the disclosure of sensitive information or even execution of fraudulent transactions. As a result, it is important to make sure an agent only travels to the correct destination and the agent's functionality will be disabled during its transmission.

Safe Transmission

Another concern in agent transport is agent safety. This includes agent integrity during transmission and the agent's ability to reach the correct destination. When the agent is being transmitted from one host to another, a virus could be implanted into the agent; functionality of the agent may be tracked, disabled or even modified by malicious users; and the data carried by the agent may be compromised too. Therefore, mechanisms must be implemented to ensure agent integrity during transmission. Moreover, in order to verify that the agent reaches the intended destination, the agent must be equipped with the ability to identify the correct receptionist throughout the handshaking process so as not to stray into unknown sites/receptionists.

Agent Traceability

One possible requirement from the owner of agents is the tracking of agents. Sometimes it is desirable to track the agent's movement as it travels, especially in a multi-agent environment. For example, if a user sends out a group of agents to search for certain products, the user or some coordinating agent may wish to track the sites visited by each searching agent so as to prevent other agents from searching the same site again. Hence, the agent should be able to inform the owner of its movement by certain means. This notification can take on a direct or indirect approach.

Efficiency

Due to the nature of the Internet, it is necessary to ensure that the agent transport protocol does not cause too much additional network traffic. In a certain sense, this is contradictory to the security requirement as security always comes with a price. What can be achieved is to improve efficiency as much as possible on the condition that a satisfactory level of security is guaranteed.

Interoperability

Since the architecture designed is used in the Internet environment where different hosts may be running in different operating system, a cross-platform language, Java, is chosen to prototype the whole architecture. In addition, the thread-safe features of Java make it an ideal language for implementing multi-thread client-server applications.

Other Issues on Agent Transport

Besides the various concerns discussed previously, there are some other issues related to the area of distributed computing. Some of these issues are availability, load-balancing management, etc. Since these issues can either be resolved by existing techniques such as server farms and application servers or have been discussed in other publications (Schoonderwoerd, 1997; Odubiyi, 1997), they are not addressed in the chapter. Applications using SAFE are responsible for service availability and load balancing.

Agent Transport Protocol

Agent transport is the process in which the body of an agent is transmitted from one host to another. The agent body contains the agent's identification information, program code and data. With the various considerations discussed previously in mind, three approaches for agent transport are proposed. Each of them has a different emphasis on issues highlighted in the previous section. In these protocols, the agent and agent receptionist (sometimes the owner's machine as well) communicate by sending messages to each other. In order to prevent SAFE from replay-attack, a timestamp and a message label are attached to every message exchanged. For message integrity and digital signing purpose, a digest of the message content with timestamp and label is calculated. This message digest is signed using the private key of the sender's certificate. In this way, if the message content were modified by any third party during transmission, the message digest would have changed. Since the digital signature is based on the message digest, the signature verification will fail. Replaying the message will be easily detected since each message has a message label and timestamp. Furthermore, digital signature cannot be forged without knowledge of the private key to the certificate; a signature on the recalculated digest by a third party is impossible. In this way, man-in-the-middle attack is prevented, while at the same time, message integrity is achieved.

As such, each message comprises of a timestamp to identify the time when the message is generated, a message digest on the message content and the timestamp, and a sender's signature of the message digest.

In the following, we describe each approach of agent transport.

Supervised Agent Transport

The first approach (as shown in Figure 1) ensures that the owner is well informed of the agent's movement and is capable of preventing a move if it wishes (agent movement fully supervised). This is useful for situations where an agent's movement is important to the owner or the owner has a need to know and control where the agent is heading before the roaming takes place. For example, the owner may have a database containing a regularly

Figure 1. Supervised Agent Transport

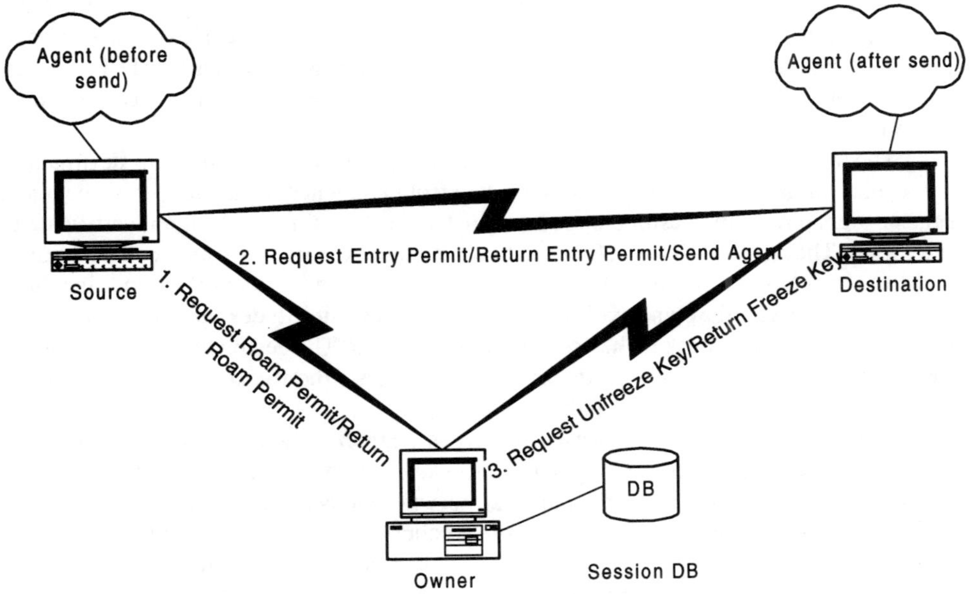

updated list of sites where the agent should not visit. In order to prevent agents from visiting such sites without placing the whole database of blacklisted sites into each agent, a supervised agent transport approach can be taken.

In the supervised agent transport, when an agent needs to roam from computer A to computer B, it will have to inform its owner of the destination. The owner will issue a roaming permit to the agent if the roaming request is granted. The roaming permit contains the signed roaming authorization, agent ID, destination receptionist ID as well as an encrypted freeze key. The roaming authorization is a statement issued by the agent owner authorizing the roaming operation. It is digitally signed with the owner's private key. The agent ID and destination receptionist ID combine to limit the validity of the permit to the specified agent with its destination receptionist specified. In this way, only the requesting agent can make use of the permit and the permit can only be used to roam to the destination specified. The freeze key is generated by the agent owner to protect sensitive data/functions. To prevent the key from being exposed to eavesdroppers, the key is encrypted with the public key from the agent's certificate.

At the same time, an entry permit from the destination host is required. The entry permit is a proof that the agent is allowed to enter the destination site and will be used in later stages of handshaking to help the agent register itself into the destination host. Besides this, an entry permit contains other information that will help to unfreeze the agent upon reaching the destination. Furthermore, the issuer can embed in the permit the agent's access privileges when it reaches the destination. This piece of information can be used by the agent to request access to different service zones in the destination.

The agent can only start roaming after both a roaming permit and an entry permit are issued. Before roaming, a roaming agent will use its private key to decrypt the freeze key from the roaming permit, and use the freeze key to encrypt/freeze its sensitive modules/data before transmission. In this way, the agent virtually disables itself before being transmitted. Anyone that intercepts the agent during its transmission will only get a paralyzed version of the agent that has no more than the standard functionality. Both sensitive functions and important data are 'frozen' and will not be known to any unauthorized party. The freeze key is immediately discarded after the freeze operation and before the agent leaves the source receptionist.

The frozen agent is sent to the destination receptionist. After reaching the destination, the agent will have to request the unfreeze key from its owner. To achieve this, the agent sends a signature of the destination receptionist and the destination's digital certificate to the owner. The agent owner will first verify if the digital certificate from the destination is valid and matches descriptions of the intended destination and the validity of the signature. If everything is okay, the owner will encrypt the freeze key using its destination receptionist's public key, and send it back to the destination receptionist. The destination receptionist can then decrypt the freeze key with its private key and pass the freeze key to the agent for decrypting the frozen sensitive module/data.

Note that the public key is not used directly as the freeze key here, but rather, the public key is used to encrypt a freeze key and the freeze key is used to encrypt the agent. There are a few rationales behind this. Firstly, public key cryptography is a very expensive operation, and hence, not suitable for encrypting a large amount of information. Since the agent body contains a large amount of code/data, it is not economical to use public key cryptography for agent body encryption. Therefore, a freeze key is generated to encrypt the agent body (using symmetric key algorithm). The freeze key, a much smaller piece of information, is encrypted using a public key algorithm. The other reason not to use the issuer's public key for encrypting the agent body is to protect the private key of the issuer. Under public key cryptography, to decrypt a piece of information encrypted by public key, the corresponding private key must be used. If this information is the agent's body, the decryption can only take place at the location where the private key is located. However, the encrypted agent body is at the destination host. If the encrypted agent body is sent to the agent owner for decryption, how to send the decrypted agent back to destination becomes another problem. Besides, the transmission of encrypted agent body to and fro may introduce too much additional network traffic. Therefore, the public key is not directly used to encrypt the agent body.

Unsupervised Agent Transport

As the name suggests, the second approach (shown in Figure 2) uses unsupervised notification to improve the efficiency of the transmission. The owner of an agent is no longer directly involved in the transmission process. When an agent needs to roam from computer A to computer B, it will send out a notification to the owner (it can be in the form of e-mail). However, it does not wait for the owner's acknowledgment and starts to transmit itself immediately. Compared with the previous approach, the agent only needs an entry permit from the destination receptionist to start transmission.

Since there is no roaming permit involved, the destination receptionist will generate the freeze key and encrypt it using the agent's public key. When the agent reaches the destination, the corresponding unfreeze key can be retrieved from the destination receptionist's database to unfreeze the agent. If the agent is abducted by any other party, it will become useless without the unfreeze key. (The only exception is the agent owner who can unfreeze the agent using a master key.) [Schneier, 1993]

Figure 2: Unsupervised Agent Transport

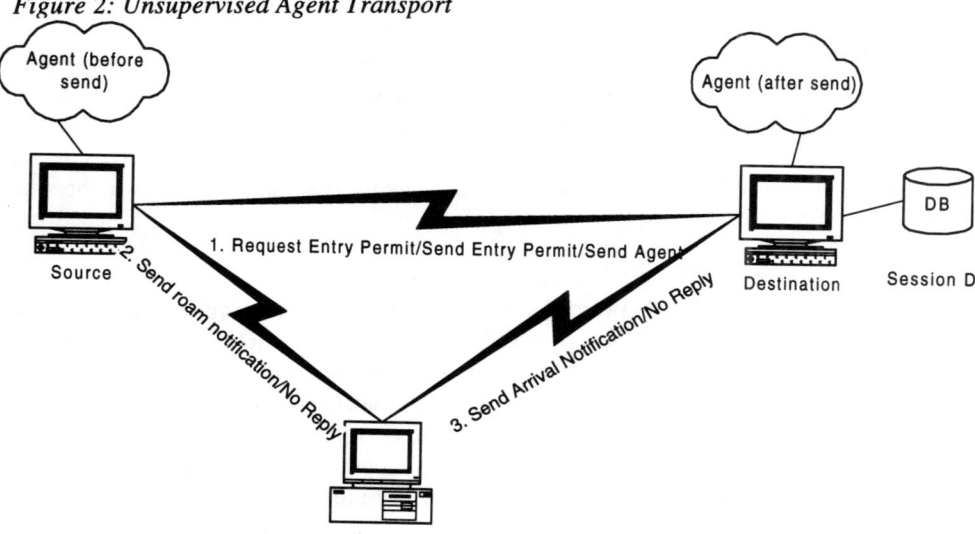

Bootstrap Agent Transport

The main difference between the supervised and the unsupervised approach is on the agent owner's role in the transport process. From the dimension on the method of transport, both the supervised and unsupervised approaches use a standardized transport algorithm. In order to provide enhanced security and greater flexibility, a third approach – bootstrap agent transport—is proposed (Figure 3).

In this approach, an agent contacts the destination receptionist and sends over a child-transport agent. The transport agent contains transport modules that are used to receive and unfreeze the parent agent in later stages of agent transport. Each individual agent has the

Figure 3: Bootstrap Agent Transport

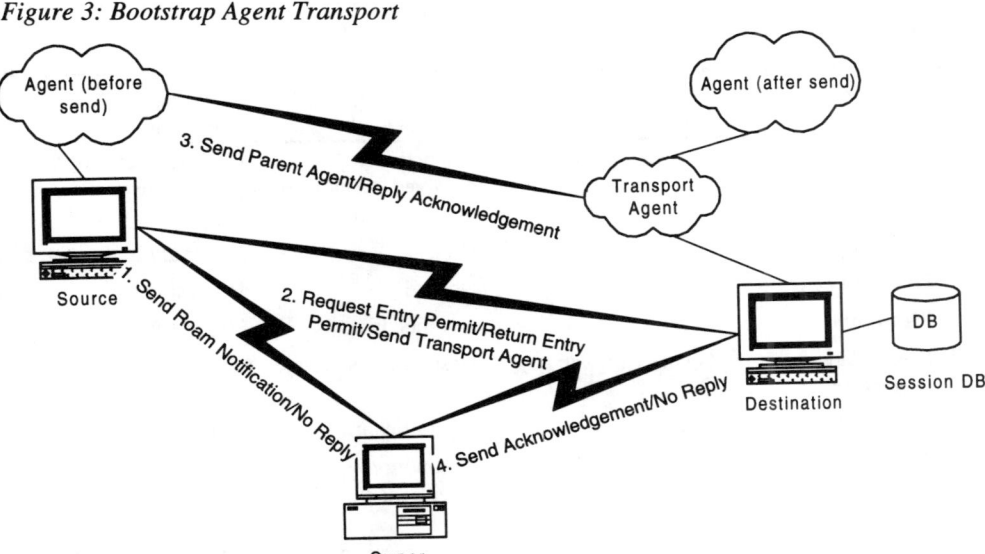

ability to customize a transport protocol and implement it as a black box in the transport agent.

Once the transport agent reaches the destination, it requests the necessary resource from the destination machine (e.g. memory space) and establishes a connection with the parent agent. The parent agent can then freeze itself and send a copy of itself to the transport agent. The transport agent unfreezes the incoming agent and passes the control to its parent at the new location. The parent agent on the source machine may optionally cease to operate once the transport process is over.

Comparison of the Three Protocols

Some of the differences between the three protocols are summarized in Table 1. From the table, it can be concluded that supervised transport approach proactively involves the agent owner in the transport process, while the unsupervised approach does not directly involve the agent owner. The advantage of involving the agent owner is to allow more owner control over the roaming process. Authorization to agent roaming, which will be discussed in a later section, is not possible if the agent owner is not directly involved in the transport process. Furthermore, even if the agent is abducted, with the agent trail, owners will have no difficulty locating the culprit (traceability).

However, for certain applications with less stringent security requirements, the need to trace an agent's movement may be overcome by the need for efficiency. Thus, without the agent owner's direct involvement in the agent transport, the roaming process can be more efficient since each message exchange is time consuming. The ability to cut down message exchange and waive the need to wait for message reply will greatly reduce the round-trip time in agent transport.

On the other hand, there may be applications that have extremely strict security requirements or other special requirements. The bootstrap agent transport protocol is designed to allow maximum flexibility and customizable security to agents, which the previous two protocols are unable to offer. Each agent can implement its proprietary transport algorithm in the transport agent. Once the transport agent is sent to the destination

Table 1: Comparison of Three Agent Transport Protocols

Difference	Supervised Approach	Unsupervised Approach	Bootstrap Approach
Owner Involvement	Actively involved, can veto agent's move	Not actively involved, cannot veto agent's move	Can take either of the previous two approaches
Efficiency	Low	High	Generally higher
Level of Security	High	Normal	Highest
Flexibility	Least	Not much	Highest flexibility
Freeze Key Protection	Owner's private key	Destination's private key	Destination's private key
Overhead	Insignificant	Insignificant	High
Agent Receiver	Destination receptionist	Destination receptionist	Destination receptionist, transport agent

under a standard protocol, it completes the remaining part of the transportation using the customized transport algorithm.

The bootstrap approach also facilitates phased-migration, i.e., migration can occur stage by stage. This is especially useful when agents are spawning child agents with certain functionality to a remote host for specific tasks. The bootstrap transport approach allows the transport agent to receive only the required modules from its parent agent and reconstruct a minimal agent with the necessary functionality to complete a task.

However, there are a number of drawbacks with bootstrap transport. First, the roaming agent has to be equipped with transport capability (fatter agent). In the other two approaches, an agent does not need to carry modules related to transport with them. These modules are provided by the receptionists as standard modules. With the bootstrap transport approach, the agent and all its child agents will have to carry these modules themselves. The agent's size is bigger (lower efficiency).

Other than efficiency, there are difficulties protecting the sensitive information on the transport algorithm in the transport agent. Since the transport agent is able to unfreeze its parent with the freeze key, anyone that intercepts the transport agent may discover the algorithm to unfreeze the parent agent. This exposure may threaten the black box security in the transport algorithm. Furthermore, in case the attacker is able to obtain the freeze key, the parent agent can be easily unfrozen.

One possible solution is to protect the information and algorithm in transport agents. Preventing sensitive information from leaking from the transport agents is part of the future focus of SAFE: agent protection against malicious hosts. Various approaches for agent protection are under active research.

The other way is to let the transport agent use the transport protocols implemented by a trusted third party (agent factory). In this way, the transport agent does not need to carry the sensitive algorithm with it but specify the identifier to the algorithm in its code. The destination receptionist, if it does not already have the module, will have to load the module from the trusted third party and pass it to the transport agent. Since the agent factory can implement different algorithms with various security strength, the transport agent still has the flexibility to choose an algorithm with satisfactory security strength.

SECURITY ANALYSIS OF PROPOSED AGENT TRANSPORT PROTOCOLS

To analyze the security of an agent transport protocol, different viewpoints are considered. Concerns related to agent transport are identified from the following viewpoints and their impact is studied. The protocol addresses these needs to ensure no loophole is introduced to any party in the transport process.

Agent Owner's Viewpoint

From the owner's viewpoint, there are two concerns related to agent transport. They are authorization and traceability.

Authorization

When an agent wishes to roam from one host to another, it is desirable for its owners to be aware of the agent's intention to roam and grant permission (roam permit) to the agent.

In this way, the owner can be in full control of the agent's movement whenever roaming takes place. Responding to this need, the agent transport protocol has the option to force an agent to seek its owner's approval before roaming. The need for authorization is addressed.

However, not all agent systems require such authorization. In fact, the need to get authorization limits the agent's roaming capability and flexibility. When the owner or the owner's workstation is not online, no agent will be able to roam. If the agent and the owner are only connected by a low-bandwidth line, the authorization may take a long time to come, which could significantly slow down the agent roaming process. This delay partially defeats the purpose of achieving distributive computing without having dependency on bandwidth in agent roaming. In order not to introduce additional inconvenience to agent systems that do not need to closely monitor their agents' activities, the SAFE transport protocol allows the option to bypass owner authorization during the transport process. Only an acknowledgment of the roaming event is sent to the agent owner; the agent does not need to wait for the reply from its owner before roaming on. In this way, agent roaming can take place regardless of its owner's status or owner network's availability. The efficiency of the transport is greatly improved.

Traceability

To find out where the agent has been visiting and how often it visits certain sites, an audit trail is inevitable. Such a trail may be used in auditing, analyzing the agent's behavior, and investigating agent-related disputes and so on. Furthermore, when the agent is abducted, modified or replaced without the owner's knowledge, the agent owner can easily identify who the culprit is by tracing through the audit trail.

As such, the SAFE transport protocol keeps the agent owner updated of the agent's movement in a supervised or unsupervised approach. The agent owner can record the agent's movement into its local database as the agent roams.

Agent's Viewpoint

From the agent's viewpoint, as far as agent transport is concerned, the concerns come from agent integrity, agent privacy and host identification.

Agent Integrity

Agent integrity refers to the agent's ability to remain intact during the roaming process. Any replacement, modification and deletion to the agent's code/data should be detectable by the receiving host.

This is achieved by the combined use of digital certificate and message digest. Each entity in SAFE (owner, agent, and merchant) must have a digital certificate. When the agent leaves its owner, the owner will append a message digest of the whole agent entity and generate a digital signature on the message digest using the private key of the certificate. Any party can verify the agent code's integrity by calculating the agent's message digest and verifying the signature on the message digest to see if it is really from the agent owner. Since the private key of the owner's certificate is only known to the owner, no one else can forge the owner's signature on another piece of message digest. And theoretically, once any modification is done to the agent's code, the message digest of the code will be completely different. As such, no one but the agent owner will be able to modify the agent without messing up the integrity check codes.

To protect an agent's data integrity, the data collected must be signed by the information provider (similar to agent code signing) at the collection point. When agents carry these data around, even the agent itself cannot forge the signature on the collected data.

Agent Secrecy

This mainly arises when the agent is being transmitted from one host to another. In the SAFE transport protocol, whenever an agent is about to roam, it will always 'freeze' itself with a freeze key (either from owner or destination host). Anyone that intercepts the agent as it roams will not be able to find out the agent content. When the agent reaches the destination, it will 'unfreeze' itself with the unfreeze key and resume normal operation.

As for sensitive agent data, the agent can establish a secure connection with its owner at the data collection point and send the data back to its owner. Optionally, the agent can encrypt the data using its owner's public key and carry the data with it. When the agent's task is completed, the agent can return to its owner and the agent owner can decrypt the data.

Host Identification

It is important for an agent to be able to verify the destination's identity. In other words, intelligent agents must be able to find out if the destination host is really what it claims to be. This is achieved by challenging the destination host with a random number and requesting a digital signature on the random number. To prevent man-in-the-middle attack, the random number is appended with information on the agent, destination, and a timestamp to form the complete challenge.

Merchant's Viewpoint

From a merchant's viewpoint, there are two issues related to agent transport: host protection and agent identification.

Host Protection

Whenever an agent wishes to roam to a host, the first question the host will ask is probably this: Is it safe to allow the agent to run in the local environment? Mechanisms must be put in place to protect any host from a malicious intelligent agent before agent roaming can be widely accepted by the Internet community.

There are a number of ways to protect hosts. The first and probably the most widely used technology today is the sandbox approach. Under sandbox restriction, foreign modules are not allowed to utilize any local services/resources, for example, local file I/O, printing services, directory access, etc. Furthermore, the foreign module is not allowed to communicate with external hosts except the origin of the foreign module. A typical application of sandbox restriction is the Java sandbox which places the previous restrictions on Java applets.

Sandbox restriction is, in essence, a preventive measure to protect the host since the sandbox prohibits any potentially destructive operation. The legitimate operations by intelligent agents will not be able to cause any damage to the host.

However, in case the intelligent agent needs to break the sandbox for valid reasons, the sandbox model can no longer meet the needs of intelligent agents. Therefore, a second security model, code-signing, is enforced together with the sandbox to provide more flexibility. Intelligent agents that need to break the sandbox for valid reasons must explicitly request for such privileges. To request for a privilege, an intelligent agent must have relevant sections of code signed by its owner. When the agent requests for any privilege, it will inform the hosting machine. If the host trusts the agent's owner and verifies that the signature is valid, privileges can be granted. Even if damage is done to the host afterwards, the signature leaves a cryptographic trace identifying the culprit's identity.

One other area on host protection under active research is proof-carrying code. The intelligent agent can carry some code that distinguishes whether its operation is friendly or dangerous. The host can inspect these proofs that come with the codes to decide whether the agent is friendly.

To further protect the host, certain common modules needed by most agents are imported from a trusted third party and stored by the host. Whenever the agent requires these modules, it can specify the module's global identifiers. The host will then load up the modules from its library and pass them to the agent. Since the module is implemented by a trusted third party (agent factory), the module is considered secure and will not cause any damage to the host.

Agent Identification

For one purpose or another, a host may wish to find out the true identity of an agent or make sure the agent is not masqueraded. This is achieved by requesting every agent to carry a digital certificate. The certificate should be issued by the agent owner (if the agent has more than one owner, a joint certificate may be issued). In this way, any host will be able to find out the agent's identity as well as its owner's identity.

Third Party's Viewpoint

From a third party's viewpoint, an intelligent agent should be a secure module during transmission. An intelligent agent should not be compromised by any third party through inspection, abduction, or modification.

Whenever the agent leaves one host for another, the sensitive modules/data of the agent would have been encrypted/frozen. The key to unfreezing the agent does not go with the agent body during transmission. As such, no third party would be able to discover any sensitive information by inspecting the agent's body.

As for agent abduction, a destination agent will be alerted if the agent fails to arrive during the transport process and alert both the source and agent owner. If a third party tries to replace/modify the agent during the transport process, the destination host will easily detect this by checking the agent's integrity and verifying the signature on the agent's message digest.

Architecture's Viewpoint

The concept of a third-party agent factory is introduced for a number of reasons. The first is to assist in host protection as illustrated in previous sections. The other is to reduce the agent's size. Since the most common modules of most agents are implemented by the software factory and are made available in every participating host, intelligent agents no longer need to carry these modules with them. When an agent needs to use the modules, it can request the module from the host by quoting the global identifier to the module. In this way, the overall efficiency of the agent system is greatly improved.

PROTOTYPING

A prototype of the proposed agent transport protocols is being developed to experiment with the design. The first phase on prototyping the unsupervised transport approach has been completed. To enable the prototype over multi-vendor platforms such as the Internet, Java has been chosen as the prototyping language.

In the prototype, three processes were used to simulate the source receptionist, destination receptionist and the agent sitting on the source host. The prototype demonstrated the complete process of the unsupervised transport approach. An intelligent agent residing at host A requests for an entry permit through the source receptionist to host B. After receiving the entry permit, the agent sends out a notification to its owner, freezes itself and sends itself through the source receptionist to host B. The agent receptionist in B then unfreezes the incoming agent and activates it.

CONCLUSION

SAFE is the architecture for intelligent agents to roam on the Internet infrastructure and perform e-commerce-related missions. In this chapter, we have addressed security implications incurred from roaming agents. One of the key components of SAFE is the agent transport protocol. The agent transport protocol developed provides an important security framework to make agent roaming a reality. To suit the various needs of individual agents, different approaches to agent roaming are proposed with emphasis on different concerns. The security of the transport protocol is studied from different viewpoints to ensure that the agent system does not have security holes. A prototype of agent transport using the unsupervised approach has been developed and tested successfully.

REFERENCE

Corley, S. (1995). *The application of Intelligent and Mobile Agents to Network and Service Management,* et. al, 5th International Conferences on Intelligence in Services and Networks, IS&N'98, Antwerp, Belgium, May 1998 Proceedings.

Finin, T., Weber, J. (1993). *Draft specification of the KQML agent communication language,* et al., http://www.cs.umbc.edu/kqml/kqmlspec/spec.html.

Finin T. et. al *KQML – A Language Protocol for Knowledge and Information Exchange,* CS Tech. Report CS-94-02, University of Maryland, 1994.

Gray, R. (1997). *Agent TCL: A flexible and secure mobile-agent system,* Ph.D. thesis, Dept. of Computer Science, Dartmouth College.

Guilfoyle, C. (1994). *Intelligent Agents: The new revolution in software,* OVUM, London.

Johansen, D., Marzullo, K., and Lauvset K.J. (1999), *An Approach towards an Agent Computing Environment,* ICDCS'99 Workshop on Middleware.

Kotz, D., Gray, R., Nog, S., Rus, D., Chawla, S., and Cybenko, G. (1997), *Agent Tcl: targeting the needs of mobile computers,* IEEE Internet Computing, 1(4), 58 – 67.

Odubiyi, J.B., Kocur, D.J., Weinstein, S.M., Wakim, N., Srivastava, S., Gokey, C., and Graham, J. (1997). *SAIRE – A Scalable Agent-Based Information Retrieval Engine,* Proceedings of the Autonomous Agents 97 conference, Marina Del Rey, California, U.S.A., 292 – 299.

Rus, D., Gray, R., and Kotz, D. (1997). *Trnasportable information agents.* In Michael Huhns and Munindar Singh, editors, Readings in Agents. Morgan Kaufmann Publishers, San Francisco.

Rus, D., Gray, R., and Kotz, D. (1996), *Autonomous and adaptive agents that gather information*, AAAI '96 International Workshop on Intelligent Adaptive Agents.

Schneier, B. (1993). *Applied Cryptography: Protocols, Algorithms, and Source Code in C*, John Wiley & Sons, Inc, New York.

Schneider, F.B. (1997), *Towards Fault-tolerant and Secure Agentry*, Invited paper, 11th International Workshop on Distributed Algorithms, Saarbrücken, Germany.

Schoonderwoerd, R., Holland, O., and Bruten, J. (1997), *Ant-like agents for load balancing in telecommunications networks*, Proceedings of the 1997 1st International Conference on Autonomous Agents, Marina Del Rey, California, U.S.A., pp. 209 – 216.

Thirunavukkarasu, C., Finin, T. and Mayfield, J. (1995), *Secret Agents – A Security Architecture for the KQML Agent Communication Language*, CIKM'95 Intelligent Information Agents Workshop, Baltimore.

White, D.E. (1998), *A comparison of mobile agent migration mechanisms*, Senior Honors Thesis, Dartmouth College.

Chapter XXI

The Evolving Future of Agent-Based Electronic Commerce

T. Deshani Rodrigo and Peter A. Stanski
Monash University, Australia

E-commerce technologies are continually evolving, bringing about innovative developments and resultant benefits. Herein one such visionary path for existing on-line systems to adopt is presented. An emerging set of models is discussed which combines intelligent systems, mobile code applications (MCAs) and Web-based systems. Such technologies are presented to illustrate the impact upon the numerous new value-adds for users brought about by e-commerce vendors. These are discussed in context of current developments in related fields, to expose the full gains from the integrated systems synergy. Furthermore, we conclude with an expected business model for electronic commerce in the new millennium and beyond.

INTRODUCTION

The introduction of e-commerce has revolutionized the way in which business transactions are carried out, allowing them to be processed over electronic networks. This has brought about new levels of sophistication to marketing strategies. Along this path, automation and overhead cost reductions have become evident. This trend has proven beneficial for everyone, ranging from suppliers to end-user consumers, translating to overall reduction in costs, decreasing of lead times, and increasing the speed to market of new products. These many benefits and cost reductions brought about by Web-based systems have left less technologically inclined businesses with little choice but to form a presence on the Internet. Moreover, the opportunities presented by on-line systems have also impacted most areas of business, and are continuing on this trend at a phenomenal rate.

It is estimated that companies will spend $3.8 billion on electronic commerce (e-commerce) software in 2002. This is 16 times the 1998 forecast of $235 million, made by

Copyright © 2000, Idea Group Publishing.

Forrester Research (Taggart, 1998). The exponential growth of the Internet, together with the inevitable ongoing growth in the information technology (IT) field are two key factors for significant increase in forecasts in e-commerce growth.

The introduction of e-commerce appealed to the masses, and its popularity is predominately due to its simplicity and the significant cost reductions resulting from it (Rodrigo, 1998). However, this first generation of e-commerce has its limitations. Nevertheless, newly emerging technologies, in particular agent technologies, will profoundly change the way in which e-commerce will continue to take place in the information age. Moreover, there is the potential for intelligent agents to become the most efficient sales representatives to date.

This chapter looks briefly at the limitations of e-commerce in its present form, then proceeds to discuss the next waves: second and third-generation e-commerce technologies. Some companies are already starting to realize the potential of such implementations, however, most of the work to date is in the form of research projects, not commercial applications. This is likely to change in the not too distant future, with second-generation e-commerce becoming widely used.

Third-generation e-commerce is an inevitable occurrence, although it may be years before application of such ideas are seen. However, there is little doubt that this will be the next logical step to the evolution of e-commerce, and so the likely features of this system are also briefly presented from an implementation viewpoint. In addition, the pros and cons of such systems are briefly discussed, mainly in regards to security and privacy issues. This chapter concludes with a discussion about the use of e-commerce in this way, until now unimaginable to many and touches upon some related social and legal impacts.

FIRST-GENERATION E-COMMERCE

First-generation e-commerce systems enable many business functions to be conducted without large amounts of capital investment in buildings and other infrastructures. Presently, a successful business may be conducted with a virtual shop front (Web site), using minimal staffing and resources for key functions. In this model businesses are provided with a more level playing field in which they are each judged by the appearance of their virtual shop front and the quality of goods and services supplied. In addition, the introduction of e-commerce systems has been beneficial for consumers. Prices have been driven down due to the proliferation of streamlined businesses, leading to an increase in competition.

In addition to the huge cost reductions for businesses, first generation e-commerce systems appeal to the masses due to their extravagant use of multimedia. In hindsight, these early systems employ basic uses of multimedia. Initially most sites had several linked Web pages in which they advertised their various products and services. In some cases the less interesting Web sites had predominant textual content whereas others made significant usage of flaming logo graphics, animations and the like.

Although current Web-based marketing strategies provide relatively affordable means of mass advertising, they may not necessarily be the best way in which to generate sales. These Web-based marketing strategies are often broad, unfocused, and most often do not target the right market. Many businesses often resort to the use of spam e-mail in order to target large numbers of people, many of who often have no interest at all in the product or service being offered. At times such behaviour can also have negative effects for companies, annoying people by filling up their inboxes with unwanted advertising. Also, to add to the existing problems, there are now an increasing amount of legal issues involved with spam e-mail.

Hence, the only real means of target advertising over the Web, in the age of first-generation e-commerce is by resorting to mailing lists. This once again does not guarantee that the correct markets will be targeted, and there are also difficulties involved in maintaining these mailing lists.

The benefits of e-commerce at its present state include the ability to process transactions using electronic networks, allowing goods and services to be sold via the Web. However, with each of these transactions, customers themselves have to find the product, the Web site, and then make the decision to make a purchase. Businesses are unable to do any more than simply advertise an easily navigable Web site and provide a reliable service, with an attractive 'virtual' shop front. A typical architecture of a first-generation system is shown in Figure 1. It depicts similar site responses to diverse users, and leaves item searching and product matching to the users' discretion.

Limited profiles of users may be kept by certain Web sites, gathered for example when users fill out registration forms. However, even these are poorly used mainly due to the lack of foresight for the potential use of this information. Also, some of the information gathered may be useless on its own, needing other bits of data before meaningful inferences may be made. At present each Web site has its own information about its users but they do not collaborate with other Web sites to combine information.

Furthermore, matching of users to products or services is left to the user and not done by the Web site, although this may be a proactive way in which to generate sales. The only form in which assistance is given to users is by registering Web sites with search engines (e.g. Alta Vista, Yahoo and Webcrawler), and these are often only beneficial for simple keyword searches. Advertising of a Web presence through publicity of a URL (Uniform Resource Locator) does not always provide sufficient information about the organization. Moreover, such searches often result in hundreds, if not thousands of 'hits' with users having to manually sort through them to find those that fit their purpose.

Overall, first-generation e-commerce provides users with a more convenient way in which to shop, however, does not allow businesses a highly efficient way in which to reach the correct audiences and to 'push' appropriate goods and services to customers. In the

Figure 1: First Generation E-Commerce System

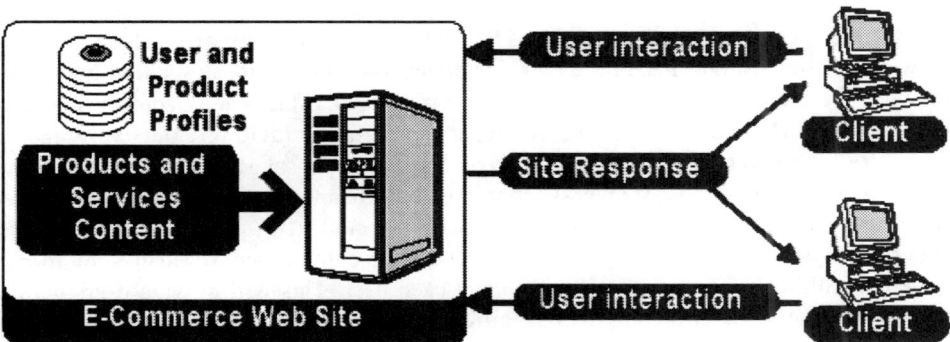

coming sections techniques for focused adverting and user notifications will be discussed, while presenting next generations of e-commerce technologies.

SECOND-GENERATION E-COMMERCE

This next wave of e-commerce has only recently reached the commercial sector, in some cases as trial research projects. These technologies use stationary agents and user profiling to further exploit the power of e-commerce systems. Stationary agents, which are further described below, are used to aid in implementing user-focused Web-based marketing strategies. These agents are used to supply users with more specific e-mails, which present a more personalized marketing technique for delivery of vendor care or value-adds (Figure 2).

Information required for such 'personalized' advertising may be done through the formation of user profiles. These may be gathered from users, either knowingly or unknowingly. For effective profiling, as much information as possible needs to be gathered. The two types of user profile acquisitions are direct and indirect. The way in which profiles may be gathered indirectly is by forming a profile based on selections that users make while visiting the site, that is, through the monitoring of user behaviour (browsing patterns) using cookies (Attwood, 1999). Unlike direct acquisition, users do not willingly provide the information about themselves. The degree of complexity, completeness, as well as depth of user profiles may significantly vary. Some profiles may include psychological factors elicited during registration, spending habits from past interactions, and even income levels derived or provided by the user. However, this may soon be a method of the past as users are exploring ways in which to 'browse undercover' such that minimal data is available from the browser (Noteboom, 1999). Alternatively, direct information extraction may include users filling out registration forms or other forms that give some information about them.

In a second-generation system, as e-site agents interact with users, they keep the goals of the business in mind while trying to satisfy and match customer needs to the products and services offered by the site. Information will be added to user profiles based on all user interactions with the system. These profiles will then be used during subsequent sessions or in real time to present users with specific information about products and services. This type of behavioral knowledge may be used for personalized e-mail advertising mail-outs or for customized Web pages. Since Web pages are created dynamically upon request, the server side agents may customize them at the time of construction. Through the use of cookies and user site logins, much of this information may be gathered and incorporated into e-mails or page contents.

These agents may resort to heuristics for finding solutions or answers for user queries. However, if suggestions made by agents do not generate sufficient sales, altering the way in which the agents operate may easily rectify this problem. This is analogous to changing the sales pitch when customers are not finding it appropriate or inviting. Effectively, agents will carry out some of the tasks traditionally carried out by a salesperson.

There is no doubt that Web based marketing will be more specific and sophisticated when user profiles are used in conjunction with the context of user activities. Second generation systems are also likely to increase the amount of multimedia used in e-commerce systems, with text and images tailored to suit each user. This will provide users with a personalized service, tailored to their specific individual needs, and also cut down on the

Figure 2: Second Generation E-Commerce System

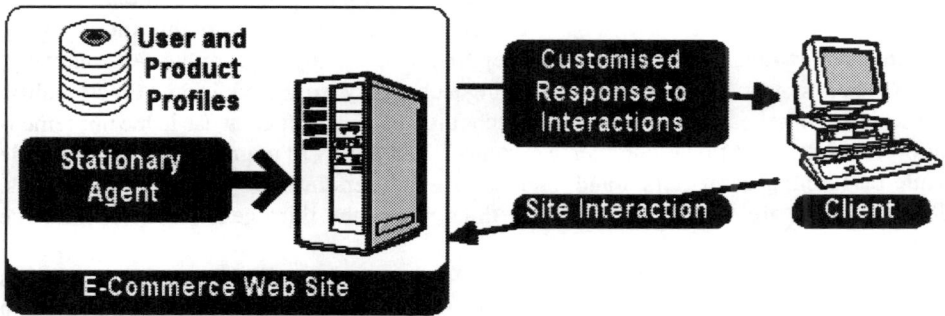

large amounts of unwanted advertising.

Consequently, these systems will be powerful as Web-based marketing will be carried out in the context of user preferences, listed in their profiles. However, the basic concepts present in these systems may be extended further to build more personalized and robust e-commerce solutions. These are discussed further in the sections below. Some background of agents needs to be presented before these third-generation systems are discussed, hence the following section presents details pertaining to agent technologies that are relevant to e-commerce systems.

AGENTS

The utilization of agent technologies, both mobile and stationary, presents a revolutionary approach to conducting business analysis and market research. Previously building the perfect sales pitch was left to highly skilled individuals who occasionally made errors of judgment and miscalculations. Now, with the adoption of agent technologies the perfect pitch is not a myth but almost a reality. The ability for dynamically developing a customized and personalized sales approach for each individual on a real-time basis is almost unimaginable. However, through accurate and personalized user profiles, together with the use of agent technologies, a much higher degree of sales confidence can be achieved by knowing the habits and shopping trends of the e-consumers. This is the primary motivation for the use of agents in e-commerce systems.

In the research field there seems to be very little consensus as to what exactly is an agent. However, one definition is that they are atomic software entities operating through autonomous actions on behalf of the user (machines & humans) without constant human intervention. Agents may also be either *mobile* or *stationary*. Each of these *classes* of agents consists of a number of agent *types* that are discussed further in the following subsections. Furthermore, all agents have various *properties*, making them more suited to perform certain functions, or suited to different applications. The BDI (Belief-Desire-Intention) model may be used for static agent reasoning, given user profiles and operational directives. These concepts are presented below in the context of e-commerce applications, for further clarification.

Classes of Agents

The agents currently being used in second-generation systems are *stationary*. Static agents primarily interact with databases containing user profiles and use this knowledge to present users with any information that they find contextually appropriate. Alternatively, *mobile* agent systems that are still an evolving technology exhibit additional functionality. These more complicated mobile software technologies will be of great use in the implementation of third-generation e-commerce systems. Their ability to migrate from node to node while performing computation and interacting with users introduces numerous benefits. Some of these are discussed in later sections where the third-generation e-commerce systems are presented.

Both types of agent technologies present technological compliments and opportunities for e-commerce Web sites. Their inclusion as a standard functionality component in commercial sites will continue to revolutionize the way in which on-line sales are made.

Types of Agents

Several types of agents currently exist, the most common being *guides, advisors, reminders, assistants* and *analyzers*. Each of these agents performs specialized functions that may be further specialized towards a specific application. These are briefly summarized below:

- Guides—Provide information and guidelines for performing tasks.
- Advisors—Make recommendations.
- Reminders—Background agents used for notification of asynchronous events.
- Assistants—Similar to guides, but work may be delegated to them (i.e., Searching, negotiating, filtering, etc.).
- Analyzers—Analyze user profiles, users do not deal directly with these.

The increased use of on-line applications will aid in making agents more acceptable by users. It is expected that an animated, interactive, and interesting-looking agent is more likely to be tolerated by a user involved in browsing, than a plain textual message. Agents may be considered to be helpers or workers to whom tasks are delegated to, and help is sought from. As discussed below, each type of agent is specifically used depending on the specialized task that needs to be performed.

Guide agents are analogous with customer care, as these agents only provide users with assistance when requested. The guide agents may also be closely associated with advisors. These agents are less intrusive and lurk in the background. They may assist users with any on-line difficulties that they may have such as with incorrectly submitted forms. Therefore, users filling in on-line purchase orders or having difficulties searching the site for a product may deal with guide agents. Their sole purpose in life is to gently handhold the users towards a goal mutually beneficial to both the user and the on-line virtual shopkeeper. Here conflicting goals need to be resolved such that users feel satisfied with the assistance, but not pressured into something they do not feel comfortable with. In real-life scenarios, this translates to customer care and service.

The *advisor* agents are less passive, supplying users with ideas and suggestions for various decisions that may be faced. They may be able to advise users as to the best product or service to purchase, based on a list of personal details and preferences that are provided. That is, the advisor may prompt the user on the best shopping criteria. Hence, the application of an advisor agent alone may boost sales and user service satisfaction. For instance, a user shopping for life insurance would contact an advisor agent to whom personal preferences for premiums, terms and coverage would be given. The agent would then provide the most suitable policy that should be considered, given the importance placed upon the policy attributes. These types of agents are key to differentiation between numerous services/ products, which on the surface appear similar, but after deeper examination reveal significant differences. These agents are likely to be appreciated by users, especially if they may be called upon as required. In addition such agents will help combat the growing number of consumer choices provided by the large number of competitive businesses that now exist, making it increasingly difficult for users to discriminate between this wide range of choices.

The trend for current lifestyles tends to be irregular and busy, hence *reminder* agents may be timely. Reminder agents may simply contact users while they are browsing, or via an e-mail, to advise them of a particular activity that needs to be performed. This may range from a virtual card shop reminding a user that it is time to send a birthday card, based on the user's purchase history, to other applications like reminding users of when an insurance policy is due for renewal. Another application of a reminder agent could be for an Internet travel agent, or a stock brokering firm which could send an e-mail notifying an interested user that the prices have dropped to their preferred levels.

Assistant agents are closest in personality to the guide agents. In contrast, these agents may carry out jobs delegated to them while the user continues to browse. That is, the user may give the assistant agent chores or tasks to do, without disturbing their browsing momentum. Hence, assistant agents help users in their browsing activities by allowing tasks to be conducted in parallel, which results in the saving of time. It is important that these assistants need to be passive when their services are not required; letting users do things at their own pace and then providing users with some other information upon their request. Furthermore, sometimes a job may not run to completion during the period of a user's site browsing. In this situation, the next time the user revisits, the job results would be available at the site. The assistant will also remind the user of this previously incomplete task. These agents are often also used for searching and filtering.

The final agent type to be discussed, the *analyzer* agent, has very little user interaction. These agents perform the difficult and tedious task of collecting and analyzing the vast amounts of data that are acquired from users, such that user profiles may be refined and fine-tuned. Some analyses may be batch processed while others may be carried out in real-time. The results of correlations in user activities and other related findings are established from user profiles. These are used to feed other system components such as the e-mailer or the above mentioned agents. These real-time or batch data processing agents require significant investment in hardware in order to perform their job efficiently. Nevertheless, the provision of the derived user information will be invaluable to the whole e-commerce system and its ongoing operations. Furthermore, the benefits associated with a set of well-tuned virtual sales agents will undoubtedly outweigh the initial costs of investment and establishment.

Agent Properties

As briefly mentioned above, all agents exhibit key properties. Some of these that are relevant to e-commerce are listed below (Franklin, 1996):

- Reactive
- Goal-Oriented
- Temporally Continuous
- Autonomous
- Mobility/Nomadic
- Communicative (multi-agent or with user)
- Flexible
- Learning/Adaptive

In addition to these properties agents also have a personality and character. These features, in combination with other agent attributes, distinguish agents from other software with similar capabilities. Both mobile and stationary agents have the same types of agent properties, with the exception of the mobility (nomadic) feature in stationary agents. However, agent properties occur to varying degrees in each class of agents. That is, some features may be predominant in stationary agents while they may not be in mobile agents. As Figure 3 depicts, all agent properties except mobility are found to be high in stationary agents while variations are found in the case of mobile agents.

In the context of e-commerce, the degree of agent properties may vary. Both mobile and stationary agents are expected to be high in reactiveness. Mobile agents are reactive depending on direct user interactions, while their stationary counterparts may react to other asynchronous, direct or indirect behavior. In the case of a mobile agent, interaction through dialogues may cause agent reactiveness, while for static agents, user browsing patterns may stimulate their reactive processing.

Generally, both classes of agents are highly goal-oriented. Mobile agents will continue to keep business goals in mind while trying to assist or prompt their users. Stationary agents also maintain their goals when generating customized e-mails and dynamic Web content.

Temporal continuity is a property that is low in mobile agents as they only execute at certain times, when the need arises. Furthermore, they suspend their execution during migration between nodes and resume execution after arriving at a new node. Alternatively, this property is high in stationary agents as they are in a continual execution mode, as long as the server node is active.

Goal-orientation and reactiveness are applicable to both mobile and stationary agents, which makes both types of agents highly autonomous. In spite of containing differing code, both classes of agents are independent and self-ruling. Moreover, they are enabled to make certain decisions and take appropriate actions pertaining to user or system interactions.

Stationary agents are considered highly communicative, while mobile agents are likely to exhibit a medium amount of communicative abilities. This is due to the latter having less code, which would give it less functionality. It is noteworthy that the communicative property does not only encompass system to user communication, but also communication among other system components or other agents.

Size restrictions are generally a non-issue for stationary agents. Hence, a larger amount of stationary code may be devoted to interaction with a variety of other systems such as local or remote databases. For the same reason, mobile agents are low in flexibility and learning/adapting, while stationary agents portray a high degree of all these properties.

Finally, as previously mentioned the only class of agents that allow mobility (nomadic) is the mobile class of agents. This property furnishes them with flexibility and functionality previously unknown to stationary agents. These benefits of mobility will be discussed in

Figure 3: Comparison of Mobile and Stationary Agent Properties

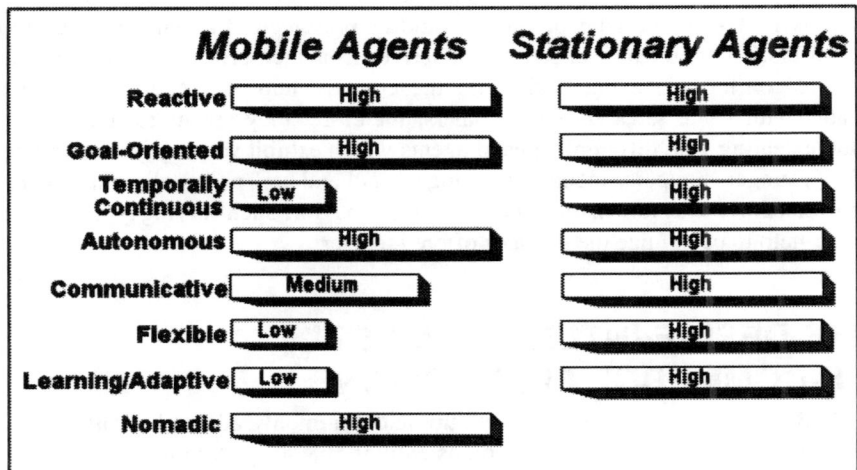

greater depth below. The following subsection continues to discuss agent properties and how they are useful in an e-commerce application.

AGENT PROPERTIES IN AN E-COMMERCE APPLICATION

In the area of e-commerce, agent attributes such as reactiveness are ideal for responding to user actions and their browsing behavior. Reacting to user behavior can feed a user's profile statistical analysis record with access data of a site's products or services. This information is much more meaningful than simply knowing that a user has accessed a particular site. Usually, server statistics have been used to measure user interests in pages. In many cases the total number of user visits to a site may have been generated by a small portion of the users, and not by the whole of the user base. In this respect statistical figures of user interest are incorrectly distributed, but could have been better established if a reactive agent had monitored user browsing trends and recorded these.

Furthermore, work proposed by Huberman and Adanic at Xerox PARC (Palo Alto Research Center), in the area of predicting user site visits and new information discovery may prove instrumental in streamlining user browse paths to selected pages and products (Huberman and Adamic, 1998).

Combined with the learning and adaptive agent behavior, the agent's flexibility in restructuring their sales pitch to meet the user's current frame of mind may be crucial. The ability to discover that a user visits a particular product's page could be indicative of their interest in it. By restructuring the information at run-time, the page could be regenerated such that the user has more of an incentive to purchase that product or service. This could be done by providing a personalized "deal" where the e-business constructs a package composed of the users core product along with some free products which further appeal to the user (by examining their personal profile).

To complete the set of agent attributes the personality of an agent may also prove of interest to users. Guide and advisor agents could be presented in a manner which most appeals to users. This could be user selected or derived from their profile, such that the most friendly and comfortable agent deals with the e-user. Shoppers generally feel more comfortable with some sales staff than others, therefore, they are more likely to feel comfortable dealing with different types of agents which exhibit varying types of personalities. For younger shoppers, agents presenting a "cool and hip" personality may be more appealing than those of a more mature and adult-like behavior. Such varying types of agents will further help to customize the services offered to users.

BELIEF-DESIRE-INTENTION MODEL FOR E-COMMERCE APPLICATIONS

BDI (Belief-Desire-Intention) is a mature and commonly adopted architecture for intelligent agents. BDI agents are autonomous entities able to work in teams and react to changing environmental conditions (Busetta and Ramamohanarao, 1998).

Beliefs, desires and intentions of agents form what is known as the BDI model. The BDI model is used for agent reasoning and is fundamental to many aspects of stationary agents and profile management. Agents are programmed with beliefs, desires and intentions. These are recalled and applied in order to make various decisions given the current context, such that a defined goal is reached.

Agents are programmed with beliefs, depending on what they need to do and achieve. Beliefs indicate to agents what data and information is known in the current context. User and product profiles in e-commerce systems may provide agents with the necessary beliefs required for their operation. Desires of agents reflect their end goals, that is, the life mission of the agent. Some of these may be to provide users with a highly customized and personalized service, or to sell a product. The third and final portion of the model is the intention. The intention component outlines how agents may go about obtaining their goals, within a given framework. However, this goal(s) may dynamically change as users decide upon a new direction or change their minds.

The continual change of user motives has often resulted in loss of sales through frustration on the part of the sales staff. However, in this model, the agents will always strive towards reaching their goals. Despite potentially lengthy user-to-agent interactions, these will never aggravate these virtual shop assistants. Furthermore, with the firm goals of closing a sale, the collection of BDI agents will collectively seek to entertain, dazzle and inform the user until a purchase is made.

Furthermore, unlike in every day environments, agents may periodically follow up on past customers with timely and accurate after-sales service. These may include marketing information or just a "thank you for shopping with us" e-mail. This becomes even more of a holistic e-business which cares, when reminder notices such as "your water filter is due to be changed" or "the item is in stock now" notices become the norm. Effectively, a whole company image may be forged through the use of the above-mentioned agent technologies, while striving ahead of the competitors.

Consequently, BDI-enabled agents may be the only way in which businesses will be able to keep up with a continually expanding global market. These agents will be able to continue to keep in touch with the numerous customers, while helping to maintain a good company profile. Therefore, a company may soon be as good as its software agent technologies.

THIRD-GENERATION E-COMMERCE

Future e-commerce models are an enhancement of the second-generation models, together with the use of interactive and optionally intelligent mobile agents (Figure 4). Mobile agents are most likely to be used for e-business to user notification and this increased interaction with users is likely to open up a window of opportunities for businesses, allowing the potential of e-commerce to be fully exploited, in more of an intelligent 'push' methodology. Hence, these third-generation systems are expected to surpass the capabilities of evolving second-generation technologies. One of the major benefits of these systems is the ability to provide customized messages and code to users in an intelligent manner. In addition, these systems are likely to have an increased use of multimedia applications, due to the browser-centric nature of this model.

Such technology would permit browsers to receive code when the user is not aware of it, and therefore permit agent mobility. It would also provide the ability to migrate the code after it has been received and utilized, such that it may continue upon its life mission (Stanski, 1999a). Effectively, mobile agents will also be able to present themselves to the user, without the user having to log onto the agent's particular Web site, that is, while the user is involved in browsing of another site (Stanski, 1999a). However, in order to implement these third-generation systems, browser-server technologies that will support such agent mobility are required (Stanski, 1999c). The details of such a technology are further discussed in Stanski (1999d).

With these technologies, agents will not have to remain dormant until a user logs into the site again, but will instead be able to approach the user when the need arises. These interactive (and intelligent) mobile agents will also enable purchases to be made at the time of informing users of various offers, and therefore increase the probability of closing a sale during the follow up.

Therefore, users may be presented with timely information, forming the basis for a successful marketing strategy. The arrival of an active agent is more likely to capture the attention of a user than a customized passive e-mail that may get lost among others in an inbox. Hence, users are more inclined to respond to messages delivered through interactive agent pop-up dialogues. Furthermore, such actions are likely to result in the closure of more on-line sales. Since the agent has the capacity to act on the user's behalf, an agreement to purchase will simplify the overall transaction, allowing the user to resume their interrupted work after a mouse click. This has also the potential for impulse buying, as a user is more likely to agree to an interrupting dialogue box that is brought to the foreground than to any other form of advertising. Such impulse buying as a result of mobile agents is analogous to impulse buying when watching infomercials.

In addition, these third-generation systems are expected to be data mining enabled, such that local user profiles and those of other companies may be examined. That is, user profiles, previously held by individual sites as described in second generation systems, may be used across various applications as well as various Web sites. This predicted sharing of information between competing or collaborating organizations is known as "coopetition"

Figure 4: Third Generation E-Commerce System

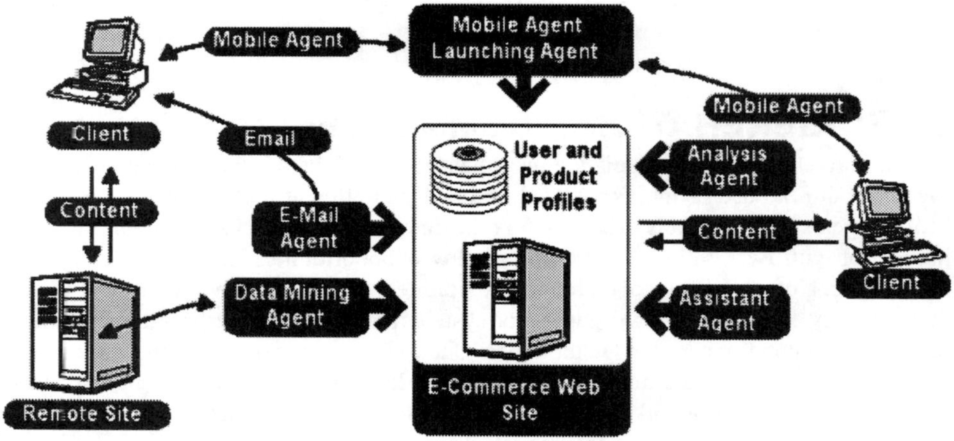

(Taggart, 1998). Such practices are likely to bring about many benefits for businesses, but also have many implications.

With the inclusion of the above additional features, third-generation systems will aid in taking the notion of electronic commerce a step further, allowing its potential to be fully exploited. The synergy created through the mixture of complementing technologies shall revolutionize the user and vendor relationships beyond any previously imaginable boundaries.

POTENTIAL PROBLEMS AND CHALLENGES FOR THIRD-GENERATION SYSTEMS

The foremost challenges faced in implementing third-generation systems are technology related. As mentioned above, browser-server technologies are required before intelligent and interactive mobile agents may be used for e-commerce applications. However, this challenge may be overcome through continual research in the field (Stanski, 1999c). In addition to software requirements, technological security issues will also play an important role in e-commerce, since mobile agents will need to be regulated at the user's desktop (Vitek et al., 1996). It will be vital that the utilization of mobile agents does not compromise system integrity and user privacy. Agent identification and the ticketing of mobility certificates are likely to assist in achieving these objectives (Le, 1997).

Furthermore, there is additional scope for malicious intent expressed through agents. For instance, mobile agents if developed with a rogue life mission may also be viewed as nomadic viruses. Virus agents, junk agents and dishonest impersonator agents are potential problems that also need to be addressed (Chess, 1996). Until these issues are at least partially addressed, the third generation of e-commerce systems will continue to be elusive until more workable solutions become available.

As mentioned, third-generation e-commerce systems will enable businesses to data mine rich sets of user information. Hence, such infrastructures have their benefits, but also have great potential to be misused. Profile gathering, both direct and indirect, and their usage has many social and legal implications. There are also many privacy issues associated with the sharing of information, to the degree that is suggested above. Therefore, prior to any commercial implementations of these technologically advanced systems, it is crucial that some regulations are in place to protect users from potential privacy abuse. There is no doubt that this area needs to be regulated in order to protect users from being abused by businesses thrilled with the idea of being able to have such a global reach at their fingertips.

Already there is growing pressure by Web users to have more privacy laws in place, giving them more protection when Web browsing (Berst, 1999; Noteboom, 1999). The momentum of these campaigns, such as the Privacy First Campaign will only continue to increase as more users are made aware of the current vulnerability of Web browsers (Anchordesk, 1999). Presently in the United States, a push to introduce an Online Privacy Protection Act of 1999 is sought to regulate such behavior (Berst, 1999). It may be assumed that this is the initial wave of many similar regulations to follow worldwide. Consequently, there is little doubt that some sort of regulations will be imposed by local governments (Enbysk, 1999), but the problems associated with international privacy rulings will continue as is currently the case.

In the past, only the governments have had the ability to data mine rich sets of user information ranging from payroll systems, bank accounts, travel habits and domestic census information. With the current evolving technologies for e-commerce, governments will no longer be the only organizations to build an individual's profiles from their shopping and living habits. It is still difficult to establish the extent of the impact brought about by user profiling, but the ability to attain such information will initially create user fear. Therefore, without any guarantees against potential abuse, it is unlikely users will willingly embrace third-generation systems. Even with the current systems, users are increasingly becoming aware of the practice of indirect profile acquisition. Hence, unless users are convinced that businesses will not betray their trust and abuse them, the acceptance of future e-commerce systems may not eventuate.

SUMMARY

As shown in this chapter, despite the advantages of the introduction of e-commerce technologies, first-generation systems have their limitations and do not fully exploit the potential capabilities of these systems.

For e-businesses, the advanced systems that are offered by second and third-generation e-commerce would undoubtedly be welcome, due to the phenomenal power that they hold. Businesses will be able to carry out the functions of marketing and selling in a manner that previously has never been dreamt of. In addition, the current extravagant advertising budgets may be slashed, helping to greatly reduce the costs of doing business. These continual improvements can reform Web-based marketing strategies for all e-companies that decide to employ these systems.

Further improvements are to be brought about by future third-generation systems. These interactive and intelligent systems are likely to increase the power and functionality of e-commerce systems through the use of mobile agent technologies.

However, various problems and challenges need to be overcome before third-generation systems will become a reality. These consist of technological challenges, as well as issues related to privacy that ultimately lead to the user acceptance of the technology. Users will initially be wary of businesses being able to obtain so much information about them, giving them a sense of vulnerability. Hence, users may at first be extremely cautious of the Web once these systems are deployed. However, once these initial hurdles are overcome, it is expected that future e-commerce systems will be advantageous to both users and businesses.

It is simply a matter of 'when' and not 'if' the above developments in e-commerce will eventuate. Therefore, the major challenge that lies in the hand of businesses is to establish a sense of trust from users and ensure that this trust is maintained. In order for e-commerce to continue to proceed along the current successful path, the ideas and concepts must be sold to users, and they must feel comfortable with the technology, knowing that they will not be abused by giving into it. Acceptance is paramount, as a technologically powerful system without a client base is likely to prove of limited demand.

REFERENCES

Anchordesk. (1999). Petition: *If *You* Can't Protect Your Privacy Online - Who Can?* [Online]. Available: http://www.zdnet.com/anchordesk/privacyfirst/.

Attwood, C. (1999). *Online Privacy Guide.* [Online]. Available: http://www.zdnet.com/zdhelp/stories/main/0,5594,2245224,00.html.

Berst, J. (1999, March 24). *Privacy First: How to Protect Ourselves From Electronic Invasion.* [Online]. Available: http://www.anchordesk.com/a/ad1tlt0324ba/3216.

Busetta, P. & Ramamohanarao, K. (1998, February 27-March 1). *An Architecture for Mobile BDI Agents.* Proceedings of the ACM Symposium on Applied Computing (SAC'98).

Chess D., Harrison, C. & Kershenbaum, A. (1996). *Mobile Agents: Are They a Good Idea?.* Second International Workshop on Mobile Object Systems 1996 (MOS'96), Lecture Notes In Computer Science (LNCS) 1222, 25-47, Springer.

Enbysk, L. (1999, April 20). *Congress Mulls Privacy.* [Online]. Available: http://www.zdnet.com/anchordesk/story/story_3309.html.

Franklin, S. & Graesser, A. (1996). Is it an Agent, or Just a Program?: A Taxonomy for Autonomous Agents. *Proceedings of the Third International Workshop on Agent Theories, Architectures, and Languages*, Springer-Verlag, 1996.

Huberman, B.A. & Adamic, L.A. (1998). Novelty and Social Search in the World Wide Web. *Xerox Palo Alto Research Center*, available from CORR database.

Le, P.D., Srinivasan, B., Le, H.P., Price, R. & Mohammed, S. (1997). *Abstract Ticket to Support Mobile Users.* 2nd Australian Workshop on Mobile Computing & Databases & Applications (MCDA97), 102-107.

Noteboom, N. (1999, March 24). *Seven Ways to Protect Your Privacy Online - Right Now.* [Online]. Available: http://www.zdnet.com/anchordesk/story/story_3214.html.

Rodrigo, D.T. (1998). *Internet Service Providers: Characteristics and Challenges.* Honours Thesis, Department of Management Science and Information Systems, Auckland University, 3-4.

Stanski, P.A. (1999a). *Models, Trends and Design Patterns in Mobile Code Systems.* Submitted to PART'99 Conference, Melbourne, Australia.

Stanski, P.A. (1999b). *Future Directions in Mobile Code, Applets, Agents and Browser Integration.* Submitted to MDDS'99 Workshop at DEXA'99, Florence.

Stanski, P.A. (1999c). The Bright Future of Internet Based Mobile Agents. *PC Update*, 38-

39, ISSN 1031-8202.

Stanski, P.A. (1999d). *The Architecture of the PESOS Browser Server.* Proceedings of PDPTA'99 Conference, Las Vegas, Nevada, 896-901.

Taggart, S. (1998). Building the Perfect Pitch. *Business 2.0, October 1998*, 112-114

Vitek, J., Serrano, M. and Thanos, D. (1996). *Security and Communication in Mobile Object Systems.* Lecture Notes in Computer Science (LNCS) 1222, 177-199, Springer.

Chapter XXII

The Use of the Internet by Terrorists and its Impact upon Electronic Commerce

Matthew Warren
Deakin University, Australia

William Hutchinson
Edith Cowan University, Australia

INTRODUCTION

In the developed world, the influence of information systems can now be seen in most operational areas of business. A significant result of these advances is that organizations have become increasingly dependent upon the availability of systems and reliant upon the data that they hold.

In recent years the Internet has grown from a solely military/academic network to one that can be used by business or individuals. In the years since the first WWW applications were developed, there has been an explosion in the global use of the Internet. With this growth has come an increasing usage of the medium by criminal and terrorist groups (Rathmell, 1997).

The term terrorist or terrorism is a highly emotive term. Generally it is used to denote "revolutionaries who seek to use terror systematically to further their views or to govern a particular area" (Warren, 1998). 'Cyber-terrorism' is a different form of terrorism since physical systematic terror does not usually occur (although it can if it causes disruption to a critical system), but a widespread destruction of information resources can. The problem of defining the term 'terrorist' relates to the fact that a terrorist group could easily be perceived as a resistance group carrying out lawful or morally legitimate actions. In the context of the chapter the term cyber-terrorist/terrorism will refer to all terrorist/resistance groups in order to give a neutral perception of their activities and aims.

Another new term related to the Information Society is 'electronic commerce.' The notion of 'electronic commerce' is proposed as a means of drawing together a wide range of business support services. It includes such elements as inter-organizational e-mail; on-line directories; trading support systems for commodities, products, customised products and custom-built goods and services; ordering and logistic support systems; settlement

Copyright © 2000, Idea Group Publishing.

support systems; and management information and statistical reporting systems (Warren et al, 1999).

Business around the world has become more of a target of cyber terrorism due to the fact that they are increasingly dependent upon information technology (Howard, 1997). Therefore there are many more high technology targets to prey upon. Increasingly in the future, businesses will use electronic commerce and on-line systems as a method of conducting trade. These on-line methods are very vulnerable to attacks. In a recent, informal survey of Australian IT managers (Hutchinson and Warren, 1999), 80% of replies said that their sites had never been attacked, 66% do not feel their competitors would attack their site, and 66% had no policy about dealing with an attack.

This chapter will explain why and how cyber-terrorists attack these services. The aims of the chapter are to:
- describe the background of cyber-terrorism;
- describe what cyber-terrorism is;
- describe the vulnerabilities of electronic commerce to cyber-terrorism;
- discuss the future of electronic commerce and cyber-terrorism.

DEVELOPMENT OF CYBER-TERRORISM AND CURRENT STATUS

The term 'information warfare' (IW) is used in the context of cyber-terrorism. One definition of IW is that it relates to the struggle for control over information activities. The reason for the IW's recent rise to prominence is the perception that human activities are now much more reliant on information than in the past. Therefore, these information activities are a more tempting and significant target than in the past (Rathmall, 1998). Offensive information warfare operations produce win-lose outcomes by altering the availability and integrity of information resources to the benefit of the offence and to the detriment of the defence (Denning, 1999).

The term 'cyber-terrorist' is a recent addition to the computer security vocabulary and is used to describe a number of different individuals and groups. The convergence of the new technological and socio-political trends suggests that cyber-terrorism may be the terrorist activity of the future. If warfare is going to be conducted in cyber-space and if the combatants of the future are going to be irregulars, then cyber-terrorism is the logical paradigm of future conflict (Schwartau, 1996). Cyber-terrorists will be the 'irregular troops' of future cyber-wars, as they will attack what they see as more accessible targets. Cyber-terrorists will attack electronic commerce systems, since they will represent an easier target than conventional government or military systems. In the future this will result in some dramatic occurrences and will make the computer security sector re-think its strategy towards cyber-terrorist attacks.

CYBER TERRORISTS ON THE INTERNET

We are now facing a situation where terrorist/resistance groups are now developing Internet sites and using Internet technologies. At the moment, the areas where terrorist/resistance groups are using the Internet consist of:

Propaganda/Publicity

Terrorist/resistance groups have difficulty in relaying their political messages to the general public without encountering censorship, they can now overcome this by using the Internet. Different terrorist groups/political parties use the Internet for a variety of different reasons. The following are examples:

- Irish Republican Information Service (Irish Republican Information Services, 1999) is a service offering news articles (their interpretation) relating to the troubles in Northern Ireland. Sinn Fein also offer their own site containing information about Sinn Fein, the armed struggle, policy documents, paper subscription, links to other sites, etc;
- Zapatista Movement. They have several sites (Zapatista Movement, 1999), detailing their struggle against the Mexican authorities. These sites offer information directly from the Zapatista Movement, i.e. communiques from the general command of the Zapatista Army of National Liberation;
- Third world terrorist/resistance groups have a cyber presence. The Tamil Tigers now have a voice through TamilNet (Eelam Web, 1999), which includes general information, electronic newsletters and electronic magazines putting forward their points of view. Terrorist groups from Peru, Philippines, Turkey, Columbia and the Middle East also have dedicated Internet sites serving as propaganda tools.

Information Dissemination

It is also possible that groups may publish sensitive information about a particular country. Sinn Fein supporters in the USA made public on the Internet details about British Army establishments within Northern Ireland (Tendler, 1996); an example of this is shown by Figure 1.

Figure 1: Screen Shot Illustrating British Military Forces

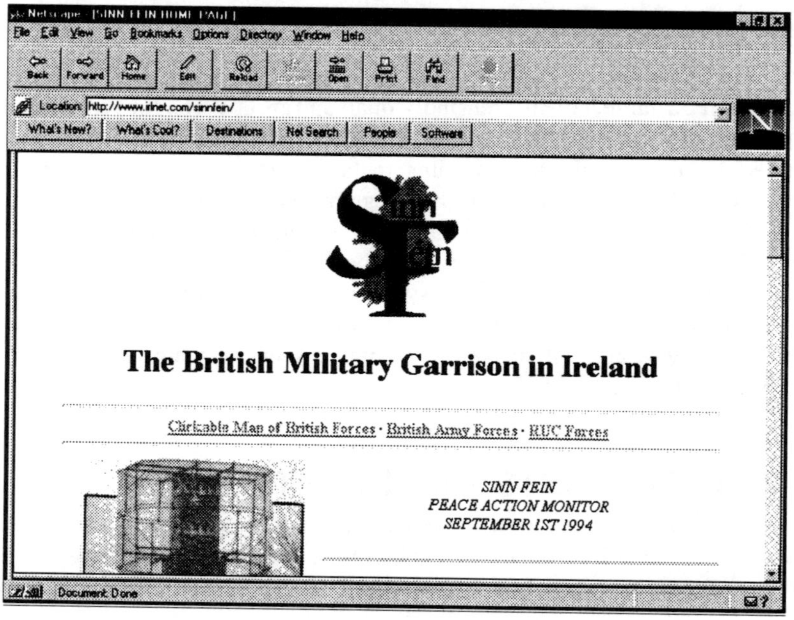

Information is widely available on the Internet about engaging in conventional terrorist activities. The 'Terrorist Handbook' (Authors Unknown, 1994) contains details for beginners on how to make explosives and weapons. The information contained within this document would assist any potential terrorists to develop their own bombing campaign.

It also is possible for terrorist/resistance group members on the Internet to have anonymous electronic re-mailers (Malik, 1996). This shields their identity from public view. Once they have acquired an anonymous identity, any messages that are sent to this anonymous identity are re-routed to their e-mail addresses. Individuals are also able to access e-mail worldwide via the introduction of Web-based e-mail systems or by using mobile communication links. The Internet has become a part of the armory of the cyber-terrorist.

THE DEVELOPMENT OF CYBER-TERRORIST GROUPS

Research has shown that terrorist/resistance groups are now using the Internet for many different purposes, these groups are now learning how to use more complex and diverse technologies of the Internet in order to further advance their causes (Warren and Furnell, 1999). When viewed from the perspective of skills and techniques, there is little to distinguish cyber terrorists from the general classification of hackers. Both groups require and utilise an arsenal of techniques in order to breach the security of target systems. From a motivational perspective, however, cyber terrorists are clearly different, operating with a specific political or ideological agenda to support their actions (Warren and Furnell, 1999). This in turn may result in more focused/determined efforts to achieve their objectives and more considered selection of suitable targets for attack. However, the difference does not necessarily end there and other factors should be considered. Firstly, the fact that cyber terrorists are part of an organised group could mean that they have funding available to support their activities. This in turn would mean that individual hackers could be hired to carry out attacks on behalf of a terrorist organisation (effectively subcontracting the necessary technical expertise) (Warren and Furnell, 1999). In this situation, the hackers themselves may not believe in the terrorist's 'cause,' but will undertake the work for financial gain.

CYBER-TERRORISM AND ELECTRONIC COMMERCE

Earlier in the chapter we discussed what cyber-terrorists are and the way in which they operate. Electronic commerce sites represent easy targets; security is usually not as tight as in secured, military systems (Howard, 1997). The systems tend to be always on-line via the Internet. Any damage to the systems creates publicity for the terrorists and losses to the businesses concerned (either through physical damage, credibility, or financial loss). The most common attack methods currently available include:

Password Sniffing/Cracking Software

This is one of the simplest and most common method attacks, using software packages such as Brute (PC based), Passfinder (Mac based), and Crack V4.1 (Unix based). These software packages run in a number of ways, e.g., accessing a system via a File Transfer Protocol (FTP) port and trying to determine password files. Another method is to use software that systematically uses a combination of passwords on a Unix password file until one is successful. There are now even commercial companies that offer a password cracking service — payment is only sought if a successful cracking occurs, for example:

US$40 to crack CuteFTP passwords;
US$40 to crack Euroda passwords;
US$250 to crack Winzip passwords.

A cyber-terrorist might use this software or service in order to gain passwords for further usage or to gain access to systems or data.

Spoofing Attacks

IP (Internet Protocol) spoofing was first associated with Kevin Mitnick (Littman, 1997) and his attacks by infiltrating networks. It works by forging the 'From' address so that the message appears to have originated from somewhere other than its actual source. Normally, the false address is that of a site which is trusted by the receiving host so that the packet will be accepted and acted upon, in some cases allowing an intruder to penetrate right through a firewall (Denning, 1999). Another type of spoofing is known as Web spoofing. This is where an attacker sets up a fake Web site to lure users in hopes of stealing their credit card numbers or other information. One hacker set up a site called MICROS0FT.com, using the number zero in place of the letter 'O', which many users might type by mistake (See Figure 2). Users might find themselves in a situation that they do not notice they are using a bogus Web-site and give their credit card details.

A cyber-terrorist may use these techniques in a number of ways: cracking passwords; setting up false Web-sites with the intent to defraud—thus raising funds or creating

Figure 2: Example of WWW.MICROS0FT.COM

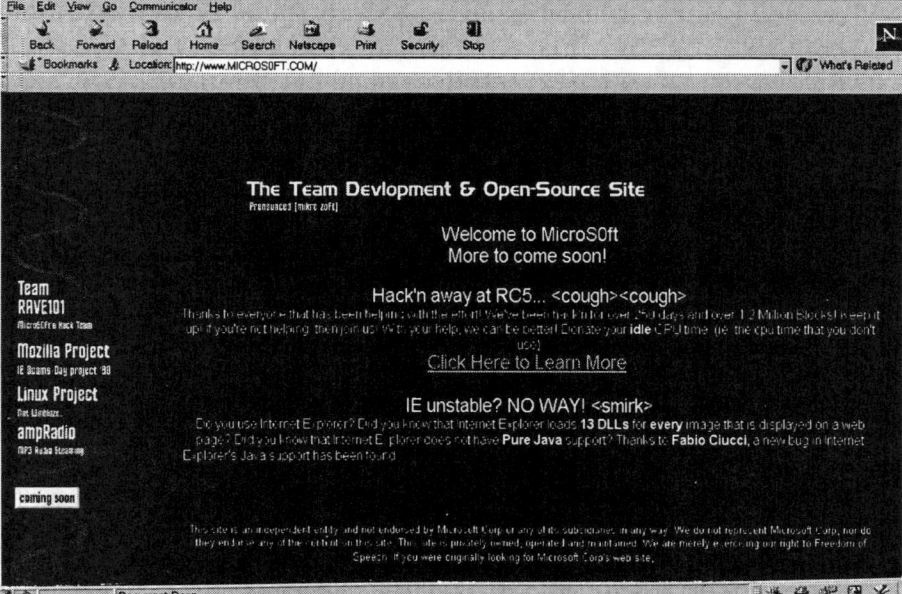

misinformation, e.g., pretending the Web-site is an official government Web-site.

It is possible to protect against bogus Web sites. The secure sockets layer tool that comes packaged with most Web browsers cannot determine a fake web site. The way to overcome this problem is to add authentication software between the client and server so that the client can be sure it is connecting to the correct Web site. An alternative is the use of 'digital signatures'. These are basically electronic IDs that include a public key and the name and address of the user, all digitally signed and encrypted with a private key. These IDs are proof of identity and that a message has not been tampered with (Mulschlegel, 1997).

Denial of Service Attacks

A denial-of-service attack results when access to a computer or network resource is intentionally blocked or degraded as a result of malicious action taken by another user. These attacks do not necessarily damage data directly or permanently (although they could), but they intentionally compromise the availability of the resources (Howard, 1997). These types of attacks tend to affect the availability of computer systems for legitimate usage. These forms of attacks can include e-mail bomb attacks, sending thousands of emails to a particular computer system until that system crashes. The software required to carry out denial-of-service attacks is widely available on the Internet.

Another commonly used denial-of-service attack is the Ping O'Death ('Ping' messages are used to determine the whether another machine on a network is active). The Ping O'Death can crash or reboot a computer by sending a 'ping' message of greater than 65,536 bytes, the default size is 64 bytes. Router updates have nearly eliminated these problems (Mulschlegel, 1997). These sorts of attacks would commonly be carried out by cyber-terrorists with a low level of expertise. The reason for this is that these attacks require very little technical skill level, and the software is freely available on the Internet. Denial-of-service attacks could be very effective against an Internet-based company, since they rely

Figure 3: Results of a PHAIT Attack

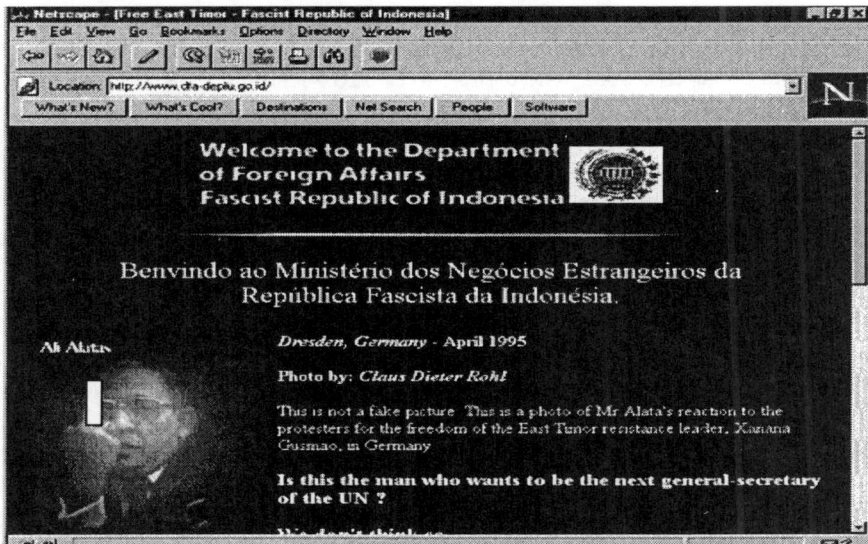

Figure 4: Successful Hack of a Fur Company Web Site

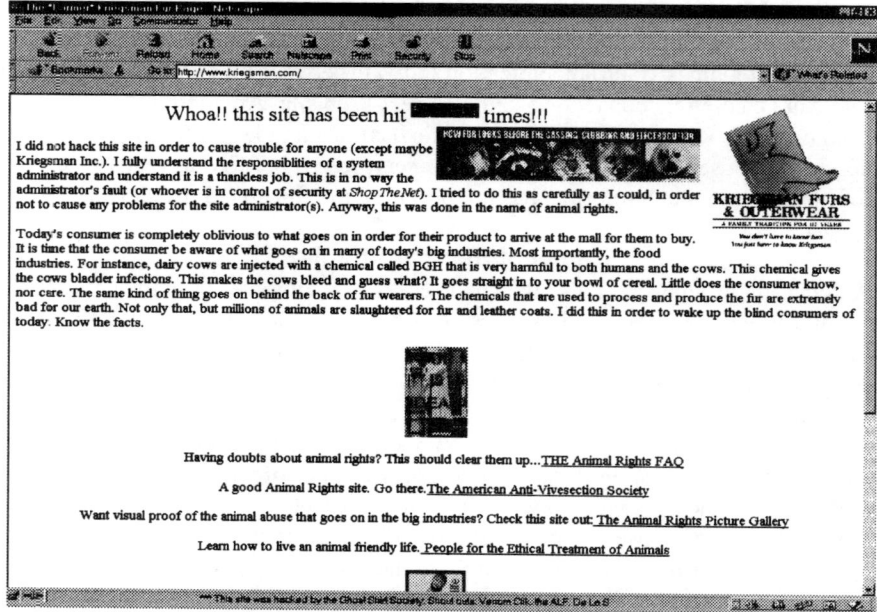

on on-line connectivity. These sort of attacks could easily disrupt electronic commerce on-line mechanisms (Howard, 1997).

Direct Attack

A direct attack would take the form of hacking into a computer system and rewriting or stealing information. Some recent examples have that hackers operate for political purposes, as shown by the Portuguese hacker group called PHAIT (Portuguese Hackers Against Indonesian Tyranny). They have rewritten Indonesian government and commercial Web sites in order to protest about East Timor situation (see Figure 3). Since 1997 the group has hacked and defaced (according to their sources): 20 government systems, 14 commercial systems, one academic system and another nine minor government systems. Their current campaign is still ongoing at the time of writing.

Anti-fur hackers have also attacked fur company Web sites in order to get their message to the general public (as shown by Figure 4).

Another method of hacking is more concerned with attacking computers files and destroying, modifying or extracting data. These types of hacking attacks may be less apparent to organizations, as they may not realise they have been a victim. Cyber-terrorists would use hacking as an extensive part of their 'attack strategy' against electronic commerce. By hacking Web sites, cyber-terrorists will gain a global audience for their political message and they will also be able to discredit the security of the companies using the on-line service (Warren, 1998). It should also be remembered that hackers are available for hire on the open market and therefore their services can be easily acquired (Denning, 1999).

By actually hacking the data contained within the system, sales can be disrupted, or data altered. This would help to harm the organization's effectiveness or allow fraud to take place. National research within Australia has shown that the main concern that users have about electronic commerce is security (DIST, 1998). Cyber-terrorist attacks on commercial sites could easily damage users' belief in secure transactions. Overnight, the newly developed electronic commerce marketplace could disappear.

THE NEW SECURITY WEAKNESS

One of the first electronic commerce security studies has confirmed that organizations conducting e-commerce experience far more security breaches than those that do not conduct e-commerce (Briney, 1999). The survey of 745 U.S. organizations showed that their major e-commerce concerns were:

Hacking	19%
E-mail security	17%
Malicious code (viruses)	12%
Secure e-commerce	11%
Secure remote access	11%

The survey also showed that organizations conducting e-commerce are 57% more likely to experience a proprietary information leak and 24% are more likely to experience a hacking-related breach than an organization not using electronic commerce (Briney, 1999). Electronic commerce applications are now beginning to attract the attention of hackers; in the future cyber terrorists will also be attracted. The reason why terrorist groups would attack e-commerce businesses are (Warren, 1998):

- an effective attack would could cause embarrassment for the victim company and result in loss of business and customers through a lack of confidence;
- the on-line facilities used by e-commerce applications can easily be disrupted by denial of service attacks;
- attacks upon a particular countries e-commerce businesses could result in political pressure being placed by those organizations upon their countries government;
- any successful attack would cause publicity well beyond any damage that was actually caused.

RESPONDING TO THE THREAT OF CYBER-TERRORISM

The seriousness with which the issue is taken can be illustrated by recent activities by national governments. For example, in the United States, concern over IT-related threats has led to the establishment of the National Infrastructure Protection Centre (NIPC). It is a US$64 million facility, employing some 500 staff across the country, with representatives taken from existing agencies such as the Secret Service, the CIA, NASA, the National Security Agency, the Department of Defense and several others. The role of NIPC is to "detect, deter, assess, warn of, respond to, and investigate computer intrusions and unlawful acts" that threaten or target U.S. critical infrastructures such as telecommunications, energy, banking and finance, water systems, government operations and emergency services (NIPC, 1998).

Without appropriate control, it is possible that measures could be introduced that are harmful to society in different ways. For example, the complete regulation or monitoring of our use of IT systems could lead to the emergence (some would say extension) of a 'surveillance society' in which technology is used to erode individual rights and freedoms in the name of the wider public good (Davies, 1996). It can already be seen that the activities of cyber-terrorists ultimately have the effect of restricting freedoms for the rest of us. For example, despite some concessions, the United States continues to maintain a relatively restrictive policy on the use of cryptographic technologies. One of the stated reasons for control is to prevent unregulated use of strong encryption techniques by terrorist organizations (FBI, 1998).

SOLUTIONS AND RECOMMENDATIONS

The on-line framework in which electronic commerce operates is the greatest vulnerability that it faces. The weapons to attack electronic commerce services are easily available on the Internet. Security administrators must ensure that they have the latest security installed to protect their systems. However, this is not enough. Pro-active and dynamic security procedures and counter-measures must be put in place. Hiding behind a seemingly impenetrable security wall will not guarantee protection. Criminal and terrorist groups have the initiative at the moment. This must be taken away from them.

It is difficult to predict the future strategies of cyber-terrorism. We are now seeing the first terrorist groups carrying out denial-of-service attacks, such as the Tamil Tigers denial of service attack against Sri Lankan embassies (Associated Press, 1998). We have also seen the first instance of a terrorist trying to buy detailed plans of the American National Computer Network Infrastructure (McKay, 1998) via the Internet.

CONCLUSION

It is now becoming more widely accepted that groups have the ability to attack targets using cyber-terrorist techniques, such as the IRA (Irish Republican Army) and the City of London (Berger, 1997). But in this case the political cease-fire stopped the development of the IRA cyber strategies any further.

Within the last few years, there has been continued development of cyber-terrorist capabilities in these organizations (Associated Press, 1998; McKay, 1998; Tender, 1996). The potential of these groups in a decade can only be postulated. In the future information society, these irregular forces will be looking for easy targets, and unfortunately the proliferation of electronic commerce has made many more sites prime targets for terrorist attacks.

REFERENCES

Associated Press. (1998, May 6). "First cyber terrorist action reported", USA.
Authors Unknown. (1994). *The Terrorists Handbook*, USA.
Berger, S. (1997, May 25). IRA has technology to wipe out the City. *The Sunday Telegraph*, UK.

Briney, A. (1999, July). Study Confirms Increased Security Risks of E-Commerce, *Information Security Magazine*, ICSA, USA.

Davies, S. (1996). *Big Brother – Britain's web of surveillance and the new technological order*. Pan Book Ltd, London, UK, ISBN 0-330-34931-7.

Denning, D. (1999). *Information Warfare and Security*, Addison Wesley Longman Inc, USA, ISBN 0-201-433303-6.

DIST (Department of Industry, Science and Tourism). (1998). *Stats – Electronic Commerce in Australia (Public Report)*, Commonwealth of Australia, Australia.

EelamWeb (1999). [On-line]. http://www.eelamweb.com/

FBI. (1998). *Encryption: Impact on law Enforcement*. Information Resources Division, Federal Bureau of Investigation, Virginia, USA.

Howard, J. (1997). PhD thesis. *An Analysis Of Security Incidents On The Internet*, Carnegie Mellon University, USA.

Hutchinson, H and Warren, M (1999). The attitude and practice of Australian Information Technology managers toward Cyber-Vigilantism, *InfoWarCon10*, Washington, USA.

Irish Republican Information Services (1999). [On-line]. http://joyce.iol.ie/~saoirse/

Littman, J. (1997). *The Watchman – The Twisted Life and Crimes of Serial Hacker Kevin Poulsen*. Little, Brown & Company Limited, USA, ISBN 0-316-52857-9.

Malik, I. (1996). *Computer Hacking: detection and protection*. Sigma Press, UK, ISBN 1-85058-538-5.

McKay, N. (1998, 16 October). "Cyber Terror Arsenal Grows", Wired News, [On-line]: http://www.wired.com/news.

Mulschlegel, F. (1997). Cyber Attacks: Detection and Prevention, *InfoWarCon 97*, pp B2 3-14, Brussels, Belgium.

NIPC. (1998). Mission Statement, National Infrastructure Protection Centre. [On-line]. http://www.fbi.gov/nipc/nipc.htm

Schwartau, W. (1996). *Information Warfare: Chaos on the Electronic Superhighway*. Thunder's Mouth Press, New York, USA.

Tendler, S. (1996, 25th March). "Ulster security details posed on the Internet", *The Times*, UK.

Rathmall, A. (1997). Cyber-terrorism: The Shape of Future Conflict?, *Royal United Service Institute Journal*, October, 40-46, UK.

Rathmall, A. (1998). Information Warfare: Implications for Arms Control, *Bulletin of Arms Control*, No.29, 8-14, UK.

Warren, M. (1998). Cyber Terrorism, *IFIP TC11 International on Information Security (SEC 98)*, pp 429-438, Budapest, Hungary.

Warren, M., Coldwell, J., Willey, A., Hutchinson, D. and Moosajee, D. (1999). A Training System relating to Australian Electronic Commerce, *Euromedia 99*, 250-254, Munich, Germany.

Warren, M and Furnell, S.M, (1999). Cyber-Terrorism - a new threat for the next millennium, *Australian Institute of Computer Ethics Conference 99*, 416-425, Melbourne, Australia.

Zapatista Movement (1999). [On-Line]. http://www.ezln.org/

Chapter XXIII

The Law Vis-À-Vis Electronic Commerce

Assafa Endeshaw
Nanyang Technological University, Singapore

INTRODUCTION

A great deal of uncertainty surrounds the impact of the continuing growth of electronic commerce (e-commerce) on existing law. While commercial law has evolved over the centuries in response to the development of trade in goods and services, within or across nations,[1] the emergence of an electronic medium ('cyberspace') as an additional avenue for trade has pushed to the fore many questions: whether and how an adaptation of existing law would be possible, appropriate or sufficient to catch up with the problems thrown up by the new medium. For one thing, the nature and effects of transactions that would ordinarily have been taken for granted had they occurred on non-electronic media confound established notions of commercial law. Secondly, the unpredictability of the ultimate consequence of such transactions to the respective trading partners, who would be more likely to come from different jurisdictions, prompts scrutiny of pre-existing, widely accepted formulations in domestic trade law, custom and treaty among nations.

A major feature of the emergent situation is that the impact of e-commerce on the law has not been across the board, simply because e-commerce has not been developing evenly. Most transactions to date relate to the purchase of computer hardware or software or the supply of information of various types: plain news, financial data, entertainment, education, travel, advertisements, health and DIY tips. These items have one characteristic, namely the buyers' lack of interest in, or disregard of, any need to have to conduct checking or inspection prior to purchase or, at any rate, before delivery. In light of the general uncertainty surrounding the status of the online buyer and seller, the relevant law and of how it might be applied on behalf of a buyer claiming redress, the purchase of "safe" items acquires a precautionary significance. In other words, the very nature of the items involved in the transactions seems to rule out any fundamental failure that could surface at a later stage and necessitate the intervention of the law to resolve the consequences of that failure. Obviously, once money has passed from the buyer to the seller, the path to recovery of that money, let

Copyright © 2000, Idea Group Publishing.

alone further damages as would be expected under normal contract law, could be too complicated for the buyer to understand or pursue.

What makes the plight of an on-line buyer who seeks redress intractable is that solutions to on-line legal disputes are only just evolving in bits and pieces. New rules have begun to emerge in the form of statutory reforms in single jurisdictions or through case decisions on disputes arising from on-line transactions. However, the ambit and applicability of the evolving laws tend to be subject to time, the nature of the concrete problems they are meant to address, as well as the diverse contexts. Consequently, pre-existing laws have not undergone modification or replacement by the emergence of e-commerce in all respects, to the same extent, nor in every jurisdiction.

This chapter explores the nature of legal changes that have been propelled by the onset of e-commerce and the likely course of future developments. First, we present a brief summary of the impacts on contract law followed by a discussion on the liabilities arising from on-line transactions. Then, the focus is on issues of security and privacy of transactions. Finally, we cover the incipient forms of dispute resolution in e-commerce. The conclusion affirms that the law as applied to e-commerce is still in continuous flux and will take more time to acquire a definite shape. In particular, it underscores the urgency of meeting with the ever-apparent demand for an international treaty or agreement, at least parallel to existing treaties in contracts or sales.

CONTRACT LAW

The most important area of law that has been put to the test by the growth of e-commerce is, not surprisingly, contract law. It needs no emphasis that contract law is the foundation of commercial law.[2] However, the degree of change effected on existing rules of contract law or, even, the level of understanding of the problems that the new medium presents to contract law is not readily apparent across jurisdictions. So far, some elements of case law have been modified; a few statutory authorities have been amended but nothing comprehensive has surfaced in any country. Most changes have occurred in the U.S. prompted by the rising use of e-commerce in interstate trade. The rules developed in the context of interstate trade have had to be re-examined to accommodate e-commerce. Nevertheless, no approach has been adopted to consummate all efforts through an international solution.

In the area of new legislation, the UNCITRAL Model Law on Electronic Commerce has set the pace for all nations. Essentially, the Model Law provides for assimilation of electronic forms of contracting as well as electronic evidence to non-electronic ones; in short, it equates electronic (offers, acceptances and evidence for such) to non-electronic forms without indicating whether the legal consequences that arise will also be the same or different. While the assimilation of electronic forms of communications is a step in the right direction, it is submitted that the absence of any provision on the legality or validity of transactions is a major deficiency of the Model Law.[3]

The attempt to come up with a legislative solution to this problem has taken, in the U.S., the form of amending the Uniform Commercial Code, by introducing a new Article 2B. The draft has undergone various revisions (starting from 1996) partly because of the disparate views expressed to improve it and the lack of common understanding about its intended coverage.[4] The latest draft was issued on February 1, 1999.[5] An April 7, 1999 press release by the two bodies engaged in the work, the National Conference of Commissioners on Uniform State Laws and the American Law Institute, indicated that the draft Uniform Electronic Transactions Act will replace the relevant sections of the proposed Article 2B. This change is purportedly because the area relating to formal aspects electronic transactions "does not presently allow the sort of codification that is represented by the Uniform Commercial Code."[6] In terms of the substance of the proposed amendment, the Article encompasses the whole range of contract law rules (formation,[7] construction,[8] performance,[9] remedies,[10] authentication,[11] and, surprisingly too, choice of law and forum[12]). Thus it goes beyond merely the assimilation of non-electronic forms of contracting to electronic ones and the provisions for authentication that one finds in laws of other nations. If the draft becomes adopted by the various states in the U.S., it will represent a major influence on the efforts of other countries which are seeking legislative solutions.

Identification and Authentication of the Parties

One of the major problems that contracting on the Net faces is the difficulty of establishing the identity of the party who is on the other side of the transaction. The exchange of valuables which is at the heart of contract law loses meaning if the parties exchanging them do not exactly know that there is somebody at the other side who is what she claims to be. This is not necessarily because of any need to know the other person's particulars or in view of future business prospects, but to be sure that if anything goes wrong the party claiming redress knows how to get to or communicate with that other party. In contract law terms, the innocent party should have sufficient information about the party in default or alleged breach of the contract so as to pursue her claims against that party successfully.

The problem of not being able to establish the identity of a person transacting on the Net readily is made worse by the use of 'remailers' or 'anonymizers.' These are software programs which can cloak the identity of a contracting party by either removing or replacing the actual address from which a party is sending messages so that it becomes impossible to trace that party. From a practical angle, where such software is used, the party that pays for goods on the Net but does not receive the goods will not be able to establish if the seller is real or a phantom or whether she is residing at the specified origin of the electronic communication of acceptance or notice of delivery.

Another way in which a party may be prevented from establishing the identity of the other side is "spoofing," that is the use by the latter party of the identity or account of another person to masquerade as that other person. This is done not only by faking the identity of another party, but also by altering or falsifying e-mails so that the identity of a non-transacting party is assumed. There are several spy programs that monitor the keystrokes of people to imitate their identity and misrepresent them. It is therefore vital for contracting parties to know, and have confidence, that the other party is genuine and fits the description that she has supplied about herself during the transaction.

The common use of passwords as a means of identity authentication has been found to be deficient, open as it is to deliberate or inadvertent disclosure, hacking or some other means of intervention or eavesdropping. Among the more reliable emerging forms of authentication of parties employing electronic means of transactions is the use of digital signature technology. Biometric techniques (such as fingerprinting, handwriting or voice recognition, retinal, or hand-geometry scanning) are still in a process of development or immensely expensive to adopt at the moment.

A digital signature is a data string generated by an algorithm using information supplied by the signer. The most common form of encryption (known as public key cryptography) involves possession of two keys by the sender, one 'private' and another 'public', and the encryption of a message or document by the sender using his private key to be decrypted by the receiver using a copy of the public key. The private key is solely at the disposal of the sender of messages while the public key is also in the custody of the certification authority (CA) which makes it available to parties which conduct transactions with the public key owner and seek to establish the identity of that owner and integrity of its messages in the transaction. The public key is maintained by a trusted third party, (CA), playing the role of archivist and registrar. The CA will require establishing the identity and other particulars of parties in possession of public keys in order to guarantee the reliability of those public keys.

During the electronic transaction, the signature created with a sender's private key identifies the sender as the originator and proves that the message was not tampered with since it left the sender. In order to check the identity and integrity of an electronic message, the recipient needs to know the public key of the sender. So long as the recipient of the message has access to a copy of the public key, generally based on a prior arrangement with the sender and her CA, the recipient can establish whether the "hash value" of the received message (that is a numerical quantity computed from the contents of that message) is the same as that sent with message. A fraudulent message will have a different hash value thus alerting the recipient.

A whole host of regulations and guidelines have emerged across the world to institutionalise the workings of CAs and to clarify the rights and liabilities of all parties in the authentication process. Legislation has been issued or proposed in the main industrial nations, including many states of the U.S., Japan and the EU (1998)[13], to standardise the use of digital signatures and the operations of CAs. Unfortunately, there is no uniformity between national laws, either in the substance of the rights and liabilities or in the formalities of operations of CAs. A mixture of public, semi-public and private CAs has been allowed to operate, sometimes side by side, in many nations. The establishment of government-based CAs has been justified as a necessary step in the building up of trust in e-commerce.

A key problem in the use of digital signatures is adequacy of safeguards for public keys and the maintenance of their continued validity and currency. It is sometimes possible for the public key to expire or to be abandoned by the registrant or for changes to be made if it becomes unusable (owing to security breaches and the like). Unless CAs undertake to provide foolproof, safekeeping and management services and become responsible for any resulting liability for failure to carry out these critical tasks, the authentication process will be discredited and lose its value. These problems add to the other main problems of legal efficacy of transactions to which we now turn.

The Legality or Validity of Transactions

The conclusion of a formally complete contract for the delivery of goods and services online is the starting point and not the end of a commercial transaction. As well as the form (the making of a valid offer and acceptance, the identification of the object of the contract and the price), the content of the contract, its terms, must be in accord with legal requirements. These relate to mistake, misrepresentation, competition law, false or misleading trade descriptions and illegality in general. The latter includes gambling, pornography, offences against the state, and property such as computer crime, information theft and other forms of fraud.

The effects of mistake and misrepresentation on a contract are uncomplicated. A mistake affecting both parties is likely to make the contract either void or unenforceable since their expectations from the contract cannot materialise. However, where a party's (usually the buyer's) consent to a contract is obtained through misrepresentation of the key facts about the subject matter of the contract, that party is permitted under the law to cancel the contract and seek compensation for any damages (including expenses) she sustained.

The other strands of legality of contracts just mentioned will require special attention by all parties engaged in e-commerce because the Internet has the potential to become a means of subverting domestic laws and making them less relevant or even totally inapplicable. A good example is an occurrence in France during the 1997 elections; under existing French electoral law, opinion polls are required to be kept secret during the week before a parliamentary vote. However, this was evaded through anonymous postings on Web sites by thousands of Internet users. As *Le Monde* stated in its editorial "From here on, it is the globalization of communications that renders the law obsolete."[14]

The determination of the specific types and grounds for illegality of contracts is an exercise of constitutional and judicial authorities in each nation. To date, there are no international standards that establish forms of illegality acceptable for all nations, even for groups of them. The various forms of illegality adopted in each nation are contrived by reference to what each nation views to be the 'public (or judicial) policy', or 'ordre public' (in continental European law) that it considers to be reflecting its interests. Consequently, national laws on contractual illegality or terms that prejudice public policy in some way or other would have more differences than similarities because of the concrete contexts within which the national authorities operate.

The debate has been going on, for instance, in the U.S. as to whether the potential of the Internet for the promotion and operation of gambling should be addressed in a new law. One U.S. Senator was reported to have said "Yes, we know we are facing a challenge with enforcement, but society does need to say what is right and wrong even when it is hard to enforce. It's still a crime, even though it's in a new venue."[15] As the Internet is rendering previous control mechanisms through licensing ineffective, the search is going on to find formula[16] to keep the youth and rouges, whether in the U.S. or any location abroad, from engaging in unauthorised gambling. But the task is not easy; as one commentator put it, "No matter how serious the potential problems, Internet gambling is here to stay, growing explosively and impossible to stop."[17] Some nations have even adopted it as a means of gaining revenue.[18]

As an illustration of the nature of the problem of illegality, we pick up an important aspect, namely competition law. The criteria for determining unfair or anti-competitive practices in the formation of contracts, as well as in general business transactions, are not the same across nations. The furthest progress has been achieved in the U.S., through its antitrust laws and the EU in view of the single-market initiative. However, most nations generally outlaw certain practices (that are in restraint of trade or free economic activities) without adopting similar yardsticks or scopes. Some nations still do not recognise any form of anti-competitiveness.

By contrast, most nations have roughly similar rules regarding deception or misrepresentation of some sort among parties in business or commercial transactions. Apart from criminal sanctions that take care of these malpractices, there are civil remedies that allow rejection of the contract but order the award of damages to the party affected by the misrepresentation. Indeed, these measures have often been tied to schemes for the protection of consumers and have, thereby, found increasing significance among the laws prohibiting illegality.

It is not possible to go through other forms of illegality in the limited space available here. It must be stated, however, that the lack of cross-jurisdictional agreement on what constitutes illegality and its scope in terrestrial commercial law is bound to prevail in e-commerce too with all the uncertainties that follow. It is not unthinkable that the same transaction might be illegal under the laws of one state while it remains fully valid elsewhere. This may perhaps explain why the major international sales conventions avoid the subject altogether, considering the diversity of national solutions and the stakes that each nation has in not abandoning determination of illegality in its own narrow interests. It goes without saying that contractual illegality is one of the areas of e-commerce law that needs international solution.

ONLINE LIABILITY

In spite of the myth of 'the World Wild Web'—in other words, an electronic frontier where no laws apply—unwittingly spread about the Internet, on-line commercial transactions do not operate in the void. The Internet is merely an additional avenue of communication, trade and general interaction within and among groups of nations, businesses and individuals which are interconnected. Consequently, the protection of legal interests recognised in realspace can only be regarded as extended to the Internet as well unless the latter makes such protection less effective or totally obsolete. Moreover, liabilities arising from tampering or infringement of those legal interests protected in realspace will be dealt with under the existing laws in so far as they remain applicable. Thus the protection on the Internet of legal interests such as intellectual property, privacy and information is an important aspect of e-commerce. Any violation of these interests will be a source of liability for wrongdoers.

Intellectual Property

The well-known laws of intellectual property (patents, copyright, trademarks and industrial designs) and other allied rights in the form or substance of information (confidentiality) face a measure of shake-up resulting from the advance of information technology. The principal impact on all types of intellectual property (IP), particularly on those relating to forms and texture (copyright, trademarks and industrial designs) originates from the 'dematerialisation' of information or 'decoupling' from the material substructure that the information used to subsist or be deposited in. Although the protection granted under IP has always been distinctly earmarked for the information or 'expression' rather than the material medium embodying such information or used for the expression, the possibility offered by information technology to de-link completely the information from the material background, indeed to make electronic impulses the new medium of expression, has thrown some long-standing conceptions into chaos.

The proliferation of the new medium of creativity, namely the use of digitisation, has thus reopened long-solved issues of copyright requirements of subsistence, originality and fixation. Even while these issues are being tackled, the capability provided by digitisation and the communication technologies, including the Internet, to transmit data and information to virtually any spot on the globe and transform them into anything at all has shaken up the protection and enforcement mechanisms developed over the centuries.

Where an earlier work in the ordinary, that is non-electronic, media becomes digitised, the possibility of manipulating the latter and transferring it into something similar rips apart the protection given under current law to specific forms. While the translation or adaptation of any work is covered under the copyright belonging to the original author, the complete transformation possible through digitisation confounds the application of those legal principles. Obviously, prohibiting any tampering with the digital format will not work nor make any sense as the consequence would be to grant unlimited monopoly rights over bits and bytes which are the common stock available in any digital medium. Thus digital "sampling" of music, that is manipulating sound from existing works (a note or two) or from an audience or the surrounding to recreate sound or alter lines of a specific music, prompts the question whether unauthorised sampling should be considered an infringement? Though the process is akin to reverse engineering or experimenting in the fields of patents or software programming, the adverse impact of the new form on the earlier sources for the 'sampling' militates against accepting it as permissible under existing IP. Yet, in the absence of any practical means of thwarting it, any rejection of 'sampling' will only remain declaratory in significance.

In the area of trademark, the rise of domain names has proved to be somewhat a menace. The use of a domain name not only as an indictor of on-line presence (a Web site address) but also of goods and services overlaps or clashes with established functions of trademarks: a link to the source or quality of goods or services in geographically delimited compartments (in realspace). The problem has been pronounced with respect to famous marks as they have worldwide significance and criss-cross national borders in the creation of market niches for their owners. However, the possibility for overlaps and the concurrent use of similar marks, whether or not famous, in a single territory or in many that normally would have been acceptable in trademark law is no longer possible for domain names.

Firstly, domain names represent exclusive addresses that no one else but the registrant occupies and utilises. Unless different levels of hierarchy are adopted in the registration of domain names, once a domain name has been assigned to an entity, a third party cannot use it again. In a sense, the domain name system (DNS) provides an absolute monopoly right to the registrant.

Secondly, the possibility of varying domain names by inserting alphanumeric characters into a pre-registered name spawns confusion among consumers though the technical address on the Internet (known as the Internet Protocol) will be in order. Thus the apparent monopoly granted in the DNS can be compromised by the parallel layers of registration that are in place. Added to this is the unauthorised use of others' trademarks as domain names, a practice dubbed "cybersquatting." All this boils down to an unavoidable clash between the two forms of value indicators. Unfortunately, recent progress in the improvement of the registration system (particularly through the establishment of the Internet Corporation for Names and Numbers, ICANN) have not embraced the resolution of these intractable problems.

Overall, the potential for digital technology to be deployed in infringing intellectual property rights has been viewed with alarm and consternation, naturally by proprietors. No wonder that some have even proclaimed the end of copyright. Save a few who have argued that the Internet has outlived property in information and in all things that are amenable to digitisation,[19] the vast majority insist on finding better means of protecting intellectual property (mainly trademarks and copyright) which pertain to information placed on the Internet.

Lately, technological means of thwarting infringement have come on the market. One such technology detects unauthorised copying of proprietary matter (music, film and the like available online) and provides details of addresses of those doing so.[20] Another technology that might help prevent unauthorised copying of digital music is a software that creates a "virtual" envelope for the digital content and allows the user only such limited time that he bought or rented it for. The technology consists of an encryption system with a security lock and encoded with a set of rules.[21] Another technology intended to be introduced by five major consumer electronics companies—IBM, Hitachi, NEC Corporation, the Pioneer Electronic Corporation and Sony— is the embedding of a "watermark", an indelible binary code, in each frame of a digital music recording. The digital watermark is expected to prevent unauthorized copying.[22]

The World Intellectual Property Organization has produced the 1996 Copyright Treaty which effectively seeks to amend (in the form of a Protocol) the Berne Convention for the protection of copyright. Articles 11 and 12 prohibit tampering with or removal of the use of technological devices that prevent infringement. Some of the member nations such as the U.S. have started to pass national laws to incorporate the changes. The U.S. passed the Digital Millennium Copyright Act on October 12, 1998, among other things, to prohibit the use of code-cracking devices in infringement of copyright or tampering with technologies that protect software from piracy. On the other hand, the Act grants exemption to SPs from liability for transmitting material which might be infringing copyright though they would be expected to act when they have reason to believe that there is infringement.

Misappropriation or Theft of Information

The protection of economically valuable data or information, whether proprietary or not, from competitors or potential misuse is an important aspect of the growth and market power of modern companies. A range of civil and criminal law remedies are available in national legislation to safeguard such information. The more well-known type of loss of information is through plain theft by an insider or a hacker. In the context of the Internet, there are programs that are capable of retrieving information from a computer, without the user's knowledge, and sending it to a hacker's own site. Any encrypted protective device will be broken by the hacker first before files are stolen. Such programs obviously pose a serious risk of loss of valuable data or information. Other forms of loss of information are disclosure, whether deliberately or not, by employees or contractual parties or through lapse or oversight of the company. The disgruntled employee or one who is offered bribes for passing on secrets is very much the typical miscreant.

Not unexpectedly, although any information of a confidential nature is protected from theft or unauthorised disclosure under laws of one kind of another, the specific laws in each nation differ widely. Besides the legal redress available under trade secret law, law of confidentiality or other IP laws that pertain to proprietary information, there are a range of other laws. The main legal instrument increasingly being adopted by nations is computer misuse or crime law. Some have added to this still other laws targeting specific aspects of theft of information. In the U.S., the Electronic Communication Privacy Act 1986 forbids interception of wire, oral or electronic communication, divulging or screening content. The doing of any of these is illegal. The U.S. Economic Espionage Act of 1996 was issued to punish theft of trade secrets (defined in the broadest of terms to include any information of whatever type kept secret and possessing value by that fact).

There have been sporadic pronouncements by courts of certain nations (the U.K., U.S. and even Malaysia) to consider information as being subject matter for protection on the basis of its economic value alone. Yet, the lack of adequate justification for such an approach has stopped it from emerging as a trend, let alone become adopted as a general legal rule across jurisdictions. Indeed, some courts have vacillated often between granting and refusing recognition to a blanket protection of information that does not qualify for such a privilege reserved at the moment for proprietary forms alone.

Consumer Protection

On-line contracts replicate standard forms which have long been viewed as veritable scourges for consumers. By definition, such forms specify terms and conditions that the on-line seller or supplier of goods and services determines unilaterally and without any room for the buyer to bargain for or change them in any way. A consumer will generally be expected to supply her details, including her credit card information and delivery address, and hence make payments first even before she has have had the chance to inspect, test or examine the goods as allowed under the sales law. The fact that even the making of any offer of purchase by the consumer is conditional on supplying details required by the seller and not necessarily the other way round (that is the address, legal standing and financial liquidity of the seller) and the express agreement of the consumer to terms and conditions points to the great leverage the seller has against the consumer. A consumer who refuses to agree to the express terms and conditions (by clicking on the 'I agree' buttons on the seller's Web page) will simply be refused further access to the Web page unless she engages in e-mail communications with the respective 'customer information' or "helpline," if any, that the seller may provide.

To make matters worse, the spectrum of laws and institutions that have been evolving since the 1960s to sustain the hapless consumer may simply be sidestepped or become ineffective as the standard terms and conditions are usually expressed with little or no regard for their requirements or consent. The one-sided nature of online contracts and the confusion in the type of laws and institutions that may or may not have any authority to intervene on behalf of the consumer has not helped stave off the latter's plight.[23]

On the other hand, the potential misuse of information supplied by consumers to online suppliers of goods and services makes them wary of disclosing their details opting, instead, to keep away from engaging in on-line purchases. Yet, information may be gathered on consumers even if they refuse to supply it themselves. Apart from those collecting information in their professional capacity and dealing in them, cookie files help in obtaining information on users. These are files written on a user's hard drive during visits to cookie-compatible Web sites and allow tracking of the activities of a user, visits to sites and the like. The 'click stream,' that is the profile of a person's visits over time, may be used by businesses to market their products or services, but can be sold to other marketers too.

One consequence of consumers' fear of invasion of their privacy and misuse of information they supply while transacting on the Internet is that consumers do not flock onto the Internet and on-line businesses cannot hope to make money. Hence there have been calls for legislative intervention by governments as well as continued attempts to work out private schemes that generate trust among consumers. We will examine below the legislative and other measures proposed or undertaken within the general bounds of security.[24]

Ironically, consumer protection has been enhanced by the fact that communities of people interact and exchange their experiences on Net purchases or other transactions. The immediacy of their reactions, particularly their dislikes of what is on offer on the Net, might rebound on businesses that cannot accede to consumer requirements or look after their tastes. Hence, open criticisms or appraisals of products and services might squeeze or expand the chances of doing business on the Net. Ultimately, businesses will be forced to cut down on aspects of their business that have not found favour with customers.

Indeed, some businesses already cater for diverse interests of consumers even before the complaints start appearing on the Net. Thus Amazon.com not only provides books but also information about authors, reviews from the media and related information about other book authors. Consequently, a community of devoted customers and a profile of their needs and tastes is acquired by Amazon.com, which might be used to expand sales and continue to have an edge over rival booksellers, online or not.

Consumer protection groups have grabbed the facility for complaints in cyberspace. The creation of forums for e-mail-based complaints by consumers dissatisfied with advertisements, goods or services or to expose violators of self-regulatory codes of ethics is growing. Web portals such as Yahoo! routinely provide a space for consumer complaints. A new technological solution by a California-based software producer (called "Third Voice")[25] also promises to offer the possibility of posting comments on sites which the site owners will not be able to remove. The advantage of the postings is that, apart from the absence of consent by the site owners and possibility of censorship, they will be viewed by other users too and thus pressurize the site owners to conform to consumer demands or established industry standards.

Liability for Negligence

In every situation where the conduct of any person, whether though action or inaction, results in harm to another person, the law attaches consequences. Under the general duty imposed by the law on all persons not to cause any harm to others, a breach of the standard normally expected in the given circumstances will entitle the victim to claim civil remedies against the wrongdoer—cessation of the harm and compensation for the harm caused. The types of civil wrongs that might lead to civil sanctions are endless but we will concentrate on the most important ones here. The two major sources of negligent liability are defective goods and false or misleading information (more often called "misstatements").

The action against suppliers of defective goods has become a major plank of consumer protection as it entitles consumers who have suffered from the defects to claim under the various product liability laws. Earlier on, establishing the liability of the provider of services or goods had placed a burden on consumers because they would have to prove faulty performance or manufacturing by the alleged wrongdoer. This has now been replaced in many industrial nations by strict liability laws which provide, essentially, for compensation to the buyer or consumer in all cases where the supplier could not prove that it was not at fault. Needless to say, the victim needs to prove that the alleged wrongdoer was the source of the goods and that the harm originated from the specified goods.

The liability for defective physical goods cannot acquire any more significance on the Internet than it has in realspace. However, if digital goods become defective and result in some harm to persons or property, there are obvious grounds for product liability law to be relevant. Suppliers of digital goods who do not take adequate care as to the quality of the goods and the freedom from any defects, whether inherent to the goods (e.g. bugs) or because of extraneous problems (such as viruses), will be liable in the ordinary way.

Liability for misstatements affects all purveyors of information (advertisers, professionals, consultants) or others who engage in this activity relying on their expertise or competence. The standard of duty of care for these categories is the reasonably competent professional or consultant. In all cases where the information supply failed to live up to that standard, the victim who relied on such information and suffered as a result will be able to claim compensation.

The range of persons who might become liable or claim compensation is defined under the law. Those who cause the harm in their own capacity (individuals, companies, self-employed persons, or independent contractors) are obviously liable on their own account. Where, however, the liability springs from a wrongdoer's activity under the direction of some principal, the wrongdoer will not become liable on his own (thus called vicarious liability). Such happens under relations of agency or in employment. There is also the situation where the victim may have been partly instrumental in his harm (hence known as contributory liability or infringement), and therefore the responsibility might be shared.

We will briefly touch on the special problem of on-line service providers (SPs), the fact that they are vehicles for the display, transmission and exchange of information, goods and services. The obvious question is then whether they should not be liable for the content they fail to supervise, check offending material. Arguments have been levelled against imposing such a liability on SPs, for instance, for defamation or infringement of IP and the like because the speed or volume of information or transactions may be such that it may not be possible for them to exercise editorial control. A counter-argument presented to this is that the best person to do any control would be the SP.

On the practical side, monitoring the network may slow it down to such an extent that subscribers will clog it to a standstill or that the SP would find it unprofitable to run the service. Then there are limitations of expertise and knowledge by SPs. Thus, as far as copyright or trademark infringement is concerned, how could the SP know who owns what and who is the infringer? In any case, the use of encryption might shut the SP's efforts to detect what is going on? On the other hand, to make SPs liable for everything that passes through their systems will be akin to requiring them to know what is going on every minute.

The more acceptable solution seems to be the decision in the U.S. cases of *Cubby* v *Compuserve* (1991) and *Stratton Oakmont Inc.* v *Prodigy* (1996). In the first case Compuserve, an SP, had created and run an electronic forum to which had been posted material allegedly defaming the plaintiff. The court relied on the absence of any editorial control by Compuserve to rule against the plaintiff. The court found the reverse in the *Prodigy* case, i.e., responsibility rested with the SP as a publisher, simply because it held itself out as having better editorial control than its competitors. If at all it is an indication of the general trend to protect SPs, the UK defamation law has endorsed the U.S. approach. Otherwise imposing a requirement on carriers of having the relevant knowledge or introducing filtering materials that might infringe or offend will be such a heavy burden that only SPs with greater resources will be able to shoulder it.

As regarding the likely claimants, the law is complicated. All claims are supposed to be among the circle of people who would have been in the "path" of the wrongdoer's acts or omissions and that a reasonable person in the wrongdoer's position would have foreseen that they might be in his path. Now, from a layperson's point of view, this is a rule full of ifs and buts. Translated into ordinary language, this means that the courts will hold the key to determination of the real claimants. Applied to the Internet, it is not possible to hazard a guess as to whether they would readily hold a purveyor of information or supplies liable on the strength of it Web presence alone. The mountain of information available, the anonymity with which parties can operate on the Net, might persuade the courts that any reliance by the victim of any information would be unjustified. In any case, the specific law that would serve as a measure of liability may not be clear, much less its relevance to the claimed wrongdoing, the defendant. Perhaps, the borderless frontier might have transformed the already difficult law of liability in realspace into something of a nightmare for potential victims?

On-line 'Trespass'

The pervasive use of spamming (or Internet 'junkmail'), that is unsolicited mass e-mailing, has become a cause for concern because of the costs to consumers and the jamming impact on the speed of access of networks. As one commentator put it, "junk e-mail is a costly and time-consuming challenge. Spam assaults have been known to hobble Internet service providers for days and force them to devote as much as half their equipment to handling the flood of e-mail."[26] Inevitably, courts have begun to deal with spamming. In *Cyber Promotions, Inc.* v. *America Online* (1996), the latter's actions of blocking unsolicited e-mail advertisements held not to violate the First Amendment. Sending spam to networks that do not allow it might be considered an illegal form of trespass if the decision by a California state court in April 1999 stands. The case concerned an ex-employee of Intel's who, after being fired, sent unsolicited e-mail messages to other workers criticising the company about its compensation and other policies.[27]

A number of states in the U.S. (California, Washington, Nevada, and Virginia) have already issued legislation that outlaws spamming. If the trend continues, other countries might also follow suit. It is likely that a law might be passed in the U.S. Congress to curb spam though free speech advocates may yet be able to overturn these laws as being unconstitutional. In the meantime, the use of technological solutions is gaining acceptance. Some Internet service providers block spam outright although in the U.S. this has provoked the ire of civil liberties groups asserting constitutional (First Amendment) rights. Thus filtering technology is being used by many including Microsoft to block unwanted messages by known spammers.

Defamation on the Web

The display, transmission or supply of information likely to cast aspersion on the reputation of individuals or companies will be subject to libel laws as such information will be considered published, though in an electronic form. Traditional tests of libel are that false information was attributed to a plaintiff and that it was published maliciously, or at least without regard to its consequence to the plaintiff. While establishing the falsehood is a straightforward affair, the issue of publication may be somewhat tricky. Except where the electronic statement is put on a Web page and accessible to anyone, with or without a password, the communication of private messages through email may not necessarily be construed as 'publication'—very much in line with current legal rules on the sending of private letters to single addressees. However, it is doubtful if forwarding of the email by the recipient to others, or the fact that it can be read by other people besides the recipient, can be taken as 'publication.'

A further problem for those claiming redress is the establishment of loss of reputation by reference to the set of persons before whom the plaintiff had reputation prior to the publication of the falsehood. The strictness of the requirement of identifiable (not to say, a closed circle of) persons to gauge the resulting harm may deprive an action against on-line defamation any biting teeth. Neither the persons nor the harm could be proved easily as the community in reference to whom harm is assessed may not be easily ascertainable. A decision that mere publication would justify injunction and damages will only turn the law on its head.

Assuming one has proved publication, the next issue to determine is the culpability of the respective persons engaged in on-line publishing. All those involved in the process might be liable unless they can show that they were not aware of the libellous falsehood nor that they had been negligent in any way. The extent to which various actors in the creation or dissemination of information might be liable will hence rest on the degree of control and authority they possess on the content of the information.

The law of defamation has generally placed full responsibility on those who initiate, compile and publish the information wilfully or without taking adequate safeguards against any falsehood. Distributors, publishers and other carriers have been exempted from *prima facie* liability as their regular duties do not demand scrutiny of the content that they transmit; indeed, were that to be the case, their time and resources will be utterly consumed by such an onerous obligation. Consequently, the exception for carriers has been recognised in Internet defamation, as it has been in realspace, to protect service providers whether general access or specific content such as on-line publishers.

Two famous U.S. decisions, *Cubby* v *Compuserve* (1991) and *Stratton Oakmont Inc.* v *Prodigy* (1996) concerned the issue of whether the service provider was not party to defamatory material placed on its system because of the editorial control it had or should have exercised, respectively. In *Prodigy*, the dispute arose from a contribution to an electronic forum provided and closely controlled by the service provider. Prodigy had expressed to the public that it supervised the forum and had even screened out certain offensive messages. In *Compuserve*, on the other hand, the service was merely provision of space for the uploading of an electronic magazine, the contents of which it did not vet. In both of them, the courts' ruling was nevertheless based on the level of control that the service provider had or could have had; hence Prodigy was found to be liable whereas Compuserve was not.

In the UK, the Defamation Act 1996 seems to have explained any doubts about the liability of various persons involved in electronic publications. Section 1 provides such a defence to a person who was not the author, editor or publisher of the statement complained of but took reasonable care in relation to its publication, and did not know, and had no reason to believe, that what he did caused or contributed to the publication of a defamatory statement. The "secondary publishers" are defined in such a way as to grant them a defence from liability. Thus an author is an "originator" (excluding those who did not give consent for the statement to be published); an editor is one who has "editorial or equivalent responsibility for the content of the statement or the decision to publish it; a publisher is a commercial publisher whose business is issuing material to the public.[28] All other persons engaged in processing, distributing or selling material containing the statement are not to be considered as any of the three categories of persons who are *prima facie* liable.[29]

Lawsuits over alleged occurrences of defamation on the Web have put to the test the traditional legal notion of jurisdiction. The fact that the Internet is a borderless phenomenon has meant that the exposure of the defamatory information will span nations and not remain confined to the site it was mounted on. Such an expansive view is causing headaches to companies that use the Internet to advertise or sell their products. The problem for the courts has therefore been to redefine what constitutes jurisdiction as far as defamation is concerned. A lawsuit filed in California in 1997 was decided in favour of Vermont-based plaintiffs who claimed that a negative comment about their company sent by e-mail to an employee of Pacific Northwest Bell in Washington amounted to defamation because the message could be read by anyone on the system. "While modern technology has made nationwide commercial transactions simpler and more feasible, even for small businesses, it must broaden correspondingly the permissible scope of jurisdiction exercisable by the courts," reasoned the California court. Jurisdiction in the U.S. is normally based on state long-arm statute and the Due Process Clause of the United States Constitution.

The jurisdictional disputes in the U.S. have relied on interpretation of a 1984 Supreme Court decision in which a woman residing in New York State had sued an Ohio-based magazine, *Hustler*, in a New Hampshire court for libel.[30] The court decided that the magazine company "continuously and deliberately exploited the New Hampshire market," thus making it possible to be sued there.[31] If the courts follow this precedent, presumably anyone who operates a Web page could be sued in any jurisdiction in which that page can be accessed.

Decisions of the courts in other countries have to be awaited to determine whether a consensus is emerging on the issue of jurisdiction. Until that is done, the possibility of concurrent liabilities in multiple jurisdictions cannot be ruled out, nor the potential crippling effects on the activities of on-line stores. The unsettling situation for businesses on the Web needs to be resolved, again, through an international instrument that defines knotty problems such as this and others.

Taxation

The taxation of e-commerce is a vexatious problem because it is difficult to establish the residence of buyers and sellers, or of where the transaction took place. The international nature of the Internet brings into conflict various issues that used to be treated routinely under domestic law with a level of certainty. The taxable basis of the transaction (goods, services or persons—both natural and legal) and the jurisdiction(s) to which it must be submitted will differ according to which domestic law one subjects it to. The nature of the problem resembles that presented by the direct selling to nations other than those in which the seller is registered. While the taxable goods or services are supposed to be those generated or provided in a given nation, Internet transactions will by and large entail the transmission of goods or services from wherever they may have been sourced to the buyers wherever they might be. Who could say, hence, that the goods or services were provided in the single state interested in the tax revenues? Considerations of the promotion of export usually leads to the removal of any taxation, other than customs duty; could taxation on the Net consequently be assessed in general terms rather than any linkages to the direct or indirect nature, whether the taxable items are consumed in the 'producing' nation or exported? Moreover, the incidence of taxation might be multiplied by any shift in taxability to the receiver of the goods or services on the pretext that the seller is not registered in the given state or not subject to its jurisdiction in any way. Should the buyer or receiver of the goods or services be made to pay taxes, the possibility that the seller's state may also impose taxes could deter buyers from purchasing from such a source, preferring instead to buy from other sellers who pay the taxes themselves. In other words, the potential for multiplicity of taxation will operate as a differentiating factor for buyers that take their custom to Net sites.

The fact also that no government will be willing, in principle, to implement taxation laws of other nations—on the theory that they result from the exercise of the sovereign power of each nation and therefore constitutional in nature—leaves this aspect of e-commerce in limbo. If nations do insist on taxing Net transactions according to their domestic laws, the ultimate consequence will be, at one end, the proliferation of multiple taxation of the same transaction and at another end, the absence of any.

On the other hand, some transactions that occur in a jurisdiction may not be taxed at all because the parties do not reside there. Thus the provision of services by a business which has no physical presence in a jurisdiction may not be taxed at the service provider's end. The reverse of this may be more quixotic where businesses operate in multiple jurisdictions (a virtual presence) but have no physical or registered address. The growing divestment of businesses from national and realspace requirements will heighten this problem. Under current EU law, registration of businesses for value-added tax (VAT) in the member state they operate in is a requirement but should the business provide goods and services on the Net to EU buyers from Web sites hosted beyond the EU, the problem is apparent.

Then there are the obvious problems of tax avoidance which are magnified by the nature of the technology. Web operators may have their revenues stashed away at foreign banks that have low tax rates; the nature of the transaction they engage in may be disguised through encryption thus making it difficult to assess whether there may be anything taxable.

In terms of substantive issues, the still generally unresolved problem of whether digital products constitute goods or services will require a solution to provide a sound basis for taxation on the Net, just as much as in the ordinary way. The EU has expressed an intention in 1998 to treat the taxation of downloaded software as services.

Out of concern for the development of e-commerce (perhaps not entirely out of altruism—because the U.S. stands to gain from the expansion of e-commerce to the rest of the world considering that currently it is the biggest e-commercial nation), the U.S. Senate passed the Internet Tax Freedom Act in October 1998. The Act provides for leaving the Internet tax-free for most types of transactions in the next three years, the establishment of a body to work out a formula for Internet taxation.

The Organization for Economic Cooperation and Development (OECD) nevertheless came out at the Ottawa conference with a scheme extending current principles of taxation, hence without any need to impose any new taxes. Taxation is proposed to take place at the point of consumption, while digitized products would be treated on the value of the content. The issue of presence for taxation purposes was postponed for later.

In general, the argument as to whether and what forms of taxation should be imposed on Net transactions will continue to rage since the pros and cons do not seem to have won; those against mainly pointing to the need to boost e-commerce and not curtail it by exacting financial burdens when it is too early to judge how it will fare; those for taxation alluding to the erosion of taxation and the necessity to get to grips with it before it becomes overwhelming.[32]

SECURITY AND PRIVACY OF TRANSACTIONS

The security of the Internet is the single most important issue that still plagues its value for e-commerce, if not for other things too—exchange of information or views, a fast mode of communication. Despite the general declarations of safety and security of the Internet, largely emanating from businesses with vested interests, the veracity of the likely risk has been established in various ways. The vulnerability of systems, even those as closely guarded as those of the Pentagon, to intrusion was discovered when a security audit was conducted by the Information Warfare Division of the Defense Information Agency into 15,000 Pentagon systems. It was found that intrusion was possible into nine out 10 of the systems using publicly available techniques.[33] The vulnerability of established codes to being cracked by determined hackers was demonstrated when the key to decode the Data Encryption Standard (DES) used to protect electronic financial transactions (money transfers and ATMs) was discovered in a contest after testing only about 25% of the possible combinations.[34]

Added to these problem are U.S. objections to the export of sophisticated encryption systems for use in all kinds of on-line communications that need security. U.S. objections emanate from the perennial fear of compromising national security, enabling crime to proliferate and become undetectable, etc. Linked to the alleged threat of information warfare by terrorists, foreign espionage agents or governments, the U.S. seeks to forestall the development of any capability through the use of more sophisticated encryption systems. One proposed U.S. solution has been to require some form of key recovery scheme to be in place for the stated purposes of national security and prevention of crime. The campaign against such a solution in the U.S. and the U.S. courts' intervention declaring legislation to be unconstitutional has so far led to an impasse. By contrast, the OECD issued the 1997 Guidelines for Cryptography Policy allowing for freedom to use any method of cryptography.

Security and Modes of Payment

The development of electronic money, digital cash or forms of micropayment, as opposed to the current predominant method of credit card transactions, is still being awaited. The comparative ease and convenience for both sellers and buyers of using micropayment forms as they navigate the WWW to sample items offered for sale, and pick and choose as they cruise through the malls has been widely noted.[35] Since buyers will only be paying through infinitesimally less valuable bits of electronic tokens, the expectation is that they will avoid the fear of losing a substantial amount of money that credit card payments may lend themselves to. Besides, the removal of third-party intervention (the credit card issuer or more) in the payment transaction shortcuts and hastens the turnover at the same time as reducing the costs and tripartite tangle of liability inherent in this payment form.

As we said, the use of digital forms of payment has yet to be answered not only in practice (particularly by devising and configuring the requisite technology, including the prevention of repeated payments with the same e-cash, 'digital coin' or whatever through an appropriate clearance system) but also through the promulgation of statutory authority or adaptation of case law where the former is slow in coming. Since the underlying problems associated with e-payment relate to security and privacy, these have to be addressed in national laws both in a specific form as well as in connection with general issues of data security and protection.

The use of digital coupons for use over the Internet that can be redeemed within a given time frame is one of the new technologies available to promote sale of goods or services. Another is a system for allowing personal and household bills to be presented and paid electronically. Visa and MasterCard have set technical standards for secure electronic transactions (SET).[36] Under SET, each credit card holder will be issued a digital certificate by his bank to authenticate her identity to a seller, and a seller's identity is similarly authenticated by its bank. The buyer's credit card detail is encrypted so that the seller cannot have any access to it.

Data Security

The dangers that the new technologies pose for people through their capacity for monitoring and surveillance, in intercepting messages including credit card details, are too well known and we have referred to them earlier. The main aspects of data security have been identified as privacy (or confidentiality), accuracy and accessibility. Prevention of intrusion into information systems is only a first step in the security of data as, if that fails or detection of intrusion is impossible, the misuse of data becomes the main concern. Most national laws have incorporated the first part into computer misuse or crime legislation (as well as laws prohibiting the interception of communications). The protection of data has been taken care of, for the most part, under data protection laws, like in the EU.

Standards and modes of payment and security of information exchanges generally are emerging through the efforts of private businesses or organisations which have sought to act without waiting for governments or any other international agencies. International agencies too have set in motion several initiatives. The UNCITRAL, for one, has come out with suggestions for a platform of e-commerce. In all cases, the parallel efforts and activities by more and more regulatory-cum-facilitative bodies, the industries concerned and governments are producing means of safe transactions.

In terms of legislative attempts in relation to privacy, the EU Privacy Directive appears to be the driving force for all nations, including the U.S. The U.S. does provide though the Electronic Communication Privacy Act 1986, as referred to above, a level of protection for personal data. By making interception of wire, oral or electronic communication or divulging or screening content a criminal offence, the Act prevents such means of obtaining information.

Personal privacy has now become reinforced by the issue of anti-stalking laws (in four states of the U.S. and in the UK) both in real space as well as in cyberspace. The California cyber-stalking law has been put to the test in a case where a person rebuffed by a woman he met at church after his romantic advances posted ads in her name on various Internet sites describing her fantasies of wanting to be gang-raped. He supplied personal details on her such as addresses and contact numbers whereupon six men turned up at her door at various times. He was charged with stalking, computer fraud and solicitation of sexual assault.[37]

Individual companies have also started to make an impact by their imposition of standards on their clients, denying them cooperation or business if they do not observe those standards. Thus IBM, considered to be the second-biggest advertiser on the Internet, has decided to refrain from advertising on Web sites that do not post clear privacy protection policies. Such policies need to state to visitors what information is being collected about them and "how it will be used, sold, or otherwise disseminated for marketing purposes."[38]

DISPUTE RESOLUTION IN E-COMMERCE

The most important issues in the resolution of disputes, whether in real or cyberspace, are the determination of the law applicable to the dispute and the jurisdiction (of the court) to which it must be submitted. Obviously, these two issues defy easy solution in cyberspace, arising mainly from the fact that it is not contained within any national territory. The international nature of the Internet means that every dispute will arise and needs resolution in that context. Regardless of the possible attempts of some nations to extend their national jurisdictions under the rubric of some doctrine or other, declaring any nation's laws as applicable or having the jurisdictional power to resolve any disputes will have no real impact.

It is well known that current conflicts of laws rules may be used to find a solution to the two main issues. Thus the rules may indicate to the seller's or buyer's law and courts as being the governing law and having jurisdiction to try the dispute.[39] However, this may not be necessarily the case in all situations, indeed in the majority of situations, or become acceptable by or desirable to the parties. We have already argued this point, above, when we took up the special difficulties that e-commerce poses to consumers, particularly in the matter of legal redress for defective performance.

On the other hand, using current conflicts of laws rules, it is perfectly possible to arrive at the laws and jurisdictions of many nations with parallel or equally valid claims in the dispute; moreover, the complexity in the process of determination of which nations' laws will have the "closest and most proximate" connection with the dispute at hand (contract or tort) suggests that on-line disputes demand a special regime that is capable of supplying easier and faster solutions befitting the nature of the new technology.

It is submitted that unless a major international treaty sorts out this problem, the various national attempts to find solutions within the framework of their requirements and interests, albe it international or global, only amount to 'usurpation' of a momentary nature. Should an agreement later emerge to harmonize such national laws, it will surely represent some sort of a stumbling block to what can now be a straightforward effort.

CONCLUSION

There is an important common thread running through the various aspects of e-commerce law examined in this chapter. The emerging legal regime for e-commerce suffers from a major problem in the disparity among the national laws. In a nutshell, the type and scope of transactions covered under, and remedies provided by, national "e-commerce laws" is not the same across jurisdictions. For instance, the regulation of CAs is based on national perceptions or requirements while the transactions they are likely to have impacts on will generally be cross-national. U.S. experiences in this direction have not been enlightening either in that the main concern so far has been interstate electronic trade and all solutions appear to have that imprint and inherent limitation. As a matter of fact, the legal and institutional framework emerging in U.S. interstate e-commerce has been neither coherent nor uniform.⁴⁰ Obviously, if the leading e-commerce nation is not showing the way in the legal field that it has done in the technological, the confused state of affairs is likely to persist for more years to come.

Another aspect of the emergent legal regime coming out of this chapter is the attempt of various groups to build up support for a global solution to legal as well as other problems relating to e-commerce. The self-help efforts as well as self-regulatory practices will no doubt add to the drive to make e-commerce as stable, predictable and safe as realspace commerce has been. Moreover, other major players such as to cite some of them, the World Wide Web Consortium (W3C), the Electronic Commerce Association, and the Internet Law and Policy Forum (IPLF), the Internet Engineering Task Force (IETF), the International Organization for Standardisation (ISO) engage in producing solutions at a global level. This has been helped by the U.S. government's position enunciated in the 1997 document, 'Framework for Global Electronic Commerce'. The U.S. government has expressed its wish to defer to private business initiative rather than legislation though it somehow declared at the same time support for the creation of a Commercial Code.

Finally, a recurrent theme in this chapter has been the need to work out an internationally acceptable legal regime for e-commerce,[41] in view of the disparities in emerging national laws and the insufficiency of attempts by private organisations. However, the shape of the international legal instruments that are increasingly being felt as indispensable for e-commerce is not very clear yet, perhaps reflecting the inchoate state of Internet technology and e-commerce.

ENDNOTES

1 For a good account of this see Clive M. Schmithoff, "The Law of International Trade, its Growth, Formulation and Operation", in Chia-Jui Cheng, ed., *Clive M. Schmitthoff's Select Essays on International Trade Law* (Dorecht, Boston, London, 1988) at pp.137-169. For an argument as to the appropriateness of the combination of new customary rules and a treaty to harness the new developments, see Assafa Endeshaw, "The Proper Law of Electronic Commerce", *Information and Communications Technology Law,* (Vol. 7, No.1, March 1998).

2 R.M Goode, *Commercial Law*, Penguin Books, 1995, at p.12.

3 See Endeshaw, note 1, above, at pp.11-2.

4 See, generally, Michael Froomkin, "Article 2B as Legal Software for Electronic Contracting - Operating System or Trojan Horse?" 13 *Berkeley Tech. L.J.* 1023 (1998); available online from *Lexis-Nexis*.

5 Available at <http://www.law.upenn.edu/library/ulc/ulc_frame.htm>

6 *Ibid*.

7 Part 2, Sections 2B—201ff of the April 1999 draft of the new Article 2B, Uniform Commercial Code.

8 Part 3, Sections 2B-301ff, *ibid*.

9 Part 6, Sections 2B—601ff, *ibid*.

10 Part 7, Sections 701ff, *ibid*.

11 Sections 2B—113ff, *ibid*.

12 Sections 2B-107 and 108, respectively, *ibid*.

13 Proposal for European Parliament and Council Directive on a Common Framework

for Digital Signatures, (1998) 297.
14   *Associated Press*, 31 May, 1997, quoted in Edupage (*educom@educom.unc.edu*), I June 1997.
15   *USA Today*, 5 June 1997, quoted in Edupage (*educom@educom.unc.edu*), 5 June 1997.
16   John C. Henry, "Federal panelists call for more limits on legal gambling", *The Houston Chronicle*, May 19, 1999, Section A, p. 2
17   Robert A. Rankin, "Legislation is unlikely to stop Web gambling", *The Houston Chronicle*, May 16, 1999, Section A, p. 2
18   *Ibid.*
19   The most notable being John Perry Barlow, "The Economy of Ideas: Selling Wine Without Bottles", *Wired*, Issue 2.03, March 1994; available online at www.hotwired.com.
20   It was reported that a new company called Intersect, is marketing a product named MusicReport which uses Audio Video Scan technology to search for media formats commonly used to deliver video and audio over the Internet and report on the details of the culprits. *Inforworld Electric* of 3 June 1997; quoted in Edupage (educom@educom.unc.edu), 5 June 1997.
21   Chuck Philips, "Universal Music to Test Piracy Protection", *The Los Angeles Times*, 4 May 1999, Section: Business; Part C; p. 9.
22   Rob Fixmer, "Companies Agree on Plan For Digital Watermarks", *The New York Times*, 17 February 1999, Section C, p. 2, column 1.
23   For an extended discussion of the impasse in consumer protection law in cyberspace, see Assafa Endeshaw, "Consumer Protection in Cyberspace: Back to *Caveat Emptor?*" *Consumer Law Journal* (forthcoming)
24   For the private schemes for creation of trust, see *ibid.*
25   "Start-Up Is Unveiling Software to Let Users Annotate Web Sites", *The Wall Street Journal* April 17, 1999, p. B13. Available online from the Dow-Jones Interactive.
26   Stephen Buel, "Spam War Takes New Turn", *San Jose Mercury News*, March 29, 1999, no p.; available online from Lexis-Nexis.
27   Greg Miller, "Court Bars Fired Intel Worker's Mass E-Mails" *The Los Angeles Times*, 29 April 1999 Section: Business, Part C, p. 1
28   Section 2, Defamation Act 1996.
29   Section 3, *ibid.*
30   Reported in Edupage (*educom@educom.unc.edu*), 1997.
31   *Ibid.*
32   The estimate of $20 billion in lost revenues for the states and local governments in the US by 2002 seems staggering. See Michael Janofsky, "States in Fine Fiscal Health, But a Revenue Threat Looms", *The New York Times,* December 31, 1998, Section A, p. 12, column 5
33   Sharon Machlis, "Security experts: Hacker detection is key; You cant keep them out, so shut them down", *Computerworld*, 3 March, 1997, p. 59
34   Don Clark, "Group Cracks Financial-Data Encryption Code", *Wall Street Journal*, 19 June, 1997, Section A, p.3
35   See, for example, D. Muller, "Survey: Selected Developments In The Law Of Cyberspace Payments", 54 The Business Lawyer 403, November, 1998.

36 Details are available at <http://www.setco.org>.
37 Greg Miller and Davan Maharaj, "N. Hollywood Man Charged In 1st Cyber-Stalking Case", *The Los Angeles Times,* 22 January 1999, Part A; p. 1.
38 Jon G. Auerbach, "To Get IBM Ad, Sites Must Post Privacy Policies", *Wall Street Journal* 31 March 1999, p. B1 Available online from the Dow-Jones Interactive.
39 The EU has recently proposed (for a future voting by government representatives) the governing law to be that of the place where the transaction originated where it has not been already covered by EU rules. But this does not answer the further question of what is originating: Offering or inquiring, putting up stuff on websites? See *E-Commerce Times* 05/11/99
40 Froomkin, note 4, above, *ibid.*
41 For a broad exposition of how changes in contract law should be made, *on an international scale*, in light of the advent of electronic commerce, see Endeshaw, note 1, above, at pp.10-12.

REFERENCES

Endeshaw, Assafa (1998). The Proper Law of Electronic Commerce, *Information and Communications Technology Law,* 7(1), 5.

Endeshaw, Assafa (1999). Consumer Protection in Cyberspace: Back to *Caveat Emptor? Consumer Law Journal* (forthcoming)

Froomkin, Michael (1998). Article 2B as Legal Software for Electronic Contracting - Operating System or Trojan Horse? 13 *Berkeley Tech. L.J.* 1023.

Goode, R.M. (1995). *Commercial Law*, Penguin Books.

Muller, D. (1998), Survey: Selected Developments In The Law Of Cyberspace Payments, 54 *The Business Lawyer* 403.

Schmithoff, Clive M. (1988). The Law of International Trade, its Growth, Formulation and Operation", in Chia-Jui Cheng, ed., *Clive M. Schmitthoff's Select Essays on International Trade Law* (Dorecht, Boston, London).

Chapter XXIV

The Challenge of the Law to Electronic Commerce: The European Union Initiative

Séverine Dusollier and Laetitia Rolin Jacquemyns
University of Namur, Belgium

INTRODUCTION

In the Communication on Electronic Commerce of 1997[1], the European Commission stressed that *"in order to allow electronic commerce operators to reap the full benefits of the Single Market, it is essential to avoid regulatory inconsistencies and to ensure a coherent legal and regulatory framework for electronic commerce."*

The electronic marketplace has a crucial need to know *"the rules of the game"*[2] in order to carry out electronic commerce. Therefore, the regulatory framework has to be clear, stable and predictable, both to enable e-commerce operators to face all challenges raised by the development of new products and services and to ensure the trust and confidence of consumers in the new electronic supermarket. These are the main objectives of the legislative action of the European Commission[3] which has, in recent years, laid the foundations for a consistent setting of the legal scene for electronic commerce in Europe. It is worth recalling that the action of the Commission has been and should be guided by the key principles of the EC Treaty, particularly by the concern for the Internal Market and the enhancement of the circulation of products and services. A clear consequence is that any regulatory intervention of the Commission should be directed to a further harmonization or clarification of the existing rules in order to lift the uncertainties and discrepancies in national policies which might impede the free circulation of electronic goods and services. Other key concerns of the European Commission are to refrain from over-regulating electronic markets and businesses and to remain open to a self-regulatory approach and alternative dispute resolution. This last guideline is particularly followed in the recent Draft Directive on electronic commerce[4].

The European Commission couples its legislative efforts with an overwhelming number of R&D projects that are developing new tools, technologies and services for electronic commerce. Within this framework, the ECLIP (Electronic Commerce Legal Issues Platform) project seeks to set up a platform on the legal issues of electronic commerce

Copyright © 2000, Idea Group Publishing.

with the objective of providing legal support to EC-funded RTD projects on any issue of law linked to electronic commerce, thereby stimulating expertise and increasing general awareness of the existing or recommended legal framework of electronic commerce[5].

Other objectives of ECLIP consist in analyzing the current European legal framework and the technology available to be taken into account when launching an electronic commerce initiative, and of ensuring the early integration of the legal requirements in technological tools. This enables the lawyers to develop a techno-legal thinking that integrates technological features in legal solutions and principles. The ECLIP project promotes general and specific awareness among developers of legal issues on electronic commerce through publications, workshops, conferences, and animation of Web sites.

One key aim of the project is to produce a global overview of the legal aspects of electronic commerce with a view to making recommendations to the EC. Such recommendations have already been addressed to the Commission in the field of user protection, privacy-enhancing technology, privacy-compliant browsers, alternative dispute resolution, labelling systems, electronic contracting and digital copyright protection.

ECLIP started in 1998 and is likely to go on until the end of 2002. Its main partners are five university research centers specialized in information technology law, i.e. the University of Namur (Belgium), the Queen Mary and Westfield College of London, the University of Münster (Germany), the University of the Balearic Islands (Spain) and the University of Oslo[6].

The purpose of this chapter is to provide an outline of the regulatory framework[7] that the European Union has started to set up for electronic commerce. Some issues that the European policymaker has to consider particularly are the key questions that any e-commerce developer has to cope with in the different steps of the development of his activity, from the establishment of his business, the advertising and promotion of his products, the selling of goods and services, to delivery and payment. These are the different sections we will address.

THE EUROPEAN REGULATORY FRAMEWORK AT A GLANCE

A key measure for preventing the Member States from adopting a fragmented approach in the field of regulation of information society is the Directive of June 29, 1998 laying down a procedure for provision of information in the field of technical standards and regulations[8] (hereafter the 'Transparency Directive'). This text imposes Member States to notify the Commission and other Member States of any draft rules and regulation activity they undertake in the field of information society services. This transparency mechanism launches a process of making comments and giving opinions on aspects of the draft which may hinder trade, the free movement of service or the free establishment of service providers, which can lead to a postponing or modification of the proposed measure. This directive also lays down a definition of the information society services which will be used by subsequent relevant directives, i.e., *"any service normally provided for remuneration, at a distance, by electronic means and at the individual request of a recipient of services"*[9].

Other key legislative acts are the Directive on the protection of consumers with respect to distance contracts[10] (hereafter the 'Distance Contracts Directive), the Directive on the legal protection of services based on, or consisting of conditional access[11] (hereafter the

'Conditional Access Directive'), the Directive on the legal protection of databases[12] (hereafter the 'Database Directive'), and the Directive on the protection of personal data[13]. The European Union is in the process of adopting a number of other relevant directives such as the Proposal for a Directive concerning the distance marketing of consumer financial services[14] (hereafter the financial services Draft Directive), the Proposal for a Directive on certain legal aspects of electronic commerce in the internal market[15] (hereafter the 'E-commerce Draft Directive'), the Proposals for a Directive on the business of credit institutions[16] and for a Directive on electronic money[17] (hereafter the 'electronic money Draft Directives'), the Proposal for a Directive on a common framework for electronic signatures[18] (hereafter the 'Electronic Signature Draft Directive), the Proposal for a Directive on the harmonization of certain aspects of copyright and related rights in the Information Society[19] (hereafter the 'Copyright Draft Directive') and the proposal for a Directive aimed at establishing a clear regulatory framework for the marketing of financial services at a distance within the Single Market (hereafter the 'Financial services Draft Directive[20]'). Although such texts are not yet enacted and thus might be subject to further modifications, they already highlight the position of the European legislators. We also note that most of the above-mentioned Directives are minimum harmonization Directives, which means that the Member States remain free to transpose the text in a more consumer protective way in their national legal framework. Therefore, for the purpose of this overview, attention should be paid to the fact that main provisions will not be binding as such, either because they are still in a draft stage or because the European States may transpose them in a slightly different way. Nevertheless, we think that this outline might be of some interest to anyone who seeks a better understanding of the process and views of the European policy in that field.

Non-binding texts, such as Communications, Recommendations or Resolutions can also be of great importance in understanding the concerns and inclinations of the European legislator. They will be mentioned and considered where relevant.

APPLICATION OF EUROPEAN REGULATORY FRAMEWORK TO E-COMMERCE TRANSACTIONS

A first point of this chapter would be to define in which cases the European regulatory framework is applicable to electronic business. Determining which national regulations apply to e-commerce transactions is one of the most difficult and delicate questions of transglobal electronic networks. Legislative and case law answers are rare. One difficulty arises from the fact that some activities can occur in different territories, from setting up a Web site, technical management, business management, hosting, access to network, to the making of contracts, commercial communications and delivery. The key question is to know with which national policies the activity has to comply. This is a matter for the national courts to determine—if they have jurisdiction over the litigation—and which law is applicable, by using rules of international private law. This field of law has been early on the object of the European harmonization. Recent directives on information society have specifically addressed the issue as well.

We can infer from the present regulatory situation that e-commerce operators would be under the jurisdiction of relevant EU Member States laws in the following cases:

- In the case of contracts, the Rome Convention of 1980 on the law applicable to contractual obligations[21] would still be applicable to information society contracts. The main rule of the convention is twofold. On one hand, the parties have the freedom to choose the law applicable to the contract. It is thus useful to insert a clause specifying the law applicable to eventual litigation in electronic contracts (software license, access to databases, sales contract, etc.). When dealing with consumers, the Convention nevertheless provides a prohibition to contract outside the mandatory rules of the country where the consumer normally resides. This rule applies only if a specific publicity and/or a specific invitation was made to the consumer in his country and if he accepted it there; if the other party or his agent received the consumer's order in that country; or if transborder shopping trips have been organized by the seller. Whether advertising products or services online should be regarded as a specific publicity directed towards consumers is still controversial. Some factors, such as the language used, the use of individual e-mails, targeted advertising tailored to the profile of the consumer, and any other factual elements indicating that the advertising is specific, can imply the application of the derogation from the rule of free choice of law in the contract. In concrete terms, since most of the regulatory framework of consumer protection is mandatory in Europe, it would mean that the consumer would retain the rights granted by such protection if the law of the contract does not provide the same level of protection as that of his own country.

On the other hand, in the absence of a choice of law, the contract would be under the jurisdiction of the law of the country with which the contract has the closest connection. This connection is presumed to be with the country in which the party which has to undertake the characteristic performance of the contract has its residence. This presumption is rebuttable, i.e., subject to the proof of contrary, for instance if it appears that the contract is more connected to another country. But in the case of sales, the delivery of the product is often regarded as the characteristic performance of the contract, which would entail the application of the law of the seller, except when dealing with the consumer. In this last case, the convention imposes the application of the law of the country of habitual residence of the consumer. This would be the case for instance for a software license if the licensee intends to use the software for private purposes which fall outside his business[22].

This general rule of the Rome Convention for protecting consumers is coupled with Article 12 of the Distance Contracts Directive that states that the consumers cannot waive the rights granted to them by the national laws transposing the Directive. But above all, contractual choice of the law of a non-EU country cannot have the consequence of depriving consumers of the protection granted by the Directive, if the contract has a close connection with the territory of at least one Member State, e.g. because the consumer and the supplier are located within the Community, or the consumer is located within the Community and his order is managed and carried out by an European agent of the supplier.

- The Data Protection Directive imposes its application[23] when the processing of personal data is carried out in the context of activities of an establishment of the controller on the territory of one Member State, or when the controller, not established within the Community, makes use—for the purpose of processing personal data—of equipment, automated or otherwise, situated on the territory of one Member State, unless such equipment is used only for purposes of transit through the territory of the

Community. It is still discussed whether the use of cookies or other types of technology placed on the hardware of users and the processing of personal data should be regarded as the use of equipment within the European Community[24]. This rule of applicable law should be of great importance for e-commerce operators located outside EU, namely in the United States. Should they collect and process personal data through the use of equipment (such as a European server or a cookie), they would have to comply with the protective provisions of the personal data protection directive.

- In copyright matters, the question of applicable law is very delicate and partially unresolved[25]. Beyond contractual matters which enter the scope of the Rome Convention (see above), other rules apply to the existence and scope of protection of copyrighted material. First of all, the copyright protection will be granted under the provisions of the domestic law of the country of origin, i.e., the country where a work was first published.
Secondly, article 5(2) of the Berne Convention states that *"the extent of protection, as well as the means of redress afforded to the author to protect his rights, shall be governed by the laws of the country where protection is claimed"*. This law of the protecting country is the law of the country where the work is exploited or used. Let's take an example in electronic commerce. If a piece of music is digitized and uploaded to the Internet, the law of the country in which the uploading occurred will be applicable to the issue as to whether the uploading belongs to the exclusive right of the copyright owner. This law is the law of the protecting country. If a work is communicated through the Internet, the situation is more complex, since the act of communication could be deemed occurring anywhere in the world[26].

- Any information society service provider established in Europe to carry out e-commerce business would be under the control of the Member State where it is established. This is the solution preferred by the Draft E-Commerce Directive. This rule's objective is to determine which Member State is responsible for ensuring the legality of the activities, thereby preventing restrictions to the free circulation of information society services within the European Union. Without being a rule of determination of applicable law, it can be said that the service provider established on the territory of one Member State will have to ensure that his activity complies with the relevant regulatory framework of this State, including the applicable Community regulation.
The criterion is thus the establishment defined in Article 2 of the Draft Directive as *"the pursuit of an economic activity using a fixed establishment for an indeterminate duration"*. This definition focuses on the real nature and stability of the activity. It is also said that the presence and use of technical means and technologies required to provide the service (such as a Web site) do not constitute an establishment. This principle of country of origin would not apply[27] to intellectual and industrial property rights, emission of electronic money, direct insurance, contract obligations concerning consumer contracts and unsolicited commercial communication by e-mail. Such exemptions mean that in those cases, other countries than the country of establishment have jurisdiction over possible illicit activities.

In conclusion, the European policies can be of great importance, even for e-commerce operators established outside the European Community. This is particularly true when dealing with consumers, when collecting and processing personal data in Europe, or when exploiting copyrighted material inside the European Union.

INFRASTRUCTURE OF ELECTRONIC COMMERCE

Electronic commerce takes place in a converging environment where telephone, television and personal computers offer similar services, and creates new markets whose boundaries are fading away. This convergence of services and markets raises new legal issues, such as defining the regulatory framework to be applied thereto. Current regulations of the audio-visual sector on one hand and the telecommunications sector on the other hand are largely different and sometimes contradictory. Their convergence would not be an easy task. A recent Green Paper of the European Commission[28] on the convergence of the telecommunications, media and information technology sectors, and the implications for regulation addresses numerous challenges, such as the relevance of regulations based on scarcity of spectrum, the blurring of boundaries between public and private activities, the likely overlapping of current regulations or the key issue of access to content.

As far as telecommunication is concerned, the European Union has been engaged in a gradual process of liberalization of the sector[29] for the past 10 years. This has been fully completed as of January 1, 1998. As a result, the number of infrastructure providers and Internet access providers has continuously increased. A great number of directives constitute the architecture of this process : the services directive 90/388, satellites directive 94/46, the directive on the use of cable TV networks for already liberalized telecommunication services 95/51, the mobile and personal communications directive 96/2, and so on.

Nevertheless, exploring those documents would go beyond the frame of the present chapter.

ESTABLISHMENT OF A SERVICE PROVIDER

The European Union tends to acknowledge the establishment of an information society service provider without requiring any prior authorization or control procedure. The draft e-commerce directive would forbid Member States to provide such an authorization scheme which could impede the free establishment of e-commerce operators. This prohibition would apply to information society services, defined as "any service normally provided for remuneration, at a distance, by electronic means and at the individual request of a recipient of services". Any procedure having basically the same effect would be prohibited as well. Therefore the access to the supply of products and services on the Internet would be facilitated. The provision is without prejudice (a) to authorization schemes existing in the telecommunications field, and (b) to those which are not specifically and exclusively targeted at information society services. This last case covers the activities that require authorization or for which the operator has to justify he has the required professional qualifications, whether this activity is carried out in the real world or on the Internet. Some examples are travel agencies, insurance agencies, the sale of medicines, activity of lawyers, etc.

INFORMATION TO BE PROVIDED

Everybody knows the famous sentence: "On the Web, nobody knows that I am a dog". Indeed, in the information society age, it is not rare that a user has no idea or information about what is hidden behind the Web site he is browsing. Some Web sites prefer to stay anonymous, others neglect providing any information other than their e-mail address. A recent U.S. study carried out by the FTC showed that more than half the Web sites don't give any physical address or contact point.

With such a lack of transparency, the consumer or company might be reluctant to engage business with someone so physically invisible. In case of conflict, for instance if the delivered product is not the one requested or is defective, if the price is debited twice, one can wonder where complaints should be addressed. Is an e-mail address sufficient? And what if nobody answers to subsequent e-mails? Where can one address a formal notice?

Some techniques are developing in order to facilitate the identification and authentication of web sites and hence enhance the trust of users. Labelling web sites is one such technique, encouraged by the European Commission for that matter[30]. Labellisation results from an audit procedure assessing the compliance of the web site with a number of business, security and legal requirements. The label then posted on the Web site guarantees the compliance of the site with the requirements of which a list is hyperlinked to the label, thus enabling the user to check.

Along with the development of technical solutions from the electronic commerce market itself, the European Commission puts forward a regulatory response. Article 5 of the Draft E-Commerce Directive would compel information society services to identify themselves by providing the following information:

a) the name of the service provider;
b) the address at which the service provider is established;
c) the address of the service provider including his electronic-mail address;
d) where the service provider is registered in a trade register, the trade register in which the service provider is entered and any registration number in that register;
e) where the activity is subject to an authorization scheme, the activities covered by the authorization granted to the service provider and the coordinates of the authority providing this authorization;
f) as concerns the regulated professions, the professional body or similar institution with which the service provider is registered and the professional title granted in the Member State of establishment, the applicable professional rules in the Member State of establishment, and the Member States in which the information society services are regularly provided;
g) in the case where the service provider undertakes an activity that is subject to VAT, the VAT number he is registered under with his fiscal administration.

The information in question must be easily accessible in a direct and permanent manner to the recipients and competent authorities. It is said in the comments of this article that an icon or logo inserted on the Web pages with a hyperlink to a page containing the information would be sufficient to meet the requirement.

Supplementary information should be given to consumers when contracting online. It will be examined below.

COMMERCIAL COMMUNICATIONS

The European Union has given particular consideration to the legal issues arising from on-line commercial communications, both from a consumer protection's point of view and from a business-to-business point of view.

In its communication of March 4, 1998 on the follow-up of the Green Paper on Commercial Communications in the Internal Market[31], the Commission has decided to refrain from adopting a binding instrument for commercial communications, whose objective would be, for instance, a harmonised prohibition of advertising of some products (e.g. tobacco, drugs, etc.), or a harmonised framework of specific requirements related, for instance to language, to information to be provided.

Instead, it proposes the application of a specific methodology to assess the possible effects and proportionality of a commercial communications measure. The application of this methodology would prevent any national restrictions on communications but those based on public interest objectives. The Commission also intends to set up a database with national and Community regulations and self-regulatory codes in this field.

The Draft E-Commerce Directive seeks to regulate further commercial communications by subjecting them to some transparency requirements. Commercial communications, defined as *"any form of communication designed to promote, directly or indirectly, goods, services or the image of a company, organisation or person pursuing a commercial, industrial or craft activity or exercising a liberal profession"*, would have to comply with the following requirements :

1. the commercial communication must be clearly identifiable as such;
2. the natural or legal person on whose behalf the commercial communication is made must be clearly identifiable;
3. promotional offers, such as discounts, premiums and gifts, where authorized, must be clearly identifiable as such, and the conditions which must be met to receive them must be easily accessible and be presented accurately and unequivocally;
4. promotional competitions or games, where authorized, must be clearly identifiable as such, and the conditions of participation must be easily accessible and be presented accurately and unequivocally.

Moreover, Article 7 of the draft states that unsolicited commercial communication by electronic mail must be clearly and unequivocally identifiable as such as soon as it is received by the recipient.

Besides, three European Directives offer consumers the possibility to oppose obtrusive commercial communications:

- the Directive on the protection of individuals with regard to the processing of personal data[32] whose Article 14 states the right of data subject to *"object, free of charge, to the processing of personal data relating to him which the controller anticipates being processed for the purposes of direct marketing";*
- another personal data protection directive has been adopted in the field of telecommunication. Its Article 12 prohibits the unsolicited calls for purposes of direct marketing, unless the consumer has given his consent;
- the Distance contracts directive lays down that *"means of distance communication which allow individual communications may be used only where there is no clear objection from the consumer".*

Both data protection and distance contracts directives establish the principle of opt-out where individual distance communications are allowed only in the absence of a clear objection from the consumer.

CONSUMER PROTECTION

A recent directive governs distance selling contracts between consumers and suppliers. In the initial version, the financial services were excluded from the scope of application of the directive. Recently, the Commission proposed a financial services draft directive that would modify the distance selling contracts directive to add the financial services that will be regulated by specific provisions. We will mention, when relevant, the specific regulations of the financial services. But it is not clear as yet how the Commission will combine both of the texts relative to distance contracts. It means that the interpretation given in this article could change rapidly concerning the financial services and their integration in the distance contract Directive.

Distance contracts cover *"any contract concerning goods or services concluded between a supplier and a consumer under an organised distance sales or service-provision scheme run by the supplier, who for the purpose of the contract, makes exclusive use of one or more means of distance communication*[33] *up to and including the moment at which the contract is concluded "*(Article 2.1.). From this definition and from the areas that are explicitly excluded from the scope of the directive[34], it appears clearly that the "on-line delivery and/or distribution of materials" is covered by the directive. Main rules laid down in the Directive are:

Prior Information: In good time prior to the conclusion of any distance contract, the consumer must be provided with information[35] concerning :
(a) *the identity of the supplier and, in cases requiring payment in advance, his address,*
(b) *the main characteristics of the goods and services;*
(c) *the price of the goods or services including taxes,*
(d) *delivery costs, where appropriate,*
(e) *the arrangements for payment, delivery or performance,*
(f) *the existence of a right of withdrawal,*
(g) *the cost of using the means of distance communication, when it isn't calculated with the basic rate,*
(h) *the period of time for which the offer remains valid,*
(i) *the minimum duration of the contract.*

Concerning the financial services, the content of the prior information is extended to add more precision regarding the price of the service and, if need be, the way to calculate it.

For contracts that are intended to be entered into on the Internet, it is best that this type of information be included on a Web site in a clearly accessible manner. An hyperlink to an information page could be sufficient on the condition that it refers to information in an on-going way and can be accessed at any stage of the Web site browsing.

Written confirmation of information: Article 5 provides: *"the consumer must receive written confirmation or confirmation in another durable medium available and accessible to him of the information referred to in Art. 4(1)(a) to (f), in good time during the performance of the contract, and at the latest on delivery.*

In any event the following must be provided :
- *written information on the conditions and procedures for exercising the right of withdrawal,*
- *the geographical address of the place of business of the supplier to which the consumer may address any complaints,*
- *information on after-sales services and guarantees which exist,*
- *the conditions for canceling the contract, whether it is of unspecified duration or of a duration exceeding one year."*

Right of withdrawal: As a rule, for any distance contract, the consumer will benefit from a period of at least seven working days in which to withdraw from the contract without penalty and without giving any reason. The supplier will then be obliged to refund the sums paid, free of charge[36]. However, an exception is provided, which will probably apply to some cases of on-line distribution of protected material: Unless the parties have agreed otherwise in respect of certain types of contracts, such as for the provision of services, if the performance has begun with the consumer's agreement, before the end of the seven working day period, for the supply of newspaper, periodicals and magazines or for the supply of audio or video recordings or computer software which were unsealed by the consumer. In the case of the financial services, the right of withdrawal is excluded for services concerning change operations, money market instruments, transferable securities, UCITS and other collective investment schemes, financial futures and options, exchange and interest rate instruments, non-life insurance from a duration under two months, and the complete fulfillment of the contract before the consumer uses his/her right of withdrawal.

Performance: Again, unless the parties have agreed otherwise, the supplier must execute the order within a maximum of 30 days from the day on which the consumer forwarded his order to the supplier[37].

ELECTRONIC SIGNATURE

Doing electronic transactions requires the acknowledgment of the formal validity of digital files and documents. Yet, most European countries still impose that documents be made or at least proven in writing and validated by a hand-written signature. On the electronic networks, the issue of the evidence and authenticity of the documents and parties has been largely discussed so far. A number of countries are in the process of enacting a legislation that provides the equal value of hand-written and digital signatures. Besides the work already done by the UNCITRAL[38] and the OECD, the European Commission has proposed in a recent draft directive the establishment of a common framework for electronic signature.

Its objective is twofold:
- to prevent Member States from denying an electronic signature legal effect, validity and enforceability on the sole grounds that it is made electronically; and,
- to ensure the free circulation of certification services and certificates within the European Union.

According to the proposal, Member Sates shall recognize the validity and the evidentiary value of electronic signatures which are based on a qualified certificate issued by a certification service provider who satisfies a number of requirements set out in the proposal. Certificates would be considered as qualified if they include certain mandatory information, such as:
- the identity of the certification service provider,
- the name of the holder and his specific attributes,
- the signature of the verification device,
- the time limit of validity,
- the electronic signature of the certification service provider,
- the identity code of the certificate.

The operators willing to engage in certification activities would have to fulfill certain conditions of trust and reliability as well. For instance, they would have to justify that they employ qualified personnel, that they take measures against forgery of certificates and confidentiality, that they have the financial ability to pay damages if they were to be found liable. They also should provide consumers with some prior information before contracting and refrain from storing private keys, except if the consent of the holder is given. These requirements will not be mandatory for the exercise of their activity but the certificates they will deliver will gain greater legal force.

Other provisions of the proposal rule the liability regime of certification service providers, data protection requirements and the guarantee of the free circulation and mutual recognition of certificates and certification services.

ELECTRONIC CONTRACTS

Acknowledging the validity of electronic transactions is the necessary complement of the legal value of the electronic signature. This issue is the follow-up of the EDI question that had arisen in the mid-1970s and has similarly showed the lack of legal recognition of the electronic contracting. Normally, the contract is formed between two parties when there is an actual consent to conclude such an agreement. The question arises whether clicking on an icon 'I accept' or 'I agree' amounts to the acceptance of the contract. Not only this question of the reality of the consent can be somewhat complex in an electronic process, but the evidence and validity of the electronic agreement can be difficult to reach in some countries which still impose formal requirements.

These are both obstacles that constitute the main background of the relevant provisions of the Draft E-Commerce Directive[39].

Article 9 requires the Member States "*to ensure that their legislation allows contracts to be concluded electronically. Member States shall in particular ensure that the legal requirements applicable to the contractual process neither prevent the effective use of electronic contracts nor result in such contracts being deprived of legal validity because of the fact they have been concluded electronically*". This article is formulated very broadly and seeks to cover any stage of the contractual process. This would mean that the Member States would have to assess and systematically review any rule which might prevent, limit or deter the use of electronic contracts. Not only the form requirements, such as an obligation to produce a 'paper', laid down in national legislation, but also any rule which might lead in practice to a difficulty to electronically contract would have to be reviewed and properly modified. The various stages of the contractual process to be considered are: the invitation to trade or the contract offer itself, negotiations, the offer or invitation to enter a contract, the conclusion of the contract, registration, cancellation or amendment of the contract, invoicing and archiving of the contract.

In concrete terms, no national provisions restricting the use of electronic media or electronic systems such as intelligent agents, weakening the legal effect of electronic contract or requiring formalities or conditions[40] that cannot be met by electronic means would be prohibited and should be adapted.

Some exemptions can be provided for instance for family law, succession contracts or contracts requiring the intervention of a notary or the registration with a public authority.

The problem of the consent to conclude the contract is ruled by a transparency and information system. Indeed, article 10 would impose that the service provider explain the manner in which the contract is formed clearly, unequivocally and prior to the conclusion of the contract. This information shall include:
- the different stages to follow to conclude the contract;
- whether or not the concluded contract will be archived and will be accessible;
- any available means of correcting handling errors.

This information shall not be mandatory between professional parties when otherwise agreed.

It will be a matter for Member States to lay down in their legislation that the different steps to be followed to conclude an electronic contract be set out so as to ensure that parties can reach a full and informed consent. Appropriate means should also be offered by the service provider for enabling the recipient of the service to identify and correct handling errors. Thus, the proposal does not specify whether automated consent carried out by intelligent agents would be valid, neither the way in which contractual terms or Web pages should be designed and presented.

Finally, the Draft Directive determines the moment when the electronic contract shall be deemed to be concluded, i.e., when the recipient of the service receives from the service provider, by electronic means, an acknowledgment of receipt of the recipient's acceptance, and confirms receipt of the acknowledgment of receipt. This latter step (confirmation of receipt) would probably be removed from the proposal in line with the amendments already adopted by the European Parliament. This will have the advantage of simplifying this intricate and rather non-practical rule. Other modifications are likely to be brought to this Article 11, since the controversy has so far been intense on that point. The acknowledgment of receipt is deemed to be received and the confirmation is deemed to have been given when the parties for whom they are destined are able to access them.

This moment of conclusion of the contract is relevant to determine the moment when the contract becomes binding for the parties, the law applicable to the contract and any other modalities of the contract which might be determined by a time criterion. This issue was already crucial in other types of contracts concluded at a distance, for instance by telephone, fax or ordinary mail. The contract was considered to be concluded at different times according to the countries, which some relate to the sending of the acceptance letter, while others focus on the time of the receipt of the acceptance. Once adopted, Article 11 will settle these discrepancies amongst national laws in Europe.

ELECTRONIC PAYMENTS

To create an adequate legal framework for the electronic payments is one of the great challenges of the Internet regulation. First of all because there are different categories of payment and secondly because those payments sometimes use complicated technologies. The main categories of payment in Europe are the electronic money instrument and the credit card. It is important to mark the difference because those instruments are not exactly regulated in the same way and are designed for rather different purposes. The credit card has the advantage of being used worldwide and the traceability of its issuer ensures it an easier acceptance on the Internet. Moreover, it offers the possibility to make payments for larger sums.

The electronic money instrument is, on the contrary, designed for small to micro-payments, the trust it can inspire relies more on the complex technology it is based on. It has the following characteristics: the payment is made offline thanks to a technology that allows the storage of monetary units on a device that could[41] be either a chip card or a computer memory.

Credit Cards

The choice of limiting the analysis to credit cards and not speaking of some other payment instruments could appear arbitrary. But it seems that they are becoming now one of the most popular payment instruments used because of the development of security features like cryptography or digital signatures and certificates. Those applications will allow the credit card number to travel through the network safely.

There is a particular European text that is of great help for understanding the regulation of credit cards when they are used for cyber payments. It is the Commission recommendation (hereafter the recommendation) concerning the transactions by electronic payment instruments[42].

We note that a recommendation is not considered as a legal binding instrument, but it remains important to analyze and understand it because the Commission will conduct a survey to decide whether the recommendation has been sufficiently implemented in the different Member States, and if not will issue a Directive that will certainly be strongly inspired by the actual recommendation.

To be included in the scope of the recommendation, the electronic payment instrument must enable the holder to perform transfers of funds or/and cash withdrawals[43]. There is no particular disposition on the quality of the issuer that is defined in Article 2 (e) as "*a person who, in the course of his business, makes available to another person a payment instrument pursuant to a contract concluded with him/her*". But he supports several obligations that relate on the one hand to the transparency of the conditions of transaction and on the other hand to the loss or theft of a payment instrument.

Prior to the transaction, to achieve the transparency, the issuer must for example[44]:
- Upon signature of the contract or in any event in good time prior to delivering an electronic payment instrument, communicate the contractual terms and conditions governing the issue and use of that electronic payment instrument to the holder. The terms indicate the law applicable to the contract.
- The terms set out in writing include at least
  a) a description of the electronic payment instrument,
  b) a description of the holder's and issuer's respective obligations and liabilities,

c) where applicable, the normal period within which the holder's account will be debited or credited,
d) the types of any charges payable by the holder.
   - the amount of any initial and annual fees,
   - any commission fees and charges payable by the holder to the issuer for particular types of transactions,
   - any interest rate which may be applied, including the way in which it is calculated;
e) the period of time during which a given transaction can be contested by the holder and an indication of the redress and complaints procedures available to the holder and the method of gaining access to them.

- If the electronic payment instrument is usable for transactions abroad (outside the country of issuing/affiliation), the following information is also communicated to the holder:
   a) an indication of the amount of any fees and charges levied for foreign currency transactions, including where appropriate the rates;
   b) the reference exchange rate used for converting foreign currency transactions, including the relevant date for determining such a rate.

There is also some information to be provided after the transaction, for example a reference for identifying the transaction, the amount debited and the related fees or charges.

But the most interesting part of the recommendation concerns the repartition[45] of the respective rights and obligations of the issuer and the holder *in case of loss or theft*. Everything is organized around the moment of the notification of the loss or theft. In fact, the issuer must ensure that appropriate means are available to enable the holder to make the required notification, including, when it is made by phone (which is currently the most common way), the provision of a proof that such a notification has been made.

Therefore, up to the time of notification, the holder bears the loss incurred as a result of the loss or theft of the electronic payment instrument up to a limit which may not exceed 150 EURO, except when he has acted with an extreme negligence or fraudulently, in that case no limit is applicable. What is meant by extreme negligence is for example the recording of his/her PIN in an easily recognisable form or late notification. After the notification, the holder is not liable anymore for the loss arising except if he acted fraudulently. But there is one specific case where that regime is not applicable. It is when the payment instrument has been used without physical presentation or electronic identification (of the instrument itself) and the recommendation adds that the use of a confidential code or any other similar proof of identity is not sufficient to entail the holder's liability.

That specific provision has to be read in relation with the common use of the credit card number and the expiration date (without any signature) as a means of payment. If that mean is used by an intrusive third party after the loss or theft of the instrument, the holder will not be liable. Certain authors argue that such provision has to be viewed as a strong encouragement from the Commission to use digital signatures and certificates.

Electronic Money Instruments

The European Commission has shown a particular interest in electronic money and is trying now to create a legal framework for its issuing that will open the electronic money business to non-bank institutions by creating lighter conditions for the access to that kind of activity[46].

Beside the issuing, other aspects of electronic money have been regulated by another European text that is actually the European Commission recommendation concerning the transactions by electronic payment instruments. The electronic money instrument is defined as a reloadable instrument other than a remote access payment instrument, whether a stored-value card or a computer memory, on which value units are stored electronically, enabling its holder to effect transactions like electronic funds transfers or cash withdrawals[47].

The legal framework applicable to the electronic money instrument is not so far from the credit card one. But, according to the special nature of the instrument (limited value and prepayment) the recommendation creates a strange system of a two levels application. The electronic money instrument is considered to have two main functions : a *payment* function and a *loading* function through remote access to the holder's account. Some dispositions are not applicable to the payment function, for example Article 6 which contains the dispositions relative to the liability of the holder. It means that the notification-based regime will not be applicable to the payment made by an electronic money instrument. But the recommendation applies fully to the loading function.

There is also some specific provision such as the obligation for the issuer to provide the holder with the possibility of verifying the last five transactions made with the instrument and the outstanding value stored thereon. That system means that there is also an obligation to provide information subsequent to the transaction, made with the electronic money instrument.

Another specific provision puts the liability on the issuer for the lost amount stored on the instrument and for a defective execution of a transaction that are attributable to a malfunction of the instrument, the equipment or any other equipment authorized for use.

VAT REGIME FOR ON-LINE SALES[48]

Unlike direct taxation, the regulation of indirect taxation is within the competencies of the European Commission. It means that it is the Commission that now faces the challenge to adapt the indirect taxation to the digital world. The central problem arises from the fact that all transactions are passing through the network and can not be counted or supervised by any authority without considerable investments in time and money.

General Notions

The following transactions shall be subject to value added tax[49]: "the supply of goods or services effected for consideration within the territory of the country by a taxable person acting as such and the importation of goods." A taxable person means "any person who independently carries out in any place any economic activity (…), whatever the purpose or results of that activity. The economic activities referred to (in paragraph 1) shall comprise all activities of producers, traders and persons supplying services, including mining and agricultural activities and activities of the professions. The exploitation of tangible or intangible property for the purpose of obtaining income therefrom on a continuing basis shall also be considered an economic activity".

Qualification of the Transaction

According to the qualification which will be given to the transaction, the burden of the tax will be supported by one or another party. The reason is that there are different rules according to the type of transaction made. There are two main categories of transactions which are the delivery of goods and the supply of services. Each of those main categories contains different subcategories such as, in the case of delivery of goods, distance selling, delivery of goods with transport by the recipient, etc.

In a communication to the Council, the Parliament and the Economical and Social Committee on Electronic Commerce and Indirect Taxation, the Commission stated the opinion that the goods ordered and delivered through the networks are to be considered as services. This communication is as yet the only action taken by a European institution to adapt the existing framework to electronic commerce.

Place of the Transaction

The general rule is that taxable services are taxed in the tax jurisdiction to which the supplier belongs[50], but this principle is subject to a lot of exceptions. The reason for the exception is to limit the "distortion of competition caused by tax differentials between tax jurisdictions in relation to purchases by those who are not permitted to set off the input tax credit[51]". The exceptions generally relate to intellectual services like transfer of copyrights or financial services.

For example, in the United Kingdom, the VAT may be chargeable on the provision of services if the place of supply is the UK. A UK customer who acquires certain intellectual services[52] may be treated as having been supplied with those services in the UK, even though the supplier may have no place of business in the UK.

Under these circumstances, a recipient (subject to the VAT) of such services would be required to charge VAT on the 'imported service' under the "reverse charge" procedure. According to this procedure, the recipient is required to account for input VAT, instead of the supplier[53].

The process of the reverse charge works only in two cases: when the supply is to a person who belongs outside of the European Union and when the supply is to a *taxable* person in another Member State and for the purpose of that person's business[54]

The system of VAT in Europe is complicated and currently allows a lot of threats by way of electronic means for the transfer of information because it seems obviously difficult to control the transactions made on an open network.

PROTECTION OF PRIVACY

Data on users and consumers are a key asset in electronic commerce. Knowing the profile and interests of potential clients enables a company to reach relevant markets and people to offer them the products and services they might be looking for. Let alone that such data can be easily collected, processed and connected to other files when they have been given by the user when browsing the Internet, with or without his knowledge, there is no need to say that the threats to the privacy of Internet users are numerous. Moreover, this threat is also one of the primary reasons why a great number of people are still reluctant to use the Web for buying goods or services.

Privacy has thus become one of the main concerns of business and of users willing to carry out electronic transactions. Privacy-enhancing technologies are developing, technical standards seek to be privacy-compliant[55] and a greater number of operators display their privacy policy on their Web pages.

The European Union has set up a coherent regulatory framework for protecting personal data and ensuring at the same time the free circulation of this data within the Internal Market. The key instrument is the Directive 95/46 on the protection of individuals with regard to the processing of personal data and on the free circulation of such data[56]. Most European countries have already transposed the Directive in their national laws. A second directive has been enacted in 1997 in the specific field of telecommunications and complements the general directive[57].

'Personal data' are very broadly defined by the data protection directive as *"any information relating to an identified or identifiable person"*. To determine whether a person is identifiable, account shall be taken of all the means reasonably likely to be used by the controller or by any other person to identify the person[58]. In an e-commerce environment, a number of data related to persons are collected and processed, for instance through conditional access systems, use of digital signatures, electronic ordering of goods or services. Other data might be considered personal as well. This could namely be the case of a fixed IP address, which leaves its trace when the user is surfing, when coupled with facilities providing other identification of the user, such as cookie or data collected by a profiling agent, e-mail address, etc. Nevertheless the question is very controversial.

The Directive imposes some obligations to the controller of the processing who is defined as the natural or legal person, public authority, agency or any other body which alone or jointly with others determines the purposes and means of the processing of personal data. These obligations are the following:

1. personal data must be processed fairly and lawfully: this implies that the purpose of the processing must be transparent and clearly explicit and that the data subject should be informed of the collecting of data related to him and of the purpose thereof.
2. personal data must be processed for legitimate purposes : the criterion of legitimacy is not fixed and is left to the appreciation of courts or national data protection institutions.
3. personal data may not be processed in a way incompatible with the purposes for which the data are collected: such purposes have to be determined at the time of collection of data and can be extended to other secondary purposes only in a compatible way: for instance, data collected in order to monitor the proper delivery of goods or performance of services ordered by a customer, should not be used for further marketing purposes, unless this purpose has been specified to the user earlier.
4. the processing of personal data can namely occur if:
    - the data subject has unambiguously given his consent;
    - the processing is necessary for the performance of a contract to which the data subject is a party or in order to take steps at the request of the data subject prior to entering into a contract;
    - The processing is necessary for the purposes of the legitimate interests pursued by the controller, except where such interests are overridden by the interests or fundamental rights or freedoms of the data subject.[59]
5. Sensitive data relative to racial or ethnic origin, political opinions, religious or philosophical beliefs, trade-union membership, health or sex-life can only be col-

lected upon strict conditions.
6. Data must be adequate, relevant and not excessive as regards the purposes for which they were collected;
7. Data must be accurate and kept up to date;
8. Data may only be kept as long as necessary.
9. The controller has to ensure the security of the data by adequate technical measures.
10. The controller must notify the processing to the national authority responsible for the supervision of the protection of personal data.

Finally, the Directive grants certain rights to the data subjects: the right to be informed of the identity of the controller and of the purpose of the processing, the right to get access to the data collected on him, the right to rectify data, the processing of which does not comply with the Directive, and the right to object to the processing for compelling legitimate reasons. This latter right does not have to be based on a justification when the purpose of the processing is marketing.

The Directive prohibits the transfer of personal data to non-EU countries, except if the country of destination guarantees an adequate level of protection, if the data subject has consented to the transfer or if the transfer is necessary to the performance of a contract to which the data subject is a party. Due to the transfrontier nature of electronic commerce, this general prohibition of transfer to third countries could be a problem. A solution for e-commerce operators concerned with the privacy of their clients is to ensure adequate safeguards with respect to the protection of personal data, for instance through contractual solutions or through codes of conduct whose principles would be compliant with the personal data directive.

COPYRIGHT PROTECTION

a) Introduction

In its Communication on the Follow-Up to the Green Paper on Copyright and Related Rights in the Information Society[60], the Commission announced that it intended to propose a number of harmonizing measures in the field of copyright and related rights with a view to adjust and further complement the existing legislative framework, where this is necessary for the proper functioning of the Internal Market and for bringing about a favorable regulatory environment for the development of the Information Society in Europe. Therefore, a draft directive on the harmonization of copyright and related rights in the Information Society was proposed by the Commission in December 1997. This Draft Directive would complete the existing copyright harmonization carried out so far in the field of protection of software and databases, harmonization of the copyright duration, neighboring rights and lending and rental rights[61], thereby forming a coherent copyright regulatory framework in Europe, ready to face the information society challenges[62].

At the same time, it implements a significant number of the new WIPO Treaty obligations (resulting from the "WIPO Copyright Treaty" and the "WIPO Performances and Phonograms Treaty" adopted at the Diplomatic Conference of Geneva in December 1996[63]) on a Community level in parallel with the ratification of these treaties by the Community. In some cases, the proposal goes beyond the provisions enacted by the WIPO Treaties by seeking to implement on a European scale former proposals submitted -but not adopted- to the Diplomatic Conference.

As set out in the Commission's Communication of November 20, 1996[64], harmonization is proposed for these elements:

The right of reproduction;

The stake of the definition of the scope of the reproduction right[65] has always been fundamental for rightholders as for other actors involved in on-line delivery of copyrighted material, such as users, telecommunications operators, access providers, etc... Actually, the on-line transmission of works or performances protected by an intellectual property right implies a number of transient and technical electronic reproductions of works. Whether such reproductions are covered by the scope of the reproduction right as defined in most Member States is still uncertain, which justifies the necessity to provide for a harmonized definition of this right of reproduction.

The definition finally adopted in the proposal is: " *the exclusive right to authorise or prohibit direct or indirect, temporary or permanent reproduction by any means and in any form, in whole or in part.*"

Such a definition conveys clearly that temporary and transient reproduction is subject to the exclusive right of the rightholder. Nevertheless, an exception to this reproduction right with regards to this particular technical reproduction is put forward in the Article 5 (1) of the proposal, which states that "*transient and incidental acts of reproduction which are an integral and essential part of a technological process, including those which facilitate effective functioning of transmission systems, for the sole purpose of enabling use to be made of a work or other subject matter, and having no independent economic significance, shall be exempted from the right set out in Article 2*".

This exception seeks to take into account the concerns of service and access providers concerning the incidental acts of reproduction. "Browsing", "caching" or transient fixations necessary for transmission through networks may thus not be restricted acts if they comply with particular requirements set out in Article 5(1)[66]. The transposition of this exception of temporary acts of reproduction will be obligatory for the Member States.

This provision applies also to the other rightholders recognized in the *acquis communautaire* (performers, Phonograms and film producers and broadcasting organizations, *sui generis* rightholders for databases) and the new WIPO Performances and Phonograms Treaty who benefit from the same level of protection for their works or other subject matter as regards the acts protected by the reproduction right.

The right of communication to the public, including making available "on-demand" over the net;

Article 3 of the proposal sets out: "*Member States shall provide authors with the exclusive right to authorize or prohibit any communication to the public of originals and copies of their works, by wired or wireless means, including making their works available to the public in such a way that members of the public may access them from a place and at a time individually chosen by them.*"

One of the main objectives of this provision is to make it clear that interactive "on-demand" acts of transmission are covered by this right. Actually, the fact that individuals may have access to such services and request their transmission individually had raised a doubt as to whether such transmission was made to the *public* and not to a private person.

This provision aims to settle this key question by providing that the *public* consists of individual *members of the public*.

The right of distribution of physical copies, including its exhaustion

Article 4(1) of the proposal provides authors with the exclusive right to authorize any form of distribution to the public—by sale or otherwise—of the originals and copies of their works. Both new WIPO treaties contain also an exclusive right of distribution, namely the right to authorize or prohibit the distribution of fixed copies as tangible objects (e.g. on paper, CD, CD ROM, tape, as opposed to on-line form). The distribution right does thus not apply to services in general or online.

The second provision sets out that the distribution right is only exhausted in the whole of the Community upon the first sale of the copy of a work in the Community, providing that the sale is made by the rightholder or with his consent. Under this principle, once an author has agreed that tangible copies of his work may be sold in one Member State, these copies can be sold throughout the EU without requiring a new authorization from the rightholder.

This latter provision finally meets the view of the Diplomatic Conference which decided that it shall be a matter for Member States to determine the existence and the conditions of the exhaustion of the distribution right. Consequently, the proposal has chosen the principle of community exhaustion while providing that the distribution right should not be exhausted after a first sale outside the European Union[67].

Exceptions to the Reproduction Right and Communication to the Public Right

Article 5 harmonizes the limitations and exceptions to the reproduction right and the communication to the public right[68]. The list set out in this provision is exhaustive, which entails that national legal systems would not be allowed to maintain any exceptions to copyright other than those enumerated. But, apart from the exception for temporary reproduction mentioned above, the implementation of these exceptions is only facultative. Thereby, it shall be a matter for each Member State to decide which exceptions it will transpose in its legislation. The harmonization foreseen by the proposal is thus relative, since after the transposition of the directive in national laws, the systems of limitations to copyright could still comprise a number of disparities from a country to another both in the actual exceptions in force as in their scope and interpretation.

The list of exceptions is very detailed and precise. The European Parliament has amended it so that a number of exceptions would be coupled with an obligation to provide the rightholders with a fair remuneration.

The list of exceptions follows:

Article 5(2) sets out five exceptions to the reproduction right:
- Article 5(2) (a) allows Member States to maintain or introduce an exception for photo print type reproduction ("reprography"), with a remuneration scheme. Such reprography is limited to techniques of reproduction allowing a paper print. So the result of the reproduction must be in paper form.
- Article 5(2) (b) allows for exceptions regarding reproduction of audio and audio-visual material for private use and for noncommercial ends, but makes a distinction between the *analogue* private copy and *digital* private copy. This last one will not prevent the use of operational, reliable and effective technical means capable of inhibiting the copy. A fair remuneration should be attributed to rightholders for both types of copy.

- Article 5(2) (c) allows Member States to exempt certain acts of reproduction from the reproduction right for archiving or conservation purposes to the benefit of establishments which are accessible to the public, which are not for direct or indirect economic or commercial advantage, such as public libraries and archives This exception does not apply to the communication to the public right. Thus, a library making a work available from a server to users online should and would require a license of the rightholder or his intermediary and would not fall within a permitted exception. It is stated in the Explanatory Memorandum that the communication of copyright-protected material via the homepage or Web site of a library will in many cases be in competition with commercial on-line deliveries of material, since perfect quality copies of any work could be made available to a large number of users, whether on-site (with a multiplicity of screens in the library) or off-site (to other libraries or remote users)[69].
- Article 5(2) (d) exempts the ephemeral fixations made by broadcasting organizations by means of their own facilities and for their own broadcasts.

Article 5(3) provides Member States with the possibility of certain limitations both to the reproduction right and to the communication to the public right in the following cases: :
- use of a work or other subject matter (such as a sound or visual recording) for the sole purpose of illustration for teaching or scientific research, as long as the source is indicated, against fair remuneration to rightholders. In any case, only the part of the use which is justified by its noncommercial purpose may be exempted from the exclusive right.
- uses to the benefit of people with a disability, which are directly related to the disability and of a noncommercial nature and to the extent required by the specific disability (handicapped persons);
- use of excerpts in connection with the reporting of current events, as long as the source is indicated, and to the extent justified by the information purpose (news reporting);
- quotations for purposes such as criticism or review, provided that they relate to a work or other subject matter which has already been lawfully made available to the public, that if possible, the source is indicated, and to the extent required by the specific purpose (quotations);
- use for the purposes of public security or for the purposes of the proper performance of an administrative or judicial procedure (public security uses and uses in administrative and judicial proceedings).

Technological Measures

The proposal conveys an on-going concern of the Commission which consists of protecting technological measures, such as anti-copy devices or electronic copyright management systems, by preventing them from being circumvented[70].

According to Article 6 of the Directive, Member States shall provide adequate legal protection against on one hand the act of circumvention itself, and on the other hand, against the so-called preparatory activities, i.e., any act of commercial distribution or promotion of devices enabling the circumvention of technical measures, therefore, any activities, including manufacture or distribution of devices of the provision of services, which (a) are promoted, advertised or marketed for the purpose of circumvention; or (b) have only limited commercially significant purpose or use other than to circumvent, or (c) are primarily designed, produced, adapted or performed for the purpose of enabling or facilitating without authority the circumvention of any effective technological measure designed to protect any copyright or any rights related.

The 'technological measures' are defined as *"any device, product or component that, in the normal course of its operation, is designed to prevent or inhibit the infringement of any copyright or any rights related to copyright as provided by law or the sui generis right"*. Technological measures shall only be deemed to be 'effective' where the access to or use of a protected work or other subject matter is controlled through application of an access code or any other type of protection process which achieves the protection objectives in an operational and reliable manner with the authority of the rightholders. This requirement of effectiveness of the measure would imply that rightholders have a duty to demonstrate the effectiveness of the technology chosen in order to obtain protection.

The provision only covers the activities and services whose main commercially significant purpose or use is to circumvent, which would ensure that general-purpose electronic equipment or service is not prohibited even if they may be used to this end.

It is worth mentioning that along with the protection conferred by this proposal, another protection for the technical copyright protection mechanisms can be found in the directive on the protection of conditional access services[71] which applies to conditional access systems to services normally offered against remuneration. Therefore, an encryption system protecting the access to an on-line entertainment service (on-line music or video) might be protected against illicit devices, enabling its circumvention on the ground of both directives.

Rights Management Information

Article 7 of the proposal gives Member States appropriate flexibility in implementing adequate legal protection against any person performing without authority any of the following acts :
- to remove or alter any electronic rights management information
- to distribute, import for distribution, broadcast, communicate or make available to the public copies of works or other subject matter

This provision conveys the similar protection laid down by WIPO Treaties in order to protect any digital information, copyright notice or identification systems attached to protected works.

PROTECTION OF DATABASES

One of the main reasons why U.S. operators would establish themselves in the European Union is the protection granted to databases. Indeed, the EU has been the first to set up a coherent regulatory framework for protecting databases of information, whether they are original or not. This has been refused by U.S. case law so far and is still discussed in the U.S. Senate, in a very controversial way.

The recent European directive on the legal protection of the databases[72] provides a double protection for databases defined as *"a collection of independent works, data or other materials arranged in a systematic or methodical way and individually accessible by electronic or other means[73]"*. First, they can be protected as such by the general rules on copyright if they constitute the author's own intellectual creation, by reason of the selection or arrangement of their content. Thus the standard of protection is defined at a European level[74].

Concerning the authorship of a database, the directive states:

"The author of a database shall be the natural person or group of natural persons who created the base or, where the legislation of the Member States so permit, the legal person designated as the rightholder by that legislation[75]. Where collective works are recognized by the legislation of a Member State, the economic rights shall be owned by the person holding the copyright. In the case of a database created by a group of natural persons jointly, the exclusive rights shall be owned jointly."[76]

The duration of the right is the same as what is provided in the general rules of copyright, thus 70 years after the death of the author.

The non-original databases shall be protected by a *sui generis* right which prevents extraction and/or reutilization of the whole or of a substantial part of the contents of that database.

This new right vests upon the *maker of a database,* which is defined in recital 41 of the directive as "the person who takes the initiatives and the risk of investing". Consequently, the rightholder may be a natural person or a legal entity.

The *sui generis* right lasts for 15 years from the date of completion of the database or from any substantial change to the contents of the database, evaluated qualitatively or quantitatively, so long as this results in the database being considered to be a substantial new investment.

LIABILITY OF ON-LINE INTERMEDIARIES

Liability for on-line intermediaries[77], such as access providers, hosting services or network operators, for infringements operated by others on the network, has always been a hot issue of the Information Society. Is an Internet access provider liable for child pornography images available on the Net? Is a BBS operator liable for copyright infringements committed by the users of his system? Is a hosting service liable for defamatory, criminal or counterfeiting material that is posted on his pages? The issue is very delicate since it can be considered as the crossroads between the legitimacy of applying the law on the web, as in the physical world, and the freedom of expression and the practical impossibility of controlling the content which are claimed by many users and intermediaries as key features of the Information Society.

The European Commission has decided to rule this matter horizontally, i.e. by imposing the same rules of liability whatever the type of infringement is: copyright, defamation, illegal and harmful content, etc... It is interesting to note that the lines of this new regime are rather similar to the U.S. Digital Millennium Copyright Act.

The proposal makes a distinction between three types of situations. In each of these situations, conditions are laid down for limiting the liability of service providers. It is worthwhile noting that this limitation of liability does not prevent injunctive relief.

- *Mere conduit* : this situation consists in the transmission on a communication network of information provided by a person who places information online or the provision of access to a communication network. The Draft specifies in Article 12 (2) that this includes also the automatic, intermediate and transient storage of the information if

this takes place for the sole purpose of carrying out the transmission. In this case, the provider carrying out this conduit shall not be held liable on condition that:
- he does not initiate the transmission,
- he does not select the receiver of the transmission, and
- he does not select and does not modify the information contained in the transmission.

- *Caching*: information stored in the intermediate and temporary cache made by a service provider would not imply his liability on condition that:
  - the provider does not modify the information,
  - the provider complies with the conditions on access to the information;
  - the provider complies with the rules regarding the updating of the information, specified in a manner consistent with industry standards,
  - the provider does not interfere with technology used to obtain data on the use of the information; and
  - the provider acts expeditiously to remove or to disable access to the information upon obtaining actual knowledge that the information at the initial source of the transmission has been removed from the network, or that access to it has been disabled or that a competent authority has ordered such removal or disablement to take place.
- *Hosting*: the hosting service provider would not be held liable for illegal activity undertaken by an user of his service, if:
  - he does not have the actual knowledge that the activity is illegal and, as regards claims for damages, is not aware of facts or circumstances from which illegal activity is apparent, and
  - upon obtaining such knowledge or awareness, he acts expeditiously to remove or disable access to the information.

On this matter of liability, the European Commission strongly encourages industry self-regulatory systems, including the establishment of codes of conduct and hotline mechanisms.

CONCLUSION

Early development of the Internet and electronic commerce has challenged the law in an unprecedented way. Scholars and legislators have wondered how the regulation could fit the new electronic environment. It has also been questioned whether the existing legal framework will be able to cover the new applications offered by the technology.

The choice of the European Institutions has been in favor of a tailored regulation and it has proceeded in a case-by-case approach. So the law, in turn, challenges electronic commerce. We note that most of those texts are of minimum harmonization, which means that the transposition in the national framework can be different from country to country, which makes things less simple than it could appear at first sight.

One of the central orientations of that way of acting is the protection of the weakest part in the transaction process: the consumer. But one can wonder if that policy will at the same time meet the needs of another important party which is the 'merchant'. A parallel question concerns the cost of consumer protection, because the implementation and the observation of all these rules require time and money. It is not sure whether the consumer indeed requires such great protection.

But it remains that some fields have to be regulated, mostly because they are common to a lot of different activities. One thinks of the regulation of electronic signatures, privacy or copyright. In those cases, the regulation is for the benefit of all actors of the Information Society. It allows business to enjoy a clearer regulatory framework in which it can operate.

ENDNOTES

1 European Commission Communication (COM(97)157) of April16, 1997, "A European Initiative in electronic commerce) available at <http://www.cordis.lu/esprit/src/ecomcom.htm>
2 M. Bangemann, "Which rule for the online world", Info., vol 1., n°1, feb. 1999, p. 11.
3 see http://www.ispo.cec.be/infosoc/legreg/actionla.html
4 see below
5 see http://www.jura.uni-muenster.de/eclip/
6 Other partners are the Professeur Herbert Burkert from the University of St-Gallen, who is also the President of the Legal Advisory Board by the European Commission, and a Belgian management company, the Bureau Van Dijk.
7 The regulatory framework or legal initiatives carried out by the European Commission were to be considered as of the end of June 1999.
8 European Council and Parliament Directive 98/34/EC, June 22, 1998, OJ L 204, 21.07.1998, as amended by the Directive 98/48/EC, July 20, 1998, OJ L 217, 05.08.1998, available at http://europa.eu.int/eur-lex/en/lif/dat/1998/en_398L0048.html
9 Article 1(2).
10 European Parliament and Council Directive 97/7/EC of May 20, 1997, OJ L 144, 4.6.1997, available at http://europa.eu.int/comm/dg24/policy/developments/dist_sell/dist01_en.html.
11. Council and European Parliament Directive 98/84/EC of November 20, 1998, OJ L320, 28.11.1998.
12 Council and European Parliament Directive 96/9/EC of March 11, 1996, OJ L77, 23.6.1996, available at http://www2.echo.lu/legal/en/ipr/database/database.html.
13 Directive 95/46/EC of the European Parliament and of the Council of 24 October 1995 on the protection of individuals with regard to the processing of personal data and on the free movement of such data, OJ 23.11.1995 No L. 281 p. 31. http://www2.echo.lu/legal/en/dataprot/directiv/directiv.html.
14 European Commission Proposal of October 14, 1998, available at http://europa.eu.int/comm/dg15/en/finances/consumer/891.htm.
15 European Commission Proposal of November 18, 1998, available at http://www.ispo.cec.be/Ecommerce/legal.htm#legal.
16 European Commission Proposal for a Directive amending Directive 77/780/EC on the coordination of laws, regulations and administrative provisions relating to the taking-up, the pursuit and the prudential supervision of the business of credit institutions of 29 July 1998.
17 European Commission Proposal for a Directive on the taking-up, the pursuit and the prudential supervision of the business of electronic money institutions of 29 July 1998

18 European Commission Proposal of May 13, 1998. available at http://www.europa.eu.int/comm/dg15/en/media/infso/com297en.pdf
19 European Commission Proposal of December 10, 1997; revised proposal on May 21, 1999, available at http://europa.eu.int/comm/dg15/en/intprop/intprop/copy2.htm
20 Information available at http://europa.eu.int/comm/dg15/en/finances/consumer/99-559.htm
21 EEC Rome Convention on the law applicable to contractual obligations, [1980] OJ L226/1
22 J. Fawcett & P. Torremans, "Intellectual Property and Private International Law", Clarendon Press Oxford, 1998, p. 579.
23 More exactly, the application of the national law of Member States having transposed it.
24 C. de Terwagne & S. Louveaux, Data protection and online networks, C.L.S.R., 08/1997, n° 13/4, pp. 234-246
25 For a detailed and thorough analysis, see Fawcett and Torremans, op.cit.
26 J. Ginsburg & M. Gauthier, The celestial jukebox and earthbound courts: Judicial competence in the European Union and the United States over copyright infringements in cyberspace, R.I.D.A., 07/1997, n° 173, pp. 61-131.
27 Annex II of the Draft e-commerce directive
28 Green Paper of December 3, 1997, followed by a Commission Communication of March 10, 1999, available at http://www.ispo.cec.be/iconvergencegp/
29 R. Preiskel, N. Higham, Liberalization of telecommunication infrastructure and cable television networks. - The European Commission's Green Paper., Tel.Pol., 07/1995, n° 19/5.; see also Baker and McKenzie, EU developments in IP, IT and telecommunications law, C.L.S.R., different articles published in 1998 and 1999.
30 A. Salaün, E-Commerce. Consumer protection - Proposals for improving the protection of online consumers, C.L.S.R., 06/1999, n° 15/3, pp. 159-167
31 available at http://europa.eu.int/comm/dg15/en/media/commcomm/commer.htm
32 Directive 95/46/EC, op.cit.
33 Defined as any means which, without the simultaneous physical presence of the supplier and the consumer, may be used for the conclusion of a contract between those parties (article 2.4). This clearly covers contracts entered into on an open network such as the Internet.
34 Article 3 1.
35 Article 4.
36 Article 6 1. and 6.2..
37 Article 7 1.
38 http://www.un.or.at/uncitral/english/sessions/wg_ec/wp-79.htm
39 For an in-depth analysis of the contractual rules in the draft directive, R. JULIA BARCELO, "A new legal framework for electronic contracts", CLSR vol 15, n°3, 1999, p. 147-158.
40 The explanatory memorandum of the Draft directive gives three examples of such formalities : the requirements as to the medium used for the contractual process (paper form, number of copies or printed contract), the requirements as to human presence, the requirements as to the involvement of third parties.
41 We note that in the particular case of the electronic money instrument, the technology

keeps changing, the applications mentioned are the actual ones but could change.
42 Commission recommendation 97/489/EC of 30 July 1997 concerning transactions by electronic payment instruments and in particular the relationship between issuer and holder, OJ, n° L 208, 02.08.97, p.52.
43 Article 1.1 and 2 (a).
44 For a complete list of obligations, see article 3 of the recommendation.
45 Article 6 and 8.
46 Commission proposal for directives on the regulation of the Commission proposal for European Parliament and Council Directives on the taking up, the pursuit and the prudential supervision of the business of electronic money institutions. The only version available on the Internet is different than the actual version that is discussed in the European Parliament. It can be found at http://europa.eu.int/comm/dg15/en/finances/general/727.htm
47 Article 1 (c).
48 For more details on the indirect taxation of the electronic commerce see L. Edwards and C. Waelde, "Law and the Internet, regulating cyberspace", Hart Publishing, 1997, p.155-170.
49 Sixth Council Directive 77/388/EEC of 17 May 1977 on the harmonisation of the laws of the Member, States relating to turnover taxes Common system of value added tax: uniform basis of assessment.
50 S. Eden, "The Taxation of Electronic Commerce", in Law and the Internet, Hart Publishing, Oxford, 1997, p.155.
51 Idem.
52 Value Added Tax Act 1994, Schedule 5.
53 S. Eden, "The Taxation of Electronic Commerce", in Law and the Internet, Hart Publishing, Oxford, 1997, p.156.
54 UK VAT Order 1992 SI 1992/3121, Art. 16; Belgian Code on VAT, article 21§3,7°.
55 see the example of the P3P (Privacy Preference Platform) developed by W3C, http://www.w3.org/Privacy/Activity.html
56 Op. cit, see note 11
57 Directive 97/66/EC of the European Parliament and the Council of 15 December 1997 concerning the processing of personal data and the protection of privacy in the telecommunications sector, OJ L24/1,
58 Recital 26 of the Data protection directive.
59 Other exemptions are provided in the directive, but they are not relevant for electronic commerce environment.
60 COM (95) 382 final of 19 July 1995.
61 Directive on the legal protection of computer programs, May 14, 1991, OJ L122, 17.5.1991; Directive on rental and lending rights and on certain neighbouring rights, November 19, 1992, OJ L346, 27.11.1992; Directive on satellite broadcasting and cable retransmission of September 27, 1993, OJ L248, 6.10.1993; Directive on the harmonization of the term of protection of copyright and certain related rights of October 29, 1993, OJ L290, 24.11.1993; Directive on the legal protection of databases of 11 march 1996, OJ. 23/6/96; Follow-up of the Green Paper on copyright and related rights of 20/11/96; available at http://europa.eu.int/comm/dg15/en/intprop/intprop/index.htm..
62 S. von Lewinski, A successful step towards copyright and related rights in the

information age : The E.C. proposal for a harmonization directive, E.I.P.R., 04/1998, n° 20/4, pp. 135-139.
63 WIPO Copyright Treaty, WIPO Performances and Phonograms Treaty, http://www.wipo.int.
64 Follow-Up to the Green Paper on Copyright and Related Rights in the Information Society, 20.11.96, COM(96) 568 final, Chapter 2, p. .9
65 Y. Gendreau, "Reproduction right and Internet", RIDA, January 1999, p. 3-81.
66 Recital 23 of the Directive. "Copyright and Related Rights in the Information Society -Proposal for Directive/Background", http://europa.eu.int/comm/dg15/en/intpropo/intprop/1100.html, p.7.
67 Recital 18 of the Proposal.
68 M. Hart, The proposed directive for copyright in the information society : Nice rights, shame about the exceptions, E.I.P.R., 05/1998, n° 20/5, pp. 169-171.
69 Directive Background, op. Cit., p. 9.
70 S. Dussollier, Electrifying the Fence : The legal protection of technological measures for protecting copyright, E.I.P.R., 06/1999, n° 21/6, pp. 285-297.
71 op.cit, see note 8.
72 op. cit. note 10.
73 Art.\icle 1 (2) of the Database Directive.
74 A. Strowel & J.P. Trialle, Le droit d'auteur, du logiciel au multimédia : droit belge, droit Européen, droit comparé, Story-Scientia, 1997, XXIV, 510 p.
75 For instance, in the employer or the person who commissioned the work will be the author.
76 Article 4 (1) of the Database Directive.
77 M. Schaeffer, C. Rasch, T. Braun, Liability of on-line service and access providers for copyright infringing third-party contents, E.I.P.R., 04/1999, n° 21/4, pp. 208-211; R. Julia-Barcelo, Liability for on-line intermediaries : An european perspective, E.I.P.R., 12/1998, n° 20/12, pp. 453-463.

About the Authors

Robert Bignall holds a B.Sc. and Ph.D. from the Flinders University of South Australia and postgraduate diplomas in Computer Science and Further Education from the University of Adelaide and the University of South Australia. He worked in education and as an IT consultant before joining academia. He was the foundation Head of the Gippsland School of Computing and Information Technology at Monash University and also serves as the Executive Director of the Monash Centre for Electronic Commerce. He was recently appointed as Pro Vice-Chancellor of Monash University's Malaysian campus and will take up this role in the year 2000. His research interests include multiple-valued logic, multimedia technologies and electronic commerce enabling technologies.

Lois Burgess is a lecturer in the School of Information Technology and Computer Science at the University of Wollongong teaching IT Strategic Planning and Business Online to Masters and fourth year students. She holds an Honours degree in Information and Communication Technology from the University of Wollongong. Ms. Burgess's research interests include strategic planning for IT, electronic commerce and service quality within the electronic trading environment. Prior to joining the University she worked for 20 years in the Australian Public Sector in Administration Management, Personnel, and training and Development. During this period she also held a number of high-level elected positions.

Joan Cooper is the foundation Professor of Technology at the University of Wollongong, and the first female professor in IT in Australia. She is Head of the School of Information Technology and Computer Science, and has over twenty years' experience within the information technology field. She is also coordinator of the Secure Electronic Commerce Research group. Her most recent work is in Electronic Commerce and Health Informatics. She has expertise in electronic commerce, IT privacy and security issues, the impact of the Internet on society and the application of IT to the health sector. She has just been appointed to the NSW Privacy Advisory Committee, established as part of the NSW Government's Privacy and Personal Information Protection Act 1998. She is one of the three founders of Australia's first inter-University Electronic Commerce research and consulting group CollECTeR (Collaborative Electronic Commerce Technology and Research).

Head of the IPR Department at the Center of Research in Computer and Law (University of Namur- Belgium), **Séverine Dusollier** has a law degree and works in e-commerce and intellectual property rights. She has been involved in the European COPEARMS project on Electronic Copyright Management Systems and in the ECLIP Project on the legal issues of e-commerce. Séverine Dusollier is preparing a Ph.D. on the "Technical means of copyright protection". She has published several articles on electronic commerce and on copyright matters. She is also a member of the International Association of Science and Technology for Development (IASTED) and of the Belgian Copyright Association.

Assafa Endeshaw graduated from London University in intellectual property policy and technology-related legal disciplines such as information technology and transfer of technology laws as well as in international trade and franchising. He was previously a legal attorney and advisor in government departments and a legal researcher and consultant in a law firm in Ethiopia. Dr. Assafa has written several articles and conference papers that have appeared in local and international publications. He has authored *Intellectual Property Policy for Non-Industrial Countries* (Dartmouth, 1996), *Intellectual Property in China: The Roots of the Problem of Enforcement* (Acumen, 1996) and (jointly) *Marketing and Consumer Law in Singapore* (1999). His areas of interest are: intellectual property, information technology (including regulation of the Internet and E-Commerce), international trade law, franchising law, transfer of technology law, consumer protection law and law and development. Currently, he is an Associate Professor of law at the Nanyang Business School of the Nanyang Technological University, Singapore.

Mariam Fergusson is a senior lecturer in the School of Computer Science, UNSW, at the Australian Defence Force Academy in Canberra. Her main areas of interest are in electronic commerce and telecommunications management. Her research has concentrated on public sector electronic commerce and on on-line payments. Over the last three years she has worked with the Australian Capital Territory government on various electronic commerce projects including Internet payment systems. Mariam has been in the information technology industry over the last 20 years and has evenly distributed the time between working as a consultant and being in the tertiary education sector.

David Gordon is a Professor of Management, has been affiliated with the University of Dallas as a faculty member of the Graduate School of Management since 1969. During this period, he has functioned in several management roles including that of Associate Dean. Currently, he serves as a Director of MBA Programs in Engineering and Industrial Management. Prior to receiving his doctorate in Industrial Engineering from the University of Oklahoma and joining GSM, Dr. Gordon held a broad range of industrial management positions.

Sheng-Uei Guan received his M.Sc. & Ph.D. from the University of North Carolina at Chapel Hill. He is currently an associate professor of the Electrical Engineering Department at National University of Singapore. Prof. Guan has also worked in a prestigious R&D organization for several years, serving as a design engineer, project leader, and manager. He has also served as a member on the R.O.C. Information & Communication National Standard Draft Committee. After leaving the industry, he joined Yuan-Ze University in Taiwan for three-and-a-half years. He served as deputy director for the Computing Center, and also as the chairman for the Department of Information & Communication Technology. Later he joined La Trobe University with the Department of Computer Science & Computer Engineering where he helped to create a new multimedia systems stream.

Thomas Gulledge is Professor of Public Policy and Engineering at George Mason University and Director of the Policy Analysis Center within the Institute of Public Policy.

He lectures in the areas of organizational informatics, electronic commerce, planning, engineering management, and enterprise integration.

Liaquat Hossain received a Bachelor of Business Administration (BBA) and MSc in Computer and Engineering Management in 1993 and 1995 from the Assumption University of Thailand. During 1995 to 1997, the Hossain was a PhD candidate at the School of Information Technology and Computer Science, The University of Wollongong, Australia. Chapter 6, partially based on Hossain's Ph.D. thesis, is titled "The Formalisation of a National Telecommunications Strategic Planning Processes (NTSPP) for the Telecos: A Case Study of Telecommunications in Thailand". The author was also invited to conduct some postdoctoral research at the Internet Telephony Interoperability Consortium (ITC), MIT-Center for Technology, Policy and Industrial Development (MIT-CTPID), Massachusetts Institute of Technology (MIT) in 1997. At present, the author is a lecturer at the Institute of Information and Mathematical Sciences of Massey University at Albany, Auckland, New Zealand. The following areas are the author's current interest: information infrastructure and economic development; impact of technological innovation on communications industry; strategic IS/IT planning under environmental uncertainty; CSFs for investing in e-commerce projects; and, national strategy for New Zealand's health information infrastructure development.

Bill Hutchinson is the Associate Head of Management Information Systems at Edith Cowan University in Western Australia. He has had over 20 years experience in information systems in the government sector, and the oil and finance industries. He has published numerous papers on system design and information warfare.

Laetitia Rolin Jacquemyns has a degree in law and is a researcher in e-commerce at the Center of research in Computer and Law (University of Namur- Belgium). She works particularly in electronic payments, financial issues, taxation and self-regulation fields. She has been involved in the European project TRANSIPOL on the use of NTIC in the transport sector in the ECLIP Project on the legal issues of e-commerce. She has written a number of articles about these topics.

Robert Johnston is a Senior Lecturer and Researcher at Monash University, Melbourne, Australia, and holds Bachelor of Science (Hons.), Master of Science, and Doctor of Philosophy degrees from Monash University. Before joining the University he consulted for many years in the areas of production and inventory management and other manufacturing systems. Since then his main research areas have been operations management, advanced supply chain systems, and electronic commerce. He has published in the *Journal of the Operational Research Society, Omega International Journal of Management Science, International Journal of Electronic Commerce*, and many conference proceedings. He can be contacted at robert.johnston@infotech.monash.edu.au.

Boon-Chye Lee is a senior lecturer in economics at the University of Wollongong. He holds degrees in Business Administration as well as a PhD from the Australian Graduate School of Management, University of New South Wales. His research interests include sovereign debt, small and medium enterprises, electronic commerce, and electronic money. His published work include articles in the *Asia-Pacific Journal of Management, Journal of*

Economics and Finance, Netnomics, and *Applied Economics Letters*, and a book, *The Economics of International Debt Renegotiation* (Westview, 1993).

Ronald M. Lee is currently Professor and Director of the Erasmus University Research Institute for Decision Information System (Euridis) in Rotterdam, the Netherlands. He is also a Research Fellow at the Wharton School, University of Pennsyvania. Previously, he was Associate Professor of Information Systems at the University of Texas at Austin, and earlier served as a research scholar at the International Institute for Applied Systems Analysis in Vienna, Austria, and as Visiting Professor of Management at the Universidade Nova de Lisboa, in Lisbon, Portugal. He has a Ph.D. in Decision Sciences (Wharton, University of Pennsylvania, 1980). Current research focuses on applications of artificial intelligence, Petri nets, and logic modeling to electronic commerce; including represenions of electronic trade procedures for international, business-to-business commerce.

Andreas Mitrakas (*andreas@globalsign.net*) LL.B., University of Athens, 1990, LL.M., Queen's University of Belfast, 1991, Ph.D., Erasmus University of Rotterdam, 1997, is Senior Legal Consultant at GlobalSign NV, (*www.globalsign.net*) a European Certification Authority and provider of Public Key Infrastructure products and services. A member of the Athens Bar Association he participates in the ETERMS WG of the International Chamber of Commerce and has authored numerous publications in electronic commerce and IT Law including the book *Open EDI and Law in Europe*, Kluwer Law International, 1997.

Teoh Kok Poh is a graduate student of the National University of Singapore. He is currently a smart card and IT consultant of SciNet Systems, a start-up system consulting firm. Before starting up SciNet Systems, Mr. Poh was the product development manager of a smart card company in Singapore. His team was actively involved in smart card-based product and system design, and engineering test for smart card. After that, he was transferred to manage the operations of a system integration company that was actively involved in design and integration of smart card and IT system, real-time system, computer networking and Internet applications.

M. A. Quaddus received his Ph.D. from the University of Pittsburgh, M.S. from University of Pittsburgh and Asian Institute of Technology, and B.S. from Bangladesh University of Engineering and Technology. His research interests are in decision support systems, group decision and negotiation support systems, multiple criteria decision Making, systems dynamics, business research methods and in the theories and applications of innovation diffusion processes. Dr. Quaddus has published in a number of journals including *Technological Forecasting & Social Change, Socio-Economic Planning Sciences, Journal of OR Society, Interfaces, Engineering Optimization, Eng Costs & Production Economics, International Journal of Management, Computers & Education* etc and contributed to several books/monographs. In 1996 he received the researcher of the year award from Curtin Business School. Currently he is an Associate Professor with the Graduate School of Business, Curtin University of Technology, Australia. Prior to joining Curtin Dr Quaddus was with the University of Technology-Sydney and with the National University of Singapore.

Syed M. Rahman is currently a Visiting Professor at North Dakota State University, Fargo USA on leave from Monash University, Australia. He is a senior faculty member at the Gippsland School of Computing and Information Technology of Monash University. He obtained his doctoral degree from Budapest Technical University in 1980. He was the head of the Department of Computer Science and Engineering of Bangladesh University of Engineering and Technology from 1986 to 1992. He supervised more than 30 research projects leading to post graduate degrees. He has published 90+ research papers. He has organized a number of international conferences and is on the program committee of a number of conferences. His main area of interest includes multimedia computing and communications, electronic commerce and security issues, image processing and retrieval, pattern recognition and distributed processing.

Mahesh S. Raisinghani is a faculty member and co-director of the E-Commerce MBA Program at the University of Dallas' Graduate School of Management. He also serves as the director of research at the University of Dallas' Center for Applied Information Technology. His primary areas of expertise are electronic commerce technology and management, strategic utilization and management of information systems, and the organizational impacts of emerging technologies. He is the chair of the Electronic Commerce track and a world representative for the International Resources Management Association, an active member of the Association of Information Systems, Decision Sciences Institute, and the International Association of Computer Information Systems. He has had numerous listings including the *Who's Who in Information Systems, Who's Who in the World* and *Who's Who Among Students in American Universities and Colleges*. Dr. Raisinghani conducts seminars in e-commerce and global information systems for executives. Professor Raisinghani's previous publications have appeared in the *Journal of Information Systems Management, International Journal of Information Management, International Journal of Materials and Product Technology, Journal of Electronic Commerce, Journal of Information Technology Theory and Application, Industrial Management and Data Systems, Electronic Commerce World, American Business Review, Minority Business News USA* and Arthur Anderson's *KnowledgeSpace*. His chapters have been published in *Annals of Cases in Information Technology Management, Managing Web-Enabled Technologies Application and Management: A Global Perspective,* and *Healthcare Information Systems: Challenges of the Next Millennium*; and has proceedings published in several regional, national and international information systems conferences in Australia, Canada, Greece, Israel, Mexico, Puerto Rico, South America and the U.S. His seven years of professional experience in information systems has taken him to Canada, China, India, Japan, Mexico, Singapore, Thailand, and U.K.

Deshani Rodrigo is completing her Masters Degree at Monash University, Australia, in the area of electronic commerce. Her research interests include performance related issues in Web systems and evolving electronic commerce technologies, in particular agent-based architectures. Her current qualifications include a Bachelor of Commerce (First Class Honors) in Management Science and Information Systems, with a major in Operations Research from The University of Auckland, New Zealand. Deshani is presently working at Monash University, developing a course in the field of electronic commerce as well as teaching in the area of system modelling and simulation. Previously she has undertaken a variety of consulting jobs and worked at The University of Auckland. She may be reached at deshani.rodrigo@csse.monash.edu.au.

Ruhul A Sarker received his Ph.D. from DalTech (former TUNS), Dalhousie University, Halifax, Canada, and is currently a Lecturer in Operations Research / Management Science at the School of Computer Science, University of New South Wales, ADFA, Canberra, Australia. Before joining UNSW, Dr. Sarker worked with the Monash University, Victoria, and the Bangladesh University of Engineering and Technology, Dhaka. In his school, he is the coordinator for postgraduate program in Operations Research and Statistics. His main research interests are mathematical modelling, evolutionary optimization, and computers and operations research Applications to real world problems. His research papers have appeared in many international journals, which include *EJOR, JORS, AMM, IJIE, IJMS, MPT,* and *Computers in Industry.*

Sen Sendjaya recently completed his M.B.A. training at Monash Mount Eliza Business School, Monash University. He also holds a management degree from Seattle University. Apart from e-commerce, his other research interests are leadership, ethics, and organization learning. Prior to his MBA training, he worked in the industry as a middle manager as well as served as a part-time lecturer at the Faculty of Economics, Petra Christian University in Indonesia.

Timothy K. Shih is a Professor and Chairman of the Department of Computer Science and Information Engineering at Tamkang University, Taiwan, R.O.C. His research interests include multimedia computing, software engineering, and formal specification and verification. He was a faculty member of the Computer Engineering Department at Tamkang University in 1986. In 1993 and 1994, he was a part-time faculty member of the Computer Engineering Department at Santa Clara University. He was also a visiting professor at the University of Aizu, Japan in the summer of 1999. Dr. Shih received his B.S. and M.S. degrees in Computer Engineering from Tamkang University and California State University, Chico, in 1983 and 1985, respectively. He also received his Ph.D. in Computer Engineering from Santa Clara University in 1993. Dr. Shih has published about 170 papers and participated in many international academic activities. Dr. Shih has received many research awards, including Tamkang University research awards, NSC research awards (National Science Council of Taiwan), and the IIAS research award of Germany. He also received many funded research grants from NSC, from the Institute of Information Industry, Taiwan, and from the University of Aizu, Japan. Dr. Shih has been invited frequently to give talks at national and international conferences and research organizations. The contact address of Dr. Shih is Department of Computer Science and Information Engineering, Tamkang University, Tamsui, Taipei Hsien, Taiwan 251, ROC. E-mail: tshih@cs.tku.edu.tw, Fax: +886 2 26209749, Phone: +886 2 26215656 x2743, http://www.mine.tku.edu.tw/chinese/teacher/tshih.htm

Chee Kheong Siew is presently the director of the Information Communication Institute of Singapore. In recent years, he led the institute to focus on innovative projects like electronic commerce, distance learning and ATM-based multimedia communication systems. He looks forward to leading ICIS to fulfill his vision of a world-class institute in teaching, research and innovation in communication software systems and networks. His research interests include electronic commerce, traffic shaping, neural networks and network performance.

James E. Skibo is currently an Adjunct Professor of Industrial Management at the University of Dallas. He holds a M.B.A. from the University of Dallas and is working on his doctorate degree at The Fielding Institute, Santa Barbara, CA. He is Director of Cooperative Advertising for the Army & Air Force Exchange Service in Dallas, Texas. His areas of expertise include business and industrial management, marketing management, and consulting.

Rainer Sommer is a member of the George Mason University research faculty. He is Associate Research Professor of Public Policy and Systems Engineering as well as the assistant director of the Policy Analysis Center of the George Mason University's Institute of Public Policy. Dr. Sommer has consulted and lectured internationally in the field of Enterprise Resource Planning systems, Integrated EC\EDI, software requirement analysis, and Enterprise Integration.

Marla Royne Stafford is Associate Professor of Marketing at the University of North Texas in Denton, Texas. She holds the Ph.D. in Marketing from the University of Georgia, and has been noted as a leading contributor to the field of advertising. Dr. Stafford's research has focused primarily on message and media effects in services advertising and the new media. Her current research investigates uses and gratifications of the World Wide Web and non-profit advertising.

Thomas F. Stafford is Visiting Assistant Professor of Information Systems at Texas Woman's University in Denton, Texas. He holds the Ph.D. in Marketing from University of Georgia and is currently pursuing doctoral studies in Information Systems at the University of Texas-Arlington. He serves on the Editorial Review Boards of *Psychology & Marketing, Journal of Consumer Affairs,* and *Journal of Marketing Education.* His research involves understanding consumer motivations and decision making and motivations for commercial activity on the Internet.

Peter A. Stanski is completing his Ph.D. at Computer Science and Software Engineering, Monash University Australia, in the area of Mobile Agents, Networks, the World Wide Web and converging technologies. His other research interests include distributed systems, mobile computing, electronic commerce, telecommunication systems and systems administration. He holds a Bachelor of Computing degree with a first class honors from Monash University, and is a member of the IEEE. In the last 9 years Peter has served as a founder and a company director, a systems architect and developer, a video games programmer, analyst, consultant, contractor and lecturer. He can be reached at peter.stanski @csse.monash.edu.au.

Ly Fie Sugianto is a lecturer at the Gippsland School of Computing and Information Technology, Monash University. Her research projects in Electronic Commerce include the development of the Electronic Commerce Implementation Adviser (eCIA) and the Web site support for Internet Commerce. She has also coauthored a number of research publications in optimization techniques, Decision Support Systems and Fuzzy Mathematics. Prior to her appointment at GSCIT, she was involved in extensive research within the Australian power industry.

Charles Trappey is Associate Dean, College of Management and Professor of Management Science at the National Chiao Tung University in Taiwan. His research interests are international marketing, consumer behavior and marketing aspects of electronic commerce.

Amy Trappey is Professor of Industrial Engineering and Engineering Management at the National Tsing Hua University in Taiwan. Her research interests are business-to-business electronic commerce, product data management, and CAD/CAM.

Klaus Turowski is assistant professor at the University of Magdeburg in the area of Business Information Systems. Prior to assuming his current position, he worked at the University of Münster. 1993 he received his Dipl.-Wi.-Ing. (diploma degree in Industrial Engineering and Management) at the University of Karlsruhe and 1997 his Dr. rer. pol. (Ph.D. in Business Information Systems) at the University of Münster. Since 1998 he is speaker of Working Group 5.10.3 *Component-oriented Business Application Systems* of German Informatics Society (GI) and co-founder of working group 5.5 *E-Commerce*. His main research interests are component-oriented software development and e-commerce techniques, especially XML/EDI and Web engineering.

Matthew Warren is a information systems lecturer at Deakin University (Department of Computing & Mathematics) (1998 +) and before that a Lecturer at the Plymouth Business School, UK (1996 - 1998). He obtained his PhD in Computer Security Risk Analysis at Plymouth University, UK (1996). He has published 40 refereed journal and conference papers. He is a member of Australian Standards Committee IT/12/4 Security Techniques and is the Australian Representative on IFIP 11 WG 11 - Security Management. He has also worked on several European Union Research projects including projects under the ADAPT, HTCA, INFOSEC and AIM schemes.

Yang Yang received his B. Eng. (Electrical) from the National University of Singapore. He is currently pursuing M. Eng. (Electrical) in the Department of Electrical Engineering at the National University of Singapore on a part-time basis. During his industrial attachment, he worked in the Information Security Group at the Institute of System Science (Singapore) on a Secure-Cash project. He went on to work to develop a smart-card-based SSL 3.0 package for the same organization. During this period, he is also involved in the development of S-One, a web-based payment solution using smart card. After his graduation from the University, Yang Yang works in the Development Bank of Singapore as an analyst/programmer.

Xun Yi is a visiting research fellow of Information Communication Institute of Singapore. In recent years, he has been working on electronic commerce research area. His main research interests center in applying software agent technologies along with cryptographic technologies to solve issues faced by electronic commerce. So far, he has published papers in this area in international journals and conferences.

Index

A

A Model of Internet Commerce
    Adoption 190
adoption and diffusion 103
advertising 22
advertising revenue 33
agent transport 326
agent transport protocols 335
APT Strategies 193
assessment methods 156
authentication 364
automated systems 138
automatic identification 42

B

bar code 42
broadband digital services 229
business process simplification 41
business-to-business electronic
    commerce 7
business-to-consumer EC 6, 43
buyer 362

C

CA 365
card acceptance device 247
catalog 25
certification authority 365
challenges for global enterprises 12
cheques 235
coaxial cable 229
commercial law 362
communications theory 218
competition 22
competition law 366
competitive advantage 163

competitive environment 65
conflicts of laws 379
consumer 370
consumer protection 371
consumer-supplier value chain 115
content-specific information 220
contract law 363
cost-benefit analysis 152, 166
credit card 235, 377
critical success factors 118
cross-docking 57
cryptographic technology 280
custom software 246
customer-supplier interaction 189
customers 22
cyber-terrorism 352
cyberspace 362
cybersquatting 368

D

data turnaround 43
debit cards 236
decision analysis 158
decision analysis approach 156
defamation 372
defective physical goods 372
defense industry supply chains 86
department store 22
diffusion model 102
digital cash 115, 236, 377
digital signature 365
digital signature technology 129
digitisation 367
Documentary Petri Nets 65
domain names 368
domestic laws 376

E

e-Commerce 2, 21, 262
e-strategic framework 116
e-strategy planning framework 115
economic cost benefit 163
EDI 42, 261, 265
EDI adoption models 193
EDI investment 153
EDIFACT 267
electronic banking 115
electronic commerce
  2, 65, 85, 102, 233, 303,
  337, 352, 383
Electronic Commerce Resource
  Centers (ECRCs) 85
electronic contracting 138
electronic contracting regulation 138
electronic crimes 321
electronic data interchange 42,
  65, 115, 152, 261, 265
electronic funds transfer 43
electronic messages 130
electronic money 236
electronic payment systems 115
electronic purchase transactions 279
electronic textbooks 134
electronic tokens 236
electronic trade 67
electronic transfer 143
encryption 365
EU Privacy Directive 378
European Commission 383
evaluated receipts settlement 47
evolution computing 304

F

fulfillment 29
functionality 24
future of electronic commerce 353

G

gambling 366
global enterprise networks 115
global Internet commerce community 189
global supply chains 66, 75
government on-line service delivery 172
graphical interface 72
gratifications 218
growth 34

H

hits 33

I

identity 364
illegality 367
Incoterms 134
Index-based search engines 283
information extraction 283
information filtering 256
information gathering 284
information planning approach 116
information retrieval 283, 303
information searches 228
information sharing 43
information society 219
infrastructure risk 164
infringement 369
integrated services digital network 159
integrated telephony 229
intellectual property 367
intelligent agents 305, 322
Intelligent gateway 58
intelligent software agents 246
interchange agreements 131, 138
intermediaries 202
"internal" interactions 102
Internal Market 383
international treaty 379
Internet 56, 218, 246, 303, 337
Internet commerce 202
investment evaluation 167
investment strategy 121
ISO authentication framework 282
IT maturity 153

J

Java 333
Java Card 248
JavaBeans 262, 274
junkmail 373
jurisdiction 376
Just-In-Time 41

K

Kanban 52

L

legacy 28
legislation 369
legislative efforts 383
liability 367

M

mass customization 262
material requirement schedules 49
MCAs 337
menu-based system 136
misrepresentation 366
misstatements 372
misuse of information 370
mobile agents 303, 344, 347
mobile code applications 337
multi-lingual interface 135
multiple linked projects 166

N

negligent liability 371
network money 236
New Zealand Government 117

O

on-line business transactions 129
on-line processing capabilities 197
on-line services 202
once-only data entry 43
open EDI 126
open system 295
operations 22
opportunities for global enterprises 9

order processing 28
organizational structure 26

P

paper-less transactions 144
passwords 364
payment 28
payments system 233
PDF417 55
personal digital assistants 259
personal privacy 378
privacy 249, 367
promotion 31
prototyping of trade scenarios 80
purchase request transaction 291
push and pull 51

R

realspace 367
Recon 137
regulatory framework 383
regulatory inconsistencies 383
reputation 374
resolution of disputes 379
retail 21
retail payments 233
retailing 202
return on investment 156
reusable models 65
reusable software 81
revenue growth 23

S

sandbox approach 333
search engines 304
Secure Electronic Transaction (SET)
    protocol 243, 289
secure sockets layer (SSL) protocol
    243
secure-roaming agent For e-commerce 322
security 137,
    144, 248, 249, 295, 321, 378
seller 362
set-up costs 149

signature 365
small to medium sized enterprises (SMEs) 57, 142, 189
smart card agent 246
software agent 270, 280
software agent technology 246, 279
software components 273
spam 373
standardization 134, 322
stored-value card 236
storefront 21
strategic advantage 23
strategic match 163
strategic opportunities 152
strategic planners 118
strict liability 371
supply chain management 89
supply chains 65
synchronicity 43

T

taxation 375
The HotWired Study 223
theft 369
Toycta Production System 52
trust and confidence 383
Trusted Third Party (TTP) services 129
twisted pair lines 229
two-dimensional bar code 54

U

unauthorised disclosure 369
uncertainty 163
UNCITRAL Model Law 363
uniform commercial code 363
universal product numbering 42
usage motivations 220
uses 218
uses and gratifications 220

V

validity 363
value chain integration 195
vendor-managed inventories 49

virtual community 257
viruses 295, 324
visitors 33
vulnerabilities 353

W

Web 337
Web-based EDI 149
Web browsing 222
Web sites 218
Web-based transactions 256
wholesale payments 233
wireless technology 229
World Wide Web 219, 321
www.aafes.com 24

X

XML 262, 270